I0114431

.

On the Proposed Crimes Against Humanity Convention

Morten Bergsmo and SONG Tianying (editors)

2014
Torkel Opsahl Academic EPublisher
Brussels

This and other books in our *FICHL Publication Series* may be openly accessed and downloaded through the web site http://www.fichl.org/ which uses Persistent URLs for all publications it makes available (such PURLs will not be changed). Printed copies may be ordered through online and other distributors, including https://www.amazon.co.uk/. This book was first published on 12 December 2014.

© **Torkel Opsahl Academic EPublisher, 2014**

All rights are reserved. You may read, print or download this book or any part of it from http://www.fichl.org/ for personal use, but you may not in any way charge for its use by others, directly or by reproducing it, storing it in a retrieval system, transmitting it, or utilising it in any form or by any means, electronic, mechanical, photocopying, recording, or otherwise, in whole or in part, without the prior permission in writing of the copyright holder. Enquiries concerning reproduction outside the scope of the above should be sent to the copyright holder. You must not circulate this book in any other cover and you must impose the same condition on any acquirer. You must not make this book or any part of it available on the Internet by any other URL than that on http://www.fichl.org/.

ISBN 978-82-93081-96-8

Dedicated to Judge Hans-Peter Kaul
for his fearless service to
international criminal law and its integrity

PREFACE BY HANS-PETER KAUL

Treaties must be taken seriously, both when they have entered into force, and when they are being made. In the third preambular paragraph of the United Nations Charter – that foundational document of our international society – all Member States commit themselves to "respect for the obligations arising from treaties". Today's international legal order – established after millions of Jews, Russians, Chinese and others were killed during World War II – depends on our commitment to this principle.

This applies in the same way to international courts. Their judges must at all times be faithful to the treaty or statute that established the international jurisdiction in question. They should not see themselves as law-makers. This is particularly important in international criminal jurisdictions. A judge may dislike an element of a crime in the statute, but he or she must respect that element by applying it pursuant to its ordinary statutory meaning.

What was perhaps seen as a *constructive ambiguity* during the negotiations of a statute – breaking a paralysing disunity and facilitating a compromise between States – may well be perceived as an *unhelpful lack of clarity* later, when the provision has to be applied in specific cases by judges who are bound to respect the wording of the statute.

Having both participated in the negotiation of the Statute of the International Criminal Court and applied this Statute as a Judge of the Court, I have witnessed first-hand the importance of fully recognising the significance of every word that is included in such an instrument with a view to honouring the complex agreement reached between law-making States. This is illustrated in particular by early decisions of Pre-Trial Chamber II in respect of the Prosecutor's request for the initiation of an investigation into the situation of Kenya and the related cases of *The Prosecutor v. William Samoei Ruto and Joshua Arap Sang* and *The Prosecutor v. Uhuru Muigai Kenyatta* on the question of the interpretation and application of certain contextual elements of crimes against humanity as set out in Article 7 of the ICC Statute.

Actors who may take part in the process to prepare a general convention on crimes against humanity should keep this in mind. Treaties are not only of cardinal importance when they have entered into force, but also when they are being made.

FOREWORD BY HANS CORELL

When I started writing these lines, I had just been informed that my long-time friend Judge Hans-Peter Kaul had passed away. It is therefore with great sadness that I am authoring this brief foreword. At the same time, in so doing, I remember with gratitude and fondness my many contacts with Hans-Peter over the years. In this particular context I recall our interaction at the international conference commemorating the tenth anniversary of the International Criminal Court, which took place at Washington University School of Law in St. Louis in November 2012. Judge Kaul's important and dedicated contribution to the development of international criminal law will long be remembered.

When I was invited to contribute this foreword, it was suggested that readers would find it particularly interesting if the foreword contained a few words about my background in international criminal law and justice from the early Commission on Security and Cooperation in Europe ('CSCE') – now Organization for Security and Co-operation in Europe ('OSCE') – mission to Croatia, up until the current initiative for a convention on crimes against humanity; my view on whether such a convention should be developed, and, if so, how it could add to the existing international legal order; and what those who will be involved in its making should keep in mind in light of past experience and new challenges. The following is an attempt to respond to this invitation.

My background in criminal law practice dates back to 1962, when I graduated from law school and joined the judiciary. In my country, Sweden, it is customary that young lawyers join the judiciary as law clerks, working with senior judges at the circuit court level. A few months later, these young lawyers are assigned to adjudicate petty criminal cases as a first step in their judicial career. This is what happened to me with the result that criminal justice became part of my daily work for more than ten years in different circuit courts and also in one of our courts of appeal.

With respect to the idea of establishing international criminal courts, I was rather doubtful in those days. Would this work? Would not the complexity of dealing with criminal cases at the national level multiply at the international level? Would not trials before international criminal courts be politicised? Was this realistic?

Later in life, I completely changed my mind. As a CSCE war crimes rapporteur in the former Yugoslavia I realised that nobody would do anything about bringing perpetrators of the crimes committed there to justice unless an international criminal tribunal was created. On 9 February 1993, Helmut Türk of Austria, Gro Hillestad Thune of Norway and I completed our task by presenting our report Proposal for an International War Crimes Tribunal for the Former Yugoslavia by Rapporteurs (Corell-Türk-Thune) under the CSCE Moscow Human Dimension Mechanism to Bosnia-Herzegovina and Croatia. The CSCE immediately forwarded the proposal to the United Nations, and later in the same month the Security Council decided, on the basis also of a proposal by a U.N. Commission, to establish the International Criminal Tribunal for the former Yugoslavia ('ICTY').

About a year later, in March 1994, I found myself in the position as Under-Secretary-General for Legal Affairs and the Legal Counsel of the United Nations. To make a long story short: during my ten years in that position, I was involved in the final steps of establishing the ICTY and later in establishing the International Criminal Tribunal for Rwanda, the Special Court for Sierra Leone, and the Extraordinary Chambers in the Courts of Cambodia. Furthermore, in 1998, I was the Representative of the Secretary-General at the Rome Conference that adopted the Rome Statute of the International Criminal Court. Consequently, when the Statute entered into force in 2002, I was also involved in the establishment of the Court.

At the conference in St. Louis in 2012, I reflected on State sovereignty in modern-day society and came to the conclusion that one of the most prominent features of this sovereignty is the responsibility to protect. This responsibility includes an obligation on States to protect their populations against grave international crimes. Therefore, the international criminal justice system must function everywhere. The whole State community must be part of this system in the future.

Making a comparison with the criminal justice system at the national level, I asked the question whether it would be possible to administer a country if all of a sudden the criminal justice system would not apply in certain municipalities or counties. The self-evident answer is that it would not. In consequence, if we look to the administration of our modern day international globalized society, the conclusion is the same. The international criminal justice system must apply in all States. This will take time. But it must be the goal.

This brings me to the Crimes Against Humanity Initiative. I must confess that I was somewhat dubious at the outset when I was invited to join its Steering Committee. Was it really necessary to elaborate such a convention after the adoption of the Rome Statute and the establishment of the International Criminal Court? On further reflection, I soon came to the conclusion that it is an anomaly that we do not have an elaborate convention on crimes against humanity when other parts of international humanitarian law are codified, notably in the 1948 Convention on the Prevention and Punishment of the Crime of Genocide and in the 1949 Geneva Conventions and their Additional Protocols.

The contribution which the Proposed Convention will make to the observance of the principle of complementarity is of particular importance. It goes without saying that a robust criminal justice system at the national level in all States is an indispensable element in a proper administration of our global society in the future. For this reason it is crucial that national criminal law in this field is as homogenous as possible. In addition, it is important that there are also provisions that assist States when they need to co-operate in bringing perpetrators to justice. The principle of *aut dedere aut judicare* is a necessary element in fulfilling the obligation to bring perpetrators of international crimes to justice.

Needless to say, the focus of the International Criminal Court must be on high-ranking officials, leaving the prosecution of low- and mid-level perpetrators to domestic courts. It is therefore imperative that prosecution at this level can be done effectively and efficiently. This also necessitates an effective inter-State co-operation relating to such prosecutions. A new convention will provide the basis for inter-State co-operation in matters relating to, for example, evidence, extradition, and transfer of proceedings.

A central element in the elaboration of a new convention on crimes against humanity is that it is seen as complementary to the Rome Statute; under no circumstances should it prejudice or be seen to prejudice the work of the International Criminal Court.

Against this background it is a great step forward that the International Law Commission of the United Nations in its meeting in 2014 decided to add the topic of "crimes against humanity" to its active agenda. A contributing factor to this decision may have been a very fruitful and interesting meeting in Geneva in May 2014, in which members of the Commission participated in discussions with members of the Initiative and others. The report from this meeting – 'Fulfilling the Dictates of Public Conscience: Moving Forward with a Convention on Crimes Against Humanity' – provides highly interesting reading.

In the Commission's work, the definition of crimes against humanity will constitute a central component. During the work of the Initiative a great majority of the more than 250 experts consulted supported the need to align any new convention with Article 7 of the Rome Statute. Let me express the hope that the Commission will proceed on the assumption that no changes in Article 7 should be made by a new crimes against humanity convention.

A critical element in the upcoming process is to promote a new convention and to convince States that are doubtful and hesitant that a new convention is the way ahead. The work instigated by the Initiative has generated an opportunity that simply must not be missed.

It is against this background that the present anthology must be warmly welcomed. It will most certainly be an important contribution to the work that now lies ahead and I do look forward to reading the articles when the volume is published.

Hans Corell
Former Legal Counsel of the United Nations

TABLE OF CONTENTS

1

A Crimes Against Humanity Convention After the Establishment of the International Criminal Court

Morten Bergsmo* and SONG Tianying**

1.1. Initiatives to Codify Core International Crimes

The International Criminal Court ('ICC') currently exercises jurisdiction over three categories of core international crimes: genocide, war crimes, and crimes against humanity. The first two were respectively codified by specialized conventions in 1948 and 1949, not long after the World War II. The success of Genocide Convention was closely associated with Raphael Lemkin, who coined the term 'genocide' and relentlessly advocated for a genocide convention.[1] The Geneva Conventions, together with their 1977 Additional Protocol I, codified war crimes by means of "grave breaches".[2] The International Committee of the Red Cross ('ICRC')

---

* **Morten Bergsmo** is Director of the Centre for International Law Research and Policy, and Visiting Professor at Peking University Law School.

** **SONG Tianying**, Legal Officer, Regional Delegation for East Asia of the International Committee of the Red Cross, holds a Master Degree in International Law and a Bachelor Degree in Law from China University of Political Science and Law. She contributed to this chapter in her personal capacity. Views expressed in this chapter do not necessarily reflect those of the ICRC.

[1] William Schabas, "Convention for the Prevention and Punishment of the Crime of Genocide", United Nations Audiovisual Library of International Law, available at http://legal.un.org/avl/ha/cppcg/cppcg.html.

[2] Geneva Convention for the Amelioration of the Condition of the Wounded and Sick in Armed Forces in the Field of 12 August 1949; Geneva Convention for the Amelioration of the Conditions of Wounded, Sick and Shipwrecked Members of Armed Forces at Sea of 12 August 1949; Geneva Convention Relative to the Treatment of Prisoners of War of 12 August 1949; Geneva Convention Relative to the Protection of Civilian Persons in Time of War of 12 August 1949 (respectively Geneva Conventions I–IV); Protocol Additional to the Geneva Conventions of 12 August 1949, and Relating to the Protection of Victims of International Armed Conflicts (Additional Protocol I).

played an indispensable role in the creation and development of the Geneva Conventions.[3]

The long lack of such a treaty for crimes against humanity is conspicuous, but has not gone unnoticed. In 2010, a group of experts convened by the Crimes Against Humanity Initiative concluded the 'Proposed International Convention on the Prevention and Punishment of Crimes Against Humanity' ('Proposed Convention'), reproduced in Annex 1 to this volume.[4] In 2014, with positive involvement of the Crimes Against Humanity Initiative, the topic 'crimes against humanity' entered the International Law Commission's active agenda.[5] This could represent a significant turning point.

During the past 70 years, from Lemkin to the ICRC, to the making of the ICC, and the recent Crimes Against Humanity Initiative, the codification of core international crimes and creation of international criminal jurisdictions have been driven by individuals and institutions with faith and expertise. States are ultimately made up of individuals in their service, who act on their behalf. Their ability and values influence to a considerable extent the contribution States make to the collective development of international criminal law.

Crafting a specialized crimes against humanity ('CAH') convention has two main regulatory aspects: one is to codify the substantive law on crimes against humanity, which, taken together with the other two categories of core crimes operational at the ICC, lays down the normative foundation for the intended protection of victims. The other aspect concerns concrete measures to prevent and punish CAH. This is not specific to crimes against humanity, and may draw on international efforts in dealing with the other core crimes or ordinary crimes. It could go beyond that, and progressively incorporate measures that may enhance the prevention and punishment. There is room for new thinking here.

---

3   ICRC, "The Geneva Conventions of 1949: Origins and Current Significance", available at https://www.icrc.org/eng/resources/documents/statement/geneva-conventions-statement-120809.htm, last accessed on 31 October 2014.

4   Leila Nadya Sadat, "A Comprehensive History of the Proposed International Convention on the Prevention and Punishment of Crimes Against Humanity", in Leila Nadya Sadat (ed.), *Forging a Convention for Crimes Against Humanity*, Cambridge University Press, Cambridge, 2011.

5   See section 2.4. of Chapter 2 below.

1.2. Towards a Distinct and Clarified Definition of Crimes Against Humanity

1.2.1. Internationalising Serious Human Rights Violations: The Unique Role of Crimes Against Humanity

The categories of core international crimes are made up of ordinary criminal acts committed with 'internationalising elements'. These elements vary between the categories. For genocide, for example, there is a special intent to destroy a protected group; for crimes against humanity, a context of attack directed against any civilian population is required; and for war crimes, there must be an association with an armed conflict. Historically, the notion of violations of laws and customs of law – and their prohibition – preceded the concepts of genocide and crimes against humanity. In its early days, crimes against humanity were closely associated with war. The term 'law of humanity' came from the 'Martens Clause' in the 1899 and 1907 Hague Conventions – an important instrument of international humanitarian law ('IHL'). The Martens Clause was restated in the 1949 Geneva Conventions and their 1977 Additional Protocols and remains a crucial IHL principle.[6] The CAH definition in the Nuremberg and Tokyo Charters requires acts committed "before or during the war".[7] The Statute of International Criminal Tribunal for Former Yugoslavia ('ICTY') retains the nexus to armed conflict, "whether international or internal in character". The Statute of International Criminal Tribunal for Rwanda ('ICTR') used a different contextual formulation: "a widespread or systematic attack against any civilian population on national, political, ethnic, racial or religious grounds". The ICTR definition eliminated the link to armed conflict, but imported a discriminatory requirement for all acts. The ICC Statute deleted both the armed-conflict nexus and discriminatory requirement.

---

[6] Geneva Convention I, Article 63; Geneva Convention II, Article 64; Geneva Convention III, Article 142; Geneva Convention IV, Article 158; Additional Protocol I, Article 1(2); Protocol Additional to the Geneva Conventions of 12 August 1949, and Relating to the Protection of Victims of Non-International Armed Conflicts (Additional Protocol II), Preamble.

[7] Charter of the International Military Tribunal ('Nuremberg Charter'), Part of the London Agreement of 8 August 1945, Article 6(c) (http://www.legal-tools.org/doc/64ffdd/); Charter of the International Military Tribunal for the Far East ('Tokyo Charter'), enacted 19 January 1946, Article 5(c) (http://www.legal-tools.org/doc/a3c41c/).

It has been argued that an armed-conflict linkage may render CAH largely redundant, since many acts may constitute CAH and war crimes at the same time.[8] Decades after the Nuremberg and Tokyo trials, CAH has evolved into a standalone category that does not need a nexus or special intent to be prosecuted. Under the ICC Statute, it achieves a contextual element increasingly distinct from war crimes and genocide, namely "a widespread or systematic attack directed against any civilian population". Crimes against humanity have eventually navigated through the complex matrix of core crimes, by accentuating its original rationale to punish serious violations committed by a State against its own nationals and their fundamental rights. Crimes against humanity transcend the traditional internationalising element of inter-State conflict, and recognize serious violations of human rights in and of themselves as being contrary to the value of humanity and thus of international concern.

The separation of crimes against humanity from other core international crimes has direct implications on the protection of victims. As more atrocities are committed within a State's border, not necessarily related to a non-international armed conflict, even less likely to an international one, the unique element in crimes against humanity reveals its value. The mass murder committed by the Khmer Rouge regime in the 1970s is a case in point.[9]

The contextual elements not only create a special area of application as compared to other core international crimes, but have another defining function to distinguish the category from ordinary crimes. The latter function is explored in great detail before the international courts. Interpretation of elements such as "State or organizational policy" and "widespread or systematic" invites sharp questions regarding the very nature and rationale of this crime. This challenge may also reign in domestic contexts, where the crime is applied by legal professionals who are used to dealing with ordinary crimes, and not familiar with the special contextual elements which can confuse even international criminal lawyers. Chapters 3 by Eleni Chaitidou and 4 by Darryl Robinson elucidate the

---

[8]   Darryl Robinson, "Defining 'Crimes Against Humanity' at the Rome Conference", in *American Journal of International Law*, 1999, vol. 93, no. 1.

[9]   Report of the International Law Commission, Sixty-fifth session, (6 May–7 June and 8 July–9 August 2013), General Assembly Official Records, Sixty-eighth session Supplement No. 10 (A/68/10), p. 140.

international and national authorities regarding the connotation of the contextual elements for crimes against humanity.

1.2.2. Enumerated Acts of Crimes Against Humanity

The enumerated acts have evolved through the post-World War II trials, the Statutes of the ICTY and ICTR, the ILC Draft Code of Crimes Against the Peace and Security of Mankind ('ILC Draft Code'), and the ICC Statute. There are two types of enumerated acts under Article 6(c) of the Nuremberg Charter: "murder [. . .] and other inhumane acts" and "persecution on political, racial, or religious grounds in execution of or in connection with any crime within the jurisdiction of the Tribunal". Article 5(3) of the Tokyo Charter followed the Nuremberg definition of crimes against humanity, except that the Tokyo Charter did not include religious persecution. Control Council Law No. 10 added "imprisonment" and "rape" to the list of acts and struck the connection of persecution with other crimes.[10] Although the subsequently adopted Nuremberg Principles followed the Nuremberg Charter formulation,[11] the ICTY and ICTR Statutes included these two acts, together with "torture", and did not require persecution to be linked to other crimes under the tribunals' jurisdiction. The ILC Draft Code added "enforced disappearance of persons" and "institutionalized discrimination", and supplemented "rape" with other forms of sexual violence, on the basis of all the acts included in the *ad hoc* tribunal statutes. It also recognized an "ethnic" ground for persecution. In 1998, the ICC Statute further expanded persecution to include "national", "ethnic", "cultural", "gender" and "other grounds that are universally recognized as impermissible under international law", yet restored the requirement of its link to other acts of crimes against humanity or crimes under the ICC jurisdiction.

In many ways the incremental path of acts of crimes against humanity tracks the reality of human rights violations. Along the path, the U.N. General Assembly declared apartheid a crime against humanity in 1966,[12] the Apartheid Convention was concluded in 1973,[13] and Torture Conven-

---

[10] Control Council Law No. 10, Article 2 (1) (http://www.legal-tools.org/doc/ffda62/).

[11] Principles of International Law Recognized in the Charter of the Nürnberg Tribunal and in the Judgment of the Tribunal, 1950 (http://www.legal-tools.org/doc/5164a6/).

[12] UNGA Res. 2202 A (XXI), 16 December 1966.

[13] International Convention on the Suppression and Punishment of the Crime of Apartheid ('Apartheid Convention'), UNGA Res. 3068 (XXVIII), 30 November 1973.

tion in 1984.[14] The Declaration on the Protection of All Persons from Enforced Disappearance[15] was made in 1992, and the Enforced Disappearance Convention[16] in 2006, after the conclusion of the ICC Statute. There have been discussions whether more acts should be included in the new convention for crimes against humanity. Chapter 9 by Christen Price suggests human trafficking may constitute crimes against humanity when certain conditions are met; for that purpose, Chapter 9 also presents a partial comparative chart of crimes against humanity definitions in various instruments. Chapter 14 by Tessa Bolton suggests to include forced marriage, but not terrorism, and sexual orientation should be an additional ground for persecution.

1.2.3. Interaction with Existing International and National Practice

There has been jurisprudence on crimes against humanity in international and national courts since the post-World War II trials. Drafting an international treaty for crimes against humanity at this time in history is assisted by the existing interpretations and definitions, and at the same time complicated by them. This is different from circumstances surrounding the conclusion of the Genocide Convention and Geneva Conventions.

In pursuing its work on crimes against humanity, the International Law Commission ('ILC') has requested States to provide information, by 31 January 2015, on the criminalisation of and jurisdiction over crimes against humanity under national law, as well as on existing judicial decisions.[17] According to a previous report submitted to the ILC, approximately one-half of United Nations Member States have national laws addressing crimes against humanity.[18] Prosecution and other measures such

---

[14] Convention against Torture and Other Cruel, Inhuman or Degrading Treatment or Punishment ('Torture Convention'), UNGA Res. 39/46, 10 December 1984.

[15] A/RES/47/133, 18 December 1992.

[16] International Convention for the Protection of All Persons from Enforced Disappearance ('Enforced Disappearance Convention'), A/61/448, 20 December 2006.

[17] Report of the International Law Commission, 66th Session (5 May–6 June and 7 July –8 August, 2014), General Assembly Official Records, 69th Session, Supplement No. 10, A/69/10, para. 34.

[18] Report of the International Law Commission, Sixty-fifth session, (6 May–7 June and 8 July–9 August 2013), General Assembly Official Records, Sixty-eighth session Supplement No. 10 (A/68/10), p. 144. See also, M. Cherif Bassiouni, "Crimes Against Humanity: The Case for a Specialized Convention", in *Washington University Global Studies Law Review*, 2010, vol. 9, p. 582.

as immigration control have been carried out in the domestic domain. Concrete examples may be found in Chapters 10 and 11 regarding Canadian and American experiences. At the international level, this crime has been dealt with by the ICC, ICTY, ICTR, the Special Court for Sierra Leone, the Special Panels for Serious Crimes in East Timor, the Extraordinary Chambers in the Courts of Cambodia, and the Nuremberg and Tokyo International Military Tribunals.[19]

A new CAH convention will need to consider existing practice, among which there are discrepancies, and the extent of understanding of the crime varies. Since a specialized CAH convention would aim for national implementation, it may have an impact on those countries that have a different definition of crimes against humanity in their national law. The need to separate crimes against humanity from ordinary crimes is equally pressing in the domestic context. It may have consequences for the scope of jurisdiction, immunity, statutory limitations, and other procedural matters which may be subject to abuse and can cause tension among States.

1.3. Prevention Measures

The Genocide Convention sets out measures for prevention. Under Article I of the Genocide Convention, States Parties "undertake to prevent" genocide. Article VIII provides that "[a]ny Contracting Party may call upon the competent organs of the United Nations to take such action under the Charter of the United Nations as they consider appropriate for the prevention and suppression of acts of genocide or any of the other acts enumerated in article III". Similarly, Article 8(1) of the Proposed Convention obligates each State Party to prevent the commission of crimes against humanity in any territory under its jurisdiction or control. Article 8(13) provides that "States Parties may call upon the competent organs of the United Nations to take such action in accordance with the Charter of the United Nations as they consider appropriate for the prevention and punishment of crimes against humanity".

Not only the text of the Genocide Convention, but subsequent interpretation by the International Court of Justice also carries weight in contemplating an obligation to prevent crimes against humanity in a fu-

---

[19]   Report of the International Law Commission, Sixty-fifth session, (6 May–7 June and 8 July–9 August 2013), General Assembly Official Records, Sixty-eighth session Supplement No. 10 (A/68/10), p. 144.

ture treaty. The case *Application of the Convention on the Prevention and Punishment of the Crime of Genocide (Bosnia and Herzegovina v. Serbia and Montenegro)* [20] is thoroughly explored in association with the Proposed Convention, from different angles, in Chapters 5, 6 and 7. The exact formulation of the scope of the obligation to prevent crimes against humanity will be of critical importance for the support by civil society and other key actors for the Proposed Convention.

Article 8(15) and (16) of the Proposed Convention resemble Article 23 of the Enforced Disappearance Convention in obligating States Parties to develop education and training sessions in order to give effect to the obligation to prevent crimes against humanity. [21]

1.4. Punishment Measures

A specialized CAH convention may consolidate the principles regarding punishment of core international crimes. The Geneva Conventions and its Additional Protocol I prescribe universal jurisdiction and an *aut dedere aut judicare* obligation for "grave breaches". [22] The Genocide Convention does not provide for universal jurisdiction, nor does it limit it. The Torture Convention and Enforced Disappearance Convention also include universal jurisdiction and the *aut dedere aut judicare* principle. [23] Subsequent State practice and international jurisprudence have visited these matters. The new CAH convention presents a good opportunity to entrench the positive developments. Chapter 7 by Julie Pasch discusses this issue in some detail.

Compared to prevention, the punishment of crimes against humanity may reference a wider range of existing conventions. Accumulative experience in punishing crimes through international co-operation may provide rich technical resources. The Proposed Convention explicitly referenced 35 international treaties or instruments, including many on transnational crimes, such as the Convention Against Corruption, U.N. Con-

---

[20] International Court of Justice, *Application of the Convention on the Prevention and Punishment of the Crime of Genocide (Bosnia and Herzegovina v. Serbia and Montenegro)*, Judgment, 26 February 2007.

[21] Proposed Convention, Explanatory Note, Article 8.

[22] Articles 49, 50, 129 and 146 respectively of the Geneva Conventions I–IV, Article 85 of Additional Protocol I.

[23] Enforced Disappearance Convention, Article 9(2); Torture Convention, Articles 5(2) and 7(1).

vention Against Transnational Crimes, Convention for the Suppression of Unlawful Seizure of Aircraft. Some of the instruments are mainly of a procedural nature, such as the European Convention on the Transfer of Sentenced Persons. For example, the Proposed Convention adopts an Annex setting out concrete terms to facilitate extradition, drawing on the Enforced Disappearance Convention and the U.N. Model Treaty on Extradition. Annex 3 on "Mutual Legal Assistance" benefits from the U.N. Convention Against Corruption. Although the scope of the new convention – whether to focus on core provisions or extend to operational details – is uncertain, the existing practice may be illuminating when weighing the possibilities.

1.5. Chapter Contributions

In Chapter 2, Leila N. Sadat, who has been leading the initiative of the Proposed Convention, answers the preliminary question why the international community should finally codify crimes against humanity in an international convention, particularly given its inclusion in the ICC Statute. She observes that the absence of a global treaty on crimes against humanity leads to accountability gaps at international and State levels, a downgrading of crimes against humanity, and overuse of the Genocide Convention as a legal tool. Sadat demonstrates how a specialized treaty may accentuate the primary role of States – including ICC non-States Parties – in comprehensively addressing the crime. She is hopeful that the International Law Commission's recent inclusion of crimes against humanity in its agenda will contribute to the eventual adoption of such a treaty.

Chapters 3 and 4 tackle the contextual elements of crimes against humanity as defined by the ICC Statute, and in turn, by the Proposed Convention. In Chapter 3, Eleni Chaitidou reviews how separate elements and components such as "widespread", "systematic", "organization", "policy", and "attack" have been interpreted and applied in ICC case law. In light of the dynamic interactions among those elements and resulting ambiguities in the current ICC jurisprudence, Chaitidou underlines the essential function of those elements as a whole, to distinguish crimes against humanity from ordinary crimes. Noting that such challenges facing the ICC may be magnified in the application of the Proposed Convention by more diversified practitioners, Chaitidou calls for clear guidance supplementary to the Proposed Convention to ensure legal certainty and transparency.

The call is echoed by Darryl Robinson in Chapter 4, who proposes a commentary on the "policy" element in connection with a new convention. He draws on national and international authorities to show that the policy element is a modest test to screen out ordinary crimes – it is below "systematic", may be implicit, and manifested by action or inaction. Robinson reiterates that an artificially heightened "policy" threshold may lead to tensions with other contextual elements and undermine the applicability of crimes against humanity.

Chapters 5 and 6 explore the prevention aspect of the Proposed Convention. In Chapter 5, María Luisa Piqué examines the State obligation to prevent "in any territory under its jurisdiction or control" as defined by Article 8(1) of the Proposed Convention. Assisted by a wide range of case law from the ICJ, ICTY, and particularly human rights systems, Piqué demonstrates how this territory-centred approach develops the scope of State obligation and at the same time limits it. Emphasising the vital role of extraterritorial obligation in preventing crimes against humanity, Piqué suggests this phrase should encompass persons, facilities and situations under the jurisdiction or control of States, in addition to territory. In Chapter 6, Travis Weber reflects on the obligation to prevent genocide as defined by the Genocide Convention and subsequently interpreted by the ICJ. He finds that similar to the Genocide Convention, States would have an independent obligation to prevent crimes against humanity under the Proposed Convention. Weber also considers whether Article 8(1) hampers effective prevention and argues it should be expanded to allow intervention. Meanwhile, he cautions against casting the net too wide: Article 8(12) inhibiting free speech should be removed or narrowed.

Chapter 7 turns to the punishment aspect of the Proposed Convention. Julie Pasch investigates jurisdiction and attendant State obligations or rights in punishing core international crimes: at the national level, the right to exercise universal jurisdiction over genocide and war crimes other than grave breaches of the Geneva Conventions has taken shape in recent decades; at the international level, the ICC's complementary jurisdiction provides an alternative forum to punish core crimes. She concludes that by including an obligation to exercise universal jurisdiction, the Proposed Convention heralds a progress in punishing crimes against humanity and core international crimes in general.

In Chapter 8, Rhea Brathwaite juxtaposes the definitions of genocide and crimes against humanity and argues the two-tier protection afforded by the prohibition of these two crimes would be strengthened with greater coherence in their protected groups. She accounts for the *ad hoc* tribunals' struggle in applying the current genocide definition, and illustrates national legislations that have readily adopted less stringent approaches than the Genocide Convention. Noting that crimes against humanity has embraced a more inclusive and flexible definition of protected groups in its evolution, the author proposes to expand the protected groups for genocide to include "other grounds universally recognized as permissible under international law".

In Chapter 9, Christen Price looks at human trafficking through the lens of crimes against humanity. The author presents the trend of recognizing human trafficking as modern slavery in human rights jurisprudence and academic writing. Where applicable, human trafficking may also fall under other enumerated acts of crimes against humanity, such as torture and crimes of sexual violence. Price deems it necessary that the contextual elements of crimes against humanity be expanded or interpreted in a way so as to include certain forms of human trafficking that are gross human rights violations committed by private actors, in peacetime, for profit.

In Chapter 10, Rita Maxwell suggests that the Proposed Convention should reinforce the principle of Responsibility to Protect ('R2P') by explicitly referring to it as the basis for State obligation to prosecute. Maxwell considers Canada's experience in exercising universal jurisdiction over core international crimes and advancing R2P, which serves as an example of implementing R2P through effective national prosecutions. She sees the Proposed Convention as an opportunity to move the R2P doctrine from an ideal to a binding legal obligation.

In Chapter 11, Mary Kate Whalen shows the complexities of the domestic prevention and punishment of crimes against humanity in the U.S. context. She revisits the two failed draft Crimes Against Humanity Acts of 2009 and 2010, and discerns controversies over issues such as inclusion of certain underlying crimes, jurisdiction, command responsibility, and immunities. Whalen also outlines existing U.S. law that may criminalize specific acts of crimes against humanity and immigration-related prosecutions as response to crimes against humanity.

In Chapter 12, Ian Kennedy warns that the Proposed Convention may erode the potential of the *aut dedere aut judicare* obligation to become customary international law if States are allowed to only criticize alleged violations instead of taking legal actions. He suggests Article 9 should affirm the custodial State's *prima facie* discretion as to whether to initiate proceedings against the alleged criminal. Meanwhile, Article 9 should explicitly provide that such discretion would be overridden by resolutions of the Security Council or another designated U.N. body supporting a crimes-against-humanity accusation. This solution would alleviate frivolous accusations by other States Parties and induce State legal actions, which may in turn contribute to the crystallization of the obligation to prosecute or extradite crimes against humanity into customary international law.

Chapter 13 looks at the *aut dedere aut judicare* principle from a Chinese perspective. SHANG Weiwei and ZHANG Yueyao offer insight into China's consistent emphasis on the State's discretion to choose between the two options – a seemingly literal interpretation which may in truth be driven by concerns over intervention. At the domestic level, China's existing law is better equipped to extradite crimes against humanity than to prosecute them. Also not to be taken lightly are China's reservations over the definition of the crime and the 'third alternative' to transfer to international judicial organs. In the course of implementing this principle, the authors consider the categorical removal of immunity in the Proposed Convention would be against China's law and policy.

In the final Chapter, Tessa Bolton critiques some controversial issues in the Proposed Convention. The author is concerned with the biology-based gender definition which eludes cultural and social variations. She also argues that forced marriage as an underlying act and sexual orientation as a ground of persecution should be explicitly included in the crimes against humanity definition – the 'constructive ambiguity' in this instance is not desirable. Reflecting on the problematic practice regarding similar human rights provisions, Bolton suggests to further clarify Article 8(12) on hate speech so as to enhance national implementation and prevent potential overreach. She also questions whether the removal of immunity *ratione personae* before national courts is a leap too far, too soon. She credits the restrained manner in which the Proposed Convention deals with terrorism and responsibility to protect, and applauds the symbolic significance of adopting universal jurisdiction obligations.

1.6. Concluding Remarks

As a specialized crimes against humanity convention assumes the primary goal of facilitating national criminal justice for core international crimes, it also faces the primary challenge of *Realpolitik* in the domestic context. It is noticed that to date only a few national prosecutions of such crimes have been carried out.[24] The inherent element of State or organizational policy in crimes against humanity compels State actors to open themselves to potential responsibility, if not when they are in power, then after they step down. In some cases, this will be a challenge. The codification process, however, not only contributes to the normative architecture of international criminal law, but, more importantly, affirms the common value of prohibition of the most serious violations against individuals and their fundamental rights. The category of crimes against humanity takes the side of vulnerable individual victims when State or organizational power comes down on them in ways so extreme that it affronts our very sense of humanity or humanness. The codification project accumulates the collective conviction that there is no backtrack *vis-à-vis* this minimum standard, that it can no longer be reversed or refuted by individual State actors.

Against this background, the project to develop a crimes against humanity convention has the capacity to mobilise broad interest and involvement around the world: to become the new 'generational' project to develop international law to protect the individual. It could give civil society renewed life at a time when the ICC has become established and more autonomous of their rallying support. The project may be perceived as a new frontline in the struggle to keep the legacy of the Nuremberg and Tokyo trials alive and healthy. As Chapter 2 elaborates, the international law category of crimes against humanity was born in response to the Nazi-State's treatment of German Jews, its own citizens. By including the category in the subject-matter jurisdiction of the Nuremberg Charter,[25] the International Military Tribunal was enabled to prosecute this victimisation as well – not only that of foreign citizens – by that bringing the outcome of the trial and the principles applied closer to the German people. Late Judge Hans-Peter Kaul – to whom this volume is dedicated – reminds us

---

[24] M. Cherif Bassiouni, "Perspectives on International Criminal Justice", in *Virginia Journal of International Law*, 2010, vol. 50, p. 305.

[25] It was also included in the Tokyo Charter, see *supra* note 7.

in his Preface that today's international legal order was "established after millions of Jews, Russians, Chinese and others were killed during World War II". Seen from this perspective, Israelis, Russians and Chinese have a greater stake in international criminal law, crimes against humanity included, than other nations.[26] The terrible sacrifices made by their relatives during World War II gave birth to the Nuremberg and Tokyo trials, to the later codification and construction of international criminal jurisdictions, and now to the process of developing a crimes against humanity convention. This begs the question of how the Proposed Convention will be received by Israel, China and Russia.

Contemporary Germany has proved to be the strongest defender of the integrity of international criminal law during the process to create the legal infrastructure of the ICC and to establish a proper Court on that basis. But, although the ICC has 122 States Parties at the time of writing, more than half of humankind stands outside, with States such as China, India, Indonesia and Russia not having accepted to be members of the Court. In the current international climate, such polarisation could be used to divide the world over international criminal law, especially on issues linked to the ICC, universal jurisdiction, State immunity and aggression. This should be a source of concern. It was in part the fundamental principles of international criminal law that united nations against the authors of World War II and its horrendous atrocities. Indeed, these principles were inherent in the rationale for the creation of the United Nations Organisation and its mandate to further develop and codify international law. This legacy can not be taken lightly.

It is in recognition of the dangers of this emerging polarisation that some have called for a consolidation of the field of international criminal law, rather "than further development at the risk of over-extension".[27] Would a process to develop a crimes against humanity convention run contrary to this call? Such a process will, by definition, entail a further construction of the normative room of international criminal law, by add-

---

[26] See LIU Yiqiang, "Exploring Peace Through Justice Should Be An Essential Element of China's Anti-Fascist War Memorialisation", Torkel Opsahl Academic EPublisher, Brussels, 2014, ISBN 978-82-93081-34-0 (https://www.legal-tools.org/en/doc/f059de/).

[27] See Morten Bergsmo and LING Yan, "On State Sovereignty and Individual Criminal Responsibility for Core International Crimes in International Law", in Morten Bergsmo and LING Yan: *State Sovereignty and International Criminal Law*, Torkel Opsahl Academic EPublisher, Beijing, 2012, ISBN 978-82-93081-35-7, p. 11 (http://www.legal-tools.org/doc/82ec96/).

ing another treaty to the discipline. On the other hand, it will not necessarily represent an expansion of the room, through new principles or their extension. And the emphasis is likely to be on the facilitation of exercise of national criminal jurisdiction over crimes against humanity.

But perceptions and the political dynamics may take a different direction. The convention project may be seen or presented as the opening of another front in the onward march of well-intentioned international lawyers, civil society activists, and some governments that link a part of their self-representation to international standard-setting. This risk should be carefully considered by those who seek to exercise leadership in the convention project. It is not sufficient that they create the impression that they are concerned with universal support for the convention. They should genuinely engage the reservations, views and proposals of States such as China, India, Indonesia, Israel and Russia, not restricted to their members in the International Law Commission or representatives in the United Nations General Assembly. Some may find that it is not easy for them to do that.

The champions of the crimes against humanity convention project will face additional risks. In the current international climate, we may see efforts to water down standards when issues are opened for the formulation of consensus. We witnessed this tendency during the negotiation of the ICC Statute itself, for example on Article 33 on superior orders or Article 7(2)(a) on the contextual requirements of crimes against humanity. Chapter 4 of this volume is a conscientious and able analysis of how to remedy negative consequences of constructive ambiguity in Article 7 of the ICC Statute. It is particularly the scope of the obligation to prevent crimes against humanity – currently expressed in Article 8(1) of the Proposed Convention – which may come under pressure in ways that will lead to results below that of the Genocide Convention as interpreted by the ICJ. This risk is discussed in detail in Chapter 5 below.

The burden on those actors who lead the process is, in other words, considerable. There is a downside to the moral and professional satisfaction which the process generates. However, the burden to prove that a new convention would add sufficient value – whether we need a crimes against humanity convention after the establishment of the ICC – does not ultimately rest on these individual actors. This question will remain open until the number of States Parties of a future convention is sufficient for it to enter into force. The community of States is the jury, and those States who will take it upon themselves to drive the process forward will have to shoulder the burden of persuasion.

The Proposed Convention while seeking to consolidate the aspiration to deal with core international crimes, also reflects a science in doing so. It shows the initiative and strength of civil society in responding to the most serious crimes of international concern. In the continuation, the initiative will have to be truly "[c]onscious that *all peoples* are united by common bonds",[28] so that a crimes against humanity convention will reinforce the "delicate mosaic"[29] of global unity, rather than contribute to the polarisation of the international society.

---

[28] See ICC Statute, first preambular paragraph (emphasis added).
[29] *Ibid.*

2

Codifying the 'Laws of Humanity' and the 'Dictates of the Public Conscience': Towards a New Global Treaty on Crimes Against Humanity

Leila Nadya Sadat*

On 17 July 2014, an historic, but little-noticed, event occurred: The United Nations International Law Commission voted to move the topic of a new treaty on crimes against humanity to its active agenda and appoint a Special Rapporteur.[1] The expectation is that the Rapporteur will prepare, and the Commission will debate, a complete set of Draft Articles which will be sent to the United Nations General Assembly in due course. This could lead to the adoption of a new global treaty on crimes against humanity, filling a normative gap that has persisted for nearly seventy years.

This chapter asks why – and whether – the international community should finally codify crimes against humanity in an international convention, particularly given its recent inclusion in the Statute of the International Criminal Court. It considers the normative foundations and practical application of crimes against humanity by international and national courts, and how a new treaty might strengthen both the preventive and punishment dimensions of national and international responses to these

---

* **Leila Nadya Sadat** is Henry H. Oberschelp Professor, Israel Treiman Faculty Fellow and Director of the Whitney R. Harris World Law Institute at Washington University School of Law. Sadat is the Special Adviser to the ICC Prosecutor on Crimes Against Humanity and Director of the Crimes Against Humanity Initiative, a multi-year project aiming at the elaborating and adoption of a new global treaty on crimes against humanity. The author thanks Madaline George, Ashley Hammet and Douglas Pivnichny for their superb assistance. Nothing in this chapter represents or should be construed as representing the views of the ICC Prosecutor or any organ of the Court. All Internet references were last accessed on 24 September 2014.

[1] Daily Bulletin, International Law Commission, 18 July 2014, 66th session, 3227th meeting, summary record, available at http://legal.un.org/ilc/sessions/66/jourchr.htm. The Rapporteur's charge is to prepare a First Report on the subject, which will begin the process of proposing Draft Articles to the Commission for its approval. The First Report would normally be circulated within the Commission and discussed at its next session in summer 2015.

crimes. Finally, given the recent challenge to the legitimacy of the International Criminal Court by States resisting its jurisdiction as well as the more existential challenge posed by sceptics of international justice writ large regarding its ultimate utility, it offers a modest defence of what one might call 'the international criminal justice project' on legal and moral grounds.

2.1. Crimes Against Humanity and Customary International Law

Crimes against humanity have been described as "politics gone cancerous",[2] or as *crimes contre l'esprit* ('crimes against the spirit')[3] that "shock the conscience of humankind". The concept emerged as a response to inhumane acts that transgressed the bounds of 'civilized' behaviour, even when committed by a government or Head of State, and particularly if carried out on a massive scale. Over time, they have become a residual category, addressing atrocities that cannot be categorized either as war crimes (because they address evils not within the purview of the laws of war or because they take place outside of armed conflict) or as genocide within the meaning of the Genocide Convention of 1948, because they do not represent the intentional destruction of one of the four groups (racial, religious, national or ethnic) it protects. They are controversial because they not only describe as *immoral* certain acts of government (and, later, non-State actors) but label them *criminal* – depriving the officials and other perpetrators accused of such crimes of defences they might wield as a function of State sovereignty. Moreover, released from their original moorings through the development of customary international law and their codification in the Rome Statute for the International Criminal Court, they have now come to represent attacks carried out not only during inter-State conflict, but in intra-State armed conflict, or even peace time, and attacks by State and non-State actors.[4]

---

2   David Luban, "A Theory of Crimes Against Humanity", in *Yale Journal of International Law*, 2004, vol. 29, p. 90.

3   M. François de Menthon, Chief Prosecutor for the French Republic, Opening Statement to the International Military Tribunal at Nuremberg, January 17, 1946, reprinted in *The Trial of German Major War Criminals by the International Military Tribunal Sitting at Nuremberg, Germany: Opening Speeches of the Chief Prosecutors* (William S. Hein & Co., Inc., Buffalo, NY: 2001).

4   Rome Statute of the International Criminal Court, Article 7(2)(a), UN Doc. A/CONF. 183/9, adopted on 17 July 1998, entered into force on 1 July 2002, in UNTS, vol. 2187, p. 90 ('ICC Statute'). Some of the early writings on crimes against humanity insisted that

The evolution from moral condemnation to positive law took nearly a century. The term 'crimes against humanity' or offenses against the 'laws of humanity' emerged in the nineteenth century to describe the evils of slavery and the slave trade.[5] Subsequently, the 'Martens Clause' in the preamble of the 1907 Hague Convention Respecting the Laws and Customs of War on Land referenced the "laws of humanity, and [...] the dictates of the public conscience"[6] as protections available under the law of nations to human beings caught in the ravages of war. The declaration of France, Great Britain and Russia of 28 May 1915 described the massacre of the Armenians in Turkey as "crimes against humanity and civilization",[7] and the United Nations Report on the Commission on the Responsibilities of the Authors of War and on Enforcement of Penalties in 1919 used the term as well.[8] In this way, it emerged as a term of art, but was not yet a legal rule capable of international (or national) enforcement. The provision in the Martens Clause was too uncertain to provide a clear basis for either State responsibility or criminal liability,[9] and it is perhaps un-

---

they were autonomous from war crimes and crimes against peace. See, *e.g.*, Eugene Aroneanu, *Le Crime Contre l'Humanité*, Dalloz, 1961, pp. 20–21.

5   Leila Nadya Sadat, "Crimes Against Humanity in the Modern Age", in *American Journal of International Law*, 2013, vol. 107, p. 337, footnote16 and sources cited. See also Sandra Szurek, "Historique: La Formation du Droit International Pénal", in Hervé Ascensio, Emmanuel Decaux and Alain Pellet (eds.), *Droit International Pénal*, Pedone, 2012, pp. 21–23.

6   Convention (IV) Respecting the Laws and Customs of War by Land, Annex, Preamble, opened for signature 18 October 1907, UKTS 9, entered into force on 26 January 1910.

7   The original language proposed was "crimes against Christianity and civilization". The term 'Christianity' was deleted at the behest of the French delegation who deemed it potentially offensive to Muslims. See Arthur Beylerian (ed.), *Les Grandes Puissances, l'Empire Ottoman et les Arméniens dans les Archives Françaises (1914–1918)*, Panthéon Sorbonne, 1983, pp. 23–29.

8   The Commission was established at the plenary session of the Preliminary Peace Conference in 1919. See, U.N. Secretary General, Historical Survey of the Question of International Criminal Jurisdiction, p. 7, U.N. Doc. A/CN.4/7/Rev.1, U.N. Sales No. V.8 (1949) ('Historical Survey'). The report can be found at "Commission on the Responsibility of Authors of the War and on Enforcement of Penalties: Report Presented to the Preliminary Peace Conference", in *American Journal of International Law*, 1920, vol. 14, p. 95; see also M. Cherif Bassiouni, *Crimes Against Humanity: Historical Evolution and Contemporary Application*, Cambridge University Press, 2011, pp. xxviii–xxix.

9   See, *e.g.*, Leila Sadat, "The Interpretation of the Nuremberg Principles by the French Court of Cassation: From Touvier to Barbie and Back Again", in *Columbia Journal of Transnational Law*, 1994, vol. 32, p. 296 (formerly Wexler).

surprising that efforts to prosecute 'crimes against humanity' following the First World War were unsuccessful.

The history of the failed efforts to conduct war crimes trials after World War I need not be recounted in detail here. The Treaty of Versailles provided for the establishment of a special tribunal to try William II of Hohenzollern, the German emperor. Two members of the Commission – Robert Lansing and James Scott Brown – both prominent members of the American Society of International Law[10] – dissented, arguing that any such trials would violate the principle of sovereignty, particularly as there was no international treaty establishing either the nature of the crime or a court with jurisdiction over it.[11] Although it was perhaps an American preoccupation at the outset, this insistence upon a *treaty* – as opposed to customary international law – as the basis for international criminal jurisdiction has persisted, differentiating, to some extent, international *criminal* law from other branches of international law in which reliance upon custom seems more natural and accepted by States. And indeed, no trial of the Kaiser took place as even States ostensibly supporting his trial, such as the Netherlands, refused his extradition, offering him refuge instead.[12]

It was not until World War II that a more serious effort to set out the specific parameters of 'crimes against humanity' in an international agreement occurred. 'Crimes against humanity' were specifically included in the Charters of the International Military Tribunals at Nuremberg[13] and Tokyo[14] after a great deal of negotiation which focused much more on the aggressive war and war crimes charges. In early drafts what became crimes against humanity were referred to as "atrocities and persecutions and deportations on political, racial or religious grounds".[15] It was not un-

---

[10] Frederic L. Kirgis, *The American Society of International Law's First Century: 1906–2006*, Brill, 2006, p. 76.

[11] Historical Survey, p. 58, see *supra* note 8.

[12] Leila Sadat, "The Proposed Permanent International Criminal Court: An Appraisal", in *Cornell International Law Journal*, 1996, vol. 29, pp. 669–670.

[13] Agreement for the Prosecution and Punishment of Major War Criminals of the European Axis, and Establishing the Charter of the International Military Tribunal ('IMT'), 8 August 1945, in UNTS, vol. 82, p. 279 ('IMT Charter').

[14] Charter of the International Military Tribunal for the Far East, 19 January 1946, amended 26 April 1946, T.I.A.S. No. 1589 ('IMFTE Charter').

[15] "Revised Draft of Agreement and Memorandum Submitted by American Delegation, 30 June 1945", in *Report of Robert H. Jackson, U.S. Representative to the International Con-*

til 31 July 1945 (the London conference convened on 26 June, and the Charter was signed on 8 August 1945) that the term 'crimes against humanity' appeared in the draft. A note by Robert Jackson indicated that the intention was to make sure that "we are reaching persecution, etc., of Jews and others in Germany as well as outside of it, and before as well as after commencement of the war".[16] Apparently Sir Hersch Lauterpacht proposed the addition to the text at a meeting with Jackson during which he put forward the idea of presenting the case against the accused under the three principal headings we know today: crimes against peace, war crimes and crimes against humanity.[17] This ensured the entry of the term 'crimes against humanity' into the international legal lexicon, and perhaps obscured the fact that this was in many ways the most revolutionary of the charges upon which the accused were indicted and convicted, given that its foundations in international law were so fragile.[18]

The proceedings at Nuremberg did not themselves focus greatly on crimes against humanity; the Tokyo trials even less so. Article 6(c) of the London Charter defined them as:

> namely, murder, extermination, enslavement, deportation, and other inhumane acts committed against any civilian population, before or during the war, or persecutions on political, racial or religious grounds in execution of or in connection with any crime within the jurisdiction of the Tribunal whether or not in violation of the domestic law of the country where perpetrated.[19]

---

ference on Military Trials, London 1945, U.S. Department of State, Publication 3080, 1949, p. 121.

[16] "Notes on Proposed Definition of 'Crimes', Submitted by American Delegation, 31 July 1945", in *Report of Robert H. Jackson, U.S. Representative to the International Conference on Military Trials, London 1945*, U.S. Department of State, Publication 3080, 1949, p. 394.

[17] Elihu Lauterparcht, *The Life of Sir Hersch Lauterpacht*, Cambridge University Press, 2010, p. 272; See also Philippe Sands, "My legal hero: Hersch Lauterpacht", The Guardian, 10 November 2010; Martti Koskenniemi, "Hersch Lauterpacht and the Development of International Criminal Law", in *Journal of International Criminal Justice*, 2004, vol. 2, p. 811; Philippe Sands QC, "Twin Peaks: The Hersch Lauterpacht Draft Nuremberg Speeches", in *Cambridge Journal of International and Comparative Law*, 2013, vol. 1, p. 37.

[18] The other was the crime of waging an aggressive war.

[19] IMT Charter, Article 6(c), see *supra* note 13. The definition in the IMFTE was similar, but removed the reference to persecution on "religious grounds". IMFTE Charter, Article 5(c), see *supra* note 14.

Although the indictment charged 20 of the 22 defendants ultimately tried at Nuremberg with crimes against humanity, it was not very specific as to what crimes the accused had committed which fell within that rubric. The prosecution's theory was essentially that the accused, by debasing the "sanctity of man in their own countries [...] affront[ed] the International Law of mankind",[20] and in all but two cases in which crimes against humanity were charged, these charges were brought in parallel with war crimes charges and often charges of crimes against peace. The judgment of the Tribunal was similarly non-specific, acknowledging that crimes against humanity were somehow different than war crimes, but providing little interpretative guidance as to their elements. The preoccupation of the Tribunal as regards the charges was evidently the final solution and Hitler's attempted extermination of European Jews. The two accused, Julius Streicher and Baldur von Schirach, who were found guilty only of crimes against humanity, were convicted, respectively, of "incitement to murder and extermination", on the basis of virulently anti-Jewish propaganda (Streicher) and of deporting Jews from Vienna (von Schirach).[21]

Following the trials, the Nuremberg Principles embodied in the IMT Charter and Judgment were adopted by the General Assembly in 1946,[22] and codified by the International Law Commission in 1950, which largely retained the Nuremberg definition of the crime.[23] In this way, 'crimes against humanity' were transformed from rhetorical flourish to a category of offences condemned by international law for which individuals could be tried and punished. During the same period, the Geneva Conventions of 1949 on the laws of war were adopted;[24] and the Genocide

---

[20] Egon Schwelb, "Crimes Against Humanity", in *British Yearbook of International Law*, 1946, vol. 23, pp. 198–199 (quoting the British Chief Prosecutor, Sir Hartley Shawcross, in his closing speech delivered on 26–27 July 1946).

[21] "Judgment of 1 October 1946, International Military Tribunal Judgment and Sentence", in *American Journal of International Law*, 1947, vol. 41, pp. 296, 310–311 ('IMT Judgment').

[22] "Affirmation of the Principles of International Law Recognized by the Charter of the Nuremberg Tribunal: Report of the Sixth Committee", U.N. GAOR, 1st Session, Part 2, 55th plenary meeting, p. 1144, U.N. Doc. A/236 (1946) (also appears as G.A. Res. 95 (I), p. 188, U.N. Doc. A/64/Add.1, 1946).

[23] "Documents of the Second Session Including the Report of the Commission to the General Assembly", in *Yearbook of International Law Commission*, 1950, vol. 2, p. 374, U.N. Doc. A/CN.4.SER.A/1950/Add.I.

[24] Geneva Convention for the Amelioration of the Condition of the Wounded and Sick in Armed Forces in the Field, 12 August 1949, in UNTS, vol. 75, p. 31 ('First Geneva Con-

Convention, covering a certain narrow category of crimes against humanity, was adopted in 1948 and entered into force in 1951.[25] No comprehensive treaty on crimes against humanity was ever proposed or negotiated, however, and customary international law often continued to link it to the commission of crimes against peace or war crimes. This requirement was not definitively removed until 1998, when the Rome Statute for the International Criminal Court finally abolished the linkage and acknowledged its autonomous nature.

Crimes against humanity under customary international law percolated into the legal systems of a handful of countries that had domesticated the crime, such as Canada, France, and Israel, and certain elements of their prohibition could be found in new international instruments prohibiting torture and apartheid.[26] Israel prosecuted Adolph Eichmann, for example,[27] and France conducted a series of trials relying essentially upon Article 6(c) of the Nuremberg Charter, convicting not only Klaus Barbie, the infamous 'Butcher of Lyon', but two French participants in the Vichy regime.[28] But these cases were the exception, not the rule, and all involved a link to World War II. Latin American jurisprudence on crimes against humanity has only more recently begun to truly develop, notably in Peru, Argentina and most recently Ecuador, following decades of

---

vention'); Geneva Convention for the Amelioration of the Shipwrecked Members of Armed Forces at Sea, 12 August 1949, in UNTS, vol. 75, p. 85 ('Second Geneva Convention'); Geneva Convention Relative to the Treatment of Prisoners of War, 12 August 1949, in UNTS, vol. 75, p. 135 ('Third Geneva Convention'); Geneva Convention Relative to the Protection of Civilian Persons in Times of War, 12 August 1949, in UNTS, vol. 75, p. 287 ('Fourth Geneva Convention').

[25] Convention on the Prevention and Punishment of the Crime of Genocide, adopted on 9 December 1948, entered into force on 12 January 1951, in UNTS, vol. 78, p. 277 ('Genocide Convention').

[26] See International Convention on the Suppression and Punishment of the Crime of Apartheid, adopted on 30 November 1973, entered into force on 18 July 1976, in UNTS, vol. 1015, p. 243; Convention against Torture and Other Cruel, Inhuman or Degrading Treatment or Punishment, adopted on 10 December 1984, entered into force on 26 June 1987, in UNTS, vol. 1465, p. 85; Organization of American States, Inter-American Convention to Prevent and Punish Torture, adopted on 9 December 1985, entered into force on 28 February 1987, OASTS 67; Council of Europe, European Convention for the Prevention of Torture and Inhuman or Degrading Treatment or Punishment, adopted on 26 November 1987, entered into force on 1 February 1989, ETS 126.

[27] *Attorney General of Israel v. Eichmann*, 36 ILR 5 (District Court of Jerusalem, 1961), *aff.* 36 ILR 277 (Israel Supreme Court, 1962).

[28] See, *e.g.*, Sadat, 1994, *supra* note 9.

sweeping amnesty laws, and a lack of political will or domestic codification under which to prosecute these crimes.[29] Scholarly articles sporadi-
cally appeared as well.[30] But even though the commission of mass atrocities continued apace during the second half of the 20th century,[31] there
was little accountability imposed upon those ostensibly responsible,
whether government officials or military leaders, rebels, insurgents or
low-level perpetrators,[32] and there was no talk of a new convention on
crimes against humanity, although the International Law Commission

---

[29] Jo-Marie Burt, "Challenging Impunity in Domestic Courts: Human Rights Prosecutions in Latin America", in Félix Reátegui (ed.), *Transitional Justice: Handbook for Latin America*, Brasilia: Brazilian Amnesty Commission, Ministry of Justice and International Center for Transitional Justice, 2011, p. 285. Many human rights violations in Latin America are charged as something other than 'crimes against humanity', however reference and discussion of such has found its way into various judgments, including that of former Peruvian president Alberto Fujimori. Jo-Marie Burt, "Guilty as Charged: The Trial of former Peruvian President Alberto Fujimori for Grave Violations of Human Rights", in *International Journal of Transnational Justice*, 2009, vol. 3, pp. 398–399. Moreover, Argentina has successfully prosecuted former generals for crimes against humanity committed in the 1970's and 1980's, while Ecuador is currently proceeding with its first crimes against humanity trial. For a comprehensive analysis of the codification of crimes against humanity in Latin American states, see Ramiro García Falconí, "The Codification of Crimes Against Humanity in the Domestic Legislation of Latin American States", in *International Criminal Law Review*, 2010, vol. 10, p. 453.

[30] See, *e.g.*, M. Cherif Bassiouni, "'Crimes Against Humanity': The Need for a Specialized Convention", in *Columbia Journal of Transnational Law*, 1994, vol. 31, p. 457; Schwelb, 1946, see *supra* note 20.

[31] A recent study suggested that between 1945 and 2008, between 92 and 101 million persons were killed in 313 different conflicts, the majority of whom were civilians. In addition to those killed directly in these events, others died as a consequence, or had their lives shattered in other ways – through the loss of property, victimization by sexual violence, disappearances, slavery and slavery-related practices, deportations and forced displacements and torture. M. Cherif Bassiouni, "Assessing Conflict Outcomes: Accountability and Impunity", in M. Cherif Bassiouni (ed.), *The Pursuit of International Criminal Justice: A World Study on Conflicts, Victimization, and Post-Conflict Justice*, Intersentia, 2010, p. 6.

[32] In 1989, the Cold War ended with the fall of the Berlin Wall and this began to change. The International Criminal Court project, which had lain fallow, was restarted with the introduction of a resolution into the General Assembly by Trinidad and Tobago, leading a coalition of 16 Caribbean nations, and the continuation of work on the Draft Code of Crimes at the International Law Commission. See "Report of the Commission to the General Assembly on the work of its Forty-Eighth Session", in *Yearbook of International Law Commission*, 1996, vol. 2, pp. 15–42, U.N. Doc. A/CN.4/SER.A/1996/Add.1; see also Leila Nadya Sadat, *The International Criminal Court and the Transformation of International Law: Justice for the New Millennium*, Martinus Nijhoff, 2002.

---

continued to work on defining the crime under customary international law.[33]

2.2. What Difference Could a Treaty Make?

The absence of a comprehensive treaty on crimes against humanity, of course, did not mean that international law did not prohibit their commission. It is well known that the Statute of the International Court of Justice identifies the sources of international law as including not only "international conventions", but "international custom, as evidence of a general practice accepted as law", and "general principles of law recognized by civilized nations".[34] While treaties are listed first, in Article 38(1)(a), followed by custom (paragraph (b)), and then general principles (paragraph (c)), it has been generally understood that the order in which the sources of law are listed in Article 38 does not establish a strict hierarchy amongst them, but instead are listed in the order in which a judge would typically consult them in addressing a particular legal question.[35] Thus, to the extent crimes against humanity remained part of customary international law but was not codified in an international convention (other than the 1945 Nuremberg Charter), it could still presumably be the basis for future prosecutions or State responsibility. At the same time, the absence of a clear definition, and the crime's continued linkage to other offenses (crimes against peace and war crimes), made it a clumsy rubric at best, and incomplete and ineffective at worst. Moreover, under the legality principle, which requires crimes to be defined prior to prosecution, and also requires them to be defined to a certain level of particularity, it is not clear that prosecuting an individual for violating customary international law – without a clear Statute defining it – is consistent with modern understandings of human rights law. Indeed, when the International Law Commission considered *not* defining the crimes in the ICC Statute, but simply list-

---

[33] The ILC took up the question of crimes against humanity as part of its work on the Draft Code of Crimes Against the Peace and Security of Mankind, which was finalized in 1996, but never adopted. See "Report of the International Law Commission on the Work of its Forth-Eighth Session", in *Yearbook of International Law Commission*, 1996, vol. 2, pp. 17, 45, UN Doc. A/CN/.4/SER.A/1996/Add.1 (Part 2).

[34] Statute of the International Court of Justice, 26 June 1946, Article 38 (1), in UNTS, vol. 33, p. 993.

[35] See, *e.g.*, Ian Brownlie, *Principles of Public International Law*, Oxford University Press, 2008, p. 5.

ing them, the nearly unanimous response of commentators was that this would violate the legality principle.[36]

Thus, while customary international law remains important to international criminal law, the norm of this sub-specialty has been to adopt treaties defining crimes and imposing obligations upon States to enact penal legislation, to prevent the crimes (in some cases), to extradite or try the offenders, and to co-operate with each other in the apprehension, trial and even incarceration of the accused. There are now more than 318 international criminal law conventions, covering twenty-four general categories of international crime including terrorism, drug trafficking, hostage taking, aircraft hijacking, environmental crimes, non-applicability of statutes of limitations, apartheid, genocide, torture, unlawful use of weapons, aggression, piracy, bribery, environmental protection, corruption, destruction of cultural property and theft of nuclear materials, each one of which contains some combination of definitional provisions, provisions for interstate co-operation and other provisions related to the enforcement of the treaty itself.[37]

A few examples may be useful to illustrate the difficulties engendered by the absence of a treaty covering crimes against humanity. In the 1990s, when war broke out in the former Yugoslavia, and the Rwandan genocide took place, the international community reached for the Nuremberg precedent only to find that it had failed to finish it. This made the task of elaborating statutes for the two new *ad hoc* Tribunals difficult and complex. The uncertainty in the law was evidenced by the texts of the Statutes for the International Criminal Tribunals for the former Yugoslavia ('ICTY') and Rwanda ('ICTR') adopted by the Security Council in 1993 and 1994, respectively, which although similar in many respects, contained different and arguably contradictory definitions of crimes against humanity. The ICTY Statute, for example, included a link to

---

[36] The International Law Commission took the position that the draft statute was primary an "adjectival and procedural instrument", and therefore did not define the crimes. 1994 Draft Statute for the International Criminal Court, Report of the International Law Commission, U.N. GAOR, 49th Session, Supplement No. 10, U.N. Doc. A/49/10 (1994). This position was criticized by most experts, and ultimately the Preparatory Committee for the Court and later the Diplomatic Conference assumed the task of setting out complete definitions of the three crimes currently in the Court's jurisdiction. See, *e.g.*, Sadat, 1996, p. 667, see *supra* note 12.

[37] Jordan J. Paust, M. Cherif Bassiouni, *et al.*, *International Criminal Law: Cases and Materials*, Carolina Academic Press, 2013, pp. 17–18.

armed conflict whereas the ICTR Statute did not. Conversely, the ICTR Statute required a persecutory or discriminatory element in its chapeau, which the ICTY Statute did not. These substantive and potentially important variations in the definition of the crime were difficult to square with the idea of universal international crimes under customary international law.[38] M. Cherif Bassiouni underscored this problem in an important but little-noticed article, in which he lamented the "existence of a significant gap in the international normative proscriptive scheme, one which is regrettably met by political decision makers with shocking complacency".[39]

At the international level, then, the absence of a clear definition led to some difficulties in the elaboration of the Statutes for the *ad hoc* international criminal tribunals.[40] Equally problematic was the inability to use national or hybrid mechanisms to pursue accountability under universal jurisdiction. A case in point is the Cambodian 'genocide'.[41] From 1975 to 1979, the Khmer Rouge regime killed an estimated 1.7 to 2.5 million Cambodians, out of a total population of seven million.[42] For the most part, individuals were killed, tortured, starved or worked to death by the Khmer Rouge not because of their appurtenance to a particular racial, eth-

---

[38] See, *e.g.*, ICTY Statute; ICTR Statute. The IMT Statutes for Tokyo, see *supra* note 12, and Control Council Law No. 10, Punishment of Persons Guilty of War Crimes, Crimes against Peace and Humanity, 20 December 1945, Official Gazette of the Control Council for Germany, No. 3, 31 January 1946, also differed slightly from the Nuremberg definition.

[39] Bassiouni, 1994, p. 457, see *supra* note 30.

[40] The Statute of the Special Court for Sierra Leone is not identical to either the ICTY, the ICTR or the ICC Statute, although it was adopted in 2002. See, Statute of the Special Court for Sierra Leone, U.N.-Sierra Leone, 16 January 2002, Article 2, in UNTS, vol. 2178, p. 149, which provides that the Court

> shall have the power to prosecute persons who committed the following crimes as part of a widespread or systematic attack against any civilian population: a. Murder; b. Extermination; c. Enslavement; d. Deportation; e. Imprisonment; f. Torture; g. Rape, sexual slavery, enforced prostitution, forced pregnancy and any other form of sexual violence; h. Persecution on political, racial, ethnic or religious grounds; i. Other inhumane acts.

[41] Gareth Evans, "Crimes Against Humanity and the Responsibility to Protect", in Leila Nadya Sadat (ed.), *Forging a Convention for Crimes Against Humanity*, Cambridge University Press, 2011 (*'Forging a Convention'*).

[42] *Cf.*, Craig Etcheson, *After the Killing Fields: Lessons from the Cambodian Genocide*, Praeger, 2005, pp. 118–120.

nic, religious or national group – the four categories to which the Genocide Convention applies – but because of their political or social classes, or the fact that they could be identified as intellectuals.[43] While theories have been advanced suggesting ways that the Genocide Convention applied to these atrocities[44] and the Co-Prosecutors in Case 2/2 at the Extraordinary Chambers in the Courts of Cambodia ('ECCC') have argued that some groups were exterminated *qua* groups – such as the Cham Muslims and the Vietnamese[45] – most experts agree that:

> [F]or all its compelling general moral authority the Genocide Convention had absolutely no legal application to the killing fields of Cambodia, which nearly everyone still thinks of as the worst genocide of modern times. Because those doing the killing and beating and expelling were of exactly the same nationality, ethnicity, race and religion as those they were victimizing – and their motives were political, ideological and class-based [...] the necessary elements of specific intent required for its application were simply not there.[46]

This raised problems at the ECCC, as Prosecutors were forced to rely upon crimes against humanity and had to prove (absent a treaty) that it did not violate the legality principle to indict the accused on that ground for their conduct in the 1970s, a laborious task given its lack of codification.[47] Likewise, prior to the ECCC's establishment, when Pol Pot was subsequently arrested in Cambodia in 1997, he could not be tried. Cambodia could not muster the political will, and other countries lacked the necessary legal infrastructure. Although many countries (such as the

---

[43]   *Cf.*, Samantha Power, *A Problem From Hell: America and the Age of Genocide*, HarperCollins, 2002, pp. 87–154.

[44]   See Hurst Hannum, "International Law and Cambodian Genocide: The Sounds of Silence", in *Human Rights Quarterly*, 1989, vol. 11, p. 82 (describing the mass atrocities in Cambodia as an 'auto genocide').

[45]   Extraordinary Chambers in the Courts of Cambodia, *Prosecutor v. Nuon, Ieng, Khieu and Ieng*, Case No. 002/19-09-2007/ECCC/OCIJ, Closing Order, No. D427, 15 September 2010, paras. 1336–1342, 1343–1349.

[46]   Gareth Evans, 2011, p. 3, see *supra* note 41.

[47]   Extraordinary Chambers in the Courts of Cambodia, *Prosecutor v. Nuon and Khieu*, Case No. 002/19-09-2007/ECCC/TC, Judgment, No. E313, 7 August 2014, paras. 16–17, 411, 416, 426, 435–436. The ECCC addressed each of the crimes against humanity alleged – murder, extermination, persecution on political grounds, and "other inhumane acts" – and determined that each was recognized "as a crime against humanity under customary international law by 1975", *ibid.*

Netherlands and Denmark) could exercise universal jurisdiction over genocide, torture, terrorism and hijacking, they could not do so over crimes against humanity because no treaty existed setting out a definition of the offense and modalities of inter-State co-operation, including procedures for extradition.[48] Pol Pot died one year later, at the age of 73, having never stood trial.[49]

Likewise, although the *Pinochet* case is often referred to as an example of the power of universal jurisdiction with respect to international crimes, the decision of the House of Lords in *Pinochet III* is more a testament to the requirement of a treaty-based definition of international crime and jurisdiction. For the Law Lords, in considering the legality of Pinochet's potential extradition from the UK to Spain for crimes he had allegedly committed in Chile, limited extradition to the crime of torture, committed after the entry into force of the Torture Convention for the UK, Spain and Chile.[50] Without the existence of a treaty – the Torture Convention in this particular case – the *Pinochet* case would not have been successfully prosecuted. Unfortunately, the limitations imposed by the Lords' reliance upon the entry into force of the Torture Convention for all three countries meant that virtually all of the most serious crimes could not be considered.[51] Likewise, in *Belgium v. Senegal*, the International Court of Justice found that Senegal had an obligation to either try or extradite former Chadian leader Hissène Habre who was indicted by a Belgian investigating judge "as the perpetrator or co-perpetrator, *inter alia* of serious violations of international humanitarian law, genocide, crimes against humanity and war crimes", but not under customary international law.

---

[48] David Scheffer, *All the Missing Souls: A Personal History of the War Crimes Tribunals*, Princeton University Press, 2012, pp. 347–349.

[49] Newsmax, "Cambodia Tribunal Convicts Khmer Rouge Leaders", available at http://www.newsmax.com/Newsfront/Cambodia-Khmer-Rouge-Verdict/2014/08/07/id/587422/. The Extraordinary Chambers in the Court of Cambodia have tried three individuals since its establishment in 2003. See Agreements between the United Nations and the Royal Government of Cambodia Concerning the Prosecution Under Cambodian Law of Crimes Committed during the Period of Democratic Kampuchea, in UNTS, vol. 43, p. 2329, 6 June 2003.

[50] *R v. Bow Street Metropolitan Stipendiary Magistrate*, Ex parte Pinochet Ugarte (No. 3), [1999] 1 A.C. 147, 154 (H.L.) (appeal taken from England).

[51] *Ibid.*, pp. 175–176, 179, 188.

Rather, it was pursuant to the express provisions of Articles 6 and 7 of the Torture Convention, which applied as both States were parties.[52]

Finally, the case of *Bosnia v. Serbia*[53] evidences the difficulty created by gaps in States' responsibility for the commission of crimes against humanity. Because ICJ jurisdiction was based on a compromissory clause in the Genocide Convention, the Court's discussion – which centred upon whether the atrocities committed in Bosnia constituted genocide – missed the point. Despite the 200,000 deaths, estimated 50,000 rapes, and 2.2 million people forcibly displaced as a result of the Serb ethnic cleansing campaign, genocide was held to have been proven only in the massacre of some 8,000 Muslim men and boys in the Srebrenica area in July 1995.[54] Although the Court recognized that crimes against humanity had been committed, it could not address them. Had a global treaty on crimes against humanity equipped the ICJ with jurisdiction, the Court could have more fully addressed Bosnia's allegations.[55]

The latter example raises one more difficulty engendered because crimes against humanity do not have their own convention – and that is a tendency to 'overuse' the Genocide Convention because it is the only tool available. This leads to confusing rhetoric and anger on the part of victim's groups who insist that the wrongs done to them constituted 'genocide', to overly technical discussions by governments and the international community as to whether a particular atrocity constitutes 'genocide' or not, which could give rise to a duty to prevent, not just a requirement of

---

[52] ICJ, *Questions relating to the Obligation to Prosecute or Extradite (Belgium v. Senegal)*, Judgment, 20 July 2012, p. 450 ("[A]ny State party to the Convention may invoke the responsibility of another State party with a view to ascertaining the alleged failure to comply with its obligations *erga omnes partes*, such as those under Article 6, paragraph 2, and Article 7, paragraph 1, of the Convention, and to bring that failure to an end.").

[53] ICJ, *Case Concerning the Application of the Convention on the Prevention and Punishment of the Crime of Genocide (Bosnia and Herzegovina v. Serbia and Montenegro)*, Judgment, 26 February 2007.

[54] *Ibid.*, para. 297.

[55] Article 26 of the Proposed Convention grants such jurisdiction. See "Proposed International Convention on the Prevention of Crimes Against Humanity", Appendix 1 in *Forging a Convention*, see *supra* note 41. The same can also be said for the actions brought to the Court by Croatia and Serbia. See *Case Concerning the Application of the Convention on the Prevention and Punishment of the Crime of Genocide (Croatia v. Serbia)*, Judgment, 18 November 2008.

---

punishment,[56] and to disappointment when an atrocity turns out to be 'only' a crime against humanity, as opposed to a genocide, which implicitly downgrades the significance of crimes against humanity as a legal and sociological category.

From the above examples, we see that the absence of a global treaty on crimes against humanity leads to several categories of difficulties: (i) an impunity gap, in which individuals are unable to be prosecuted or are prosecuted only with difficulty at both the national and international levels; (ii) a State responsibility gap, because the definition of crimes against humanity is uncertain and no compromissory clause exists to permit litigation before the ICJ (or other fora) regarding their commission; (iii) a situation of definitional uncertainty leading to difficult questions regarding whether a particular atrocity was or was not a crime against humanity; and (iv) a downgrading of crimes against humanity and overuse of the Genocide Convention as a legal tool.

2.3. Codification of Crimes Against Humanity in the International Criminal Court Statute: Necessary but not Sufficient

With the adoption of the International Criminal Court Statute in 1998, crimes against humanity were at last defined and ensconced in an international convention. The ICC definition is similar to earlier versions, but differs in important respects, such as the requirement that crimes against humanity be committed "pursuant to a State or organizational policy",[57] and the absence of any linkage to armed conflict. The addition of the policy element continues to elicit controversy, because the *ad hoc* tribunals rejected that element as a matter of customary international law.[58] Of

---

[56] See, *e.g.*, Power, 2002, see *supra* note 43; *Bosnia v. Serbia*, para. 427, see *supra* note 53 (stating "[t]he obligation on each contracting State to prevent genocide is both normative and compelling. It is not merged in the duty to punish, nor can it be regarded as simply a component of that duty").

[57] ICC Statute, Article 7(2)(a), see *supra* note 4.

[58] ICTY, *Prosecutor v. Kunarac*, Case No. IT-96-23 and IT-96-23/1-A, Appeal Judgment, 12 June 2002, para. 98. The appeals chamber noted that there was some "debate" in the jurisprudence of the Tribunal on the question whether a policy or plan constitutes an element of crimes against humanity, *ibid.*, para. 98, footnote 114. The *Kunarac* appeals chamber decision effectively ended the debate. See also, ICTY, *Prosecutor v. Vasiljević*, Case No. IT-98-32-T, Trial Judgment, 29 November 2002, para. 36; ICTY, *Prosecutor v. Naletilić and Martinović*, Case No. IT-98-34-T, Judgment, 31 March 2003, para. 234; ICTY, *Prosecutor v. Blaškić*, Case No. IT-95-14A, Appeal Judgment, 29 July 2004, paras. 100, 120, 126; ICTY, *Prosecutor v. Krnojelac*, Case No. IT-97-25-T, Trial Judgment, 15 March 2002, pa-

course, the ICC Statute *by its own terms* did not purport to represent customary law, but only law defined for the purposes of the Statute itself,[59] suggesting that perhaps it is possible for 'Rome law' to be different than customary international law outside the ICC Statute.[60] At the same time, given that the ICC Statute applies to nationals of ICC non-States Parties through the possibility of referral by the Security Council, as well as the Court's territorially based jurisdiction, most have concluded that it is difficult to support the notion of different versions of crimes against humanity law existing inside and outside the ICC Statute, and have suggested that the ICC definition has ultimately come to represent customary international law.[61]

If so, perhaps the ICC Statute is sufficient to fill the gaps identified in the preceding sections flowing from the absence of a treaty on crimes against humanity? Certainly, the negotiation of the ICC Statute arguably solved the question of definitional uncertainty and clearly gave crimes against humanity an autonomous status, definitively delinking it from war crimes and genocide. But other gaps and difficulties remain. First, the ICC Statute applies only to cases to be tried before the ICC, that is, to a handful of perpetrators from the limited number of cases that fall within the jurisdiction of the Court. Unlike the *ad hoc* tribunals, the ICC has a very broad mandate to not only assist with punishment but also prevention of atrocity crimes, in situations scattered all over the world. Given its small size and limited resources, the Court has had to be very judicious about limiting the number of cases per situation. This will leave many potential perpetrators outside the reach of the ICC Statute, and other mechanisms will be required to bring them to book.

---

ra. 58; ICTR, *Prosecutor v. Semanza*, Case No. ICTR-97-20-T, Judgment and Sentence, 15 May 2003, para. 329; ICTR, *Prosecutor v. Kajelijeli*, Case No. ICTR-98-44A-T, Judgment and Sentence, 1 December 2003, para. 827.

[59] See, *e.g.*, ICC Statute, Article 7(1) ("For the purpose of this Statute, 'crime against humanity' means [...]"). Whether it has *subsequently* come to represent customary international law is the subject of some debate, see Guénaël Mettraux, "The Definition of Crimes Against Humanity and the Question of a 'Policy' Element" and Kai Ambos, "Crimes Against Humanity and the International Criminal Court", in *Forging a Convention*, pp. 142, 279, respectively, see *supra* note 41.

[60] Leila Sadat, "Custom, Codification and Some Thoughts About the Relationship Between the Two: Article 10 of the ICC Statute", in *DePaul Law Review*, 2000, vol. 35, p. 909.

[61] Sadat, 2013, pp. 372–374, see *supra* note 5.

Second, the ICC Statute does not require States to adopt implementing legislation on the crimes within the Statute, although many have done so and the Statute assumes that they have an obligation to do so.[62] A recent study suggests that 34% of ICC States parties do not have legislation on crimes against humanity; the percentage is much higher for non-States parties.[63] Moreover, the ICC Statute provides no vehicle for inter-State co-operation, leaving gaps in mutual legal assistance, extradition and other aspects of the horizontal co-operation needed for the prosecution of atrocity crimes across State borders.

Third, the ICC Statute does not provide for State responsibility but only addresses the possible criminal responsibility of individuals, and does not explicitly impose an obligation upon States to prevent as well as punish crimes against humanity. A new treaty could do so, along the lines of the Genocide Convention, and consistently with the Responsibility to Protect.

Finally, although 122 States have ratified the ICC Statute at the time of writing, many remain outside the Rome Statute system. Just as many of these jurisdictions – like Russia, India and the United States – have ratified the Genocide and Geneva Conventions,[64] it is not impossible to imagine that they would support and ultimately ratify a new convention on crimes against humanity. Indeed, the ABA House of Delegates recently adopted – unanimously – a resolution calling for federal legislation and for the United States to take the lead in negotiating a new treaty on crimes against humanity.[65] These States could support a crimes against humanity convention, thereby agreeing to the treaty definition of the crime, agree upon the need to prevent, punish and co-operate regarding it, but still take the time they need to become comfortable with the adjudicative jurisdiction of the International Criminal Court.

Although it has recently been proposed that a new interstate mutual legal assistance convention be adopted covering all of the crimes in the

---

[62] ICC Statute, Preamble, para. 6, see *supra* note 4.

[63] Arturo J. Carrillo and Annalise K. Nelson, "Comparative Law Study and Analysis of National Legislation Relating to Crimes Against Humanity and Extraterritorial Jurisdiction", in *George Washington International Law Review*, 2014, vol. 46, pp. 8, 9.

[64] A complete list of ratifications of the Genocide and Geneva Conventions are available at https://treaties.un.org/.

[65] ABA Resolution 300, adopted on 18 August 2014, available at http://www.americanbar.org/content/dam/aba/images/abanews/2014am_hodres/300.pdf.

ICC Statute,[66] that effort has not received much attention largely because it fills only one of the gaps identified above (interstate co-operation) and, additionally, is not a realistic alternative for States not party to the ICC Statute, given that they may not have incorporated the ICC crimes into their national legislation and may not, therefore, be in a position to co-operate with other States on questions of mutual legal assistance. It also would not address many of the critical subsidiary elements required for the effective prosecution of atrocity crimes: the non-applicability of Statutes of limitation, the lifting of immunities, setting out modes of liability, and other provisions essential to establishing a comprehensive regime for the prevention and punishment of crimes against humanity.

2.4. A New Treaty for Crimes Against Humanity? The Crimes Against Humanity Initiative and the Task Now Before the International Law Commission

2.4.1. The Work of the Crimes Against Humanity Initiative

Concerned about the problems of continued impunity for the commission of atrocity crimes, in 2008, the Whitney R. Harris World Law Institute at Washington University School of Law launched the Crimes Against Humanity Initiative, with three primary objectives: (1) to study the current state of the law and sociological reality as regards the commission of crimes against humanity; (2) to combat the indifference generated by an assessment that a particular crime is 'only' a crime against humanity (rather than a 'genocide'); and (3) to address the gap in the current law by elaborating the first-ever comprehensive specialized convention on crimes against humanity.[67]

The Initiative progressed in phases, each building upon the work of the last. In 2011, the first edition of *Forging a Convention for Crimes Against Humanity* was published, which included a major study of issues that needed to be considered if a new treaty was to be elaborated, as well as a model text of a *Proposed International Convention for the Prevention*

---

[66] International Co-operation in the Fight Against the Crime of Genocide, Crimes Against Humanity and War Crimes, Draft Resolution, 28 March 2013, U.N. Doc. E/CN.15/2013/L.5.

[67] Leila Nadya Sadat, "A Comprehensive History of the Proposed International Convention on the Prevention and Punishment of Crimes Against Humanity", in *Forging a Convention*, pp. xxiii–xxiv, see *supra* note 41.

and Punishment of Crimes Against Humanity in English and in French.[68] The work was overseen by a Steering Committee of distinguished experts.[69]

During Phase II of the Initiative, papers written by leading experts were presented and discussed at a conference held at Washington University School of Law on 13–14 April 2009, and then revised for publication.[70] They addressed the legal regulation of crimes against humanity and examined the broader social and historical context within which they occur. Each chapter was commissioned not only to examine the topic's relationship to the elaboration of a future treaty, but to serve as an important contribution to the literature on crimes against humanity in and of itself.

The papers ranged from technical discussions of specific legal issues such as modes of responsibility, immunities and amnesties, enforcement and gender crimes to broader conceptual treatments of earlier codification efforts, the definition of the crime in the ICC Statute and customary international law, and the phenomenon of ethnic cleansing. Several of the papers contrasted the ICC and *ad hoc* tribunal definition of crimes against humanity and were very helpful to the discussions as the drafting effort progressed; the same can be said for the many other contributions which addressed specific topics such as crimes against humanity and terrorism, universal jurisdiction, and the Responsibility to Protect.

In discussing the scholarly work more questions were raised than answered. What was the social harm any convention would protect? Atrocities committed by the State, or a broader concept that would include non-State actors? Would a new legal instrument prove useful in combating atrocity crimes? How would any new instrument interact with the

---

[68] "Proposed International Convention on the Prevention and Punishment of Crimes Against Humanity", in *Forging a Convention*, p. 359, see *supra* note 41 ('Proposed Convention'). The Proposed Convention can also be found on p. 403 in French and on p. 503 in Spanish. These texts, as well as Arabic, Chinese, German and Russian translations, are also available at crimesagainsthumanity@wustl.edu.

[69] The Steering Committee is composed of Professor M. Cherif Bassiouni, Ambassador Hans Corell, Justice Richard Goldstone, Professor Juan Mendez, Professor William Schabas and Judge Christine Van den Wyngaert.

[70] One paper was commissioned subsequent to the April meeting based upon the emphasis in that meeting on inter-state co-operation as a principal need to adopt the Convention: Laura M. Olson, "Re-enforcing Enforcement in a Specialized Convention on Crimes Against Humanity: Inter-State Cooperation, Mutual Legal Assistance, and the *Aut Dedere Aut Judicare* Obligation", in *Forging a Convention*, p. 323, see *supra* note 41.

Rome Statute for the International Criminal Court? As the initial scholarly work was undertaken, a preliminary draft text of the convention, prepared by M. Cherif Bassiouni, was circulated to participants at the April meeting to begin the drafting process. As the Initiative progressed, nearly 250 experts were consulted, many of whom submitted detailed comments (orally or in writing) on the various drafts of the proposed convention circulated, or attended meetings convened by the Initiative either in the United States or abroad. Between formal meetings, technical advisory sessions were held during which every comment received – whether in writing or communicated verbally – was discussed as the draft convention was refined. The Proposed Convention went through seven major revisions (and innumerable minor ones) and was approved by the members of the Steering Committee in August 2010 in English (and is annexed to this volume).

The Proposed Convention has begun, not ended, the debate. Elaborated by experts without the constraints of government instructions (although deeply cognizant of political realities), it is a platform for discussion by States, the International Law Commission, civil society and academics with a view to the eventual adoption of a United Nations Convention on the Prevention and Punishment of Crimes Against Humanity. The Proposed Convention builds upon and complements the ICC Statute by retaining the Rome Statute definition of crimes against humanity but has added robust interstate co-operation, extradition and mutual legal assistance provisions in Annexes 2–6. Universal jurisdiction was retained (but is not mandatory), and the Rome Statute served as a model for several additional provisions, including Articles 4–7 (Responsibility, Official Capacity, and Non-Applicability of Statute of Limitations) and with respect to final clauses. Other provisions draw upon international criminal law and human rights instruments more broadly, such as the recently negotiated Enforced Disappearance Convention, the Terrorist Bombing Convention, the Convention Against Torture, the United Nations Conventions on Corruption and Organized Crime, the European Transfer of Proceedings Convention, and the Inter-American Criminal Sentences Convention, to name a few.[71]

---

[71] A complete list can be found in the table at the back of the Proposed Convention, reproduced in Appendices I and II of *Forging a Convention*, pp. 398–401, 445–448, see *supra* note 41.

Yet although the drafting process benefited from the existence of current international criminal law instruments, the creative work of the Initiative was to meld these and our own ideas into a single, coherent model convention that establishes the principle of State responsibility as well as individual criminal responsibility (including the possibility of responsibility for the criminal acts of legal persons) for the commission of crimes against humanity. Thus, Article 1 of the Proposed Convention reads:

> Article 1
>
> Nature of the Crime
>
> Crimes against humanity, whether committed in time of armed conflict or in time of peace, constitute crimes under international law for which there is individual criminal responsibility. In addition, States may be held responsible for crimes against humanity pursuant to principles of States responsibility for internationally wrongful acts.[72]

The Proposed Convention innovates in many respects by attempting to bring prevention into the instrument in a much more explicit way than predecessor instruments, by including the possibility of responsibility for the criminal acts of legal persons, by excluding defences of immunities and statutory limitations, by prohibiting reservations, and by establishing a unique institutional mechanism for supervision of the Convention. Echoing its 1907 forbearer, it also contains its own 'Martens Clause' in the Preamble, as follows:

> Declaring that in cases not covered by the present Convention or by other international agreements, the human person remains under the protection and authority of the principles of international law derived from established customs, from the laws of humanity, and from the dictates of the public conscience, and continues to enjoy the fundamental rights that are recognized by international law [...].[73]

Elaborating the 27 articles and six annexes of the treaty was a daunting challenge, and one that could not have been accomplished without the dedication and enthusiasm of many individuals.[74] The effort has

---

[72] Proposed Convention, Article 1, see *supra* note 68.

[73] *Ibid.*, Preamble, para. 13. Credit is due to Morten Bergsmo for this provision's inclusion.

[74] I am particularly grateful to M. Cherif Bassiouni for his extraordinary efforts in leading the drafting effort and his service as a member of the Initiative's Steering Committee, and

been well-rewarded; in 2010, more than 75 experts endorsed the objectives of the Initiative in a Declaration adopted on 12 March 2010, in Washington, D.C., as did the Prosecutors of the world's international criminal courts and tribunals in the *Kigali Declaration of the Fifth Colloquium of Prosecutors of the International Criminal Tribunals* adopted on 13 November 2009, and the *Fourth Chautauqua Declaration* adopted on 31 August 2010.[75] The Proposed Convention has now been translated into Arabic, Chinese, German, Russian and Spanish, and continues to attract discussion and debate.[76]

2.4.2. The International Law Commission Moves Forward

The International Law Commission first included the topic of crimes against humanity on its long-term work program in 2013 on the basis of a report prepared by Professor Sean Murphy.[77] The report identified four key elements a new convention should have: a definition adopting Article 7 of the ICC Statute; an obligation to criminalize crimes against humanity with national legislation; robust inter-State co-operation procedures; and a clear obligation to prosecute or extradite offenders.[78] The report also emphasized how a new treaty would complement the ICC Statute.[79]

In autumn 2013, States had an opportunity to comment on the Commission's decision to include the topic in its long-term work programme at the General Assembly Sixth Committee. Many States commented favourably on the prospect of a new crimes against humanity con-

---

equally grateful to the other members of the Steering Committee – for their leadership. Each member brought tremendous energy and expertise to the project, guiding its methodological development and conceptual design, and carefully reading, commenting upon and debating each interim draft of the Proposed Convention extensively. As with all such projects, many supported – and continue to support – the effort without being on the front pages of it, so to speak. Their contributions are noted in "Preface and Acknowledgments", in *Forging a Convention*, pp. xxvi–xxviii, see *supra* note 41.

75 "Declaration on the Need for a Comprehensive Convention on Crimes Against Humanity", reprinted in *Forging a Convention*, p. 579, see *supra* note 41; "Kigali Declaration of the Fifth Colloquium of Prosecutors of International Criminal Tribunals", *ibid.*, p. 588; "The Fourth Chautauqua Declaration", *ibid.*, p. 591.

76 For a list of the Initiative's activities, see http://crimesagainsthumanity.wustl.edu/.

77 Report to the International Law Commission, Report of the Working Group on the Obligation to Extradite or Prosecute (*aut dedere aut judicare*), 22 July 2013, U.N. Doc. A/CN.4/L.829.

78 *Ibid.*, para. 8.

79 *Ibid.*, paras. 9–13.

vention. Slovenia, for example, stated that "all efforts should be directed at filling this gap".[80] Austria, the Czech Republic, Italy, Norway, Peru, Poland and the United States also welcomed the decision.[81] A major focus was the importance of ensuring a new treaty complements the ICC Statute, as the comments of Malaysia and the United Kingdom, for example, made clear.[82] Some States questioned the need for a new treaty. For example, Iran stated that it "does not seem that [...] there is a legal loophole to be filled through the adoption of a new international instrument".[83] Other States questioning the need for a treaty included France, Malaysia, Romania and Russia.[84]

In May 2014, prior to the Commission's July session, the Proposed Convention was the basis of an Experts' Meeting held at the Villa Moynier in Geneva bringing together international justice experts and members of the International Law Commission. Participants discussed the need for a new convention, its potential content and the process of building support amongst States. These discussions are summarized in a Report

---

[80] Statement by Mr. Borut Mahnič, 68th Session of the General Assembly, 6th Committee, under agenda item 81, 30 October 2013, p. 8.

[81] Statement by Gregor Schusterschitz, 68th Session of the General Assembly, 6th Committee, under agenda item 81, 28 October 2013, p. 5; Statement by Mr. Petr Válek, 68th Session of the General Assembly, 6th Committee, under agenda item 81, 29 October 2013, p. 3; Statement by Min. Plenipotentiary Andrea Tiriticco, 68th Session of the General Assembly, 6th Committee, under agenda item 81, 29 October 2013, p. 5; Statement on behalf of the Nordic Countries by Mr. Rolf Einar Fife, 68th Session of the General Assembly, 6th Committee, under agenda item 81, 28 October 2013, pp. 3-4; Intervención de la Misión Permanente del Perú, 68th Session of the General Assembly, 6th Committee, under agenda item 81, 29 October 2013, p. 2; Statement by Ambassador Ryszard Sarkowicz, 68th Session of the General Assembly, 6th Committee, under agenda item 81, 30 October 2013, p. 5; Statement by the United States, 68th Session of the General Assembly, 6th Committee, under agenda item 81, 2013, p. 4.

[82] Statement by Ms. Sarah Khalilah Abdul Rahman, 68th Session of the General Assembly, 6th Committee, under agenda item 81, 30 October 2013, p. 1; Statement by Mr. Jesse Clarke, 68th Session of the General Assembly, 6th Committee, under agenda item 81, 28-30 October 2013, p. 5.

[83] Statement by Professor Djamchid Momtaz, 68th Session of the General Assembly, 6th Committee, under agenda item 81, 5 November 2013, p. 7.

[84] Statement by Mrs. Edwige Belliard, 68th Session of the General Assembly, 6th Committee, under agenda item 81, 28 October 2013, Part I, p. 2; Statement by Ms. Sarah Khalilah Abdul Rahman, see *supra* note 82; Statement by Mrs. Alina Orosan, 68th Session of the General Assembly, 6th Committee, under agenda item 79, October 2013, p. 5; Statement by the Representative of the Russian Federation, 68th Session of the General Assembly, 6th Committee, under agenda item 79, 2013, p. 6.

published on 17 July 2014.[85] Participants noted the long involvement of the Commission on the subject of crimes against humanity and commented upon the progressive stance of the Commission in de-linking crimes against humanity from armed conflict in its formulation of the Nuremberg Principles. In paragraph 123 of its commentary to 'Principles of International Law recognized in the Charter of the Nuremberg Tribunal and in the Judgment of the Tribunal', the Commission noted "that [crimes against humanity] may take place also before a war in connection with crimes against peace".[86] It was also observed that the Commission was nearing completion of its work on the obligation to extradite or prosecute (*aut dedere aut judicare*), and was therefore in an excellent position to take up the question of a new convention on crimes against humanity.

Following this meeting, the Commission voted, on 18 July 2014, to add the topic of crimes against humanity to its active agenda and appointed Professor Murphy as Special Rapporteur. The Rapporteur will prepare draft articles for discussion by the Commission, and comment by States.[87] Under the Commission's Statute, it can suggest further study at that point, depending upon government reaction; or the convening of a diplomatic conference to negotiate a new treaty.[88] The work could be completed in as little as four years; or could take considerably longer, depending upon the reaction of governments.[89]

2.5. How Does a New Convention on Crimes Against Humanity Fit within the International Justice Project More Generally?

Thus far, this chapter has assumed that the prevention and punishment of crimes against humanity is desirable. This section will take up just a few of the issues and controversies surrounding international criminal justice and its application and attempt to place the elaboration and adoption of a

---

[85] Leila Nadya Sadat and Douglas J. Pivnichny, *Fulfilling the Dictates of Public Conscience: Moving Forward with a Convention on Crimes Against Humanity*, 17 July 2014, Whitney R. Harris World Law Institute ('Geneva Report').

[86] Report of the International Law Commission on the Work of its Second Session, U.N. Doc. A/1316, para. 123, reprinted in *Yearbook of International Law Commission*, vol. 2, 1950, U.N. Doc. A/CN.4/SER.A/1950/Add. 1, p. 364.

[87] International Law Commission, 66th Session, Provisional Summary Record of the 3227th Meeting, A/CN.4/SR.3227.

[88] Statute of the International Law Commission, Articles 16, 17, 21 November 1947, G.A. Res. 174 (II), U.N. GAOR, 2nd Session, U.N. Doc A/RES/175(II).

[89] Geneva Report, para. 79, see *supra* note 85.

new global convention on crimes against humanity in context of the over-all picture today.

The considerable effort required to negotiate and elaborate a new global convention on crimes against humanity is only valuable if the prevention and punishment of such crimes is a useful public good, and if a new treaty would assist in such an effort. Moreover, for the International Law Commission's efforts to be successful, States must be willing to expend political capital to support a new convention on crimes against humanity, and civil society must become excited about it. A new *inter-State* convention, of course, is different than a treaty like the ICC Statute, because it is about empowering *States* to do the job of preventing, punishing and building capacity to address, atrocity crimes. It is *not* about creating a new supranational jurisdiction to do so. In this sense, then, many of the concerns that have arisen regarding the appropriateness, or not, of particular cases before the International Criminal Court, have no relevance in considering the utility of a new convention on crimes against humanity. It is also why States that have not yet accepted the adjudicative jurisdiction of the ICC Statute, but do accept the content of the substantive law,[90] might be willing to ratify a new convention on crimes against humanity.

At the same time, the reality is that – assuming a new treaty will look at least as 'progressive' as the 1984 Torture Convention or the more recently enacted terrorism treaties – the exercise of universal jurisdiction will be an option for States Parties to the treaty, under their obligation of *aut dedere aut judicare*, meaning that there may be friction between governments as to the proper outcome of a particular case (as was true in the *Pinochet* and *Habre* examples discussed above). And indeed, the *Proposed Convention* removes any defence of statutes of limitations (Article 7), imposes an obligation to prosecute or extradite (Article 9) and provides for jurisdiction if "the alleged offender is present in any territory under its jurisdiction, unless it extradites or surrenders him or her to another State [...] or an international criminal tribunal".[91] This language draws upon the language of Article 9(2) of the Enforced Disappearance Convention and Article 5(2) of the Torture Convention. Thus, many of the concerns raised as regards international criminal justice, such as the al-

---

[90] Leila Nadya Sadat and S. Richard Carden, "The New International Criminal Court: An Uneasy Revolution", in *Georgetown Law Journal*, 2000, vol. 88, p. 335.

[91] Proposed Convention, Articles 7, 9, 10(3), see *supra* note 71.

leged conflict between peace and justice or the concern that Africans are being disproportionately targeted by the ICC, to name just two, may arise in connection with the negotiation of a new global convention on crimes against humanity. And certainly, even if not specifically relevant, these concerns may influence the context in which the elaboration and negotiation of such a treaty takes place.

So what would be the purpose of a new convention, and what would its elaboration hope to bring about? First, as a legal matter, it has been asserted that as a 'core crime', crimes against humanity is a *jus cogens* norm under international law, and is, by its nature, non-derogable, meaning that States may not justify their commission (and perhaps non-State actors as well), just as they may not justify the commission of genocide through legal argument. That is, a treaty on crimes against humanity would speak to the fact that the prohibition of crimes against humanity is a fundamental rule of international law, a *grundnorm*, and of course would, in this way, support the Responsibility to Protect doctrine as well as other efforts to establish their universal prohibition and call for their protection. In terms of their prevention, a treaty mechanism could be established (and many were suggested during the conferences held by the Initiative) that could help with monitoring situations likely to turn bad, that is, to deteriorate into the kinds of widespread and systematic attacks on civilians that become crimes against humanity. Although many such mechanisms exist today, the situations in Syria, North Korea, Honduras, and many countries in Africa suggest that more needs to be done in terms of prevention. A new treaty could prohibit incitement to crimes against humanity, for example, which was omitted from the ICC Statute, and could contain provisions on capacity building and education to address the problems of lesser-developed States. The importance of crimes against humanity to atrocity crime prevention is critical: because crimes against humanity can be committed in peacetime, and because the bar to prosecution is lower for crimes against humanity than for genocide, we have seen that nearly 30% of the cases at the International Criminal Court are 'crimes against humanity only' cases, including the situations in Côte d'Ivoire, Kenya and Libya.[92] We have also seen prevention become a legal requirement under the Genocide Convention under the jurisprudence of the ICJ in *Bosnia v. Serbia*. It could be very powerful if that were true

---

[92] Sadat, 2013, pp. 356–357, see *supra* note 5.

for crimes against humanity as well. Although the Kenya case has raised difficult political problems for the International Criminal Court as two indictees in the political violence were elected to office following their indictment, leading to a firestorm of criticism from some quarters that the ICC was 'anti-African' and a threatened pull out of African Union members from the Court. However, consider the fact that following the opening of the ICC investigation and the confirmation of the case against individuals from both political parties in 2010, when Kenya subsequently held elections, they were by and large, peaceful. Did the ICC proceedings cast a shadow that helped contain the ethnic violence that had erupted so powerfully in during the 2007 elections? It is hard to know. But Kenya seems more peaceful than before.

In terms of punishment of offenders, there is no doubt that international criminal justice as a modality for the prevention and punishment of atrocity crimes has always faced scepticism. Whether it be from government officials wary of being constrained by law,[93] or by legal scholars arguing that international criminal justice may be ineffective and even harmful to the restoration of social peace,[94] since the establishment of the ad hoc tribunals 20 years ago, the international criminal justice project has always needed to articulate its objectives and establish its utility. While perhaps this is less so at the national level, the intense scrutiny of the French example evoked above, and the debates about the appropriateness of trying French perpetrators decades after the crimes were committed,[95] is an indicator that this is an issue even before national courts. Indeed, it has arisen in Latin America, where prosecutions have occurred, including Argentina, Chile, Peru, and most recently Ecuador.[96] Especially when

---

[93] See, *e.g.*, Press Release, Decision of the Meeting of African States Parties to the Rome Statute of the International Criminal Court, 14 July 2009, available at http://www.haguejusticeportal.net/Docs/Court%20Documents/ICC/African%20Union%20 Press%20Release%20-%20ICC.pdf (stating that the Union's refusal to co-operate with the ICC's request for the arrest and surrender of President Omar El Bashir of the Sudan was "a logical consequence" of the Union's position "on the manner in which the prosecution against President Bashir has been conducted, the publicity-seeking approach of the ICC Prosecutor, [and] the refusal by the UN Security Council to address the request made by the African Union [...] for deferment of the indictment against President Bashir").

[94] Mark A. Drumbl, *Atrocity, Punishment, and International Law*, Cambridge University Press, 2007.

[95] See, *e.g.*, Leila Sadat, "Reflections on the Trial of Vichy Collaborator Paul Touvier for Crimes Against Humanity in France", in *Law and Social Inquiry*, 1995, vol. 20, p. 191.

[96] See *supra* note 29.

committed by the State, crimes against humanity become political crimes, and the same push and pull extant at the international level is found at the national level as well.

These problems are magnified at the international level, however, because, unlike domestic criminal justice systems, which are taken for granted as necessary for social peace in every State in which they exist, international criminal justice is not yet a given. As one observer remarked regarding the transition of the Central European countries away from communism, "[i]t will take six months to reform the political systems, six years to change the economic systems, and sixty years to effect a revolution in the people's hearts and minds".[97] Yet the same factors that animate the need for justice at the domestic level operate in the international context: the need to recognize the sufferings of the victims, the possibility of specific or even general deterrence, and finally the need to promote rehabilitation of the offender and perhaps offer an element of retribution for the wrongs done. At the international level, international justice has two additional goals: rendering an historic and accurate account of the atrocity crimes commission and assisting with the rebuilding of a damaged and possibly war-torn society.[98] While the evidence is as yet limited in terms of whether international justice is achieving these goals, there is some anecdotal evidence that the work of the past two decades is having a positive effect,[99] States continue to ratify the ICC Statute at high rates,[100] and there have been increasing instances of domestic prosecutions and commissions of inquiry regarding atrocity crimes. When a crisis erupts and violence

---

[97] Vojtěch Cepl, "The Transformation of Hearts and Minds in Eastern Europe", in *Cato Journal*, 1997, vol. 17, pp. 229–230.

[98] "Overview of the ICC Statute of the International Criminal Court", available at http://legal.un.org/icc/general/overview.htm:

> One of the primary objectives of the United Nations is securing universal respect for human rights and fundamental freedoms of individuals throughout the world. In this connection, few topics are of greater importance than the fight against impunity and the struggle for peace and justice and human rights in conflict situations in today's world. The establishment of a permanent international criminal court (ICC) is seen as a decisive step forward.

[99] Leila Nadya Sadat, "Exile, Amnesty and International Law", in *Notre Dame Law Review*, 2006, vol. 81, pp. 998–999.

[100] As of 24 September 2014, there are 139 signatories to the Statute, and 122 ratifications. A complete list of treaty ratifications is available at https://treaties.un.org/Pages/ViewDetails.aspx?src=TREATY&mtdsg_no=XVIII-10&chapter=18&lang=en.

---

ensues, a fact-finding enquiry is likely to follow. Individuals appear interested in justice even when it is rendered decades after the alleged crimes have been committed, as demonstrated by the very high rates of attendance at the ECCC hearings (more than 135,000 individuals have visited the courtroom since it began holding hearings),[101] or the fascination in Israel and France during the prosecutions that took place of Eichmann, Barbie and Touvier. Finally, in the case of a new global convention on crimes against humanity, perhaps one of the most compelling reasons for a State to embrace it is the idea that it should not be providing sanctuary for an individual who has committed such crimes and then fled to another jurisdiction to avoid being held accountable. Just as international law does not permit States to 'harbour' terrorists, they should not be offering refuge or exile to individuals credibly accused of atrocity crimes.

A related issue regarding the utility of a new global treaty on crimes against humanity that is often raised by government officials I have met with, especially from those living in Western and developed countries least likely to need its protections is, why should we care? Of course, there is the argument of self-interest, enlightened or otherwise; there is also a moral response. The work of John Rawls offers an interesting perspective. In *A Theory of Justice*, Rawls argues that one should evaluate the fairness – justness – of social rules from behind a "veil of ignorance". Put succinctly, the idea is that everyone should choose the rules that apply to them to produce the highest payoff for the least advantaged position, as if they did not know whether or not they would be born weak or strong, poor or rich. From this original position, rules that promote social equality are the most desirable as they protect everyone. Extrapolating to the international arena, the question we might ask when considering what system of international justice we prefer, is not what system we (as a U.S. citizen, in my case) might like to maximize our freedom to do as we please, but what system would protect us if we were born in a different place and time – and unlucky enough to have been Jewish during the Holocaust, Tutsi during the Rwandan Genocide, a wearer of eyeglasses during the Khmer Rouge regime, or a Masalit or Fur tribe member in contemporary Darfur, Sudan.

---

[101] Extraordinary Chambers in the Courts of Cambodia, "ECCC surpasses 100,000 visitors milestone", last updated on 11 November 2013, 15:54, available at http://www.eccc.gov.kh/en/articles/eccc-surpasses-100000-visitors-milestone.

In terms of self-interest, a new global convention on crimes against humanity could assist in isolating leaders that are disrupting international peace and security and make the world safer for the international trade that fuels the high standard of living the developed world expects. International criminal law conventions contain key elements required for effective counterterrorism, including the duty of States to try or to extradite international criminals; the obligation of States not to give safe haven to international criminals; and the right of the international community to act together, if States are unable or unwilling to fulfil their obligations. Shoring up these obligations for the 'core crime' of crimes against humanity can strengthen both the political will and legal obligation of other States to comply with these provisions in the dozens of terrorism, trafficking, organized crime and corruption conventions that have been negotiated at the international and regional levels.

2.6. Conclusion

The Nuremberg legacy suggests that to meet the challenges of a world in which the commission of atrocity crimes is but too common, three elements are required: rules, institutions and enforcement – rules that govern human behaviour, and institutions to assist with the formulation, the application and the enforcement of those rules. Although the International Criminal Court is an important step forward in the prevention and punishment of atrocity crimes, without national enforcement, it will be of limited effect.

When beginning the Crimes Against Humanity Initiative it was daunting to ask both whether it would make a difference, and whether it represented the right step forward. While concerns remain regarding the content of any new treaty that might be negotiated as well as the relationship of any new convention with the ICC Statute, the absence of a global treaty on crimes against humanity means that we are effectively depriving our strongest institutions – national governments – of the tools they need to comprehensively address this most ubiquitous of crimes. It also leaves significant enforcement gaps, and the law may remain unclear, particularly with respect to ICC non-States Parties. The work of the Initiative over several years, as well as the decision taken by the International Law Commission, suggests that the time has come at last to remedy this normative and enforcement gap in international law.

3

The ICC Case Law on the Contextual Elements of Crimes Against Humanity

Eleni Chaitidou*

The proposed International Convention on the Prevention and Punishment of Crimes Against Humanity[1] aims to close the still-existing gap concerning this category of crimes in the normative architecture of international criminal law. It offers for the first time, outside of the context of the International Criminal Court ('ICC'), a conventional text on crimes against humanity which, it is hoped, will aid in "shoring up the capacity for national legal systems to pick up cases involving crimes against humanity".[2] Attracting particular attention is the manner in which the definition of these crimes has been articulated in the Convention and the relationship between this proposed instrument and the Rome Statute ('Statute'), the founding treaty of the ICC. Clarity is soon provided in paragraph 12 of the preamble of the Convention which makes explicit reference to "Article 7 and other relevant provisions of the Rome Statute of the International Criminal Court", thus putting a spotlight on the ICC. Indeed, Article 3 of the Convention reflects almost verbatim the statutory definition of crimes against humanity applicable before the ICC. By doing so, the Convention unequivocally pays special tribute to the final compromise on the definition of crimes against humanity that States reached in their multilateral negotiations in Rome in 1998 and cements this definition's future

---

* **Eleni Chaitidou** is Legal Officer in the Pre-Trial Division of the International Criminal Court since 2006. The views expressed herein are those of the author alone and do not reflect the views of the International Criminal Court. The author wishes to thank Gilbert Bitti and Donald Riznik who kindly commented on earlier versions, and expresses her gratitude to Erin Rosenberg and Teodora Jugrin for proof-reading the manuscript. Finally, this article is dedicated to the memory of Judge Hans-Peter Kaul.

1   For the text of the Proposed Convention, see Annex 1, or in Leila N. Sadat (ed.), *Forging a Convention for Crimes Against Humanity*, Cambridge University Press, 2011, p. 359 *et seq.*

2   Leila Sadat, "Preface and Acknowledgments", in Leila Sadat (ed.), *Forging a Convention for Crimes Against Humanity, op. cit.*, p. xxiii.

use. What was meant to be a special definition for the purpose of the ICC Statute[3] appears to have the potential of gaining universal recognition.

Reliance on this statutory definition implies that questions of interpretation that arose under the ICC Statute are also likely to arise under the Proposed Convention. It seems therefore appropriate to look to certain decisions of the ICC that provide guidance on how different components of crimes against humanity have been construed and which aspects of the definition have challenged the effective prosecution of crimes against humanity. This chapter seeks to provide an overview of one aspect of the statutory definition of crimes against humanity which has aroused much controversy in the early case law of the ICC, that of its contextual elements. The author does not claim to resolve the complex issues pervading Article 7 of the Statute, but seeks to explain some of the issues that arose in the ICC jurisprudence which may, it is hoped, offer some lessons for the application of Article 3 of the Proposed Convention.

3.1. Introduction

Crimes against humanity have been an essential part of investigatory and prosecutorial activity before the ICC from the beginning of the Court's operation. To date, 16 out of 19 cases[4] involve(d) allegations of crimes against humanity pursuant to Article 7 of the Rome Statute.[5] Indeed, the

---

[3]   See Article 10 of the Statute.

[4]   The cases are the *Prosecutor v. Thomas Lubanga Dyilo* (ICC-01/04-01/06); *Prosecutor v. Germain Katanga* (ICC-01/04-01/07); *Prosecutor v. Mathieu Ngudjolo Chui* (ICC-01/04-02/12); *Prosecutor v. Bosco Ntaganda* (ICC-01/04-02/06); *Prosecutor v. Callixte Mbarushimana* (ICC-01/04-01/10); *Prosecutor v. Sylvestre Mudacumura* (ICC-01/04-01/12); *Prosecutor v. Joseph Kony, Vincent Otti, Okot Odhiambo and Dominic Ongwen* (ICC-02/04-01/05); *Prosecutor v. Jean-Pierre Bemba Gombo* (ICC-01/05-01/08); *Prosecutor v. Ahmad Muhammad Harun and Ali Muhammad Ali Abd-Al-Rahman* (ICC-02/05-01/07); *Prosecutor v. Omar Hassan Ahmad Al Bashir* (ICC-02/05-01/09); *Prosecutor v. Bahar Idriss Abu Garda* (ICC-02/05-02/09); *Prosecutor v. Abdallah Banda Abakaer Nourain* (ICC-02/05-03/09); *Prosecutor v. Abdel Raheem Muhammad Hussein* (ICC-02/05-01/12); *Prosecutor v. William Samoei Ruto and Joshua Arap Sang* (ICC-01/09-01/11); *Prosecutor v. Uhuru Muigai Kenyatta* (ICC-01/09-02/11); *Prosecutor v. Saif Al-Islam Gaddafi* (ICC-01/11-01/11); *Prosecutor v. Laurent Gbagbo* (ICC-02/11-01/11); *Prosecutor v. Simone Gbagbo* (ICC-02/11-01/12); *Prosecutor v. Charles Blé Goudé* (ICC-02/11-02/11). The overall number of 19 cases does not factor in the two proceedings pursuant to Article 70 of the Statute.

[5]   From the outset, proceedings against *Thomas Lubanga Dyilo, Bahar Idriss Abu Garda*, and *Abdallah Banda Abakaer Nourain* concerned allegations of war crimes only. In a fourth case against *Sylvestre Mudacumura*, the Prosecutor had requested the issuance of a

Court's interventions in the situations in the Republic of Kenya, Libya and Côte d'Ivoire have focused exclusively on Article 7 crimes. One may therefore assume that, in the future, crimes against humanity will form the most important aspect of the cases before the ICC.[6]

In the first years, the interpretation and application of Article 7 of the Statute did not seem to raise any particular difficulties (see section 3.3.). The first situations contemplated by the Court, that is, the situations in the Republic of Uganda, the Democratic Republic of the Congo, the Central African Republic and Sudan/Darfur, concerned protracted armed conflict situations during which crimes were allegedly committed against civilians by, as the case may be, governmental forces, rebel movements and/or other armed groups. It was above all the Pre-Trial Chambers, assigned to issue warrants of arrest[7] and decide on the confirmation of charges,[8] that developed the applicable law before the ICC in the first set of cases emanating from the above-mentioned situations. Lacking any previous rulings on the different components of crimes against humanity pursuant to Article 7 of the Statute, the Judges resorted to the jurisprudence of the *ad hoc* tribunals and unhesitatingly borrowed relevant definitions and criteria therefrom. The elaborateness of their interpretative findings on the law was determined by the facts presented before them. But, as will be shown below, the legal determinations were also charged with ambiguity and conceptual vagueness. The fact that various Chambers cross-referenced to and relied on each other's decisions led to a first phase of consolidation of – but also a continuation of ambiguities in – the Court's jurisprudence on Article 7 of the Statute, pending the prospective contribution of the Trial and Appeals Chambers. All in all, the emerging consensus at the Court on the definition of crimes against humanity in the early years was not disturbed by critical questions.

---

warrant of arrest also involving crimes against humanity. However, Pre-Trial Chamber II rejected this request and did not include any counts of crimes against humanity in the warrant of arrest. This does not prevent the Prosecutor from re-characterizing the facts of the case as crimes against humanity in light of new evidence at the confirmation stage or from presenting a new request under Article 58 of the Statute for the issuance of a warrant of arrest involving crimes against humanity. The *Mudacumura* case will be presented in section 3.5.

6   To date, 13 out of 19 cases involve allegations of war crimes and only one case involves allegations of genocide.

7   Article 58 of the Statute.

8   Article 61(7) of the Statute.

It was only with the initiative of the former Prosecutor Luis Moreno Ocampo in November 2009 to intervene *proprio motu* in the situation in the Republic of Kenya that a discussion on the definition of crimes against humanity, and more precisely on the contextual elements of crimes against humanity, was opened for the first time (see section 3.4.). The reason for this development may be found in the fact that the Judges were confronted with a scenario which differed markedly from the situations they had hitherto examined. The events to be assessed under the purview of Article 7 of the Statute did not involve armed groups or armed rebel movements launching attacks against civilians. Rather, the criminal acts were committed by ordinary civilians, perceived to be associated with political parties, at different times and locations and with varying degrees of intensity over a period of approximately two months. Would the facts as presented at the time meet the statutory requirement of an "organizational policy" within the meaning of Article 7(2)(a) of the Statute? Concerns as to the fulfilment of this contextual element sparked a conflict of opinion within the competent Pre-Trial Chamber that was tasked with authorizing the Prosecutor's first-ever *proprio motu* investigation under Article 15 of the Statute. The disagreement remained throughout the two case proceedings that derive from this situation.

It is perhaps fair to say that the dispute over the contextual elements of crimes against humanity in the context of the *Kenya* situation was something of an eye-opener. It sensitized the prosecutorial and judicial authorities at the ICC to the need for definitional clarity of the contextual components of crimes against humanity as they have been framed in the Statute. But far more than that, the Kenya controversy seemed also to have brought about a turn in the evidentiary approach regarding crimes against humanity: some Chambers began to more rigidly scrutinize the fulfilment of each contextual legal requirement of crimes against humanity. Pre-Trial Chamber I, for example, declined to confirm any charges of crimes against humanity brought against *Callixte Mbarushimana* on the basis that there was no evidence sustaining the existence of a "policy". For the same reason, Pre-Trial Chamber II rejected a request to include allegations amounting to crimes against humanity in the warrant of arrest issued against *Sylvestre Mudacumura*. In the authorization proceedings of *proprio motu* investigations in the *Côte d'Ivoire* situation, Pre-Trial Chamber III ruled on including crimes against humanity by taking into account the *Kenya* controversy.[9] In the first case emanating from this situation, the *Laurent Gbagbo* case, the majority of Pre-Trial Chamber I adjourned the hearing on the confirmation of charges and requested the Prosecutor to consider providing further evidence or conducting further investigation, *inter alia*, with respect to the alleged "organizational policy". Finally, in the *Germain Katanga* case, Trial Chamber II proposed a new definition of "organization" within the meaning of Article 7(2)(a) of the Statute, which, in its view, accords with the object and purpose of the Statute. As one can see, the debate on the contextual elements of crimes against humanity is still very much ongoing at the Court (see section 3.5.).

3.2. The Applicable Law

Crimes against humanity belong to the category of core crimes listed in Article 5 of the Statute that are considered to be "the most serious crimes of concern to the international community as a whole".[10] Article 7 of the Statute is presumed to codify the customary law definition of crimes against humanity.[11] Despite this principled approach, which – one would assume – could have facilitated reaching an agreement without difficulty at the Diplomatic Conference in Rome, participants at the time attest to the complicated negotiations concerning the exact definition of crimes against humanity. Considerations of "constructive ambiguity" in the wording finally allowed delegations to overcome their differences and adopt, by way of compromise, the text of Article 7 of the Statute. This achievement is underlined by the introductory words in Article 7(1) of the Statute, which sets out that this definition is "for the purpose *of this Statute*" (emphasis added).

Article 7 of the Statute contains three paragraphs: Article 7(1) of the Statute encompasses the *chapeau* elements reflecting the contextual ele-

---

[9] Pre-Trial Chamber III, Corrigendum to "Decision Pursuant to Article 15 of the Rome Statute on the Authorisation of an Investigation into the Situation in the Republic of Côte d'Ivoire" ('*Côte d'Ivoire* Authorisation of Investigation'), 15 November 2011, ICC-02/11-14-Corr, paras. 43, 45, 46 and 99 (http://www.legal-tools.org/doc/e0c0eb/).

[10] Paragraph 4 of the preamble of the Statute.

[11] Report of the Preparatory Committee on the Establishment of an International Criminal Court. Volume I (Proceedings of the Preparatory Committee during March-April and August 1996), General Assembly, 51st session, Supplement No 22, A/51/22 (1996), paras. 51–54; Herman von Hebel and Darryl Robinson, "Crimes Within the Jurisdiction of the Court", in Roy Lee (ed.), *The International Criminal Court: The Making of the ICC Statute*, Kluwer Law International, The Hague, 1999, p. 91.

ments of crimes against humanity in which the individual offences, as set out in sub-paragraphs (a) to (k), are embedded. Articles 7(2) and 7(3) of the Statute contain statutory definitions in relation to selected terms used in Article 7(1) of the Statute.

Of particular interest is the statutory articulation of the context of crimes against humanity as set out in the introductory sentence of Article 7(1) of the Statute, which reads:

> For the purpose of this Statute, 'crime against humanity' means any of the following acts when committed as part of a widespread or systematic attack directed against any civilian population, with knowledge of the attack: […]

Article 7(2)(a) of the Statute provides a legal definition for the notion "attack directed against any civilian population" used in Article 7(1) of the Statute, which is as follows:

> 'Attack directed against any civilian population' means a course of conduct involving the multiple commission of acts referred to in paragraph 1 against any civilian population, pursuant to or in furtherance of a State or organizational policy to commit such attack.

In interpreting the Statute, Judges are assisted by the Elements of Crimes.[12] With respect to the current discussion, paragraph 3 of the Introduction to Crimes Against Humanity in the Elements of Crimes adds:

> "Attack directed against a civilian population" in these context elements is understood to mean a course of conduct involving the multiple commission of acts referred to in Article 7, paragraph 1, of the Statute against any civilian population, pursuant to or in furtherance of a State or organizational policy to commit such attack. The acts need not constitute a military attack. It is understood that 'policy to commit such attack' requires that the State or organization actively promote or encourage such an attack against a civilian population.

Finally footnote 6 of the Elements of Crimes stipulates on the "policy" requirement:

> A policy which has a civilian population as the object of the attack would be implemented by State or organizational ac-

---

[12] Article 9 of the Statute. According to Article 21(1)(a) of the Statute, the Court shall apply, in the first place, the Statute and the Elements of Crimes.

tion. Such a policy may, in exceptional circumstances, be implemented by a deliberate failure to take action, which is consciously aimed at encouraging such attack. The existence of such a policy cannot be inferred solely from the absence of governmental or organizational action.

A comparison of the above with other antecedent instruments reveals two significant discrepancies in wording. As has already been noted by others, any nexus requirement to the armed conflict, as found in other instruments,[13] is absent from the statutory definition of crimes against humanity. Likewise, any discriminatory grounds according to which the crimes occur[14] are also not required. Most importantly, there has been no attempt by the Court to read either of these two requirements into Article 7(1) of the Statute.[15]

Crimes against humanity are made of two components: the context and the specific acts. How they relate to each other is expressed in the chapeau of Article 7(1) of the Statute which confirms that the specific acts enlisted under Article 7(1)(a) to (k) of the Statute are to be considered as crimes against humanity "*when committed as part of* a widespread or systematic attack directed against any civilian population" (emphasis added). Hence, the specific acts are embedded into the wider contextual "attack". This requirement is commonly referred to as the nexus, linking the underlying act with the "attack".[16] The nexus requirement ensures that an individual offence is related to the "attack", excluding the possibility that it is an isolated act, unrelated to the prevailing context. Indicators, such as the "nature, aim and consequences" of the act, assist in the determination of

---

[13] See, *e.g.*, Article 6(c) of the Charter of the International Military Tribunal, as annexed to the London Agreement; Article 5 of the Statute of the International Criminal Tribunal for the Former Yugoslavia.

[14] See Article 3 of the Statute of the International Tribunal for Rwanda. A special intent element is, however, required for the crime of persecution within the meaning of Article 7(1)(h) of the ICC Statute.

[15] Therefore, it has been said that the two requirements contained in other instruments no longer form part of the customary law definition of crimes against humanity, see also Rodney Dixon, revised by Christopher Hall, "Article 7", in Otto Triffterer (ed.), *Commentary on the ICC Statute of the International Criminal Court*, C. H. Beck, München, 2008, p. 174.

[16] In the Elements of Crimes, this requirement is one of the objective conditions for establishing a crime as a crime against humanity.

whether the act formed part of the attack.[17] The Court has followed the logic of the Statute and regularly first examines and establishes the existence of such context.[18] Failure to prove a widespread or systematic attack carries the consequence that there is no need to proceed with an examination of the underlying act.[19]

The establishment of the contextual elements is also of pivotal importance for another reason. A number of crimes, such as murder or rape, do not in and of themselves bear the character of an international crime. It is the context in which they occur that 'internationalizes' them and elevates them to the category of "the most serious crimes of concern to the international community as a whole". It has therefore been argued that it is the context that, when established, confers jurisdiction on the Court and triggers the Court's intervention.[20] This consideration suggests the follow-

---

[17] Pre-Trial Chamber II, Decision Pursuant to Article 61(7)(a) and (b) of the Rome Statute on the Charges of the Prosecutor Against Jean-Pierre Bemba Gombo ('*Bemba* Confirmation of Charges'), 15 June 2009, ICC-01/05-01/08-424, para. 86 (http://www.legal-tools.org/doc/07965c/); Pre-Trial Chamber II, Decision Pursuant to Article 15 of the Rome Statute on the Authorization of an Investigation into the Situation in the Republic of Kenya ('*Kenya* Authorization of Investigation'), 31 March 2010, ICC-01/09-19-Corr, para. 98 (http://www.legal-tools.org/doc/f0caaf/); Trial Chamber II, *Jugement rendu en application de l'Article 74 du Statut* ('*Katanga* Judgment'), 7 March 2014, ICC-01/04-01/07-3436, para. 1124 ("Les actes isolés qui, par leur nature, leurs buts et leurs conséquences, diffèrent clairement d'autres actes s'inscrivant dans le cadre d'une attaque ne relèvent ainsi pas de l'Article 7-1 du Statut.") (http://www.legal-tools.org/doc/9813bb/).

[18] Pre-Trial Chamber I, Decision on the Prosecution's Application for a Warrant of Arrest against Omar Hassan Ahmad Al Bashir ('*Bashir* Arrest Warrant 2009'), 4 March 2009, ICC-02/05-01/09-3, para. 53 (http://www.legal-tools.org/doc/e26cf4/). Exceptions are the judgment of Trial Chamber II in the *Katanga* case and the confirmation of charges decision of Pre-Trial Chamber I in the *Laurent Gbagbo* case, in which the specific acts were examined before the context was established. However, this is not grounded in a departure from the understanding of crimes against humanity, but rather in an effort to use the findings on the specific crimes for the purpose of the context, see Trial Chamber II, *Katanga* Judgment; Pre-Trial Chamber I, Decision on the confirmation of charges against Laurent Gbagbo ('*Gbagbo* Confirmation of Charges'), 12 June 2014, ICC-02/11-01/11-656-Red (http://www.legal-tools.org/doc/5b41bc/).

[19] See also Pre-Trial Chamber I, Decision on the Confirmation of Charges ('*Mbarushimana* Confirmation of Charges'), 16 December 2011, ICC-01/04-01/10-465-Red, paras. 244 and 266 (http://www.legal-tools.org/doc/63028f/).

[20] Dissenting Opinions of Judge Hans-Peter Kaul, annexed to Pre-Trial Chamber II, Decision on the Confirmation of Charges Pursuant to Article 61(7)(a) and (b) of the Rome Statute ('*Ruto et al.* Confirmation of Charges'), 23 January 2012, ICC-01/09-01/11-373, p. 155, para. 25 (http://www.legal-tools.org/doc/96c3c2/); and Pre-Trial Chamber II, Decision on the Confirmation of Charges Pursuant to Article 61(7)(a) and (b) of the Rome Statute ('*Muthaura et al.* Confirmation of Charges'), 23 January 2012, ICC-01/09-02/11-382-Red,

up question about the true nature of the context and whether contextual elements of crimes against humanity are jurisdictional matters and/or matters relating to substantive law, as they form part and parcel of the definition of the crime. The answer to this query has important consequences in practice. Assuming that the context is bound up with 'jurisdiction', to what extent is the Court entitled to assess the contextual elements as a matter of accepting the Court's competence in the first place? If so, would the establishment of the context as a matter of 'jurisdiction' over a particular situation relieve the Court from later asserting its existence anew when discussing the substantive merits of a case? Which threshold is determinative for the establishment of the context: a jurisdictional threshold, such as that of "degree of certainty",[21] which is not an evidentiary threshold linked to the merits of a case,[22] or the progressively higher evidentiary

---

para. 32 (http://www.legal-tools.org/doc/4972c0/). See also Rodney Dixon, revised by Christopher Hall, 2008, *supra* note 15.

[21] *Bemba* Confirmation of Charges, para. 24, *supra* note 17; Pre-Trial Chamber II, Decision on the Prosecutor's Application for Summons to Appear for William Samoei Ruto, Henry Kiprono Kosgey and Joshua Arap Sang, 8 March 2011, ICC-01/09-01/11-1, para. 9 (http://www.legal-tools.org/doc/6c9fb0/); as recalled in *Ruto et al.* Confirmation of Charges, para. 25, see *supra* note 20; Mohamed M. El Zeidy, *The Principle of Complementarity in International Criminal Law: Origin, Development and Practice*, Brill, 2008, pp. 248–249.

[22] The formula 'attain the degree of certainty' was introduced by Pre-Trial Chamber II in the *Bemba* case without defining it. On the other hand, Pre-Trial Chamber I in the *Mbarushimana* case, refrained from making a pronouncement in the context of the suspect's challenge to jurisdiction, Pre-Trial Chamber I, Decision on the "Challenge to the Jurisdiction of the Court", 26 October 2011, ICC-01/04-01/10-451, para. 5 (http://www.legal-tools.org/doc/864f9b/). In any event, it is clear that the Court draws a distinction between preliminary procedural questions, such as those of jurisdiction and admissibility, and the merits of the case. This is supported by the fact that Chambers have declined to apply any of the already existing evidentiary thresholds pertaining to the criminal proceedings *stricto sensu* under the Statute. The same approach was followed in the context of admissibility issues which, as a concept, is also enshrined in Article 19(1) of the Statute, see, *e.g.*, Pre-Trial Chamber I, Decision on the Admissibility of the Case Against Saif Al-Islam Gaddafi, 31 May 2013, ICC-01/11-01/11-344-Red, paras. 54–55 (http://www.legal-tools.org/doc/339ee2/). Pre-Trial Chamber II, when deciding on the admissibility challenge of the Republic of Kenya did not refer to any standard at all, see Pre-Trial Chamber II, Decision on the Application by the Government of Kenya Challenging the Admissibility of the Case Pursuant to Article 19(2)(b) of the Statute, 30 May 2011, ICC-01/09-02/11-96, para. 41 ("[T]he Chamber's determination on the subject-matter of the present challenge is ultimately dictated by the facts presented and the legal parameters embodied in the Court's statutory provisions.") (http://www.legal-tools.org/doc/bb4591/).

thresholds[23] of the Statute? Which type of evidence would be considered sufficient to satisfy the relevant standards? Some of the above questions have been addressed but are not yet fully explored by the Court.

The practice of the Office of the Prosecutor suggests that contextual elements of the crimes (also) pertain to the issue of 'jurisdiction'. Indeed, during the preliminary examination of a 'situation',[24] the Prosecutor has regularly extended his/her analysis on the jurisdictional scope to a thorough legal and factual assessment of the contextual elements of the crimes, without applying any particular evidentiary threshold.[25] In fact, the opening of the investigation into the situation in Venezuela was declined on the grounds that "the available information did not provide a reasonable basis to believe that the requirement of a widespread or systematic attack against any civilian population had been satisfied".[26] The mandate of the Court, as expressed in Article 1 of the Statute, the limited resources of the Court, and the ensuing necessity for the Prosecutor to carefully select the situations in which the Court would eventually inter-

---

[23] Appeals Chamber, Judgment on the Appeal of the Prosecutor Against the "Decision on the Prosecution's Application for a Warrant of Arrest Against Omar Hassan Ahmad Al Bashir", 3 February 2010, ICC-02/05-01/09-73, para. 30 (http://www.legal-tools.org/doc/9ada8e/); *Kenya* Authorization of Investigation, paras. 28 and 34–35, see *supra* note 17.

[24] Article 53(1) of the Statute sets out the criteria for the preliminary examination. Subparagraph (a) instructs the Prosecutor to consider whether there is "a reasonable basis to believe that a crime within the jurisdiction of the Court has been or is being committed". This has been interpreted by Pre-Trial Chamber II to include all jurisdictional parameters, including *ratione materiae*, see *Kenya* Authorization of Investigation, para. 39, *supra* note 17.

[25] See the "Policy Paper on Preliminary Examinations" of 13 November 2013, paras. 36, 39 ("Accordingly, for the purpose of assessing subject-matter jurisdiction, the Office considers, on the basis of the available information, the relevant underlying facts and factors relating to the crimes that appear to fall within the jurisdiction of the Court; contextual circumstances, such as the nexus to an armed conflict or to a widespread or systematic attack directed against a civilian population, or a manifest pattern of similar conduct directed at the destruction of a particular protected group or which could itself effect such destruction"), 80 and 81 ("Phase 2 analysis entails a thorough factual and legal assessment of the crimes allegedly committed in the situation at hand with a view to identifying the potential cases falling within the jurisdiction of the Court").

[26] In the same decision, the Prosecutor also determined that, in relation to allegations of war crimes, the situation "clearly does not meet the threshold of an armed conflict", see Office of the Prosecutor, Decision of the Prosecutor Not to Open an Investigation Into the Situation in Venezuela dated 9 February 2006; see similarly the conclusion not to open an investigation into the situation in the Republic of Korea, Office of the Prosecutor, Article 5 Report, June 2014, paras. 42 *et seq.*, and 82.

---

vene justify such a reasonable approach. Likewise, in the context of 'situation'-related proceedings as to the authorization of the commencement of an investigation under Article 15 of the Statute, the analysis of the material under the rubric of 'jurisdiction' suggests that Pre-Trial Chambers also consider the contextual elements of crimes against humanity to be part of jurisdiction.[27] However, this approach changes the moment a 'case' is opened. There, the Court has deferred the assessment of the context to the discussion on the merits of the case.[28] In the context of the two *Kenya* cases, the Appeals Chamber in particular seized the opportunity to clarify this issue as a matter of principle. While it did not take a position on the proposition as to the jurisdictional nature of the context,[29] it nevertheless highlighted the risk of duplicating the discussion and cautioned against conflating the separate concepts of 'jurisdiction' with, at the time, the

---

[27] See *Kenya* Authorization of Investigation, *supra* note 17; *Côte d'Ivoire* Authorisation of Investigation, *supra* note 9.

[28] *Ruto et al.* Confirmation of Charges, para. 35, see *supra* note 20; *Muthaura et al.* Confirmation of Charges, paras. 33–34, see *supra* note 20. For a different view see Judge Hans-Peter Kaul:

> [T]he answer to the question of whether the Court has such jurisdiction is, in principle, not subject to the progressively higher evidentiary thresholds which apply at the different stages of the proceedings. [...] [A]n affirmative answer to that question is a pre-condition to the Court's discussion of the merits. Consequently, the question cannot be deferred to the merits but must be ruled upon definitively *ab initio*. In other words, the Court does not have limited jurisdiction when issuing a warrant of arrest or summons to appear; slightly more jurisdiction at the confirmation of charges stage; and jurisdiction 'beyond reasonable doubt' at trial, after the merits have been fully adjudged. The Court either has jurisdiction or does not.

See, *e.g.*, Dissenting Opinion of Judge Hans-Peter Kaul, annexed to *Ruto et al.* Confirmation of Charges, pp. 155–156, para. 26, *supra* note 20; and annexed to *Muthaura et al.* Confirmation of Charges, pp. 177–178, para. 33, *supra* note 20.

[29] Referring to the Dissenting Opinion of Judge Hans-Peter Kaul in the *Kenya* cases, in which the dissenting Judge advocated that the context relates to both the jurisdiction and the merits of the case, the Appeals Chamber replied that these arguments "do not affect the conclusion of the Appeals Chamber", see, *e.g.*, Appeals Chamber, Decision on the Appeals of Mr William Samoei Ruto and Mr Joshua Arap Sang Against the Decision of Pre-Trial Chamber II of 23 January 2012 entitled "Decision on the Confirmation of Charges Pursuant to Article 61(7)(a) and (b) of the Rome Statute" (*'Ruto et al.* Appeal Decision'), 24 May 2012, ICC-01/09-01/11-414, para. 30 (http://www.legal-tools.org/doc/6934fb/). The same finding was made in the *Kenyatta* case (ICC-01/09-02/11).

confirmation of charges process, during which this question surfaced.[30] Finally, the Appeals Judges concluded:

> [...] the interpretation and existence of an 'organizational policy' relate to the substantive merits of this case as opposed to the issue of whether the Court has subject-matter jurisdiction to consider such questions. As the Prosecutor has expressly alleged crimes against humanity, including the existence of an 'organizational policy', the Appeals Chamber finds that the Court has subject-matter jurisdiction over the crimes [...]. Whether the Prosecutor can establish the existence of such a policy, in law and on the evidence, is a question to be determined on the merits.[31]

The solution suggested above has left little flexibility for the Court to react at the stage of a 'case' – in admittedly exceptional situations where the context is controversial – in the same manner as it would during the 'situation' stage. As seen above, should the Prosecutor during the preliminary examination stage determine that the context of crimes against humanity does not exist, he/she would render a finding on 'jurisdiction'. The same applies for the Pre-Trial Chamber that reviews the Prosecutor's assessment in the context of the Article 15(4) authorization proceedings or Article 53(3)(a) review proceedings. For which reasons the same question is treated differently in the context of a 'case' is not further developed by the Appeals Chamber.[32] Rather, the Judges resolved the matter by highlighting the procedural 'context' of the cases *sub judice* in which this question arose. The consequence of the Appeals Chamber's ruling is that in 'case' proceedings any concerns as to the existence of the context must be postponed to the evidentiary discussion on the merits; the Judges cannot raise any concerns in relation to the jurisdictional test within the

---

[30] *Ibid.*, *Ruto et al.* Appeal Decision, paras. 29–30; see also Appeals Chamber, Decision on the Appeal of Mr Francis Kirimi Muthaura and Mr Uhuru Muigai Kenyatta Against the Decision of Pre-Trial Chamber II of 23 January 2012 entitled "Decision on the Confirmation of Charges Pursuant to Article 61(7)(a) and (b) of the Rome Statute" (*'Muthaura and Kenyatta* Appeal Decision'), 24 May 2012, ICC-01/09-02/11-425, paras. 35–36 (http://www.legal-tools.org/doc/b6aad9/).

[31] *Ibid.*

[32] In fact, should the Appeals Chamber entertain the question of 'jurisdiction' in the context of reviewing the Pre-Trial Chamber's relevant decisions under Article 15(4) or 53(3)(a)/53(1)(a) of the Statute, then a distinction between 'jurisdiction' and 'merits of the case' is no longer possible.

meaning of Article 19(1) of the Statute.[33] Effectively, the discussion on the context has been removed from the subject-matter jurisdiction of the Court; jurisdictional challenges under Article 19(2) of the Statute purporting an alleged absence of the context cannot be brought. Far more, the Appeals Chamber suggests that the Prosecutor's initial labelling of the crimes, which triggers the Court's intervention in the first place, be accepted unquestionably by the Judges: "As the Prosecutor has expressly alleged crimes against humanity, […] the Appeals Chamber finds that the Court has subject-matter jurisdiction over the crimes".[34] But, the actual effect of the above cited statement lies in entertaining the contextual elements at the stage of the merits, subjecting their assessment to the progressively higher thresholds of the Statute. Undoubtedly, as part of the definition of crimes against humanity, the contextual elements are inextricably intertwined with the substantive law. The case law of international courts and tribunals also supports this approach. But, whether this will prove to be a practicable and sustainable approach for the Office of the Prosecutor at the ICC still needs to be seen.[35] In the case of the *Prosecutor v. Laurent Gbagbo*, it became clear what such an assessment at the stage of the merits entails.

---

[33] "Even if the Trial Chamber were not to find, in law or on the evidence that there was an organizational policy this would not mean that the Court did not have jurisdiction over the case but rather that crimes against humanity were not committed", see *Ruto et al.* Appeal Decision, para. 30, *supra* note 29; *Muthaura and Kenyatta* Appeal Decision, para. 36, *supra* note 30.

[34] Also this statement is difficult to uphold in proceedings at the 'situation' level as the very essence of Article 15(4) and 53(3)(a)/53(1)(a) proceedings is to enquire, amongst other, into the Court's competence *ratione materiae*. Deference to the assessment of the Prosecutor is difficult to reconcile with the Pre-Trial Chamber's supervisory functions. By the same token, the argumentation advanced by the Appeals Chamber, *i.e.*, that a distinction must be made between the 'existence' and the 'contours' of the crime, must be viewed in light of the particular circumstances in which this statement was made. It borrowed this argument from the case law of other international tribunals that do not have any situation-related proceedings but deal with cases in a pre-defined situation only. Again, in the framework of Articles 15, 53(1)(a)/53(3)(a) proceedings, this argument does not carry over because a decision on the 'contours' of the crime is part and parcel of the Court's assessment, see *ibid.*, *Ruto et al.* Appeal Decision, paras. 31–32, *supra* note 29; *Muthaura and Kenyatta* Appeal Decision, para. 37, *supra* note 30. It is unfortunate that the Appeals Chamber did not analyse the potential two-fold nature of the context broadly, by taking into account the operation of the Statute as a whole.

[35] See Dissenting Opinion of Judge Hans-Peter Kaul, *supra*, note 28.

Regardless of when the components of the contextual elements are to be assessed, considerations of legal certainty require that their meaning and scope be clearly defined. As the wording of Article 3 of the Proposed Convention replicates that of Article 7 of the Statute, how the statutory provision has been interpreted and applied in the context of the various situations before the Court may be of interest. As has been pointed out in the introduction, the jurisprudence of the Court began rather harmoniously but soon was upset by a number of discordant voices. The following summary of the evolution in the interpretation of Article 7 of the Statute is meant to assist in understanding where the Court stands today. A short description of the underlying cases will introduce these developments with a view to allowing the reader to understand the various approaches taken by the Chambers.

3.3. The First Cases

The first cases involving crimes against humanity emanate from situations which share a basic factual constellation: parts of the civilian population are menaced and targeted over several years by State forces or rebel groups/armed movements, which have adopted an inhumane and toxic policy to commit an attack against the former. Regularly, civilians are targeted because of their perceived affiliation with one side of the conflict. In the scenario involving a conflict situation between armed groups, the State is weak or not in a position to assert its authority over at least parts of the territory. The armed groups have filled this gap and pursue their goals by resorting to brutal violence. Below, four representative case studies, which provided the factual basis against which the Chambers developed the analysis of the applicable law, are introduced.

3.3.1. The Facts

The first case emanates from the situation in the Republic of Uganda which was referred to the Court by the Republic of Uganda itself. It concerns *Joseph Kony, Vincent Otti, Okot Odhiambo and Dominic Ongwen*,[36]

---

[36] A warrant of arrest was issued separately for each suspect. For ease of reference, only reference to the warrant of arrest against *Joseph Kony* will be made in this chapter. A further warrant of arrest was issued against the fifth suspect *Raska Lukwiya* who was killed subsequently. Proceedings against him were terminated and the warrant of arrest ceased to have effect, see Pre-Trial Chamber II, Decision to Terminate Proceedings Against Raska Lukwiya, 11 July 2007, ICC-02/04-01/05-248 (http://www.legal-tools.org/doc/3e6d25/).

leadership members of the 'Lord's Resistance Army' ('LRA'), for whom warrants of arrest were issued on 8 July 2005[37] on account of their alleged involvement in the commission of crimes in Northern Uganda. In the respective warrants, Pre-Trial Chamber II held that there were reasonable grounds to believe that the LRA had been carrying out an insurgency against the Government of Uganda and the Ugandan Army and local defence units since at least 1987.[38] In pursuing its goals the LRA leadership purportedly devised and implemented a strategy to brutalize and target the civilian population in a "campaign of attacks".[39] The Chamber further held that the LRA, led by *Joseph Kony*, is "organized in a military-type hierarchy and operates as an army"[40] and that *Joseph Kony* had "issued broad orders to target and kill civilian populations, including those living in camps for internally displaced persons".[41] Accordingly, *Joseph Kony* and the co-suspects were believed to be responsible, *inter alia*, for the commission of crimes against humanity and war crimes in connection with six attacks during sometime in 2003 and sometime in 2004.[42]

The second case stems from the situation in the Democratic Republic of the Congo ('DRC') which was referred to the Court by the DRC itself. *Germain Katanga*, President of the Ngiti militia 'Forces de résistance patriotique en Ituri' ('FRPI') and *Mathieu Ngudjolo Chui*, allegedly a member of the 'Front des Nationalistes et Intégrationnistes' ('FNI') were brought before the Court for their alleged participation in the attack of the village Bogoro on 24 February 2003 which "resulted in the deaths of approximately 200 civilians".[43] In the decision confirming the charges, Pre-Trial Chamber I found substantial grounds to believe that the Bogoro attack occurred in the context of a "widespread campaign of military attacks" against various locations throughout Ituri "from the end of 2002

---

[37] The initial warrant of arrest against *Joseph Kony* was amended on 27 September 2005, see Pre-Trial Chamber II, Warrant of Arrest for Joseph Kony issued on 8 July 2005 as amended on 27 September 2005, ICC-02/04-01/05-53 (http://www.legal-tools.org/doc/b1010a/).

[38] *Ibid.*, para. 5.

[39] *Ibid.*, paras. 9 and 12.

[40] *Ibid.*, para. 7.

[41] *Ibid.*, para. 12.

[42] *Ibid.*, paras. 13 and 42.

[43] Pre-Trial Chamber I, Decision on the confirmation of charges ('*Katanga and Chui* Confirmation of Charges'), 30 September 2008, ICC-01/04-01/07-717, para. 408 (http://www.legal-tools.org/doc/67a9ec/).

until the middle of 2003".[44] Special mention is made in the decision to the killing of about 1,200 civilians in the village of Nyankunde.[45] The military attacks were directed against the civilian population of predominantly Hema ethnicity of the region Ituri[46] and were committed "pursuant to a common policy and an organized common plan" which aimed at, *inter alia*, specifically targeting the Hema civilians, in the context of a larger campaign of reprisals, and destroying Bogoro in order to ensure control over the route to Bunia.[47] Moreover, Pre-Trial Chamber I found that the Bogoro attack also occurred in context of an armed conflict taking place in Ituri from August 2002 until May 2003 that involved a number of local armed groups and the forces of at least one State.[48] Accordingly, both *Germain Katanga* and *Mathieu Ngudjolo Chui* were committed to trial for having committed crimes against humanity and war crimes.[49]

The third case emanates from the situation in the Central African Republic ('CAR') which was referred to the Court by that State itself. *Jean-Pierre Bemba Gombo* was charged with criminal responsibility for the commission of crimes committed by elements of his militia 'Mouvement de Libération du Congo' ('MLC') during the period of 25 October 2002 until 15 March 2003 at different localities in the CAR. In its decision on the confirmation of charges, Pre-Trial Chamber II found substantial grounds to believe that crimes had taken place in the context of a protracted confrontation between, on the one hand, the national armed forces loyal to former CAR President, Ange-Félix Patassé, assisted by MLC combatants commonly referred to as 'Banyamulenge', and, on the other, a rebel movement led by former Chief of Staff of the CAR national armed forces, François Bozizé. Other foreign armed groups were also believed to be involved in the conflict. The MLC contingent, of which *Jean-Pierre Bemba Gombo* was purportedly the commander-in-chief, was sent to the CAR in response to a call from Ange-Félix Patassé who was facing a

---

44   *Ibid.*, paras. 409–411 and 416.

45   *Ibid.*, para. 409, footnote 535.

46   *Ibid.*, para. 411.

47   *Ibid.*, para. 413.

48   *Ibid.*, paras. 239–241.

49   *Mathieu Ngudjolo Chui* was later acquitted by Trial Chamber II as it could not be established beyond reasonable doubt that he was the commander of the armed group he was associated with at the material time, see Trial Chamber II, *Jugement rendu en application de l'Article 74 du Statut*, 18 December 2012, ICC-01/04-02/12-3 (http://www.legal-tools.org/doc/120cd8/).

coup by François Bozizé. *Jean-Pierre Bemba Gombo* was committed to trial for his criminal responsibility, as military commander, for crimes against humanity and war crimes.[50]

Finally, the fourth case stems from the situation in Sudan/Darfur, which was referred to the Court by Security Council resolution 1593(2005). A case was brought against the current President of Sudan, *Omar Hassan Ahmad Al Bashir*, for his alleged responsibility in the commission of genocide, crimes against humanity and war crimes against members of the Fur, Masalit and Zaghawa groups inhabiting the Darfur region.[51] The alleged crimes took place over five years, from April 2003 to 14 July 2008, affecting hundreds of thousands of civilians. In the first warrant of arrest for *Omar Hassan Ahmad Al Bashir*, Pre-Trial Chamber I found reasonable grounds to believe that, as President, he had used the State apparatus, involving the Sudanese army and police forces, national intelligence and security services, the humanitarian aid commission and the allied Janjaweed militia group, to conduct a counter-insurgency campaign against several armed groups in the Darfur region. The campaign was believed to have as its aim the unlawful attack on the Fur, Masalit and Zaghawa civilian population of Darfur perceived to be close to armed groups opposing the government of Sudan in the ongoing armed conflict.[52] The attacks, conducted against a great number of villages and towns across large areas of Darfur,[53] were regularly introduced by air

---

[50] *Bemba* Confirmation of Charges, see *supra* note 17.

[51] *Bashir* Arrest Warrant 2009, see *supra* note 18; Pre-Trial Chamber I, Second Decision on the Prosecution's Application for a Warrant of Arrest ('*Bashir* Arrest Warrant 2010'), 12 July 2010, ICC-02/05-01/09-94 (http://www.legal-tools.org/doc/50fbab/). Prior to that, Pre-Trial Chamber I had issued warrants of arrest against *Ahmad Muhammad Harun* ('*Harun*') and *Ali Muhammad Ali Abd-Al-Rahman* ('*Kushayb*'). That case overlaps, to a great extent, with the facts of the case against the current President *Omar Hassan Ahmad Al Bashir*, but is more limited in its temporal scope, see Pre-Trial Chamber I, Decision on the Prosecution Application under Article 58(7) of the Statute ('*Harun and Kushayb* Arrest Warrant'), 27 April 2007, ICC-02/05-01/07-1-Corr (http://www.legal-tools.org/doc/e2469d/).

[52] *Ibid.*, paras. 55, 62–70, 76–78, and 83.

[53] Note was taken of the reported attacks against the towns of Kodoom, Bindisi, Mukjar and Arawala and surrounding villages in Wadi Salih, Mukjar and Garsila-Deleig localities in West-Darfur (August/September and December 2003); the towns of Shattaya and Kailek in South Darfur (February/March 2004); between 89 to 92 mainly Zaghawa, Masalit and Misseriya Jebel towns and villages in Buram locality in South Darfur (between November 2005 and September 2006); the town of Muhajeriya in the Yasin locality in South Darfur (8 October 2007); the towns of Saraf Jidad, Abu Suruj, Sirba, Jebel Moon and Silea towns

plane bombings followed by a wide line formation of attackers in tens or hundreds of vehicles and camels.[54] The localities concerned were pillaged and means of survival in the area, including food, shelter, crops, livestock, wells and water pumps, were destroyed.[55] Thousands of civilians are believed to have been killed[56] tortured,[57] raped,[58] and up to 2.7 million civilians from the Fur, Masalit and Zaghawa groups forcibly transferred into inhospitable terrain where some have died as a result of thirst, starvation and disease.[59]

3.3.2. The Early Interpretation

The above cases can be said to have laid down the foundations regarding the appropriate interpretation and application of Article 7 of the Statute. Some of the legal determinations made therein remain uncontested and are systematically applied in different situations and cases. As already explained above, the centrepiece of the Court's enquiry is the existence of the widespread or systematic "attack", without which the crimes remain ordinary crimes.[60] As also described above, the Statute assists with a definition in Article 7(2)(a) of the Statute for the component "attack", but remains silent as to the terms "widespread" and "systematic". As will be

---

in the Kulbus lovality in West Darfur (January/February 2008); and Shegeg Karo and al-Ain areas in North Darfur (May 2008).

[54] *Bashir* Arrest Warrant 2009, para. 85, see *supra* note 18.

[55] *Ibid.*, paras. 77 and 91.

[56] *Ibid.*, paras. 94 and 97. See also *Bashir* Arrest Warrant 2010, footnotes 32 and 33, *supra* note 51.

[57] *Ibid.*, *Bashir* Arrest Warrant 2009, para. 104.

[58] *Ibid.*, para. 108.

[59] *Ibid.*, para. 100. On 12 July 2010, the Chamber issued a second warrant of arrest concluding that the crime of genocide had been fulfilled by killing, causing serious bodily harm and deliberately inflicting on the Fur, Masalit and Zaghawa groups conditions of life calculated to bring about their physical destruction in whole or in part, see *Bashir* Arrest Warrant 2010, *supra* note 51.

[60] As was later acknowledged in the *Mbarushimana* case, see *Mbarushimana* Confirmation of Charges, para. 244, *supra* note 19 ("Acts such as those charged by the Prosecution under Article 7 of the Statute only qualify as crimes against humanity, pursuant to Article 7(1) of the Statute, when 'committed as part of a widespread or systematic attack directed against any civilian population, with knowledge of the attack'"); see similarly in the *Mudacumura* case, Pre-Trial Chamber II, Decision on the Prosecutor's Application under Article 58 of the Statute ('*Mudacumura* Arrest Warrant'), 13 July 2012, ICC-01/04-01/12-1-Red, para. 22 (http://www.legal-tools.org/doc/ecfae0/).

---

shown, in these cases, the Court further elicited the meaning of those qualifiers.

3.3.2.1. The "Attack"

The Judges regularly embraced the definitional specification of "attack directed against any civilian population" in Article 7(2)(a) of the Statute, but went further to concretize its meaning to the extent needed for the determination of the first cases. The "attack" as a "course of conduct" has been described largely as a "campaign or operation carried out against civilians" that, as prescribed by the Elements of Crimes, does not need to carry the features of a military attack.[61] The notions of 'campaign' or 'operation' seem to imply a certain degree of magnitude, continuity and linkage between individual acts. However, in light of the facts of the first cases, these notions have not been further elaborated upon. The "attack" is further characterized by two cumulative elements.

The "multiple commission of acts and the attack being pursuant to or in furtherance of a State or organizational policy to commit such attack" are statutory components that assist in identifying the "attack" as such.[62] The Court devoted some effort in giving those two distinct conditions appropriate meaning and effect. It is thus clear that the Court did not dispose of those conditions or consider them redundant or otherwise subsumed. At first, the "course of conduct" is conditioned upon the existence of "multiple commission of acts". In the *Bemba* case, Pre-Trial Chamber II understood this condition to mean "that more than a few isolated incidents or acts as referred to in Article 7(1) of the Statute have occurred".[63] To support a finding of this kind, consideration was given to the commission of the specific generic acts listed under Article 7(1) of the Statute.[64]

---

[61] *Bemba* Confirmation of Charges, para. 75, see *supra* note 17. This definition was later endorsed by, *e.g.*, *Katanga* Judgment, para. 1101, see *supra* note 17; Pre-Trial Chamber II, Decision Pursuant to Article 61(7)(a) and (b) of the Rome Statute on the Charges of the Prosecutor Against Bosco Ntaganda ('*Ntaganda* Confirmation of Charges'), 11 June 2014, ICC-01/04-02/06-309, paras. 22–23 (http://www.legal-tools.org/doc/5686c6/); and *Gbagbo* Confirmation of Charges, para. 209, see *supra* note 18.

[62] *Ibid.*, *Bemba* Confirmation of Charges, para. 80. This seems to also be the starting point for *Katanga and Chui* Confirmation of Charges, para. 393, see *supra* note 43.

[63] *Ibid.*, *Bemba* Confirmation of Charges, para. 81.

[64] *Ibid.*, paras. 92 and 108. As an aside, it is noteworthy that in a later case, the Court may have considered as relevant all types of acts committed during an operation, including

Given the scale and duration of the military operations carried out against the civilian population in the first cases, this sub-element of Article 7(2)(a) of the Statute equally did not attract much attention.

For an "attack" to be qualified as such under the Statute, it is not sufficient to identify a multiplicity of violent acts. It is also not sufficient that they occur in the course of a 'campaign' or 'operation'. Rather, the acts of violence, which give the "course of conduct" its identity, must be linked or brought together by way of a "policy". This requirement is expressed in the element "pursuant to or in furtherance of a State or organizational policy to commit such attack" in Article 7(2)(a) of the Statute.[65] The legal pronouncements of the Court on this particular condition in the early case law are brief and, compared to later decisions, underdeveloped. To start with, no judicial clarification is given with respect to the two notions "pursuant to or in furtherance of" and what the difference is between either of them, if any. As regards the legal requirement of a "policy", Pre-Trial Chamber II in the *Bemba* case simply suggested that the policy "implies that the attack follows a regular pattern"[66] and need not be formalized.[67] And, the same Chamber added that any attack "which is planned, directed or organized – as opposed to spontaneous or isolated acts of violence – will satisfy this criterion".[68] This latter finding is borrowed from a decision of Pre-Trial Chamber I in the *Katanga/Ngudjolo* case, which added to the above that the policy involves the use of "public or private resources".[69] As we will see below, the factor of the organized nature of the crimes or the pattern in which they occur is also used to evidence the existence of 'systematicity'. Thus, from an *evidentiary* point of view, the

---

what could be considered only as war crimes, see *Ntaganda* Confirmation of Charges, paras. 25–30, *supra* note 61.

[65] "It is the existence of a policy that unites otherwise unrelated inhumane acts, so that it may be said that in the aggregate they collectively form an 'attack'", see Herman von Hebel and Darryl Robinson, 1999, p. 97, *supra* note 11.

[66] *Bemba* Confirmation of Charges, para. 81, see *supra* note 17.

[67] *Ibid.*, para. 81; see also *Katanga and Chui* Confirmation of Charges, para. 396, *supra* note 43 ("The policy need not be explicitly defined by the organisational group"). This finding is later endorsed also by other Chambers, such as in the *Laurent Gbagbo* case, *Gbagbo* Confirmation of Charges, para. 215, see *supra* note 18.

[68] *Ibid.*, *Bemba* Confirmation of Charges, see *supra* note 17. This finding is later endorsed in, e.g., the *Kenyatta* case, see *Muthaura et al.* Confirmation of Charges, para. 111, *supra* note 20; and the *Laurent Gbagbo* case, see *ibid.*, *Gbagbo* Confirmation of Charges.

[69] *Katanga and Chui* Confirmation of Charges, para. 396, see *supra* note 43.

Court simply accepts that the "policy" can be inferred from the existence of a regular pattern/organized nature of the crimes[70] without proposing a definition or dissecting the relationship between the "policy" and the related 'systematic' requirement.[71] Chambers seem to follow the logic: "If the acts of violence follow a regular pattern, there must be a policy behind it". Pre-Trial Chamber II in the *Bemba* case, for example, relied on factors such as threatening civilians, conducting house-to-house searches, intruding into houses, and looting goods to infer such a "policy".[72] By using language pertaining to the 'systematic' prong of the Article 7(1) definition, the early case law seems to meld the two concepts[73] and indeed offers little clarity as to which meaning the Statute foresees for both distinct terms.[74]

As regards the authors of such a "policy", Pre-Trial Chambers have laconically referred to "groups of persons who govern a specific territory or […] any organization with the capability to commit a widespread or systematic attack against a civilian population".[75] The reference to the organization's 'governance' of a specific territory introduces a somewhat high threshold and is reminiscent of the discussion on the existence of

---

[70] See, *e.g.*, *Bemba* Confirmation of Charges, para. 115, *supra* note 17. It is also noted that in the decision concerning the issuance of the first warrant of arrest in the *Bashir* case, the existence of the "policy" is accepted without any further explanation, see *Bashir* Arrest Warrant 2009, paras. 76 and 83, *supra* note 18.

[71] Indeed, as was highlighted later in the *Laurent Gbagbo* case, "evidence of planning, organisation or direction by a State or organisation may be relevant to prove both the policy and the systematic nature of the attack, although the two concepts should not be conflated as they serve different purposes and imply different thresholds under Article 7(1) and 7(2)(a) of the Statute", *Gbagbo* Confirmation of Charges, para. 216, see *supra* note 18.

[72] *Bemba* Confirmation of Charges, para. 115, see *supra* note 17.

[73] See, *e.g.*, Pre-Trial Chamber I in the *Harun/Kushayb* case, which infers conversely the systematicity from the existence of a "policy", *Harun and Kushayb* Arrest Warrant, *supra* note 51, para. 62.

[74] Some clarity is later offered in the *Katanga* judgment, in which Trial Chamber II articulates that the "policy" implies "*un projet préétabli ou un plan à cet effet*", a pre-established design or plan, to attack the civilian population, the details of which may be readily identifiable only in retrospect, once the attack has unfolded, see *Katanga* Judgment, paras. 1109–1110, *supra* note 17.

[75] *Bemba* Confirmation of Charges, para. 81, see *supra* note 17. The same interpretation is to be found in *Katanga and Chui* Confirmation of Charges, para. 396, see *supra* note 43. Reference was made later to these holdings in the *Laurent Gbagbo* case, see *Gbagbo* Confirmation of Charges, para. 217, *supra* note 18.

'organized armed groups'.[76] Indeed, the Judges' interpretation of the law appears to have been influenced by the facts of the cases before them. Moreover, no particular differentiation is made between the policy of a "State" and that of an "organization". In fact, in the *Bashir* case, Pre-Trial Chamber I, when issuing the first warrant of arrest, simply refers to the "Government of Sudan policy", without further contemplating the fact that the Sudanese conflict party included also allied militia groups, which are clearly not part of the State structure.[77] Likewise, the attribution of the policy to the State or organization is also not further discussed. Again, the shortcomings of the early jurisprudence may be explained by the fact that the cases simply did not raise any particular interpretative difficulties for the Judges. It may also have helped that the cases involved charges of crimes against humanity and war crimes the latter of which necessitated the presence of 'organized armed groups' within the meaning of Article 8(2)(f) of the Statute. The basic elaboration of the Judges on this point was sufficient for the purposes of the early cases: there was simply no doubt that the LRA, FNI/FRPI, the MLC or the Sudanese governmental forces fulfilled the statutory requirement of an "organization"/"State" within the meaning of Article 7(2)(a) of the Statute.

From a legal point of view, the most uncontroversial requirement in the early jurisprudence of the Court is the target group of crimes against humanity. Contrary to what Article 7(2)(a) of the Statute announces, the constitutive features of the victimized group are not further set out. Chambers have underscored that the "attack" must have as its primary object the civilian population.[78] This collective entity has been construed to include "all persons who are civilians as opposed to members of armed forces and other legitimate combatants" of "any nationality, ethnicity or

---

[76] See, *e.g.*, *ibid.*, *Katanga and Chui* Confirmation of Charges, para. 239. However, Pre-Trial Chamber II in the *Bemba* case did not discuss the element of 'control over the territory', see *ibid.*, *Bemba* Confirmation of Charges, paras. 233–234.

[77] *Bashir* Arrest Warrant 2009, paras. 55, 83, see *supra* note 18. It is not suggested here that the involvement of private entities negates the existence of a State policy. Rather, it must be assumed that Pre-Trial Chamber I saw no need to qualify this element for the purpose of the issuance of the warrant of arrest. This question became relevant again in the context of the *Laurent Gbagbo* case (see section 3.5.).

[78] *Bemba* Confirmation of Charges, para. 76, see *supra* note 17 ("the civilian population must be the primary object of the attack and not just an incidental victim of the attack"). This was later endorsed by *Katanga* Judgment, para. 1104, see *supra* note 17.

---

other distinguishing features".[79] All the Prosecutor must demonstrate is that the "attack" was not directed against only "a limited and randomly selected group of individuals"; he or she must not provide evidence that the entire population of a geographical area was affected.[80] In the *Katanga* judgment,[81] Trial Chamber II would later add that the presence of non-civilians within the population does not deprive the collectivity of its protection as civilian.[82]

One last point: in the first cases, the "attack" was presented as consisting of a series of assaults or 'contextual attacks' against the civilian population that took place over a prolonged period of time and in various locations. The events, for which the suspect would be held accountable, formed only part of those assaults or 'contextual attacks'. This helped the Court to understand the contextual environment in which the charged incidents took place and eased the determination of "attack" and, subsequently, that of "widespread". This kind of case presentation also conformed to the reading of Article 7(1) of the Statute that considers the specific acts, the charged incidents, to be "part of" the "attack", suggesting that there may be more acts than those charged that formed the overall "attack". As would be later pronounced by Pre-Trial Chamber II in the *Ntaganda* case, "the Prosecutor is free to present further additional acts to

---

[79] *Ibid.*, paras. 76 and 78; *Katanga and Chui* Confirmation of Charges, para. 399, see *supra* note 43; Pre-Trial Chamber I in the *Bashir* case seems to exclude in addition those individuals "who, despite not being members of the said armed groups, were assisting any of them in such a way to amount to taking part in the hostilities", see *Bashir* Arrest Warrant 2009, para. 92, *supra* note 18. This jurisprudence was followed later, *e.g.*, in the *Kenyatta* case, see *Muthaura et al.* Confirmation of Charges, para. 110, *supra* note 20; and in the *Laurent Gbagbo* case, see *Gbagbo* Confirmation of Charges, para. 209, *supra* note 18. For a critical appraisal, see Leila N. Sadat, "Crimes Against Humanity in the Modern Age", in *American Journal of International Law*, 2013, vol. 107, p. 360.

[80] *Bemba* Confirmation of Charges, para. 77, see *supra* note 17.

[81] With the decision dated 21 November 2012, the Trial Chamber II severed the charges against the two accused, *Germain Katanga* and *Mathieu Ngudjolo Chui*, and announced to render its judgment against *Mathieu Ngudjolo Chui* on 18 December 2012, see Trial Chamber II, Decision on the Implementation of Regulation 55 of the Regulations of the Court and Severing the Charges Against the Accused Persons, 21 November 2012, ICC-01/04-01/07-3319 (http://www.legal-tools.org/doc/51ded0/).

[82] *Katanga* Judgment, para. 1105, para. 1105, see *supra* note 17 ("Il convient de souligner que, conformément à la jurisprudence des tribunaux *ad hoc* fondée sur l'article 50 du Protocole additionnel I aux Conventions de Genève du 12 août 1949, la population ainsi prise pour cible doit être essentiellement composée de civils, la présence en son sein de personnes ne l'étant pas n'ayant dès lors aucune incidence sur sa qualification de population civile.").

the ones charged, with a view to demonstrating that an 'attack' within the meaning of Articles 7(1) and 7(2)(a) of the Statute took place".[83]

3.3.2.2. "Widespread" or "Systematic"

According to the Statute, the mere existence of the "attack" within the meaning of Article 7(2)(a) of the Statute, does not yet satisfy all contextual elements of crimes against humanity. The "attack" must be further qualified as either "widespread" or "systematic". These two qualifiers are used disjunctively in Article 7(1) of the Statute[84] and come into play, in a second step, once the "attack" has been established. Interestingly, the Statute remains silent as to their exact meaning and has left it to the Judges to construe them.[85] But most importantly, the two qualifiers seem to correlate with the two conditions in Article 7(2)(a) of the Statute that define the "attack": "widespread" relates to the "multiple commission of acts" and "systematic" relates to "State or organizational policy". Considering that the Statute foresees a conjunctive application of the two conditions in Article 7(2)(a) of the Statute, but a disjunctive application of the two qualifiers in Article 7(1) of the Statute, it is of particular interest to trace whether these notions simply overlap in meaning and how they relate to each other.

"Widespread" is seen to connote "the large-scale nature of the attack, which should be massive, frequent, carried out collectively with considerable seriousness and directed against a multiplicity of victims".[86] The "widespread" nature of the attack has been related to either the large size of the affected geographical area or the large number of victims, ex-

---

[83] *Ntaganda* Confirmation of Charges, para. 23, see *supra* note 61.

[84] See *Bemba* Confirmation of Charges, para. 82, *supra* note 17; *Katanga and Chui* Confirmation of Charges, para. 412, see *supra* note 43.

[85] "Agreement was quickly reached among most delegations that such issues should not be addressed in the Elements and should be left to the evolving jurisprudence", see Darryl Robinson, "The Elements of Crimes Against Humanity", in Roy Lee and Håkan Friman (eds.), *The International Criminal Court: Elements of Crimes and Rules of Evidence*, Transnational Pub, 2001, p. 78.

[86] *Bemba* Confirmation of Charges, para. 83, see *supra* note 17. This finding was later endorsed in the *Laurent Gbagbo* case, see *Gbagbo* Confirmation of Charges, para. 222, *supra* note 18.

cluding isolated acts.[87] One may argue that this qualifier imports a quantitative assessment of the attack beyond the mere "multiple commission of acts".[88] Indeed, in a demonstration of this element, Pre-Trial Chamber I in the *Katanga/Ngudjolo* and *Bashir* cases, for example, draws upon the large number of victims.[89]

The term "systematic" has been understood to mean "an organized plan in furtherance of a common policy which follows a regular pattern and results in a continuous commission of acts" or a "pattern or crimes" which reflects the "non-accidental repetition of similar criminal conduct on a regular basis".[90] It "pertains to the organized nature of the acts of violence and to the improbability of their random occurrence".[91] One may argue that this qualifier imports a qualitative assessment of the "attack". In a demonstration of this element, Pre-Trial Chamber I in the *Katanga/Ngudjolo* case draws upon the pattern of the crimes and the "common policy and an organized plan".[92] Later in the *Bashir* case, the same Cham-

---

[87] *Katanga and Chui* Confirmation of Charges, para. 395, see *supra* note 43; *Harun and Kushayb* Arrest Warrant, para. 62, see *supra* note 51; *ibid.*, *Bemba* Confirmation of Charges, para. 83; *Bashir* Arrest Warrant 2009, para. 81, see *supra* note 18.

[88] Pre-Trial Chamber II later added in the *Kenya* situation that this assessment "is neither exclusively quantitative nor geographical, but must be carried out on the basis of the individual facts. Accordingly, a widespread attack may be the 'cumulative effect of a series of inhumane acts or the singular effect of an inhumane act of extraordinary magnitude'", see *Kenya* Authorization of Investigation, para. 95, *supra* note 17. This finding was quoted in the decision authorizing the commencement of the investigation into the situation in *Côte d'Ivoire*, *Côte d'Ivoire* Authorisation of Investigation, para. 53, *supra* note 9.

[89] See *Katanga and Chui* Confirmation of Charges, paras. 408–410, see *supra* note 43; and *Bashir* Arrest Warrant 2009, para. 83, see *supra* note 18.

[90] *Katanga and Chui* Confirmation of Charges, para. 397, see *supra* note 43; *ibid.*, *Bashir* Arrest Warrant 2009, para. 81. Pre-Trial Chamber II in the *Bemba* case did not provide an interpretation of this notion as it enquired only into the "widespread" nature of the attack in the case. This jurisprudence was followed later, *e.g.*, in the decision authorising the commencement of the investigation into the situation in Kenya, see Kenya Authorization of Investigation, para. 96, *supra* note 17; and in the *Katanga* case, see *Katanga* Judgment, para. 1123, *supra* note 17.

[91] *Ibid.*, *Bashir* Arrest Warrant 2009, para. 81. See also previously in *Harun and Kushayb* Arrest Warrant, para. 62, *supra* note 51. This definition was later also used by, *e.g.*, *Gbagbo* Confirmation of Charges, para. 223, see *supra* note 18.

[92] *Katanga and Chui* Confirmation of Charges, para. 413, see *supra* note 43. Indeed, in the *Harun/Kushayb* case, Pre-Trial Chamber I states: "The Chamber is also of the view that the existence of a State or organizational policy is an element from which the systematic nature of an attack may be inferred", see *ibid.*, *Harun and Kushayb* Arrest Warrant, para. 62.

ber refrains from taking into account the "policy", but refers to the five-year duration of the attack, as well as its co-ordination on the ground and the involvement of a considerable amount of military equipment.[93] The above examples regarding the application of the law further evidence that the Court in the early years, in building the tandem 'systematic/policy', has not yet clearly carved out the content of those notions so as to facilitate an appropriate examination of the law.

The ambiguity discernible in the notional determinations continued in attempts to clarify the interrelation of Articles 7(2)(a) and 7(1) of the Statute. The Chamber that first put the conditions in Article 7(2)(a) of the Statute and the qualifiers in Article 7(1) of the Statute in context was Pre-Trial Chamber I in the *Katanga/Ngudjolo* case. Having first acknowledged the requisite fulfilment of an "attack", the Chamber, in defining the notion "widespread", draws upon the "policy" requirement in Article 7(2)(a) of the Statute and suggests that the latter "ensures that the attack, even if carried out over a large geographical area or directed against a large number of victims, must still be thoroughly organized and follow a regular pattern".[94] By the same token, in the context of determining the notion "systematic", it introduces the requirement of "multiplicity of victims"[95] and holds that the latter "ensures that the attack involve[s] a multiplicity of victims of one of the acts referred to in Article 7(1) of the Statute".[96] These explanations are somewhat surprising. In a seemingly 'unitary approach', the Chamber takes into consideration all factors laid out in Article 7(1) and (2)(a) of the Statute at an equal level and combines them crossways. In doing so, the Chamber appears to turn the disjunctive wording in Article 7(1) of the Statute into a cumulative formulation requiring that the "attack" be eventually both "widespread" *and* "systematic".[97] This, however, is contrary to the explicit wording of the Statute. It also contradicts the reported agreement of the negotiators to encapsulate in Article 7(2)(a) of the Statute a low, and in Article 7(1) of the Statute a

---

[93] *Bashir* Arrest Warrant 2009, para. 85, see *supra* note 18.

[94] *Katanga and Chui* Confirmation of Charges, para. 396, see *supra* note 43.

[95] It is assumed that in this context the Chamber sought to draw upon the component of "multiple commission of acts" within the meaning of Article 7(2)(a) of the Statute.

[96] *Katanga and Chui* Confirmation of Charges, para. 398, see *supra* note 43.

[97] Critically seen by Sadat, 2013, p. 359, see *supra* note 79. See also on this point William Schabas, "Article 7", in William Schabas (ed.), *The International Criminal Court: A Commentary on the Rome Statute*, Oxford University Press, 2010, p. 149.

high threshold test.[98] The undifferentiated application of Articles 7(1) and 7(2)(a) of the Statute was therefore misleading. Besides, having already accepted the Article 7(2)(a) conditions of "multiple commission"/"State or organizational policy" when identifying the "attack" at the lower level – prior to its qualification as "widespread" or "systematic" – cumulatively, their re-assessment was not necessary.

Pre-Trial Chamber II in the *Bemba* case follows a clearer structure in adopting a 'two-step approach', dissociating the discussion about the Article 7(1) conditions from the one regarding the qualifiers in Article 7(2)(a) of the Statute.[99] It enquires first into the "attack", which is contingent upon the fulfilment of the cumulative conditions of Article 7(2)(a) of the Statute, and only thereafter, in a second step, examines the higher-levelled disjunctive qualifiers of "widespread" or "systematic". At that second stage, no reference to the Article 7(2)(a) conditions is possible as the Article 7(2)(a) conditions do not reach the threshold of the Article 7(1) qualifiers. In conclusion, a "widespread" or "systematic" attack will regularly embrace the cumulative requirements of Article 7(2)(a) of the Statute at a lower level.

Many of the above key findings and definitions have retained their relevance and have found their way into the Court's jurisprudence on crimes against humanity. Indeed, some have proven to be sufficiently precise and flexible so as to be applied in a variety of cases up until today. But, the ostensible consolidation in the Court's jurisprudence is also accompanied by ambiguities and vague conceptions. The notions in Article 7(2)(a) of the Statute are underdeveloped, at times used interchangeably;

---

[98] "The result is a conjunctive, but low-threshold, test which must be met before establishing one of the disjunctive, but more onerous, requirements of 'widespread' or 'systematic'. See Herman von Hebel and Darryl Robinson, 1999, pp. 96–97, *supra* note 11.

[99] Pre-Trial Chamber I in the *Bashir* case also presented its analysis in this fashion, see *Bashir* Arrest Warrant 2009, paras. 83–85, *supra* note 18. The same approach was later adopted by Trial Chamber II in the *Katanga* case, see *Katanga* Judgment, paras. 1097, 1098, *supra* note 17:

> La première étape de ce raisonnement a trait à l'analyse de *l'existence* d'une attaque [...]. La deuxième étape porte sur la *caractérisation* de l'attaque, en particulier, sur la question de savoir si celle-ci était généralisée ou systématique. Cette démarche, essentielle pour établir l'existence d'un crime contre l'humanité, ne devrait, en principe, intervenir que si la première étape a été concluante.

and Pre-Trial Chamber I in the *Laurent Gbagbo* case, *Gbagbo* Confirmation of Charges, para. 207, see *supra* note 18.

the crucial relationship between Article 7(2)(a) and 7(1) of the Statute remains obscure. It was therefore perhaps to be expected that in the following situation in which the Court intervened, the Court would struggle over a component of the contextual element that up until the end of 2009 was deemed the least problematic element of crimes against humanity.

3.4. The Kenya Situation: What is an "Organization" Within the Meaning of Article 7(2)(a) of the Statute?

By the end of 2009, the long-standing *acquis* on crimes against humanity was challenged unexpectedly. The impetus came from the first-ever Article 15 *proprio motu* initiative of the Prosecutor to commence an investigation into the situation in the Republic of Kenya. Absent any referral from a State Party or the Security Council, former Prosecutor Luis Moreno Ocampo had approached Pre-Trial Chamber II with the request to authorize such an investigation. On 31 March 2010, Pre-Trial Chamber II confirmed, by majority, that there was a "reasonable basis to proceed" with the investigation. To this end, it reviewed, on the basis of Article 15(4) of the Statute, the Prosecutor's assessment of the Article 53(1)(a) to (c) criteria, which also included a provisional assessment of the crimes both in terms of law and fact.[100] It confined the authorization to only the investigation of crimes against humanity[101] and limited *ratione temporis* the incidents to be investigated.[102] The Prosecutor commenced the investigation thereafter.

3.4.1. The Facts

The facts were the following: presidential elections were held in the Republic of Kenya in late December 2007. Soon after the announcement of the election results on 27 December 2007, the perceived rigging of elections sparked violence that lasted from 27 December 2007 to 28 February

---

[100] *Kenya* Authorization of Investigation, paras. 36–39, 71, see *supra* note 17.

[101] As a consequence, if the Prosecutor discovered information during the investigation that demonstrated the existence of other crimes, the Prosecutor would have been obliged to come back to the Pre-Trial Chamber and request anew authorization to investigate those crimes. *Ibid.*, paras. 208–209.

[102] The Chamber took issue with the Prosecutor's "ambiguous" determination of the temporal scope of the situation, and limited the crimes to be investigated from the time the Statute entered into force *vis-à-vis* the Republic of Kenya until the moment that the Prosecutor's request was lodged. The authorization did not extend to prospective crimes. This temporal delimitation gives the situation a clearly defined temporal scope, *ibid.*, paras. 204–207.

2008 and ultimately included six out of eight provinces of the country. The Majority of Pre-Trial Chamber II acknowledged instances of spontaneous or opportunistic crimes after the announcement of the election results, but considered a number of incidents to have been "planned, directed or organized by various groups including local leaders, businessmen and politicians associated with the two leading political parties" as well as members of the police.[103] Those incidents "differed from one region to another, depending on the respective ethnical composition and other region-specific dynamics".[104] Nevertheless, the Chamber believed that some incidents fell into the following three categories of "attacks": (i) the initial violence was attributed to the group of supporters of the 'Orange Democratic Movement' ('ODM') who directed their attacks against perceived supporters of the 'Party of National Unity' ('PNU') supporters.[105] These acts of violence were alleged to have been orchestrated by ODM politicians, businessmen and Kalenjin leaders;[106] (ii) retaliatory attacks by those previously attacked against those who were believed to be responsible for the initial violence.[107] These attacks were allegedly directed by Kikuyu leaders, businessmen and PNU politicians;[108] and (iii) violent acts committed by the police, including the use of "excessive force, partiality or collaboration with the attackers, and deliberate inaction by the police".[109] The organized nature of these attacks was inferred from a series of reported meetings, inflammatory rhetoric and propaganda, and the "strategy and method employed" in some of the attacks.[110] The violence in Kenya resulted in about 1,133 to 1,220 people being killed, about 3,561 being injured and between 268,330 to 350,000 persons being forcibly displaced.[111] According to the Prosecutor, the perpetrators were ordi-

---

[103] *Ibid.*, para. 117.

[104] *Ibid.*, para. 103.

[105] *Ibid.*, para. 104.

[106] *Ibid.*, para. 123.

[107] *Ibid.*, para. 105.

[108] *Ibid.*, para. 127.

[109] *Ibid.*, para. 106.

[110] *Ibid.*, paras. 118–122 and 124–126.

[111] *Ibid.*, para. 131. The Chamber also noted that the displaced population fell to 150,671 persons as of 21 April 2008 and 138,428 persons as of 13 May 2008, see *ibid.*, para. 159.

nary civilians, "gangs of young men armed with traditional weapons" who were believed to be associated with the two main political parties.[112]

Unlike in the situations previously discussed, the crimes are not carried out by armed groups and do not occur in the context of an ongoing armed conflict. The protagonists in the conflict are different groups of individuals across the country, who make their appearance as a group only during the material time and are believed to interact on a horizontal level. The reason for their various appearances lies in the power struggle within the tiers of the political elite that has flared up in the aftermath of an intense election period. Both political sides seek to resolve the situation to their advantage by, *inter alia*, resorting to violent means. The general political situation is unstable and paralyzed; society is deeply divided. Law enforcement agencies do not perform their functions in an orderly fashion. Information indicates that they are overwhelmed by the situation on the ground, or they are seen to either take part in the violence or induce an environment of criminality and lawlessness.

As regards the legal discussion that followed, only one issue became a bone of contention between the Judges of the Pre-Trial Chamber. It concerned the construction of the notion 'organizational policy' and, in particular, the concept of "organization" within the meaning of Article 7(2)(a) of the Statute. This was due to the fact that the notion "organization" as interpreted by the Pre-Trial Chambers in the early cases was not suitable to cover this scenario. Indeed, the chaotic and dynamic situation on the ground did not allow for the easy identification of a "group of persons who govern a specific territory". But then, what qualifies as an "organization" within the meaning of Article 7(2)(a) of the Statute? The question of whether the facts of the situation, as presented by the Prosecutor at the time, fulfilled all the legal requirements pursuant to Article 7 of the Statute was also a topic of controversy leading finally to a dissenting opinion in these proceedings.

3.4.2. The Majority's Decision of 31 March 2010

With regard to the interpretation of the contextual elements, the Majority of Pre-Trial Chamber II follows to a great extent the definitions as estab-

---

[112] Office of the Prosecutor, Request for Authorization of an Investigation Pursuant to Article 15, 26 November 2009, ICC-01/09-3, paras. 74, 83 and 86 (http://www.legal-tools.org/doc/c63dcc/).

lished in earlier rulings of the Court. However, with the allegation that both political sides had formed an "organization", particular attention was paid to determining this concept in legal terms. The Majority began its analysis by noting that the Statute does not provide any criteria for the determination of an "organization" within the meaning of Article 7(2)(a) of the Statute. What was clear to the Judges of the Majority was that the Statute, by including the term "organization", did not exclude non-State actors.[113] Rather, in their view, "organizations not linked to a State may, for the purposes of the Statute, elaborate and carry out a policy to commit an attack against a civilian population".[114] The decisive part of their ruling is captured in the following:

> Whereas some have argued that only State-like organizations may qualify, the Chamber opines that the formal nature of a group and the level of its organization should not be the defining criterion. Instead, as others have convincingly put forward, a distinction should be drawn on whether a group has the capability to perform acts which infringe on basic human values.[115]

The Chamber conceded that this determination can only be made on a case-by-case basis and offered a non-exhaustive list of factors that may assist in such a determination:

> (i) whether the group is under a responsible command, or has an established hierarchy; (ii) whether the group possesses, in fact, the means to carry out a widespread or systematic attack against a civilian population; (iii) whether the group exercises control over part of the territory of a State; (iv) whether the group has criminal activities against the civilian population as a primary purpose; (v) whether the group articulates, explicitly or implicitly, an intention to attack a civilian population; (vi) whether the group is part of a larger group, which fulfils some or all of the abovementioned criteria.[116]

The Majority opted for a flexible approach, making the existence of an "organization" dependent on its capability "to infringe basic human values". It was perhaps the accentuation of the human rights component in

---

[113] *Kenya* Authorization of Investigation, para. 92, see *supra* note 17.
[114] *Ibid.*
[115] *Ibid.*, para. 90 (footnote omitted).
[116] *Ibid.*, para. 93 (footnotes omitted).

this formula that triggered controversy within the Chamber. The organization's capacity to commit an "attack directed against any civilian population" was not the starting point, but rather any violation of basic human rights. But, the question must be posed: are not crimes against humanity the most serious and grave form of human rights violations?

3.4.3. The Dissenting Opinion

The dissenting member of the Chamber, Judge Hans-Peter Kaul, agreed with the Majority's assumption that an "organization" is an entity different from a "State". Like his colleagues, he considered that the "organization" can be any "private entity (a non-State actor) which is not an organ of a State or acting on behalf of a State".[117] While all Judges therefore agreed on what an "organization" is *not*, the question of defining its contours proved to be more difficult and brought about the divide. Judge Kaul responded to the Majority's proposition of the "organization" as follows:

> I read the provision such that the juxtaposition of the notions 'State' and 'organization' in Article 7(2)(a) of the Statute are an indication that even though the constitutive elements of statehood need not be established those 'organizations' should partake of some characteristics of a State. Those characteristics eventually turn the private 'organization' into an entity which may act like a State or has quasi-State abilities. These characteristics could involve the following: (a) a collectivity of persons; (b) which was established and acts for a common purpose; (c) over a prolonged period of time; (d) which is under responsible command or adopted a certain degree of hierarchical structure, including, as a minimum, some kind of policy level; (e) with the capacity to impose the policy on its members and to sanction them; and (f) which has the capacity and means available to attack any civilian population on a large scale.

> In contrast, I believe that non-state actors which do not reach the level described above are not able to carry out a policy of this nature, such as groups of organized crime, a mob,

---

[117] Dissenting Opinion of Judge Hans-Peter Kaul, annexed to Pre-Trial Chamber II, Decision Pursuant to Article 15 of the Rome Statute on the Authorization of an Investigation into the Situation in the Republic of Kenya ('Dissenting Judge Kaul *Kenya* Authorization of Investigation'), 31 March 2010, ICC-01/09-19-Corr, p. 107, para. 45 (http://www.legal-tools.org/doc/f0caaf/).

groups of (armed) civilians or criminal gangs. They would generally fall outside the scope of Article 7(2)(a) of the Statute. To give a concrete example, violence-prone groups of persons formed on an ad hoc basis, randomly, spontaneously, for a passing occasion, with fluctuating membership and without a structure and level to set up a policy are not within the ambit of the Statute, even if they engage in numerous serious and organized crimes. Further elements are needed for a private entity to reach the level of an 'organization' within the meaning of Article 7 of the Statute. For it is not the cruelty or mass victimization that turns a crime into a *delictum iuris gentium* but the constitutive contextual elements in which the act is embedded.

In this respect, the general argument that any kind of non-state actors may be qualified as an 'organization' within the meaning of Article 7(2)(a) of the Statute on the grounds that it "has the capability to perform acts which infringe on basic human values" without any further specification seems unconvincing to me. In fact this approach may expand the concept of crimes against humanity to any infringement of human rights. I am convinced that a distinction must be upheld between human rights violations on the one side and international crimes on the other side, the latter forming the nucleus of the most heinous violations of human rights representing the most serious crimes of concern to the international community as a whole.[118]

Given Judge Kaul's clarification that the "organization" is *different* from a State, some words must be devoted to his proposition that it be nevertheless 'State-like'. His conception of a 'State-like organization' is best understood when read with his further elaboration on the *raison d'être* of crimes against humanity. Perhaps the most telling consideration in this context is his emphasis on the particular threat for the civilian population that, in the past, typically emanated from the criminal policy that the State adopted, involving various segments of the State apparatus. It was not so much the large-scale commission of crimes, but the existence of an '(inhumane) policy' that called for the intervention of the international community. He found this particular threat to be exemplified in historic precedents, such as the crimes committed by Nazi Germany, the

---

[118] *Ibid.*, pp. 110–112, paras. 51–53 (footnotes omitted).

'killing fields' of the Khmer Rouge, the 1988 mass poisoning of Kurds in Halabja and the horrendous mass crimes committed in Rwanda and the former Yugoslavia. He subjected the actions of non-State actors to the same standard. In his words:

> The Statute [...] further accommodates new scenarios of threats which may equally shake the very foundations of the international community and deeply shock the conscience of humanity. Such policy may also be adopted and implemented by private entities. However, it follows from the above that the private entity must have the means and resources available to reach the gravity of systemic injustice in which parts of the civilian population find themselves.[119]

Hence, according to Judge Kaul, the "organization" would come under the purview of the ICC Prosecutor if it implemented a policy that constituted such an extraordinary threat of 'systemic injustice' for the civilian population – as opposed to any human rights violations – that the intervention of the international community became imperative. In this sense he considered the "organization" to be 'State-like'.

Judge Kaul also contradicted the Majority in its analysis of the factual narrative which has been summarized above. Disagreeing with the Majority's categorization of the violence, he concluded, in essence, that there were several centres of violence erupting at different times and for different reasons.[120] According to him, the perpetrators were not organized in one "organization" that met "the prerequisites of structure, membership, duration and means to attack the civilian population". He also found no support for the existence of a "policy" that could have unified the different acts of violence into one attack, as suggested by the Majority. Judge Kaul also rejected the allegation of the existence of a State policy involving law enforcement agencies and the military. His summary of the situation is captured in this verdict: "In total, the overall picture is charac-

---

[119] *Ibid.*, p. 118, para. 66.

[120] "Albeit the motives of the perpetrators are not decisive and may vary, it nevertheless sheds light on the question of the existence of a possible policy", see *ibid.*, p. 159, para. 148. This idea was later reiterated in the *Laurent Gbagbo* case, see *Gbagbo* Confirmation of Charges, para. 214, see *supra* note 18 ("The Chamber observes that neither the Statute nor the Elements of Crimes include a certain rationale or motivations of the policy as a requirement of the definition. Establishing the underlying motive may, however, be useful for the detection of common features and links between acts.").

---

terized by chaos, anarchy, a collapse of State authority in most parts of the country and almost total failure of law enforcement agencies".[121]

Reading the main decision and the dissent, one cannot help but notice that the two approaches share common ground in law. Both sides differ in their proposal of the generic formula that seeks to capture the essence of the "organization". But, both agree that the overall generic definition cannot be applied without the help of certain factors. In this regard, it is somewhat astonishing that both sides of the debate, in an effort to delineate the contours of such an entity, chose similar factors that would, taken altogether, demonstrate the existence of the "organization" according to their respective definition. Upon closer inspection, the factors they would look for would give the group a more formal and structured shape. It seems that they are in agreement that only a somewhat structured entity is able to implement the policy of the "organization" in the first place. Factors such as the structure of the group,[122] the means and resources at its disposal to carry out an "attack",[123] as opposed to human rights violations, and an aspect of duration,[124] are important aspects both sides pay heed to. The reference to responsible command and hierarchical structures is not an attempt to introduce through the back door a link to the armed conflict,[125] but simply highlights that the "organization" would qualify under the Statute with respect to the commission of both war crimes and crimes against humanity, signalling the threat that emanates from such entities. As a consequence, it seems that while the Judges in their actual assessment apply similar factors, the objective they set would lead them to different results: should the capability of the "organization" meet the threshold of human rights violations or should it rather reach the level of

---

[121] *Ibid.*, Dissenting Judge Kaul *Kenya* Authorization of Investigation, pp. 160–162, paras. 149–153.

[122] The Majority proposes to consider "whether the group is under responsible command, or has an established hierarchy". The dissenting Judge equally considers factors of responsible command or the adoption of "certain degree of hierarchical structure", including some sort of policy level (see respective quotations above).

[123] Both, the Majority and the dissenting Judge agree that the organization must possess the necessary means to carry out a widespread or systematic attack against the civilian population (see respective quotations above).

[124] The Majority refers in its list of factors to "whether the group exercises control over part of the territory of a State", which could be argued involves the aspect of duration. Likewise, the dissenting Judge would consider whether the organization existed for a prolonged period of time (see respective quotations above).

[125] This argument is put forth by Sadat, 2013, pp. 370–371, *supra* note 79.

the most serious forms of human rights violations, namely international crimes? The Majority adopted an all-inclusive approach, putting crimes against humanity on par with human rights violations. The dissenting Judge, on the other hand, raised the question of a possible demarcation line, contemplating the further consequences in case an overly generous approach was adopted:

> There is, in my view, a demarcation line between crimes against humanity pursuant to Article 7 of the Statute, and crimes under national law. There is, for example, such a demarcation line between murder as a crime against humanity pursuant to Article 7(1)(a) of the Statute and murder under the national law of the Republic of Kenya. It is my considered view that the existing demarcation line between those crimes must not be marginalized or downgraded, even in an incremental way. I also opine that the distinction between those crimes must not be blurred.
>
> Furthermore, it is my considered view that this would not be in the interest of criminal justice in general and international criminal justice in particular. It is neither appropriate nor possible to examine and explain in this opinion all the potential negative implications and risks of a gradual downscaling of crimes against humanity towards serious ordinary crimes. As a Judge of the ICC, I feel, however, duty-bound to point at least to the following: such an approach might infringe on State sovereignty and the action of national courts for crimes which should not be within the ambit of the Statute. It would broaden the scope of possible ICC intervention almost indefinitely. This might turn the ICC, which is fully dependent on State cooperation, in a hopelessly overstretched, inefficient international court, with related risks for its standing and credibility. Taken into consideration the limited financial and material means of the institution, it might be unable to tackle all the situations which could fall under its jurisdiction with the consequence that the selection of the situations under actual investigation might be quite arbitrary to the dismay of the numerous victims in the situations disregarded by the Court who would be deprived of any access to justice without any convincing justification.[126]

---

[126] Dissenting Judge Kaul Kenya Authorization of Investigation, p. 88, paras. 9–10, see *supra* note 117.

The above conflict of opinion continued to permeate the two cases emanating from the Kenya situation and the two positions remained apart. The response of outside observers mirrored by and large the divide within the Chamber.[127] An old discussion revived whether to abandon altogether the "policy" requirement, inextricably linked with the State or "organization", in line with the jurisprudence of the *ad hoc* tribunals.[128] Bound by the dictate of article 21(1)(a) of the Statute, this was never an option for the Court. For this would mean abandoning a requirement that was purposefully included in the statutory definition, and which ensured acceptance of the Statute by States.[129] Quite to the contrary, as will be shown in the following section, discussion at the Court would now centre on the difficulties in proving the existence of a "policy" and a Trial Chamber proposing a new formula of the concept of "organization" within the meaning of Article 7(2)(a) of the Statute.

3.5. After Kenya: Search for an Appropriate Interpretation of the Contextual Elements of Crimes Against Humanity

As explained at the beginning, the juridical debate in the *Kenya* situation on the boundaries of Article 7 of the Statute opened a wider discussion on and a more stringent application of Article 7 of the Statute. Three exemplary case studies will illustrate the problems encountered.

---

[127] Claus Kress, "On the Outer Limits of Crimes Against Humanity: the Concept of Organization Within the Policy Requirement: Some Reflections on the March 2010 ICC Kenya Decision", in *Leiden Journal of International Law*, 2010, vol. 23, p. 855 *et seq.*; William Schabas, "Prosecuting Dr Strangelove, Goldfinger and the Joker at the International Criminal Court: Closing the Loopholes", in *Leiden Journal of International Law*, vol. 23, 2010, p. 847 *et seq.*; Gerhard Werle and Boris Burghardt, "Do Crimes Against Humanity Require the Participation of a State or a 'State-like' Organization?", in *Journal of International Criminal Justice*, 2012, vol. 10, p. 1151 *et seq.*; Charles Jalloh, "Situation in the Republic of Kenya", in *American Journal of International Law*, 2011, vol. 105, p. 540 *et seq.*; Darryl Robinson, "Essence of Crimes against Humanity Raised by Challenges at ICC", in EJIL Talk! Blog, 27 September 2011, available at www.ejiltalk.org.

[128] Arguing for it, Matt Halling, "Push the Envelope – Watch it Bend: Removing the Policy Requirement and Extending Crimes against Humanity", in *Leiden Journal of International Law*, 2010, vol. 23, p. 827 *et seq.* Arguing against it, Katrin Gierhake, "Zum Erfordernis eines 'ausgedehnten oder systematischen Angriffs gegen die Zivilbevölkerung' als Merkmal der Verbrechen gegen die Menschlichkeit", ZIS 11/2010, p. 676 *et seq.*, available at www-zis-online.com; Kai Ambos, "Crimes Against Humanity and the ICC", in Leila N. Sadat (ed.), *Forging a Convention for Crimes Against Humanity, op. cit.*, pp. 285–286.

[129] "Moreover, explicit recognition of this policy element was essential to the compromise on crimes against humanity", see Herman von Hebel and Darryl Robinson, 1999, pp. 96–97, *supra* note 11.

3.5.1. The Mbarushimana and Mudacumura Cases: No Evidence of a "Policy"

In the *Callixte Mbarushimana* and *Sylvestre Mudacumuara* cases it was the "policy" requirement that caught the Chambers' attention. Both cases stem from the DRC situation. They share great similarities in terms of the factual narrative, but were presented separately by the Prosecutor. Eventually, in the *Mbarushimana* case, Pre-Trial Chamber I declined to confirm the charges of crimes against humanity,[130] and in the *Mudacumura* case, Pre-Trial Chamber II declined to issue a warrant of arrest[131] for those crimes. The two cases are presented in what follows.

Callixte Mbarushimana was charged for having contributed "in any other way" to the commission of crimes against humanity and war crimes by the 'Forces Démocratiques pour la Liberation du Rwanda' ('FDLR') in a number of attacks[132] in the Kivu provinces of the DRC from about 20 January to 31 December 2009. The FDLR, a hierarchically structured armed group,[133] allegedly launched in January 2009, "a campaign aimed at attacking the civilian population and creating a 'humanitarian catastrophe' in the Kivu provinces"[134] in order to primarily "extort concessions of political power for the FDLR from the DRC and Rwandan government in exchange for ceasing to commit crimes against civilians".[135] The attacks against the civilian population had been ordered purportedly by the FDLR leadership, including *Mudacumura*.[136] *Mbarushimana* was believed to have been associated with the FDLR since at least 2004[137] and to have

---

[130] *Mbarushimana* Confirmation of Charges, see *supra* note 19.

[131] *Mudacumura* Arrest Warrant, see *supra* note 60.

[132] The Chamber took as basis for its analysis the incidents in Remeka (late January and late February 2009); Busheke (late January 2009); Kipopo (12–13 February 2009); Mianga (12 April 2009); Luofo and Kasiki (18 April 2009); Busurungi and neighbouring villages (28 April 2009 and 9–10 May 2009); Manje (20–21 July 2009); a village in Masisi territory (second half of 2009); Ruvundi October 2009); Mutakato (2–3 December 2009); Kahole (6 December 2009); Pinga (12 and 14 February 2009); Miriki (February 2009); Malembe (11–16 August and 15 September 2009), see *Mbarushimana* Confirmation of Charges, fn. 565, see *supra* note 19.

[133] *Ibid.*, *Mbarushimana* Confirmation of Charges, paras. 104–106.

[134] *Ibid.*, para. 6.

[135] *Ibid.*, para. 243.

[136] Office of the Prosecutor, Document Containing the Charges, 15 July 2011, ICC-01/04-01/10-311-AnxA-Red, para. 111 (http://www.legal-tools.org/doc/5d47ff/).

[137] *Mbarushimana* Confirmation of Charges, para. 2, see *supra* note 19.

---

held several positions within the group, lastly as the FDLR's first Vice President *ad interim* in 2010.[138] His contribution to the crimes laid in issuing press releases on behalf of the FDLR organization in the aftermath of operations and engaging in international negotiations, thus "[transforming] the FDLR's crimes on the ground into political capital".[139]

Likewise, a warrant of arrest for *Mudacumura* had been sought by the Prosecutor for his alleged criminal responsibility in the commission of war crimes and crimes against humanity committed by the FDLR in the Kivu provinces between 20 January 2009 and the end of September 2010. *Mudacumura* was believed to have issued an order "to create 'a chaotic situation in Congo' by way of a 'humanitarian catastrophe'",[140] in which "[c]ivilians were killed, abducted, raped, subjected to cruel treatment or mutilated and homes were destroyed" and which "also caused population displacement".[141]

In the view of both Pre-Trial Chambers, the cardinal point was whether the FDLR order to "create a humanitarian catastrophe" existed from which the "policy" to attack the civilian population could be inferred. Accordingly, both Chambers embarked on an assessment of this order's evidentiary validity. On the basis of the evidence presented, however, both Chambers denied such an allegation.

In the *Mbarushimana* case, the Majority of Pre-Trial Chamber I highlighted the inconsistencies in the evidence in relation to the existence of the FDLR order as alleged by the Prosecutor and, consequently, denied the existence of a "policy".[142] But as this case involved both allegations of crimes against humanity and war crimes, the Chamber went further to enquire into whether any of its findings relating to the commission of war crimes could be of assistance in determining the existence of Article 7 crimes.[143] The Chamber's findings on war crimes encompassed five at-

---

[138] *Ibid.*, para. 5.

[139] *Ibid.*, para. 8.

[140] *Ibid.*, para. 25.

[141] *Ibid.*

[142] *Ibid.*, paras. 263, 266–267. Upon examination of the entirety of the evidence, the dissenting Judge arrived at a different result. In particular, she did not attach so much importance to the inconsistencies contained in the evidence, but asked that they be resolved at trial, see Dissenting Opinion of Judge Sanji Mmasenono Monageng, annexed to the decision of the Chamber, pp. 152 –160.

[143] The Majority of the Chamber nevertheless did not confirm any of the charges as (i) it was not convinced, having rejected the policy of attacking the civilian population, that the

tacks (out of twenty-five originally alleged by the Prosecutor) during which crimes, involving civilians, had been committed. However, the Majority of the Chamber remained unconvinced that those five attacks "scattered over a 6 month period"[144] evidenced the existence of a policy,[145] not even that they were part of a "course of conduct".[146] This latter statement is somewhat opaque as it appears that the Majority Judges moved away from the discussion on the "policy" and now questioned the very existence of the entry requirement of a "course of conduct" within the meaning of Article 7(2)(a) of the Statute. Putting an emphasis on the fact that (only) five attacks occurred over a period of six months could be misunderstood as introducing some kind of quantitative benchmark for accepting an overall "attack" that must be exceeded in order to reach the low threshold of Article 7(2)(a) of the Statute. But perhaps the Majority simply suggested that the five attacks it looked into did not display any signs of coherence and continuity which would qualify them as one 'campaign' or 'operation'.[147] Or perhaps they meant to say that *in the absence* of a "policy" to attack the civilian population, which would otherwise link the attacks "scattered" over a period of six months, the five attacks remain apart and cannot be viewed as forming a coherent and interrelated course of action. Be it as it may, the Chamber's Majority then continued its analysis regarding the objective of those five attacks and concluded that they were of retaliatory nature in which both military objectives and, as the case may be, individual civilians not taking part in the hostilities were tar-

---

FDLR leadership constituted a group acting with a common purpose featuring an element of criminality; and (ii) that *Mbarushimana* provided any contribution to the commission of such crimes, "even less a significant one" within the meaning of Article 25(3)(d) of the Statute, see *ibid.*, *Mbarushimana* Confirmation of Charges, paras. 291–292.

[144] *Ibid.*, para. 265.

[145] *Ibid.*, para. 263.

[146] "Indeed, although the Chamber has found substantial grounds to believe that acts amounting to war crimes were committed on 5 out of the 25 occasions alleged by the Prosecution, the evidence submitted is, nevertheless, insufficient for the Majority to be convinced, to the threshold of substantial grounds to believe, that such acts were part of a course of conduct amounting to an 'attack directed against the civilian population' within the meaning of Article 7 of the Statute" (footnote omitted), see *ibid.*, para. 264.

[147] Pre-Trial Chamber I would remark subsequently in the *Laurent Gbagbo* case: "[S]ince the course of conduct requires a certain 'pattern' of behaviour, evidence relevant to proving the degree of planning, direction or organisation by a group or organisation is also relevant to assessing the links and commonality of features between individual acts that demonstrate the existence of a 'course of conduct' within the meaning of Article 7(2)(a) of the Statute", *Gbagbo* Confirmation of Charges, para. 210, see *supra* note 18.

geted. In these particular circumstances, it concluded that it failed to see that those attacks formed "part of any larger organized campaign specifically designed to be directed against the civilian population".[148] The quotation encapsulates the Majority's concern that the civilian population was not the primary target of the attacks. Whether the remark of the "larger organised campaign" related to the legal requirement of the "course of conduct" or to the alleged "policy" is open to interpretation. It is difficult to follow the Majority Judges' argumentation as it amalgamates in its reasoning the different legal requirements of Article 7(2)(a) of the Statute. Moreover, it is also worth noting that apart from the alleged order, the Chamber did not look into the organized nature of the crimes as a potential indicator for accepting a "policy", as it had done on previous occasions.

Pre-Trial Chamber II in the *Mudacumura* case conducted the same analysis on the basis of an expanded evidentiary record[149] at the stage of issuing a warrant of arrest.[150] That Chamber accepted that the FDLR was an "organization" that was responsible for the commission of multiple acts affecting the civilian population.[151] Similar to Pre-Trial Chamber I, however, it rejected the allegation that a "policy" existed to attack the civilian population as such. It highlighted the contradictory nature of the evidence at hand and the fact that some attacks were of a retaliatory nature affecting, as the case may be, both military objectives and civilians not taking part in the armed hostilities.[152] As the Chamber summarized, the "failure to observe the principles of international humanitarian law does not in itself, particularly in the context of the circumstances of the present case as portrayed in the material submitted, reveal the existence of such policy".[153] Like Pre-Trial Chamber I, this Chamber also did not look into the organized nature of the crimes as a potential indicator for accepting a "policy", as it had done in previous cases.

The above two cases did not raise particular problems of law in respect of the requisite "policy" element, but highlight the necessity of establishing and the difficulty in proving an alleged "policy". They further

---

[148] *Mbarushimana* Confirmation of Charges, para. 265, see *supra* note 19.

[149] *Mudacumura* Arrest Warrant, para. 28, see *supra* note 60.

[150] Article 58 of the Statute.

[151] *Mudacumura* Arrest Warrant, paras. 23–25, see *supra* note 60.

[152] *Ibid.*, para. 26.

[153] *Ibid.*

illustrate the relationship between the "policy" and the remaining legal requirements in Article 7(2)(a) of the Statute. The "policy" to attack the civilian population cannot be assumed without more from the armed confrontation between armed groups affecting also civilians. Rather, as has been emphasized since the early case law of the Court, the civilian population must be the primary object of the "attack" and not just an incidental victim thereof.[154] The two cases also show that the enquiry into the "policy" is independent from that of an "organization". In fact, the existence of an "organization" that fulfils even the requirements of an organized armed group within the meaning of Article 8 of the Statute does not automatically imply the existence of a "policy". Also, the existence of an armed conflict has proven to be irrelevant in this context. However, the most interesting point was raised in the *Mbarushimana* decision insofar as the Chamber apparently conflated the discussion on the "policy" with that of the "attack". But this argumentation may be motivated by the actual definition of "attack" which is circular. Indeed, Article 7(2)(a) of the Statute suggests that the compound notion of "attack" is composed of several sub-elements which in concert give shape to the "attack". However, the sub-element "policy" itself is linked again with the term "attack", it in fact seeks to demonstrate: "Attack directed against any civilian population means [...] policy to commit such attack".

3.5.2. The Gbagbo Case: Was There an "Attack"?

Doubts as to the existence of the "policy" element of crimes against humanity also surfaced in the *Laurent Gbagbo* case. The pre-trial phase of this case was longer compared to other cases before the Court, as the Judges, before rendering their final decision on the confirmation of charges, adjourned the confirmation of charges hearing requesting the Prosecutor to consider further investigating particular aspects which affected the entire case. The factual background of this case, as it was pleaded before the adjournment of the confirmation of charges hearing, is briefly summarized as follows: since 2002, Côte d'Ivoire has been divided in a government-controlled South and a rebel-controlled North.[155] Ongoing peace efforts culminated in presidential elections held in late October/November

---

[154] *Bemba* Confirmation of Charges, para. 76, see *supra* note 17.

[155] Office of the Prosecutor, *Document amendé de notification des charges*, 25 January 2013, ICC-02/11-01/11-357-Anx1-Red, para. 3 (http://www.legal-tools.org/doc/fd7407/).

2010. Soon after the elections, however, a power struggle broke out between the two candidates, the incumbent *Laurent Gbagbo* and his political rival Alassane Ouattara. Both took the oath of office and formed respective governments.[156] The Prosecutor alleged that immediately after these events, *Laurent Gbagbo* implemented a "policy" to retain power by all means, including through widespread and systematic attacks directed against the civilian population perceived to support his opponent Alassane Ouattara that lasted between 27 November 2010 and 8 May 2011.[157] The "policy" was purportedly implemented by 'pro-Gbagbo forces', a conglomerate involving different State structures, such as the army and the police, and private entities, including the youth militia and mercenaries.[158] The Prosecutor also averred that the implementation of the "policy" was discussed in a series of meetings.[159] The situation on the ground is further characterized by the presence of an Ouattara-loyal armed group named *'commando invisible'* in the capital Abidjan, which engaged in fighting with the Ivorian armed forces.[160] Thousands of people demonstrated in the streets of Abidjan, demanding that *Laurent Gbagbo* step down.[161] By the end of February 2011, the Prosecutor assessed that the situation had reached the level of an armed conflict, as Ouattara-loyal forces advanced from the North to the South, reaching the capital on 31 March 2011. As of this moment, the Ivorian army became weaker due to a significant number of defections, and *Laurent Gbagbo* supposedly turned to the youth militia members and mercenaries for support.[162] On 11 April 2011, the power struggle was decided in favour of Alassane Ouattara as forces loyal to

---

[156] *Ibid.*, para. 7.

[157] *Ibid.*, paras. 4, 9 and 13.

[158] *Ibid.*, para. 5. It is worth recalling that during the Article 15 process, the Prosecutor had argued that the crimes had been committed pursuant to a State policy. She changed her position when requesting the issuance of warrant of arrest. The then competent Pre-Trial Chamber III accepted this legal characterisation of the facts but noted that "at a later stage in the proceedings, it may be necessary for the Chamber to revisit the issue of whether the attack by the pro Gbagbo forces during the post-electoral violence (...) were committed pursuant to a state policy", see Pre-Trial Chamber III, Decision on the Prosecutor's Application Pursuant to Article 58 for a warrant of arrest against Laurent Koudou Gbagbo, 30 November 2011, ICC-02/11-01/11-9-Red, para. 48 (http://www.legal-tools.org/doc/36dcad/).

[159] *Ibid.*, paras. 39–41.

[160] *Ibid.*, para. 22.

[161] *Ibid.*, para. 8.

[162] *Ibid.*, para. 14.

him, together with the backing of the French *Opération Licorne*, arrested and put *Laurent Gbagbo* under house arrest.[163] The Prosecutor alleged that an estimate of more than 700 killings, 40 rapes, 520 arbitrary arrests, and 140 serious injuries are attributed to the activities of the pro-Gbagbo forces during that time throughout the country.[164] The victims, perceived pro-Ouattara supporters, were allegedly identified based on ethnic, religious or national grounds. Houses were marked and roadblocks erected to identify possible targets.[165] What is of importance for the current discussion is how the Prosecutor sought to demonstrate the existence of an "attack" within the meaning of Article 7(2)(a) of the Statute: four incidents, which were charged, and an additional 41 'contextual' incidents were presented as constituting this requirement.[166] With the exception of a few incidents taking place in the western part of the country, most of the incidents referred to occurred in the capital of Côte d'Ivoire, Abidjan. The Prosecutor also argued that the four charged incidents alone, in and of themselves, were sufficient to establish the existence of a widespread or systematic attack.[167]

The Majority of Pre-Trial Chamber I decided to adjourn the hearing and to request the Prosecutor to consider providing further evidence or conducting further investigation,[168] in particular, with respect to the contextual element of 'organizational policy', affecting all charges against *Laurent Gbagbo*.[169] The Majority Judges were not yet satisfied that the evidence underpinning the factual allegations of the 45 contextual incidents constituting the "attack" was of sufficient probative value and specificity to allow the Chamber to reach the same conclusions as the Prosecutor. As a matter of guidance, the Chamber's Majority provided a cata-

---

[163] *Ibid.*, para. 15.

[164] *Ibid.*, paras. 13 and 20.

[165] *Ibid.*, para. 21.

[166] *Ibid.*, paras. 20, and 23–29.

[167] Office of the Prosecutor, Prosecution's submission on issues discussed during the Confirmation Hearing, 21 March 2013, ICC-02/11-01/11-420-Red, para. 30 (http://www.legal-tools.org/doc/fae772/).

[168] Article 61(7)(c)(i) of the Statute.

[169] Pre-Trial Chamber II, Decision adjourning the hearing on the confirmation of charges pursuant to article 61(7)(c)(i) of the Rome Statute ('*Gbagbo* Adjourning Decision'), 3 June 2013, ICC-02/11-01/11-432 (http://www.legal-tools.org/doc/2682d8/); Pre-Trial Chamber II, Dissenting Opinion of Judge Silvia Fernandez de Gurmendi, ICC-02/11-01/11-432-Anx-Corr (http://www.legal-tools.org/doc/9a3b94/).

logue of issues that the Prosecutor was free to take into account when considering the Chamber's request. Those issues concerned in particular the organizational structure of the "pro-Gbagbo forces", the "policy" allegedly adopted in meetings, information on the contextual incidents that would allow considering them as an expression of the policy, and the presence and activities of all armed groups opposing the 'pro-Gbagbo forces' at the material time. The adjournment decision was appealed and ultimately upheld by the Appeals Chamber.[170]

With this case, some further key findings have been added to the discussion of the contextual elements of crimes against humanity at the ICC. The first issue concerns the Pre-Trial Chamber's approach to consider *all* 'contextual' incidents, regardless of whether they were charged, to be, as a matter of law, part of the "facts and circumstances" of the case within the meaning of Article 74(2), second sentence, of the Statute[171] thus subjecting them to the relevant evidentiary threshold.[172] This can be interpreted as a consequence of the Appeals Chamber ruling in the *Kenya* cases, in which that Chamber considered the contextual elements of crimes against humanity to be part of the merits of the case, which by implication, requires meeting the evidentiary threshold applicable at the respective stage of the proceedings.[173] The dissenting Judge, on the other hand, argued that only the four charged incidents needed to be proven as the remaining 41 'contextual' incidents are "neither contextual elements nor underlying acts within the meaning of Article 7(1)(a) of the Statute.

---

[170] Appeals Chamber, Judgment on the appeal of the Prosecutor against the decision of Pre-Trial Chamber I of 3 June 2013 entitled "Decision adjourning the hearing on the confirmation of charges pursuant to article 61(7)(c)(i) of the Rome Statute" (*'Gbagbo* Adjournment Appeal Decision'), 16 December 2013, ICC-02/11-01/11-572 (OA 5) (http://www.legal-tools.org/doc/1bffda/).

[171] "For example, the individual incidents alleged by the Prosecutor in support of her allegation that there was an 'attack directed against any civilian population' are part of the facts and circumstances for the purposes of Article 74(2) of the Statute and therefore must be proved to the requisite threshold of 'substantial grounds to believe'. This is especially so in this case in which the Prosecutor identifies particular incidents that *constitute* the attack against the civilian population. In other words, the incidents are 'facts' which 'support the [contextual] legal elements of the crime charged'", see *Gbagbo* Adjourning Decision, para. 21, *supra* note 169.

[172] "The standard by which the Chamber scrutinizes the evidence is the same for all factual allegations, whether they pertain to the individual crimes charged, contextual elements of the crimes or the criminal responsibility of the suspect", see *ibid.*, para. 19.

[173] For example, *Muthaura and Kenyatta* Appeal Decision, paras. 33–36, see *supra* note 30.

They are not facts underlying the elements of crimes against humanity but [...] merely serve to prove, together with all available evidence, the attack".[174] The Appeals Chamber did not follow this differentiation as it did not mirror the manner in which the context had been pleaded by the Prosecutor throughout the confirmation process. Also the attempt to qualify the 'contextual' incidents as "subsidiary facts" or alike was equally not followed.[175] Indeed, the Appeals Judges confirmed the relevance of *all* 45 contextual incidents for establishing the attack, as originally argued by the Prosecutor in the document containing the charges.[176]

The above classification of the contextual elements as part of the 'facts and circumstances' of the case has, naturally, significant consequences for the pleading of facts and the ensuing evidentiary discussion. Indeed, the presentation of a series of 'contextual' incidents begs the legitimate question of whether *all* incidents *must be proven* against the requisite applicable threshold, thereby imposing on the Prosecutor an exacting investigative exercise. The Majority of Pre-Trial Chamber I acknowledged this dilemma and explicated that in this particular case,

> the Prosecutor must establish to the requisite threshold that a *sufficient number of incidents* relevant to the establishment of the alleged 'attack' took place. This is all the more so in case none of the incidents, taken on their own, could establish the existence of such an 'attack' (emphasis added).[177]

What follows from this statement is that only a sufficient number of proven incidents, viewed as a whole, will demonstrate a 'campaign or operation' against the civilian population. Indeed, this is in line with earlier jurisprudence of the Court, insofar as the "attack" has always been demonstrated by a series of events which have been subjected to the req-

---

[174] Pre-Trial Chamber I, Dissenting Opinion of Judge Silvia Fernandez de Gurmendi, ICC-02/11-01/11-432-Anx-Corr, para. 41.

[175] "The Appeals Chamber notes that [articles 67(1)(a) and 61(3) of the Statute, rule 121(3) of the Rules and regulation 52 of the Regulations of the Court] do not distinguish between 'material facts' and 'subsidiary facts'", see *Gbagbo* Adjournment Appeal Decision, para. 37, *supra* note 170.

[176] "The Appeals Chamber notes that the factual allegations in question describe a series of separate events. Therefore, it is not immediately obvious that there is any distinction between the four Charged Incidents and the 41 Incidents in terms of their relevance to establishing an attack against a civilian population", *ibid.*, para. 46.

[177] *Gbagbo* Adjourning Decision, para. 23, see *supra* note 169. This was later acknowledged by the *Gbagbo* Adjournment Appeal Decision, para. 47, *ibid.*

uisite threshold. This flexible approach also assists in not conflating the context with the individual charged incidents. The Majority's interest in the 'contextual' incidents was perhaps also driven by the fact that, unlike in previous cases, the "attack", as portrayed by the Prosecutor, did not involve a sequence of large-scale military operations like, for example, in the *Bashir* case or assaults in the *Kenya* cases, which are in themselves compound events of a certain intensity over a prolonged period of time. Rather, as described in the Prosecutor's document containing the charges,[178] the incidents were smaller in scope[179] and occurring at times of unrest and political turmoil with the involvement of a high number of different actors affiliated with both conflict parties on the ground. Importantly, in situations where several groups act on the ground, the question of attributing the act of violence to the pertinent conflict party also becomes crucial.

As regards the Chamber's evidentiary expectations, the Majority drew a distinction between those incidents that formed the charges and those which were relevant for the context. It clarified:

> [I]n order to be considered relevant as proof of the contextual elements, the information needed may be less specific than what is needed for the crimes charged but is still required to be sufficiently probative and specific so as to support the existence of an 'attack' against a civilian population. The information needed must include, for example, details such as the identity of the perpetrators, or at least information as to the group they belonged to, as well as the identity of the victims, or at least information as to their real or perceived political, ethnic, religious or national allegiance(s).[180]

What can be distilled from these sentences is that the Chamber would accept less detailed information as long as it reveals in a generic fashion the groups to which the perpetrators and the victims belonged. In other words, not any violent act by whoever against whomever would suffice to evidence the Prosecutor's proposition that 'pro-Gbagbo forces' attacked ci-

---

[178] Reference is made to the Prosecutor's presentation of the 'contextual' incidents in the document containing the charges, see ICC-02/11-01/11-357-Anx1-Red, paras. 23–29, *supra* note 155.

[179] Apart from the charged incidents, the other incidents involved, *e.g.*, only one, two or nine victims. Other incidents involved "several" persons.

[180] *Gbagbo* Adjourning Decision, para. 22, see *supra* note 169.

vilians.[181] These allegations must be proven with evidence of sufficient probative value. Which types of evidence this would necessitate is a matter to be determined by the Chambers, but should not go so far as to establish an obligation upon the Prosecutor to gather evidence that would meet the standard of proving the incident as if it were charged.

Finally, some discussion arose as to whether the policy requirement related to the "attack" or to the incidents which constitute the "attack". This was grounded in the Majority Judges' statement that, on the basis of the evidence at hand, the incidents as described made it difficult to discern whether the "perpetrators acted pursuant to or in furtherance of a policy to attack a civilian population".[182] Indeed, the adjournment decision can be read to establish that the "policy" be proven for each incident.[183] However, the "policy" requirement in Article 7(2)(a) of the Statute relates to the "attack" and may be inferred from an overall assessment of all underlying incidents or assaults, taken together.[184] At the same time, however, one cannot deny that if the overall "attack" is committed pursuant to or in furtherance of a "policy", then the constituent elements of such an "attack", that is, a sufficient number of incidents, must be the expression of such a "policy". If none or only a few incidents are linked to the alleged "policy", how could the inference be reasonably made that the overall "attack" *is* pursuant to that "policy"? This becomes even more crucial, in case several groups are involved in an incident. For only those incidents can form the basis of the "attack" which were committed by those perpetrators associated with the alleged "policy". In other words, if two opposing conflict parties commit violent acts during a specific period of time in pursuance of their respective policies, it would be illogical to take into account

---

[181] "Moreover, many of these incidents are described in very summary fashion, making it difficult for the Chamber to determine whether the perpetrators acted pursuant to or in furtherance of a policy to attack a civilian population as required by Article 7(2)(a) of the Statute", *ibid.*, para. 36.

[182] *Ibid.*

[183] *Ibid.*, paras. 36 and 44; Dissenting Opinion of Judge Silvia Fernandez de Gurmendi, ICC-02/11-01/11-432-Anx-Corr, paras. 47–48.

[184] See also paragraph 2 of the Introduction to Crimes Against Humanity in the Elements of Crimes which reads, in the relevant part: "[T]he last element should not be interpreted as requiring proof that the perpetrator had knowledge of all characteristics of the attack or the precise details of the plan or policy of the State or organization".

the entirety of violent acts, regardless of whether the crimes were committed by one side or the other.[185]

The Prosecutor considered the Chamber's request and reverted to the Chamber after having conducted further investigation. It is worth noting that in the amended document containing the charges, the Prosecutor sought to prove the existence of the "attack" on the basis of 39 incidents in Abidjan, including the four charged incidents, and added further information.[186] The pre-trial phase concluded with the confirmation of the charges against *Laurent Gbagbo*.[187] It seems that the initial evidentiary difficulties in the Prosecutor's case record were resolved eventually to the satisfaction of the Majority of the Chamber.[188]

3.5.3. The Katanga Case: A New Attempt to Define the "Organization"

The last case study of this overview is the 7 March 2014 *Katanga* judgment of Trial Chamber II[189] which is discussed only with respect to two

---

[185] A different appreciation was proposed by the *amici curiae* in this case who cited the following comparison: "One can be convinced of a 'forest' without evidence of the nature and location of particular 'trees'", see Amicus Curiae Observations of Professors Robinson, deGuzman, Jalloh and Cryer, 9 October 2013, ICC-02/11-01/11-534, para. 42 (http://www.legal-tools.org/doc/16ef11/). However, as explained above, the existence of a 'forest' as such is not at stake as the 'forest' in a conflict situation involving several actors is always further specified. What needs to be proven is that the 'forest' consisted predominantly of, *e.g.*, oak trees. Only if a sufficient number of oak trees are identifiable, can the 'forest' be overall assessed as an 'oak forest'.

[186] Office of the Prosecutor, *Document amendé de notification des charges*, 13 January 2014, ICC-02/11-01/11-592-Anx1, para. 56 (http://www.legal-tools.org/doc/11fec9/).

[187] *Gbagbo* Confirmation of Charges, see *supra* note 18.

[188] Judge van den Wyngaert dissented from the Majority decision but expressed disagreement with regard to the Majority's findings regarding the individual criminal responsibility of *Laurent Gbagbo*, see Dissenting Opinion of Judge van den Wyngaert, annexed to Pre-Trial Chamber I, Decision on the confirmation of charges against Laurent Gbagbo, 12 June 2014, ICC-02/11-01/11-656-Anx (http://www.legal-tools.org/doc/f715a5/). With regard to the 'contextual' incidents, she confirmed that "[t]he several incidents supporting the crimes against humanity allegation are now better supported by evidence" but indicated that "the previously identified problem regarding reliance upon anonymous hearsay remains", see *ibid.*, para. 2.

[189] On 7 March 2014, *Germain Katanga* was convicted by a Majority of two Judges of Trial Chamber II to 12 years imprisonment for having contributed "in any other way" to the crime of murder as crime against humanity and war crimes in the context of the attack on Bogoro village. He was acquitted of the charges involving rape and sexual slavery as

issues concerning the context of crimes against humanity.[190] In general, the Majority of Trial Chamber followed by and large the Court's jurisprudence in the early cases. One detail that catches the reader's attention is the Trial Chamber's factual analysis in relation to the "attack". Unlike Pre-Trial Chamber I, which, as set out above, assumed the existence of a 'widespread attack' consisting of many operations, including the Bogoro attack, throughout the region of Ituri in the period end of 2002 to mid-2003, the Trial Chamber reduced its factual examination of the "attack" to the 24 February 2003 Bogoro event only.[191] In so doing, the Trial Chamber accepted the Prosecutor's proposition that the charged incident, the Bogoro attack, alone would suffice to establish the overall "attack".[192] However, it did not go so far as to qualify the Bogoro attack as "widespread", but confirmed its "systematic" nature.[193] There is no impediment in law to rely on a single incident for the establishment of a "widespread or systematic attack" and, consequently, the Prosecutor may present the charged incident as actually constituting the "attack". But the single-day attack against Bogoro village also demonstrates that the threshold of Article 7(1) of the Statute is not as stringent as some may fear. In fact, the Court's authority to intervene in numerous situations may not be limited so much by the legal requirements of Article 7 of the Statute but it will be defined by the Prosecutor's exercise of prosecutorial discretion in the selection of events to be investigated which must be fair and transparent, lest it raises criticism.

But, the more noteworthy contribution of the Judges to the ongoing discussion on crimes against humanity at the Court was its attempt to delineate afresh in legal terms the contours of the "organization" within the

---

crimes against humanity and war crimes as well as the use of children under the age of 15 years to participate actively in hostilities as a war crime.

[190] *Katanga* Judgment, see *supra* note 17; Minority Opinion of Judge Christine van den Wyngaert, 7 March 2014, ICC-01/04-01/07-3436-AnxI (http://www.legal-tools.org/doc/9b0c61/); Concurring opinion of Judges Fatoumata Diarra and Bruno Cotte, 7 March 2014, ICC-01/04-01/07-3436-AnxII (http://www.legal-tools.org/doc/c815e4/). For a comprehensive analysis of the judgment, see Carsten Stahn, "Justice Delivered or Justice Denied? The Legacy of the Katanga Judgment", in *Journal of International Criminal Justice*, 2014, vol. 12, pp. 809–834.

[191] *Ibid., Katanga* Judgment, para. 1133 *et seq.* However it took other attacks into consideration to infer, *e.g.*, the "policy", or the pattern of violence, see *ibid.*, paras. 1151 and 1154.

[192] *Ibid.*, para. 1128.

[193] *Ibid.*, paras. 1157–1162.

---

meaning of Article 7(2)(a) of the Statute. This was done, despite the fact that the qualification of the respective organized armed group FRPI as an "organization" did not risk to be viewed differently – from a legal point of view – given the Court's long-standing jurisprudence in relation to similarly structured organizations. [194] Nevertheless, the Majority of Trial Chamber II undertook to further the discussion by integrating into their exegesis of the law the controversy that arose within Pre-Trial Chamber II in the context of the *Kenya* situation and by proposing a definition of their own. They clearly reject the requirement that the non-State actors possess 'quasi-State' structures or even a hierarchical set-up.[195] Their suggestion for an alternative definition is as follows:

> On peut ainsi se demander si le fait que l'organisation soit normativement rattachée à l'existence d'une attaque, au sens de l'article 7-2-a, est de nature à influer sur la définition des caractéristiques qu'elle doit présenter. Pour la Chambre, le rattachement du terme organisation à l'existence même de l'attaque, et non pas au caractère systématique ou généralisé de celle-ci, suppose que l'organisation dispose de ressources, de moyens et de capacités suffisantes pour permettre la réalisation de la ligne de conduite ou de l'opération impliquant la commission multiple d'actes visés à l'article 7-2-a du Statut. Il suffit donc qu'elle soit dotée d'un ensemble de structures ou de mécanismes, quels qu'ils soient, suffisamment efficaces pour assurer la coordination nécessaire à la réalisation d'une attaque dirigée contre une population civile. Ainsi,

---

[194] As a side, it is noted that the Prosecutor, in the latest Article 53(1) Report concerning the opening of the investigation in the Central African Republic II, assessed that the Séléka movement, an organized armed group within the meaning of Article 8 of the Statute, also satisfies the criteria of an "organization" within the meaning of Article 7 of the Statute:

> A responsible command, hierarchical structure, and the group's capability to coordinate and carry out a widespread and systematic attack, described above in the discussion of Séléka as an organized armed group for purposes of article 8 of the Statute, also satisfy many of the criteria mentioned above for establishing Séléka as an organization for the purposes of Article 7. The Pre-Trial Chambers have also identified a group's control over territory of a State as a factor that may assist in the determination of whether a group qualifies an organization within the meaning of Article 7(2)(a) of the Statute. In this regard it is notable that Séléka was already in control of almost half of the territory of the CAR by December 2012 [...] (footnotes omitted).

See Office of the Prosecutor, Article 53(1) Report, 24 September 2014.

[195] *Katanga* Judgment, paras. 1120 and 1122, see *supra* note 17.

comme cela a été indiqué précédemment, l'organisation con-
cernée doit disposer des moyens suffisants pour favoriser ou
encourager l'attaque sans qu'il y ait lieu d'exiger plus. En effet, il est loin d'être exclu, tout particulièrement dans le con-
texte des guerres asymétriques d'aujourd'hui, qu'une attaque
dirigée contre une population civile puisse être aussi le fait
d'une entité privée regroupant un ensemble de personnes
poursuivant l'objectif d'attaquer une population civile, en
d'autres termes d'un groupe ne disposant pas obliga-
toirement d'une structure élaborée, susceptible d'être qualifiée de quasi-étatique.

Le fait que l'attaque doive par ailleurs être qualifiée de gé-
néralisée ou de systématique ne signifie pas, pour autant, que
l'organisation qui la favorise ou l'encourage soit structurée
d'une manière telle qu'elle présente les mêmes caracté-
ristiques que celles d'un État. Pour la Chambre, ce qui
compte avant tout ce sont, une nouvelle fois, les capacités
d'action, de concertation et de coordination, autant
d'éléments essentiels à ses yeux pour définir une organisation qui, en raison même des moyens et des ressources dont
elle dispose comme de l'adhésion qu'elle suscite, per-
mettront la réalisation de l'attaque.[196]

The Trial Chamber approaches the determination of "organization"
from two angles. On the one hand, it gives weight to the placement of the
"organization" in Article 7(2)(a) of the Statute, linking it to the existence
of the "attack", but not to its qualification as "widespread" or "systematic". Mindful of the negotiation history of Article 7 of the Statute, this may
be interpreted as the Chamber's intention not to subject the "organization"
to an overly stringent test as the determination of the "attack" was to be
analysed against a lower threshold than the determination of its qualifiers.
On the other hand, associating the "organization" with the "attack" rather
than the 'basic human values' test proposed by Pre-Trial Chamber II, the
Trial Judges gave the impression to assess the quality of the "organization" against a higher threshold. When it comes to the description of the
entity's features, the Judges proposed some generic criteria it would look
into, such as the organization's capacities for action, mutual agreement
and co-ordination as well as its membership and the means and resources

---

[196] *Ibid.*, paras. 1119–1120.

at its disposal.[197] Those factors are even less defined and stringent than those proposed by Pre-Trial Chamber II. In the end, this all-inclusive conception of the "organization" does not draw any contours and allows all kinds of "organizations" to come under the purview of the Statute. Be that as it may, the facts of the case clearly exceeded the generic test of the Chamber, as the Ngiti militia, also called FRPI, constituted in the view of the Chamber an organized armed group under humanitarian law.[198]

3.6. Conclusions

This chapter presented a selection of issues concerning the interpretation and application of the contextual elements of crimes against humanity under Article 7 of the ICC Statute and the manner in which they have been addressed jurisprudentially. As the case law of the ICC suggests, the Court has yet to dissect some of the legal components of the context, weed out ambiguities, and provide its understanding on their interrelation. This is essential for the Court's future success in prosecuting those who bear the greatest responsibility for having committed crimes against humanity.

Despite the jurisprudential legacy of other international(ised) criminal tribunals, the Court still struggles over concretizing certain notions which are essential components of the contextual definition of crimes against humanity. For example, does the component of "course of conduct" already presuppose a certain linkage of the acts, as implied in the *Mbarushimana* case? If so, what is the difference between "course of conduct" and the "policy"? Does the determination of "organization" within the meaning of Article 7 of the ICC Statute require the fulfilment of some minimum conditions or shall it remain a concept to be affirmed only on a case-by-case basis? The early cases, such as the *Bemba* case and the *Katanga/Ngudjolo* case, the *Kenya* debate and Trial Chamber II's views in the *Katanga* judgment display three different perceptions on this point. What are the criteria according to which a "policy" is attributed to

---

[197] The Chambers argumentation to link the "organization" only with the "attack" within the meaning of Article 7(2)(a) of the Statute appears therefore, at first, peculiar as the "attack", which the "organization" co-ordinates, in the end must be either "widespread" or "systematic" within the meaning of Article 7(1) of the Statute. Inevitably, this may have consequences on the capacities, resources, means and membership of such an "organization". It also shows the interrelation of the components contained in Articles 7(1) and 7(2)(a) of the Statute which cannot be viewed in isolation.

[198] *Katanga* Judgment, paras. 1139–1141, see *supra* note 17.

the entity devising and implementing it? What is the meaning of and the interrelation between "policy" and "systematic"? Is it simply a matter of different thresholds or do they carry a different meaning? When can a Chamber infer from the existence of a recurrent pattern of behaviour the existence of a "policy" and when is this inference no longer sufficient? The *Bemba* and *Bashir* cases, on the one hand, and the *Mbarushimana* and *Mudacumura* cases, on the other hand, follow a different approach in their pertinent analysis of the facts.

But the discussion over the contextual elements of crimes against humanity involves more than delineating the individual boundaries of each component. The different components should not be assessed in isolation but must be appraised as components of an ensemble. Retaining a relatively low threshold for one or more components will inevitably have consequences for the entire construction of Article 7 of the Statute. At the same time, raising the bar too high has the potential of narrowing down the applicability of said provision. Where to strike the balance? The Court seems to favour a more elastic, inclusive interpretation of the law. Any fears that Article 7 of the Statute was framed too restrictively are unfounded. Indeed, the Court's approach is defendable as long as a demarcation line between crimes against humanity and ordinary crimes can be discerned. Another very important aspect pertains to the application of the law to the facts which must be sound and transparent. When assessing the facts of a case, due regard must also be paid to the historical, political and social circumstances existing at the time. The legal appreciation of the facts must correspond as much as possible to 'reality' on the ground.

Those who will apply Article 3 of the Proposed Convention will not be spared of the above questions. Indeed, unlike the ICC Statute, the Convention, if entered into force, will be interpreted and applied by a plethora of national judges, prosecutors, and counsel all around the world who may have a different understanding of the law and the *raison d'être* of crimes against humanity. Legal certainty about the concept as such and the different components of the definition will assist in the creation of a worldwide understanding of crimes against humanity and avoid, it is hoped, disputes over borderline cases. Any boundaries to the concept of crimes against humanity must stem from the *law*; the authority of national courts to intervene in a particular situation must be limited by the *legal* requirements of the definition. A supplementary text to the Convention, such as the Elements of Crimes to the ICC Statute, could be a tool to achieve such clarity. But, most importantly, appropriate guidance could be found in the jurisprudence of the ICC which, it is hoped, will gradually grow and put the concept on a robust fundament.

4

The Draft Convention on Crimes Against Humanity: What to Do With the Definition?

Darryl Robinson[*]

4.1. Overview of the Chapter

A centrally important and influential feature of the Draft Convention will, obviously, be its definition of crimes against humanity. For reasons that will be canvassed below, it is most likely that the Draft Convention will use the definition from Article 7 of the Rome Statute. There are however significant legitimate concerns about aspects of Article 7, most particularly the 'policy element'. Accordingly, it is highly desirable that the commentary to the Draft Convention mitigate the concerns by explaining some key terms in accordance with pertinent authorities. This chapter proposes some such clarifying commentary.

The Article 7 definition features the now-iconic contextual element of a 'widespread or systematic attack directed against a civilian population'. The definition of 'attack', in Article 7(2)(a), requires a 'State or organizational policy'. This raises legitimate questions about the relationship between 'policy' and 'systematic', whether they are duplicative, and whether the policy element will complicate and restrict crimes against humanity prosecutions. This chapter will look both at the logical structure of Article 7 and at past authorities to show that 'policy' is, and must be, different from and less demanding than 'systematic'. The authorities will show some of the concrete ways in which 'policy' is more modest.

---

[*] Associate Professor, Queen's University, Faculty of Law. This research was facilitated by a research grant from the Social Sciences and Humanities Research Council of Canada as well as the Antonio Cassese Prize for International Criminal Law Studies. I am grateful for the very helpful assistance of Gillian MacNeil. This chapter draws at points on a related chapter, Darryl Robinson, "Crimes Against Humanity: A Better Policy on 'Policy'", in Carsten Stahn (ed.), *The Law and Practice of the International Criminal Court*, Oxford University Press, Oxford, 2015. That chapter raises concerns about trends in some early ICC cases – and notes the better trajectory of later cases – whereas this chapter proposes commentary for the Draft Convention on crimes against humanity.

The proposed commentary draws on national jurisprudence and other authorities, showing that the policy element is an *in limine* filter screening out situations of unconnected ordinary crimes. It should not be elevated to a major barrier to legitimate prosecutions. Such commentary would be valuable not only in relation to the Draft Convention, but also for customary law, by showing the consistency of authorities in support of a workable definition.

4.2. Introduction

The Draft Convention is a welcome initiative for many reasons. War crimes and genocide are subjects of treaty obligations, whereas the third core crime – crimes against humanity – lacks the same clarity of enforcement obligations. This is particularly regrettable given that crimes against humanity are of the greatest contemporary relevance (as they do not require armed conflict or special genocidal intent). A convention would remove ambiguities about the obligation to prosecute and about jurisdictional rules. It would 'tighten the net' by creating and strengthening a network of co-operation and prevention. Given that governmental authorities have accepted strong obligations in relation to financial crimes, it would be ironic and unacceptable that we do not establish similar obligations in relation to, for example, the extermination of hundreds of human beings. A convention would complement the ICC Statute system by emphasizing the 'horizontal' obligations of States to respond to crimes against humanity and to assist each other in doing so. And most elusively but perhaps most importantly, it could help instill a sense of responsibility to prevent, in the same vein as U.N. Member States recognize in connection with crimes of genocide.

The definition of crimes against humanity has been a matter of great uncertainty and fluctuation, largely because there has not yet been a general convention on crimes against humanity. Since the 1990s, there has been a convergence around the notion of a 'widespread or systematic attack directed against any civilian population'. But instruments still differ in subtle ways. For example, the Statute of the International Criminal Tribunal for the former Yugoslavia ('ICTY'), adopted in 1993, requires the presence of armed conflict. The Statute of the International Criminal Tribunal for Rwanda ('ICTR'), adopted in 1994, drops the requirement of armed conflict but requires discriminatory motive. The ICC Statute, adopted in 1998, drops both the requirement of armed conflict and of discriminatory motive, but it requires a "State or organizational policy".

The most plausible options for the Draft Convention are either to adhere to the ICC Statute definition or to advance a new definition. Both options have advantages and disadvantages. The advantage of a new definition is that it would allow international lawyers to remove or rewrite the aspects of Article 7 that they regard as the most problematic. The most frequently-mentioned candidate for rewriting is the 'policy element', which is seen by many scholars and jurists as an unnecessary impediment to prosecution. Some lawyers would also seek to make other changes, such as removing the term 'civilian', in order to include crimes against combatants, or remove the requirement of awareness of the surrounding context.

At this time, the arguments for crafting a new definition are widely seen to be outweighed by the benefits of using the established definition in Article 7. First, to re-open and re-negotiate the definition would take an indeterminate amount of time and would have unforeseeable results. Indeed, a definition negotiated in the current international climate may be more restrictive, rather than more progressive, which is contrary to the aim of most of those who might prefer a new definition. Second, the ICC Statute definition was developed by States with broad participation, and thus is familiar to them and more likely to be accepted by them. Third, many States have already incorporated the ICC Statute definition into national laws; adhering to that definition thus simplifies implementation of the new convention. Fourth, to introduce another definition would increase the problems of fragmention. It is desirable to avoid the complication of having one definition for some obligations and another definition for other obligations. Fifth, Article 7 is already regarded in some authorities as having the status of customary international law.[1] Accordingly, it

---

[1] See examples cited in Leila Sadat, "Crimes Against Humanity in the Modern Age", in *American Journal of International Law*, 2013, vol. 107, no. 2, p. 373. For other examples, see England and Wales Court of Appeal (Civil Division), *SK (Zimbabwe) v. Secretary of State for the Home Department*, [2012] EWCA Civ 807, [2012] 2 Cr App R 28, Judgment, 19 June 2012; European Court of Human Rights (Grand Chamber), *Case of Streletz, Kessler and Krenz v. Germany*, Judgment, 22 March 2001, Application nos. 34044/96, 35532/97 and 44801/98, ECHR 2001-II, p. 409, concurring opinion of Judge Loucaides, p. 453; International Criminal Court (Trial Chamber II), *Prosecutor v. Germain Katanga*, Jugement Rendu en Application de l'Article 74 du Statut, 7 March 2014, ICC-01/04-01/07-3436, para. 1100 ('*Katanga* Judgment').

seems highly likely that the Draft Convention will simply use the Article 7 definition.

Adopting the Article 7 definition does not mean however that the legitimate and widely shared concerns about the policy element should be neglected. On the contrary, the concerns about the definition should be addressed in accompanying commentary. This approach reaps the benefits of using the established definition while also seizing the opportunity to mitigate the main concerns. There are at least four advantages to this approach. First, commentary can facilitate acceptance by those who are concerned about the dangers of mis-interpretation or over-extension of the policy element. Second, the commentary can facilitate prosecution and make the convention more effective, by demonstrating how the policy element has been understood and applied. Third, by drawing on national and international authorities, many of which are not well known, the commentary can help show that there is considerable harmony in the different authorities, and thus reduce the current fragmentation in the law. Fourth, as International Law Commission ('ILC') commentary is often used to aid in interpretation and as a guide to customary law, it will be of assistance not only in relation to the convention but also for national and international courts applying crimes against humanity law for any reason.

This chapter will focus only on contextual elements, and in particular, the policy element. There are other aspects of the definition that could arguably benefit from clarification. For example, in my view, it would be desirable to clarify that the term 'civilian' includes all persons no longer taking part in hostilities.[2] Others might want to clarify the term 'organiza-

---

[2] The ICTY has interpreted 'civilian' as having the same meaning as in Article 50 of Additional Protocol I, and thus as excluding prisoners of war and persons *hors de combat.* There are reasons to doubt this transplant from the detailed international humanitarian legal regime of the Geneva Conventions. The ICTY approach means, *e.g.*, that large-scale torture of prisoners of war would not constitute a crime against humanity. This departs from important international case law. Arguably, 'civilian' should be given its previous and broader meaning of any person no longer participating in hostilities, since the purpose of the term is to exclude lawful attacks on military objectives. The ICTY relied on the principle of distinction, but the principle of distinction would also prohibit the massacre of prisoners of war. For discussion see Robert Cryer *et al.*, *An Introduction to International Criminal Law and Procedure*, Cambridge University Press, Cambridge, 2014, pp. 240–242. Arguably it would also be desirable to recall the proposition that in peacetime, all persons are 'civilians'.

tion'.[3] However, it could well be argued that these matters are best left to jurisprudence. Commentary should be parsimonious. Accordingly, the proposed commentary will focus on the policy element, because (1) it is the element which has raised the most concerns, (2) it is the most frequently misunderstood, and (3) it is the subject of quite consistent yet little-noticed jurisprudence. Thus, it is the issue for which it is most beneficial to highlight and draw attention to the authorities.

This chapter will: touch lightly on the issue of the customary law status of the policy element (primarily to explain that the proposed commentary is apt regardless of one's view on that question) (section 4.3.); examine the problem with the policy element and the desirability of commentary (4.4.); and then explain the proposed comments along with their supporting authorities (4.5.). The proposed comments are that:

- The term 'policy' is not equivalent to the term 'systematic'. 'Policy' does not necessarily require deliberate planning, direction or orchestration; it requires only that some State or organization must have at least encouraged the attack, either actively or passively.

- The purpose of the policy element is to screen out 'ordinary crime', that is, acts of individuals on their own unconnected criminal initiatives.

- A policy need not be expressly stated or formalized, and need not involve the highest levels of a State or organization. A policy may be implicit. The existence of a policy can be inferred from the manner in which the acts occur. In particular, it can be inferred from the implausibility of coincidental occurrence.

- While a policy will typically be manifested by the actions of a State or organization, it may also be manifested by a deliberate failure to act which is consciously aimed at encouraging an attack.

---

[3]   There is currently a debate about the meaning of 'organization', and whether the organization must be 'State-like' or whether it more broadly encompasses non-State organizations with capacity to inflict harm. ICC jurisprudence is converging on the latter view. Both views have merit, although I also incline to the latter view. It is possible that better and more refined tests for 'organization' are yet to be discovered, and thus I would not seek to entrench any test at this point.

4.3. Differing Plausible Views on Customary Status

The customary law status of the policy element is hotly debated and credible arguments are available on all sides. Scholarly opinion as to the customary status of the element has gone through cycles. Prior to the 1990s, the comparatively few scholars interested in crimes against humanity seemed to regard policy as a requirement.[4] In the 1990s, as the element was recognized in the *Tadić* decision and the Rome Statute, popular scholarly opinion moved quite decisively against the element.[5] More recently, there has been a resurgence, with scholars such as Luban, Schabas, Kress, Ambos and Wirth arguing that the element has support in precedents and is conceptually important.[6] At this time, it is difficult to ascertain which is the minority and majority view.

For the purposes of this chapter, it is not necessary to resolve the customary law question. This chapter starts from the premise that the Rome Statute definition will likely be used in the Draft Convention, and asks what commentary should be included to ameliorate concerns about the policy element.

Nonetheless, I must at least lightly touch on the question, because some readers may feel that the policy element is so clearly against cus-

---

[4] Joseph Keenan and Brendan Brown, *Crimes Against International Law*, Public Affairs Press, Washington, 1950; M. Cherif Bassiouni, *Crimes Against Humanity in International Law*, Martinus Nijhoff Publishers, Dordrecht, 1992.

[5] Margaret McAuliffe deGuzman, "The Road From Rome: The Developing Law of Crimes Against Humanity", in *Human Rights Quarterly*, 2000, vol. 22, no. 2, p. 335; Phyllis Hwang, "Defining Crimes Against Humanity in the ICC Statute of the International Criminal Court", in *Fordham International Law Journal*, 1998, vol. 22, no. 2, p. 457; Guénaël Mettraux, "Crimes Against Humanity in the Jurisprudence of the International Criminal Tribunals for the Former Yugoslavia and Rwanda", in *Harvard International Law Journal*, 2002, vol, 43, no. 1, p. 237.

[6] See, *e.g.*, Claus Kreß, "On the Outer Limits of Crimes Against Humanity: The Concept of Organization Within the Policy Requirement: Some Reflections on the March 2010 ICC *Kenya* Decision", in *Leiden Journal of International Law*, 2010, vol. 23, no. 4, p. 855; William Schabas, "State Policy as an Element of International Crimes", in *Journal of Criminal Law and Criminology*, 2008, vol. 98, no. 3, p. 953; M. Cherif Bassiouni, "Revisiting the Architecture of Crimes Against Humanity: Almost a Century in the Making, with Gaps and Ambiguities Remaining − The Need for a Specialized Convention", in Leila Nadya Sadat (ed.), *Forging a Convention for Crimes against Humanity*, Cambridge University Press, 2011, p. 43; Kai Ambos and Steffen Wirth, "The Current Law of Crimes Against Humanity", in *Criminal Law Forum*, 2002, vol. 13, no. 1, p. 1; David Luban, "A Theory of Crimes Against Humanity", in *Yale Journal of International Law*, 2004, vol. 29, no. 1, p. 85.

tomary law that the decision to use Article 7 will seem incomprehensible. In particular, I must briefly address the ICTY *Kunarac* case, because many scholars and jurists regard that case as determinative of the customary law question. In *Kunarac*, the ICTY Appeals Chamber declared rather categorically that there is "nothing" in customary law that required a policy element and an "overwhelming" case against it.[7] An assertion by the ICTY Appeals Chamber is always entitled to great weight as an indicator of custom. I would however advocate some caution in this instance. As many scholars have noted, that assertion appeared only in a thinly-reasoned footnote; the authorities it cited are actually either silent on or indeed contrary to the Chamber's assertion; and many authorities in favour of the policy element are simply ignored.[8] Furthermore, there is more to customary law than just ICTY/ICTR jurisprudence. For example, the Rome Statute, reflecting a simultaneous statement of a great many States purporting to reflect customary law, is also entitled to some weight.[9] There is also a long tradition of national and international case and other expert bodies that must be taken into account.[10]

---

[7] International Criminal Tribunal for the former Yugoslavia (Appeals Chamber), *Prosecutor v. Kunarac et al.*, Judgment, 12 June 2002, IT-96-23 and IT-96-23/1-A, para. 98. The reasoning of the Chamber is almost identical to that in Mettraux, 2002, pp. 270–282, see *supra* note 5.

[8] For scholarly commentary critical of the Chamber's claims about the past authorities, see Schabas, 2008, see *supra* note 6; Kreß, 2010, pp. 870–871, see *supra* note 6; Bassiouni, 2011, p. xxxiii, see *supra* note 6 (describing it as a "gross misstatement of precedent"); Charles Jalloh, "What Makes A Crime Against Humanity A Crime Against Humanity", in *American University International Law Review*, 2013, vol. 28, no. 2, pp. 397–340; Matt Halling, "Push the Envelope – Watch It Bend: Removing the Policy Element and Extending Crimes Against Humanity", in *Leiden Journal of International Law*, 2010, vol. 23, no. 4, pp. 829–831.

[9] Richard Baxter, "Multilateral Treaties as Evidence of Customary International Law", in *British Yearbook of International Law*, 1965, vol. 41, p. 275.

[10] I review some of the authorities in Darryl Robinson, "Crimes Against Humanity: Reflections on State Sovereignty, Legal Precision and the Dictates of the Public Conscience", in Lattanzi and Schabas (eds.), *Essays on the ICC Statute of the International Criminal Court*, Volume I, il Sirente, Fagnano Alto, 1999, pp. 152–164. Some relevant cases include: Nuremberg Military Tribunal, *United States v. Brandt et al.* (the Medical Case), Judgment, 19 August 1947, 2 Trials of War Criminals Before the Nuernberg Military Tribunals Under Control Council Law No. 10, p. 181 (crimes must be "ordered, sanctioned or approved"); Nuremberg Military Tribunal, *United States v. Altstötter et al.* (the Justice Trial), Judgment, 3 Trials of War Criminals Before the Nuernberg Military Tribunals Under Control Council Law No. 10, p. 982 ("organized or approved"); Dutch Court of Cassation, *Public Prosecutor v. Menten*, (1987), International Law Reports, vol. 75, Judgment, 13 January 1981 pp. 362–363 ("concept of crimes against humanity requires [...] consciously

My own view is that, given the paucity, inconsistency and frequent vagueness of previous authorities, a fair observer will not find the authorities at this time decisively conclusive one way or the other. Many national cases, international cases, and other expert bodies indicate that a policy is needed, and many do not. Looking at this pattern of sparse authorities, a capable jurist could plausibly highlight those passages that seem to require a policy, or those passages that seem not to. Speaking for myself, I incline to the view that the element *is* custom. For me, given the indeterminacy of the 'ascending' analysis (the sources), what tilts the balance in favour is the conceptual, 'descending' analysis, that is, that the element is valuable for the coherence of the concept, as discussed in section 4.5.2.

However, you do not need to agree with me on the custom question for the purposes of this chapter. For example, you might be agnostic and agree that the case against the policy element is not so overwhelming as to warrant the disadvantages of re-opening and re-negotiating the definition, risking support, and increasing the fragmentation of the law. Alternatively, you may be firmly convinced that the element is not custom and that it is a legislative imposition. In that case, the fact remains that the element appears in the ICC Statute, in the national legislation of many countries, and will likely appear in the Draft Convention, and thus must be interpreted. Thus, you should be all the more supportive of clarifications intended to prevent the element from being interpreted as a major obstacle. Accordingly, regardless of our respective positions on the customary law question, we have an overlapping interest in commentary to clarify the element.

---

pursued policy"); Supreme Court of Canada, *R. v. Finta*, [1994] 1 S.C.R. 701, Judgment, 24 March 1994, p. 814 ("what distinguishes a crime against humanity from any other criminal offence [...] is [...] pursuance of a policy"); High Court of Australia, *Polyukhovich v. Commonwealth ("War Crimes Act case")*, [1991] HCA 32; (1991) 172 CLR 501, Judgment, 14 August 1991, para. 53 (exclude "isolated acts [...] unconnected with a larger design"); as well as expert bodies, such as Commission of Experts for Yugoslavia, *Final Report of the Commission of Experts Established Pursuant to Security Council Resolution 780 (1992)*, United Nations, 1994, para. 84 ("must be part of a policy"); Commission of Experts for Rwanda, *Final Report of the Commission of Experts established pursuant to Security Council Resolution 935 (1994)*, United Nations, 1994, para. 135 ("official policy"); Gay J. McDougall, Contemporary Forms of Slavery: Systematic Rape, Sexual Slavery and Slavery-like Practices During Armed Conflict; Final Report submitted by Ms. Gay J. McDougall, Special Rapporteur, United Nations, 1998, para. 39 ("policy, plan or design").

4.4. The Problem With 'Policy' and the Desirability of Commentary

A recurring and persistent problem with 'policy' is that one of the best-known connotations of the term implies something highly formal and official. In this connotation, it conveys something adopted at a high level, such as by a Cabinet or board of directors, and then promulgated to lower levels. In this sense, the word implies something more than mere orders or deliberately turning a blind eye to crimes: it suggests something special, momentous, deliberate and sanctified, more akin to a manifesto, programme or platform. However, that is not the only ordinary meaning of the term. Indeed, the "chief living sense" of the term simply connotes "a course of action adopted as expedient".[11] It is something the State or organization is deliberately doing – or encouraging others to do.

Among the understandable concerns raised about the policy element are that it might get interpreted to require direct proof of internal machinations and secret plans, or that it might be equated with 'systematic', contradicting the disjunctiveness of the threshold test. All of these concerns are legitimate. Indeed, the dangers have even come to pass in some particular decisions (see sections 4.5.1 and 4.5.3 below).

The concerns can be resolved if the policy element is interpreted in accordance with the national and international authorities, including those on which it was based. The problem, however, is that many of those authorities – including national cases and international expert bodies – are not well known. Thus, the very real risk is that judges, at the ICC or in national courts, will inject their own assumptions and reactions to the word 'policy', and thereby inadvertently create new and onerous requirements. Thus commentary drawing attention to the often overlooked but highly informative web of authorities on the modest role of the policy element can help to maintain the consistency and effectiveness of the law.

As I will strive to demonstrate below, the term 'policy' is a juridical term of art, adopted from *Tadić* and other sources. Its modest purpose is to screen out 'ordinary crime', that is, unconnected crimes committed by diverse individuals acting on their own separate criminal initiatives. The element does this by making explicit the logical corollary of excluding

---

[11] *Oxford English Dictionary*, vol. XII, Oxford University Press, Oxford, 1989, p. 27. The *Katanga* Judgment of the ICC helpfully refers as well to the ordinary meaning in French dictionaries; such as "*mani.r e concertée de conduire une affaire*". *Katanga* Judgment, para. 1108, see *supra* note 1.

unprompted individual crimes: to wit, they must be directed or encouraged by something *other than isolated individuals*, that is, a State or organization. It delineates the minimum required degree of 'collectivity', so that the acts can be described in the aggregate as an 'attack'.

Four important features of the policy element, which have been consistently emphasized in the jurisprudence, help to underscore and serve this modest purpose. I will expand on these features below. First, the term 'policy' is not used in a bureaucratic sense: a policy *need not be formalized*, need not be stated expressly, and need not be defined precisely.[12] In other words, it may be implicit. Second, a policy *need not implicate the highest levels* of a State or organization, although it does require more than the acts of one or two agents acting against instructions.[13] Third, a policy may be manifested by State or organizational action or by deliberate inaction to encourage crimes where a State or organization has a duty to intervene.[14] Fourth, and most importantly, a policy *may be inferred* from the manner in which the acts occur. It is satisfied by showing the improbability that the acts were a random, coincidental occurrence.[15] These four features are mutually connected and consistent with the purpose of excluding ordinary random crime. Numerous scholars have noted these features of the policy element.[16] Some of the jurisprudence will be reviewed below.

---

[12] See below, section 4.5.3, for authorities.

[13] See, *e.g.*, International Criminal Tribunal for the former Yugoslavia (Trial Chamber), *Prosecutor v. Dragan Nikolić*, Review of the Indictment Pursuant to Rule 61 of the Rules of Procedure and Evidence, 20 October 1995, IT-94-2-R61, para. 26; International Criminal Tribunal for the former Yugoslavia (Trial Chamber), *Prosecutor v. Blaškić*, Judgment, 3 March 2000, IT-95-14-T, para. 205 (*'Blaškić'*).

[14] See below, section 4.5.4 for authorities.

[15] See below, section 4.4.1 for authorities.

[16] Machteld Boot, Rodney Dixon and Christopher Hall, "Article 7", in Otto Triffterer (ed.), *Commentary on the ICC Statute of the International Criminal Court*, C. H. Beck, München, 2008, p. 236 ("policy need not be formalised, and can be deduced from the manner in which the acts occur [...] In essence, the policy element only requires that the acts of individuals alone, which are isolated, uncoordinated, and haphazard, be excluded"); Kriangsak Kittichaisaree, *International Criminal Law*, Oxford University Press, Oxford, 2001, pp. 97–98 (excludes individuals acting on own initiative without direction or encouragement from a State or organization, not formal, not express, not highest level, infer from circumstances); Cryer *et al.*, 2014, pp. 235–239, see *supra* note 2 (exclude random criminality of individuals, infer from manner); Ambos and Wirth, 2002, pp. 30–34, see *supra* note 6 (policy excludes ordinary crimes, may be implicit and may be passive); Sadat, 2013, pp. 354, 372, see *supra* note 1 (exclude uncoordinated, haphazard, random acts);

The term 'policy', for all its faults, helps to convey a subtle difference from mere 'attribution'. Under the normal rules of attribution in international law, acts would still be attributed to the State or organization, even if they were carried by one or two agents acting against the wishes of their State or organization.[17] Crimes against humanity, by contrast, require slightly *more* involvement or implication of the State or organization. The degree to which the State or organization must be implicated has not yet been perfectly delineated in jurisprudence. We do know at least that it is intermediate between two points. On the one hand, the requisite link is more than just the acts of one or two rogue agents acting against orders. On the other hand, it does not require the involvement of the highest levels of the State or organization.[18] And, of course, claims by a State or organization that acts are purely a matter of 'rogue' agents or 'a few bad applies' must be scrutinized with care. One would look at repetition or patterns of similar acts, a failure to respond to the acts, and so on, in order to deduce the true state of affairs.[19]

Note that I am not advancing a 'progressive', 'liberal' or creative interpretation of the policy element.[20] The points I would highlight are *already established* in national and international authorities with significant consistency, and these are the authorities on which Article 7 was based. Because many of the authorities are often unknown or overlooked, it is valuable to highlight them.

Simon Chesterman, "An Altogether Different Order: Defining the Elements of Crimes Against Humanity", in *Duke Journal of Comparative and International Law*, 2000, vol. 10, no. 2, p. 316 ("policy requirement reiterates the position that isolated and random acts cannot amount to crimes against humanity"); Yoram Dinstein, "Crimes Against Humanity After Tadić", in *Leiden Journal of International Law*, 2000, vol. 13, no. 2, p. 389 (need policy element to exclude spontaneous, fortuitous crimes).

[17] ILC Draft Articles on State Responsibility, Articles 4 and 7.

[18] *Nikolić*, see *supra* note 13; *Blaškić*, see *supra* note 13.

[19] Commission of Experts for Yugoslavia, 1994, paras. 84–85, see *supra* note 10; Special Court for Sierra Leone (Appeals Chamber), *Prosecutor v. Issa Hassan Sesay, Morris Kallon, Augustine Gbao* ('RUF Case'), Judgment, 26 October 2009, SCSL-04-15-A, para. 723, finding declared norms of the Revolutionary United Front ('RUF') prohibiting rape, unauthorised looting, killings or molestation to be "a mere farce intended to camouflage" the planned atrocities.

[20] Of course, such terms are always admittedly relative, as they depend on one's view of the *lex lata*. For one who is convinced of a more restrictive and formalistic concept of 'policy', the propositions here will indeed appear 'progressive' or 'liberal' interpretations. However, the argument here is for an affirmation of the existing authorities.

4.5. Proposed Commentary

4.5.1. The Term 'Policy' Must Not Be Conflated With 'Systematic'

The first proposed clarification is as follows: *The term 'policy' is not equivalent to the term 'systematic'. 'Policy' does not necessarily require deliberate planning, direction or orchestration; it requires only that some State or organization must have at least encouraged the attack, either actively or passively.*

The confusion between the terms 'policy' and 'systematic' is a recurring and quite understandable problem, seen both in jurisprudence and in scholarly discourse. The confusion is understandable, because Article 7 is a rather complex provision. Article 7 refers both to 'policy' and to 'systematic', which certainly sound similar. Both terms deal with the *collective* dimension of the crimes – the connectedness, co-ordination or orchestration of the crimes. The confusion is all the more understandable given that a few passages in early authorities have even equated 'policy' with 'systematic'.[21]

Nonetheless, the terms cannot be equivalent. Equating the terms would generate a contradiction within Article 7. Article 7(1) provides that 'widespread' and 'systematic' are disjunctive alternatives. Since Article 7(2)(a) requires 'policy' in all cases, to equate policy with systematic would amount to requiring systematicity in all cases, thereby contradicting the disjunctive test. It is a basic tenet of contextual interpretation that we try to read provisions coherently, that is, avoid unnecessary contradictions. In this instance, contradiction is very easily avoided if 'policy' is understood to be a more modest test. That understanding also conforms to the bulk of national and international authorities on the policy element, as well as the intent of the drafters.

To equate the terms not only creates a contradiction within Article 7 but also within other authorities as well. The very same authorities that introduced the now-hallowed 'widespread or systematic' test – for exam-

---

[21] The ILC Draft Code refers to 'systematic' as referring to a "preconceived plan or policy". International Law Commission, "Draft Code of Crimes Against the Peace and Security of Mankind With Commentaries", in *Yearbook of the International Law Commission*, 1996, vol. II, Part Two, United Nations, New York, 1998, p. 47 ('ILC Draft Code'). That understanding has been echoed in some cases; see, *e.g.*, International Criminal Tribunal for Rwanda (Trial Chamber II), *Prosecutor v. Kayishema and Ruzidana*, Judgment, 21 May 1999, ICTR-95-1-T, para. 123.

ple, the *Tadić* decision and the ILC Draft Code – also expressly coupled it with a policy element as an additional requirement.[22] We should not lightly adopt an interpretation that renders those authorities self-contradictory as well. We should strive to understand them coherently.

The non-contradictory interpretation is also supported by the bulk of national and international authorities, which reveal a much more modest threshold for the policy element. 'Systematic' requires active orchestration, planning and directing the crimes; cases have referred to factors such as recurring patterns, use of resources, and involvement of high-level authorities.[23] By contrast, 'policy' does not require active orchestration; it is also satisfied by implicit support or encouragement, including deliberate inaction to encourage crimes.[24] Policy does not require high level involvement, can be implicit, and can be inferred from the improbability of random occurrence.[25] The delineation between 'policy' and 'systematic' will be further specified in future jurisprudence.[26] In addition to the differing degrees of planning and engagement, there may also be differences in the involvement of high-level authorities[27] or the responsibilities of the organization.[28]

---

[22] See below, section 4.5.2.

[23] More recent Tribunal cases are settling on the test of 'organized nature of the acts of violence and the improbability of their random occurrence'. See, *e.g.*, International Criminal Tribunal for Rwanda, *Prosecutor v. Nahimana*, Judgment and Sentence, 28 November 2008, ICTR-99-52-A, para. 920; International Criminal Tribunal for the former Yugoslavia (Trial Chamber), *Prosecutor v. Kunarac et al.*, Judgment, 22 February 2001, IT-96-23-T and IT-96-23/1-T, para. 429; *Blaškić*, para. 203, see *supra* note 13.

[24] As Kai Ambos and Steffen Wirth have noted, a key to distinguishing 'policy' from 'systematic' is that policy does not require active orchestration but can include encouragement through deliberate passivity. Ambos and Wirth, 2002, pp. 28, 31–34, see *supra* note 6.

[25] Tribunal jurisprudence recognizes 'improbability of random occurrence' as part of the definition of 'systematic'; however, as I argue here, improbability of random occurrence must be part of all crimes against humanity, since truly random crime is not a crime against humanity. Thus, the remainder of the systematic test (*e.g.*, organized nature of the acts) is doing the real work and must be fleshed out.

[26] As I argue here, given the inadequacy of 'improbability of random occurrence' as a definition of 'systematic', the requirement of 'organized nature' will need to be further elaborated in jurisprudence.

[27] *Blaškić*, para. 203, see *supra* note 13.

[28] It is arguable that the 'systematic' test should require a 'State-like' entity, with some power or authority. This would absorb some of the insights of scholars such as Claus Kreß and William Schabas. Any organization committing widespread crimes would fall within the definition, whereas non-widespread crimes would reach the threshold only where system-

Many scholars have noted that 'policy' must be a lower threshold than 'systematic', (1) in order to follow the authorities, (2) in order not to negate the disjunctive test, and (3) in order not to negate the position of the vast majority of delegations at the Rome Conference, who accepted only a moderate limitation to the disjunctive test.[29]

Early ICC experience has demonstrated the value of the proposed commentary. Some early ICC decisions have described the policy element in the same terms as the 'systematic' threshold. Some decisions have suggested for example that the policy element requires that the attack be "thoroughly organized", follow a regular pattern, and involve public or private resources.[30] That, however, is the early test for 'systematic' from Tribunal jurisprudence.[31] Fortunately, more recent cases have been clearer in distinguishing the test for 'attack' from the 'widespread or systematic' character of the attack, and thus that 'policy' must be a lower threshold

---

atically organized by a State or organization with a responsibility to protect civilians. This argument will be developed in a future work.

[29] Ambos and Wirth, 2002, pp. 28, 31–34, see *supra* note 6; Hwang, 1998, p. 503, see *supra* note 5 (need for future ICC judges to recall 'policy' is not 'systematic', but merely requires State or organizational involvement; not formal and can be inferred); deGuzman, 2000, pp. 372–374, see *supra* note 5 (interpreting 'policy' as 'systematic' would contradict Article 7 and erase the position of the vast majority of States); Timothy McCormack, "Crimes Against Humanity", in Dominic McGoldrick, Peter Rowe and Eric Donnelly (eds.), *The Permanent International Criminal Court: Legal and Policy Issues*, Hart Publishing, Oxford, 2004, pp. 186–189; David Donat-Cattin, "A General Definition of Crimes Against Humanity Under International Law: The Contribution of the ICC Statute" in *Revue de Droit Pénal et des Droits de l'Homme*, 1999, vol. 8, p. 83; Wiebke Rückert and Georg Witschel, "Genocide and Crimes Against Humanity in the Elements of Crimes", in Horst Fischer, Claus Kreß and Sascha Rolf Lüder (eds.), *International and National Prosecution of Crimes Under International Law*, Berlin Verlag Arno Spitz, Berlin, 2001, p. 71; Sadat, 2013, p. 359, see *supra* note 1.

[30] International Criminal Court (Pre-Trial Chamber I), *Prosecutor v. Katanga*, Decision on the Confirmation of Charges, 30 September 2008, ICC-01/04-01/07-717, para. 396 ('*Katanga* Confirmation Decision'); International Criminal Court (Pre-Trial Chamber I), *Situation in the Republic of Côte d'Ivoire*, Decision Pursuant to Article 15 of the ICC Statute of the Authorisation of an Investigation into the Situation in the Republic of Côte d'Ivoire, 3 October 2011, ICC-02/11-14-Corr, para. 43; International Criminal Court (Pre-Trial Chamber III), *Prosecutor v. Gbagbo*, Decision on the Prosecutor's Application Pursuant to Article 58 for a Warrant of Arrest Against Laurent Koudou Gbagbo (Public redacted version), 30 November 2011, ICC-02/11-01/11-9-Red, para. 37 ('*Gbagbo* Arrest Warrant Decision').

[31] See, *e.g.*, International Criminal Tribunal for Rwanda (Trial Chamber I), *Prosecutor v. Akayesu*, Judgment, 2 September 1998, ICTR-96-4-T, para. 580 ('*Akayesu*').

---

than 'systematic'.[32] The ICC's early experience shows how the confusion is understandable, and supports the view that other courts, including national courts, could benefit from the educative function of the proposed commentary.

4.5.2. The Purpose of the Policy Element Is Simply to Screen Out Ordinary Crime

The second proposed comment recalls the narrow purpose of the element. *The purpose of the policy element is to screen out 'ordinary crime', that is, haphazard or unco-ordinated acts of individuals on their own unconnected criminal initiatives.*

4.5.2.1. History and Purpose

It is widely accepted that the concept of crimes against humanity does not include 'ordinary' patterns of crime – the random, unconnected acts of individuals carrying out their own criminal designs.[33] The policy element delivers on this assurance, by excluding the haphazard, coincidental crimes of individuals, carried out without any source directing or encouraging them.

Different deliberative bodies have noticed over the years that the 'widespread or systematic' test does not actually suffice to exclude ordinary crime. At the Rome Conference, a significant number of States, including the P-5 and many Asian and Arab States, raised precisely this concern about the disjunctive 'widespread or systematic' test.[34] The concern arises because 'widespread or systematic' is disjunctive, and 'widespread' does not necessarily imply any connection between crimes. Crimes in a city or region could easily be 'widespread' but unconnected;

---

[32] Helpful cases such as the *Gbagbo* Confirmation Decision and the *Katanga* Judgment, see *supra* note 1 are discussed below in 4.5.3.

[33] The proposition that isolated or random acts of individuals do not constitute a crime against humanity is so frequently noted that it hardly needs a citation, but a few examples include: International Law Commission draft Code, 1996, p. 47, see *supra* note 21; *Kunarac*, Trial Judgment, 2001, see *supra* note 23; International Criminal Tribunal for the former Yugoslavia (Trial Chamber), *Prosecutor v. Tadić*, Judgment, 7 May 1997, IT-14-94-1-T, para. 648 ('*Tadić* Trial Judgment').

[34] See, *e.g.*, Herman von Hebel and Darryl Robinson, "Crimes Within the Jurisdiction of the Court", in Roy Lee (ed.), *The International Criminal Court: The Making of the ICC Statute*, Kluwer Law International, The Hague, 1999, pp. 79, 92–98.

this would be 'rampant crime', not a crime against humanity. Like-minded delegations responded that an aggregate of truly random, unconnected crimes would not constitute an 'attack'. Agreement was reached to retain the disjunctive 'widespread or systematic' test, provided that the definition of 'attack' explicitly delivers on the assurance that unconnected crimes are excluded.

The Rome Conference was not the first time that the over-inclusiveness problem had been noticed. Both the *Tadić* decision of the ICTY and the 1996 ILC Draft Code of Crimes suggested a solution. The *Tadić* decision employed the term 'policy' to explain the idea that an attack is not composed of "isolated, random acts of individuals",[35] and "cannot be the work of isolated individuals alone".[36] The *Tadić* decision equated the policy element with the requirement recognized by the ILC in the 1996 draft Code of Crimes, that an attack must be "instigated or directed by a Government or by any organization or group".[37] Both *Tadić* and the ILC draft Code described this requirement as *additional to* the 'widespread or systematic' test. At the Rome Conference, a Canadian compromise proposal advanced Article 7(2)(a), explicitly based on and footnoting to these passages in *Tadić* and the ILC Draft Code.[38]

The purpose of the policy element has been well-articulated by the Supreme Court of Peru in the *Fujimori* case. The policy element

> requires only that *the casual acts of individuals acting on their own, in isolation, and with no one coordinating them, be excluded* [...] Such common crimes, even when committed on a widespread scale, do not constitute crimes against humanity, unless they are at least *connected in one way or another* to a particular State or organizational authority: they must at least be tolerated by the latter.[39]

---

[35] *Tadić* Trial Judgment, para. 653, see *supra* note 33.

[36] *Ibid.*, para. 655.

[37] *Ibid.*; ILC Draft Code, Article 18, p. 47, see *supra* note 21.

[38] Darryl Robinson, "Defining 'Crimes Against Humanity' at the Rome Conference", in *American Journal of International Law*, 1999, vol. 93, no. 1, p. 43.

[39] Sala Penal Especial de la Corte Suprema (Peru), *Barrios Altos, La Cantuta and Army Intelligence Service Basement Cases*, Case No. AV 19-2001, Judgment, 7 April 2009, para. 715 (citing Kai Ambos); translation available in *American University International Law Review*, 2010, vol. 25, no. 4, p. 657 (emphasis added).

4.5.2.2. Elaboration on the Inadequacy of Widespread or Systematic

It is worthwhile to pause a moment here to examine a common counter-argument. It is frequently asserted that the 'widespread or systematic' test is by itself sufficient to exclude random, isolated crime,[40] and thus that the policy element is not needed to perform that function.[41] Appreciating the gap in the 'widespread or systematic' test will help illuminate the role and purpose of the policy element, which is to fill that gap.

While the 'systematic' branch succeeds in excluding random criminal activity, because it requires that the crimes be organized, the problem is that the alternative branch, 'widespread', merely requires scale. Consider for example a State with high crime, such as South Africa today, which faces thousands of murders each year. The number of crimes easily satisfies the 'widespread' requirement. Murders satisfy the base crime requirement. The crimes are committed against 'civilians', satisfying another element. Recall that *a single crime* committed within the requisite context qualifies as a crime against humanity.[42] Thus, any person committing a single murder within that context satisfies the act and linkage requirements. The perpetrators are also aware of the surrounding context (that is, widespread crime against civilians).

Thus, if we do not have a policy element or some equivalent, and we apply the elements for crime against humanity, we will find that all elements are met. If we apply the tests literally, then each and every serious crime committed in a context of rampant serious crime would consti-

---

[40] See, *e.g.*, International Criminal Tribunal for Rwanda (Trial Chamber I), *Prosecutor v. Bagilishema*, Judgment, 7 June 2000, ICTR-95-1A-T, para. 78; International Criminal Tribunal for Rwanda (Trial Chamber II), *Prosecutor v Kayishema and Ruzindana*, Judgment, 21 May 1999, ICTR-95-1-T, para. 123; Mettraux, 2011, pp. 153–155, see *supra* note 40; Halling, 2010, pp. 840–841, see *supra* note 8; Boot, Dixon and Hall, 2008, pp. 179–180, see *supra* note 16.

[41] Halling, 2010, p. 841, see *supra* note 8 ("redundant check"); Boot, Dixon and Hall, 2008, p. 179, see *supra* note 16 ("superfluous"); Guénaël Mettraux, "The Definition of Crimes Against Humanity and the Question of a 'Policy" Element'", in Leila Nadya Sadat (ed.), *Forging A Convention for Crimes Against Humanity*, Cambridge University Press, Cambridge, 2011, p. 153 ("redundant and unnecessary").

[42] Thus, the common argument that no ordinary perpetrator could commit crimes on a 'widespread' scale, and thus that 'widespread or systematic' suffices to exclude ordinary crime, misses the point. 'Widespread' only applies to the contextual element. Committing a single crime within that context is all that is needed.

tute a crime against humanity.[43] The test fails to delineate crimes against humanity from ordinary crimes and fails to delineate the scope of international jurisdiction.

Most jurists will agree that the 'high crime rate' scenario is not a crime against humanity. The most typical rejoinder to this example would be that unconnected crimes are not an "attack directed against the civilian population". That reaction is correct. But then the next question is: "Can you articulate the specific requirement within your definition of 'attack' that actually excludes those unconnected acts?" The answer to that question is the first key to the riddle of crimes against humanity. Some legal element is needed to actually do the job of screening out unconnected ordinary crime. The solution adopted in Article 7 (and, *inter alia*, the ILC Draft Code of Crimes) is the policy element. There may conceivably be other solutions. But understanding the problem helps (1) to understand the purpose of the policy element and (2) to avoid inflating it beyond its narrow purpose.

4.5.2.3. The Resulting Concept of CAH

The foregoing discussion sheds light on the concept of a crime against humanity. The hallmarks are *atrocity* (the prohibited acts), *scale* and *collectivity*.[44] It is well-recognized that there must be a high degree of *either* scale ('widespread') *or* collectivity ('systematic'). The more subtle and less-appreciated feature is that there must at least be *some minimal degree of both* scale and collectivity before we can sensibly say that there was an 'attack' on a civilian population. Where there is insignificant scale − not even 'multiple' crimes − then there is no crime against humanity. And where there is no collectivity − coincidental, haphazard crimes − then there is no crime against humanity.

---

[43] There are solutions other than a policy element. For example, one could require that the population be targeted on prohibited grounds, which would exclude most random 'ordinary' crimes; however the re-introduction of specific grounds, motives or special intents also raises difficulties.

[44] On the conceptual importance of this collective or 'associative' element, see Luban, 2004, *supra* note 6; Kirsten Fisher, *Moral Accountability and International Criminal Law*, Routledge, Abingdon, 2012, pp. 22−25; Richard Vernon, "Crimes Against Humanity: A Defence of the Subsidiarity View", in *Canadian Journal of Law and Jurisprudence*, 2013, vol. 26, no. 1, p. 229.

The task of Article 7(2)(a) is to fulfil this less-obvious, less-recognized, yet still important function. It is an *in limine* test, screening out contexts that lack the minimum necessary scale and collectivity. Article 7(2)(a) avoids the absurdities of a purely disjunctive approach to scale and collectivity. The 'multiple acts' requirement screens out crime that has no scale. The policy requirement screens out crime that has no collectivity. Once these minimal standards are both met, then a prosecutor must prove a *high degree* of *either* scale (widespread) or collectivity (systematic).

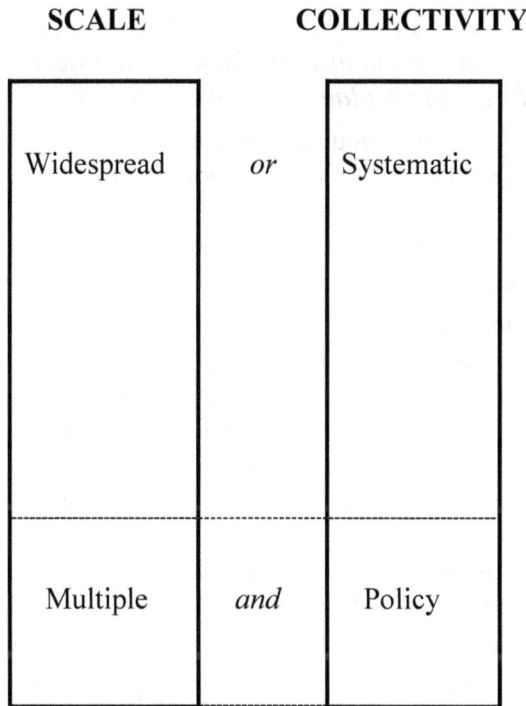

SCALE		COLLECTIVITY
Widespread	*or*	Systematic
Multiple	*and*	Policy

An interesting theory that can aid in understanding the policy element has been advanced by David Luban. Luban argues that crimes against humanity concern our human nature as social and political animals. We live socially and we form organizations. Crimes against humanity are when our organizational nature turns against us, and people work together to commit atrocities; they are "politics gone cancerous".[45]

---

[45] Luban, 2010, see *supra* note 6.

Whereas genocide focuses on the group nature of the victims, the law of crimes against humanity is engaged by the group nature of the perpetrators. The link to a State or organization reflects the minimum requisite 'associative' dimension.

4.5.3. A Policy May Be Implicit, and Can Be Inferred From the Manner in Which the Acts Occur

The third proposed commentary is as follows: *A policy need not be expressly stated or formalized, and need not involve the highest levels of a State or organization. A policy may be implicit. The existence of a policy can be inferred from the manner in which the acts occur. In particular, it can be inferred from the implausibility of coincidental occurrence.*

These propositions recur consistently in the authorities. They are essential to address concerns that the policy element might require proof of secret plans or some formalistic adoption. Some early ICC cases demonstrate the dangers of precisely these mis-intepretations, although fortunately more recent ICC cases are reflecting the global jurisprudence.

The seminal *Tadić* decision, on which Article 7(2)(a) was based, emphasized that the "policy need not be formalized and can be deduced from the way in which the acts occur".[46] Indeed, this very passage was part of the proposal at the Rome Conference introducing Article 7(2)(a) and explaining its terms. Other Tribunal cases have repeatedly affirmed these features. Cases affirm that the "policy need not be explicitly formulated"[47] and that it need not be conceived at the highest levels.[48] The *Blaškić* decision is particularly instructive. In addition to confirming that "[t]his plan [...] need not necessarily be declared expressly or even stated clearly and precisely",[49] the decision provides a valuable list of factors from which one may infer a policy, including repetition of the acts, the scale of the acts, and the overall political background.[50]

---

[46] *Tadić* Trial Judgment, para. 653, see *supra* note 33.

[47] See, *e.g.*, International Criminal Tribunal for the former Yugoslavia (Trial Chamber), *Prosecutor v. Kupreškić*, Judgment, 14 January 2001, IT-95-16, para. 551; International Criminal Tribunal for the former Yugoslavia (Trial Chamber), *Prosecutor v. Kordić and Čerkez*, Judgment, 26 February 2001, IT-95-14/2-T, para. 181.

[48] *Blaškić*, para. 205, see *supra* note 13.

[49] *Ibid.*, para. 204.

[50] *Ibid.*

Similarly, ICTR cases consistently held that a policy need not be adopted formally,[51] and the Sierra Leone Special Court had little difficulty inferring a policy from the manner in which the acts occurred. Of course, after the *Kunarac* decision, these Tribunals now hold that the policy element is not required.[52] Nonetheless, the earlier cases are helpful statements about the features of the policy element, especially as they in turn are based on other national and international jurisprudence.[53]

Expert bodies and national cases, many of which are not as well known as the Tribunal cases, can valuably enrich our picture of the global approach. For example, the 1994 Commission of Experts on crimes in former Yugoslavia recognized the policy element.[54] The Commission inferred the policy from the circumstances:

> There is sufficient evidence to conclude that the practices of "ethnic cleansing" were not coincidental, sporadic or carried out by disorganized groups or bands of civilians who could not be controlled by the Bosnian-Serb leadership.[55]

Notice here that policy is deduced by assessing the alternative hypothesis of coincidental, sporadic, uncontrolled crimes. Even more valuably, the Commission noted:

---

[51] See, *e.g.*, *Akayesu*, see *supra* note 31, para. 508; International Criminal Tribunal for Rwanda (Trial Chamber I), *Prosecutor v. Rutaganda*, Judgment and Sentence, 6 December 1999, ICTR-96-3-T, para. 68; International Criminal Tribunal for Rwanda (Trial Chamber I), *Prosecutor v. Musema*, Judgment and Sentence, 27 January 2000, ICTR-96-13-T, para. 204. *Akayesu* and later cases note that a policy need not be adopted formally by a State. It is now well accepted that a policy may also be that of a non-State organization.

[52] *Kunarac* Appeal Judgment, see *supra* note 7, para. 98; International Criminal Tribunal for Rwanda (Trial Chamber III), *Prosecutor v. Semanza*, Judgment and Sentence, 15 May 2003, ICTR-97-20-T, para. 329 (citing *Kunarac*); Special Court for Sierra Leone (Trial Chamber I), *Prosecutor v. Fofana*, Judgment, 2 August 2007, SCSL-04-14-T, para. 113 (citing *Kunarac*).

[53] As was correctly noted in International Criminal Court (Pre-Trial Chamber II), *Situation in the Republic of Kenya*, Decision Pursuant to Article 15 of the ICC Statute on the Authorisation of an Investigation into the Situation in the Republic of Kenya, 31 March 2010, ICC-01/09, para. 86. The early ICTY jurisprudence on policy was a helpful summation of other national and international jurisprudence. See also Sadat, 2013, pp. 372–373, see *supra* note 1.

[54] Commission of Experts for Yugoslavia, 1994, para. 84, see *supra* note 10.

[55] *Ibid.*, para. 142. See also para. 313, inferring policy behind ethnic cleansing, rape and sexual assault, based on frequency of occurrence and the consistent failure to prevent or punish such crimes.

It should not be accepted at face value that the perpetrators are merely uncontrolled elements, especially not if these elements target almost exclusively groups also otherwise discriminated against and persecuted. Unwillingness to manage, prosecute and punish uncontrolled elements may be another indication that these elements are, in reality, but a useful tool for the implementation of a policy of crime against humanity.[56]

National courts have also recognized that a policy may be implicit and can be inferred from circumstances. An Argentine court in the famous *Junta* trial demonstrates with admirable clarity how policy is inferred from the improbability of coincidence:

The operative system put in practice [...] was substantially identical in the whole territory of the Nation and prolonged over time. It having been proved that the acts were committed by members of the armed and security forces, vertically and disciplinarily organized, *the hypothesis that this could have occurred without express superior orders is discarded.*[57]

Similarly, a more recent case against Jorge Rafael Videla held:

It having been proved that the events were directly committed by members of the army, the State Intelligence Secretariat, the Buenos Aires Provincial Police [...] organised vertically and disciplinarily, it does not appear probable − in this stage − that they could have been committed without orders from hierarchical superiors.[58]

The same approach of inferring policy was also taken in the recent Guatemalan case against General Rios Montt.[59]

---

[56] *Ibid.*, para. 85.

[57] Cámara Nacional de Apelaciones en lo Criminal y Correccional Federal de Buenos Aires, *'Causa No. 13/84 (Juicio a las Juntas Militares)'*, Sentencia, 9 December 1985, Second Part, para. 3(c), available at http://www.derechos.org/nizkor/arg/ causa13/cap20.html, last accessed at 28 April 2014 (emphasis added).

[58] Juzgado Federal de San Isidro, *Causa N° 1.285/85, 'Videla, Jorge Rafael y otros s/ presunta infracción a los arts. 146, 293 y 139, inc. 2do. del Código Penal'*, Judgment, 13 July 1998.

[59] *Tribunal de Alto Riesgo A, Sentencia C-01076-2011-00015 (Rios Montt, Rodriguez Sanchez) Of. 2o*, Judgment, 2 May 2011, Folio 697, available at http://paraqueseconozca. blogspot.com/, last accessed at 28 April 2014:

A court in Bosnia and Herzegovina, applying a provision identical to Article 7(2)(a) in a crime against humanity case, provided a helpful list of factors from which to infer policy:

> The following factual factors are considered with regard to establishing the existence of a policy to commit an attack: *concerted action* by members of an organization or State; *distinct but similar acts* by members of an organization or State; *preparatory acts* prior to the commencement of the attack; prepared acts or steps undertaken during or at the conclusion of the attack; the existence of political, economic or other strategic *objectives* of a State or organization furthered by the attack; and in the case of omissions, *knowledge of an attack or attacks and willful failure to act.*[60]

Similarly, in *Sexual Minorities Uganda v. Scott Lively*,[61] a US court upheld the contrast between isolated or sporadic acts versus policy:

> one ought to look at these atrocities or acts in their context and verify whether they may be regarded as part of an overall policy or a consistent pattern of inhumanity, or whether they instead constitute isolated or sporadic acts of cruelty or wickedness.[62]

> [T]he army carried out these massacres using the same pattern of conduct, which is verified by the actions carried out in each of the communities. This circumstance is very important because it is evidence of prior planning and the implementation of that planning. Why do we say this? It is important because, as has been shown, the violent acts against the Ixil [people] was not a spontaneous action but the concretization of previously prepared plans which formed part of a State policy towards the elimination of that group.

Judgment annulled pending appeal against the rejection of a defence motion to recuse two trial judges: Corte de Constitucionalidad, 20 May 2013, decision available at http://www.right2info.org/resources/publications/constitutional-court-judgment-5.20.2013, last accessed 28 April 2014.

[60]   Court of Bosnia and Herzegovina, *Prosecutor v. Mitar Rašević and Savo Todović*, Case No. X-KR/06/275, Verdict, 28 February 2008, available at http://www.legal-tools.org/en/doc/6a28b5/, last accessed 28 April 2014 (emphasis added).

[61]   United States District Court for the District of Massachusetts, *Sexual Minorities Uganda v. Lively*, 2013 U.S. Dist. LEXIS 114754, Order, 14 August 2013.

[62]   See also United States District Court for the Eastern District of California, *Doe v. Alvaro Rafael Saravia*, 348 F. Supp. 2d 1112, Judgment, 23 November 2004, para. 260 (same quote).

While this was a civil law case, it relied on criminal law authorities, and on this point the court referred to the late Antonio Cassese.

As can be seen, the available authorities draw the contrast between (a) crimes with State or organizational support or encouragement versus (b) crimes that are 'haphazard', 'coincidental', 'random', 'sporadic', and carried out by 'uncontrolled and uncontrollable elements'. They have not required direct proof of formal adoption of policy or internal workings of organizations. They have quite easily inferred policy where the events speak for themselves. It can usually be seen readily that the crimes are not a mere crime wave but rather must have involved behind-the-scenes direction, support or encouragement.

4.5.3.1. The Gbagbo Adjournment Decision Shows the Value of Clarification

An early ICC case shows the potential dangers of neglecting this jurisprudence. The case against Laurent Gbagbo, the former President of the Ivory Coast, concerned large-scale killings, assaults and rapes, committed by pro-Gbagbo State forces and youth militia, against civilians who were perceived to support the rival candidate to Gbagbo.[63] The case presented by the Prosecutor focused on four incidents, involving over 294 crimes against civilians, and also referred to 41 other incidents.

To establish the policy element, the Prosecutor had offered a significant amount of direct evidence (witnesses, police records, photographs, videos) as well as indirect evidence. The evidence attested to: repeated attacks by pro-Gbagbo forces against civilians supportive of his political opponent; the failure of police to intervene; the participation of police in crimes; preparation for atrocities, such as policemen bringing condoms to the site where they raped female protestors; measures to identify supporters of the opposition; public statements of leaders of the pro-Gbagbo inner circle; internal instructions; prior warnings that unarmed demonstrators would be killed; and witness reports that perpetrators indicated that they were targeting victims because of their opposition to Gbagbo.[64]

---

[63] See International Criminal Court, "Document Amendé de Notification des Charges", 13 July 2012, ICC-02/11-01/11-184-AnxI-Red (available in French only) ('*Gbagbo* DCC'). The attacks overall involved over 1,300 victims; the four charged incidents involved over 294 crimes against civilians.

[64] *Ibid.*, paras. 21, 37, 40, 44, 50, 81–84.

Nonetheless, the majority was not satisfied of a policy from this evidence. In June 2013, a majority of Pre-Trial Chamber I adjourned the confirmation hearing to allow the Prosecutor to collect and present additional evidence.[65] The majority requested additional evidence about specific meetings at which the policy was adopted and its internal promulgation; for example:

> How, when and by whom the alleged policy/plan to attack the 'pro-Outtara civilian population' was adopted, including specific information about meetings at which this policy/plan was allegedly adopted, as well as how the existence and content of this policy/plan was communicated or made known to members of the 'pro-Gbagbo forces' once it was adopted.[66]

The majority also requested additional evidence about the co-ordination, structure and operating methods of the 'inner circle' of the pro-Gbagbo forces.[67]

By requesting such specific evidence, after declaring the proffered evidence to be inadequate, the majority appears to have in mind heightened legal and evidentiary requirements for the policy element. There are three main concerns with the majority approach.

First, the majority's approach appears to reflect a formalized, bureaucratic conception of the policy element. The requests relate to specific *meetings* at which a policy was *adopted*, dates of such meetings,[68] inner workings and internal communication of the policy to the rank and file. That conception is somewhat understandable, given that one common sense of the word 'policy' does indeed connote something official and formally adopted, perhaps by a Cabinet or board of directors, and then promulgated to the levels below. But it contradicts the meaning of the juridical term 'policy' as elaborated in the authorities, which emphasize that it need not be formalized, express, formally adopted, and so on.

---

[65] See International Criminal Court (Pre-Trial Chamber I), *Prosecutor v. Laurent Gbagbo*, Decision Adjourning the Hearing on the Confirmation of Charges Pursuant to Article 61(7)(c)(i) of the ICC Statute, 3 June 2013, ICC-02/11-01/11-432 ('*Gbagbo* Adjournment Decision').

[66] *Ibid.*, para. 44.

[67] *Ibid.*, for the evidence that was provided on the pro-Gbagbo forces, the inner circle, its membership, its control, and its meetings, see *Gbagbo* DCC, paras. 59–86, *supra* note 63.

[68] *Gbagbo* Adjournment Decision, para. 44, see *supra* note 65.

Second, the majority approach is not only in conflict with past jurisprudence, it is also undesirable practically and normatively. Practically, direct proof of formal adoption would usually be difficult to obtain. In the absence of written minutes, which will surely be rare, the approach almost mandates insider testimony for any crime against humanity case. Normatively, there does not seem to be a good principled reason to restrict crimes against humanity to crimes that were bureaucratically endorsed at the highest level. Doing so is not required by any available theory of crimes against humanity. Indeed, the paradigm of adopting policies at meetings seems to reflect a culturally specific concept of organizations, and does not reflect the diverse types of human organizations that may orchestrate mass crimes.

Third, another problem with the majority's approach is that it is epistemologically over-cautious and rarified. The majority indicated its reservations about the inferences it was asked to draw,[69] and thus requested direct evidence of formal adoption. However, the crucially important point is that a policy will *almost always be a matter of inference*. This is why past jurisprudence emphasizes that a policy can be inferred from the manner in which the acts occur. It is understandable for a diligent judge to ask: "How can I be sure there is a State or organizational policy unless I have proof of the adoption of the policy?" The answer is that we don't need the 'smoking gun'. *We can prove 'P' (policy) by proving the implausibility of 'not-P'.* In other words, we can infer the policy element from the sheer absurdity of the rival hypothesis, which is that these hundreds of crimes, committed by pro-Gbagbo forces against anti-Gbagbo forces, with perpetrators making statements indicative of a common purpose and co-ordination, were actually just a coincidence. It is implausible that this was a simple 'crime wave' of individual acts occurring without any State or organizational co-ordination or at least encouragement.

4.5.3.2. Subsequent ICC Cases Adhere to Global Jurisprudence

Happily, the *Gbagbo* adjournment decision was not the last word in that case. After assessing the additional evidence proferred by the Prosecutor, Judge Hans-Peter Kaul sided in favour of confirmation, thereby forming a new majority. Moreover, as the majority confirmation decision shows, Judge Kaul appears to have reconsidered and modified some of his views

---

[69] *Ibid.*, para. 36.

on the policy element. The result is one of the most careful and helpful discussions of the policy element to date in ICC jurisprudence, reflective of the approach of other national and international authorities. The confirmation decision will be one of the most important aspects of the valuable legacy left by Judge Kaul.

The *Gbabgo* confirmation decision affirms that the requirements of 'attack' are less demanding than the requirements of 'widespread or systematic', and thus that policy is less demanding than 'systematic'.[70] It also holds that "there is no requirement that a policy be formally adopted" and that evidence of planning is relevant but not required.[71]

Subsequently, the *Katanga* trial chamber judgment provided an even more careful and thorough analysis of Article 7(1), 7(2)(a) and the policy element. *Katanga* correctly distinguished between the test for 'attack' and the test for 'widespread or systematic'.[72] The decision notes that a policy need not be formalized[73] and can be manifested by action or deliberate inaction to encourage crimes.[74] The chamber rightly noted that that it would be relatively rare that a State or organization intending to encourage an attack would adopt and disseminate an established plan to this effect.[75] Thus, in most cases, it would be necessary to *deduce* the policy from, for example, the repetition of acts, preparatory activities, and orchestrated or co-ordinated activities.[76]

These and other cases show that the ICC is aligning with the broader web of global authorities.[77] Nonetheless, the deviations in some early

---

[70] International Criminal Court (Pre-Trial Chamber I), *Prosecutor v. Laurent Gbagbo*, Decision on Confirmation of Charges Against Laurent Gbagbo, 12 June 2014, ICC-02/11-01/11-656, paras. 208, 216.

[71] *Ibid.*, paras. 210, 215, 216.

[72] *Katanga* Judgment, paras. 1097–1098, 1101, see *supra* note 1.

[73] *Ibid.*, para. 1108.

[74] *Ibid.*, paras. 1107–1108.

[75] *Ibid.*, para. 1109 : « Il est relativement rare, même si on ne peut l'exclure, que l'État ou l'organisation qui entend encourager une attaque contre une population civile adopte et diffuse un projet préétabli ou un plan à cet effet. »

[76] *Ibid.*, para. 1109.

[77] Pre-Trial Chamber II held in the *Bemba* confirmation decision that the "policy need not be formalised. Indeed, an attack which is planned, directed or organized – as opposed to spontaneous or isolated acts of violence – will satisfy this criterion". International Criminal Court (Pre-Trial Chamber II), *Prosecutor v. Bemba*, Decision Pursuant to Article 61(7)(a) and (b) of the Rome Statute on the Charges of the Prosecutor Against Jean-Pierre Bemba Gombo, 15 June 2009, ICC-01/05-01/08-424, para. 8. Pre-Trial Chamber I made

cases show that even an institution specializing in international core crimes may not be aware of all the nuances of national and international precedent. The challenges are even greater for national courts that deal relatively rare with such crimes, and thus commentary would be of value.

4.5.4. A Policy May be Manifested by Action or Inaction

The final proposed commentary is the following: *While a policy will typically be manifested by the actions of a State or organization, it may also be manifested by a deliberate failure to act which is consciously aimed at encouraging an attack.*

Throughout the authorities since World War II, many different verbs have been used to describe the requisite link between the State or organization and the attack. Those verbs have included: *direct, instigate, promote, encourage* (including by deliberate inaction*), acquiesce, tolerate, approve, condone, countenance* and *endorse*. It is arguably premature to ascertain precisely what linkage or attitude is required. What is however crucial to convey is that the linkage can be *passive* (for example, acquiesce, tolerate, condone, countenance, implicitly approve, encourage by inaction). Most crimes against humanity prosecuted to date have involved *action*: the agents of the State or organization have directly carried out atrocities. Nonetheless, a consistent thread in the authorities is that passive encouragement or approval can suffice. Indeed, inaction can be relevant in two different ways. First, if agents of a State or organization commit crimes and the State or organization fails to respond, that is an indication of a policy of encouragement. Second, and perhaps more rarely, a State or an organization with a duty to prevent crimes may observe crimes committed by *private actors* against a target group, and deliberately refrain from responding in order to encourage further crimes.

The ICC Elements of Crimes acknowledge policies of passivity, but they do so in a circuitous manner. The introduction to the elements for crimes against humanity says that a State or organization must "actively

---

the identical observation in the confirmation decision. *Katanga* Confirmation Decision, para. 396, see *supra* note 30: "The policy need not be explicitly defined by the organisational group. Indeed, an attack which is planned, directed or organised – as opposed to spontaneous or isolated acts of violence – will satisfy this criterion". And Pre-Trial Chamber III held in the *Gbagbo* arrest warrant decision that a policy "need not be explicitly defined or formalised". *Gbagbo* Arrest Warrant Decision, para. 37, see *supra* note 30.

---

promote or encourage" the attack.[78] A footnote again reiterates that a policy "would be implemented by State or organizational action".[79] Only then
do the Elements finally acknowledge that "such a policy may, in exceptional circumstances, be implemented by a deliberate failure to take action, which is consciously aimed at encouraging such attack".[80] Thus, to
read only the text, without reading the footnote, would give one an incomplete picture of the provision.

During the deliberations, some delegations had raised an understandable concern about terms like 'tolerate', 'condone' or 'countenance'.[81] The concern was that, if such terms are used too loosely, then
any time a State was not succeeding in particular crimes, the court might
leap to an assumption of policy, without considering other explanations,
such as lack of knowledge or inability to respond. An early attempt to address this concern was to require State or organizational 'action'.[82] However, later deliberations revealed that this solution was too crude. A majority of delegations grew concerned about its incompatibility with authorities indicating that a deliberate failure to respond to private actors
could suffice. Thus, different formulas emerged to capture State or organizational inaction, where it was not a matter of mere *ineffectiveness* but
rather *deliberate* inaction in order to encourage the crimes. Thus, to infer
policy, one would need to consider not only the inadequacy of the State's
response but also whether the State had knowledge of the crimes and capacity to respond.[83]

The Element provision certainly has an unusual structure, with the
text seemingly requiring 'action' and then a footnote acknowledging inaction. It is also unusual that the point that was of greatest importance to the
majority of delegations appears in only a footnote. This was agreed on the
penultimate day as a package to allow for the consensus adoption of the

---

[78] ICC Elements of Crimes, Introduction to Crimes Against Humanity, para. 3.

[79] *Ibid.*, note 6.

[80] *Ibid.*

[81] A more detailed account of the history is available at Roy Lee *et al.* (eds.), *The International Criminal Court: Elements of Crimes and Rules of Procedure and Evidence*, Transnational Publishers, Ardsley, 2001, pp. 74–78.

[82] *Ibid.*

[83] This is re-inforced by an additional sentence, proposed by Turkey: "The existence of such
a policy cannot be inferred *solely* from the absence of governmental or organizational action" (ICC Elements, footnote 6, emphasis added). Thus, as noted, one must consider
whether the State had knowledge and capacity to act.

Elements.[84] While the format is curious, the text and the footnote, read together, are adequately consistent with other authorities.

Other national and international authorities provide additional illumination, and they are clear that State or organizational passivity can suffice. The *Kupreškić* decision of the ICTY reviewed World War II jurisprudence concerning policies of inaction. That jurisprudence referred to "explicit or implicit approval or endorsement" and required that crimes be "approved of or at least condoned or countenanced by a governmental body".[85] The 1954 ILC Draft Code referred to crimes "by the authorities of a State or by private individuals acting at the instigation or *with the toleration* of such authorities".[86] The *Fujimori* decision, referred to above, requires that the crimes must be "*connected in one way or another* to a particular State or organizational authority: they must *at least be tolerated* by the latter".[87] The following passage from the Commission of Experts on former Yugoslavia was already cited above, but is equally pertinent and insightful with respect to encouragement by inaction:

> Unwillingness to manage, prosecute and punish uncontrolled elements may be another indication that these elements are, in reality, but a useful tool for the implementation of a policy of crime against humanity.[88]

Finally, as scholars such as Kai Ambos and Steffen Wirth have noted, the possibility of policy by inaction is not only supported by authorities, but is also important for the logical construction of Article 7, since 'policy' must be distinguished from 'systematic'. 'Systematic' requires State or organizational action, because the crimes must be planned and orchestrated, whereas 'policy' includes, *inter alia*, passive encouragement. Thus widespread crimes committed by private actors, where State authorities deliberately fail to maintain law and order in order to encourage the crimes, can be a crime against humanity.[89]

---

[84] See Roy Lee *et al.*, 2001, pp. 74–78, *supra* note 81.

[85] *Kupreškić* Judgment, paras. 554–555, see *supra* note 47.

[86] International Law Commission, "Draft Code of Offences Against the Peace and Security of Mankind", in *Yearbook of the International Law Commission*, 1954, vol. II, United Nations, New York, 1960, p. 112.

[87] *Barrios Altos, La Cantuta and Army Intelligence Service Basement Cases*, para. 715 (citing Kai Ambos) (emphasis added), see *supra* note 39.

[88] Commission of Experts for Yugoslavia, 1994, para. 85, see *supra* note 10.

[89] Ambos and Wirth, 2002, pp. 31–34, see *supra* note 6.

4.6. Conclusion

The Draft Convention is a welcome initiative. One of its many potential contributions is to help clarify and harmonize the definition. Clarifying commentary would be valuable (1) to mitigate legitimate concerns about Article 7 and thereby bolster acceptability of the Convention; (2) to increase the effectiveness of the Convention by forestalling restrictive misinterpretations; (3) to reduce fragmentation of the law of crimes against humanity, by showing that many diverse national and international authorities converge in regarding 'policy' as a modest test, that does what it is generally agreed that crimes against humanity should do, namely to exclude ordinary crimes.

5

Beyond Territory, Jurisdiction, and Control: Towards a Comprehensive Obligation to Prevent Crimes Against Humanity

María Luisa Piqué[*]

5.1. Introduction and Overview

This chapter considers the scope of the obligation to prevent crimes against humanity that the proposed International Convention on the Prevention and Punishment of Crimes Against Humanity[1] ('Proposed Convention') would impose on States Parties were it to become law.

The scope of States' positive obligations pursuant to the text of the Proposed Convention is mainly regulated by Article 8(1), according to which such obligations are meant to be observed within each State Party's "territory under its jurisdiction or control".

In the first part of the chapter, I address in turn why there should be a specialized Convention on Crimes Against Humanity, the relationship between international human rights law and international criminal law,

---

[*] **María Luisa Piqué** has a law degree from the University of Buenos Aires, Faculty of Law, and an LL.M. from Georgetown University Law Center. She has served as a member of the team that prosecuted several members of the Argentinean Armed and Security Forces involved in crimes against humanity committed during the 1976–1983 military dictatorship, in the Navy's Mechanics School (ESMA) and within the Operation Condor – the coordinated repressive effort of the Southern Cone military governments. Currently, she is a law professor of Constitutional and Criminal Law at Universidad de Buenos Aires, and a prosecutor of gender violence cases. She would like to thank Professors Morten Bergsmo and David Luban for their inspiration, encouragement, and useful comments, and she would also like to acknowledge the invaluable help of Michelle Ueland and Alexis Paddock, of the ESL Writing Center of Georgetown University Law Center. She would also like to acknowledge the enlightening comments to the draft done by Kiki A. Japutra and SONG Tianying. The usual disclaimer applies. All the Internet references were last accessed on 2 September 2014.

[1] This Proposed Convention is the result of the project to study the need for a comprehensive convention about crimes against humanity, which started in the spring of 2008 within the Whitney R. Harris World Law Institute of Washington University School of Law and it was named "the Crimes against Humanity Initiative". For more details see Chapter 2 of this volume. The text of the Proposed Convention is reproduced in Annex 1.

and the positive and negative obligations of States created by international criminal law. Then, I deconstruct the phrase "territory under its jurisdiction or control" and analyse the way it impacts the scope of States' obligations under the Proposed Convention, particularly in their obligation to prevent crimes against humanity.

The chapter next describes how this provision would represent progress regarding the prevention of crimes against humanity, particularly because it would reach situations in which States currently are not under the obligation to prevent those crimes. However, I also explain how that progress would be outweighed by the negative consequences such a provision could have – meaning those that involve a restrictive interpretation of the obligation to prevent crimes against humanity.

Finally, I argue that the obligation to prevent crimes against humanity should not be territory-centred. Rather, it should encompass persons, facilities or situations under the jurisdiction or control of States, and be constructed in a similar fashion to the obligation to prevent genocide, according to the International Court of Justice's ('ICJ') interpretation of the Convention for the Prevention and Punishment of the Crime of Genocide of 1948 ('Genocide Convention') in the *Case Concerning the Application of the Convention on the Prevention and Punishment of the Crime of Genocide* ('*Genocide* case').[2]

5.2. Why Should There be a Specialized Convention on Crimes Against Humanity?[3]

The condemnation of crimes against humanity is not novel. It can be traced to Article 6(c) of the Charter of the International Military Tribunal that sat at Nuremberg ('Nuremberg Charter') and to the Genocide Convention that followed.[4] Those precedents paved the way for further inter-

---

[2] ICJ, Judgment, 26 February 2007, para. 166.

[3] This account stems from Leila Nadya Sadat, *A Comprehensive History of the Proposed International Convention on the Prevention and Punishment of Crimes against Humanity*, Washington University Law, 2010, available at http://law.wustl.edu/harris/CAH/docs/CompHistoryFinal12-01-10.pdf.

[4] Although it is still unknown how the actual denomination of crimes against humanity was selected by the drafters of the Nuremberg Charter, it is worth noting that in 1915, France, Great Britain and Russia denounced the Armenian genocide committed by the Ottoman government as "crimes against civilization and humanity". That same phrase appeared in 1919 within a failed proposal to try the perpetrators of the Armenian genocide. See David

national treaties that condemned specific manifestations of crimes against humanity[5] and declared the non-applicability of statutory limitations in the investigation and prosecution of acts falling within that category.[6]

The Nuremberg Charter articulated the international community's repudiation of war crimes, crimes against humanity and crimes against peace committed by major war criminals of the European Axis countries during World War II. The Genocide Convention, in turn, was the first international treaty of general application that systematized atrocious crimes and obliged its contracting parties to punish and prevent them.[7]

However, those steps in the struggle against mass atrocity turned out to be insufficient. Not only are some groups left unprotected (such as those based on political or cultural affiliations, or gender distinctions, see Chapter 8 below), but also the scope of the obligations imposed on States is restrictive.[8] As a result, "only a fraction of the millions of victims over the past six decades has benefited from the provisions of the Genocide Convention".[9]

As of 2011, the most comprehensive codification of crimes against humanity can be found in Article 7 of the Rome Statute of the International Criminal Court ('ICC Statute'). However, the application of Article 7 is limited to situations within the jurisdiction of the ICC.[10] Furthermore,

---

Luban, "A Theory of Crimes Against Humanity", in *Yale Journal of International Law*, 2004, vol. 29, p. 85.

[5] At the international level, the treaties that have entered into force are the "International Convention on the Suppression and Punishment of the Crime of Apartheid" ('Apartheid Convention'), adopted and opened for signature, ratified by General Assembly (UNGA) resolution 3068 (XXVIII) of 30 November 1973, entered into force 18 July 1976; the "Convention against Torture and Other Cruel, Inhuman or Degrading Treatment or Punishment" ('Torture Convention'), UNGA resolution 39/46 of 10 December 1984, entered into force 26 June 1987; and the "International Convention for the Protection of All Persons from Enforced Disappearance" ('Enforced Disappearance Convention'), UNGA Resolution A/RES/61/177 of 20 December 2006, entered into force on 23 December 2010 (Doc. A/61/488. C.N.737.2008). There are also other treaties at the regional level.

[6] "Convention on the Non-Applicability of Statutory Limitations to War Crimes and Crimes against Humanity", UNGA resolution 2391, entered into force on 11 November 1970, U.N. GAOR, 23d Sess., Supp. No. 18, at 40, U.N. Doc. A/7218 (1968).

[7] Sadat, 2010, p. 3, para. 7, *supra* note 3.

[8] *Ibid.*

[9] *Ibid.*

[10] For instance, extermination, imprisonment, persecution and widespread sexual violence including rape, sexual slavery, enforced prostitution and forced pregnancy. See *ibid.*

apart from the obligations of co-operation that States Parties to the ICC Statute have *vis-à-vis* the ICC, they are not obligated by the Statute to prevent crimes against humanity.

It is especially interesting to notice that expert consultations held regarding the Proposed Convention[11] underscored the fact that sometimes it is difficult to get the attention of the international community to react against the commission of crimes against humanity.[12] Particularly, the experts agreed that "unless a crime was described as 'genocide,' its commission somehow seemed less of a problem and required no international response".[13] Thus, many participants in those discussions felt frustrated with the "semantic indifference" to the commission of crimes against humanity, which has taken the lives of millions of persons.[14]

With those evils in mind, the drafters acknowledged that it would be very important for the Convention to be, on the one hand, an instrument for the prosecution and punishment of those responsible for the commission of crimes against humanity and, on the other hand, an instrument recognizing the importance of prevention.[15] As regards prevention, it was suggested that a focus on education and capacity-building among States could be a starting point in "operationalizing" the 'Responsibility to Protect' norm ('R2P').[16]

Codifying crimes against humanity and prescribing attendant State obligations, with an ambition of universality, represent significant progress propelled by past struggles and future prevention. As such, the Proposed Convention deserves dedicated commitment to its development, in the interest of eradication of crimes against humanity.

5.3. Relationship Between International Human Rights Law and International Criminal Law

International criminal law and human rights law are closely tied together. Clarifying their relationship, in particular, their similarities and differences, is important to discerning the nature and scope of State obligations

---

[11] Regarding those discussions, and which experts were invited, see Sadat, *supra* note 3.
[12] *Ibid.*, p. 8, para. 24.
[13] *Ibid.*
[14] *Ibid.*
[15] *Ibid.*, para. 56.
[16] *Ibid.*, para. 57.

in each of these two areas of law, as well as the beneficiaries of those obligations.

The development of human rights law has eroded the international law paradigm according to which international law was only concerned about the relations among States. Now, international law is also concerned with the way States treat their own citizens and subjects,[17] and human rights treaties are meant to reflect that concern and limit State action.

In a similar fashion, the surfacing of international criminal law reflects the international community's view that some grave violations of human rights, or "gross violations",[18] deserve specific, and harsher, treatment. In fact, not all human rights violations are international crimes,[19] international criminal law is the last resort for the protection of human rights.

What are, then, the criteria to differentiate between human rights violations that amount to international crimes, and those that do not? According to David Luban, the condemnation, at least intuitively, stems from the need to distinguish between "civilized and uncivilized conduct", and to claim that whereas some "torments and humiliations" cross the line,[20] others, such as the suppression of the free press or the denial of the

---

[17] Luban, 2004, pp. 34–35, *supra* note 4.

[18] For instance, according to Bassiouni, the proscription against crimes against humanity protects the following rights: life, liberty, and personal security; freedom from torture and from cruel, inhuman or degrading treatment or punishment; freedom from slavery and forced labor; freedom from arbitrary arrest and detention; a fair criminal trial; equal treatment; freedom of movement, religion, opinion, expression, and association; the right to a family; and recognition as a person before the law. See M. Cherif Bassiouni, "The Proscribing Function of International Criminal Law in the Process of International Protection of Human Rights", in *Yale Law Journal of World Public Order*, 1982, vol. 9, pp. 200–201.

[19] None of the three most important human rights instruments – the "Universal Declaration of Human Rights" ('UDHR') (adopted by the UNGA on 10 December 1948), the "International Covenant on Civil and Political Rights" ('ICCPR') (adopted and opened for signature, ratification and accession by UNGA resolution 2200A (XXI) of 16 December 1966, and entered into force 23 March 1976), and the "International Covenant on Economic, Social and Cultural Rights" ('ICESCR') (adopted and opened for signature, ratification and accession by UNGA resolution 2200A (XXI) of 16 December 1966, and entered into force 3 January 1976) – contain criminal enforcement provisions. See David Luban, Julie O'Sullivan and David Stewart, *International and Transnational Criminal Law*, Aspen Publishers, 2010, p. 34.

[20] Luban, 2004, p. 101, *supra* note 4.

right to own real property, do not.[21] In Luban's words, "[t]he atrocities and humiliations that count as crimes against humanity are, in effect, the ones that turn our stomachs, and no principle exists to explain what turns our stomachs".[22]

Whereas all the rights enshrined in human rights conventions are applicable within a State's territory, it is not always the case when the State is operating abroad. In situations like that, the spectrum of enforceable rights "may be limited by the scope of the State's authority or control in the circumstances".[23] These differences in the scope of obligation, depending on where the State is acting, also have to do with the scope of beneficiaries of human rights treaties, which is usually restricted to persons within a State's territory or subject to its jurisdiction.

The extraterritorial applicability of human rights treaties has, thus, proven to be more problematic and controversial. One reason for this is that not all those rights established by the human rights treaties were, by their nature, intended to be applicable extraterritorially.[24] Whereas some fundamental principles must always be respected,[25] other provisions – such as States' obligation to respect free press – are not suitable for their extraterritorial application.

Notwithstanding that debate, there seems to be a general consensus that States are prohibited to do abroad what they are barred from committing within their own territories under human rights treaties, particularly if that entails gross violations of human rights.

This approach to an extraterritorial application of human rights treaties has been recognized by international and regional human rights bodies such as the Human Rights Committee ('HRC'), the European Court of Human Rights ('ECtHR'), the International Court of Justice ('ICJ'), and the Inter-American Commission of Human Rights ('IACHR').

---

[21] *Ibid.*

[22] *Ibid.*

[23] John Cerone, "Jurisdiction and Power: The Intersection of Human Rights Law and the Law of Non-International Armed Conflict in an Extraterritorial Context", in *Israel Law Review*, 2007, vol. 40, footnote 72, p. 437.

[24] Theodor Meron, "Extraterritoriality of Human Rights Treaties", in *American Journal of International Law*, January 1995, vol. 89, p. 80.

[25] According to Meron, among those fundamental principles would be the prohibition of the arbitrary taking of life, the duty of humane treatment of persons in detention, the prohibition of inhuman or degrading treatment or punishment, and essential due process, see *ibid.*

For instance, the HRC interpreted Article 2 of the International Covenant on Civil and Political Rights ('ICCPR'), according to which States Parties are obligated to respect and ensure human rights "to all individuals within its territory and subject to its jurisdiction" in the context of complaints concerning the kidnapping, torture and imprisonment in a clandestine detention centre in Argentina of Uruguayan citizens, perpetrated by Uruguayan officials during the late 1970s.[26] The HRC stated that Uruguay could be held accountable for "violations of rights under the Covenant which its agents commit upon a territory of another State".[27] The reason for this was that it would be "unconscionable" to interpret Article 2 as barring States Parties from violating the rights protected in the Covenant on their own territory, but allowing them to violate them on the territory of another State.[28]

This position was later reaffirmed by the HRC in the General Comment No. 31, entitled 'The Nature of the General Legal Obligation Imposed on States Parties to the Covenant',[29] where it Stated that a State Party was compelled to respect and ensure human rights "to anyone within the power or effective control of that State Party, even if not situated within the territory of the State Party".[30]

In turn, the ECtHR has taken a similar approach, although its application was somewhat erratic. In the *Cypriot* cases[31] the Court had to de-

---

[26] *Sergio Rubén López Burgos v. Uruguay*, Communication No. 52/1979, 6 June 1979, CCPR/C/13/D/52/1979 para. 176; and *Lilian Celiberti de Casariego v. Uruguay*, Communication No. 56/79, CCPR/C/13/D/76/1976, both views were adopted on 29 July 1981.

[27] See *Sergio Rubén López Burgos v. Uruguay, ibid.*, paras. 12.1. and 12.3.

[28] *Ibid.*

[29] Adopted on 29 March 2004 (2187th meeting), CCPR/C/21/Rev.1/Add.13 (General Comments).

[30] *Ibid.*, para. 10.

[31] By "Cypriot cases" I mean those cases concerning human rights violations in Northern Cyprus after Turkey's invasion, 20 July 1974. In short, as a result of those military operations, Turkey seized a significant part of Cyprus' territory (around 40%). In November 1983, the Turkish Republic of Northern Cyprus ('TRNC') was proclaimed in the territories occupied by Turkey – although it was condemned and not recognized by the international community. Turkey, however, did not lose control over the territory of Northern Cyprus when the TRNC was proclaimed. That control was still exercised both directly (by Turkish soldiers on duty in Cyprus) and indirectly through the government of the TRNC which was a "puppet government" dependent on Turkey (see Michal Gondek, *The Reach of Human Rights in a Globalising World: Extraterritorial Application of Human Rights Treaties*, Intersentia, 2009, pp. 126–131).

termine whether human rights violations in Northern Cyprus were capable of falling within the 'jurisdiction' of Turkey under the European Convention for the Protection of Human Rights and Fundamental Freedoms ('ECHR') even though they had occurred outside its national territory. The ECtHR held that the responsibility of States Parties could be involved, on the one hand, due to acts of their authorities, whether performed within or outside national boundaries, which produce effects outside their own territory and, on the other hand, when as a consequence of military action – whether lawful or unlawful – a particular State Party exercises effective control of an area outside its national territory. In that case, the controlling State is under the obligation to secure, in such an area, the rights and freedoms protected by the ECHR.[32]

Regarding the ICJ, it has concluded that the ICCPR is applicable "in respect of acts done by a State in the exercise of jurisdiction outside its own territory".[33]

Finally, within the Inter-American System of Human Rights, the IACHR has noted that, occasionally, "the exercise of its jurisdiction over acts with an extra-territorial locus will not only be consistent with, but

---

[32]   ECtHR, *Loizidou v. Turkey*, Preliminary Objections, 23 March 1995, Series A, No. 310, para. 62. See also, ECtHR, *Case of Cyprus v. Turkey*, Judgment, 10 May 2001, Reports of Judgments and Decisions 2001-IV, para. 77 (maintaining the *Loizidou* precedent and adding that Turkey's jurisdiction over Northern Cyprus should be considered to reach the securing of the entire range of substantive rights protected by the ECHR, and that violations of those rights are imputable to Turkey). But see also the *Banković and others v. Belgium and others*, Admissibility decision, 12 December 2001, Application No. 52207/99, ECHR 2001-XII ('*Banković* case'), which involved a complaint filed against NATO by the victims of a missile launched on 23 April 1999 by a NATO aircraft against the buildings of a Serbian radio station in Belgrade. In that case the ECtHR changed its position. Specifically, it denied the ECHR's protection to the victims of that act because the positive obligation to secure "the rights and freedoms defined in Section I of this Convention" was only extraterritorial in very restricted exceptions, and this case was not one of them. In a later decision, though, (*Issa and others v. Turkey*, Admissibility Decision, 30 May 2000, Application No. 31821/96), the ECtHR implicitly overruled *Banković* and held that a State could be held accountable for violating human rights protected by the ECHR of persons who were in other State's territory, but who also happened to be under the former State's authority and control through its agents operating – whether lawfully or unlawfully – in the latter State. In those circumstances, the ECtHR went on, responsibility stemmed from Article 1 of the ECHR, which could not be interpreted so as to allow a State Party to perpetrate violations of the Convention abroad that they were barred from committing in their own territory.

[33]   ICJ, *Legal Consequences of the Construction of a Wall in the Occupied Palestinian Territories*, Advisory Opinion, 9 July 2004, I.C.J. Reports 2004, p. 136, para. 111.

---

required by, the norms which pertain [...]".[34] Given the fact that every person is entitled to individual rights because of human nature, American States are obliged to "uphold the protected rights"[35] of the American Declaration of the Rights and Duties of Man of any person under its authority and control, even if the State Party is acting beyond its national boundaries.[36]

5.4. Positive and Negative Obligations of States Created by International Criminal Law

States can be subjected to different kinds of obligations under human rights and international criminal law. Some of them are treaty-based, and others can be inferred from international custom. Those obligations can be categorized as 'positive' or 'negative' depending on the kind of State conduct they require (actions or omissions).

In the human rights law field, the negative category obligates States to respect rights or to refrain from encroaching on them, whereas the positive category obligates States to ensure rights, or to take measures in order to secure human rights. While the former are obligations of 'result', the latter are obligations of 'conduct'. Consequently, they are ruled by different standards.[37]

When a State affirmatively violates a human right it is also breaching an obligation of 'result'. Thus, the responsibility for the violation is manifest and immediate. In turn, when such conduct is not attributable to a State but to the action of non-State actors, the question of whether a particular State has breached its positive obligation ("to ensure") under human rights law "will be determined by the quality of the State's response to this conduct, generally governed by the State's 'best efforts' standard".[38]

---

[34] IACHR, *Coard et al. v. the United States*, Report No. 109/99, Case No. 10.951, 29 September 1999, para. 37.

[35] *Ibid.*, para. 37.

[36] See also, IACHR, *Rafael Ferrer-Mazorra et al.* (United States), Report No. 51/01, Case No. 9903, 4 April 2001, IACHR Annual Report, 2000, OEA/Ser.L/V/II.111, Doc. 20 rev., para. 178; *Saldano case* (Argentina), Report No. 38/99, 11 March 1999, in IACHR Annual Report, 1998, OEA/Ser.L/V/II.102, Doc. 6 rev., paras. 15-20.

[37] See John Cerone, 2007, p. 416, *supra* note 23.

[38] *Ibid.* See also, Inter-American Court of Human Rights, *Case of Velásquez-Rodríguez v. Honduras*, Judgment, 29 July 1988, Ser. C, no. 4 (1988), para. 172: "[I]n principle, any violation of rights recognized by the Convention carried out by an act of public authority or

As for international criminal law conventions, they create obligations with a similar structure to that of human rights treaties. Within the category of negative obligations is the prohibition against committing those crimes in and of themselves. In turn, positive obligations usually compel States Parties to prosecute or extradite those who commit the offences defined therein. Some of them, moreover, impose on States the duty to prevent the commission of those crimes in the first place.[39]

Admittedly, regarding the negative obligation, international criminal law conventions do not expressly include the prohibition to commit those crimes.[40] However, that obligation underlies all of them, notwithstanding where the State is acting (within or beyond its territory). There would be no reason for imposing a "jurisdiction threshold on a negative State obligation to refrain from doing harm".[41] And this is particularly so where international crimes are concerned.

Firstly, this approach was endorsed by the ICJ in the *Genocide* case,[42] where it found that, even if not explicitly, the Genocide Convention prohibits States Parties from committing genocide. That assertion was grounded on the fact that genocide is labelled by Article I of that Convention as "a crime under international law". If States Parties had agreed to such a categorization, they must logically refrain from committing that crime.[43]

---

by persons who use their position of authority is imputable to the State. However, this does not define all the circumstances in which a State is obligated to prevent, investigate and punish human rights violations, nor all the cases in which the State might be found responsible for an infringement of those rights. An illegal act which violates human rights and which is initially not directly imputable to a State (*e.g.*, because it is the act of a private person or because the person responsible has not been identified) can lead to international responsibility of the State, not because of the act itself, but because of the lack of due diligence to prevent the violation or to respond to it as required by the Convention".

39   See Articles I and VII, Genocide Convention; Articles IV (a), VI, and VIII, Apartheid Convention; Articles 2.1, 11, and 16, Torture Convention; Articles 12.4, 17, 22, 23, and 25, Enforced Disappearance Convention. See *supra* note 5.

40   For instance, none of the international treaties mentioned in *supra* note 39 provides expressly that States Parties will not commit those international crimes.

41   Marko Milanović, "From Compromise to Principle: Clarifying the Concept of State Jurisdiction in Human Rights Treaties", in *Human Rights Law Review*, 2008, vol. 8, no. 3, p. 446.

42   See *supra* note 2, paras. 166, 167.

43   *Ibid.*

The ICJ also took into account the obligation to prevent genocide set out in Article I of the Genocide Convention. If States are under the obligation to "employ the means at their disposal [...] to prevent persons or groups not directly under their authority from committing an act of genocide"[44], it would be at least "paradoxical" to allow them to commit such acts "through their own organs, or persons over whom they have such firm control that their conduct is attributable to the State concerned under international law".[45]

Secondly, the prohibition against international crimes (such as genocide, war crimes, and crimes against humanity), has *jus cogens* status.[46] That is to say, its hierarchical position is above all other principles, norms and rules of international and domestic law.[47] Consequently, it is a peremptory norm that is accepted by the whole international community as a norm that cannot be derogated from and can only be modified by another law of the same character.[48] Furthermore, the prohibition against the commission of the said crimes is absolute or *erga omnes*,[49] the conse-

---

[44] *Ibid.*

[45] *Ibid.*

[46] See M. Cherif Bassiouni, *Crimes against Humanity in International Law*, Kluwer Law International, 1999, p. 210; see also Payam Akhavan, "The Origin and Evolution of Crimes Against Humanity: an Uneasy Encounter between Positive Law and Moral Outrage", in Morten Bergsmo (ed.), *Human Rights and Criminal Justice for the Downtrodden. Essays in Honour of Asbjørn Eide*, Martinus Nijhoff Publishers, 2003, p. 3 ("The prohibition against crimes against humanity is, beyond doubt, one of the most fundamental norms of international law. It is widely considered as a part of *ius cogens* [...]"). This has also been recognized in international tribunals, see International Criminal Tribunal for the former Yugoslavia ('ICTY'), *Prosecutor v. Kupreškić et al.*, Judgment, 14 January 2000, Case No. IT-95-16-T, para. 520 ("Furthermore, most norms of international humanitarian law, in particular those prohibiting war crimes, crimes against humanity and genocide, are also peremptory norms of international law or *jus cogens*, i.e. of a non-derogable and overriding character") and all the cases that are quoted there. For a review of the recognition of the norms that have been considered *ius cogens*, see Sandesh Sivakumaran, "Impact on the Structure of International Obligations", in Menno Kamminga and Martin Scheinin (eds.), *The Impact of Human Rights Law on General International Law*, Oxford University Press, 2009, pp. 133–150.

[47] Cherif Bassiouni, 1999, p. 210, *supra* note 46.

[48] Vienna Convention on the Law of Treaties, signed at Vienna on 23 May 1969, entered into force on 27 January 1980. United Nations, Treaty Series, vol. 1155, p. 331, Article 53.

[49] See ICJ, *Case Concerning Barcelona Traction, Light and Power Company, Limited (Belgium v. Spain)*, Judgment, 5 February 1970, new application: 1962, ICJ Reports 1970, p. 3 and its famous *obiter dictum* in para. 33. In that case, the ICJ recognized that any State could hold a legal interest in the protection of "principles and rules concerning the basic

---

quence of which is that any State can claim to have a legal interest in its protection.

Thirdly, this also have been acknowledged by the Restatement (Third) of the Foreign Relations Law of the United States §702 (1987), according to which "[a] State violates international law if, as a matter of State policy, it practices, encourages or condones: a) genocide; b) slavery or slave trade; c) the murder or causing the disappearance of individuals; d) torture or other cruel, inhuman, or degrading treatment or punishment [...]".

However, as we shall see, the positive obligations – particularly the obligation to prevent – can become a thorny issue. I will delve into these topics in the following sections.

5.5. The Obligation to Prevent under the Proposed Convention

The negative obligation that implicitly stems from the Proposed Convention is to refrain from committing crimes against humanity, which, as shown above, does not have territorial limits.[50]

The positive obligations that the Proposed Convention would impose on States if it became law can be divided into three groups: (1) the obligation to investigate, prosecute and punish crimes against humanity; (2) the obligation to prevent crimes against humanity; and (3) the obligation to co-operate with other States in the fulfilment of their obligations. This chapter focuses on the obligation to prevent crimes against humanity.

The scope of the obligations is shaped by Article 8(1) of the Proposed Convention.[51] It is important to analyse closely the wording of that

---

rights of the human person", which include, according to the Court, the prohibition of acts of aggression, of genocide, and the protection from slavery and racial discrimination (the last two are particular manifestations of crimes against humanity).

[50] In line with the criteria set by the ICJ in the *Genocide* case, the prohibition to commit crimes against humanity may be inferred from the object and purpose of the Proposed Convention, from some specific provisions regarding State responsibility and the obligation to prevent, and from the characterization of crimes against humanity as "international crimes". In turn, Article 8 imposes on States Parties the obligation to prevent and to punish crimes against humanity. In addition, even if the worldwide scope of the prohibition against crimes against humanity was questioned, those crimes committed by a State acting abroad would, as Professor Luban notes, simultaneously constitute war crimes, and therefore, they would amount to international crimes anyway. Luban, 2004, p. 94, *supra* note 4.

[51] Article 8(1) in full provides: "Each State Party shall enact necessary legislation and other measures as required by its Constitution or legal system to give effect to the provisions of

provision – particularly, the meaning of the terms 'territory', 'jurisdiction' and 'control', which serve as a threshold requirement regarding the positive obligations of States. I will also delve into the interaction of those words and the way they shape the obligation to prevent crimes against humanity.

The selection of the words 'territory', 'jurisdiction' and 'control' in a provision like this is not random. In fact, many international law conventions and particularly human rights treaties have provisions similar to Article 8(1) shaping the boundaries of the obligations of States under the treaty.[52] Moreover, the way those words have been interpreted within human rights treaties by international, regional and domestic bodies has had a major impact on their extraterritorial applicability.[53]

Bearing in mind the debate that has arisen regarding the interpretation of 'territory', 'jurisdiction', and 'control', it is worth exploring the Proposed Convention in order to see if its wording may give any clues about their possible meaning and reach in Article 8(1).

As for 'territory', the provisions of the Proposed Convention "shall apply to all parts of federal States without any limitations or exceptions".[54]

Regarding 'control', although it is used in other provisions of the Proposed Convention, they do not seem linked with its use in Article 8(1), as they refer to very specific and limited situations: (1) the control of one person towards another in the crime of torture;[55] (2) the responsibility of commanders and other superiors;[56] or (3) the physical control over a person by a State for purposes of prosecution or extradition.[57] Thus, those

---

the present Convention and, in particular, to take effective legislative, administrative, judicial and other measures in accordance with the Charter of the United Nations to prevent and punish the commission of crimes against humanity in any territory under its jurisdiction or control".

[52] For a review of all the uses of the word 'jurisdiction' in human rights treaties, see, *e.g.*, Milanović, 2008, pp. 411–448, *supra* note 41. See also Gondek, 2009, *supra* note 31, and in particular, Chapter II.

[53] Gondek, 2009, p. 367, *supra* note 31.

[54] Article 20, Proposed Convention.

[55] *Ibid.*, Article 3(2)(e).

[56] *Ibid.*, Article 5(1), (2).

[57] *Ibid.*, Article 10(2)(a) , (5).

other uses do not provide any insights into interpreting 'control' or clarifying either of the other two words under study.

In turn, in-depth analysis of the different appearances of the term 'jurisdiction' throughout the Proposed Convention is worthwhile because it may illuminate the meanings that 'jurisdiction' in Article 8(1) is susceptible to.

Article 10 of the Proposed Convention encompasses a general provision about jurisdiction and the extent of States' obligations to prosecute and punish crimes against humanity.[58] 'Jurisdiction' appears many times throughout the article, although with a seemingly different meaning than in Article 8(1):

1. Persons alleged to be responsible for crimes against humanity shall be tried by a criminal court of the State Party, or by the International Criminal Court, or by an international tribunal having jurisdiction over crimes against humanity.

2. Each State Party shall take the necessary measures to establish its competence to exercise jurisdiction over persons alleged to be responsible for crimes against humanity:

   (a) When the offense is committed in any territory under its jurisdiction or onboard a ship or aircraft registered in that State or whenever a person is under the physical control of that State; or

   [...]

3. Each State Party shall likewise take such measures as may be necessary to establish its competence to exercise jurisdiction over the offense of crimes against humanity when the alleged offender is present in any territory under its jurisdiction, unless it extradites or surrenders him or her to another State in accordance with its international obligations or surrenders him or her to an international criminal tribunal whose jurisdiction it has recognized.

---

[58] In fact, many international human rights treaties include articles similar to Article 10 of the Proposed Convention, obligating States to criminalize and prosecute certain conduct. For a review of all of them, see Milanović, 2008, pp. 426–427, *supra* note 41.

4. The present Convention does not preclude the exercise of any other competent criminal jurisdiction compatible with international law and which is exercised in accordance with national law.

5. For purposes of cooperation, jurisdiction shall be deemed to exist whenever the person responsible for, or alleged to be responsible for, crimes against humanity is present in the State's territory or the State Party is in a position to exercise physical control over him or her.[59]

In Article 10(2), 'jurisdiction' is used in its general meaning under international law: "The capacity of a State under international law to prescribe or to enforce a rule of law"[60] or, to put it differently, to regulate the conduct of physical and legal persons, and to enforce such regulations.[61]

In line with Article 10(2) of the Proposed Convention, States would be under the obligation to import crimes against humanity into their domestic criminal law, and to establish their competence – through the necessary legislation – in order to investigate, prosecute and punish crimes against humanity whether they are committed in their own territory, or by their nationals, or if the victim is a national of that State.

Moreover, the Proposed Convention does not preclude States from exercising their criminal jurisdiction according to the 'protective principle' or even in a universal fashion, as both of them are compatible with international law.[62]

---

[59] Article 10, Proposed Convention. As a matter of fact, the protective principle and universal jurisdiction are already included in Article 10(2)(c), Article 8(8) and Article 9 of the Proposed Convention.

[60] Restatement (Second) of Foreign Relations Law of the United States: Jurisdiction Defined, 2010, § 6.

[61] Gondek, 2009, p. 47, *supra* note 31. Basically, the determination of the principles according to which States may exercise their jurisdiction is based on the functions that they can exercise legitimately: "States consist, at bottom, of territory and people; and so, it will come as no surprise that the two fundamental bases for jurisdiction are territorial and personal – and, thus, giving place to the 'territorial' and 'active personality' principles. In addition, international law recognizes other bases for the legitimate exercise of jurisdiction. As it is acknowledged that States have a legitimate interest in securing their borders and currency, among other interests, the protection of those interests represents another basis for jurisdiction". Lastly, regarding some specific atrocity crimes, international law also recognizes the power of States to assert jurisdiction if the perpetrator is located within its territory. See Luban, O'Sullivan, and Stewart, 2010, p. 171, *supra* note 19.

[62] See Article 10(4), Proposed Convention.

The above-mentioned meaning of 'jurisdiction', however, is not the only one that the term has within some sections of Article 10. Paragraphs one and four of Article 10 do not use 'jurisdiction' as a State's competence to prescribe, adjudicate, or enforce, but rather regarding the competence of the ICC or any other international tribunal created by the international community to try persons alleged to be responsible for crimes against humanity.[63]

In turn, the reference to 'jurisdiction' in Article 8(1) could well be interpreted as serving a different purpose, and thus having a different meaning than 'jurisdiction' as used in Article 10(1), 10(2) and 10(4). The question about what 'jurisdiction' can mean within that context has two possible and mutually exclusive answers.

On the one hand, it could be said that 'jurisdiction', as used in Article 8(1), refers to the meaning that term denotes within general international law – that is to say, the authority to make and enforce the law. In fact, that has been the way that the ECtHR has interpreted a similar clause of the ECHR – Article 1[64] – in the *Banković* case.

On the other hand, it could also be argued that 'jurisdiction' in Article 8(1) has a different meaning, closer to the one that 'jurisdiction' has within human rights conventions, where provisions of the like are very common.

According to the latter viewpoint 'jurisdiction' should not be understood as it is within general international law, but as referring "to a particular kind of factual power, authority or control that a State has over a territory, and consequently over persons in that territory".[65] In that context, 'jurisdiction' serves as a condition for assessing the existence of a particular obligation of a State regarding a particular victim – or potential victim – of a human rights violation because of his or her presence in a certain

---

[63] In this sense, 'jurisdiction' can be said to be "that which deals only with the scope of application of the supervisory mechanism under a particular treaty, most notably with the competence of a treaty body to examine individual petitions", Milanović, 2008, p. 414, *supra* note 41. I will not delve into this particular meaning of 'jurisdiction' because it is not controversial, and also because it is not relevant for the purpose of my argumentation.

[64] Article 1 of the ECHR provides that "[t]he High Contracting Parties shall secure to everyone within their jurisdiction the rights and freedoms defined in Section I of [the] Convention".

[65] Milanović, 2008, p. 428, *supra* note 41.

territory.[66] Thus, the purpose served by this meaning of jurisdiction is to determine the applicability of a human rights treaty to a particular State conduct, the legality or illegality of that conduct being irrelevant.[67]

Within international human rights law, provisions such as Article 8(1) of the Proposed Convention and Article 1 of the ECHR, containing the "territory under its jurisdiction or control" (or similar wording) requirement, are conditions to be satisfied "in order for treaty obligations to arise in the first place".[68] In other words, the concept of jurisdiction is a tool to establish whether a particular State is obligated under a particular treaty. Once that determination has been made, it is necessary to establish whether that State breached those obligations, in which case the act would be considered internationally wrongful and would entail that State's responsibility.[69]

To sum up, throughout the Proposed Convention, 'jurisdiction' appears many times and it is susceptible to at least three different meanings.[70] What is the meaning of 'jurisdiction' in Article 8(1)?

In Article 8(1), 'jurisdiction' is used as an alternative to 'control'. The conjunction 'or' links the two alternatives. Thus, the drafters were thinking about two different situations: One, a certain territory is under the 'jurisdiction' of a State; and the other, a certain territory is under its 'control'. Thus, 'jurisdiction' and 'control' are presupposed to be mutually exclusive, the main difference between those situations being presence or lack of legal competence (or 'jurisdiction' in the sense used in general international law).

---

[66] See also Gondek, 2009, p. 16, *supra* note 31, who differentiates between both meanings of 'jurisdiction', one of them being "the legal competence of a State to legislate, adjudicate and enforce the law" ('jurisdiction' as it is understood in international criminal law) and the other being "a given location" ('jurisdiction' as it is used in human rights treaties).

[67] *Ibid.*, p. 56.

[68] Milanović, 2008, p. 416, *supra* note 41.

[69] *Ibid.*, p. 441.

[70] Article 10(3), in fact, is a very good example, as it simultaneously in the same sentence embraces them: (a) 'jurisdiction' as used in general international law, specifically, to prescribe ("Each State Party shall… establish its competence to exercise jurisdiction over […]"); (b) 'jurisdiction' regarding the *rationae materiae, personae, loci* competence of an international court ("an international criminal tribunal whose jurisdiction it has recognized […]"); and (c) 'jurisdiction' as used in human rights law ("[…] when the alleged offender is present in any territory under its jurisdiction […]").

The addition of 'control' to the wording of such a clause is novel. Within human rights treaties, provisions concerning the scope of its applicability refer to 'jurisdiction' (either over persons or over territories, or both, depending on the convention) but none of them include any word alluding to factual power (as opposed to legal competence) such as 'control'.[71]

The addition of 'control' to the language of Article 8(1) of the Proposed Convention can be interpreted as a reaction against some restrictive approaches to the applicability of human rights treaties among some international and regional tribunals. Those restrictive interpretations usually stem from the conflation of 'jurisdiction' as understood in international law and 'jurisdiction' as used in human rights law.[72]

Due to that confusion, it has been asserted – most notably, by the ECtHR – that the obligations of States under human rights treaties are essentially territorial and that the extraterritorial application of those conventions is exceptional.[73] The consequence of that interpretation was that

---

[71] The "International Convention on the Elimination of All Forms of Racial Discrimination", adopted and opened for signature and ratification by UNGA resolution 2106 (XX) of 21 December 1965, and entered into force on 4 January 1969, states in Article 3 that "States Parties [...] undertake to prevent, prohibit and eradicate [racial segregation and apartheid] in territories under their jurisdiction". The ICCPR, in Article 2(1) provides that each State Party undertakes "to respect and to ensure to all individuals within its territory and subject to its jurisdiction the rights recognized in the present Covenant", without discrimination. The Torture Convention, in different provisions confines States Parties' obligations to prevent torture and other cruel treatments to the territory under their 'jurisdiction', see for instance Articles 2, 11, 16(1). For an overview of all the jurisdictional clauses in human rights treaties, see Gondek, 2009, pp. 11–18, *supra* note 31, and Milanović, *supra* note 41.

[72] Most notable by the ECtHR in the *Banković* case, and by the ICJ, 2004, para. 109, *supra* note 34. However, as noted by Milanović, the ICJ, different from its European counterpart, "[...] gave no special significance to this supposedly primarily territorial notion of jurisdiction as warranting a restrictive approach to Article 2(1) of the ICCPR [...] [and] found both the ICCPR and the ICESCR, as well as the CRC, applicable to the occupied Palestinian territories". It is important to highlight that one of the judges of the ECtHR, Judge Loucaides, delivered two separate opinions in the cases *Assanidze v. Georgia* (Judgment, 8 April 2004, Application No. 71503/01, Reports of Judgments and Decisions 2004-II) and *Ilaşcu v. Moldova* (Judgment, 8 July 2004, Application No. 48787/99, Reports of Judgments and Decisions 2004-VII), defining 'jurisdiction' – as it is usually used in human rights treaties – as the exercise of State authority.

[73] It is worth noting that this attachment to territory as the main basis for jurisdiction is not obvious. International law recognizes other bases according to which jurisdiction may be exercised. Territoriality is a sole basis only regarding the enforcement jurisdiction, but not legislative or adjudicative jurisdiction. Still, 'territory' as a basis for determining the scope

some applications concerning violations of rights in the ECHR were declared inadmissible with the argument that the alleged violations had not been committed within the jurisdiction of the respondent State or States.[74]

Accordingly, it seems that the drafters of the Proposed Convention recognized that boiling down the concept of 'jurisdiction' to the territory of the obligated State could have undesirable consequences and be understood as a blank check for States to do abroad what they cannot do within their boundaries, and added 'control' as a way of widening the scope of the positive obligations.

At the same time, though, this interpretation entails that, in the Proposed Convention, 'jurisdiction' is used as in general international law. Otherwise it would not have been necessary to add the word 'control' because 'jurisdiction' as understood in human rights law already involves the exercise of factual power over a person or a territory.

Another argument advocating for the interpretation that the Proposed Convention refers to 'jurisdiction' as understood in general international law is the focus on the territory – rather than, for instance, persons, or facilities, or property, or situations – that the Proposed Convention has regarding the positive obligations. In fact, the exercise of jurisdiction to prescribe, to adjudicate and to enforce according to the territorial principle is the epitome of jurisdiction. Nobody can object to a State's regulation or enforcement of its legislation within its own territory.

Consequently, in order to determine whether States are under the obligation to prevent crimes against humanity under the Proposed Convention, 'jurisdiction' in Article 8(1) should be interpreted as it is in gen-

---

of human rights treaties has been privileged. See Gondek, 2009, pp. 370–371, *supra* note 31.

[74] The decision of the ECtHR in the *Banković* case, already mentioned, is considered to be the first case in which such an approach was adopted. See Ralph Wilde, "Triggering State Obligations Extraterritorially: The Spatial Test in Certain Human Rights Treaties", in *Israel Law Review*, 2004, vol. 40, p. 515. See also Milanović, p. 423, *supra* note 41, who asserts that:

> In its pre-Banković case law, the Court did not base its interpretation of Article 1 ECHR on the general international law doctrine of jurisdiction. No Oppenheims, Brownlies, Casseses or Pellets were ever cited by the Court, and for good reason – exercising 'effective overall control' over a territory does not mean that the State is necessarily exercising its 'jurisdiction' – as general international law speaks of the term- over the inhabitants of that territory.

eral international law – 'legal competence' – and exclusively according to a territorial basis (because it refers to 'territories' under the 'jurisdiction' or 'control' of States Parties), and 'control' is meant to encompass those situations where States exercise some kind of factual power over a territory without any legal competence.

Nevertheless, is this resolution of the issue of jurisdiction in the Proposed Convention effective in guaranteeing strong protection against crimes against humanity?

5.6. Advantages and Disadvantages of the Wording of Article 8(1), Specifically with the Phrase "Territory within Its Jurisdiction or Control"

At first glance, such an obligation to prevent crimes against humanity represents significant progress, as it would embrace situations in which States typically are not bound by any obligation regarding the prevention of crimes against humanity.

The scope of Article 8(1) reaches situations where States have control over a territory even if they do not have jurisdiction over it (for instance, due to illegal military operations that are being performed in another State's territory) and *vice versa* (cases where States, although having jurisdiction over a territory, do not have control over what is happening there).

The first type of cases (control without jurisdiction) could arise in situations such as the one depicted by the ICJ in the case *Armed Activities on the Territory of the Congo*.[75] In that case, the ICJ found that Uganda was the occupying power in Ituri, DRC, at the relevant time and that it was under the obligation to "secure respect for the applicable rules of international human rights law and international humanitarian law, to protect the inhabitants of the occupied territory against acts of violence, and not to tolerate such violence by any third party".[76] If the Proposed Convention became law, a State Party in Uganda's situation would also be under the obligation to prevent the commission of crimes against humanity against the inhabitants of Ituri, notwithstanding who is perpetrating those crimes.

---

[75] ICJ, *Armed Activities on the Territory of the Congo (Democratic Republic of the Congo v. Uganda)*, Judgment, 19 December 2005, I.C.J. Reports 2005, p. 168.

[76] *Ibid.*, para. 178.

The other type of cases (jurisdiction without control) could arise in situations such as the one depicted by the ECtHR in its decision in the *Ilaşcu and Others v. Moldova and Russia* case.[77] In that case, the Court acknowledged that the Moldovan government did not exercise authority (control) over one region of the national territory (Transnistria) because of its secession.[78] Even in the absence of effective control over that region, the Court found Moldova to be under a positive obligation "to take the diplomatic, economic, judicial or other measures that it is in its power to take and are in accordance with international law to secure to the applicants the rights guaranteed by the [ECHR]".[79] According to Article 8(1) of the Proposed Convention, Moldova would also be under the obligation to prevent the commission of crimes against humanity in the Transnistrian region independently of who commits the crimes.

Despite the positive consequences that the wording of Article 8(1) of the Proposed Convention would have regarding the obligation to prevent crimes against humanity, the selection of the words 'territory', 'jurisdiction' and 'control', and the interaction among them, could still have unsatisfactory aspects.

First and foremost, 'control' is a tricky concept, as it has been interpreted in many different ways within international law and serves many different purposes.

In Article 8(1) of the Proposed Convention, 'control' is the criterion for determining whether that State is under the obligation to prevent crimes against humanity regarding acts that take place beyond its jurisdiction. This use of 'control' is not unusual within international human rights case law.[80] However, in those cases 'control' has been used as a test in order to determine the State's jurisdiction over territories where human rights violations took place or over victims of those violations. Under that interpretation, 'control' is not a stand-alone concept regarding the limits of States obligations. It is a requisite in order to prove the existence of jurisdiction.[81]

---

[77] See *supra* note 72.

[78] *Ibid.*, para. 330.

[79] *Ibid.*, para. 331.

[80] See, for instance, the 'Cypriot cases' of the ECtHR.

[81] Still, it is likely that this interpretation of control as a test for determining jurisdiction may have been due to the fact that those human rights treaties at stake have as a threshold requirement 'jurisdiction' over a person or territories, but not 'control'. Thus, it seems that

For instance, the ECtHR has used the 'effective control' test to determine if a State Party to the Convention was under the (positive) obligation to secure the rights and freedoms of the ECHR in an occupied territory.[82] Specifically, the ECtHR applied this test *vis-à-vis* human rights violations in Cyprus, and found that Turkey was indeed exercising "effective control", which could be exercised "directly, through its armed forces, or through a subordinate local administration".[83] In the decision about the merits,[84] the ECtHR maintained this position – although it changed the test slightly to "effective overall control".[85]

At the same time, 'control' has also served as a rule for attributing a wrongful act to a State under the rules of State responsibility. However, that is a different operation than asserting that certain acts fall within the jurisdiction of a certain State. In fact, the former evaluation can only be done after the latter – and only if it has been demonstrated that the State had jurisdiction regarding a specific international obligation.

The ICJ, in the *Nicaragua* case[86] applied two different tests using the word 'control' in order to determine the United States' responsibility over the paramilitary activities of non-State actors (*los contras*) in Nicaragua's territory. The first test was the one of "complete control"[87] by a State of non-State actors, according to which it should be determined whether that State exercises such a level of control over those actors so that the latter could be considered agents of the former.

If that level of control or dependence is not satisfied, the second test is applied: whether a particular obligation perpetrated by a non-State actor was conducted under the 'effective control' of a particular State.[88]

---

those tribunals were trying to widen the scope of 'jurisdiction' because, as understood in international law, it can be very restrictive.

[82] *Loizidou v. Turkey*, Preliminary Objections, see *supra* note 32.

[83] *Ibid.*, para. 62.

[84] *Loizidou v. Turkey*, Judgment, 18 December 1996, Reports 1996-VI.

[85] *Ibid.*, para. 56.

[86] ICJ, *Military and Paramilitary Activities in and against Nicaragua (Nicaragua v. United States of America)* ('*Nicaragua* case'), Judgment, 27 June 1986. I.C.J. Reports 1986, p. 14.

[87] *Ibid.*, para. 109.

[88] *Ibid.*, para. 115. The ICJ also used these same tests in the *Genocide* case (see *supra* note 2). Bolstering its decision in the *Nicaragua* case (*supra* note 85), it found that the Bosnian-Serbian militias did not completely depend on Serbia, nor did Serbia have complete control over them. Consequently, they could not be equated, for legal purposes, with organs of the Serbia State, or as acting on behalf of Serbia (paras. 391–395). It also found that the

'Control' has also been used for another test, applicable to a different situation. In the *Tadić* case,[89] the Appeals Chamber of the ICTY had to determine in which cases and upon which criteria, forces fighting against the central authority of the same State where they live and operate may be deemed to act on behalf of a foreign power, thereby rendering a seemingly internal armed-conflict, international. This is a very significant issue, as it has many consequences regarding the applicable international humanitarian law rules.

The Appeals Chamber found that, in order to attribute the acts of armed forces to a State, there should be enough evidence regarding the 'overall control' exercised by that State over the group, not only by providing it equipment or financing, but also by "coordinating or helping in the general planning of its military activity".[90] According to the Appeals Chamber, "it is not necessary that, in addition, the State should also issue, either to the head or to members of the group, instructions for the commission of specific acts contrary to international law".[91] In its reasoning, the Appeals Chamber expressly rejected the 'effective control' test crafted by the ICJ in the *Nicaragua* case.[92]

To sum up, different levels of control have been used in international case law as criteria for several (and distinct) determinations in order

---

perpetrators of the Srebrenica genocide had not acted following instructions, or under direction or 'effective control', of Serbia, in which case those acts could be attributed to Serbia (paras. 400–407).

[89] ICTY, Appeals Chamber, *Prosecutor v. Tadić*, Judgment, 15 July 1999, Case No. IT-94-1A.

[90] *Ibid.*, para. 131.

[91] *Ibid.*

[92] *Ibid.*, paras. 115-130. For an in-depth analysis of this particular aspect of the *Tadić* decision, see Marko Milanović, "State Responsibility for Genocide", in *European Journal of International Law*, 2006, vol. 17, p. 585. According to Milanović, the rational used in that decision was incorrect because the ICTY applied a criterion established for determining State responsibility in order to decide an issue of international humanitarian law (the nature of the armed conflict between Bosnian Serbs and Bosnian Muslims). The ICJ in the *Genocide* case (*supra* note 2, paras. 404-405) also criticized the ICTY's rational in *Tadić*. Specifically, it stated that "[t]he ICTY was not called upon in the *Tadić* case, nor is it in general called upon, to rule on questions of State responsibility, since its jurisdiction is criminal and extends over persons only [...] the ICTY presented the 'overall control' test as equally applicable under the law of State responsibility for the purpose of determining [...] when a State is responsible for acts committed by paramilitary units, armed forces which are not among its official organs. In this context, the argument in favour of that test is unpersuasive".

to establish jurisdiction of a particular State under human rights treaties *vis-à-vis* a human rights violation, to establish the attribution of a wrongful act to a particular State under the rules of State responsibility, and to determine the international character of an armed conflict.[93] Still, as the ICJ held in the *Genocide* case,[94] even if all those formulations contain the word 'control', logic does not require the same test to be adopted in resolving different issues. The degree and nature of a State's control and authority can very well, and without logical inconsistency, be different depending which issue is at stake. Even with this clarification, the different tests and meanings of control can be conflated and confused, as it happened in the *Tadić* case.

Another unsatisfactory aspect of the wording of Article 8(1) of the Proposed Convention is the selection of the term 'territory'.

Such selection of word seems to be a consequence of the use of 'jurisdiction', when determining the scope of applicability of human rights treaties, as understood in general international law. This focus on territory, however, could limit the reach of the obligation to prevent crimes against humanity in a way that would undermine the spirit and purpose of the Proposed Convention. And even the addition of 'control' is not enough to counterbalance those negative consequences.

One example of situations that would be excluded from the scope of the proposed convention because of the selection of the word 'territory' are the cases of 'extraordinary renditions' – sadly very popular nowadays within the U.S.'s 'Global War on Terror'.[95]

Extraordinary renditions, when committed within the background required by the definition of crimes against humanity (as part of a widespread or systematic attack directed against any civilian population) could be characterized as a specific manifestation of crimes against humanity –

---

[93] Gondek, 2009, p. 168, *supra* note 31.

[94] *Genocide* case, para. 168, *supra* note 2.

[95] Article 1(3)(e), Proposed Convention. Among the cases that can be mentioned is that of Maher Arar, a Syrian-born, Canadian citizen who was detained during a layover at J.F.K. Airport in September 2002 and, after being held in solitary confinement, was rendered to Syrian intelligence authorities, renowned for the use of torture, under the label of being a member of Al Qaeda. In Syria, Maher Arar was interrogated and tortured, and held without charges. Almost one year later he was released because Syrian authorities could not find connections to terrorism or criminal activities. See the information of the case at the web site of the Center for Constitutional Rights, available at http://ccrjustice.org/ourcases/current-cases/arar-v-ashcroft.

"imprisonment [...] in violation of fundamental rules of international law",[96] and torture[97] (if that were the case).

Let us imagine a case where State 'A' renders a prisoner – independently of the legality of his or her imprisonment – to State 'B', where he or she is interrogated under torture by officials of 'B'. Notwithstanding the breach of the (negative) obligation not to commit crimes against humanity by 'A' should the imprisonment be illegal, was 'A' also under the (positive) obligation to prevent the individual from being tortured by officials of 'B'? 'A' could argue, consistent with Article 8(1) of the Proposed Convention, that 'B' is a territory neither under its jurisdiction, nor under its control.

That is why it is important to take into account that in some situations, States should be under the obligation to prevent the commission of crimes against humanity against *persons* under their jurisdiction – even if those crimes were committed in territories which are neither under their jurisdiction, nor under their control.

Other situations that would be excluded from the scope of the Proposed Convention because of the territorial requirement are also inspired by the 'Global War on Terror'.

According to some documents that have been released,[98] many detainees have been subjected to practices in Iraq that could amount to crimes against humanity by their fellow nationals of the Armed and Security Forces. Specifically, those reports document deaths, beatings, burnings, lashings, and other kinds of physical violence that may have been occurring on a regular basis. The American forces in Iraq, however, have rejected the responsibility to investigate those crimes. Particularly, according to America's policy, which was made official by a Pentagon spokesman,[99] American forces were under the sole obligation to immediately report abuses, and to ask the Iraqis authorities to conduct an investigation. However, this strategy was futile. As the article informs,

---

[96] However, not all cases of extraordinary renditions start as an imprisonment in violation of international law. In fact, it could be stated that Arar's detention was not "in violation of fundamental rules of international law", as he was allegedly detained by American officers in an American airport.

[97] Article 3(1)(f), Proposed Convention.

[98] See "Detainees Fared Worse in Iraqi Hands, Logs Say", *New York Times*, print edition of 23 October 2010, p. A8.

[99] *Ibid.*

> [e]ven when Americans found abuse and reported it, Iraqis often did not act. One report said a police chief refused to file charges "as long as the abuse produced no marks." Another police chief told military inspectors that his officers engaged in abuse "and supported it as a method of conducting investigations."[100]

If this Proposed Convention were in force, and ratified by the U.S., would the American forces be under the obligation to take all the necessary measures in order to prevent those crimes? The answer to this question is not at all easy. Clearly, Iraq is no longer under the jurisdiction of the U.S. But, is it under its control? Although it could be argued that, when those acts took place, the U.S. was exercising some kind of control over the Iraq territory, that is also very debatable, and the burden of proof over victims alleging the U.S.'s violation of the obligation to prevent crimes against humanity would be very difficult to reach.

However, if the Proposed Convention contained other concepts apart from 'territory' – such as persons, facilities, situations – the U.S.'s obligation to prevent crimes against humanity would be easier to defend.

Article 1 of the ECHR can provide an example of alternative language. That article provides that States Parties undertake to secure to everyone within their jurisdiction the rights and freedoms defined in the Convention. That is to say, it does not emphasize the national territory of the States Parties, but rather the persons that may be under their jurisdiction. Along these lines, the now-defunct European Commission on Human Rights has stressed the importance of focusing on the jurisdiction or control exercised by officials of a State Party over persons, rather than over territories, when determining the extraterritorial applicability of the ECHR.[101] In the *Cypriot* cases, the Commission suggested a test according to which the ECHR was applicable to persons or property that came "under actual authority and responsibility" of Turkish agents, "not only

---

[100] *Ibid.*

[101] See European Commission on Human Rights, *Turkey v. Cyprus*, App. No. 8007/77, 13 Eur. Comm'n H.R. Dec. and Rep., p. 85, particularly para. 19, and the reports mentioned there. For a complete overview of that report and, in general, of the Commission's position on the Cyprus cases, see Gondek, 2009, pp. 126–132, *supra* note 31.

when that authority is exercised within their own territory but also when it is exercised abroad".[102]

5.7. In Favour of an Extraterritorial Obligation to Prevent Crimes Against Humanity

The significance of this attempt to promote an international convention condemning and fostering prevention of crimes against humanity is substantial. Whereas since 1948 we have had a treaty dealing with genocide, and genocide prevention,[103] crimes against humanity have "essentially lingered in the fog of customary law",[104] apart from their appearance at the Nuremberg Trials and in some regional prosecutions. Their codification in 1998 in the ICC Statute has represented an important, though limited, development, as the ICC Statute only regulates situations within its jurisdictional boundary.

As a consequence, even when the definition of crimes against humanity covers most of the gravest human rights violations,[105] and it was constructed to describe appalling atrocities such as the Armenian Genocide and the Holocaust, the lack of an international treaty condemning and obligating States to prevent them "meant that the concept was virtually impotent in a legal sense".[106] The want of a special treaty has also contributed to downplaying crimes against humanity when compared to gen-

---

[102] *Turkey v. Cyprus, ibid.*, para. 19. Still, the ECtHR, restricted the meaning of Article 1 of the ECHR, resorting to the meaning that 'jurisdiction' has within general international law (which has a strong focus on territory) and thus departing from the wording of Article 1 (that does not mention 'territory' at all). This became crystal clear in the *Banković* decision. Even more, according to that ruling, those exceptional situations in which the ECHR could be applied extraterritorially are also mainly territorial – concretely, the focus is on those territories of another State Party under the control of the respondent State, rather than on the persons who are under the control over the respondent State. See Gondek, 2009, p. 178, *supra* note 31.

[103] In 1948, when States drafted and signed the Genocide Convention, they confirmed that genocide is a crime under international law and undertook the obligation to prevent and punish it (Article I). In addition, the Convention provides a specific mechanism regarding the obligation to prevent: any State Party may appeal to the competent organs of the UN, so that they take the appropriate action under the UN Charter for the prevention and suppression of genocide (Article VIII).

[104] William A. Schabas, "Darfur and the 'Odious Scourge': The Commission of Inquiry's Findings on Genocide", in *Leiden Journal of International Law*, 2005, vol. 18, pp. 883–884.

[105] *Ibid.*, p. 884.

[106] *Ibid.*

ocide, and buttressed the idea that genocide "sits at the apex of a pyramid of criminality"[107] whereas crimes against humanity are not as serious crimes.[108]

The creation of an international treaty thus serves the function, among many others, of pronouncing the international community's condemnation of those crimes and their perpetrators, and States' commitment to prevent and eradicate crimes against humanity. Of course, we all know that the creation of an international treaty will not stop those atrocities from one day to the next – as the Genocide Convention failed to prevent or suppress genocides that took place after 1948, and human rights treaties have failed to prevent gross human rights violations. However, a comprehensive treaty on crimes against humanity can provide, at the very least, a crucial advocacy tool for human rights activists, international organizations, potential or current victims of crimes against humanity, and States interested in eradicating those crimes. It can also be a useful tool for setting the agenda, mobilizing and empowering potential and actual victims of crimes against humanity, and litigating against States and individuals that engage in those practices. In other words, the establishment of authoritative principles in an international treaty is "a crucial element in empowering individuals to imagine, articulate, and mobilize as rights holders".[109]

It is true that the legal concept of crimes against humanity and its condemnation as an international crime, already exists through customary international law, and thus, is binding for all nations. Still, an international treaty can be more effective in raising awareness about the gravity of these crimes. As has been said, "[w]hile international custom can have a direct effect even without implementing legislation [...] it would be much harder to mobilize domestic audiences to demand implementation of international custom than a ratified treaty".[110] The reason for this is that the ratification of international treaties "provides at least the color of local

[107] William A. Schabas, "Genocide Law in a Time of Transition: Recent Developments in the Law of Genocide", in *Rutgers Law Review*, 2008, vol. 61, p. 191.

[108] According to Schabas, another consequence of the "impunity gap" – or lack of systematization of crimes against humanity – was the "enlargement" of the definition of genocide in order to include conducts that square better in the crimes against humanity definition. *Ibid.*

[109] Beth Simmons, *Mobilizing for Human Rights. International Law in Domestic Politics*, Cambridge University Press, 2009, p. 351.

[110] *Ibid.*, p. 364.

ownership of specific human rights obligations".[111] However, that cannot be said about customary international law.

Still, the language of Article 8(1) of the Proposed Convention, and in particular the creation of a territory-limited obligation to prevent, could be read as reinforcing the idea that genocide is the most serious international crime and consequently trivializing crimes against humanity. The reason for this is that, in the midst of the increasing acknowledgment of an extraterritorial obligation to prevent genocide that can be tracked to at least since the turn of the century, the international community would be creating a more restrictive obligation where crimes against humanity prevention is concerned. This disparity could misconstrue the seriousness of crimes against humanity.

Regarding international efforts to prevent genocide, the U.N. Secretary General, on 13 July 2004, appointed a Special Adviser on the Prevention of Genocide, with the mandate of carrying out some activities (such as a careful verification of facts and serious political analyses and consultations) in order to enable the U.N. to act in a timely fashion in order to prevent genocide.[112]

In May 2006, the U.N. Secretary-General appointed an Advisory Committee on Genocide Prevention, integrated by renowned international figures, with the function to assist the Special Adviser on the Prevention of Genocide. On 31 August 2007, the Advisory Committee suggested a modification of the title of the Special Adviser to "Special Advisor on the Prevention of Genocide and Mass Atrocities".[113] However, that attempt failed. The Security Council took several months to respond to the letter

---

[111] *Ibid.*

[112] See letter dated 12 July 2004 from the Secretary-General addressed to the President of the Security Council, S/2004/567. The specific mandate of the Special Advisory was to (a) collect existing information, in particular from within the UN system, on massive and serious violations of human rights and international humanitarian law of ethnic and racial origin that, if not prevented or halted, might lead to genocide; (b) act as a mechanism of early warning for the Secretary-General, and through him to the Security Council, by bringing to their attention potential situations that could result in genocide; (c) make recommendations to the Security Council, through the Secretary-General, on actions to prevent or halt genocide; (d) liaise with the UN system on activities for the prevention of genocide and work to enhance the UN capacity to analyse and manage information relating to genocide or related crimes.

[113] See William A. Schabas, *Genocide in International Law: The Crime of Crimes*, Cambridge University Press, 2009, p. 576.

proposing that change, and eventually accepted an upgrade of the Adviser's position (to that of Under Secretary-General level) but maintained its denomination as "Special Adviser on the Prevention of Genocide".[114] The inclusion of 'mass atrocities' would have brought certain crimes against humanity that fall short of genocide, such as the extermination of a civilian population that do not belong to any of the protected groups, within the mandate of the Special Adviser. However, the failure of that attempt can be read as demonstrating that the Security Council upholds the hierarchy among international crimes, with genocide being 'the apex'.

Meanwhile, in the *Genocide* case, the ICJ held that a particular State (Serbia) had failed to comply with the "normative and compelling"[115] international obligation to prevent genocide from being committed in another State's territory (Bosnia), which stems from Article I of the Genocide Convention. That obligation, according to the ICJ, is an extraterritorial one. Thus, it is compelling for a State "wherever it may be acting or may be able to act" in an appropriate manner to comply with it.[116] That is why Serbia could be held responsible for failing to prevent genocide in other countries – Bosnia and Herzegovina.

The ICJ, however, clearly stated the limitations of its decision which, it asserted, did not purport to establish a precedent applicable to all cases where a treaty instrument, or other binding legal norm, creates an obligation for States to prevent certain acts, or to find whether there is a general obligation on States to prevent the commission by other persons or entities of acts contrary to certain norms of general international law. On the contrary, the Court circumscribed the scope of its decision to determining "the specific scope of the duty to prevent in the Genocide Convention, and to the extent that such a determination is necessary to the

---

[114] *Ibid.*

[115] *Genocide* case, para. 427, *supra* note 2. The ICJ also addressed the issue regarding compliance, by Serbia, of the obligation to punish genocide.

[116] *Ibid.*, para. 183. Still, extraterritorial prevention of genocide is not an absolute, nor a one-size-fits-all obligation. In order to determine whether a State has complied with its duty to prevent, many factors should be taken into account in a case-by-case assessment, because the obligation varies greatly from one State to another, depending on their power to persuade or capacity to influence those persons involved in the commission or the planning of genocide to refrain from that activity. That capacity to influence in a particular case will be measured in accordance with the geographical distance and the political relations and other bonds between the obligated State and the place where the genocide is about to take place. Paras. 430, 433.

decision to be given on the dispute before it". Consequently, the language of the decision does not allow in and of itself the extension of the extraterritorial obligation to prevent genocide to crimes against humanity.

This supposed distinction between genocide and crimes against humanity should be debated and revisited. Although the very nature of the crime of genocide is heinous – the "intentional physical destruction on an ethnic group"[117] – that is not a valid argument in order to treat crimes against humanity more lightly. In many significant ways, crimes against humanity resemble genocide.

To begin with, it is important to look closer at the historical origins of both categories of crimes. At the London Conference, where the procedures for the Nuremberg trials were set, the drafters selected the phrase "crimes against humanity" in order to encompass not only the atrocities that the Nazis had committed against foreign populations, but also against their fellow citizens. At that time, there was a *lacuna* within international humanitarian law because crimes committed by a State against its own citizens were not condemned or prohibited by international norms. In other words, "the idea that a government would use its resources to murder its own people had not been anticipated adequately by the laws of war".[118]

The concept of genocide was conceived approximately at the same time by Raphael Lemkin, a survivor of the Holocaust who made the goal of his life to commit Nations to prevent, suppress and condemn genocide (a word that he coined to describe the Ottoman atrocities against the Armenian and the Nazi atrocities against the Jews). His efforts to have genocide acknowledged as an international crime turned out to be fruitful after the Nuremberg Tribunal's refusal to condemn the Nazi leaders for the crimes committed against their own people before the outbreak of the war. It was, in part, a reaction to the decision that in 1948 States condemned genocide as an international crime "whether committed in time of peace or in time of war" (Article I of the Genocide Convention). Since

---

[117] *Ibid.* In fact, Schabas is one of the scholars who asserts that the genocide label must be reserved for the "arguably most heinous crimes against humanity", which, according to him, is the intentional physical destruction of an ethnic group (*ibid.*). In that same article, Schabas describes other positions, according to which genocide is not necessarily the most serious international crimes. Of course, by asserting that genocide is more atrocious that other crimes against humanity, by no means does he minimize the latter's gravity. However, the differentiation could contribute to that effect, as it has been showed above.

[118] Luban, 2004, p. 93, see *supra* note 4.

then, and until the 1990s, crimes against humanity and genocide existed in parallel as two different categories of international crimes. Genocide was narrowly defined, but included acts committed in peacetime, whereas crimes against humanity were defined more broadly, but they were restricted by the requirement that they be committed in connection with war.[119]

That being said, the legal concept of crimes against humanity comprises "the most severe and abominable acts of violence and persecution":[120] murder (Article 3(1)(a)), extermination (Article 3(1)(b)), enslavement (Article 3(1)(c)), deportation (Article 3(1)(d)), imprisonment "in violation of fundamental rules of international law" (Article 3(1)(e)), torture (Article 3(1)(f)), sex crimes (including rape, sexual slavery, enforced prostitution, forced pregnancy, and forced sterilization) (Article 3(1)(g)), forced disappearance (Article 3(1)(i)), and the crime of apartheid (Article 3(1)(j)) (these crimes are usually clustered into the shorthand category of 'crimes of the murder type'),[121] and persecution based on political viewpoints, race, national origin, ethnicity, cultural backgrounds, religious beliefs, and gender (Articles 3(1)(h) and 3(3)) (these latter crimes are usually labelled as 'crimes of the persecution type').[122]

All those particular manifestations of crimes against humanity, in order to be characterized as such, have to be committed "as part of a widespread or systematic attack" and have to be directed "against any civilian population" (Article 3(1)).

In turn, the ICC Statute's definition of genocide [123] consists of committing specific acts – killing, seriously harming, inflicting conditions of life calculated to physically destroy, prevent birth and forcibly transferring children – directed against the members of one of the protected

---

[119] Schabas, 2008, p. 162, *supra* note 107.

[120] Luban, 2004, p. 98, see *supra* note 4. The Proposed Convention's definition of crimes against humanity (Article 3) is exactly like the definition of the ICC Statute (Article 7). From now on, I will refer to it as the Proposed Convention. However, the remarks made in this chapter regarding Article 3 of the Proposed Convention, also apply to Article 7 of the ICC Statute.

[121] *Ibid.*

[122] *Ibid.* According to Luban, whereas "'crimes of the murder type' are the most appalling evils that people have devised to visit on the bodies of others, 'crimes of the persecution type' are the most extreme humiliations to visit on their spirit" (p. 100).

[123] ICC Statute, Article 6.

groups (national, ethnic, racial, or religious groups), provided that they are committed with the specific intent "to destroy, in whole or in part" one of those groups, as such.

From that description, it is possible to pinpoint many similarities between crimes against humanity – at least those acts that belong to the 'murder type' – with genocide. In fact, the differences between both legal definitions can be boiled down to: a) the protected groups; b) the specific intent; and c) the policy element.

First, whereas crimes against humanity protect civilian populations – whatever group the civilians belong to – genocide protects the members of specific groups: national, ethnic, religious or racial groups. Moreover, in the specific case of the crime of persecution, the legal definition of crimes against humanity widens the scope of protected groups, adding political affiliation, culture, and gender. In David Luban's words, while the targets of genocide are "groups viewed as collective entities, with a moral dignity of their own", crimes against humanity target civilian popu-lations "viewed not as unified metaphysical entities but simply as collec-tions of individuals whose own human interests and dignity are at risk and whose vulnerability arises from their presence in the target population".[124]

Secondly, while the crime of genocide requires a specific intent or 'mens rea' (the intent to destroy in whole or in part one of the protected groups, as such), the definition of crimes against humanity only requires, where 'mens rea' is concerned, that the perpetrator acts with "knowledge of the attack" (Article 3(1)); his or her internal motives are irrelevant.

Finally, another difference between both legal definitions stems from the requirement that crimes against humanity be committed "as part of a widespread or systematic attack" and "pursuant to or in furtherance of a State organizational policy to commit such attack" (Article 3(2)(a)) – the so-called 'policy element'. Thus, although the material acts of crimes against humanity are necessarily carried out by specific persons, their per-formance is within a political organization.[125]

In contrast, neither the definition of genocide in the Genocide Con-vention nor the definition in the ICC Statute encompasses such an ele-ment. This difference between crimes against humanity and genocide may be relevant in some situations. As it has been described by David Lu-

---

[124] Luban, 2004, p. 98, *supra* note 4.
[125] *Ibid.*

ban,[126] a single person can commit genocide if, for instance, he dissemi-nates a deadly disease with specific intent (to destroy, in whole or in part, one of the protected groups). However, as he would be acting on his own, he could not be charged with the crime against humanity of extermination because of the absence of the 'policy element'.[127]

In short, it can be said that while the legal definition of genocide concentrates on the "collective character of the victim", the definition of crimes against humanity emphasizes "the collective character of the per-petrator".[128] Still, those differences are not significant enough to justify disparate treatment regarding prevention.

To illustrate this assertion, consider an extermination of a civilian population (Article 3(1)(b)) that takes place in a particular country, in a widespread or systematic fashion. If the attack is based on ethnic, reli-gious, racial or national categories, objectively, that crime not only amounts to the crime against humanity of extermination, but also to geno-cide.[129] The missing element would be the lack of the specific intent among the perpetrators, either because the motives of the perpetrators are unknown, ambiguous, or different from the specific intent required by genocide (for instance, the perpetrators do not care about the fate of the group of civilians that they are assaulting, but about gaining more power or more territories).

In such a situation, from the outside the international community most likely will only be aware of the existence of that attack. Although some States may have more details about the underpinnings of the con-flict, the real internal motives of the perpetrators are likely to surface once the deeds are committed or even during the post-facto investigations that eventually may be conducted. Even though the special intent of genocide is very significant in relation to the prosecution of individual perpetrators

---

[126] Ibid.

[127] Luban, ibid., in footnote 45, mentions a real-life example, involving Abba Kovner, a Hol-ocaust survivor, resistance fighter in the Vilna ghetto, who in 1945 attempted to poison the Hamburg water supply in revenge for the Holocaust. He confessed that his purpose was to kill six million Germans. He also observes that, unfortunately, "the possibility of a lone terrorist aiming to wipe out a population by introducing biological agents is all too imagi-nable". Still, some scholars argue that the policy element is also crucial regarding the crime of genocide (see, for instance, Schabas, 2005, pp. 876–877, supra note 104).

[128] Luban, 2004, p. 98, supra note 4.

[129] Ibid., p. 97.

and to the moral condemnation of his or her conduct, there is no reason to differentiate among crimes against humanity and genocide regarding prevention on that ground. The international community should not be concerned with the reason why criminals are exterminating a civilian population, but only that civilians are being exterminated, period.

Moreover, when an attack against a civilian population is launched, it is hard to know in advance how it will progress. In fact, an attack that starts as a massive illegal detention of civilians for whatever reason could easily evolve into genocide (the killing or extermination of the members of a national group, for instance). However, there is a high risk that, while the attack is taking place, and the real motives of the perpetrators are not clear, the international community will engage in an abstract debate about whether an imminent or actual attack against civilians amounts to genocide, "when the debate *should* be about how to avert or arrest it as soon as possible",[130] regardless of its legal categorization.

Another argument in favour of widening the scope of the obligation to prevent crimes against humanity has to do with the 'policy element' or the 'organized, policy-based decision' to commit the crimes.[131]

One of the main consequences of the policy requirement is that those crimes can only be committed by States (through their agents, or through groups with some kind of State support) or, at most, by a group acting and organized as a State, holding territory and resources under its control.

Given that feature of crimes against humanity, narrowing the obligation to prevent crimes against humanity to territories within the jurisdiction or control of each State would be pointless because States would already be under the obligation not to commit those crimes. Therefore, such an obligation to prevent is redundant, but for very particular situations in which a non-State actor is sufficiently organized and equipped as to be equated to a State. In Michael Reisman's telling metaphor, to obligate States to prevent crimes against humanity within their own territories is like "solemnly assigning the proverbial fox to guard the henhouse, and

---

[130] W. Michael Reisman, "Acting Before the Victims Become Victims: Preventing and Arresting Mass Murder", in *Case Western Reserve Journal of International Law,* 2007–2008, vol. 40, p. 84.

[131] Luban, 2004, p. 98, *supra* note 4.

then pretending that meaningful measures have been taken to protect the roost".[132]

The "Responsibility to Protect" ('R2P Report'), launched in December 2001 by the International Commission on Intervention and State Sovereignty ('ICISS'), that addresses the question of when, if ever, coercive – and in particular military – action against another State is a proper measure in order to protect people at risk in that other State,[133] is consistent with this idea – that some manifestations of crimes against humanity are as grave as genocide, and that both categories of crimes deserve the attention and reaction from the international community.

In fact, one of the issues dealt with in that report is in what cases military action would be appropriate for dealing with conflicts and mass atrocities, when other means of preventing it have failed. Specifically, the intervention would be justified if its purpose was to halt or avert "*large scale loss of life*, actual or apprehended, *with genocidal intent or not*, which is the product either of *deliberate State action*, or State neglect or inability to act, or a failed State situation" or "*large scale 'ethnic cleansing'* actual or apprehended, whether carried out by *killing, forced expulsion, acts of terror or rape*" (emphasis added).[134]

It is interesting how many elements both descriptions and the Proposed Convention's definition of crimes against humanity have in common; indeed, the former list fits well with the latter. Furthermore, the Commission has expressly stated that those broad situations that might deserve military intervention would typically include crimes against humanity and war crimes involving large-scale killing or ethnic cleansing.[135]

5.8. Concluding Remarks

Notwithstanding the limitations that Article 8(1) would impose on the obligation to prevent crimes against humanity, it cannot be denied that the whole Proposed Convention strongly emphasizes the need to prevent those heinous crimes. That emphasis is significantly relevant if we consider that, until recently, the international community has addressed

---

[132] Reisman, 2007–2008, p. 62, *supra* note 130.

[133] International Commission on Intervention and State Sovereignty, *Responsibility to Protect*, p. VII, available at http://responsibilitytoprotect.org/ICISS%20Report.pdf.

[134] *Ibid.*, p. 32.

[135] *Ibid.*, p. 33.

crimes against humanity through punishment of the perpetrators and, in some instances, through compensation to the victims. However, those strategies have failed to deter subsequent episodes of crimes against humanity.[136] Thus, it is particularly important to focus on the need to develop effective strategies to prevent crimes against humanity.

Clearly, any strategy about prevention has to be grounded on the belief that those crimes are preventable. Those crimes do not happen from one day to the next, but rather are the conclusion of a long and usually bloody process. Moreover, mass killings, persecutions, torture, and similar acts, committed within a context of an attack against a civilian population, take time, communication, organization, and resources. Thereby, there are many steps that can be taken in order to deter perpetrators and to address the conflict, that fall short of using force. Acknowledging that prevention of crimes against humanity is feasible is the necessary starting point of any debate on the issue, and one of the most salient merits of the Proposed Convention is that it reinforces and commits to that idea and triggers a much needed debate about the issue.

The limitation of the obligation to prevent crimes against humanity on those territories under the jurisdiction or control of the States Parties could be defended with reasonable arguments, such as the sovereign rights of other States or lack of control of areas beyond their borders.[137] These concerns deserve attention, as each country, in most cases, is the most appropriate entity to deal with its internal conflicts and to reinforce its institutions to foster rule of law and human rights.

However, we also have to take advantage of the space for debate that the Proposed Convention has triggered, in order to link crimes against

---

[136] Since WWII, that is to say, after the Nazi leaders were convicted in Nuremberg of crimes against humanity, "nearly 50 [genocides and political mass murders] have happened; [...] these episodes have cost the lives of at least 12 million and as many as 22 million non-combatants, more than all victims of internal and international wars since 1945". See Barbara Harff, "No Lessons Learned from the Holocaust? Assessing Risks of Genocide and Political Mass Murder since 1955", in *American Political Science Review*, 2003, vol. 97, no. 1, pp. 57–73. See also, *e.g.*, Reisman, 2007–2008, p. 57, *supra* note 130, arguing that there is no evidence that any prosecution has served to prevent any subsequent mass killing, and that the "international human rights movement has celebrated the trials at Nuremberg as a vindication of human rights and as a milestone on the road to installing a regime for international protection. The celebration tends to obscure the fact that no efforts were made to arrest or prevent the genocide that had led to the Nuremberg Trials".

[137] Gondek, 2009, pp. 57–58, *supra* note 31.

---

humanity prevention with the rest of the developments within international law and, in particular human rights law, that clearly are intended to obligate States to prevent genocide extraterritorially, to protect civilians from attacks by their own government, and to hold States accountable for the human rights violations committed beyond their territories. Only with this linkage will crimes against humanity be regarded for what they are: heinous international crimes committed against civilians by those (State authorities) that are supposed to take care of them. The international community owes this debate and this acknowledgment not only to itself, but also to the millions of victims of mass atrocities throughout history.

6

The Obligation to Prevent in the
Proposed Convention Examined in Light of the
Obligation to Prevent
in the Genocide Convention

Travis Weber[*]

6.1. Introduction

This chapter will examine and critique certain provisions in the Proposed International Convention on the Prevention and Punishment of Crimes Against Humanity ('Proposed Convention')[1] which specifically relate to the obligation to prevent crimes against humanity. This critique will be made in light of the provisions relating to the obligation to prevent genocide in the Convention on the Prevention and Punishment of the Crime of Genocide ('Genocide Convention'),[2] and subsequent developments pertaining to this obligation in international law.

Section 6.2. of this chapter compares the text of provisions impacting the obligation to prevent under the Genocide Convention with the text of similar provisions in the Proposed Convention. Section 6.3. discusses how the obligation to prevent might take shape under the Proposed Con-

---

[*]   **Travis Weber** currently serves as the Director of the Center for Religious Liberty at the Family Research Council in Washington, D.C., where he focuses on international and domestic legal and policy issues concerning human rights law and religious liberty. He formerly worked in private practice as a litigator bringing constitutional and civil rights cases primarily in the U.S. federal court system, and also has experience as criminal defense counsel. Travis graduated with an LL.M. in International Law (with distinction) and a Certificate in International Human Rights Law from Georgetown University Law Center, and obtained his J.D. from Regent University School of Law. He also served as an aviator and officer in the U.S. Navy after graduating from the U.S. Naval Academy with a B.S. in Economics. This writing has been undertaken in a personal capacity. All views expressed are his own, and do not necessarily reflect the views of the Family Research Council. All the Internet references were last accessed on 21 September 2014.

[1]   International Convention on the Prevention and Punishment of Crimes Against Humanity, proposed draft August 2010, see Annex 1.

[2]   Convention on the Prevention and Punishment of the Crime of Genocide, 9 December 1948, in UNTS, vol. 78, p. 277, entered into force on 12 January 1951.

---

vention in light of how it has developed under the Genocide Convention, including a discussion of how case law has impacted the existence and scope of an independent obligation to prevent.[3] Section 6.4. makes recommendations regarding the text of provisions impacting the obligation to prevent in the Proposed Convention after reviewing the obligation to prevent under the Genocide Convention.

6.2. Overview and Comparison of Provisions Informing the Obligation to Prevent in the Genocide Convention and Proposed Convention

6.2.1. Genocide Convention

Language regarding the obligation to prevent genocide appears in several places in the Genocide Convention. The word 'prevention' appears in the title of the Convention. In addition, Article I provides that genocide is an international crime that States Parties "undertake to prevent". And Article V requires States Parties to enact the "necessary legislation to give effect to the provisions" of the Genocide Convention domestically to ensure that genocide is punished. Lastly, Article VIII provides that States Parties may call upon the organs of the United Nations to take action to prevent genocide.

6.2.2. Proposed Convention

In comparison, the Proposed Convention contains more detailed language regarding the obligation to prevent. The word 'prevention' appears in the title, but the obligation to prevent is also mentioned three times in the preamble of the Proposed Convention, with elaboration on how it is to be fulfilled.[4]

Tracking the language in Article I of the Genocide Convention, Articles 1 and 2 of the Proposed Convention provide that crimes against

---

[3]   The term "independent obligation to prevent" here refers to the obligation to prevent as a stand-alone obligation under international law for States Parties to the Genocide Convention, as opposed to merely describing a goal or aim of States Parties to the Genocide Convention. See *infra* section 6.3.1.1. The "independent obligation to prevent" is discussed as it relates to a possible similar "independent obligation to prevent" under the Proposed Convention. However, it is only one aspect or part of the "obligation to prevent" discussed more generally throughout this chapter.

[4]   Proposed Convention, Preamble, paras. 6, 9, 11, see *supra* note 1.

humanity are international crimes and that Parties will "undertake to prevent" crimes against humanity. But the Proposed Convention goes further, stating that parties agree "[t]o cooperate, pursuant to the provisions of the present Convention, with other States Parties to prevent crimes against humanity",[5] and "[t]o assist other States Parties in fulfilling their obligations in accordance with Article 8 of the present Convention".[6]

Both conventions include language requiring domestic legislation. Article 8 of the Proposed Convention, however, is much broader in scope than the corresponding Article 5 of the Genocide Convention. Article 8 states that,

> [e]ach State Party shall enact necessary legislation and other measures as required by its Constitution or legal system to give effect to the provisions of the present Convention and in particular, to take effective legislative, administrative, judicial and other measures in accordance with the Charter of the United Nations to *prevent* and punish the commission of crimes against humanity in any territory under its jurisdiction or control.[7]

The "necessary legislation and other measures" is similar to the "necessary legislation" in Article V of the Genocide Convention, and punishment is mentioned in both conventions. But the Proposed Convention also includes "to prevent", language that is not present in Article V of the Genocide Convention.

Article 8 of the Proposed Convention is also different in that it details lengthy obligations under a section titled "Prevention". Of these, the only provision carried over from Article VIII of the Genocide Convention is a provision allowing States Parties to call on U.N. organs to take action, which appears in paragraph 13 of Article 8 of the Proposed Convention. Beyond this shared provision, the Proposed Convention additionally provides that,

> 12. Each State Party shall endeavor to take measures in accordance with its domestic legal system to prevent crimes against humanity. Such measures include, but are not limited to, ensuring that any advocacy of

---

5   *Ibid.*, Article 2(2)(a).

6   *Ibid.*, Article 2(2)(d).

7   *Ibid.*, Article 8(1) (emphasis added).

national, racial, or religious hatred that constitutes incitement to discrimination, hostility, or violence shall be prohibited by law.

[...]

14. States Parties may also call upon the competent organs of a regional organization to take such action in accordance with the Charter of the United Nations as they consider appropriate for the prevention and punishment of crimes against humanity.

15. States Parties shall develop educational and informational programs regarding the prohibition of crimes against humanity including the training of law enforcement officers, military personnel, or other relevant public officials in order to:

    (a) Prevent the involvement of such officials in crimes against humanity;

    (b) Emphasize the importance of prevention and investigations in relation to c crimes against humanity;

16. Each State Party shall ensure that orders or instructions prescribing, authorizing, or encouraging crimes against humanity are prohibited. Each State Party shall guarantee that a person who refuses to obey such an order will not be punished. Moreover, each State Party shall take the necessary measures to ensure that persons who have reason to believe that crimes against humanity have occurred or are planned to occur, and who report the matter to their superiors or to appropriate authorities or bodies vested with powers of review or remedy are not punished for such conduct.[8]

In brief, these provisions require States Parties to: (1) prohibit speech advocating national, racial, or religious hatred constituting incitement to discrimination, hostility, or violence; (2) educate security personnel about crimes against humanity; and (3) prohibit orders to carry out crimes against humanity, with protection being granted to those who refuse to obey, or report, such orders. While both conventions allow States Parties to call on U.N. organs to take action, the Proposed Convention

---

[8] *Ibid.*, Article 8(12) and (14)–(16).

further provides that States Parties may ask regional organizations to do the same.

Finally, the Proposed Convention also provides for a committee to aid in prevention,[9] a provision absent from the Genocide Convention.

6.3. Predictions for the Obligation to Prevent in the Proposed Convention in Light of the Obligation to Prevent in the Genocide Convention

An examination of the obligation to prevent in the Proposed Convention consists of three separate analyses: (1) whether an independent obligation to prevent exists; (2) if it exists, what is its scope; and (3) the extent to which this obligation is affected by domestic legislation criminalizing acts leading to crimes against humanity. The independent obligation to prevent very likely exists under the Proposed Convention just like it was found to exist under the Genocide Convention. Its scope, however, is somewhat different from that under the Genocide Convention. Finally, the provisions referring to domestic criminal legislation in the Proposed Convention are significantly different from the corresponding provisions of the Genocide Convention.

6.3.1. Whether There Exists an Independent Obligation to Prevent

The Genocide Convention is generally considered to invoke the independent obligation to prevent. It is very likely that the Proposed Convention will also invoke the independent obligation to prevent, considering the similarity of the language in the two conventions, and the close relation between the crimes of genocide and crimes against humanity.

6.3.1.1. International Case Law Supports Finding an Independent Obligation to Prevent under the Proposed Convention

The International Court of Justice ('ICJ'), in *Application of the Convention on the Prevention and Punishment of the Crime of Genocide (Bosnia and Herzegovina v. Serbia and Montenegro)* ('*Bosnia and Herzegovina* case'),[10] held there is an independent obligation to prevent genocide under

---

9   *Ibid.*, Article 19(4)–(10).

10 International Court of Justice, *Application of the Convention on the Prevention and Punishment of the Crime of Genocide (Bosnia and Herzegovina v. Serbia and Montenegro)*, Judgment, 26 February 2007.

the Genocide Convention. In this case, the ICJ addressed both the nature and scope of this obligation.

The ICJ stated, regarding the nature of the obligation, that the "undertaking" to prevent genocide under the Genocide Convention is "not merely hortatory or purposive", but is an unqualified obligation to prevent genocide that is distinct from other provisions of the Genocide Convention.[11] The Court found support for the independent obligation to prevent in the universal condemnation of genocide and the civilizing purpose of the Genocide Convention.[12] The Court also looked to the drafting history of the Genocide Convention, particularly how the drafters agreed to detach "undertake to prevent" from "in accordance with the following Articles", observing that,

> [the] movement of the undertaking from the Preamble to the first operative Article and the removal of the linking clause ("in accordance with the following Articles") – confirm that Article [I] does impose distinct obligations over and above those imposed by other Articles of the [Genocide] Convention. In particular, the Contracting Parties have a direct obligation to prevent genocide.[13]

Thus, in the Court's view, the obligation to prevent was no longer tied to other provisions in the Genocide Convention, and the Genocide Convention invoked a direct and independent obligation to prevent.

Because of the similarity between the two conventions and their respective subject matter, the Proposed Convention, were it to become law, would very likely be seen to include an independent obligation to prevent. However, this argument has weaknesses. First, although the ICJ noted the presence of the obligation to prevent in other treaties, it stated there is not a general obligation to prevent applicable in the same way to multiple treaties, and confined itself to interpreting the obligation to prevent under the Genocide Convention specifically.[14] Second, the Proposed Convention necessarily lacks a drafting history, which the ICJ used to find an independent obligation to prevent in the Genocide Convention.

---

11 *Ibid.*, para. 162.
12 *Ibid.*, paras. 161–62.
13 *Ibid.*, para. 165.
14 *Ibid.*, para. 429.

Nevertheless, it is likely that the ICJ's reasoning supports a finding of an independent obligation to prevent in the Proposed Convention. As with genocide, there exists universal condemnation of crimes against humanity, and like the Genocide Convention, the Proposed Convention has a "civilizing" purpose. Moreover, the Proposed Convention includes the phrase "undertake to prevent" in Article 2, where it is detached from any "in accordance with" language that would result in it only applying to immediately subsequent provisions.[15] Thus, despite the ICJ's statements regarding each convention being interpreted differently, it seems likely that the Proposed Convention will be found to include an independent obligation to prevent crimes against humanity.

6.3.1.2. Other Provisions of the Proposed Convention May Preclude the Independent Obligation to Prevent

The next question is whether the Proposed Convention contains provisions precluding any useful analogy to the finding of an independent obligation under the Genocide Convention. Although Articles 1 and 2 of the Proposed Convention appear to support an independent obligation to prevent, the question is whether they are limited by other provisions of the Proposed Convention not present in the Genocide Convention.

The most significant of these new provisions in the Proposed Convention is Article 8(1), which requires that a State Party "take effective legislative, administrative, judicial and other measures in accordance with the Charter of the United Nations to prevent and punish the commission of crimes against humanity *in any territory under its jurisdiction or control*".[16]

One question is whether the drafters of the Proposed Convention intended to use this language – which is not present in the Genocide Convention – to foreclose an independent obligation to prevent. Even if that was their intent, such a goal would be difficult to accomplish. The core grounds upon which the ICJ found the independent obligation to prevent

---

[15] Although after "undertake to prevent", Article 2 continues "and to investigate, prosecute, and punish those responsible for such crimes", such language very likely still allows the "undertake to prevent" to remain detached. This additional language does not diminish the independent obligation to prevent as when "undertake to prevent" immediately proceeds "in accordance with other Articles" or some similar language.

[16] Proposed Convention, Article 8(1) (emphasis added), see *supra* note 1.

were the civilizing purpose of the convention and the "undertake" language in Article 1, grounds essentially unchanged in the Proposed Convention. The Article 8 language regarding territory is not present in the corresponding Article V of the Genocide Convention, which only requires States Parties "to enact, in accordance with their respective Constitutions, the necessary legislation to give effect to the provisions of the present Convention".[17] Article V of the Genocide Convention also does not require that "legislative, administrative, judicial, and other measures" be taken. But the fact that the ICJ found the independent obligation to prevent based on other provisions of the Genocide Convention suggests that the same independent obligation to prevent will be found in the Proposed Convention without needing to base such a finding on Article 8, and will also be found whether or not the word 'prevent' is included in Article 8.

The more difficult question is whether the drafters intended the language "in any territory under its jurisdiction or control" to limit the obligation to prevent in the Proposed Convention. While this question appears to be answered in the affirmative, limitations on the obligation to prevent affect the *scope* of the obligation to prevent (to be addressed later in this paper), not questions of whether the independent obligation to prevent *exists*. At a minimum, Article 8 does not eliminate the independent obligation to prevent under the Proposed Convention.

6.3.2. The Scope of the Independent Obligation to Prevent

6.3.2.1. The Scope of the Obligation to Prevent Defined in the *Bosnia and Herzegovina* Case Partially Defines the Scope of the Obligation in the Proposed Convention

6.3.2.1.1. The Scope of the Obligation to Prevent in the *Bosnia and Herzegovina* Case

The ICJ, in the *Bosnia and Herzegovina* case, outlined a rather expansive definition of the obligation to prevent under the Genocide Convention. The duty to prevent places States under a 'positive obligation' to act to prevent genocide,[18] and incurs on any "State Party which, in a given situation, has it in its power to contribute to restraining in any degree the

---

[17] Genocide Convention, Article V, see *supra* note 2.

[18] *Application of the Convention on the Prevention and Punishment of the Crime of Genocide (Bosnia and Herzegovina v. Serbia and Montenegro)*, para. 432, see *supra* note 10.

commission of genocide".[19] The obligation to prevent stands alone and "has its own scope".[20]

> [This obligation] is both normative and compelling. It is not merged in the duty to punish, nor can it be regarded as simply a component of that duty. It has its own scope, which extends beyond the particular case envisaged in Article [VIII], namely reference to the competent organs of the United Nations, for them to take such action as they deem appropriate. *Even if and when these organs have been called upon, this does not mean that the States Parties to the Convention are relieved of the obligation to take such action as they can to prevent genocide from occurring*, while respecting the United Nations Charter and any decisions that may have been taken by its competent organs.[21]

The obligation to prevent applies "wherever [a State] may be acting or may be able to act in ways appropriate to meeting the obligations in question. The extent of that ability in law and fact is considered",[22] as follows: the obligation to prevent is determined by conduct, not result. The obligation of a State in prevention is not to succeed, but rather "to employ all means reasonably available" in the prevention of genocide. A State must "manifestly [...] take all measures [...] within its power" to prevent genocide, and "which might have contributed to preventing the genocide".[23]

What is "reasonable" conduct within a State's power? The answer hinges on "the capacity to influence effectively the action of persons likely to commit, or already committing, genocide".[24] The capacity to influence depends "on the geographical distance of the State concerned from the scene of the events, and on the strength of the political links, as well as links of all other kinds, between the authorities of that State and the main actors in the events".[25] But this capacity to influence is limited by international law, so "a State's capacity to influence may vary depending

---

19 *Ibid.*, para. 461.

20 *Ibid.*, para. 427.

21 *Ibid.*, para. 427 (emphasis added).

22 *Ibid.*, para. 183.

23 *Ibid.*, para. 430.

24 *Ibid.*

25 *Ibid.*

on its particular legal position vis-à-vis the situations and persons facing the danger, or the reality, of genocide".[26] Thus the requirement of "reasonable" action does not exceed the limits of international law. It is highly fact-specific and changes with the circumstances. Finally, a State cannot escape the obligation to engage in such reasonable conduct by claiming that even if it did everything possible, genocide would still have occurred.[27]

A State can only have breached its obligation to prevent if genocide actually occurs, and "a State's obligation to prevent, and the corresponding duty to act, arise at the instant that the State learns of, or should normally have learned of, the existence of a serious risk that genocide will be committed".[28] From then on, "if the State has available to it means likely to have a deterrent effect on those suspected of preparing genocide, or reasonably suspected of harbouring specific intent (*dolus specialis*), it is under a duty to make such use of these means as the circumstances permit".[29]

The ICJ's interpretation requiring a State to "take all measures [...] within its power", and to act in accordance with its "capacity to influence" appears to suggest that the obligation to prevent is greater for more powerful nations that can do more to prevent crimes against humanity. Parts of the ICJ's opinion appear to support this view, and suggests a subjective standard that will vary from State to State – which in turn will result in a more robust obligation to prevent. This would appear to contravene the "each State's vote is equal" principle which still largely defines the U.N. Even though some U.N. bodies accord more influence to certain States (for example, the permanent members of the Security Council), any obligation to prevent executed through consensus at the U.N. to the exclusion of other methods and mechanisms risks failure due to gridlock and disagreement among at least some of the large number of U.N. Member States (or due to gridlock within the Security Council). This in turn would result in an obligation to prevent which is not very 'potent'.[30]

---

[26] *Ibid.*

[27] *Ibid.*

[28] *Ibid.*, para. 431.

[29] *Ibid.*

[30] William Schabas, *Genocide in International Law*, Cambridge University Press, 2009, p. 525.

Therefore, the obligation to prevent must be fulfilled according to each State's ability. While it is understandable why the U.N. holds up the "each State's vote is equal" principle within its decision-making, each State's power, leverage, and action is not equal in the international community. A State's relative power in the international arena undoubtedly affects its capacity to influence other States on a variety of matters, including the prevention of crimes against humanity. Therefore, in addition to acting within U.N. bodies, States can take bilateral or multilateral measures against offending States as part of their obligation to prevent crimes against humanity in those States. These measures may include economic sanctions against offending States, freezing funds of those States' officials, and a variety of other measures which do not need to be taken within U.N. bodies. States may even act through regional organizations such as the North Atlantic Treaty Organization or the Organization of American States. Finally, States may condemn other States' action on their own or through some type of joint statement even if there is insufficient support for a U.N. General Assembly resolution on the matter. Such bilateral and multilateral action helps ensure a more robust obligation to prevent, and prevents it from becoming a mere 'paper tiger'.[31]

To summarize, the obligation to prevent arises from the moment the State learned or should have learned there was a serious risk of genocide being committed, and entails actions that a State can take, within the bounds of international law, when it has the capacity to influence possible perpetrators of genocide by conducting itself in a way likely to have a deterrent effect on the perpetrators.

6.3.2.1.2. Differences Between the Text of the Two Conventions Affect the Scope of the Independent Obligation to Prevent Described in the *Bosnia and Herzegovina* Case as Applied to the Proposed Convention

The Proposed Convention differs somewhat from the Genocide Convention in its scope of the obligation to prevent. Considering the similarities between the two conventions, it would follow that any independent obligation to prevent in the Proposed Convention has a scope similar to that of the obligation to prevent in the Genocide Convention. But the ICJ's

---

[31] Morten Bergsmo, Comments in 'International Crime of Genocide' class, Georgetown University Law Center, Washington, D.C., 18 October 2010.

determination of scope under the Genocide Convention was grounded solely on the "undertake to prevent" language, while the Proposed Convention contains additional language in Articles 2 and 8 that may impact the scope of the obligation to prevent.

Both Article V of the Genocide Convention and Article 8(1) of the Proposed Convention provide for "necessary legislation" to give effect to their provisions. But Article 8(1) further provides that States Parties shall "in particular, take effective legislative, administrative, judicial and other measures in accordance with the Charter of the United Nations to *prevent* and punish the commission of crimes against humanity *in any territory under its jurisdiction or control*".[32] Thus all Article 8(1) measures are limited by territory and the U.N. Charter. Furthermore, under Article 2 of the Proposed Convention, States Parties are obligated to "cooperate" with other states to prevent crimes against humanity. These specifications and modifications add detail to the independent obligation to prevent derived from Articles 1 and 2.

Article 8 would not limit the independent obligation to prevent if the drafters intended for Article 8 to apply only to domestic law-making efforts, for the obligation would still permit intervention and other international efforts as governed by Articles 1 and 2. Support for this argument is found in the fact that the drafters left the "undertake" language in Article 2, which, according to the ICJ, is the foundation of the independent obligation to prevent. If the drafters had wanted to impact this obligation, they would have removed this language or included explicit language to the effect that Article 8 limited Article 2. Under this interpretation, while the specific actions prescribed in Article 8(1) apply to areas under a State's jurisdiction and control, an independent obligation to prevent still applies extraterritorially.

Another interpretation would suggest that the inclusion of language in Article 8 ensuring that measures are taken in accordance with the U.N. Charter positively shows that the provision applies not only to domestic measures, but also to international action and other scenarios implicating the U.N. Charter. The provision ensuring compliance with the U.N. Charter acknowledges what the ICJ recognized in the *Bosnia and Herzegovina* case – that intervention must occur within the bounds of the international legal framework. Regardless, either of these interpretations

---

[32] Proposed Convention, Article 8(1) (emphasis added), see *supra* note 1.

ensures international and transnational accountability by preventing perpetrators of crimes against humanity from being able to hide behind State
sovereignty with impunity.

However, the language of Article 2 – "States Parties to the present
Convention undertake to prevent crimes against humanity and to investigate, prosecute, and punish those responsible for such crimes" – includes
language on investigation, prosecution, and punishment, which is not
found in Article I of the Genocide Convention. The inclusion of these
terms, which are very similar to those used in Article 8, suggests that the
Article 2 obligation to prevent is intertwined with the Article 8 obligation
to prevent. By including this language in Article 2, the drafters possibly
intended to limit the scope of any obligation to prevent arising out of the
"undertake to prevent" language in Article 2.

The problem with this view, however, is that it undercuts accountability under international law, and allows perpetrators of crimes against
humanity to hide behind State sovereignty. Perhaps the drafters of the
Proposed Convention are attempting to achieve a broader consensus
among States by limiting the obligation to prevent to a State's own territory.[33] If the obligation to prevent in the Proposed Convention only extends
to areas under a State's territorial jurisdiction and control, then a State
Party to the Proposed Convention would not be obligated to take any action to prevent crimes against humanity in any territory not under its jurisdiction and control. It would not even be obligated to take lesser action,
such as notifying the appropriate U.N. entities of potential crimes against
humanity. Yet such passivity seems incongruent with the whole purpose
of international criminal law – holding individual perpetrators to account
and preventing them from hiding behind the shield of State sovereignty.

Moreover, the 'territorial interpretation' would seem incongruent
with other sections of the Proposed Convention providing for States Parties to call on the appropriate U.N. bodies to prevent crimes against humanity. These crimes would presumably not be occurring in a State's own
territory, for a State would likely have no need to call on the U.N. to prevent crimes in its own territory. Rather, a reasonable interpretation is that
the drafters of Article 8 would like to fight impunity for crimes against
humanity, but are being realistic in light of the challenges observed re-

---

[33] Morten Bergsmo, Comments in 'International Crime of Genocide' class, see *supra* note
31.

garding extraterritorial enforcement of the Genocide Convention and other international criminal law instruments. Nevertheless, if the Proposed Convention sacrifices enough extraterritorial application (a crucial aspect of ensuring compliance with human rights treaties) in an attempt to be "realistic", it is hard to see how it avoids being gutted of its core aim of ensuring accountability across national borders.[34]

Given the similarity of the conventions and their subject matter, the ICJ's description of the obligation to prevent genocide in the *Bosnia and Herzegovina* case is very instructive and applicable to the obligation to prevent crimes against humanity in the Proposed Convention. While the ICJ noted that it would interpret conventions separately and on their own merits,[35] the fact that the Court looked to the isolated language of Article 1 of the Genocide Convention suggests that it would also look to the isolated language of Article 2 of the Proposed Convention to find a similar obligation to prevent. Therefore, the Proposed Convention likely also includes an expansive, independent obligation to prevent, especially considering the "civilizing" purpose of both conventions and the similarity of their respective subject matter. While some of the textual differences discussed above could be used to support a more limited obligation to prevent, the balance of the provisions point toward a strong, independent, extraterritorial obligation to prevent.

6.3.2.1.3. Implications for an Extraterritorial Obligation to Prevent in the Proposed Convention: Sudan and Other Situations of Application

An expanded independent obligation to prevent in the Proposed Convention would place obligations on States Parties to prevent more of the human rights violations consistently occurring around the world. Ascertaining that a human rights crisis has occurred is not always that difficult. It can be more difficult, however, to ascertain facts quickly and with precision sufficient to properly label, categorize, and classify various human rights violations or criminal activity. This is the case for a variety of reasons, but primary obstacles include geographical challenges and limited media access to areas where human rights violations may occur – obsta-

---

[34] *Ibid.*

[35] *Application of the Convention on the Prevention and Punishment of the Crime of Genocide (Bosnia and Herzegovina v. Serbia and Montenegro)*, para. 429, see *supra* note 10.

cles which only increase as a regime seeks to conceal its actions. Genocide can be one of the most difficult acts to definitively establish quickly due to its numerous elements. By the time acts of genocide have been established, it is often too late to do anything to stop them.

In the last several years alone, numerous situations have developed around the world which may or may not have witnessed genocide, but very likely included the commission of crimes against humanity. For example, the civil war in Syria, and Boko Haram's actions in Nigeria, are but two more recent examples in which a case can more easily be made that human rights violations have amounted to crimes against humanity, even if not genocide. While some may have quibbled about whether genocide has occurred in Sudan (or at least made a conscious choice to avoid recognizing it as such), it is even less plausible to deny that crimes against humanity have occurred there. An independent obligation to prevent in the Proposed Convention would place obligations on States Parties to take measures to prevent such atrocities.

If crimes against humanity are actually occurring in these locations, it is very likely that other nations would be obligated in their "conduct" to "employ all means reasonably available"[36] to stop them, even though these locations are outside of their territory. Whatever the likelihood that genocide has occurred in Sudan, the likelihood that crimes against humanity (containing one less element) have occurred there is greater. Thus, while nations shrugged off their obligation to prevent genocide in Sudan by avoiding the conclusion that genocide was actually occurring,[37] they will not be able to so easily dodge the same conclusion regarding crimes against humanity.[38] Assuming that any of the crimes defined in Article 3 of the Proposed Convention – murder, extermination, forcible transfer, rape, or persecution (among others) as part of a widespread or systematic attack against civilians, with knowledge the acts are occurring – are oc-

---

[36] *Ibid.*, para. 430.

[37] See Duncan Currie, *Powell's Darfur Declaration: Why Foggy Bottom Took So Long to Characterize the Sudanese – and Rwandan – Atrocities as "Genocide"*, Weekly Standard, 15 September 2004, http://www.weeklystandard.com/Content/Public/Articles/000/000/004/627ismid.asp.

[38] See, *e.g.*, Rami G. Khouri, *Whose Crimes Against Humanity?*, Opposite Editorial, New York Times, 17 July 2008, available at http://www.nytimes.com/2008/07/17/opinion/17iht-edkhouri.1.14574302.html.

curring in Sudan,[39] States Parties to the Proposed Convention taking no action would much more likely be in violation of the obligation to prevent than they would be under the Genocide Convention. Moreover, considering that the obligation may vary from State to State, States Parties with more influence over Sudan, such as those with strong economic ties,[40] might have a greater obligation to prevent crimes against humanity.

It does not necessarily follow that States will fulfill their obligation to prevent under the Proposed Convention in this manner. States have been hesitant to invoke their obligation to prevent under the Genocide Convention by calling the acts in Sudan genocide, and they will likely be equally as hesitant to invoke their obligation to prevent in the Proposed Convention by calling these acts crimes against humanity. If, however, the obligation to prevent only extends to areas under a State's jurisdiction and control, only Sudan (and possibly any States with armed forces controlling its territory) would be obligated to prevent crimes against humanity. But as mentioned above, such a result undercuts the very purpose of international criminal law – individual accountability.

Interestingly, the prevention of genocide in Sudan and other States may be directly influenced in another manner by the existence of a Proposed Convention with an obligation to prevent. As Juan Mendez, former U.N. Special Advisor on the Prevention of Genocide, noted, the Special Advisor's office could have provided the U.N. Security Council with advance warning of possible genocide, and of deteriorating situations, that would enable States to better fulfill their obligation to prevent.[41] But this access to the U.N. Security Council did not materialize, and the loss of services to populations was not satisfactory to the Security Council as an early indication of possible genocide.[42] The Special Advisor's office thereafter attempted to use more serious indicators such as the loss of life.[43] But the problem with this and similar indicators is that they may

---

[39] *Ibid.*

[40] Gwen Thompkins, *Chinese Influence in Sudan Is Subtle, Complicated*, NPR, 29 July 2008, available at http://www.npr.org/templates/story/story.php?storyId=92282540.

[41] Juan Mendez, Former U.N. Special Advisor on the Prevention of Genocide, Comments in 'International Crime of Genocide' class, Georgetown University Law Center, Washington, D.C., 18 October 2010.

[42] *Ibid.*

[43] *Ibid.*

develop too late in the progression of events to prevent genocide once they are recognized.[44]

As mentioned above, atrocities not meeting all the criteria of genocide cannot be called genocide. But if States wait until genocide has occurred to describe acts as genocide, they have by then violated their obligation to prevent genocide.[45] Nevertheless, States are not to blame under this framework, for while events are still developing on the ground, these often 'merely' constitute crimes against humanity. The Proposed Convention may help solve this conundrum, for if events are characterized as crimes against humanity, their occurrence could trigger an obligation to prevent events which could later develop into genocide. Although the occurrence of crimes against humanity may be too late for their own prevention, triggering an obligation to prevent at this point will at least aid in the prevention of genocide and fulfilment of the obligation to prevent under the Genocide Convention.

Regardless of its exact contours, the scope of the obligation to prevent under the Proposed Convention is very likely an extraterritorial one, in keeping with the expansive scope of the obligation to prevent under the Genocide Convention, and States would be obligated in their "conduct" to "employ all means reasonably available" to prevent crimes against humanity (within the bounds of international law). This obligation to prevent would be implicated more often than that of the Genocide Convention due to the number of human rights crises which may not be definitely established as genocide but certainly constitute crimes against humanity. Another advantage of an expanded independent obligation to prevent under the Proposed Convention is that even if it is not always successful in preventing crimes against humanity, it will help prevent genocide by ensuring human rights violations are stopped before they reach the point of genocide.

6.3.2.2. The Responsibility to Protect May Impact the Scope of the Obligation to Prevent in the Proposed Convention

The scope of the obligation to prevent is also affected by the more recently developing humanitarian doctrine known as the Responsibility to Pro-

---

[44]   *Ibid.*
[45]   *Ibid.*

tect populations from mass atrocities. According to the U.N. Report of the High-Level Panel on Threats, Challenges, and Changes, there is an

> [...] emerging norm that there is a collective international Responsibility to Protect, exercisable by the Security Council authorizing military intervention as a last resort, in the event of genocide and other largescale killing, ethnic cleansing or serious violations of international humanitarian law which sovereign Governments have proved powerless or unwilling to prevent.[46]

It might be suggested that the Responsibility to Protect should permit State action outside of the U.N. Charter and its decision-making bodies. For if a State has a 'positive obligation'[47] to "contribute to restraining in any degree the commission of genocide",[48] can it really fulfil this obligation while always acting within the U.N. framework? Is it nonsensical to claim that the 'positive obligation' to attempt to prevent these horrible international crimes is fulfilled by taking a public international stance in word only and not in action? Moreover, especially in light of the Responsibility to Protect, it would appear difficult to argue that the obligation to prevent is satisfied merely by continuing to protest a deadlocked U.N. Security Council which refuses to act. Imagine that this protesting nation borders a State where genocide is likely to take place, and can deploy armed forces which would certainly be able to stop whatever action is taking place, and yet the Security Council still refuses to act. A nation that acted in such a situation would appear to be fulfilling its obligation to prevent, especially considering the "civilizing" purposes of the Genocide and Proposed Conventions.

However, the ICJ in the *Bosnia and Herzegovina* case appears to suggest the opposite, for despite its broad and powerful statements regarding the obligation to prevent, the ICJ limits itself by subjecting the obligation to prevent to the U.N. framework. At least one U.N. legal advisor has publicly offered her support of this view when she stated that the Responsibility to Protect consists only of those actions able to be executed within

---

[46] U.N. High-Level Panel on Threats, Challenges, and Change, *Report: A More Secure World: Our Shared Responsibility*, 2 December 2004, U.N. Doc. A/59/565, available at http://www.unrol.org/files/gaA.59.565_En.pdf.

[47] *Application of the Convention on the Prevention and Punishment of the Crime of Genocide (Bosnia and Herzegovina v. Serbia and Montenegro)*, para. 432, see *supra* note 10.

[48] *Ibid.*, para. 461.

the confines of the legal authority of the U.N. Charter, that there is no Responsibility to Protect independent of the U.N. Charter, and that actions taken by a State outside of this framework would be illegal under international law.[49] Many recognize that working within the U.N. framework will likely delay action to prevent crimes against humanity. Nevertheless, currently only "extreme" views of the Responsibility to Protect would authorize action outside of the U.N. framework.[50]

While the obligation to prevent still must be fulfilled within the bounds of international law, increased acceptance of the Responsibility to Protect may help shift the normative meaning of the obligation to prevent toward approval of intervention. Although the Responsibility to Protect is a 'collective' responsibility, not a right of unilateral intervention, the collective is shaped by the views of individual States when they recognize their own individual Responsibility to Protect. As the Responsibility to Protect becomes more widely accepted, a more interventionist view of the obligation to prevent may become more widespread. Ultimately, to the extent that the Responsibility to Protect supports and bolsters the independent obligation to prevent under the Genocide Convention, it will likely similarly support and bolster an independent obligation to prevent under the Proposed Convention.

6.3.2.3. The Obligation to Prevent May Constitute Customary International Law

If the obligation to prevent in Article I of the Genocide Convention is found to constitute customary international law,[51] such a shift would likely impact the obligation to prevent under the Proposed Convention. Finding the obligation to prevent to be customary international law could create potential liability for States before the ICJ if a State was found in violation of the obligation to prevent.[52] If a customary international law obligation is found and is considered in light of the obligation to prevent in the Genocide and the Proposed Conventions, the obligation to prevent

---

49 Patricia O'Brien, U.N. Under-Secretary-General for Legal Affairs and U.N. Legal Counsel, Address at Georgetown University Law Center, Washington, D.C., "Peace, Justice, and the Rule of Law", 13 October 2010.

50 Schabas, 2009, p. 531, see *supra* note 30.

51 *Ibid.*, p. 524.

52 *Ibid.*

would remain as it is or expand in scope, as the contours of the new customary international law obligation are drawn, and found to either overlap
or depart from the boundaries of the obligation to prevent contained in the
Genocide and Proposed Conventions.

6.3.2.4. The Obligation to Prevent May Include the Obligation to Promote Democracy

The expansive and still largely undefined obligation to prevent might include the obligation to promote democracy to the extent that democracy
aids in the prevention of genocide and crimes against humanity. If it is
true that mature, developed democracies do not commit genocide against
their own populations,[53] the obligation to prevent could include the obligation of each State, independently and in co-operation with other States,
to help develop democracies around the world. This is a realistic goal, as
illustrated by the post-World War II transformation of Germany and Ja-
pan from battered dictatorships to advanced democracies, and of many
other nations from belligerent authoritarian regimes to mature democracies.[54] The obligation to prevent could also include the obligation to deter
possible acts of genocide by warning and threatening political, economic,
and military repercussions against potential perpetrators,[55] which fits
neatly with the 'capacity to influence' requirement of the ICJ.[56] Finally,
the obligation to prevent could include actually taking political, economic,
and/or military action,[57] such as sanctions, which of course would have to
comply with international law and the U.N. legal framework. Democracy
promotion is arguably part of the obligation to prevent genocide, and
therefore is arguably part of the obligation to prevent crimes against humanity.

---

[53] Neal Riemer, "The Urgent Need for a Global Human Rights Regime", in Neal Riemer
(ed.), *Protection Against Genocide: Mission Impossible?*, Praeger Publishers, 2000, pp. 5–
6.

[54] *Ibid.*, pp. 148–150.

[55] *Ibid.*, pp. 6–7.

[56] *Application of the Convention on the Prevention and Punishment of the Crime of Genocide
(Bosnia and Herzegovina v. Serbia and Montenegro)*, para. 430, see *supra* note 10.

[57] Riemer, 2000, p. 7, see *supra* note 53.

6.3.3. The Obligation to Prevent as Satisfied by Enacting Domestic Legislation Prohibiting Certain Preparatory Acts

In a major departure from the Genocide Convention, the Proposed Convention requires not only the "necessary" implementing legislation,[58] but also domestic legislation in order to prevent crimes against humanity, requiring States to "endeavor to take measures" to "*prevent* crimes against humanity", including, but "not limited to, ensuring that any advocacy of national, racial, or religious hatred that constitutes incitement to discrimination, hostility, or violence shall be prohibited by law".[59] Two aspects of this domestic legislation will be examined: (1) its similarities with how the Convention Against Torture ('CAT') also addresses prevention through domestic legislation, and (2) how domestic measures outlawing hate speech and advocacy impact free speech laws and policies.

6.3.3.1. Similarities with the CAT in Enacting Domestic Prevention Measures

The language pertaining to domestic legislation regarding crimes against humanity in the Proposed Convention is closer to the language regarding 'territorial' legislation on torture in the CAT than it is to any provision in the Genocide Convention. Article 2(1) of the CAT provides that "[e]ach State Party shall take effective legislative, administrative, judicial or other measures to prevent acts of torture in any territory under its jurisdiction".[60] On its face, this language about prevention is almost identical to Article 8(1) of the Proposed Convention – yet this provision refers to territory under a State's "jurisdiction or control", whereas the CAT just refers to "jurisdiction". This difference provides slightly broader liability for entities under the Proposed Convention who may be controlling a territory yet not have it under their jurisdiction. In addition, Article 2(1) bears similarities to Article 8(12) – placed specifically in a "prevention" section of the Proposed Convention – which provides that "[e]ach State Party shall endeavor to take measures in accordance with its domestic legal system to prevent crimes against humanity". Moreover, the commentary on the CAT confirms that the obligation to prevent in the CAT refers

---

58 Proposed Convention, Article 8(1), see *supra* note 1.

59 *Ibid.*, Article 8(12) (emphasis added).

60 Convention Against Torture and Other Cruel, Inhuman or Degrading Treatment or Punishment, 10 December 1984, Article 2(1), in UNTS, vol. 1465, p. 85.

to preventing torture in territory under a State's control by taking measures to ensure government actors do not torture, and by enacting legislation criminalizing torture[61] – measures just like those in Articles 8(1) and 8(12).

It could be argued that reference to the CAT is not useful because the nature of the act of torture is very different from that of crimes against humanity or genocide. This difference weakens any useful comparison between the Proposed or Genocide Conventions and the CAT. While the preventative legislation aspect of the obligation to prevent in the Proposed Convention is best understood by reference to the CAT, this aspect of the obligation to prevent fundamentally differs from other methods of applying the obligation to prevent, such as intervention or economic sanctions. The obligation to prevent in the intervention context lends itself to making sense of preventing genocide or crimes against humanity, while it is more difficult to understand how intervention would prevent torture. Torture is not a crime usually considered to require intervention by neighbouring States. Theoretically, intervention or the threat of intervention could prevent a State from engaging in acts of torture, but more likely, due to torture usually being conducted by a government or group with established political authority, it can be better prevented by a request to that government. Moreover, torture is usually conducted in secret, while crimes against humanity and genocide occur in plain view of anyone present in the geographical area. Additionally, the nature of a single act of torture contrasts with the nature of an act constituting a crime against humanity or genocide. This difference in the natures of these crimes reveals how the latter are simply more conducive than torture to being stopped by intervention. A State could agree to not torture, and quickly thereafter retract its promise. Crimes against humanity and genocide are essentially defined by their large-scale nature. They usually occur across a large area and require planning and preparatory activity. They also require momentum to start and take a longer time to stop. Once they are stopped by intervention, they are stopped for some time, while torture may be conducted on an "on again, off again" basis. Thus, the similar natures of genocide and crimes against humanity make comparisons between the two very useful, but the strained comparison to the act of torture demands careful scrutiny when

---

[61] Manfred Nowak and Elizabeth McArthur, *The United Nations Convention Against Torture: A Commentary*, Oxford University Press, 2008, pp. 87–125.

comparing any legal instruments of crimes against humanity or genocide with those of torture.

Despite these differences, however, the similarity between these provisions in the Proposed Convention and CAT would likely lead to them being interpreted in a similar fashion. The success and appeal of the 'territorial' legislation provision in the CAT strengthens the argument for deferring to the CAT when interpreting the almost identical Article 8(1) of the Proposed Convention, and it is also helpful to look to the CAT in considering how Article 8(12) may work in practice. While these specific CAT and Proposed Convention provisions may be interpreted similarly, the impact of the CAT provisions does not eliminate the independent obligation to prevent in the Proposed Convention, which exists for the many reasons discussed earlier in this chapter.

6.3.3.2. The Impact of Domestic Measures Prohibiting Hate Speech

The requirement that States outlaw hate speech understandably attempts to attack the root of the problem, but is likely to have difficulty gaining support among States with more vigorous free speech laws and policies, and distracts the focus of the Proposed Convention from the essence of addressing crimes against humanity – prevent the murderous acts themselves.

Article 8(12) of the Proposed Convention contains extensive requirements to outlaw incitement of various forms, stating: "Each State Party shall endeavor to take measures in accordance with its domestic legal system to prevent crimes against humanity. Such measures include, but are not limited to, ensuring that any advocacy of national, racial, or religious hatred that constitutes incitement to discrimination, hostility, or violence shall be prohibited by law". The Genocide Convention lacks such extensive provisions directly impacting free speech; Article III(c) makes punishable the "[d]irect and public incitement to commit genocide". In a similar provision, Article 4(2)(e) of the Proposed Convention provides that a "person shall be criminally responsible and liable for punishment for a crime against humanity if that person [...d]irectly and publicly incites others to commit crimes against humanity". In Article 8(12), the Proposed Convention significantly broadens requirements for domestic legislation. Article 4(2)(e) sufficiently directs States to ensure that speech leading to crimes against humanity is outlawed. Article 8(12) is unnecessarily broad, and will likely cause the Proposed Convention to encounter significant opposition. States' legal regimes may differ in this respect, but individual free speech rights have a long and storied history in many States' legal and political systems, and indeed, in international human rights frameworks. Those States should not be expected to abandon their policies in order to be able to approve of the language, albeit well-intentioned language, of the Proposed Convention in this regard. In addition, the consensus of States regarding domestic and international criminal law overwhelmingly focuses on punishing *acts* – not *speech*. If a *crimes* against humanity convention – by its very terms dealing with criminal acts – is to be accepted with credibility by a large number of these States, its focus must remain on the core criminal acts themselves, and must not expand criminal law to cover ancillary concerns.

The criminal acts the Proposed Convention aims to eliminate – murder, extermination, slavery, torture, rape, *et cetera* – are horrible acts that need to be prevented and punished, and the prohibition of certain types of speech in Article 8(12) only distracts from preventing and punishing these truly horrible crimes. This is not to say that all speech is without effect; it is just a distraction from the laudable and necessary aim of the Proposed Convention – preventing the core human rights violations constituting crimes against humanity.

In addition, while Article 8(12) only requires that States "endeavour" to outlaw certain types of speech, the word "endeavour" may not be of much consolation to States as the sole barrier between them and a Proposed Convention requirement that drastically alters their free-speech laws and policies. The United States is the most obvious example of a State that might oppose Article 8(12), but other nations have free speech laws advancing a variety of worthy policies, and States should be wary about conceding individual free speech rights and thus minimizing the necessary purpose they serve in free democracies – even for the noble purpose of the Proposed Convention. Although the inclusion of "endeavour" would seem to alleviate apprehension about compliance by not setting a rigid requirement, the downside of this flexibility is that it will allow States to avoid compliance with the Proposed Convention, and States are often tempted to avoid compliance with international agreements after they have made a public show of supporting them. Yet this "endeavour" language provides the flexibility to achieve consensus on the Proposed Convention; indeed, for this reason it was likely intended to be a 'constructive ambiguity' in Article 8(12).[62] But such language does not impart clarity, which is needed to set firm standards that will lead to true accountability in international criminal law as it pertains to crimes against humanity.

There are further unanticipated consequences of restricting free speech as the Proposed Convention does. Not only will provisions like Article 8(12) cause a chilling effect on speech, but in the future these provisions might be used to target unsuspecting groups who are not speaking or acting in any way similar to the regimes around the world that the Proposed Convention is intended to target today. In other words, the lack of precision in the language will bring unintended consequences. Who is to decide what "advocacy" means in the context of Article 8(12)? Who is to decide what "hatred" means? Who is to decide what "incitement" means? Who is to decide what "discrimination" means? International agreements are almost always in danger of being used for political purposes, and depending on what group or government is interpreting these terms, a large number of diverse groups and entities may be implicated by this provision of the Proposed Convention, while not engaging at all in any action like that of the regimes the Proposed Convention is intended to target today.

Fulfilling the obligation to prevent by criminalizing certain actions preparatory to crimes against humanity is an aspect of the obligation to prevent in the Proposed Convention that is not present in the Genocide Convention. In this way, the obligation to prevent in the Proposed Convention is expanded significantly beyond its scope in the Genocide Convention. Yet Article 4(2)(e) is sufficient to ensure that speech leading to crimes against humanity is outlawed. Article 8(12) is likely to encounter significant opposition, and only distracts from the core purpose of the Proposed Convention.

6.4. Recommendations

Several provisions in the Proposed Convention impacting the obligation to prevent should be modified. First, revisions should be taken as necessary to ensure that the obligation to prevent is not limited to a State's own territory. If Article 8(1) is considered to inform the independent obligation to prevent (which as discussed earlier includes the potential for interven-

---

[62] Morten Bergsmo, Comments in 'International Crime of Genocide' class, see *supra* note 31.

tion), the Proposed Convention would impose no obligation to intervene in other States to prevent crimes against humanity because Article 8(1) is limited territorially. Therefore, Article 8(1) should be clarified so as to not territorially limit the independent obligation to prevent as supported by other provisions of the Proposed Convention.

Not requiring States to hold other States accountable would gut any international agreement on crimes against humanity. This result is all the more nonsensical when considered in light of the harsh provisions for domestic legislation in Article 8(12). Some may think the Article 8(12) provisions will ensure that intervention is never required. But that is an untested assumption. It has certainly not proven to be true, and if anything, may have been proven false; many States have thorough domestic criminal law frameworks that they just ignore. Such a domestic limitation is not in the Genocide Convention, and has not been tested under that convention. Perpetrators of crimes against humanity, especially perpetrators who are top government officials, will likely find a way around any rules which on paper are designed to constrain their behavior. While sanctions and similar actions may put some pressure on perpetrators, only the threat of intervention from other States can serve as an effective enforcement mechanism for international agreements on issues like crimes against humanity. Thus, provisions affecting the obligation to prevent need to be re-written to remove any territorial limitations on the scope of the obligation to prevent in the Proposed Convention.

Second, the provisions of Article 8(12) prohibiting certain types of speech should be modified. As mentioned above, there are concerns surrounding the prevention of crimes against humanity by criminalizing hate speech. Advocates desiring to stamp out any flicker of speech that could flame up into crimes against humanity will likely support Article 8(12), but advocates of free speech will likely view it as unnecessarily restrictive in accomplishing its goal of preventing crimes against humanity. States are justified in their wariness about conceding individual free speech rights and thus minimizing the necessary purpose they serve in free democracies, and should not be expected to abandon their policies in order to be able to approve of the language, however well-intentioned, of the Proposed Convention in this regard. Thus, the inclusion of Article 8(12) in the Proposed Convention will make consensus among States with different free speech policies that much more difficult.

Rather than eliminating Article 8(12) in its entirety, one solution would be editing it to prohibit more limited, narrow categories of speech. For example, a provision prohibiting only direct incitement to harm could be accomplished by striking out "discrimination" and "hostility", leaving only "incitement to violence". This revision would allow a range of speech, while still serving to prohibit the more proximate cause of crimes against humanity – physical violence. Such language would likely even be acceptable under the very pro-free speech constitutional jurisprudence of the United States. A further modification, for example, would be to add 'to any person' after 'violence', thus clarifying exactly what type of violence is prohibited regarding advocacy to crimes against humanity – violence committed against people (as opposed to criticizing views or beliefs). Although States with more vigorous free speech policies will still want to use great care and detailed language when drafting their implementing legislation, these simple modifications to the Proposed Convention will likely bring Article 8(12) into general alignment with the views of pro-free speech States, and also will likely satisfy the immediate concerns of other free speech advocates. Such modifications will help build consensus around the Proposed Convention, while at the same time making enforcement easier by streamlining and limiting prohibited activity.

6.5. Conclusion

Examining the obligation to prevent in the Proposed Convention in light of the obligation to prevent in the Genocide Convention leads to several conclusions. Like the Genocide Convention, the Proposed Convention would very likely be found to contain the independent obligation to prevent. Just as it is under the Genocide Convention, the scope of this obligation is quite expansive under the Proposed Convention. However, the Proposed Convention contains various provisions pertaining to prevention that are not present in the Genocide Convention, and these provisions may modify the scope of the obligation to prevent under the Proposed Convention. The crux of this uncertainty is in the possible application of certain provisions to the obligation to prevent which would only require action in a State's own territory or area under its control, a limitation not present in the Genocide Convention. The Proposed Convention also contains provisions for legislation to prevent crimes against humanity, which lack corresponding provisions in the Genocide Convention. It is unclear exactly how these provisions affect the independent obligation to prevent in the

Proposed Convention. At a minimum, these provisions subject the contours of the obligation to prevent under the Proposed Convention to uncertainty by adding an entirely new aspect to the obligation.

Although the issue of genocide is the object of many speeches and much public attention, the obligation to prevent contained in the Genocide Convention has been coolly embraced and rarely invoked in practice. This is reason to think the obligation to prevent in the Proposed Convention will be treated the same way. It is important to ensure a vigorous and expansive independent obligation to prevent in order to help fight impunity. Thus, any language pertaining to "territory" which would limit the option of intervention (taken within the bounds of international law) as it relates to the obligation to prevent should be removed from the Proposed Convention. At the same time, the contours of the obligation to prevent described elsewhere in the Proposed Convention should be sharpened and made more limited; specifically, the overly broad prohibitions on speech in Article 8(12) should be narrowed or removed. These modifications will help achieve a broader consensus on the Proposed Convention while at the same time adding 'teeth' to the obligation to prevent, which in turn advances the core aim of the Proposed Convention – ensuring world-wide accountability for perpetrators of crimes against humanity.

7

State Obligation to Punish Core International Crimes and the Proposed Crimes Against Humanity Convention

Julie Pasch[*]

7.1. Introduction

The Proposed Convention on the Prevention and Punishment of Crimes Against Humanity ('Proposed Convention') is intended to create a legal instrument to address one of the major international crimes not yet covered by a specialized convention. Should it be adopted, the Proposed Convention would take its place alongside the 1949 Geneva Conventions and their 1977 Additional Protocols[1] and the Convention on the Prevention and Punishment of the Crime of Genocide ('Genocide Convention')[2] in regulating State action regarding serious human rights violations, in particular, 'core' international crimes.

State action to suppress core international crimes can take many forms. Aspects of a convention focusing on prevention may include provisions addressing domestic legislation, State action and humanitarian

---

[*] **Julie Pasch**, B.A., International Studies, Rhodes College; J.D., Certificate in Refugee and Humanitarian Emergencies, Georgetown University Law Center. The author would like to thank Professor Morten Bergsmo, Amy Cheung, Lisa DeGray, Kiki A. Japutra, Ian Kennedy, Gerard Lynch, and SONG Tianying for their thoughtful comments and suggestions. All Internet references were last accessed on 27 August 2014.

[1] Geneva Convention for the Amelioration of the Condition of the Wounded and Sick in Armed Forces in the Field of 12 August 1949; Geneva Convention for the Amelioration of the Conditions of Wounded, Sick and Shipwrecked Members of Armed Forces at Sea of 12 August 1949; Geneva Convention Relative to the Treatment of Prisoners of War of 12 August 1949; Geneva Convention Relative to the Protection of Civilian Persons in Time of War of 12 August 1949 (respectively Geneva Conventions I–IV); Protocol Additional to the Geneva Conventions of 12 August 1949, and Relating to the Protection of Victims of International Armed Conflicts (Additional Protocol I); Protocol Additional to the Geneva Conventions of 12 August 1949, and Relating to the Protection of Victims of Non-International Armed Conflicts (Additional Protocol II).

[2] Convention on the Prevention and Punishment of the Crime of Genocide, in UNTS, vol. 78, p. 277, entered into force on 12 January 1951 (http://www.legal-tools.org/doc/498c38/).

---

intervention. Important factors with regard to prosecution may include jurisdiction and referral provisions. This chapter will explore one aspect of State obligations to prevent and punish international human rights violations under the aforementioned conventions and the Rome Statute of the International Criminal Court ('ICC Statute'), by focusing on jurisdiction and the attendant State obligations or rights.

This chapter first outlines existing State obligations to punish genocide and war crimes and their implementation at the national level. It then examines the mechanism provided by the ICC in punishing core international crimes and accompanying State obligations. Throughout the above analysis, the chapter considers the impact of the existing practice on the formation, interpretation and application of the obligation to punish in the Proposed Convention. It contemplates to what extent the Proposed Convention would crystalize and develop State obligations to repress core international crimes at national and international level, some sixty years after World War II and the Holocaust.

7.2. State Obligation to Punish Genocide

State obligations concerning genocide are part of customary international law.[3] This status determines the obligations of States even if they are not parties to the Genocide Convention. The wide acceptance of the convention's definition of genocide is evidenced by the Statutes of the ICC and the *ad hoc* tribunals.[4] There is also evidence that the prohibition of genocide has become a *jus cogens* norm.[5]

In Article I of the Genocide Convention, States undertake to "prevent and punish" genocide. Article V requires States to enact the necessary legislation to effectuate the Genocide Convention, and to provide effective penalties for persons found guilty of genocidal acts.

---

[3]   Steven Ratner and Jason Abram, *Accountability For Human Rights Atrocities In International Law: Beyond The Nuremberg Legacy*, Oxford University Press, 2001, p. 41.

[4]   See, *e.g.*, Rome Statute of the International Criminal Court, 1 July 2000, Article 6 (http://www.legal-tools.org/doc/7b9af9/); Statute of the International Criminal Tribunal for the Former Yugoslavia (as of September 2009), adopted on 25 May 1993, Article 4 (http://www.legal-tools.org/doc/b4f63b/); Statute of the International Criminal Tribunal for Rwanda as Amended on 1 January 2007, Article 2.

[5]   Ratner and Abrams, 2001, see *supra* note 3. See also International Court of Justice, *Barcelona Traction, Light and Power Company (Belgium v. Spain)*, Judgment, 5 February 1970, para. 34.

Article VI confers jurisdiction. Jurisdiction for trials is limited to a tribunal of the State where the act was committed or an international penal tribunal if the appropriate States have accepted its jurisdiction. Under Article VI of the Genocide Convention, States must punish acts of genocide that occur on their territory. The Convention does not address any obligations toward acts of genocide occurring extraterritorially.[6] Although the *Ad Hoc* Committee and the Sixth Committee explicitly rejected a universal jurisdiction provision that appeared in one of the drafts, most States considered the convention as non-exclusive regarding jurisdiction and not precluding extraterritorial jurisdiction.[7] Many States Parties to the Genocide Convention have enacted legislation creating universal jurisdiction over genocide.[8]

National courts subsequently interpreted Article VI of the Genocide Convention as not prohibiting the application of the principle of universal jurisdiction to genocide.[9] The European Court of Human Rights in upholding Germany's exercise of universal jurisdiction over genocide, recognizes that pursuant to Article I of the Genocide Convention, States Parties are under an *erga omnes* obligation to prevent and punish genocide, the prohibition of which forms part of the *jus cogens*. In view of this, the European Court reasons that the purpose of the Genocide Convention, as expressed notably in Article I, does not exclude extraterritorial jurisdiction for the punishment of genocide under national law.[10] Similarly, Judge Lauterpacht of the International Court of Justice ('ICJ') holds that Article I of the Genocide Convention is intended "to permit parties, within the domestic legislation that they adopt, to assume universal jurisdiction over the crime of genocide", in his Separate Opinion to Order of 13 September

---

[6] Genocide Convention, Article VI.

[7] Report of the Ad Hoc Committee on Genocide, 1948, U.N. Doc. E/794/Corr.1, pp. 11–12; Report of the Sixth Committee, Genocide: Draft Convention and Report of the Economic and Social Council, 1948, 3rd Sess., U.N. Doc A/760.

[8] See the summary made by the European Court of Human Rights, *Case of Jorgić v. Germany (Application no. 74613/01)*, Judgment, 12 July 2007, para. 53. These States are: Spain, France, Belgium, Finland, Italy, Latvia, Luxembourg, the Netherlands, Austria, Denmark, Estonia, Poland, Portugal, Romania, Sweden and Switzerland, Russia, the Slovak Republic, the Czech Republic, and Hungary.

[9] William Schabas, *Genocide in International Law: Crime of Crimes*, Cambridge University Press, 2009, pp. 426–443.

[10] European Court of Human Rights, *Case of Jorgić v. Germany (Application no. 74613/01)*, Judgment, 12 July 2007, para. 68.

1993 in the *Case Concerning the Application of the Convention on the Prevention and Punishment of the Crime of Genocide (Bosnia and Herzegovina v. Yugoslavia (Serbia and Montenegro))* ('*Bosnia and Herzegovina case*').[11]

In the 2007 judgment of the *Bosnia and Herzegovina case*, the ICJ clarifies the extraterritorial reach of the prevention aspect of State obligations under Article I of the Genocide Convention. The ICJ held that under the Genocide Convention, Yugoslavia should ensure that any military units and organizations and people within its control did not commit any acts of genocide. It further clarified that the obligation is one of "conduct" rather than result: a State cannot be under an obligation to *succeed* in preventing genocide.[12] The obligation to prevent, and the duty to act arises when the State learns (or should have learned) of the existence of a serious risk that genocide will be committed.[13] At that time, if States have a means of deterrent, they are under a duty to use those means as circumstances allow. The obligation to prevent varies from State to State, and depends upon the State's capacity to influence persons likely to commit genocide.[14] Interestingly, in 1993, Bosnia declared its intention to begin proceedings against the UK for failing in its obligation to prevent genocide.[15] The case (or more appropriately, the idea) was subsequently dropped, but it does indicate that States had contemplated that the obligation to prevent in the Genocide Convention extended beyond the State's territory.

Against this background, it can be said that under Article I, while States Parties have an extraterritorial *obligation* to prevent genocide, they have discretion to exercise other grounds of jurisdiction over genocide than what is mandated under Article VI, such as the universal jurisdiction – it is a *right*, not an obligation. As will be discussed below, this is a more

---

[11] International Court of Justice, *Application of the Convention on the Prevention and Punishment of the Crime of Genocide (Bosnia and Herzegovina v. Yugoslavia)*, Provisional Measures, Order of 13 September 1993, Separate Opinion of Judge Lauterpacht, p. 443.

[12] International Court of Justice, *Application of the Convention on the Prevention and Punishment of the Crime of Genocide (Bosnia and Herzegovina v. Serbia and Montenegro)*, Judgment, 26 February 2007, para. 456.

[13] *Ibid.*, para. 430.

[14] *Ibid.*, para. 461.

[15] Statement of Intention by the Republic of Bosnia and Herzegovina to Institute Legal Proceedings Against the United Kingdom Before the International Court of Justice, 15 November 1993, U.N. Doc. A/48/659-s/26806, 47 UNYB 465.

limited view of jurisdiction than what is found in the Proposed Convention.

Article VIII allows States Parties to call on the U.N. to take appropriate action to suppress genocide. It provides for a possible forum to challenge a State's inaction towards punishing genocide.

The evolution of the obligation to punish genocide illustrates experience and lessons learnt for punishing core international crimes in general. In this sense, the Proposed Convention draws on and amplifies what is envisaged in the Genocide Convention; the latter is substantially shorter and does not go into as much detail.

7.3. State Obligation to Punish War Crimes

Similar to the Genocide Convention, the Geneva Conventions and their 1977 Additional Protocols reflect customary law of State obligations to prevent and punish war crimes.

7.3.1. Jurisdiction over 'Grave Breaches' and Other Violations of IHL

The Geneva Conventions and Additional Protocol I explicitly set out State obligation to exercise universal jurisdiction over 'grave breaches' of those instruments.[16] States Parties are obliged to enact necessary legislation to provide effective penal sanctions for persons committing grave breaches. States also have an obligation to search for persons alleged to have committed grave breaches, and either to bring them before their own courts or to hand them over for trial in another State, even if the individual is *not* located in the State's territory: "When engaging troops in military operations abroad, States have a duty to use their military personnel thus deployed to search for individuals accused of war crimes".[17] Prior to the 1990s there were no prosecutions based solely on the universality princi-

---

[16]   Articles 49, 50, 129, 146 respectively of the Geneva Conventions I–IV, Article 85 of Additional Protocol I; for acts constituting grave breaches, see Articles 50, 51, 130, 147 respectively of the Geneva Conventions I–IV, Article 85 of Additional Protocol I.

[17]   Laurence Boisson de Chazournes and Luigi Condorelli, "Common Article 1 of the Geneva Conventions Revisited: Protecting Collective Interests", in *International Review of the Red Cross*, No. 837, 2000.

ple, but since then the pattern has changed, with prosecutions proceeding without protest from other States.[18]

Regarding other violations of the Geneva Conventions or Additional Protocol I than grave breaches and violations of the Additional Protocol II, there are no requirements for prosecution or extradition. It is possible that customary law would recognize universal jurisdiction for other war crimes beyond grave breaches.[19] According to the International Committee of the Red Cross ('ICRC'), States must take whatever measures necessary to prevent and suppress all violations of international humanitarian law ('IHL'). Such measures may include military regulations, administrative orders and other regulatory measures. However, criminal legislation is deemed the most appropriate and effective means of dealing with all serious violations of IHL.[20]

The differences in State jurisdiction for 'grave breaches' and other violations have given rise to interesting questions regarding whether international law can be read to give States universal jurisdiction over all war crimes. A number of States have already enacted criminal law to punish violations of Article 3 common to the Geneva Conventions and Additional Protocol II which apply to non-international armed conflict. States have recently been more willing to prosecute atrocities committed abroad, even when crimes were not committed by or against their citizens. After the creation of the International Criminal Tribunals for Yugoslavia ('ICTY') and Rwanda ('ICTR'), States started to prosecute perpetrators found in their territory on the basis of domestic statutes implementing the Geneva Conventions.[21] Processes in many of these States have led to convictions and thus affirmative findings of jurisdiction.[22]

---

[18] Ratner and Abrams, 2001, p. 164, see *supra* note 3.

[19] See, *e.g.*, Sonja Boelaert-Suominen, "Grave Breaches, Universal Jurisdiction and Internal Armed Conflicts: Is Customary Law Moving Towards a Uniform Enforcement Mechanism for all Armed Conflicts?", in *Journal of Conflict and Security Law*, 2000, vol. 5, no 1, p. 63; and Cedric Ryngaert, "Universal Jurisdiction over Genocide and Wartime Torture in Dutch Courts: An Appraisal of the Afghan and Rwandan Cases", in *Hague Justice Journal*, 2007, vol. 2, no. 2, p. 13.

[20] ICRC Advisory Service on International Humanitarian Law, "Penal Repression: Punishing War Crimes", available at http://www.icrc.org/eng/assets/files/other/penal_repression.pdf.

[21] Ratner and Abrams, 2001, p. 180, see *supra* note 3.

[22] *Ibid.*

In the Dutch case against *Abdullah F.*, the Hague District Court considered the question of whether a bystander State, having no connection with the alleged violations except the presence of the accused, could exercise jurisdiction.[23] The Court concluded that it could, basing its reasoning on a resolution from 17th Commission of the *Institut de Droit International* that stated in part:

> Universal jurisdiction may be exercised over crimes identified by international law as falling within that jurisdiction in matters such as genocide, crimes against humanity, grave breaches of the 1949 Geneva Conventions for the protection of war victims or other serious violations of international humanitarian law committed in international or non-international armed conflict.[24]

The Dutch court's approach allows universal jurisdiction over all war crimes, not just grave breaches.[25] Though the court's response is by no means the only possible one on this issue, it does acknowledge the development of customary law and add to it with this decision.[26]

States have also relied on universal jurisdiction to charge some of the former leaders of South and Central American regimes, notably Augusto Pinochet in Spain. These cases, particularly when they involve foreign nationals accused of Common Article 3 violations, indicate a move toward universal jurisdiction for all war crimes, and the general lack of international outcry over the States' unilateral actions suggests that States tacitly agree that such jurisdiction is proper. According to the ICRC, States have the *right* to vest universal jurisdiction in their national courts over war crimes other than grave breaches, not an obligation.[27]

State obligation to provide judicial assistance in criminal matters is specifically considered in Article 88(1) of Additional Protocol I, which stipulates that "the High Contracting Parties shall afford one another the

---

[23] LJN: BA9575, District Court The Hague, 09/750001-06, case against Abdullah F., 25 June 2007.

[24] Resolution of the Seventeenth Commission, Universal criminal jurisdiction with regard to the crime of genocide, crimes against humanity and war crimes, 26 August 2005, para. 3(a); *cited in* Ryngaert, 2007, p. 17, see *supra* note 19.

[25] Ryngaert, *ibid.*

[26] For discussion of the *Abdullah F.* case, *see* Ryngaert, *ibid.*

[27] ICRC Customary International Humanitarian Law Study, Rule 157, available at http://www.icrc.org/customary-ihl/eng/docs/v1_rul_rule157.

greatest measure of assistance in connection with criminal proceedings brought in respect of grave breaches of the Conventions or of this Protocol". Article 89 of Additional Protocol I further states that in the event of serious violations of the Protocol, States parties undertake to act, jointly or individually, in co-operation with the United Nations and in conformity with the Charter of the United Nations. Although for violations of IHL other than grave breaches, customary law does not establish an absolute obligation to co-operate, but rather an expectation that States should make every effort to do so, in good faith and to the extent possible.[28]

7.3.2. State Obligation to "Ensure Respect"

Common Article 1 of the 1949 Geneva Conventions provides that States parties undertake to "ensure respect for the present Convention". The same provision is repeated in Article 1 (1) of Additional Protocol I in relation to respect for the provisions of that Protocol. It seems that State obligations to punish war crimes go beyond the situation where the State itself is party to a conflict. In the commentary to common Article 1, the ICRC states that the obligation to "ensure respect" is "not limited to behaviour by parties to a conflict, but includes the requirement that States do all in their power to ensure that international humanitarian law is respected universally".[29] However, no specific course of action is identified.

Historically, two peaceful methods have been adopted in this respect: diplomatic protest and collective measures.[30] Diplomatic protests have taken multiple forms, but generally materialize as bilateral protests, protests in international fora, or through resolutions of international organizations. Though diplomatic protests do not always specifically relate to violations of the Geneva Conventions, they have on occasion referred

---

[28] ICRC Advisory Service on International Humanitarian Law, "Cooperation in Extradition and Judicial Assistance in Criminal Matters", available at http://www.icrc.org/eng/assets /files/2014/cooperation-in-extradition-and-judicial-assistance-in-criminal-matters-icrc-eng.pdf.

[29] ICRC Customary International Humanitarian Law Study, Rule 144, available at http://www.icrc.org/customary-ihl/eng/print/v1_cha_chapter41_rule144#refFn_11_2, citing Jean S. Pictet (ed.), *Commentary on the Third Geneva Convention*, ICRC, Geneva, 1960, p. 18; Yves Sandoz, Christophe Swinarski, Bruno Zimmermann (eds.), *Commentary on the Additional Protocols*, ICRC, Geneva, 1987, para. 45.

[30] *Ibid.*

to common Article 1 and the duty of States to ensure respect for international humanitarian law.[31]

Collective measures have included such actions as "holding international conferences on specific situations, investigating possible violations, creating *ad hoc* criminal tribunals and courts, creating the International Criminal Court, imposing international sanctions and sending of peacekeeping or peace-enforcement troops".[32] In 1990, U.N. Security Council called on States Parties to the Fourth Geneva Convention to ensure respect by Israel for its obligations, in accordance with Article 1 of that Convention.[33] In relation to the same conflict, the U.N. General Assembly has adopted several resolutions to the same effect.[34] Other international organizations have likewise called on their Member States to respect and ensure respect for international humanitarian law, in particular the Council of Europe, North Atlantic Treaty Organization, the Organization of African Unity and the Organization of American States.[35] These examples cover a wide range of State involvement and demonstrate that States may interpret their obligations to be quite different depending on the specifics of the situation.[36]

The way universal jurisdiction to prosecute war crimes has expanded and State obligation to "ensure respect" of IHL unfolded over time sheds lights on how State obligations to suppress crimes against humanity under the Proposed Convention may take shape. It is important to note that in the fairly recent past, Common Article 1 was seen as a "stylistic" clause, "devoid of real legal weight".[37] The Proposed Convention will cer-

---

[31] *Ibid.*

[32] *Ibid.*

[33] U.N. Security Council Res. 681.

[34] U.N. General Assembly, Res. 32/91 A, Res. 37/123 A, Res. 38/180 A and Res. 43/21.

[35] ICRC Customary International Humanitarian Law Study, Rule 144, available at http://www.icrc.org/customary-ihl/eng/docs/v1_rul_rule144#Fn_44_6, citing Council of Europe, Parliamentary Assembly, Res. 823, Res. 881, Res. 921 and Res. 948; Council of Europe, Committee of Ministers, Declaration on the Rape of Women and Children in the Territory of Former Yugoslavia; NATO, Parliamentary Assembly, Resolution of the Civilian Affairs Committee; OAU, Conference of African Ministers of Health, Res. 14 (V); OAS, General Assembly, Res. 1408 (XXVI-O/96).

[36] For discussion of the possible State actions, *see* Umesh Palwankar, "Measures available to States for fulfilling their obligation to ensure respect for international humanitarian law", in *International Review of the Red Cross*, 1994, No. 298, p. 9.

[37] Boisson de Chazournes and Condorelli, 2000, footnote 4, see *supra* note 17.

tainly benefit from the historical development of State obligations under the Geneva Conventions, and similarly, it is also likely that some elements of the Proposed Convention will develop more weight than initially contemplated as time progresses.

7.4. State Obligations under the ICC Statute

7.4.1. The Jurisdiction of the ICC

The creation of the ICC provided another forum to adjudicate international crimes. The ICC Statute creates jurisdiction over 'core' crimes – genocide, crimes against humanity, war crimes and, yet to be finalized, aggression. Amendment provisions allow for other crimes to be added at a later date. The decision to limit the court's jurisdiction to the 'core' crimes was in many ways political: those crimes are generally of great concern and benefit from a clear status under customary international law, and the drafters believed that adding other crimes might impede acceptance of the ICC Statute.[38] Generally the definitions of the core crimes are consistent with those found in international law, though in certain incidences they reflect progression in defining gender-related offenses as crimes and expanding the definition of war crimes.

The ICC may only exercise jurisdiction if the State where the offense occurred or the State of which the person committing the crime was a national is a party to the ICC Statute or has accepted the ICC's jurisdiction for the specific crime.[39] This notably gives the ICC jurisdiction over nationals of non-party States if the State where the offense occurred has consented, which was one of the main reasons the United States refused to ratify the ICC Statute.[40] It has been argued, however, that this jurisdiction is not overreaching because the crimes covered by the ICC Statute are subject to universal jurisdiction.[41] The ICC may also exercise jurisdiction over a situation referred to the Prosecutor by a State Party or by the U.N.

---

[38] *Ibid.*, p. 212.

[39] ICC Statute, Article 12.

[40] John P. Cerone, "Dynamic Equilibrium: The Evolution of US Attitudes Toward International Criminal Courts and Tribunals", in *The European Journal of International Law*, 2007, vol. 18, no. 2, pp. 292 and 296.

[41] Compare Leila Nadya Sadat and Richard Carden, "The New International Criminal Court: An Uneasy Revolution", in *Georgetown Law Journal*, 2000, vol. 88, p. 381, with Alfred P. Rubin, "A Critical View of the Proposed International Criminal Court", in *Fletcher Forum of World Affairs*, 1999, vol. 23, p. 139.

Security Council acting under Chapter VII of the U.N. Charter, or the Prosecutor has initiated an investigation on his or her own accord.[42] The Security Council referral is of particular importance because Chapter VII resolutions are binding on all U.N. Member States; allowing the ICC to exercise jurisdiction in those cases arguably extends jurisdiction to all U.N. Member States regardless of their membership to the ICC Statute.[43] Non-party States are only obligated to co-operate with the ICC if they enter into *ad hoc* or other co-operation agreements.[44] However, the Security Council referral may lead to an obligation to co-operate of all U.N. Member States if the Security Council resolution "specifically requires" so.[45]

7.4.2. The Principle of Complementarity

The principle of complementarity governs the relations between national jurisdictions of States Parties and jurisdiction of the ICC. The preamble of the ICC Statute states that effective prosecution of international crimes must be ensured by taking measures at the national level, and that "it is the duty of every State to exercise its criminal jurisdiction over those responsible for international crimes". Both the preamble and Article 1 declare the ICC's jurisdiction "shall be complementary to national criminal jurisdictions". The ICC Statute also lays down conditions relating to the exercise of jurisdiction, as concrete means of implementation of the principle of complementarity. Under Articles 17 and 18, a case will be inadmissible if a State having jurisdiction is investigating or prosecuting the case, or has declined to prosecute, unless the State is unwilling or unable genuinely to carry out the prosecution. Finally, a case is inadmissible if a prosecution would constitute double jeopardy or if the case "is not of sufficient gravity" to justify prosecution before the court.

---

[42] ICC Statute, Articles 12–15.

[43] Tiffany de Waynecaurt-Steele, "The Contribution of the Statute of the International Criminal Court to the Enforcement of International Law in the Light of the Experiences of the ICTY", in *South African Yearbook of International Law*, 2002, vol. 27, p. 29. As of June 2014, the Security Council has referred two situations to the ICC Prosecutor: Darfur, Sudan and Libya. Neither Sudan nor Libya is State Party to the ICC Statute.

[44] *Ibid.*, de Waynecaurt-Steele.

[45] *Ibid.*, de Waynecaurt-Steele cites the U.N. Security Council Resolution establishing the International Criminal Tribunal for the former Yugoslavia as an example: S/RES/821, 28 April 1993.

This distinguishes the ICC from the ICTY and the ICTR in terms of jurisdiction – the latter have primacy over national courts. The ICC Statute recognizes that States have the first responsibility and right to prosecute international crimes. The principle of complementarity is based both on respect for the primary jurisdiction of States and on considerations of efficiency and effectiveness, since States will generally have the best access to evidence and witnesses and the resources to carry out proceedings. This affirmative duty to implement domestic legislation is a significant obligation for States. It is important in the context of jurisdiction because the ICC relies so heavily on complementarity; whereas the Geneva Conventions and the Genocide Convention allow for either a State or an appropriate international body to take jurisdiction, the ICC Statute is much more specific about when the ICC may and may not take jurisdiction.

7.4.3. States Parties' Obligation to Provide International Co-operation

In addition to a general duty to exercise national jurisdiction over core international crimes, States Parties also undertake to provide international co-operation for cases before the ICC. The duty to co-operate generally is noted in Article 86: "States Parties shall, in accordance with the provisions in this Statute, cooperate fully with the Court [...]". States are required to adopt domestic laws that permit co-operation with the ICC.[46] In addition, specific provisions, such as those covering the arrest and surrender of individuals, govern acts of co-operation. States bear obligations to aid the ICC Prosecutor's investigations. Upon receiving arrest requests, States must take steps to arrest the person in accordance with the national law and the ICC Statute. After ensuring that the warrant applies to the individual and that the proper procedures have been followed and rights respected, the State must promptly deliver the person to the ICC.[47] The ICC can request any evidence necessary to determine the truth. But the ICC Statute also contains provisions for the protection of information that the State believes would prejudice its national security interests, including an

---

[46] ICC Statute, Article 88. For a discussion of how various States have implemented their obligations to co-operate into domestic law, *see* Valerie Oosterveld, Mike Perry, and John McManus, "The Cooperation of States with the International Criminal Court", in *Fordham International Law Journal*, 2001, vol. 25, no. 3, p. 767.

[47] ICC Statute, Article 59.

obligation that the ICC consult with the State concerned and allowing for the use of *in camera* or *ex parte* proceedings.[48]

Despite the specific circumstances envisaged in the ICC Statute, understanding of the court's jurisdiction is still evolving, and likely will continue to evolve as more situations are referred to the Court and those that have already been referred move through the judicial process. One such evolution will likely be the determination of when a State is "unwilling" or "unable" to prosecute under Article 17(3). Demonstrating that a State is unwilling to prosecute requires a substantial showing. The State must either shield the accused from criminal responsibility, delay the proceedings unjustifiably, or conduct biased proceedings.[49] Similarly, the standard for inability to prosecute is a high one: substantial collapse or unavailability of the judicial system.[50] Given this high threshold, States' limitations in resources (a common problem in many States just emerging from conflict) may become a basis for the ICC to expand its jurisdiction while continuing to adhere to the principle of complementarity.[51]

The ICC Statute is an interesting juxtaposition with the Geneva Conventions and the Genocide Convention because it implements an alternate jurisdiction for investigating and prosecuting core international crimes. It does not purport to challenge the jurisdiction of States (in most cases) to prosecute crimes domestically; instead, it offers an alternative court through which States may exert their obligations to punish violations of international criminal law.

7.5. State Obligation to Punish Crimes Against Humanity under the Proposed Convention

Prior to the drafting of the Proposed Convention, the international definitions and State responsibility toward crimes against humanity mainly developed through customary international law.[52] The modern idea of crimes against humanity was first set out in the Charter of the International Military Tribunal ('IMT Charter'), which defined crimes against hu-

---

[48]   ICC Statute, Articles 69 and 72.

[49]   Anja Seibert-Fohr, "The Relevance of the ICC Statute of the International Criminal Court for Amnesties and Truth Commissions", in A. von Bogdandy and R. Wolfrum (eds.), *Max Planck Yearbook of United Nations Law*, Koninklijke Brill N.V., 2003, p. 18.

[50]   ICC Statute, Article 17(3).

[51]   For discussion of these issues, *see* de Waynecaurt-Steele, p. 16, see *supra* note 43.

[52]   Ratner and Abrams, 2001, p. 47, see *supra* note 3.

manity only "in connection with" other crimes.[53] Crimes against humanity have slowly developed an identity separate from war crimes – the U.N. Human Rights Commission approved a definition without the nexus, followed by two General Assembly Committees.[54] The link was not found in the statutes of the ICTR or the ICC.[55] The Proposed Convention retains this separation by specifically recognizing that "crimes against humanity may be committed in time of armed conflict and in time of peace".[56]

Under the Proposed Convention, States have a clear obligation not to commit crimes against humanity themselves. States are also obligated *not* to provide aid or assistance to facilitate the commission of crimes against humanity by another State.[57] Violation of those prohibitions may give rise to the responsibility of States for internationally wrongful acts.[58] This obligation is similar to the ones regarding genocide and war crimes.[59]

State obligations in prosecuting crimes against humanity begin in the preamble to the Proposed Convention, where the commitment to prosecute and punish the perpetrators is "emphasiz[ed]".[60] It declares that "it is the duty of every State to exercise its criminal jurisdiction over those responsible for international crimes, including crimes against humani-

---

[53] Article 6(c) of the IMT Charter defines crimes against humanity as:

> [M]urder, extermination, enslavement, deportation, and other inhumane acts committed against any civilian population, before or during the war, or persecution on political, racial or religious grounds in execution of or in connection with any crime within the jurisdiction of the Tribunal, whether or not in violation of the domestic law of the country where perpetrated.

[54] United Nations Commission on Human Rights, Report on the Twenty-Third Session, UN ESCOR, 42d Sess., Supp. No. 6, U.N. Doc. E/4322-E/CN.4/940, para. 144.

[55] ICTR Statute, Article 3; ICC Statute, Article 7.

[56] Proposed Convention, Article 1, Explanatory Note.

[57] Proposed Convention, Article 8, Explanatory Note; see also *Bosnia and Herzegovina Case*, Judgment, paras. 425–438, see *supra* note 12.

[58] Proposed Convention, Preamble; Explanatory Note 1 of Article 8.

[59] *Bosnia and Herzegovina Case*, Judgment, para. 166, where the ICJ states that "the effect of Article I is to prohibit States from themselves committing genocide", see *supra* note 12; International Court of Justice, *Military and Paramilitary Activities in and against Nicaragua (Nicaragua v. United States of America)*, Judgment, 27 June 1986, para. 46, where the ICJ states that the United States was "under an obligation not to encourage persons or groups engaged in the conflict in Nicaragua to act in violation of the provisions of Article 3 common to the four 1949 Geneva Conventions".

[60] Proposed Convention, Preamble, para. 5.

---

ty".[61] The Explanatory Note cross-references several other international treaties and instruments, including the ICC Statute, indicating that in many instances the ideals stated in the preamble are not far removed from those already existing in international law.[62]

The punishment of crimes against humanity under the Proposed Convention comprises similar aspects with those in the Genocide Convention and Geneva Conventions, such as national legislation, scope of jurisdiction and international co-operation. But the Proposed Convention entails greater details and certainty for those obligations.

Article 2, addressing the object and purposes of the Proposed Convention, outlines State obligation to punish crimes against humanity. Paragraph 1 declares that "the States Parties to the present Convention undertake to prevent crimes against humanity and to investigate, prosecute, and punish those responsible for such crimes". Paragraph 2 formulates several obligations: co-operation with other States, fair and effective investigations, prosecutions, and punishments, co-operation with the ICC and other tribunals, and assistance to other States in fulfilling their obligations.

Article 8 requires States to enact necessary legislation and undefined "other measures" to give effect to the Proposed Convention. The ensuing obligations require States to make crimes against humanity a criminal offense as well as a military one, provide for appropriate punishments, and ensure military commanders and superiors are held responsible in accordance with other provisions of the Proposed Convention.[63] States are also responsible to ensure through both legislation and administrative measures that victims have access to justice and the right to appropriate reparations.[64]

States also have investigation and prosecution obligations under Article 8. When States receive information that a person who has committed or is alleged to have committed crimes against humanity may be present in its territory, the State is required to investigate. It is not stated what level of certainty is necessary to trigger an investigation, although based on the repeated references to "measures under domestic law" it would be logical to assume that the information must meet the minimum standards

---

[61] *Ibid.*, para. 9.

[62] Proposed Convention, Preamble, Explanatory Note.

[63] Proposed Convention, Article 5.

[64] *Ibid.*, Article 8(5).

set out in domestic law. States are required to take this action, though the measures taken can be mitigated by the domestic law of the State concerned. Once the investigation is completed and the alleged perpetrator is located, States are required to ensure that the person will be available for prosecution or extradition where necessary. The remainder of the investigation and prosecution obligations addresses matters such as the protection of witnesses and access to justice for victims.

The Proposed Convention explicitly recognizes universal jurisdiction as an obligation – "[e]ach State Party shall take necessary measures to establish its competence to exercise jurisdiction over crimes against humanity when the alleged offender is present in any territory under its jurisdiction".[65] Article 10 also lists other grounds of jurisdiction, including territorial jurisdiction, positive and negative personal jurisdictions. States Parties may only be relieved of the obligation to prosecute by extraditing the alleged offender to another State or to the ICC or other recognized international criminal tribunals, pursuant to the principle *aut dedere aut judicare*.[66] The Explanatory Note points out that States not party to the ICC Statute do not have an obligation to extradite to the ICC, but may co-operate.[67] It should be noted that where there is no request for extradition from another State, and extradition to an international court is not possible, States parties are *obligated* to exercise universal jurisdiction over crimes against humanity.

Back in 1995, the Appeals Chamber of the ICTY has already declared in the *Tadić* case that "universal jurisdiction [is] nowadays acknowledged in the case of international crimes".[68] Likewise, the Trial Chamber of the ICTY in the *Furundžija* case found that:[69]

> It has been held that international crimes being universally condemned wherever they occur, every State has the right to prosecute and punish the authors of such crimes. As stated in general terms by the Supreme Court of Israel in *Eichmann*, and echoed by a USA court in *Demjanjuk*, "it is the universal

---

[65] *Ibid.*, Articles 9(1) and 10(3).

[66] *Ibid.*, Articles 8(9).

[67] *Ibid.*, Article 9, Explanatory Note.

[68] ICTY, *Prosecutor v. Tadić*, Case No. IT-94-1, Decision on the Defence Motion for Interlocutory Appeal on Jurisdiction, 2 October 1995, para. 62.

[69] ICTY, *Prosecutor v. Furundžija*, Case No. IT-95-17/1-T, Judgment, 10 December 1998, para. 156.

character of the crimes in question [i.e. international crimes]
which vests in every State the authority to try and punish
those who participated in their commission".

The affirmation of universal jurisdiction by the Proposed Convention seems to be a progressive development of international law. The movement from 'right' to 'obligation' is not only significant for the punishment of crimes against humanity, it is symbolic to the punishment of core international crimes in general.

In terms of State obligation to co-operate in the punishment of crimes against humanity, the Proposed Convention includes concrete provisions dealing with evidence, extradition, mutual legal assistance, transfer of criminal proceedings and enforcement of punishment.[70]

Article 25 addresses interpretation, stating that terms in the Proposed Convention should be interpreted "in the light of internationally recognized human rights standards and norms". While the Explanatory Note references only the Vienna Convention and the regional human rights conventions, it also notes that interpretation should be in accordance with specific obligations established by treaties regarding different human rights conventions. With this provision, it becomes possible to look to the other human rights treaties for evidence of how certain aspects of the Proposed Convention should be interpreted, if not specifically stated in the text.

For those who believe State obligations in these areas already exist under customary international law, the Proposed Convention serves the important purpose of codification. Depending on how the Proposed Convention is received and used by States and international judicial organs, it is possible that the provisions regarding State obligation to punish crimes against humanity could eventually become binding on States not party to the Convention.

Though the drafters of the Proposed Convention drew on the existing instruments to punish international crimes, such as the Genocide Convention and ICC Statute, for inspiration, in many respects the Proposed Convention expands State obligations to punish. This can partially be attributed to the passage of time; a new Genocide Convention would likely take into account lessons learned from the genocide in Rwanda, for example. Perhaps most importantly, interpretation of the Proposed Conven-

---

[70]   Proposed Convention, Article 8(D).

tion can benefit from the subsequent State practice and interpretations of international judicial organs.

7.6. Conclusion

The Proposed Convention builds on the State obligations to punish already codified in the Genocide Convention, the Geneva Conventions and their 1977 Additional Protocols, and the ICC Statute. Its very existence indicates the solidifying of the customary law regarding crimes against humanity. Crimes against humanity have long been considered one of the core crimes of international concern (and are referred to as such in the ICC Statute); the Proposed Convention would be the most formal indication that States must take them as seriously as they do war crimes and genocide.

The Genocide Convention and the Geneva Conventions, written and adopted in the years after World War II, contain more generalized requirements and often leave it to States Parties to determine the best methods of compliance. The Proposed Convention, though still leaving room for the differences in States' domestic legal systems, has more exacting requirements, similar to those found in the ICC Statute. This is hardly surprising, as the Explanatory Notes to the Proposed Convention indicate that the drafters drew on a number of international human rights instruments.[71]

Developments of jurisdiction for genocide and war crimes following the adoption of relevant treaties show that international law is moving slowly toward expanding jurisdiction to punish human rights violations. The Proposed Convention confirms this trend. Universal jurisdiction seems to be developing in a way that allows it to cover more crimes or 'less serious' crimes (to the extent that any international human rights violation can be considered 'less serious'). The international community has also allowed States with more limited connections to international crimes to exercise jurisdiction, for example by allowing countries to prosecute foreign nationals located in the State's territory for crimes committed elsewhere, and to which the State has no connection. It is possible that as customary law and case law develop, universal jurisdiction for serious

---

[71] *See, e.g.*, Proposed Convention, Preamble, Explanatory Note, which references the Genocide Convention, the ICC Statute, and the Enforced Disappearance Convention, among others. Other international instruments are referenced throughout the text.

human rights violations may become a firmly established facet of international law.

State actions regarding crimes against humanity have been covered by customary law and other instruments for some time now – the Proposed Convention is a welcome addition to the ever-expanding body of international human rights law and international criminal law. The focus on State obligations in the Proposed Convention, particularly compared to differing focuses in the other instruments, indicates that the role of States in punishing serious human rights violations has become perceptively more prominent in the years since World War II. Though the obligation to prosecute is limited by the lack of humanitarian intervention provisions in the Proposed Convention and other instruments, it can only be hoped that the gradual strengthening of State responsibility will lead to fewer international human rights violations.

Other measures within the existing legal framework have been taken to address failure to punish international crimes. Such measures include diplomatic protests and collective actions, as illustrated by the interpretation of the obligation to "ensure respect" for IHL. Mere statement of an obligation to punish core international crimes is insufficient; efforts should be made to seek appropriate fora to challenge State inaction when there is an international obligation to punish.

8

Towards Greater Coherence in International Criminal Law: Comparing Protected Groups in Genocide and Crimes Against Humanity

Rhea Brathwaite[*]

8.1. Introduction

Raphael Lemkin, a preeminent jurist, tirelessly campaigned to bring awareness to a crime so heinous, he believed that a new word had to be created to define it. Genocide comes from the Greek *genus* which means race or kind and *-cide* which means killing.[1] Although its definition has since been moulded in international law, the kinds of groups envisaged by the 1948 Genocide Convention have remained static.[2] In contrast, the scope of groups protected against persecution in the definition of crimes against humanity has gradually evolved in the past decades. In early 1945, the creation of genocide and crimes against humanity were conceived to address crimes perpetrated by the Nazi regime. They were not identical in scope, but neatly overlapped, and could to some extent be used interchangeably. In the context of new situations, new judgments, and new formulations, both the definition of genocide and crimes against humanity

---

[*] **Rhea Brathwaite** holds a Bachelor's degree in Law (LL.B.) (Hons) from University College London and a Master's degree in International Legal Studies (LL.M.) from Georgetown University Law Center. She joined the Inter-American Development Bank (IDB) in January 2012 where she worked as a Legal and Procurement Consultant for the Haiti Country Department. She currently works as a Modernization of the State Consultant for the Institutional Capacity of the State Division supporting its transparency and accountability work. Before joining the IDB, she gained work experience from the Organization of American States, Scotiabank, and private law firms. Throughout her career in the private sector and international organizations, she has developed experience in topics such as anti-corruption, transparency, and access to information in Latin America and the Caribbean. All Internet references were last accessed on 27 August 2014.

1 Douglas Harper Online Etymology Dictionary, available at http://www.etymonline.com/index.php?search=genocide.

2 Convention on the Prevention and Punishment of the Crime of Genocide, adopted by Resolution 260 (III) A of the U.N. General Assembly on 9 December 1948, entered into force on 12 January 1951 ('Genocide Convention').

have evolved. Expanding the protected groups of both crimes may help in strengthening the two layers of protection available for individuals belonging to groups. International law regarding crimes against humanity has reflected a movement away from the idea of a closed list of groups. The definition of genocide must do the same in order to better protect group members and avoid judicial inconsistencies.

This chapter will first compare the evolution of perceptions of groups in the definitions of crimes against humanity and genocide and the difference between the two (section 8.2.). In section 8.3., I compare the arguments for and against expanding the scope of protected groups regarding genocide. Possible solutions will be proposed that seek to reflect the evolution of international law. Following this section, the implications of a possible solution for the Genocide Convention will be discussed as it relates to the definition of crimes against humanity in the Proposed Crimes Against Humanity Convention (annexed to this volume), before concluding by reaffirming the importance of modifying the definition of genocide.

8.2. The Evolution of Protected Groups in International Law: Comparing Crimes Against Humanity and Genocide

As William A. Schabas has remarked, the "enumeration of the groups protected by the [Genocide] Convention's definition of genocide is perhaps its most controversial aspect".[3] The definition of genocide as set out in the Genocide Convention is deemed by some as "exceedingly narrow".[4] Taking the U.N. Convention Relating to the Status of Refugees as an example, it has recognized the protection of many other groups beyond the four groups enumerated in the Genocide Convention.[5] It protects members "of a particular social group and or political opinion", producing the paradox that "people fleeing from genocide are recognized as refugees while those unable to flee from the same genocide are not acknowledged as being its

---

[3] William A. Schabas, "Groups Protected by the Genocide Convention: Conflicting Interpretations from the International Criminal Tribunal for Rwanda", in *ILSA Journal of International and Comparative Law*, 2000, p. 375.

[4] Kurt Jonassohn, "What is Genocide?", in Helen Fein (ed.), *Genocide Watch*, Yale University Press, 1991, p. 1.

[5] The United Nations Convention Relating to the Status of Refugees, entered into force on 22 April 1954.

victims".[6] Not only is there inconsistency between the Genocide Convention and the U.N. Convention Relating to the Status of Refugees, there is also inconsistency if one compares the protected groups in the Genocide Convention with those in crimes against humanity. There is in this author's opinion a need to broaden the kinds of groups protected by the Genocide Convention to avoid such inconsistencies. International law is moving away from strict categorizations of protected groups and the Genocide Convention would benefit from doing the same.

The definition of 'crimes against humanity' has evolved significantly during its history. The precise words 'crimes against humanity' were probably first coined in the Nuremberg Charter by Robert Jackson, a United States Supreme Court Justice after consultation with Sir Herbert Lauterpacht, an eminent international lawyer from the United Kingdom.[7] Even prior to that, the idea of crimes against humanity was in use. In the 1899 Hague Convention, the expression 'laws of humanity' or the 'Martens Clause' was used, rather than 'crimes against humanity' as such.[8] The Hague Convention does not define them, but simply states that civilians and belligerents are protected by these laws. An attempt was made to use the 'laws of humanity' against Turkish individuals for their 1915 slaughter of Armenians, but that proposal was not followed through.[9] The United States objected that there were not at the time agreed-upon 'laws of humanity'.[10]

We have since seen several definitions of crimes against humanity in international law. Article 6(c) of the Nuremberg Charter of 1945 states:

> Crimes against humanity: namely, murder, extermination, enslavement, deportation, and other inhuman acts committed against any civilian population, before or during the war, or persecutions on political, racial or religious grounds in execution of or in connection with any crime within the juris-

---

[6]   Jonassohn, see *supra* note 4, p. 9.

[7]   David Luban, Julie R. O'Sullivan, David P. Stewart, *International and Transnational Criminal Law*, Aspen Publishers, 2010.

[8]   The Hague Convention of 1899(II) Respecting the Laws and Customs of War on Land, enacted on 29 July 1899.

[9]   Luban *et al.*, see *supra* note 7.

[10] *Ibid.*

diction of the Tribunal, whether or not in violation of the domestic law of the country where perpetrated.[11]

Some aspects of this definition should be noted. First, the crimes are committed against any civilian population. Second, there are two kinds of crimes against humanity, the murder type, and the persecution type, based on group membership. Third, the acts are criminalized whether or not in violation of the domestic law of the country where perpetrated.

Control Council Law No. 10 ('CCL No. 10') enacted the offenses of the Nuremberg Charter in Germany. Crimes against humanity were defined in Article II (c):

> Crimes against Humanity. Atrocities and offenses, including but not limited to murder, extermination, enslavement, deportation, imprisonment, torture, rape, or other inhumane acts committed against any civilian population, or persecutions on political, racial or religious grounds whether or not in violation of the domestic laws of the country where perpetrated.[12]

For purposes of this comparison, it is noteworthy that CCL No. 10 adds crimes to the murder type such as imprisonment, torture and rape. The groups enumerated of the persecution type do not change.

The International Criminal Tribunals for the Former Yugoslavia ('ICTY') and Rwanda ('ICTR') have different definitions of crimes against humanity. The ICTY Statute defines crimes against humanity as follows:

> The International Tribunal shall have the power to prosecute persons responsible for the following crimes when committed in armed conflict, whether international or internal in character, and directed against any civilian population:
>
> (a) murder;
> (b) extermination;
> (c) enslavement;
> (d) deportation;

---

[11] Agreement for the Prosecution and Punishment of the Major War Criminals of the European Axis and Charter of the International Military Tribunal, enacted on 8 August 1945, London.

[12] Control Council Law No. 10, Punishment of Persons Guilty of War Crimes, Crimes against Peace and against Humanity, enacted on 20 December 1945.

    (e)   imprisonment;

    (f)   torture;

    (g)   rape;

    (h)   persecutions on political, racial and religious grounds;

    (i)   other inhumane acts.[13]

This definition copies that of CCL No. 10. It does not add anything in terms of protected groups. The ICTR Statute is similar to the ICTY Statute, but adds that the attack on the civilian population must be based on national, political, ethnic, racial or religious grounds, eliminating the war nexus. The ICTR's definition seems to say that even crimes of the murder type must be based on group discrimination.[14] The requirement has been dropped in subsequent definitions of crimes against humanity. The persecution type crimes already had a discriminatory intent requirement.[15] The Rome Statute of the International Criminal Court ('ICC Statute') defines crimes against humanity as follows:

> 1. For the purpose of this Statute, "crime against humanity" means any of the following acts when committed as part of a widespread or systematic attack directed against any civilian population, with knowledge of the attack:
>
>   (a)   Murder;
>
>   (b)   Extermination;
>
>   (c)   Enslavement;
>
>   (d)   Deportation or forcible transfer of population;
>
>   (e)   Imprisonment or other severe deprivation of physical liberty in violation of fundamental rules of international law;
>
>   (f)   Torture;

---

[13]   Article 5, Statute of the International Tribunal for the Prosecution of Persons Responsible for Serious Violations of International Humanitarian Law Committed in the Territory of the Former Yugoslavia since 1991, adopted on 25 May 1993 by Resolution 827 ('ICTY Statute').

[14]   Article 3, Statute of the International Criminal Tribunal for the Prosecution of Persons Responsible for Genocide and Other Serious Violations of International Humanitarian Law Committed in the Territory of Rwanda and Rwandan Citizens Responsible for Genocide and Other Such Violations Committed in the Territory of Neighbouring States, between 1 January 1994 and 31 December 1994, adopted on 8 November 1994 by resolution 955 (1994) ('ICTR Statute').

[15]   Luban *et al.*, see *supra* note 7.

(g)   Rape, sexual slavery, enforced prostitution, forced pregnancy, enforced sterilization, or any other form of sexual violence of comparable gravity;

(h)   Persecution against any identifiable group or collectivity on political, racial, national, ethnic, cultural, religious, gender as defined in paragraph 3, or other grounds that are universally recognized as impermissible under international law, in connection with any act referred to in this paragraph or any crime within the jurisdiction of the Court;

(i)   Enforced disappearance of persons;

(j)   The crime of apartheid;

(k)   Other inhumane acts of a similar character intentionally causing great suffering, or serious injury to body or to mental or physical health.[16]

Finally, the United Nations International Law Commission ('ILC') voted on 30 July 2013 to add the elaboration of a treaty on 'crimes against humanity' to its long-term work programme.[17] Chapter 2 above elaborates in some detail on the significance of the Commission's involvement with this issue. The definition set out in the Proposed Crimes Against Humanity Convention repeats the formulation of the ICC Statute.[18]

For our purposes, it is important to note that the definition of the ICC Statute and the Proposed Convention adopts additional crimes of the murder type such as forcible transfer of population, sexual slavery, forced prostitution or pregnancy, and forced sterilization, enforced disappearances and apartheid. The persecution type crimes have also expanded to include persecution on grounds of nationality, culture, gender, ethnicity, or "other grounds that are universally recognized as impermissible under international law". Gender means "the two sexes, male and female, within the context of society".[19]

---

[16]   Article 7, Rome Statute of the International Criminal Court, adopted on 17 July 1998.

[17]   For more information on the addition of 'crimes against humanity' to the work programme of the ILC at its sixty-fifth session in 2013, see the Report of the International Law Commission, available at http://legal.un.org/ilc/reports/2013/All_languages/A_68_10_E.pdf.

[18]   Proposed International Convention on the Prevention and Punishment of Crimes Against Humanity, see Annex 1.

[19]   Article 7(3), ICC Statute.

Genocide's evolution differs from that of crimes against humanity. Lemkin, the Polish jurist who coined the word 'genocide', first conceived of it as:

> a coordinated plan of different actions aiming at the destruction of essential foundations of the life of national groups with the aim of annihilating the groups themselves [...] genocide is directed against the national group as an entity and the actions involved are against individuals, not in their individual capacity but as members of the national group.[20]

Lemkin envisaged 'national' group not in relation to the nature of the group but rather he envisaged 'national' to be used in relation to the nature of the persecution.[21] He therefore saw genocide as "a multi-faceted attack on the existence of a human group and identified eight features of the crime, including political, social, cultural, economic, biological, physical, religious and moral genocide", but noted that physical, biological and cultural genocide were its most accepted forms.[22] However, although Lemkin had a broad conception of the forms the persecution may take, he had a narrow conception of the nature of the groups themselves which should be protected, which is similar to that of the Genocide Convention.[23]

Genocide became part of international law shortly thereafter. It was not envisaged as a separate crime until the Genocide Convention, but rather it was thought of as a part of crimes against humanity.[24] The word 'genocide' was used in the Nuremberg trial, but instead of explicitly using this term to convict the perpetrators, the judges called the killing of the Jewish people a crime against humanity.[25] The Genocide Convention gives genocide a distinct status. The United Nations General Assembly passed a unanimous resolution which condemned genocide and confined itself to four enumerated groups, national, ethnic, racial and religious.[26]

---

[20] David L. Nersessian, "The Razor's Edge: Defining and Protecting Human Groups under the Genocide Convention", in *Cornell International Law Journal*, 2003, p. 297.

[21] Schabas, 2000, see *supra* note 3, p. 376.

[22] Nersessian, 2003, see *supra* note 20, p. 297.

[23] For example, Lemkin opposed the addition of political groups to the four groups enumerated in the Convention. Schabas, 2000, see *supra* note 3, p. 377.

[24] *Ibid.*

[25] *Ibid.*

[26] General Assembly Resolution 96, The crime of genocide, A/RES/96(I), 11 December 1946.

Subsequently, the sub-committee of the Sixth Committee explicitly made mention of "racial, religious, political and other groups".[27] There is no explanation why "political and other groups" were added in the beginning, in any case these conditions were debated and omitted in the ultimate text of the Genocide Convention.[28] An exhaustive list of the four groups, national, ethnic, racial and religious was included, and in 1948, the Genocide Convention was adopted unanimously.[29] Article II of this Convention defines the crime as such:

> In the present Convention, genocide means any of the following acts committed with intent to destroy, in whole or in part, a national, ethnical, racial or religious group, as such:
>
> (a) Killing members of the group;
>
> (b) Causing serious bodily or mental harm to members of the group;
>
> (c) Deliberately inflicting on the group conditions of life calculated to bring about its physical destruction in whole or in part;
>
> (d) Imposing measures intended to prevent births within the group;
>
> (e) Forcibly transferring children of the group to another group.[30]

The Genocide Convention protects groups and individuals in so far as they are group members but "the real object of protection is the group itself".[31] For that reason an individual must be part of a protected group in order to claim protection under the Genocide Convention, even if the actor's intention is to destroy this individual in relation to the destruction of a protected group.[32] This means that, if we take the Rwandan genocide as an example, Hutus who are killed, when the ultimate intention was to kill

---

[27] Report of the Sixth Committee of the General Assembly of the United Nations, A/231 – 10, December 1946.

[28] *Ibid.* For the debates, see *infra* section 8.2.

[29] "Developments in the Law – International Criminal Law", in *Harvard Law Review*, 2001, vol. 114, p. 2010.

[30] Genocide Convention, see *supra* note 2.

[31] Nersessian, 2003, p. 298, see *supra* note 20.

[32] *Ibid.*, p. 299.

Tutsis, cannot claim that there was genocidal intent directed towards them.[33]

The drafters oscillated between narrowing the definition in order to reprimand the actors of the holocaust and broadening it in order to fit future situations. This tension may have led to the narrowing of protected groups, as one commentator has said, "what was left out of the convention is as important as what was included".[34] As will be seen below, the omission of certain groups, such as tribal groups, has led to problems in its application. Since the Genocide Convention has been enacted the International Law Commission has sought to enlarge the enumerated groups and make the number of protected groups non-exhaustive.[35] It has since abandoned this project. The ICC Statute could have also been an excellent vehicle for enlarging the number of protected groups, but the final version simply repeats the groups enumerated in the Genocide Convention.[36]

If we compare these two crimes, it is easy to see that crimes against humanity have evolved in a different direction in comparison to genocide. The kinds of acts of the murder type have evolved and so have the protected groups in the crime of persecution. The disparities between the two are most noticeable in relation to the ICC Statute. For persecution as a crime against humanity defined under Article 7, the all-encompassing group based on "other grounds that are universally recognized as impermissible under international law" allows for the future evolution of persecution to include groups that international law may one day deem acceptable for protection. The emphasis on 'universality' allows for a certain measure of consensus amongst States on future protected groups. It is uncertain what the threshold for universality may be, but the fact that the

---

[33] Ibid.

[34] Developments in International Criminal Law, 2001, see supra note 29, p. 2011.

[35] Yearbook 1951, Vol. I, 90th meeting, pp. 66–68; Yearbook 1951, Vol. II, p. 136; "Fourth report on the draft Code of Offences against the Peace and Security of Mankind", by Doudou Thiam, Special Rapporteur, U.N. Doc. A/CN.4/398 (1986), Article 12(1); Yearbook 1989, Vol. 1, 2099th meeting, p. 25, para. 42; Yearbook.1989, Vol. 1, 2100th meeting, p. 27; Yearbook 1989, Vol. 1, 2102nd meeting, p. 41; "Report of the Commission to the General Assembly on the work of its forty-first session", U.N. Doc. A/CN.4/SER.A/1989/Add.l (Part 2), p. 59; Yearbook 1991, Vol. 1, 2239th meeting, p. 214; Yearbook 1991, Vol. 1, 2251st meeting, pp. 292–293; "Report of the Commission to the General Assembly on the work of its forty-third session", U.N. Doc. A/CN.4/SER.A/199 I/Add. I (Part 2), p. 102.

[36] Article 6, ICC Statute.

definition of crimes against humanity allows for changing circumstances is progressive.

The same cannot be said for the Genocide Convention which has actually decreased the coverage it allots to protect victim groups. The desire to address the perpetrators of the holocaust is admirable, but the narrow restrictions have required judges to stretch definitions or invent new interpretations in order to accommodate unforeseen victim groups. The judicial gymnastics that judges are bound to participate in have led to inconsistencies amongst tribunals and may have also handicapped the utility of genocide. The hesitation to add more groups to the kinds of groups protected by the Genocide Convention stems from various arguments which will be addressed below.

8.3. The Need for Change

There are several arguments raised by those who believe that the protection of groups in the Genocide Convention and other international law instruments dealing with genocide is sufficient. First of all, there is the argument that changing the definition of genocide may be politically impossible. Second, there is fear that changing the definition of genocide may lead to spurious claims due to the indeterminacy of some kinds of groups. Third, it has been argued that situations envisaged by the expanded definition of genocide are already covered by crimes against humanity. Finally, reluctance also comes from the belief that so far, the expansive interpretation of protected groups by international criminal tribunals has proved to be satisfactory.

8.3.1. Existing Political Will to Expand the Scope of Protected Groups

Many hold that changing the international instruments may be too difficult due to political considerations. The Genocide Convention was signed with unanimous consent. The political will to change the definition after so many years may lead to disagreement about its scope. The Genocide Convention was signed when there were fewer countries to deal with. In addition there are those who believe that opening up the Genocide Convention may deteriorate its scope and protection: although it may not be perfect, changing the convention may be worse than leaving it as it is.

Although it is a legitimate concern, countries are in effect broadening the protection they afford when enacting the Genocide Convention in their domestic law. The political will certainly exists to broaden the kinds of groups protected amongst those States that have ratified the convention. States have widened the scope of the convention, showing their willingness to go beyond the text to protect victims that the Genocide Convention may not have envisaged, and also reflecting their view that the Genocide Convention is inadequate in this particular area. Some of the countries with this view include France which has interpreted the enumerated groups as "national, ethnic, racial or religious group", or a group determined by "any other arbitrary criterion"; Canada also has a broad definition which simply requires "an identifiable group of persons"; and Georgia's statute contains the four enumerated groups and adds or any other group "united by any other mark".[37]

8.3.2. Selection of Enumerated Protected Groups

Inclusion of the notion of cultural genocide was rejected due to fears that it would lead to spurious claims, which would detract from the legitimacy of the convention's goals, in particular, physical extermination of the groups.[38] The reason for the omission of cultural genocide is mostly the uncertainty that it engendered.[39] The scope of the Genocide Convention was confined to essentially physical acts.

Cultural genocide has been defined as such by UNESCO:

---

[37] France: Penal Code Journal Officiel, 6 August 2014, Article 211–1; Canada: An Act respecting the criminal law (R.S.C. 1985, c. C-46, as amended), Article 318 (2); Georgia: The Criminal Code of Georgia, Article 407.

[38] Developments in International Criminal Law, 2001, p. 2012, see *supra* note 29.

[39] This is because cultural genocide does not mean physical destruction of the group. For example, the Secretariat and Ad Hoc Committee Drafts of the Convention on the Prevention and Punishment of the Crime of Genocide considered that it included: "the systematic destruction of books printed in the national language or of religious works or prohibition of new publications", the "systematic destruction of historical or religious monuments or their diversion to alien uses, destruction or dispersion of documents and objects of historical, artistic, or religious value and of objects used in religious worship", and also "prohibiting the use of the language of the group in daily intercourse or in schools, or the printing and circulation of publications in the language of the group". Convention on the Prevention and Punishment of the Crime of Genocide, the Secretariat and Ad Hoc Committee Drafts, available at http://www.preventgenocide.org/law/convention/drafts/.

> An ethnic group is denied the right to enjoy, develop and transmit its own culture and its own language, whether individually or collectively [...] cultural genocide is a violation of international law equivalent to genocide which was condemned by the United Nations Convention on the Prevention and Punishment of the Crime of Genocide.[40]

Even though the instrument states that cultural genocide is a violation of international law tantamount to genocide, the Genocide Convention has not been modified to include cultural genocide. It must be noted though that some commentators prefer to designate the suppression of culture accompanied by mass killings as cultural genocide, not the suppression of culture alone.[41] This is because it would seem inappropriate to place on the same level the suppression of culture and physical exterminations. There is also a threshold that must be reached. Most suppression of culture probably would not fall under the realm of cultural genocide. Shaw admits that cultural genocide is often confused and many times superfluous because taken along with the physical element of genocide, it may simply be said to be the cultural dimension of genocide. It seems that any genocide would have some cultural element. He therefore divides the suppression of culture into three groups and states that,

> it is better to refer to cultural suppression as it relates to pre-genocidal denial of culture, the cultural dimension of genocide [is] suppression that is part of a broader genocidal process, and unintentional group destruction for cases where groups are destroyed by disease and famine that are originally unintended.[42]

Cultural genocide itself is hard to apply in concrete situations, thus the drafting members of the Genocide Convention were right to leave it out.

Political genocide was also left out of the convention, but it should have been included as it does not lead to spurious claims. Political genocide was omitted due to a compromise to accommodate the Soviet Union. Although it was debated extensively and agreed upon in the drafting stag-

---

40 Declaration of San Jose, Meeting of Experts on Ethno-Development and Ethnocide in in Latin America, UNESCO, San Jose, 11December 1981, available at http://unesdoc.unesco. org/images/0004/000499/049951eo.pdf.

41 Shaw, 2007, p. 66, see *supra* note 4.

42 *Ibid.*

es, it was ultimately regarded to be too controversial by governments feeling vulnerable to claims of genocide. During the debates there were claims that political groups were not stable and permanent, and therefore their inclusion was anathema to their aims.[43] In addition, it was claimed that political groups were joined by choice and therefore were different from groups one simply belonged to. It did not fit in with the other enumerated groups in the convention. The Soviet delegate seized on the indeterminacy of political groups, calling them "not scientific".[44]

As will be seen below, the other groups of the Genocide Convention are neither stable nor permanent with the exception of race and possibly ethnicity. The political genocide in the draft Genocide Convention was discussed extensively due to its controversial nature and the reluctance of countries to be bound. Shaw states that the main difference between political groups and the other groups in the Genocide Convention is that political groups are associations, national, ethnical and racial groups are communities.[45] Political groups represent social groups and are power organizations which mobilize power to enter into conflict while communities focus on cohesiveness rather than conflict.[46] Shaw makes it clear though that these divisions are not rigid and political groups can become communities, yet they are simply unprotected in the Genocide Convention.[47]

8.3.3. Insufficient Function of Crimes Against Humanity

Schabas claims that the four terms of the Genocide Convention "not only overlap, they also help to define each other, operating much as four corner posts that delimit an area in which a myriad of groups covered by the convention find protection".[48] For those groups such as political groups that cannot fit within the 'goal posts' of the enumerated groups, Schabas in his book 'Genocide: The Crime of Crimes' claims that the *lacuna* can

---

43 Summary Records of the meetings of the Sixth Committee of the General Assembly, 21 September –10 December 1948, Official Records of the General Assembly.

44 *Ibid.*

45 Shaw, 2007, p. 70, see *supra* note 4.

46 *Ibid.*

47 *Ibid.*

48 Schabas, 2000, p. 385, see *supra* note 3.

be filled by crimes against humanity in the Rome Statute of the International Criminal Court and other international human rights instruments.[49]

David Nersessian has stated that using persecution to criminalize political genocide (for example) is first of all, not possible because genocide and persecution are cumulative offenses.[50] In order to be cumulative, the ICTY Appeals Chamber states in *Krstić* case that "there must be separate conduct satisfying a distinct element".[51] Nersessian argues that there are five different elements between these two offenses: (a) the *actus reus* of the chapeau; (b) the *mens rea* of the chapeau; (c) victim classifications; (d) 'policy' element of the offenses; and (e) the requirement that persecution be committed in conjunction with some other international crime. The differences between the two crimes preclude using persecution instead of genocide in practice. Crimes against humanity cannot be an alternative to genocide because they "cover different legal ground".[52]

Second of all, using persecution instead of the concept of political genocide is against the principle of fair-labelling of criminal offenses.[53] The crime of persecution "is not sufficient to respond to the criminality inherent in destroying a political group as such".[54] The principle of fair-labelling is the aim to ensure that "widely felt distinctions between kinds of offences and degrees of wrongdoing are respected and signalled by the law, and that offences are subdivided and labelled so as to represent fairly the nature and magnitude of the law-breaking".[55] This argument is premised upon the assumption that genocide is a more serious crime than crimes against humanity. Even Schabas, who calls genocide "the crime of crimes", would agree that genocide is a more serious crime, and therefore, treating actions that should be labelled as genocide as crimes against hu-

---

[49] William A. Schabas, *Genocide in International Law: The Crime of Crimes*, 2000, pp. 103–104.

[50] See generally, David L. Nersessian, "Comparative Approaches to Punishing Hate: The Intersection of Genocide and Crimes Against Humanity", in *Stanford Journal International Law*, 2007, vol. 43, pp. 249–251.

[51] ICTY, *Prosecutor v. Krstić*, Appeal Judgment, 19 April 2004, Case No. ICTY-98-33-A, para. 217.

[52] See generally, Nersessian, 2007, p. 255, see *supra* note 50. Nersessian's treatise need not be covered in depth for the purposes of this argument.

[53] *Ibid.*

[54] *Ibid.*

[55] James Chalmers and Fiona Leverick, "Fair labelling in criminal law", in *The Modern Law Review*, 2008, vol. 71, no. 2.

---

manity is unfair to the victims.[56] It also attaches a lighter moral burden on the perpetrator due to the significantly lower social stigmatization of persons who have committed crimes against humanity compared to those who have committed genocide.

8.3.4. Problematic Judicial Interpretations of the Enumerated Groups

Kurt Jonassohn remarked that, it is amazing that in practice, "none of the victim groups of those genocides that have occurred since its adoption falls within its restrictive specifications".[57] This statement may still hold some truth today. Creative judicial interpretation has stepped in to fill the gap between the restrictions on the kinds of groups that may be protected and has helped to give the impression of diminishing the inadequacy of the Genocide Convention's definition. Those that believe that judicial interpretation of the Genocide Convention is adequate point to the advent of subjective and objective interpretations of each of the protected groups and the criteria of stability and permanence.

The *Akayesu* case was the first genocide trial before an international criminal tribunal after the adoption of the Genocide Convention. There the ICTR was challenged by the definition of 'ethnical group', which means having different culture and language.[58] The groups in question, Tutsis and Hutus, share the same language and the same culture. In order to accommodate the specificity of the situation, an ICTR Trial Chamber found that the intention of the drafters of the Genocide Convention "was patently to ensure the protection of any stable and permanent group", and therefore its application was not limited to the four enumerated groups. It found that there were a number of objective factors which distinguished the Tutsis as a distinct stable and permanent group.[59] In effect, it ignored

---

[56] Schabas, 2000, see *supra* note 49.

[57] Jonassohn, 1991, see *supra* note 4; Kurt Jonassohn, Karin Solveig Bjornson, *Genocide and Gross Human Rights Violations: In Comparative Perspective*, Transaction Publishers, 1998, p. 9.

[58] ICTR, *Prosecutor v. Akayesu*, Appeal Judgment, 1 June 2001, Case No. ICTR-96-4-A, para. 702.

[59] ICTR, *Prosecutor v. Akayesu*, Trial Judgment, 2 September 1998, Case No. ICTR-96-4-T, para. 511. It stated:

> On reading through the travaux preparatoires of the Genocide Convention (Summary Records of the meetings of the Sixth

the four enumerated groups, and went beyond the unambiguous language of the Genocide Convention, because it saw a need for a broader definition which would encompass the situation at hand.

In the *Kayishema* case, the ICTR used the aforementioned definition of an ethnic group and stated that the Tutsis did not comply with the objective definition of an ethnic group enunciated by the *Akayesu* Trial Chamber, but rather, they complied with a purely subjective definition, because they were viewed as having a distinct ethnicity by the Rwandan government.[60] The judges in the *Rutaganda* case admitted there was a lack of "generally and internationally accepted precise definitions" of the protected groups, and therefore each group could only be defined according to their political, social and cultural context.[61] In addition, the ICTR admitted that defining the protected groups was essentially a subjective exercise rather than an objective one. The subjective definition was not enough though, it also had to be accompanied by objective factors and the stability and permanence requirement. It concluded the Tutsis complied with all the requirements, after examining the relevant evidence.[62]

The ICTY first dealt with the definition of protected groups in the *Jelisić* case.[63] It found that using objective criteria to define the protected groups may not comport with those affected by the classification, and in addition there were not any appropriate objective criteria. It also stated that the criteria of stability and permanence, or at least groups which "in-

---

Committee of the General Assembly, 21 September–10 December 1948, Official Records of the General Assembly), it appears that the crime of genocide was allegedly perceived as targeting only "stable" groups, constituted in a permanent fashion and membership of which is determined by birth, with the exclusion of the more "mobile" groups which one joins through individual voluntary commitment, such as political and economic groups. Therefore, a common criterion in the four types of groups protected by the Genocide Convention is that membership in such groups would seem to be normally not challengeable by its members, who belong to it automatically, by birth, in a continuous and often irremediable manner.

[60] ICTR, *Prosecutor v. Kayishema and Ruzindana*, Case No. ICTR-95-1-T, Trial Judgment, 21 May 1999, paras. 34–35, 98.

[61] ICTR, *Prosecutor v. Rutaganda*, Case No. ICTR-9 6-3-T, Trial Judgment, 6 December 1999, para. 55.

[62] *Ibid.*, para. 56.

[63] ICTY, *Prosecutor v. Jelisić*, Case No. IT-95-10, Trial Judgment, 14 December 1999.

---

dividuals belong regardless of their own desires" should be used.[64] Therefore the *Jelisić* case embraced a purely subjective method of viewing the
protected groups, which differs from that embraced by the ICTR in the
Rutaganda case.

The inappropriateness of using the convention's definition of genocide has been shown repeatedly in practice. Both the ICTY and the ICTR
have struggled to interpret the protected groups in the Genocide Convention in a manner that provides protection to victims. The problem is that
the drafters of the Genocide Convention may not have envisaged the
kinds of groups that subsequently fell victim of these crimes. Already
there are problems with interpreting the Genocide Convention. New situations may arise that are outside the present scope of the Genocide Convention, and a corresponding interpretation may not be readily available.

These findings add a new category to the enumerated groups in the
Genocide Convention, as Paul Magnarella notes, by allowing stable and
permanent groups which are not in the convention to be protected. The
use of the *travaux preparatoires* is controversial in itself. It has been criticized for many reasons, including the fact that it is against "widely-
accepted international authority". Use of the *travaux preparatoires* is only
available to rectify a manifestly absurd or conflicting treaty construction
or for confirming a plain-text interpretation.[65] The judges go beyond this
by simply applying the *travaux preparatoires*. It has also been condemned
because the *travaux preparatoires* are a work of compromise amongst
States and statements by States were not supposed to have binding effect.[66]

Use of the criteria of stability and permanence to explain the existence of the four groups is also legally inconsistent. The *travaux preparatoires* included political groups, which are neither stable nor permanent.
They were eliminated at the last minute as a compromise to ensure the
maximum number of adherents possible. In addition, the criterion of stability simply does not apply to the groups enumerated in the convention.
The Universal Declaration of Human Rights recognizes the right to

---

64 *Ibid.*, para. 69.
65 *Ibid.*, Nersessian.
66 *Ibid.*

change one's nationality or religion.[67] These groups cannot be said to be stable and permanent.

The *Rutaganda* and *Kayishema* judgments use the ethnical protected group to justify protection of the Tutsis, even though admittedly the members of both groups speak the same language and have the same culture.[68] Since then, the debate has raged on whether objective criteria or subjective criteria are adequate for resolving whether or not a group is distinct. The International Commission for Darfur, for example, used a purely subjective approach in determining whether there was a separate group.[69] The *Krstić* case then states that the criterion that must be used is one that combines both subjective and objective approaches.[70]

These contrasting approaches are not only unsatisfactory on their own, they have also led to a divergence amongst tribunals that has not been resolved. The differing interpretations of the Genocide Convention by the ICTY and the ICTR are a direct result of the lack of an expansive enumeration of protected groups which covers situations facing the tribunals. It has led to confusion and inconsistency amongst tribunals. Tribunals' attempts to interpret "may undermine the international community's confidence in the tribunals as competent bodies of criminal justice adjudication".[71]

Consistency amongst the differing tribunals is necessary, but that may be impossible since the differing tribunals are, by way of creative judicial law-making, attempting to respond to the demands before them, based on the political, social and cultural context of the situation; a task which they are ill-equipped to undertake due to the sparse language of the Genocide Convention. It may be easier to achieve consistency by simply enlarging the kinds of groups that may be protected in the Genocide Convention or the ICC Statute in order to ensure consistency and restore confidence in the tribunals' competence.

---

[67] Article 18, Universal Declaration of Human Rights, available at http://www.legal-tools.org/doc/de5d83/.

[68] See *supra* notes 60 and 61.

[69] Report of the International Commission of Inquiry on Darfur to the United Nations Secretary-General Pursuant to Security Council Resolution 1564 of 18 September 2004.

[70] See *supra* note 51.

[71] Developments in International Criminal Law, 2001, p. 2021, see *supra* note 29.

Not only are the decisions of the ICTY and ICTR inconsistent, they could also be amenable to political pressure. The resultant confusion due to the ambiguity of the Genocide Convention may mean that the United Nations and individual States may take advantage of the discretion of these international tribunals, especially since these international tribunals could be amenable to political pressure not only from the international organization that enacts them but also from the host country. The United Nations may exert pressure on tribunals, and tribunals may be tempted to bend the law as not doing so may defeat the whole purpose of the creation of the tribunals. If the tribunal could not find that genocide had occurred, it would put in jeopardy its existence. Another case illustrates the political pressure it is under from the host country. The ICTR attempted to release Jean-Bosco Barayagwiza, a suspect because of his excessive detention, but Rwanda threatened to not co-operate with the ICTR if that happened. It had to claim to have received "new facts" which shone a negative light on Barayagwiza and meant that he could not be released.[72] It has been argued that,

> the tribunals' susceptibility to political pressure raises concerns about whether they are the institutions best equipped to define 'ethnical groups' [...] to reduce their susceptibility to external pressure and to enhance their credibility, it is crucial that the tribunals place an even higher priority on achieving consistency.[73]

8.4. Viable Solutions

It has been suggested that making precedent binding would solve the problem of inconsistent judicial interpretation.[74] This is not enough. The best solution is to have a broader enumeration of groups that reflects the world we live in today, and that is able to adapt to future situations, but leaves little room for judicial interpretation. Certainty is desirable. Vagueness of international criminal offenses may contravene the principle of lenity. Unsatisfactory and controversial decisions cannot form the basis of accusing suspected criminals. A legislated solution that takes better

---

[72] *Ibid.*, p. 2022–2023.
[73] *Ibid.*
[74] *Ibid.*, p. 2024.

account of the conditions of the world we live in is the best solution to this problem.

Modifying the Genocide Convention may be a possible solution to this international problem. Additionally, changing the ICC Statute is equally beneficial. The ICC Statute will be used in future International Criminal Court cases. Judges are obliged to apply it. It would eliminate the excessive exercise of judicial discretion which has led to divergent interpretations of the protected groups and once and for all provide them with more certainty.

The definition of genocide may also be altered by individual States. States have attempted to alter the scope of the Genocide Convention by widening the number of protected groups when introducing it into their domestic legislation, with the view to provide better protection to their population. In principle, going beyond the protection afforded by international law is not against international law.[75] Although this is commendable, it is still not a substitute for change on the international level.

Now that the medium to execute the necessary change has been discussed, the question remains, how should the definition of genocide be changed textually?

Adding specific types of groups may expand protection and strengthen certainty at the same time. Among others, it has been demonstrated that political genocide should be included in a possible definition of genocide. The downside of this approach is that it may not be enough to deal with future situations, and may be as restrictive as the Genocide Convention is in the future.

An all-encompassing approach may provide more comprehensive protection to victim groups. The French formulation which includes the enumerated groups in the Genocide Convention and adds to them an additional group determined by "any arbitrary criterion" may be used. It certainly would cover future situations where a group is targeted and the group is not specifically enumerated in a legislative document. At the same time, such an open formulation may be against the principle of lenity. The principle of lenity states that "a citizen is entitled to fair notice of what sort of conduct may give rise to punishment. Courts must strictly

---

[75]   Luban *et al.*, see *supra* note 7.

construe penal statutes to avoid violating the rights of the accused".[76] If an open group is used, it may contravene due process rights because it may be so broad and vague that the suspected perpetrator would not have been able to foresee the criminal liability.

A further formulation eliminating any modifiers on the word 'group' and only relying on defining a group based on the perpetrator's perception should be dismissed.[77] Although this may be easier, there should still be some indication that this is how the group see themselves. For example, if one mistakenly kills someone that one thinks is one's own father, one is not liable for patricide. In the same way that we cannot ascribe criminal liability purely based on the perpetrator's mistaken perception in criminal law, we should not be able to ascribe liability based purely on the perpetrator's perception in international criminal law.

A better approach is found in the ICC Statute in relation to crimes against humanity which criminalizes persecution of groups based on enumerated grounds and "other grounds that are universally recognized as impermissible under international law". Accordingly, this chapter proposes the chapeau of the genocide definition be changed to:

> Genocide means any of the following acts committed with intent to destroy, in whole or in part, any identifiable group on national, ethnical, racial, religious, political or other grounds that are universally recognized as impermissible under international law.

If this formulation is adopted on domestic and international levels, it would allow national and international courts to identify groups protected against genocide on the basis of applicable international law treaties and customary law. Since this formulation relies on international law it should not be against the principle of lenity and it also enables genocide to always be at the forefront of protecting new groups that international law deems deserving of protection. In addition, as discussed above, politi-

---

[76] *McNally v. United States*, 483 U.S. 350, 107 S. Ct. 2875, 97 L. Ed. 2d 292 (1987). *McBoyle v. United States*, 283 U.S. 25, 27, 51 S.Ct. 340, 75 L.Ed. 816 (1931). See also *United States v. Santos*, 128 S. Ct. 2020, 553 U.S. 507, 170 L. Ed. 2d 912 (2008) which states "the rule of lenity [...] vindicates the fundamental principle that no citizen should be held accountable for a violation of a statute whose commands are uncertain, or subjected to punishment that is not clearly prescribed".

[77] Jonassohn, 1991, see *supra* note 4, p. 19. Jonassohn and Bjornson, 1998, see *supra* note 57.

cal groups should be added to the formulation, as the inclusion of this group does not lead to spurious claims.

8.5. Two Tiers of Protection: Towards Greater Coherence of Protected Groups for Crimes Against Humanity and Genocide

This chapter posits that the scope of groups protected against the crime of genocide should mirror that in the definition of crimes against humanity. If indeed the definition of genocide is widened to include "political groups or other grounds that are universally recognized as impermissible under international law", how would it impact or change the protection afforded to victim groups in general? As stated above, the Proposed Crimes Against Humanity Convention incorporates the definition of crimes against humanity under Article 7 of the ICC Statute. The Proposed Convention, were it to come into force, will strengthen a universal definition for crimes against humanity and extend the reach of the rule of law on crimes against humanity beyond the ICC and international tribunals.[78] Such a legal framework establishing protection against crimes against humanity will be structurally parallel to that of genocide, which comprises the Genocide Convention and the ICC Statute. With the expanded definition of protected groups for genocide, these frameworks promise a two-tier protection for victim groups. As alluded to above, the two tiers of protection are not mutually replaceable; instead, together they will form a more comprehensive response to mass atrocities.

The protection afforded to groups under the framework of crimes against humanity differs from that of genocide, in two significant ways. First, the intent requirement for persecution as crimes against humanity differs from that of genocide. Second, the proposed formulation for genocide, while expanding the scope of groups in the current legal framework, still encompasses less groups than what is enumerated in Article 3 of the Proposed Convention and Article 7 of the ICC Statute. With regards to differences in intent, in the case of genocide, the intent required is the intent to destroy. Destroy in this case means "the material destruction of a group either by physical and biological means and not the destruction of the national, linguistic, religious, cultural or other identity of a particular

---

[78] Gregory H. Stanton, "Why the World Needs an International Convention", in Leila Nadya Sadat (ed.), *Forging a convention for crimes against humanity*, Cambridge University Press, 2011.

group", according to the ICTR.[79] Destroy is part of the mental element, thus genocide occurs if crimes are committed with the intent to destroy a group, even if the destruction does not materialize.

The *mens rea* specifically required for persecution as crimes against humanity is lower than that of genocide. In order to convict, there must be an intent to discriminate on prohibited grounds in conjunction with other acts which are also usually criminal. The intent to destroy is not necessary.[80]

The ICTY Trial Chamber in the *Kupreškić* case (quoted by the ICJ in the *Bosnia-Herzegovina case*) highlights the similarities and differences between persecution and destruction:

> persecution as a crime against humanity is an offence belonging to the same genus as genocide. Both persecution and genocide are crimes perpetrated against persons that belong to a particular group and who are targeted because of such belonging. In both categories what matters is the intent to discriminate: to attack persons on account of their ethnic, racial, or religious characteristics […] while in the case of persecution, the discriminatory intent may manifest itself in a plurality of actions including murder, in the case of genocide, that intent must be accompanied by the intent to destroy in whole or in part the group to which the victim belongs.[81]

The *Kupreskic* Trial Chamber saw genocide as an extreme and inhuman form of persecution. In other words, the protection afforded by the Proposed Convention and Article 7 of the ICC Statute as regards crimes

---

[79] ICTR, *Prosecutor v. Kamuhanda*, Case No.ICTR-95-54A-T, Trial Judgment, 22 January 2004, para. 627; ICTR, *Prosecutor v. Semanza*, Case No. ICTR-97-20-T, Trial Judgment, 15 May 2003, para. 315; ICTR, *Prosecutor v. Gacumbitsi*, Case No. ICTR-2001-64-T, Trial Judgment, 17 June 2004, para. 253; ICTR, *Prosecutor v. Muhimana*, Case No. ICTR-951B-T, Trial Judgment, 28 April 2005, para. 497; Van den Herik, Larissa, "The Meaning of the Word 'Destroy' and its Implications for the Wider Understanding of the Concept of Genocide", in H. G. Van Der Wilt, Harmen van der Wilt, Jeroen Vervliet (eds.), *The Genocide Convention: The Legacy of 60 Years*, Martinus Nijhoff Publishers, 2012.

[80] M. Cherif Bassiouni, *Crimes Against Humanity: Historical Evolution and Contemporary Application*, Cambridge University Press, 2011, p. 401.

[81] International Court of Justice, *Case Concerning Application of the Convention on the Prevention and Punishment of the Crime of Genocide (Bosnia-Herzegovina v. Serbia and Montenegro)*, Judgment, 26 February 2007, para. 188; ICTY, *Prosecutor v. Kupreškić et al.*, Case No. IT-95-16-T, Trial Judgment, 14 January 2000, para. 636.

against humanity is a lower form of protection. Genocide is a higher form of protection. Together they create two distinct levels of protection.

Regarding the number of enumerated groups, the crimes against humanity framework includes cultural and gender grounds, while the proposed formulation for genocide does not. However, the proposed incorporation of "other grounds that are universally recognized as impermissible under international law" means that in the future genocide could encompass these groups. In other words, under the proposed formulation, protection outside of the four groups plus political groups depends on the progress of international law. For example, although there have been some developments that point to acceptance of cultural or social genocide, an ICTY Trial Chamber has said that,

> customary international law limits the definition of genocide to those acts seeking the physical or biological destruction of all or part of the group. Hence, an enterprise attacking only the cultural or sociological characteristics of a human group in order to annihilate these elements which give to that group its own identity distinct from the rest of the community would not fall under the definition of genocide.[82]

As stated above, not only is cultural genocide hard to apply in concrete situations, it is not a part of customary international law. However this does not mean that international law cannot evolve to encompass cultural genocide and other groups. Adding "other grounds that are universally recognized as impermissible under international law" allows for enough flexibility for the definition to evolve with the times. If in fact international law evolves to encompass the same groups as crimes against humanity, it would truly create two tiers of protection. However, it must be remembered that application of the definition of crimes against humanity still requires complying with its chapeau elements, in particular the existence of a widespread or systematic attack against a civilian population, which also limits its application.

8.6. Conclusion

This chapter has argued that there is a need for greater coherence in international criminal law, by broadening the protected groups for genocide so that it reflects those for crimes against humanity. It compared the differ-

---

[82] ICTY, *Prosecutor v. Krstić*, Case No. IT-98-33-T, Trial Judgment, 2 August 2001, para. 580.

ences in the development of the definitions of crimes against humanity and genocide. It examined closely the arguments of the detractors and supporters of an expanded genocide definition. It also attempted to show why adding 'political groups' and 'other grounds that are universally recognized as impermissible under international law' is a satisfactory solution and viewed this solution in light of the emerging legal framework for crimes against humanity comprising the Proposed Crimes Against Humanity Convention and the ICC Statute. It underlined that together with the Proposed Convention, the new formulation for groups protected against genocide is conducive to a comprehensive, two-tier protection of groups under international criminal law.

As the United Nations International Law Commission considers the Proposed Crimes Against Humanity Convention, they will deliberate on whether the embodied definition of crimes against humanity is flexible enough to encompass situations not envisaged by the drafters without contravening the principle of lenity. This chapter argues that the wide protection afforded to groups by the crimes against humanity definition must be lauded.

Years after the Genocide Convention was enacted, the protection afforded to victim groups has not changed. Genocide must evolve in the same manner as the evolution of crimes against humanity or become limited in its usefulness. Judicial interpretation has not only led to inconsistent judgments but has undermined confidence in the international system. A legislative approach that allows for greater development, which protects victim groups, and which does not contravene the principle of lenity is needed.

9

The Proposed Convention on Crimes Against Humanity and Human Trafficking

Christen Price*

> Before atrocities are recognized as such, they are authoritatively regarded as either too extraordinary to be believed or too ordinary to be atrocious.[1]

9.1. Introduction

There are two reasons that human trafficking deserves legal attention: (1) it is a gross human rights abuse, and (2) it occurs on a massive, transnational scale. Sexual slavery exemplifies this, as a form of human trafficking "distinct from its composite crimes which include rape, torture and unlawful detention because it represents the culmination of all these acts through the complete deprivation of personal autonomy".[2] This deprivation of the victim's autonomy occurs thus:

> The method by which a trafficker reduces a woman to submission also secures maximum profits [...] crowded, unsanitary working conditions and sleep deprivation from working up to twenty hours day are important tools for "breaking the psychological stability of the women", and they accrue massive income for the trafficker [...]. The effect of this process is to completely dehumanize trafficked women in the eyes of traffickers, clients, and the woman herself.[3]

Additionally, victims are often invisible and unable to seek help:

---

* **Christen Price** received his J.D. in 2012 from Georgetown University Law Center, with a Certificate in Transnational Legal Studies. He currently practices primarily in the areas of employment law, international trade, and commercial litigation. All Internet references were last accessed on 2 September 2014.

[1] Catherine MacKinnon, *Are Women Human? And Other International Dialogues*, The Belknap Press of Harvard University, Cambridge, MA, 2006, p. 3.

[2] Alison Cole, "Reconceptualizing Female Trafficking: The Inhuman Trade in Women", in *Women's Rights Law Reporter*, 2005, vol. 26, no. 97, pp. 97–98.

[3] *Ibid.*, p. 105.

> The controlled environment of violence, exhaustion, and isolation induces a state of personal emergency. The conditions under which a trafficked woman is detained cause her to believe her life is constantly in danger.[4]

> [Victims (often, but not necessarily, women)] are trafficked into a foreign country, with their traffickers having taken their official documents. A woman is deterred from seeking help by her status as an illegal immigrant and prostitute. She may also have a distrust of public authority or knowledge of organized crime's power to bribe corrupt officials. Brain-washing by the traffickers in an isolated and confined environment reinforces these fears, her family may be threatened and she may be in debt to the trafficker as well.[5]

Fully aware of the limitations of researching in a relatively new field whose subject is illegal activity, slavery scholar Kevin Bales estimates that there are 27 million slaves in the world today (in contrast to much higher estimates by other human rights groups).[6] If this estimate is correct, then "[t]here are more slaves alive today than all the people stolen from Africa in the time of the transatlantic slave trade".[7] Much of that slavery is concentrated: "The biggest part of that 27 million, perhaps 15–20 million, is represented by 'bonded labour' in India, Pakistan, Bangladesh, and Nepal".[8] No country, however, is free of it; for example, there are an estimated 3,000 household slaves in Paris alone.[9] Slavery generates an estimated $13 billion in profits yearly.[10]

This chapter argues that human trafficking is often a form of slavery and is in any case a serious human rights violation. It will further examine the extent to which human trafficking is covered by the Proposed International Convention on the Prevention and Punishment of Crimes

---

[4] *Ibid.*

[5] *Ibid.*

[6] Kevin Bales, *Disposable People: New Slavery in the Global Economy*, University of California Press, Berkeley and Los Angeles, CA, 2004, pp. 8–9. See also the 2013 United States Department of State, Trafficking in Persons Report, p. 7, available at http://www.state.gov/j/tip/rls/tiprpt/index.htm.

[7] Bales, 2004, p. 9, *ibid.*

[8] *Ibid.*

[9] *Ibid.*, p. 3.

[10] *Ibid.*, p. 23.

Against Humanity ('Proposed Convention', see Annex 1).[11] Finally, it argues that there is both a legal and a practical case for broadening the Proposed Convention's definition of crimes against humanity to include certain forms of human trafficking that the Proposed Convention currently seems to exclude, regardless of whether the abuses are committed by private actors, in peace time, or for profit.

The focus of this chapter will be on human trafficking as it relates to slavery; however, human trafficking also encompasses, to varying degrees, other acts[12] that may constitute crimes against humanity: torture, rape, and sexual slavery particularly. Thus, the analysis of crimes against humanity also applies to these other crimes, in addition to slavery. Furthermore, for the sake of conciseness, the legal arguments will mostly focus on international tribunals and treaties rather than on customary international law. Finally, this chapter will not engage the debate on whether 'human trafficking' or 'trafficking in persons' is the more appropriate term, and will use the two interchangeably.

9.2. Trafficking in Persons as a Serious Human Rights Violation

This section will demonstrate that trafficking in persons can be slavery, and is in any case a serious human rights violation, whether it amounts to slavery, torture, sexual violence, or another crime.

9.2.1. Trafficking in Persons as Slavery

9.2.1.1. Definitions of Trafficking in Persons

The following definitions of 'human trafficking' are from an international treaty and a national jurisdiction's anti-trafficking law. Both definitions focus on the coercion and control aspects of human trafficking, treating them as central to slavery, suggesting that slavery need not involve legal ownership, in contrast to the chattel slavery of the transatlantic slave trade.[13]

---

[11] Proposed International Convention on the Prevention and Punishment of Crimes Against Humanity, Washington University School of Law, Whitney R. Harris World Law Institute, Crimes Against Humanity Initiative, August 2010, see Annex 1.

[12] See, *e.g.*, Article 7(1), Rome Statute of the International Criminal Court, A/CONF.183/9, 1 July 2002 ('ICC Statute').

[13] Bales, 2004, pp. 14–15, see *supra* note 6.

The Palermo Protocol is an agreement supplementing the U.N. Convention against Transnational Organized Crime, and defines trafficking in persons as:

> recruitment, transportation, transfer, harbouring or receipt of persons, by means of the threat or use of force or other forms of coercion, of abduction, of fraud, of deception, of the abuse of power or of a position of vulnerability or of the giving or receiving of payments or benefits to achieve the consent of a person having control over another person, for the purpose of exploitation. Exploitation shall include, at a minimum, the exploitation of the prostitution of others or other forms of sexual exploitation, forced labour or services, slavery or practices similar to slavery, servitude or the removal of organs [...].[14]

The victim's consent to exploitation is irrelevant if any of the above means are used, and a lower threshold is set for exploitation of children:

> The recruitment, transportation, transfer, harbouring or receipt of a child for the purpose of exploitation shall be considered trafficking in persons even if this does not involve any of the means set forth in subparagraph (a) of this article.[15]

Another definition of human trafficking comes from the United States' Trafficking Victims Protection Act. Under the U.S. federal anti-trafficking statutes, severe forms of trafficking in persons is defined as "sex trafficking in which a commercial sex act is induced by force, fraud, or coercion, or in which the person induced to perform such act has not attained 18 years of age", or "the recruitment, harboring, transportation, provision, or obtaining of a person for labor or services, through the use of force, fraud, or coercion for the purpose of subjection to involuntary servitude, peonage, debt bondage, or slavery".[16]

---

[14] Article 3(b)–(c), Protocol to Prevent, Suppress and Punish Trafficking in Persons, Especially Women and Children, Supplementing the United Nations Convention against Transnational Organized Crime ('Palermo Protocol'), 25 December 2003, available at http://www.ohchr.org/EN/ProfessionalInterest/Pages/ProtocolTraffickingInPersons.aspx.

[15] Article 3(a), Palermo Protocol, *ibid.*

[16] The Trafficking Victims Protection Act of 2000, Sec. 103(8) ('TVPA'); The William Wilberforce Trafficking Victims Protection Reauthorization Act of 2008, Sec. 222 ('TVPRA'); Trafficking Victims Protection Reauthorization Act of 2013, available at http://www.state.gov/j/tip/laws/index.htm.

Commercial sex acts and involuntary servitude fall under the statutes, and are defined respectively, as "any sex act on account of which anything of value is given to or received by any person", and "a condition of servitude induced" through "any scheme, plan, or pattern intended to cause a person to believe that, if the person did not enter into or continue in such condition, that person or another person would suffer serious harm or physical restraint", or "the abuse or threatened abuse of the legal process".[17]

This chapter will rely on the above two definitions, particularly with respect to their commonalities; their differences are not relevant to the question of whether human trafficking is slavery and a serious human rights abuse and when it should be considered a crime against humanity.

9.2.1.2. Two Clarifications

Reluctance to classify human trafficking as slavery may be due to the conflation of human trafficking with human smuggling and slavery with legal ownership. First, trafficking people is distinct from smuggling them; human smuggling, while illegal, may or may not involve exploitation. These two terms were used interchangeably in the past, but are now recognized as different acts. This is illustrated by the adoption of the Protocol Against the Smuggling of Migrants by Land, Sea and Air ('Smuggling Protocol') supplementing the Organized Crime Convention, which does not include exploitation in its definition of smuggling.[18] Thus, the relevant international instruments distinguish between human trafficking and human smuggling, reinforcing that they are separate crimes.

Second, the legal understanding of slavery is becoming increasingly consistent with Bales' definition, "the total control of one person by another for the purpose of economic exploitation".[19] Slavery, while more severe than substandard and illegal labour practices such as child labour or sharecropping, is not necessarily ownership in the traditional sense; it

---

[17] *Ibid.*

[18] Tom Obokata, "Trafficking of Human Beings as a Crime against Humanity: Some Implications for the International Legal System", in *International and Comparative Law Quarterly*, 2005, vol. 54, no. 2, p. 446. Article 3(a), Smuggling Protocol, 28 January 2004, available at https://treaties.un.org/doc/Publication/UNTS/Volume%202241/v2241.pdf.

[19] Bales, 2004, p. 9, see *supra* note 6.

is instead defined by control: "Slaveholders have all the benefits of ownership without the legalities".[20]

Modern slavery is distinct from traditional chattel slavery not only because it is based on coercion rather than ownership, but slaves today are more disposable. The world population has more than tripled since World War II and the greatest population increases have been in those areas where there are currently the greatest numbers of slaves; life becomes cheaper.[21] The laws of supply and demand mean that when there is a massive increase in the number of potential slaves, they are cheap:

> Buying a slave is no longer a major investment, like buying a car or a house (as it was in the old slavery); it is more like buying an inexpensive bicycle or a cheap computer. Slaveholders get all the work they can out of their slaves, and then throw them away.[22]

In the antebellum American South, a field slave would cost around $40,000 to $80,000 in today's U.S. dollars, yet "[s]laves generated, on average, profits of only about 5 per cent per year".[23] In contrast, modern slaves are so cheap that free workers must compete with them (which was not the case in the American South), and slaves are responsible for their own maintenance.[24] This is compounded by the fact that, for example, debt slaves in India generate profits of over 50 per cent per year and a child sex slave in Thailand can generate profits of as much as "800 per cent a year".[25]

Thus, modern slavery's victims are even more vulnerable in relation to the perpetrators: "When slaves cost a great deal of money, that investment had to be safeguarded through clear and legally documented ownership. Slaves of the past were worth stealing and were worth chasing down if they escaped", but now they are disposable, with little incentive to keep them alive for very long, as there was in the American South.[26] These realities of modern slavery show how antebellum slavery in the American South is an inappropriate model for understanding modern slavery, and

---

[20] *Ibid.*, p. 5.

[21] *Ibid.*, p. 12.

[22] *Ibid.*, p. 14.

[23] *Ibid.*, p. 16.

[24] *Ibid.*, pp. 16–17.

[25] *Ibid.*, pp. 17–18.

[26] *Ibid.*, pp. 14–15.

---

also how current legal definitions of human trafficking clearly target modern slavery.

9.2.1.3. Recent Jurisprudence

Recent court decisions as well as scholarship make a similar connection between human trafficking and slavery. In *Rantsev v. Cyprus and Russia*, the European Court of Human Rights ('ECtHR') shifted its approach to slavery by "recognizing human trafficking as slavery and articulating distinct duties of when a state must act to combat this crime generally and in individual cases".[27] The complainant in the case alleged that Cyprus and Russia had failed to protect Ms. Rantseva from human trafficking and to adequately investigate her death.[28] The ECtHR "referred to its previous case law defining the concepts of slavery, servitude, and forced and compulsory labor", even though Article 4 (which articulates the right to be free from slavery and forced labor) does not mention the term 'human trafficking'.[29]

The ECtHR referenced its own *Siliadin v. France* decision, where it had "concluded that the victim's treatment in a human trafficking context had amounted to servitude and forced and compulsory labour, but it had fallen short of slavery".[30] In contrast, the ECtHR in *Rantsev* looked to the ICTY's jurisprudence on slavery, "which concluded that the traditional concept of slavery, closely linked to the right of ownership, had now evolved to include a range of contemporary forms of slavery", and "delineated specific characteristics of a situation similar to slavery, such as the lack of free movement of a person, control over such movement to deter escape, confinement to a place or physical environment, presence of elements of psychological control, control of sexuality, and forced labor".[31]

---

[27] Roza Pati, "States' Positive Obligations with Respect to Human Trafficking: The European Court of Human Rights Breaks New Ground in *Rantsev v. Cyprus and Russia*", in *Boston University International Law Journal*, 2011, vol. 29, no. 79, pp. 82–83.

[28] European Court of Human Rights, *Rantsev v. Cyprus and Russia*, Application No. 25965/04, Judgment, 7 January 2010, para. 2.

[29] Pati, 2011, p. 93, see *supra* note 27. See also *Rantsev v. Cyprus and Russia*, 2010, *op. cit.*, paras. 275–276.

[30] Pati, 2011, pp. 93–94 (citing ECtHR, *Siliadin v. France*, Application No. 73316/01, Chamber Judgment, 26 July 2005, paras. 120, 129), see *supra* note 27.

[31] *Ibid.*, p. 94; *Rantsev v. Cyprus and Russia*, 2010, paras. 279–281, see *supra* note 28.

Thus, the ECtHR recognized that human trafficking "by its very nature and aim of exploitation, is an exercise of powers attached to ownership", and is the "modern form of the old worldwide slave trade".[32] The ECtHR decided that human trafficking's abuses were obvious enough that further discussion of whether it was slavery was unnecessary: "It concluded that human trafficking as defined in article 3(a) of the Palermo Protocol falls within the scope of article 4, and it dismissed Russia's objection on the grounds of lack of jurisdiction *ratione materiae*".[33]

9.2.2. Slavery as a Serious Violation of Human Rights

Having argued for a strong connection between slavery and its modern form, human trafficking, this section will now turn to the status of slavery as an international crime and human rights violation, by looking at its status under international law. First, slavery violates *jus cogens* norms under international law. *Jus cogens* norms are the fundamental, non-optional norms that the international community has adopted regarding severe human rights abuses such as genocide, slavery, and torture; crimes with *jus cogens* status are always prohibited, the prohibitions may not be derogated from, and no treaty or custom may override them.[34] This means that slavery is

> prohibited at all times, in all places […] peremptory norms supersede any treaty or custom to the contrary. *Jus cogens* norms constitute principles of international public policy, and serve as rules "so fundamental to the international community of states as a whole that the rule constitutes a basis for the community's legal system […]".[35]

This does not mean that *jus cogens* norms are completely uncontroversial or that there is no disagreement about which crimes meet the criteria; however, *jus cogens* status is a concept that has 'symbolic value',

---

[32] *Rantsev v. Cyprus and Russia*, 2010, para. 280, see *supra* note 28.

[33] Pati, 2011, p. 94, see *supra* note 27; *Rantsev v. Cyprus and Russia*, 2010, *op. cit.*, para. 281.

[34] See, *e.g.*, Special Rapporteur Gay J. McDougall's Final Report of 22 June 1998, "Systematic Rape, Sexual Slavery and Slavery-like Practices During Wartime", E/CN.4/Sub.2/1998/13, p. 4; Kelly D. Askin, "Prosecuting Wartime Rape and Other Gender-Related Crimes under International Law: Extraordinary Advances, Enduring Obstacles", in *Berkeley Journal of International Law*, 2003, vol. 21, no. 288, p. 293.

[35] Askin, 2003, *op. cit.*, p. 293.

even if it is problematic.[36] Petsche argues that *jus cogens* is "of limited relevance for the actual practice of international law [...]. Rather, its usefulness lies in the way it envisions the international legal order. Such vision, as we have seen, consists of a normative system based on fundamental values, characterized by a hierarchy of norms, and not entirely dependent on the consent of the subjects of international law".[37]

In any case, whether *jus cogens* is practically useful or only symbolically valuable, there seems to be little dispute that slavery is on the list. So at best, the prohibition against slavery is an international imperative of the highest order; at a minimum, its condemnation is symbolically significant, because *jus cogens* status is reserved for the worst abuses of human rights.

Although *jus cogens* status may only be of limited help in establishing slavery's human rights legal status, other forms of international law clearly prohibit it. As will be discussed below, slavery can be a crime against humanity under certain circumstances[38] and the right to be free from slavery is guaranteed under numerous human rights instruments, including the Universal Declaration of Human Rights,[39] the International Convention on Civil and Political Rights,[40] the Supplementary Convention on the Abolition of Slavery, the Slave Trade, and Institutions and Practices Similar to Slavery,[41] and the European Convention on Human Rights.[42] Additionally, criminal law instruments such as the Palermo Protocol and the Convention for the Suppression of the Traffic in Persons and of the Exploitation of the Prostitution of Others prohibit slavery as well.[43]

---

[36] Markus Petsche, "*Jus Cogens* as a Vision of the International Order", in *Penn State International Law Review,* 2010, vol. 29., no. 233, p. 237.

[37] *Ibid.*, p. 273.

[38] See, *e.g.*, Article 7(1), ICC Statute, see *supra* note 12.

[39] Article 4, Universal Declaration of Human Rights, 1948.

[40] Article 8, International Covenant on Civil and Political Rights, entered into force on 23 March 1976.

[41] Supplementary Convention on the Abolition of Slavery, the Slave Trade, and Institutions and Practices Similar to Slavery, entered into force on 30 April 1957.

[42] Article 4, European Convention on Human Rights, entered into force on 3 September 1953.

[43] Convention for the Suppression of the Traffic in Persons and of the Exploitation of the Prostitution of Others, entered into force on 25 July 1951.

For the above reasons, trafficking in persons is a serious human rights violation that often constitutes outright slavery, which is a *jus cogens* violation and an international crime by treaty.

9.3. Trafficking in Persons as a Crime Against Humanity

This section examines the status of trafficking in persons as a crime against humanity by listing several definitions of crimes against humanity, and comparing the definition of trafficking in persons to that of crimes against humanity in the Proposed Convention.

9.3.1. Defining 'Crimes Against Humanity'

This section considers how crimes against humanity have been defined both in the statutes of international criminal tribunals, the Proposed Convention, and the jurisprudence of the international tribunals. Recent international criminal tribunals have employed definitions of crimes against humanity that are similar to the International Law Commission's ('ILC') definition in the Draft Code of Crimes against the Peace and Security of Mankind. The following chart compares the largely similar acts covered by crimes against humanity in different statutes, and demonstrates some of the ways that the ICC Statute follows the ILC's Draft Code definitions.

ICC Statute[44]	ICTY Statute[45]	ICTR Statute[46]	Law on ECCC[47]	SCSL Statute[48]		ILC Draft Code[49]
Murder	Murder	Murder	Murder	Murder		Murder
Extermination	Extermination	Extermination	Extermination	Extermination		Extermination
Enslavement	Enslavement	Enslavement	Enslavement	Enslavement		Enslavement
Deportation or forcible transfer of population	Deportation	Deportation	Deportation	Deportation		Arbitrary deportation or forcible transfer of population

---

[44] Article 7(1), ICC Statute, see *supra* note 12.

[45] Article 5, Statute of the International Criminal Tribunal for the Former Yugoslavia ('ICTY'), adopted on 25 May 1993, as amended on 7 July 2009.

[46] Article 3, Statute of the International Criminal Tribunal for the Prosecution of Persons Responsible for Genocide and Other Serious Violations of International Humanitarian Law Committed in the Territory of Rwanda and Rwandan Citizens Responsible for Genocide and Other Such Violations Committed in the Territory of Neighbouring States, between 1 January 1994 and 31 December 1994 ('ICTR'), adopted on 8 November 1994, as amended on 14 August 2002.

[47] Article 5, Law on the Establishment of Extraordinary Chambers in the Courts of Cambodia for the Prosecution of Crimes Committed during the Period of Democratic Kampuchea ('ECCC'), with inclusion of amendments as promulgated on 27 October 2004.

[48] Article 2, Statute of the Special Court for Sierra Leone ('SCSL'), signed on 16 January 2002.

[49] Article 18, Draft Code of Crimes against the Peace and Security of Mankind ('ILC Draft Code'), 1996.

ILC Draft Code	Arbitrary imprisonment	Torture	Rape, enforced prostitution and other forms of sexual abuse	Forced disappearance of persons
SCSL Statute	Imprisonment	Torture	Rape, sexual slavery, enforced prostitution, forced pregnancy and any other form of sexual violence	
Law on ECCC	Imprisonment	Torture	Rape	
ICTR Statute	Imprisonment	Torture	Rape	
ICTY Statute	Imprisonment	Torture	Rape	
ICC Statute	Imprisonment or other severe deprivation of physical liberty in violation of fundamental rules of international law	Torture	Rape, sexual slavery, enforced prostitution, forced pregnancy, enforced sterilization, or any other form of sexual violence of comparable gravity	Enforced disappearance of persons

	Persecution	Other inhumane acts	
ILC Draft Code	Persecution on political, racial, religious or ethnic grounds	Other inhumane acts which severely damage physical or mental integrity, health or human dignity, such as mutilation and severe bodily harm	Institutionalized discrimination on racial, ethnic or religious grounds involving the violation of fundamental human rights and freedoms and resulting in seriously disadvantaging a part of the population
SCSL Statute	Persecution on political, racial, ethnic or religious grounds	Other inhumane acts	
Law on ECCC	Persecutions on political, racial, and religious grounds	Other inhumane acts	
ICTR Statute	Persecutions on political, racial, and religious grounds	Other inhumane acts	
ICTY Statute	Persecutions on political, racial, and religious grounds	Other inhumane acts	
ICC Statute	Persecution against any identifiable group or collectivity on political, racial, national, ethnic, cultural, religious, gender as defined in paragraph 3, or other grounds that are universally recognized as impermissible under international law, in connection with any act referred to in this paragraph or any crime within the jurisdiction of the Court[50]	Other inhumane acts of a similar character intentionally causing great suffering, or serious injury to body or to mental or physical health	The crime of apartheid

---

[50] Article 7(3) of the ICC Statute provides: "For the purpose of this Statute, it is understood that the term 'gender' refers to the two sexes, male and female, within the context of society. The term 'gender' does not indicate any meaning different from the above".

The following chart looks at the chapeau elements for crimes against humanity in the foregoing statutes:

SCSL Statute[51]	[...] the following crimes as part of a widespread or systematic attack against any civilian population
Law on ECCC[52]	[...] any acts committed as part of a widespread or systematic attack directed against any civilian population, on national, political, ethnical, racial or religious grounds
ILC Draft Code[53]	[...] any of the following acts, when committed in a systematic manner or on a large scale and instigated or directed by a Government or by any organization or group
ICTY Statute[54]	[...] the following crimes when committed in armed conflict, whether international or internal in character, and directed against any civilian population
ICTR Statute[55]	[...] the following crimes when committed as part of a widespread or systematic attack against any civilian population on national, political, ethnic, racial or religious grounds
ICC Statute[56]	[...] the following acts when committed as part of a widespread or systematic attack directed against any civilian population, with knowledge of the attack. 'Attack directed against any civilian population' means a course of conduct involving the multiple commission of acts referred to in paragraph 1 against any civilian population, pursuant to or in furtherance of a State or organizational policy to commit such attack".

The SCSL Statute, Law on ECCC, ICTR Statute, and ICC Statute all include the concept of 'widespread or systematic attack'; only the ICTY Statute's definition requires a nexus to an armed conflict.[57] The ILC Draft Code definition requires that the crimes be committed in a "widespread or systematic" fashion, but is the only definition that leaves out the concept of 'attack' as an element. The ICC Statute follows the ILC Draft Code definition except for the 'attack' requirement. The Proposed Convention employs definitions very similar to the ones in the foregoing charts, particularly the ILC and the ICC Statute, defining crimes against

---

[51] Article 2, SCSL Statute, see *supra* note 48.
[52] Article 5, Law on ECCC, see *supra* note 47.
[53] Article 18, ILC Draft Code, see *supra* note 49.
[54] Article 5, ICTY Statute, see *supra* note 45.
[55] Article 3, ICTR Statute, see *supra* note 46.
[56] Article 7(1), 7(2)(a), ICC Statute, see *supra* note 12.
[57] Article 5, ICTY Statute, see *supra* note 45.

humanity as "any of the following acts when committed as part of a wide-spread or systematic attack directed against any civilian population, with knowledge of the attack", where the acts include:

a) Murder;

b) Extermination;

c) Enslavement;

d) Deportation or forcible transfer of population;

e) Imprisonment or other severe deprivation of physical liberty in violation of fundamental rules of international law;

f) Torture;

g) Rape, sexual slavery, enforced prostitution, forced pregnancy, enforced sterilization, or any other form of sexual violence of comparable gravity;

h) Persecution against any identifiable group or collectivity on political, racial, national, ethnic, cultural, religious, gender as defined in paragraph 3, or other grounds that are universally recognized as impermissible under international law, in connection with any act referred to in this paragraph or in connection with acts of genocide or war crimes;

i) Enforced disappearance of persons;

j) The crime of apartheid;

k) Other inhumane acts of a similar character intentionally causing great suffering, or serious injury to body or to mental or physical health.[58]

Two definitions that are particularly relevant to this chapter are en-slavement, which is defined as "the exercise of any or all of the powers attaching to the right of ownership over a person and includes the exercise of such power in the course of trafficking in persons, in particular women and children", [59] and "attack directed against any civilian population" which means "a course of conduct involving the multiple commission of acts referred to in paragraph 1 against any civilian population, pursuant to or in furtherance of a State or organizational policy to commit such attack

---

[58] Article 3(1), Proposed Convention, see *supra* note 11.

[59] *Ibid.*, Article 3(2)(c).

[…]".[60] Additionally, torture is defined as "the intentional infliction of severe pain or suffering, whether physical or mental, upon a person in the custody or under the control of the accused; except that torture shall not include pain or suffering arising only from, inherent in or incidental to, lawful sanctions",[61] removing it from the domain of exclusively State-perpetrated abuses.[62]

Thus, it appears that slavery, and by extension, human trafficking, is an international crime and a predicate crime for crimes against humanity; the next section will examine how human trafficking does and does not fall under the definition of crimes against humanity proposed in the Proposed Convention.

9.3.2. Comparing Trafficking in Persons to the Definition of Crimes Against Humanity in the Proposed Convention

9.3.2.1. Acts Covered

When the above definitions of enslavement, torture and rape are compared to the realities of human trafficking, it is clear that at least those acts and occasionally murder are committed in the course of human trafficking and fall into the categories of acts that the Proposed Convention intends to prohibit. The difficulty is in establishing when those acts, committed in the course of human trafficking, meet the other criteria for crimes against humanity, as defined in the Proposed Convention.

9.3.2.2. Widespread or Systematic

Under one interpretation of the phrase 'widespread or systematic', given the high number of estimated trafficking victims[63] and the fact that organized crime groups (whether a full organization or an informal association of pimps) are heavily involved in human trafficking,[64] such conduct is often both widespread and systematic. Cole, for example, concludes:

---

[60] *Ibid.*, Article 3(2)(a).

[61] *Ibid.*, Article 3(2)(e).

[62] These definitions of "attack directed against any civilian population", "enslavement", and "torture" all follow the definitions of the same terms in Article 7 of the ICC Statute.

[63] Bales, 2004, pp. 8–9, see *supra* note 6.

[64] See, *e.g.*, Amy O'Neill Richard, *International Trafficking in Women to the United States: A Contemporary Manifestation of Slavery and Organized Crime, DCI Exceptional Intelli-*

This is evident in the initial element of the crime, which is
drafted in the disjunctive form of 'widespread or systematic
attack', demonstrating that the 'attack' requires 'a large-scale
action involving a substantial number of victims [...] or that
it was conducted with a high degree of orchestration and
methodical planning.' In specific cases, this requirement
would turn on the facts. In conceptual terms, the estimates
placing trafficked women in the millions suggest that at least
the first clause of this requirement is satisfied.[65]

In contrast, the ICTR in *Akayesu* defined 'widespread' as "massive,
frequent, large scale action, carried out collectively with considerable seriousness and directed against a multiplicity of victims", and systematic as
"thoroughly organised and following a regular pattern on the basis of a
common policy involving substantial public or private resources".[66]

This definition is narrower than Cole's, as it requires that the conduct in question be either collective or based on a common policy. However, it is important to note that neither the ICTR Statute nor the ICTY
Statute contains an explicit policy requirement.[67] Moreover, both the
ICTR and the ICTY have subsequently stated that while the existence of a
plan or policy is "evidentially relevant", it is no longer legally necessary
for defining crimes against humanity.[68] I will argue below that 'widespread or systematic' should follow the ILC Draft Code, ICTR, and ICTY
definitions and exclude the policy requirement.

9.3.2.3. "Attack Directed Against Any Civilian Population"

While victims of trafficking are almost invariably part of a civilian population, it is not clear whether the "attack" is fulfilled by forms of trafficking unconnected to armed conflict, terrorism, political uprising, or State

---

gence Analyst Program: An Intelligence Monograph, Central Intelligence Agency, 1999,
p. 3.

[65] Cole, 2005, p. 115, see *supra* note 2. I disagree, as will be noted, that Cole's understanding
of human trafficking as widespread and systematic meets the Convention's requirement of
an *attack* that is widespread and systematic.

[66] ICTR, *Prosecutor v. Akayesu*, Case No. ICTR-96-4-T, Judgment, 2 September 1998, para.
580.

[67] ICTY Statute; see *supra* note 47; ICTR Statute, see *supra* note 48.

[68] See, *e.g.*, ICTY, *Prosecutor v. Kunarac*, Case No. IT-96-23/IT-96-23/1-A, Judgment, 12
June 2002, para. 98; ICTR, *Prosecutor v. Muhimana*, Case No. ICTR- 95-1B-T, Judgment,
28 April 2005, para. 527.

---

action. While the definition of "attack directed against any civilian population" as a "course of conduct"[69] may technically cover human trafficking, given the historical (though no longer necessary) connection between crimes against humanity and armed conflict, the term may make lawyers and judges less likely to interpret human trafficking as a Proposed Convention violation when it is committed by private actors and unconnected to any armed conflict, genocide, or other uprising, notwithstanding Article 1's clarification that crimes against humanity may be committed in peacetime.[70]

The phrase is defined by the Convention as "a course of conduct involving the multiple commission of acts referred to in paragraph 1 against any civilian population, pursuant to or in furtherance of a State or organizational policy to commit such attack [...]".[71] This is similar to the ICC Statute definition.[72] The term "pursuant to or in furtherance of an organizational policy", which, taken together with "attack", seems to indicate State action, or at least an entity trying to act like a State (for example, rebel groups recruiting soldiers); it is not clear that traffickers could be characterized as having a policy of enslaving people. They enslave people because it is a business (which is quite distinct from the reasons that States and State-like private entities usually commit crimes against humanity), and they may or may not operate as part of an organization.

Cole thinks that trafficking of women fulfils the ICC Statute definition of "attack directed against any civilian population" (which is virtually identical to the Proposed Convention's), considering:

> The Elements of Crimes, adopted by the Preparatory Commission in accordance with Article 9 of the ICC Statute, provides in the introduction to the explanation of Article 7 that 'acts need not constitute a military attack'. This confirms that the notion of CAHs has evolved from the Nuremberg precedent and can be perpetrated in peacetime. Furthermore, by choosing to explain the phrase, rather than focusing on individual words, it is submitted that 'attack' is to be construed in the broader context of the sentence. The apparent militancy of the word 'attack' is removed by the

---

69 *Ibid.*, Article 3(2).

70 *Ibid.*, Article 1.

71 *Ibid.*, Article 3(2)(a), (c).

72 Article 7, ICC Statute, see *supra* note 12.

explanation in Article 7(2) referring to 'a course of conduct'.[73]

While an attack, strictly speaking, can be a course of conduct, if one wanted to remove the militancy of a word historically associated with militancy, one would probably do away with the word "attack" altogether, or at least make its meaning unambiguous. In any case, Cole's interpretation does not account for the limitations imposed or implied by the reference to State and organizational policy.

9.3.2.4. Knowledge of the Attack

This element is fact-bound; presumably, given the need for transnational criminal networks to facilitate cross-border human trafficking, traffickers are often aware of one another. "Knowledge of the attack" would have to be determined on a case-by-case basis, but would likely be met in many cases under a broad definition of "attack". That said, "knowledge of the attack" turns on how "attack" is defined. Because of the current ambiguities in defining both "attack against any civilian population" and "widespread or systematic", the Proposed Convention probably does not cover trafficking in persons when the crime is not committed by State or State-like actors.

9.4. Certain Forms of Trafficking in Persons Should be More Clearly Covered by the Proposed Convention on Crimes Against Humanity

This section examines several conceptual hurdles to expanding the Proposed Convention's definition in light of feminist critiques and international jurisprudential shifts, and responds to several practical objections.

9.4.1. Conceptual Hurdles

There are three major conceptual hurdles that are important to the traditional understanding of international law and make it difficult for human trafficking to be classed as a *per se* crime against humanity, assuming that it is widespread or systematic, including the distinction between: (1) public and private spheres, (2) State and non-State actors, and (3) war and peacetime. The war and peacetime distinction has been completely dis-

---

[73] Cole, 2005, p. 115–116, see *supra* note 2.

mantled in the definitions of crimes against humanity, and the State/non-State actor emphasis has been largely dismantled as well, although the language of "State or organizational policy" may imply private individuals behaving like States (such as rebel armies' actions).[74] However, the public/private distinction remains, exemplified by Cassese's definition of an international crime. Feminist critiques have emerged in response to this distinction, and human rights jurisprudence is slowly shifting in their direction.

9.4.1.1. Transnational but not International Crimes

Cassese argues that trafficking in persons is not an international crime. On the contrary,

> [...] it is characteristic of such crimes that when perpetrated by private individuals, they are somehow connected with a state policy or at any rate with "system criminality". On this score international crimes are thus different from criminal offences committed for personal purposes (private gain, satisfaction of personal greed, desire for revenge, etc.) as is the case with ordinary criminal offences [...] or such other crimes that have a transnational dimension but pursue private goals, such as piracy, slave trade, trade in women and children, counterfeiting currency, drug dealing, etc.[75]

Similarly, Bassiouni argues that crimes against humanity should not be defined to include any internationalized domestic crime:

> Crimes against humanity should be defined in a way that focuses on the organizational policy of the harmful conduct aimed at civilians. This excludes collateral harmful conduct to civilians occurring as a collateral consequence of organized crime activities whose purpose is unjust enrichment.[76]

---

[74] See, *e.g.*, the definition of torture under both the ICC Statute and the Proposed Convention.

[75] Antonio Cassese, *International Criminal Law*, Oxford University Press, 2008, p. 54.

[76] M. Cherif Bassiouni, *Crimes Against Humanity: Historical Evolution and Contemporary Application*. Cambridge University Press, 2011, p. 13. The risk that crimes against humanity might be used to prosecute organized crime indiscriminately is tempered by the requirement that the crimes be "widespread or systematic", and the ICC would not necessarily be required to prosecute, due to the principle of complementarity. Moreover, slavery, unlike some of the other crimes committed by organized criminal networks, such as theft

Bassiouni argues that the perpetrators of crimes against humanity must at least be acting more like State actors (rather than private actors) and seems sceptical about including non-State actors in the definition of crimes against humanity.[77]

Bassiouni and Cassese's analyses rest on a series of questionable assumptions about the distinctions discussed earlier; distinctions which manage to hide the human rights violations more often experienced by women and children. In addition to the feminist critiques below, there are at least three problems with Cassese and Bassiouni's position.

First, it is not clear that it is appropriate to characterize the violence suffered by human trafficking victims as a "collateral consequence" of organized criminal activity. Human trafficking, for one thing, is different from other forms of organized crime, because human beings are the commodity, rather than illicit drugs or weapons. Thus, sex trafficking is not like a murder committed by a gang member in the course of a drug deal gone bad. The "collateral consequence", as Bassiouni would phrase it, of abuse that sex trafficking victims experience is not criminal conduct incidental to the central criminal moneymaking activity; it *is* the central criminal moneymaking activity – perpetrators of sex trafficking profit from sexual violence directly.

Second, the very concerns that drove international law to seek to hold State actors accountable – the egregiousness of the crimes, the abuse of power used to commit them, and the impunity with which they were committed – are all present in private actors' perpetration of severe forms of trafficking in persons. The distinguishing factor for both Bassiouni and Cassese appears to be not severity or scale, but action in concert with State or State-like organizational policy. Particularly given the similarities between the acts committed in human trafficking (as detailed in section 9.1.) and torture (which the Proposed Convention does not define in terms of State action), it seems problematic to argue that severe human rights abuses should not be criminalized at the highest international level as long as they are committed for profit.[78] One can argue, when evaluating such

---

or extortion, is distinguishable as one of the very few crimes that already has *jus cogens* status.

[77] *Ibid.*, pp. 10–13, and 40–42.

[78] Whether severe forms of trafficking in persons can meet the current 'widespread or systematic' criteria (regardless of how these terms are defined) is a separate, and completely valid, question. This argument is directed only at the assumption that the private goals of

abuses, that the State's abuse of power is an aggravating factor without insinuating that the profit motive is a mitigating factor.

Third, the line between State and non-State actors is often blurry, particularly in jurisdictions with dysfunctional criminal justice systems. In some legal systems, where there is effectively no rule-of-law protection for the average person, the investigative, protective, and prosecutorial functions of the criminal justice system are privatized.[79] This means that only those who can afford to pay private persons can meaningfully access that system, and it is often those with money who additionally control and corrupt the public justice system as well.[80] Some traffickers even receive police protection.[81] While a powerful trafficker manipulating a criminal justice system for his own ends is a far cry from a State doing so as a matter of official policy, the trafficker still acts with impunity and his victims are similarly without recourse.

9.4.1.2. Feminist Critiques

In addition to not accounting for the realities of dysfunctional public justice systems and powerful people confining themselves to private criminal goals, the bias toward State or State-like action also fails to account for the dynamic of gender. The classic feminist critique by Catherine MacKinnon argues that the public/private distinction is often evidence of gender bias:

> The state is only one instrumentality of sex inequality. To fail to see this is pure gender bias. Often this bias flies under the flag of privacy, so that those areas that are defined as inappropriate for state involvement, where the discourse of human rights is made irrelevant, are those "areas in which the majority of the world's women live out their days".[82]

For example, Dillon notes that,

> [...] violations of women's rights tend to take place in the 'private' sphere. Domestic violence, honor killings, female

---

certain criminal activity are sufficient to exclude that activity from crimes against humanity even if the 'widespread or systematic' criteria are met.

[79] Gary Haugen and Victor Boutros, *The Locust Effect*, Oxford University Press, Oxford, 2014, pp. xiv–xv.

[80] *Ibid.*, pp. xiv–xv, and 1–28.

[81] *Ibid.*, pp.73–74, 82–83, and 135.

[82] MacKinnon, 2006, p. 23, see *supra* note 1.

---

genital mutilation, child marriage, and similar forms of 'invisible' suffering are implicitly separated from the more 'serious' public world of unlawful detentions and forced confessions.[83]

Thus, "violence experienced most often by women, no matter how systematic or obvious to officials in the states in which the women reside, is treated as a criminal (as opposed to a human rights) matter, to be dealt with by the respective state's law enforcement".[84]

MacKinnon specifically discusses torture as an example, but her analysis easily applies to slavery, especially sex trafficking: "Internationally, torture has a recognized profile. It usually begins with abduction, detention, imprisonment, and enforced isolation, progresses through extreme physical and mental abuse, and may end in death. The torturer has absolute power [...]. Life and death turn on his whim. Victims are beaten, raped, shocked with electricity, nearly drowned, tied, hung, burned, deprived of sleep, food, and human contact".[85]

To define torture only in terms of State abuse of power (or even private individuals imitating a State) is to enforce a double standard that excludes much of gendered violence: "Why isn't this political? The abuse is neither random nor individual. The fact that you know your assailant does not mean that your membership in a group chosen for violation is irrelevant to your abuse. It is still systematic and group-based".[86]

Dillon echoes the feminist critique, but also applies it to private crimes against children, particularly the commercial sexual exploitation of children, saying that it is not seen for the human rights violation that it is, because

> [...] the international human rights community seems for the most part caught in a conceptual warp that focuses overwhelmingly on state violence against largely male political prisoners or, in the alternative, on victims of abuses suffered in the course of armed conflict.[87]

---

[83] Sara Dillon, "What Human Rights Law Obscures: Global Sex Trafficking and the Demand for Children", in *UCLA Women's Law Journal*, vol. 17, no. 121, 2008, p. 123.

[84] *Ibid.*, p.133.

[85] MacKinnon, 2006, p. 17, see *supra* note 1.

[86] *Ibid.*, p. 22.

[87] Dillon, 2008, p. 123, see *supra* note 83.

The abuses child victims suffer are analogous to both torture and slavery:

> [Many children are victimized] often ending up with their health destroyed, victims of HIV/AIDS and other sexually transmitted diseases. Younger and younger children are sought with the expectation that clients will not be exposed to HIV. Prostituted children can be raped, beaten, sodomized, emotionally abused, tortured, and even killed by pimps, brothel owners, and customers.[88]

Unless we condition ourselves to think of victims of human rights abuses to be either harmed in war or male political prisoners, it is impossible not to see child sex slavery as a gross human rights abuse.[89]

A definition of crimes against humanity that excludes human trafficking, even if it is 'widespread or systematic', from consideration if it is done for private gain is a definition unjustifiably biased toward the ways that men experience the abuse of power, because

> the state is not all there is to power. To act as if it is produces an exceptionally inadequate definition for human rights when so much of the second-class status of women, from sexual objectification to murder, is done by men to women without express or immediate or overt state involvement.[90]

9.4.1.3. Recent Jurisprudence

Slowly, international criminal and human rights jurisprudence is shifting towards an understanding of women's human rights that is more responsive to some of these feminist concerns. For example, although gender-based violence against women has been illegal under certain laws for over hundreds of years, enforcement was extremely minimal until recently.[91] In the *Akayesu* case the ICTR explicitly compared rape to torture:

> [...] analogized aspects of the crimes of rape and torture, noting that rape "is a form of aggression" and the elements of the crime "cannot be captured in a mechanical description of objects and body parts". The Chamber noted that "[l]ike torture, rape is used for such purposes as intimidation,

---

[88] *Ibid.*, p.128.

[89] *Ibid.*, pp.122–124.

[90] MacKinnon, 2006, p. 23, see *supra* note 1.

[91] Askin, 2003, pp. 299–300, see *supra* note 34.

degradation, humiliation, discrimination, punishment, control or destruction of a person. Like torture, rape is a violation of personal dignity, and rape in fact constitutes torture" when all of the elements of torture are satisfied.[92]

The ECtHR has also found domestic and sexual violence constituted torture under the European Convention on Human Rights. In *Aydin v. Turkey*, the European Court ruled that the accumulation of acts of physical and mental violence and the especially cruel act of rape to which the applicant was subjected amounted to torture in breach of Article 3 of the ECHR. In *M.C. v. Bulgaria*, the ECtHR found the State in breach of Article 3 for failure to investigate the applicant's case of rape, and for failure to meet the requirements inherent in the State's positive obligations to "establish and apply effectively a criminal-law system punishing all forms of rape and sexual abuse".[93] In *A. v. the United Kingdom*, the ECtHR found that the State's failure to protect a child from violence in a domestic context amounted to a violation of Article 3, the prohibition of torture; the Court explicitly said that the State's responsibility included protecting private individuals from other private individuals.[94] Thus, in at least some human rights and/or international criminal law courts (including one that has jurisdiction over crimes against humanity), there has been some undermining of the public/private distinction as a way of determining an international crime or human rights abuse, particularly as torture was also once defined in terms of State action.

9.4.2. Practical Objections

In addition to theoretical objections to classifying certain forms of human trafficking as international crimes, potential practical objections could be raised to this proposal; namely, that the appropriate treaty already exists in the form of the Palermo Protocol, or that universal jurisdiction is a better solution than the Proposed Convention for combatting slavery.

---

[92] *Ibid.*, pp. 319–320 (citing *Prosecutor v. Akayesu*, 1998, para. 687).

[93] Iveta Cherneva, "Recognizing Rape as Torture: The Evolution of Women's Rights Legal Protective Techniques", in *Intercultural Human Rights Law Review*, 2011, vol. 6, no. 325, pp. 329–330, citing ECtHR, *Aydin v. Turkey*, Application No. 23178/94, Judgment, 25 September 1997, p. 86; ECtHR, *M.C. v. Bulgaria*, Application No. 39272/98, Judgment, 4 December 2003, pp. 182–185.

[94] ECtHR, *A. v. U.K.*, Judgment, Application No. 3455/05, 19 February 2009, pp. 22 and 24.

Although the Palermo Protocol regarding human trafficking is already in force, it is insufficient as a response to deal with human trafficking for at least three reasons. First, as a criminal law, it does not cover all of the actors involved in the abuse; only those involved in the actual transport and facilitators, not, to use the example of sex trafficking, the customers. Thus, it does nothing directly to address the demand.[95]

Second, as a form of law, it has no real enforcement mechanism.[96] If the Proposed Convention clearly covered human trafficking and became international law, then the classification would create a jurisdictional basis for enforcement and at least raise the priority of national government efforts to combat trafficking. No one expects another member to eradicate ordinary crime, but genocide and crimes against humanity are another matter, carrying greater expectations for enforcement. The lack of enforcement is evidenced in the absence of an 'extradite or prosecute clause' such as those for international crimes and the fact that this is an optional protocol to an organized crime treaty.

Third, international crimes have broader modes of liability, which is particularly helpful for addressing a crime that is also a business, because it allows prosecutors to better target all of the relevant actors, including those who may be more removed from the day-to-day trafficking activities, but who profit from them. These modes of liability, set forth in the Proposed Convention in Articles 4 and 5, include individual liability, joint perpetration ("with or through another"), ordering, soliciting, or inducing perpetrators (even if the crime is only attempted), aiding, abetting and other assistance to perpetrators, and intentional contributions to "to the

---

[95] To be clear, this does not mean that buyers should ordinarily be prosecuted for crimes against humanity (any more than most ordinary crimes should be so prosecuted), but it is important that they not be *de facto* excluded from potential liability by definition. Increasingly, human rights advocates and legal practitioners are recognizing buyers' participation in commercial sexual exploitation offenses against children as human trafficking offenses, rather than prostitution-related criminal offenses. See, *e.g.*, Shared Hope International, "Demanding Justice Benchmark Assessment," 2013, pp. 5–13. One example of this trend at the domestic level is the U.S. federal court decision which held that the U.S. sex trafficking statute (18 U.S.C. §1591) covered buyers of trafficked victims. Eighth Circuit, *United States v. Jungers*, 7 January 2013, 702 F.3d 1066. See also *supra* section 9.4.1.2. regarding human rights violations against women and children.

[96] The Proposed Convention does not create independent ICC jurisdiction, but Article 2(c) provides that a State Party that is already a party to the ICC Statute must co-operate with the ICC. Also, both the Palermo Protocol Articles 5–7, and the Proposed Convention in Article 2 rely primarily on States Parties to enforce the treaty requirements domestically.

---

commission or attempted commission of such a crime by a group of persons acting with a common purpose", to further a criminal purpose involving crimes against humanity or simply with the knowledge that such is the group's purpose.[97] It is not clear that perpetrators of human trafficking ought to be spared additional modes of liability largely because they are committing abuses for money.

Cohen argues that slavery is a *per se* international crime warranting universal jurisdiction; both because of its gravity and because of the impunity that surrounds it in much of the world.[98] This proposal is not inconsistent with universal jurisdiction, and if States decide that universal jurisdiction over slavery is a better and more workable solution than ICC prosecution, it will be easier to justify universal jurisdiction if slavery is clearly considered a crime against humanity, even when committed by private actors, in peacetime, and for profit.

When governments fail to prosecute atrocities, the issue is either one of capacity or political will (or both). If the issue is capacity, then identifying widespread and systematic human trafficking as a crime against humanity will justify either prioritization of resources to prosecute or international involvement. If the issue is political will, then this will also justify international involvement. Governments like Mauritania, for example, which currently turn a blind eye to slavery and then declare that it does not exist,[99] might be forced to change.

In light of the above theoretical and practical justifications for including severe forms of human trafficking as a crime against humanity *per se*, the Proposed Convention should be amended to remove or redefine the "attack against any civilian population" phrase to reflect the ILC Draft Code definition, making the only criteria enslavement (as defined by the Palermo Protocol and the TVPRA) that is either widespread or systematic (without being an organizational policy) and committed against civilians.

---

[97] Article 4, Proposed Convention, see *supra* note 11.

[98] Miriam Cohen, "The Analogy Between Piracy and Human Trafficking: A Theoretical Framework for the Application of Universal Jurisdiction", in *Buffalo Human Rights Law Review*, 2010, vol. 16, no. 201, p. 206.

[99] Bales, 2004, pp. 81, 108–112, see *supra* note 6.

9.5. Conclusion

Many forms of human trafficking are sufficiently abusive to constitute slavery (and possibly torture as well), yet are effectively excluded from the Proposed Convention on Crimes Against Humanity because they do not clearly satisfy the "widespread or systematic" and "attack directed against a civilian population" elements as currently defined by the Proposed Convention. Although crimes against humanity once were defined in relation to armed conflict and government actors, this is no longer the case, as the international community already recognizes that such abuses may be committed by private actors and in peacetime.

This chapter simply argues that the abuses may also be committed by private actors, in peacetime, for profit, and that these facts neither diminish the abuse nor present a valid distinction in light of modern human rights law, international criminal law, and human rights jurisprudence. The definitions of "widespread and systematic" and "attack directed against a civilian population" in the Proposed Convention should be expanded accordingly or interpreted in a way to reflect that private persons can commit crimes against humanity while pursuing private goals.[100]

The implications of expanding the definition of crimes against humanity in the Proposed Convention are: (1) a symbolic recognition of a human rights violation that disproportionately affects women and children and is often incorrectly viewed as a crime that ranks below crimes against humanity; (2) affirmation that the international community's responsibility to prevent it is greater than the responsibility to prevent transnational organized crime generally; and (3) practical legal tools (through the modes of liability) to combat it more effectively. Moreover, as both national and international jurisdictions seek to prevent and punish international crimes, placing human trafficking in that category will provide a powerful impetus to consistently enforce the laws against what is already almost universally criminalized and acknowledged as a great moral wrong.

---

[100] This is not to argue that the definition of crimes against humanity should be expanded to include every human trafficking offense, but that scale, severity, and impunity should be the operative factors, not whether the crime was committed as part of State or organizational policy (though of course such a State policy would be *per se* impunity).

10

The Responsibility to Protect and to Prosecute: Reflections on the Canadian Experience and Recommendations for the Proposed Crimes Against Humanity Convention

10.1. Introduction

As one of the principal architects of the Responsibility to Protect ('R2P'), Canada has distinguished itself as a voice which has significantly advanced the doctrine toward wider acceptance in the global community. The Canadian government played an important role in establishing the International Commission on Intervention and State Sovereignty ('ICISS') which introduced R2P in 2001.[1] Canada's leadership also led to the establishment of a dedicated non-profit research organization, the Canadian Centre for the Responsibility to Protect.[2] The importance of the doctrine has been recognized by the international community as "the most influential intellectual contribution" to the contemporary debate on the dilemma of intervention and as a watershed event in international discussions of humanitarian intervention.[3] Proliferation of the doctrine has led some to conclude that there is an emerging international customary norm

---

[*] **Rita J. Maxwell** is an Assistant Crown Attorney with the Ministry of the Attorney General in Toronto practicing in criminal law. She completed an LL.M. at Georgetown Law Centre in international human rights and criminal law and was a Visiting Professional at the International Criminal Court in 2011. She is a guest lecturer in international criminal law at the University of Toronto Faculty of Law and Osgoode Hall Law School. The opinions expressed in this chapter are those of the author alone. All Internet references were last accessed on 22 September 2014.

[1] The Canadian Centre for the Responsibility to Protect, "International Commission on Intervention and State Sovereignty: Responsibility to Protect Report", available at http://www.responsibilitytoprotect.org/ICISS%20Report.pdf ('ICISS Report').

[2] *Ibid.*

[3] Siobhán Wills, "Military Interventions on Behalf of Vulnerable Populations: The Legal Responsibilities of States and International Organizations Engaged in Peace Support Operations", in *Journal of Conflict Security Law*, 2004, vol. 9, pp. 387 and 388.

that recognizes this obligation on States. But just how a State can implement preventative and responsible measures to further R2P has yet to be clearly identified.[4] One of the reasons for this is that there are misconceptions about the scope and meaning of R2P as being primarily a doctrine related to military interventions.[5]

This chapter will argue that there is another way to accomplish R2P, short of military intervention, which has critical deterrent value against those who would commit crimes against humanity. Yet, currently, the world's most powerful tool in response to the perpetration of crimes against humanity and other core crimes, the International Criminal Court ('ICC'), does not establish universal jurisdiction over the core crimes of genocide, crimes against humanity and war crimes.[6] Moreover, it is a complementary court, meaning that it falls to countries to pursue prosecutions against those who commit international crimes.[7] Prosecutions at the national level, this chapter will argue, have become one of the most influential ways in which a nation can promote protection of human rights and prevention of violations everywhere. This message is amplified where countries prosecute persons alleged to have committed core crimes who are present in their territory, regardless of the perpetrator's nationality or where the crimes took place. Prosecutions, this chapter will argue, are the key to realizing the full potential of R2P.

Integral to effectively combating impunity under the Proposed Convention on the Prevention and Punishment of Crimes Against Humanity ('Proposed Convention', see Annex 1) is its adoption of universal jurisdiction obligating States Parties to prosecute anyone suspected of crimes against humanity who sets foot on the State's territory. As this chapter will discuss, many countries, including Canada, have taken an aggressive stance in prosecuting crimes against humanity, reflecting acceptance among many nations that perpetrators of these crimes must be

---

4   Carsten Stahn, "Responsibility to Protect: Political Rhetoric or Emerging Legal Norm?", in *American Journal of International Law*, 2007, vol. 101, no. 1, p. 99.

5   Barbara Barbour and Brian Gorlick, "Embracing the Responsibility to Protect: A Repertoire of Measures Including Asylum for Potential Victims", in *International Journal of Refugee Law*, 2008, vol. 20, no. 4, p. 533.

6   ICC Statute of the International Criminal Court, 1 July 2002, Articles 11–14 ('ICC Statute').

7   *Ibid.*, Article 17.

brought to justice and that prosecutions are an essential component to prevention and protection of people from mass atrocities.

However, the Proposed Convention also represents an important opportunity to give greater meaning to R2P (beyond political rhetoric) by cementing the relationship between R2P and the obligation of States to prosecute crimes against humanity.[8] Effective and efficient prosecutions are the key to advancing meaningful implementation of R2P. The Proposed Convention has the ability to enhance this mandate, but requires reinforcement in several key ways. With this framework in place, there is an opportunity to solidify the doctrine of the responsibility to protect as a concept which is linked to the obligation to prosecute. As this chapter will address, more express language throughout the Proposed Convention linking prosecutions with the doctrine of R2P will help move the doctrine from an ideal to a more binding legal obligation. Moreover, specific requirements for States Parties to account for the presence of suspected criminals in their territory, and specific action plans for dealing with these individuals should be clearly spelled out in the Proposed Convention. This will bring publicity to the issue of true compliance and accountability for States Parties under the Proposed Convention. Language in the Proposed Convention requiring this reporting should make explicit reference to the obligation to prosecute and the responsibility to protect as the basis for such a reporting requirement.

The chapter will proceed in three parts. First, it considers the relationship between the R2P doctrine and the obligation of States to prosecute *jus cogens* crimes, in particular crimes against humanity. This section will review the historical development of the R2P doctrine, focusing on Canada's pivotal involvement in the discourse and development, and argue that the doctrine of R2P is clearly meant to encompass a variety of measures which accomplish the dual mandates of protection and prevention. This section also looks at the treaty and customary law foundations of the obligation to prosecute. Second, it explores Canada's historical and current experience in prosecuting international crimes, highlighting Canada's bold legislative initiative to criminalize and prosecute crimes against humanity. This section also includes a brief review of Canada's prosecu-

---

8. Washington University School of Law, "Proposed International Convention on the Prevention and Punishment of Crimes Against Humanity Convention", Whitney R. Harris World Law Institute Crimes Against Humanity Initiative, Article 8, see Annex 1.

tions under the Crimes Against Humanity and War Crimes Act [9] ('CAHWCA'). Finally, the chapter turns to the Proposed Convention and the impact of the draft on the doctrine of R2P and States Parties' obligation to prosecute.

10.2. The Relationship Between R2P and the Obligation to Prosecute

10.2.1. The Obligation to Prosecute: Its Origins

The obligation to prosecute crimes against humanity has become generally accepted, and is often viewed as an obligation to extradite or try a suspect.[10] Prosecutions promote a sense of closure for victims and signal worldwide condemnation for human rights violations, thereby acting as a powerful deterrent.[11] Obligations to prosecute come from two sources: (1) treaty obligations, and (2) as part of customary international law. These two origins will be briefly reviewed before considering the connection between the obligation to prosecute and R2P, in the context of crimes against humanity.

10.2.1.1. Treaty-Based Origins of the Obligation to Prosecute

Numerous international treaties and conventions create an obligation to prosecute individuals for specific violations of human rights, some doing so explicitly, while others implying the obligation. The Convention Against Torture and Other Cruel, Inhuman or Degrading Treatment or Punishment[12] ('CAT Convention') is an example of a treaty which explicitly obliges States Parties to prosecute violations. Parties to the CAT Convention are required to "ensure that all acts of torture are offences under

---

[9]   The Crimes Against Humanity and War Crimes Act, 24 June 2000, S.C. 2000, c. 24 ('CAHWCA').

[10] Naomi Roht-Arriaza, "The Pinochet Precedent and Universal Jurisdiction", in *New England Law Review*, 2001, vol. 35, no. 2, p. 311.

[11] Naomi Roht-Arriaza, "Comment, State Responsibility to Investigate and Prosecute Grave Human Rights Violations in International Law", in *California Law Review*, 1990, vol. 78, no. 2, pp. 449 and 461. Also see Diane F. Orentlicher, "Settling Accounts: The Duty to Prosecute Human Rights Violations of a Prior Regime", in *Yale Law Journal*, 1991, vol. 100, no. 8, pp. 2537 and 2542–2544.

[12] Convention Against Torture and Other Cruel, Inhuman or Degrading Treatment or Punishment, 10 December 1984, in UNTS, vol. 1465, p. 113, Article 2.

their criminal law" and that any person alleged to have committed torture found within the territory "shall [...] submit the case to its competent authorities for the purpose of prosecution", in the event the individual is not extradited.[13]

Similarly, the Convention on the Prevention and Punishment of the Crime of Genocide ('Genocide Convention') obligates States Parties to prosecute genocide.[14] Articles I and VI of the Genocide Convention underscore the obligation to prosecute, mandating that persons "committing genocide or any of the other acts enumerated in Article III shall be punished" and that "[p]ersons charged with genocide or any of the other acts enumerated in article III shall be tried by a competent tribunal".[15]

These are certainly not the only human rights instruments which impose a mandatory duty to prosecute. The Inter-American Convention on the Forced Disappearance of Persons as well as the International Convention Against the Taking of Hostages also include an obligation to prosecute.[16] Many instruments which do not incorporate the obligation to prosecute explicitly, do so implicitly. Provisions in the International Covenant on Civil and Political Rights and the European Convention for the Protection of Human Rights and Fundamental Freedoms are two good examples of instruments which contain implicit obligations to prosecute.[17]

10.2.1.2. Customary Law Origins of the Obligation to Prosecute

Jus cogens norms are norms of customary law and have the special character of being preemptory and binding on all States. Crimes against humanity have reached the status of *jus cogens* crimes, as discussed by Mohammed El-Zeidy:

---

[13] *Ibid.*, Article 7.

[14] Convention on the Prevention and Punishment of the Crime of Genocide, 9 December 1948, S. Treaty Doc. No. 81-1 (1989), in UNTS, vol. 78, pp. 277 and 280.

[15] *Ibid.*, Articles I and III.

[16] Inter-American Convention on Forced Disappearances of Persons, U.N. ESCOR, Commission on Human Rights, 47th Session, U.N. Doc. E/CN.4/1991/49., Article 6; International Convention Against Taking of Hostages, 17 December 1979, in UNTS, vol. 1316, p. 205, T.I.A.S. 11, 081.

[17] International Covenant on Civil and Political Rights, 23 March 1976, in UNTS, vol. 999, p. 171, Article 2; European Convention for the Protection of Human Rights and Fundamental Freedoms, 3 September 1953, in UNTS, vol. 213, p. 222; see also Orentlicher, 1991, pp. 2569–2570, *supra* note 11.

> Th[e] legal basis [for saying that genocide, war crimes, and crimes against humanity have achieved jus cogens status] can be found in international pronouncements, or what can be called international *opinio juris*, that reflect the recognition that these crimes are deemed part of general customary law. Language in preambles [...] or other provisions of treaties applicable to these crimes, also indicate that these crimes have a higher status in international law. Another indication is the large number of States that have ratified treaties related to these crimes [...]. The writings of scholars and diplomats further buttress this legal foundation.[18]

The legal imperative to prosecute *jus cogens* crimes such as crimes against humanity is also clear. The evolution of the obligation in customary international law and treaty-based law has established an affirmative duty on countries to investigate, prosecute and provide remedies for grave breaches of human rights.[19] A contemporary example of the obligation can be found in the ICC Statute. The Preamble of the ICC Statute confirms there is an "absolute duty to prosecute" international crimes of concern to the international community and that their "prosecution must be ensured by taking steps at the national level".[20] Moreover, the ICC Statute imposes clear obligations on States Parties to prosecute or extradite and co-operate with the ICC in its investigation and prosecution of alleged perpetrators of grave international crimes.[21] How does the obligation to prosecute relate to States Parties' responsibility to protect and prevent *jus cogens* crimes? This requires consideration of the development of the doctrine.

10.2.2. Canada's Role in the Development of the Responsibility to Protect Doctrine

The world's failure to act in the face of mass atrocities has prompted soul-searching among many U.N. Member States. Canada, in particular, has been publicly and sharply criticized for its failure to respond to the geno-

---

[18] Mohamed M. El-Zeidy, "The Principle of Complementarity: A New Machinery to Implement International Criminal Law", in *Michigan Journal of International Law*, 2002, vol. 23, pp. 869 and 947–948.

[19] For a comprehensive review of the evolution of the obligation to prosecute, see Roht-Arriaza, 1990, pp. 462–498, *supra* note 11.

[20] ICC Statute, Preamble, see *supra* note 6.

[21] *Ibid.*, Articles 17, and 86–102.

cide in Rwanda and targeted attacks on civilian populations in Kosovo and Srebrenica.[22] As a response to this failure, Canada committed itself to conducting a focused assessment on initiatives to create a moral imperative to act, a doctrine which came to be known as the 'Responsibility to Protect' or 'R2P'.[23] R2P can be defined as an international security and human rights norm to address the international community's failure to prevent and stop genocide, war crimes, ethnic cleansing and crimes against humanity.[24]

In 2000, Canada announced the establishment of ICISS, during the U.N. Millennium Summit which generated a landmark ICISS Report, which set out the central thesis of R2P:

> (S)overeign states have a responsibility to protect their own citizens from avoidable catastrophe – from mass murder and rape, from starvation – but that when they are unwilling or unable to do so, that responsibility must be borne by the broader community of states.[25]

The ICISS aimed to reconcile traditional notions of State sovereignty with a national imperative (and ideally international consensus) that individual States have a responsibility to protect populations from genocide, war crimes, ethnic cleansing and crimes against humanity. The ICISS's report provided a valuable framework for fostering international consensus on the responsibility and set in motion a paradigm shift in the debate about humanitarian intervention, maintaining that sovereignty contains a dual mandate of respecting the sovereignty of States while also protecting the dignity of people within the State.[26]

R2P was adopted by a panel of experts appointed by then U.N. Secretary-General Kofi Annan, stating "there is growing acceptance that while sovereign Governments have the primary responsibility to protect their own citizens from catastrophes, when they are unable or unwilling to

---

22 Romeo Dallaire, *Shake Hands with the Devil: The Failure of Humanity in Rwanda*, Carroll & Graf Publishers, 2005; see also National Post, "Canada's Responsibility to Protect Darfur", 16 October 2007.

23 ICISS Report, see *supra* note 1. See also Ministry of Foreign Affairs and International Trade Canada, "Responsibility to Protect", 24 June 2010.

24 ICISS Report, p. viii, see *supra* note 1.

25 *Ibid*. See also background documents from the Coalition on the Responsibility to Protect at http://www.responsibilitytoprotect.org.

26 ICISS Report, paras. 1.35 and 2.14, see *supra* note 1.

do so that responsibility should be taken up by the wider international community".[27] The Canadian roots of ICISS and the dissemination of the report gave Canada a strong voice at the 2005 World Summit to advocate for broader acceptance of the R2P doctrine. Put simply, the R2P framework envisaged by ICISS included three parts: (i) the responsibility to prevent, (ii) the responsibility to react, and (iii) the responsibility to rebuild, with prevention as the single most important dimension of the responsibility to protect.[28]

Canada was instrumental in getting R2P principles included in the World Summit Outcome Document, representing the first global consensus on the responsibility of individual States and the international community to protect populations vulnerable to mass atrocities.[29]

The Summit Outcome document established a four-part approach to R2P:

a) each individual state has the primary responsibility to protect its population from genocide, war crimes, ethnic cleansing and crimes against humanity, including a responsibility to prevent;

b) the international community should assist states to exercise this responsibility and ensure early warning capabilities are established and maintained;

c) a complementary responsibility for the international community to protect populations from genocide, war crimes, ethnic cleansing and crimes against humanity, through diplomatic, humanitarian and other peaceful means through the UN and Chapters VI and VIII of the UN Charter;

d) on a case-by-case basis, where means are inadequate and national authorities manifestly fail to protect their

---

[27] Report of the Secretary-General's High-Level Panel on Threats, Challenges and Change, "A More Secure World: Our Shared Responsibility", A/59/565, 2 December 2004, para. 201.

[28] *Ibid.*, xii; see also Emma McClean, "The Responsibility to Protect: The Role of International Human Rights Law", in *Journal of Conflict and Security Law*, 2008, vol. 13, pp. 123, 131.

[29] UNGA, "World Summit Outcome Document", 15 September 2005, UNGA Res. 60/1, U.N. Doc A/60/150 ('World Summit Outcome Document').

> populations, the international community must take action, pursuant to Chapter VII of the UN Charter.[30]

The inclusion of R2P in the 2005 World Summit Outcome document marked a definitive step forward for the doctrine. Then Canadian Prime Minister Paul Martin commented:

> It [R2P] is a powerful norm of international behaviour [...] [this week] we have taken a very important step to that end. We are proud the R2P has Canadian lineage, that it is now a principle for all the world.[31]

Similar sentiments were expressed by other world leaders, including from Rwandan President Paul Kagame:

> Never again should the international community's response to these crimes be found wanting. Let us resolve to take collective actions, in a timely and decisive manner. Let us also commit to put in place early warning mechanisms and ensure that preventive interventions are the rule rather than the exception.[32]

The World Summit consensus was further endorsed by the U.N. Security Council in resolution 1674 on the Protection of Civilians in Armed Conflict.[33]

In 2009, U.N. Secretary-General Ban Ki-moon re-affirmed the three pillars of the doctrine and stressed that R2P is not a "new code for humanitarian intervention".[34] The Secretary-General also affirmed his commitment to making R2P a policy, not just an aspiration. This commitment led to the appointment of a special advisor to the Secretary-General with a focus on R2P, several days of debate in the General Assembly (involving 92 Member States) on R2P, and the Secretary-General's report entitled 'Implementing the Responsibility to Protect'.[35]

---

[30] *Ibid.*, see also ICCIS Report, *supra* note 1.

[31] World Summit Excerpts, "Responsibility to Protect – Engaging Civil Society", available at http://www.responsibilitytoprotect.org.

[32] *Ibid.*

[33] General Assembly, Resolution 1674, 28 April 2006, U.N. Doc. S/Res/1674.

[34] Report of the Secretary-General, "Implementing the Responsibility to Protect", A/63/677, 12 January 2009.

[35] *Ibid.*, see also Secretary-General, "Letter addressed to the President of the Security Council Regarding the Nomination of Edward Luck to the Position of Special Advisor to the Secretary-General with a focus on R2P", 7 December 2007, U.N. Doc. S/2007/721; see also UNGA Res. 63/308, 14 September 2009 ('UNGA Res. 63/308').

The U.N. General Assembly adopted a resolution to "take note of the report of the Secretary-General" and continue to consider the doctrine of the responsibility to protect.[36]

Yet even with these key pronouncements and the emergence of R2P as a widely endorsed concept within the international community, whether these documents create binding legal obligations under international law remains an open question.[37] As such, there remains a need to codify the concept of R2P in an international convention to ensure that R2P takes its rightful place as a legal obligation on countries to act in the face of mass atrocities. The obligation to 'act' requires broad interpretation. Creating a direct link between R2P and the obligation to prosecute is an essential component of elevating the principle to a legal obligation, as will be discussed next.

10.2.3. The Perfect Marriage: Linking Prosecutions and the Responsibility to Protect

With the R2P doctrine gaining ground in the international arena, implementation of the norm has become a central feature of the dialogue. Criminal prosecutions define and publicize international rules of behaviour and deter future abuses, and in doing so, serve a vital function in advancing R2P. Through transnational law litigation, States develop criminal and immigration responses to violations of human rights law at the national level. Commentators have pointed out that there is an important relationship between domestic and international law, with domestic institutions enforcing international obligations.[38] The Pinochet extradition battle is an excellent example of the role that criminal prosecutions can play as part of transnational law litigation. Widespread publicity over Spain's attempts to prosecute Pinochet prompted an important shift in public perceptions of accountability for human rights abuses and catalysed domestic prosecutions.[39]

---

[36] UNGA Res. 63/308, see *supra* note 35.

[37] Stahn, 2007, p. 101, see *supra* note 4.

[38] Beth Stephens, "Translating Filartiga: A Comparative and International Law Analysis of Domestic Remedies for International Human Rights Violations", in *Yale Journal of International Law*, 2002, vol. 27, no. 1.

[39] *Ibid.*, see also Roht-Arriaza, 2001, pp. 311–312, see *supra* note 10.

In his keynote address to the Crimes Against Humanity Initiative – Hague Inter-sessional Experts' Meeting in June of 2009, Gareth Evans (International Crisis Group) set out the overarching goal of the Initiative: to enshrine the 'responsibility to protect' as a norm of customary international law.[40] That is to say,

> [...] winning and consolidating genuine international acceptance and recognition of this concept as a new global norm, and, even more importantly, achieving its effective application in practice as new conscience/shocking situations continue to arise.[41]

If the goal of the Crimes Against Humanity Initiative, and the Proposed Convention, is to work towards making 'responsibility to protect' a customary norm and elevate crimes against humanity, through legal remedies, to the dominant legal concept, one has to look critically at how the Proposed Convention can define and link the dual mandates of the obligation to prosecute and the responsibility to protect. The Proposed Convention presents an important opportunity to codify the responsibility to protect by linking it to the well-accepted obligation to prosecute. Moreover, as will be addressed in the last part of this chapter, the principle of universality will be indispensable to the effectiveness of the Proposed Convention.

Canada provides an excellent reference point for the discussion. As will be discussed, Canada's history and current efforts in prosecuting crimes against humanity illuminates areas where the Proposed Convention can be enhanced and provide decisive direction to States about the link between R2P and the obligation to prosecute.

10.3. Canada's Historical and Current Experience in Prosecuting and Extraditing Suspected Violators of Human Rights

Canada views itself as a champion of global human rights. Former Minister of Justice, Irwin Cotler, captured the priority of human rights as follows:

> Canada has a reputation world-wide for being a leader in ensuring that there is no safe haven for individuals involved in

---

[40] Gareth Evans, "Keynote Address at the Crimes Against Humanity Initiative Hague Inter-sessional Experts Meeting", 11–12 June 2009.

[41] *Ibid.*

> crimes against humanity or war crimes, regardless of when
> or where these crimes took place.[42]

Canada has shown commitment to the doctrine of R2P through implementation of 'soft' measures aimed at studying and understanding R2P. Administratively and institutionally, Canada has experienced growth in the development of bodies and programmes aimed at studying prevention and protection, including the Canadian All-Party Parliamentary Group for Prevention of Genocide and other Crimes Against Humanity, the Crimes Against Humanity Program (Department of Justice), the Responsibility to Prevent Coalition, and the Montreal Institute for Genocide and Human Rights Studies. Yet, in as much as Canada has been a champion of human rights, it has a long and difficult history in prosecuting war criminals and other human rights violators. In that sense, it has seized on the importance of involving civil society in enhancing and advancing the mandate.

10.3.1. Canada's History in Prosecuting Violators of Human Rights

Until 1949, Canada had no specific criteria for rejecting immigrants, included suspected Nazi war criminals or the German military.[43] In 1949, a prohibition was introduced to include past members of the Nazi party, the SS and other regular armed forces and collaborators.[44] But, in 1962, these specific exclusions were removed from Canada's immigration policies. It was later suggested that Joseph Mengele, an infamous Nazi war criminal, had applied to immigrate to Canada in 1962 and that Canadian officials had been informed of it at the time.[45]

It was not until 1985 that the issue of Mengele's continued presence in Canada was raised in the House of Commons, prompting the establishment of the Deschenes Commission, mandated to investigate the charge that a significant number of Nazi war criminals had emigrated to Canada.[46] While the Deschenes Commission found the ultimate number of war criminals in Canada to have been exaggerated in early estimates, it

---

[42] National Post, "Ottawa Targets 86 War Thugs", 5 May 2004, A1.

[43] Grant Purves, "War Crimes: The Deschenes Commission", Political and Social Affairs Division, Government of Canada.

[44] *Ibid.*

[45] *Ibid.*

[46] *Ibid.*

did identify several suspected war criminal and made recommendations about how to bring them to justice.[47]

To bring these war criminals to justice, the Deschenes Commission recommended amendments to the Criminal Code to make prosecutions of war criminals possible in Canada and amendments to the Extradition Act to facilitate removal of individuals.[48] In 1987, the Canadian Government amended the Criminal Code to allow the exercise of jurisdiction over crimes against humanity and war crimes committed outside Canada by deeming that such crimes took place in Canada.

However, prosecutions of suspected war criminals in Canada did not meet with much success. Four prosecutions were launched between 1987 and 1994, none of which led to a conviction. The confirmation of the acquittal of Imre Finta by the Supreme Court of Canada in March 1994 gave the hardest and final blow to what had been a long overdue but laudable effort by Canada to address the issue of impunity.[49] From this point on, criminal prosecutions stopped being a focal option, and immigration measures became the preferred solution for dealing with suspects of international crimes found in Canada.[50]

10.3.2. New Horizons: The Crimes Against Humanity and War Crimes Act

More recently, Canada has taken a proactive approach to prosecuting war criminals. The CAHWCA is Canada's enacting legislation which officially criminalizes genocide, crimes against humanity and war crimes, and empowers Canadian courts to prosecute those alleged to have committed

---

[47] The Deschenes Commission compiled a master list of possible suspects totaling 774. A total of 341 were found never to have landed or resided in Canada, 21 had landed but left, 86 had died in Canada, and 4 could not be located. It could not find evidence of war crimes in a further 154 cases. The Commission ultimately recommended that 606 files be closed. The Commission could not find *prima facie* evidence of war crimes in a further 97 cases, but believed evidence might exist in Eastern Europe. The Commission found *prima facie* evidence of war crimes in only 20 cases.

[48] Purves, see *supra* note 43; see also Criminal Code of Canada, 1985, R.S.C., c. C-46; Extradition Act, 1999, S.C., c. 18.

[49] *R.* v. *Finta*, 1995, 1 S.C.R. 701.

[50] See *Oberlander* v. *Canada*, 2004, 241 DLR (4th) 146; *Obodzinsky* v. *Canada*, 2001, 278 NR 182; *B(A)* v. *Canada*, 2001, 269 NR 381; *Canada* v. *Nemsila*, 1996, 120 FTR 132; *Arica* v. *Canada*, 1995, 182 NR 392; *Gonzalez* v. *Canada*, 1994, 115 DLR (4th) 403; *Sivakumar* v. *Canada*, 1993, 163 NR 197.

these core crimes. With the enactment of CAHWCA[51] on 24 June 2000, Canada became the first country in the world to incorporate the obligations of the ICC Statute into its national law. To ensure that Canada can co-operate fully with ICC proceedings, the CAHWCA also amended existing Canadian laws including the Criminal Code,[52] Extradition Act[53] and Mutual Legal Assistance in Criminal Matters Act.[54]

The CAHWCA has important symbolic value and legislative authority to hold people accountable for grievous acts of genocide, war crimes, and crimes against humanity, such as enslavement, deportation, imprisonment, torture, and sexual violence. The CAHWCA provides that genocide, crimes against humanity, and war crimes are indictable offences under Canadian criminal law, whether committed inside or outside of Canada.[55] The CAHWCA established universal jurisdiction over core international crimes, allowing Canada to prosecute anyone present in Canada for the crimes listed in the CAHWCA, regardless of the individual's nationality or where the crimes were committed. Article 8 of the CAHWCA sets out the jurisdiction of the act:

> 8. A person who is alleged to have committed an offence under section 6 or 7 may be prosecuted for that offence if:
>
>   (a)   at the time the offence is alleged to have been committed,

---

[51]   CAHWCA, see *supra* note 9.

[52]   Criminal Code of Canada, see *supra* note 48.

[53]   Extradition Act, see *supra* note 48.

[54]   Mutual Legal Assistance in Criminal Matters Act, 1985, R.S.C., c. 30.

[55]   CAHWCA, Articles 4 and 6, see *supra* note 9. Article 4 governs offences committed within Canada while article 6 governs offences committed outside of Canada, but both share common definition for crimes against humanity, as including:

> murder, extermination, enslavement, deportation, imprisonment, torture, sexual violence, persecution or any other inhumane act or omission that is committed against any civilian population or any identifiable group and that, at the time and in the place of its commission, constitutes a crime against humanity according to customary international law or conventional international law or by virtue of its being criminal according to the general principles of law recognized by the community of nations, whether or not it constitutes a contravention of the law in force at the time and in the place of its commission.

      (i)   the person was a Canadian citizen or was employed by Canada in a civilian or military capacity,

      (ii) the person was a citizen of a state that was engaged in an armed conflict against Canada, or was employed in a civilian or military capacity by such a state,

      (iii) the victim of the alleged offence was a Canadian citizen, or

      (iv) the victim of the alleged offence was a citizen of a state that was allied with Canada in an armed conflict; or

  (b) after the time the offence is alleged to have been committed, the person is present in Canada.[56]

The CAHWCA has further provisions to prosecute even when the accused is absent from Canada:

9. […]

  (1) Proceedings for an offence under this Act alleged to have been committed outside Canada for which a person may be prosecuted under this Act may, whether or not the person is in Canada, be commenced in any territorial division in Canada and the person may be tried and punished in respect of that offence in the same manner as if the offence had been committed in that territorial division.

  (2) For greater certainty, in a proceeding commenced in any territorial division under subsection (1), the provisions of the Criminal Code relating to requirements that an accused appear at and be present during proceedings and any exceptions to those requirements apply.[57]

The CAHWCA clearly establishes a very wide scope of jurisdiction over crimes against humanity and implements universal jurisdiction in its broadest sense.[58] It allows Canadian courts to initiate prosecutions against

---

[56] CAHWCA, Article 8, see *supra* note 9.

[57] CAHWCA, Article 9, see *supra* note 9.

[58] Antonio Cassese, *International Criminal Law*, Oxford University Press, Oxford, 2003, p. 285. See also Xavier Philippe, "The Principles of Universal Jurisdiction and Complemen-

anyone for crimes against humanity, regardless of the nationality of the perpetrator, the victims, where the crime took place or when the crime occurred.

Moreover, the CAHWCA provides a clear articulation of Canada's obligation to arrest and surrender persons sought by the ICC for genocide, crimes against humanity, and war crimes, removing all grounds for refusing requests to surrender accused persons to the ICC, in particular on the grounds of immunity under customary international law. This is critical, as top suspects continue to evade accountability before the ICC by asserting functional immunity. The ICC's pursuit of the President of the Sudan, Mr. Omar Al-Bashir, has been frustrated by the position taken by Malawi that there is a conflict between Mr. Al-Bashir's right to immunity under customary international law and obligations to the ICC under Article 98 of the ICC Statute to surrender accused persons.[59]

In this regard, Canada has taken an aggressive stance, enshrining the responsibility to prosecute and the obligation to surrender accused to the ICC on request, within its domestic legislation, underscoring its commitment to ending impunity.

10.3.3. The Trial and Conviction of Désiré Munyaneza

Although the CAHWCA was adopted in 2000, it was tested out for the first time in the prosecution of Désiré Munyaneza ('Munyaneza').[60] On 19 October 2005, Munyaneza, a Rwandan immigrant living in Toronto, became the first person to be arrested and charged with an offence under the CAHWCA. Munyaneza was charged with two counts of genocide, two counts of crimes against humanity, and three counts of war crimes for actions allegedly committed in Rwanda in 1994.[61] Munyaneza was accused

---

tarity: How do the Two Principles Intermesh?" in *International Review of the Red Cross*, 2006, vol. 88, no. 862, pp. 379–380.

[59] ICC, *Prosecutor v. Al Bashir*, Decision Pursuant to Article 87(7) of the ICC Statute on the Failure by the Republic of Malawi to Comply with the Cooperation Requests Issued by the Court with Respect to the Arrest and Surrender of Omar Hassan Ahmad Al Bashir, 12 December 2011, paras. 41–43.

[60] *R. v. Munyaneza*, 2009, QCCS 2201 (CanLII), available at http://canlii.ca/t/240j1.

[61] *Ibid.*, paras. 68–69, 108–109, and 129–130.

of leading a militia whose members raped and killed dozens of Tutsis, and of orchestrating a massacre of 300–400 Tutsis in a church.[62]

Munyaneza's trial began in March of 2007 and saw 66 people giving testimony, most whose identity was hidden.[63] On 22 May 2009, Munyaneza was convicted of all charges and is the first person to have been convicted under the CAHWCA. On 29 October 2009, Munyaneza was sentenced to life in prison with no chance of parole for 25 years.[64] Mr. Munyaneza's conviction was upheld by the Quebec Court of Appeal on 7 May 2014 and an appeal to the Supreme Court of Canada has not yet been sought.[65]

From a Canadian perspective, the case of Munyaneza was historic. As the trial judge commented: "Trials for crimes against humanity are extremely rare outside of international criminal tribunals".[66] It was the first case under the CAHWCA and signalled a return to a more aggressive stance regarding alleged war criminals found on Canadian territory.[67] It also had an impact on victims of the Rwandan genocide living in Canada, who had waited for over a decade for justice. Rwandan Jean-Paul Nyilinkwaya was quoted as saying, following the convictions: "The fact that he (Munyaneza) was found guilty is a very big boost for the survivors. Everybody there is desperate for justice".[68] Another observer and genocide survivor, César Gashabizi, commented: "I'm very happy he was found guilty, I want to thank and congratulate Canada. We have been waiting for this. Nobody comes to Canada to hide".[69]

Moreover, after a difficult debut in prosecuting war criminals, the Munyaneza conviction acts as an affirmation of the usefulness of the CAHWCA and sends a strong message to the international community

---

[62] *Ibid.,* paras. 588–591. See also BBC, "Canada Jails Rwandan War Criminal", 29 October 2009.

[63] *R.* v. *Muyaneza,* see *supra* note 60.

[64] *R.* v. *Munyaneza,* 2009, QCCS 4865 (CanLII), available at http://canlii.ca/2b84z; see also "Canada jails Rwandan War Criminal", *supra* note 62.

[65] *R.* v. *Munyaneza,* 2014 QCCA 906 (CanLII), available at http://canlii.ca/t/g6vlf.

[66] *R.* v. *Munyaneza,* para. 10, see *supra* note 60.

[67] Fanny Lafontaine, "Canada's Crimes Against Humanity and War Crimes Act on Trial: An Analysis of the Munyaneza Case", in *Journal of International Criminal Justice*, 2010, vol. 8, no.1, pp. 269 and 270.

[68] "Canada Jails Rwandan War Criminal", see *supra* note 62.

[69] CBC, "Quebec court convicts Munyaneza of war crimes in Rwanda", 22 May 2009.

about Canada's position *vis-a-vis* prosecuting human rights violators. As Professor Bruce Broomhall noted:

> The international community has already made great strides in establishing global standards for prosecuting war crimes, notably through the creation of the International Criminal Court [...].
>
> But the ICC focuses on major players, such as presidents and generals, and they don't always reach down to the level of Mr. Munyaneza, who was a local actor in his hometown of Butare [...].
>
> That's where courts like those in Canada have to pick up the slack.[70]

Anyone who is present in Canada and alleged to have committed crimes against humanity, genocide, war crimes and other international criminal acts can be prosecuted in Canada.

This is not to say, however, that Canada is a perfect model of implemented universal jurisdiction over crimes against humanity. The CAHWCA is, in many ways, still in its infancy. The Munyaneza prosecution represents the only prosecution under the CAHWCA since its inception.[71]

Moreover, Canada has demonstrated what some would argue is an over-reliance on administrative remedies, such as removal of suspected war criminals from the country or immigration policies which block entry of suspected human rights violators.[72] Specifically, the Department of Justice in collaboration with the Royal Canadian Mounted Police and the Canadian Board Services Agency created the War Crimes Program in

---

[70] *Ibid.*

[71] A second Rwandan, Jacques Mungwarere, was charged with "an act of genocide" under the CAHWCA on 7 November 2009. The Royal Canadian Mounted Police alleges that he committed this act in the western Rwandan city of Kibuye, and that his case is connected to that of Munyaneza.

[72] To date, there has been one citizen revocation case in Canada under section 18 of the Citizenship Act. Branko Rogan, a former reserve police officer at a detention centre in Bileca in Bosnia-Herzegovina, sought citizenship in Canada in 1994. Mr. Rogan's citizenship was revoked after a hearing in which the presiding judge concluded that he knowingly participated in the inhumane treatment of Muslim prisoner in the detention centre in Bileca. See Department of Justice, "War Crimes and Crimes Against Humanity – Court Proceedings", available at http://www.justice.gc.ca/eng/cj-jp/wc-cdg/succ-real.html.

1998.[73] While the interdepartmental body represented a significant development in Canada's commitment to ending impunity, it is conceded that prosecution of suspected war criminal is reserved for only a fraction of the cases.[74] While these measures serve the purpose of keeping war criminals off Canadian soil, they do very little to serve the broader objectives of accountability and each State Party's obligation to prevent and protect against crimes against humanity. To that extent, the doctrine of R2P continues to be an ideal, rather than a governing principle, even in a country like Canada, which figured so prominently in its development.

Therefore, while the CAHWCA is a good illustration of a nation's capacity to build legislative infrastructure which promotes R2P, there is still a need for acknowledgment of R2P in an international treaty to advance the doctrine as a customary norm around which domestic legislation addressing crimes against humanity should be shaped. The Proposed Convention is the vehicle through which the doctrine can gain that needed momentum.

10.4.1.2. Other Examples of Implemented Universal Jurisdiction over Crimes Against Humanity

Canada is not alone in its recognition of universal jurisdiction over core international crimes. Indeed, Germany has been principled and aggressive in its approach to universal jurisdiction over such crimes. The German government opted for autonomous implementation of the ICC Statute into domestic law, implementing two comprehensive laws covering substantive and procedural matters: the Code of Crimes Against International Law (*Völkerstrafgesetzbuch*, 'VStGB')[75] and the ICC Implementation Act.[76] The VStGB provides for unlimited universal jurisdiction and incorporates crimes in the ICC Statute into domestic law. Section 6 of the German Criminal Code provides that "German criminal law shall apply,

---

[73] Royal Canadian Mounted Police, "Eleventh Annual Report: Canada's Program on Crimes Against Humanity and War Crimes, 2007–2008", available at http://www.rcmp-grc.gc.ca/pubs/wc-cg-eng.htm.

[74] *Ibid.*

[75] Bundersgesetzblatt, Teil I (2002), p. 2254 ('BGBL 2002'). The *travaux* can be found in Bundesministerium der Justiz, *Arbeitsentwurf eines Gesetzes Zur Einfuhrung Des VstGB*, 2001; Sascha Rolf Lüder, Thomas Vormbaum (eds.), *Materialien zum Völkerstrafgesetzbuch: Dokumentation des Gesetzgebungsverfahrens*, LIT Verlag, 2002.

[76] *Ibid.*

regardless of the law of the place of their commission, to a wide variety of criminal acts committed abroad, including (1) genocide [...]".[77] Further, section 6(9) of the German Criminal Code allows for the application of German criminal jurisdiction for acts covered by "an international agreement binding on the Federal Republic of Germany [...] if they are committed abroad".[78] With the entry into force of the VStGB, the universal jurisdictional regime for international core crimes within the meaning of Articles 5 to 8 of the ICC Statute was established.

Several prosecutions have taken place of individuals involved in crimes committed in the former Yugoslavia in German courts. Novislav Djajić, a member of the Bosnian Serbian army, was convicted in May of 1997 and sentenced to five years imprisonment for aiding and abetting manslaughter.[79] Maksim Sokolović was sentenced to nine years in prison for his role in aiding and abetting genocide and grave breaches of the Geneva Conventions, in November 1999.[80] Djuradj Kusljić was convicted of genocide in December 1999, receiving a life sentence,[81] as did Nicola Jorgić, for genocide and murder, in 1997.[82]

Other nations have also made impressive in-roads in exercising universal jurisdiction over those suspected of crimes against humanity, war crimes and genocide, including the Netherlands, Belgium, Demark and Spain.[83]

---

[77] *Ibid*, Section 6, entitled "Acts Abroad against Internationally Protected Legal Interests".

[78] *Ibid.*

[79] A summary of the trial of Mr. Djajic can be found at http://www.trial-ch.org/en/trial-watch/profile/db/legal-procedures/novislav_djajic_135.html.

[80] A summary of the trial of Mr. Sokolovic can be found at http://www.trial-ch.org/en/trial-watch/profile/db/facts/sokolovic_maksim_139.html.

[81] A summary of the trial of Mr. Djuradj can be found at http://www.trial-ch.org/en/trial-watch/profile/db/facts/kusljic_djuradj_140.html.

[82] A summary of the trial of Mr. Jorgic can be found at http://www.trial-ch.org/en/trial-watch/profile/db/legal-procedures/nikola_jorgic_283.html.

[83] For a comprehensive discussion of countries' exercise of universal jurisdiction, see J. Rikhof, "Fewer Places to Hide: The Impact of Domestic War Crimes Prosecutions on International Impunity", in *Criminal Law Forum*, 2009, vol. 20, no. 1, pp. 20–28.

This broad concept of universal jurisdiction is based on the notion that all nations have an obligation to protect fundamental interest through criminal law for serious international crimes.[84]

10.4. Harnessing the Potential: Universal Jurisdiction and R2P Under the Proposed Convention

10.4.1. Universal Jurisdiction Under the Proposed Convention

The need for a convention to directly address prevention and punishment of crimes against humanity was clearly captured by the Steering Committee of the Crimes Against Humanity Initiative ('CAH Initiative'), including:

1) that the ICC Statute condemns crimes against humanity and requires States to put an end to impunity by ensuring their prosecution and punishment, but *does not provide for universally effective inter-state cooperation*;

2) that there currently exists no international treaty for inter-state cooperation in the *prosecution and punishment* of crimes against humanity; and

3) that crimes against humanity continue to undermine peace and security and have been a source of untold suffering and a threat to human civilization.[85]

While the ICC has made tremendous strides in holding perpetrators accountable for their crimes, there are clear jurisdictional and admissibility limitations on the Court. The Court has no police force or prison system. The ICC relies on States Parties that have ratified or acceded to the ICC Statute to adopt legislation enabling co-operation with it. Furthermore, States Parties only have an obligation to arrest and surrender a person to the Court if the Court submits a request to the State to do so.[86] In keeping with the principle of complementarity, the ICC is the court of last resort, which carries with it, an expectation that States Parties will estab-

---

[84] Kai Ambos, "Prosecuting Guantanamo in Europe: Can and Shall the Masterminds of the 'Torture Memos' be Held Criminally Responsible on the Basis of Universal Jurisdiction?", in *Case Western Reserve Journal of International Law*, 2009, vol. 42, p. 421.

[85] Washington University, Declaration on the Need for a Comprehensive Convention on Crimes Against Humanity, 12 March 2010, Whitney R. Harris World Law Institute Steering Committee ('Declaration') (emphasis added).

[86] *Ibid.*, Article 89.

lish courts, criminalize offences, take evidence, effect arrests and surrenders and impose penalties for core crimes.[87] Therefore, it is imperative to establish mechanisms to mandate States not only to co-operate with the ICC, but also devote the necessary resources to undertake investigations and prosecutions at a domestic level. While establishing legislation, courts and dedicated staff to investigate and prosecute crimes against humanity is a costly undertaking, an overall low risk of prosecutions contributes to the continued commission of crimes against humanity worldwide. Strengthening inter-State enforcement applicable to these crimes is therefore essential.

The potential of the Proposed Convention to provide a strong framework for both the prosecution of these crimes and the advancement of R2P is significant. Unquestionably, the use of universal jurisdiction in the Proposed Convention sets the groundwork for international acceptance that crimes against humanity are *jus cogens* crimes giving rise to a duty to prosecute. Universal jurisdiction refers to jurisdiction established over a crime without reference to the place of perpetration, the nationality of the suspect or the victim or any other recognized linking point between the crime and the prosecuting State.[88] The basis for universal jurisdiction is rooted in the notion that every State has an interest in prosecuting crimes which shock the conscience of humanity:

> The alleged crime is an attack on the fundamental values of the international community as a whole (i.e., a violation of jus cogens or a species of law that is very close to that genus however described, such as *erga omnes* obligations), so that the crime is a matter of universal concern, considered as such by the international community as a whole, and that every State in the world has an interest in prosecuting the perpetrator.[89]

The suggestion that universal jurisdiction be incorporated into the Proposed Convention garnered support among experts in the field, with consensus at a meeting in May 2014 that the Proposed Convention should

---

[87]   *Ibid.*, Article 88.

[88]   Henry J. Steiner, Philip Alston and Ryan Goodman, *International Human Rights in Context: Law, Politics, Morals*, Oxford University Press, 2007, p. 1161.

[89]   YEE Siehno, "Universal Jurisdiction: Concept, Logic, and Reality", in *Chinese Journal of International Law*, 2011, vol.10, no. 3, p. 505.

provide the widest possible scope of jurisdiction.[90] Specifically, it was
suggested that the Proposed Convention should require States to take
measures to exercise universal jurisdiction.[91] A review of the relevant sections of the Proposed Convention reflects this firm commitment to universal jurisdiction.

The preambular language of the Proposed Convention alludes to
the concept of universal jurisdiction:

> Recalling that it is the duty of every State to exercise its
> criminal jurisdiction over those responsible for international
> crimes, including crimes against humanity,
>
> Recalling the contributions made by the statutes and juris-
> prudence of international, national and other tribunals estab-
> lished pursuant to an international legal instrument, to the af-
> firmation and development of the prevention and punishment
> of crimes against humanity,
>
> Recalling that crimes against humanity constitutes crimes
> under international law, which may give rise to the responsi-
> bility of States for internationally wrongful acts [...].[92]

Similarly, Article 2 of the Proposed Convention suggests a broad
obligation on States to "investigate, prosecute, and punish those responsible for such crimes".[93]

Article 9 of the Proposed Convention captures the traditional *aut
dedere aut judicare* principle, creating the general obligation of States
Parties to either take action to prosecute suspected perpetrators, or extradite to another State Party, the ICC or another international criminal tribunal whose jurisdiction it has recognized.[94]

Article 10, covering the obligation of States Parties to establish
competence to exercise jurisdiction over persons alleged to be responsible
for crimes against humanity, defines the jurisdiction on traditional bases:
(a) the place where the crime occurred, or the territoriality principle, (b)

---

[90] Leila Sadat and Douglas Pivnichny, "Fulfilling the Dictates of Public Conscience: Moving
Forward with a Convention on Crimes Against Humanity", 2014, available at
http://law.wustl.edu/harris/documents/Final-CAHGenevaReport-071714.pdf.

[91] *Ibid.*, p. 19.

[92] Proposed Convention, Preamble, see *supra* note 8.

[93] *Ibid.*, Article 2.

[94] *Ibid.*, Article 9.

the nationality of the offender, or the nationality principle, and (c) the nationality of the victim, or the passive personality principle.[95] But importantly, Article 10(3) also incorporates broad language of universal jurisdiction mandating States Parties to take measures to establish competence to exercise jurisdiction over crimes against humanity over alleged offenders present in any territory under its jurisdiction.

The broad jurisdictional reach of the Proposed Convention is underscored by Article 8 which sets out implementation responsibilities as follows:

> Each State Party shall enact necessary legislation and other measure as required by its Constitution or legal system to give effect to the provisions of the present Convention and, in particular, to take effective legislative, administrative, judicial and other measures in accordance with the Charter of the United Nations to prevent and punish the commission of crimes against humanity in any territory under its jurisdiction or control.[96]

In this sense, the Proposed Convention adopts similar language to that seen in Article 8 of the CAHWCA which gives authority for Canadian courts to prosecute anyone suspected of crimes against humanity when they set foot on Canadian soil, even if that person is not a Canadian national, the crimes were not committed on Canada soil, and the victims of the crime are not Canadians.

Universal jurisdiction meets a number of key objectives of the Proposed Convention, in particular, the recognition of the seriousness of crimes against humanity and the responsibility of States Parties to take action to prosecute and supports the 'no safe haven' mandate against those who have committed crimes against humanity.

---

[95] *Ibid.*, Article 10; see also Steiner *et al.*, 2007, see *supra* note 88.
[96] Proposed Convention, Article 8, see *supra* note 8.

10.4.2. Advancing the Doctrine of R2P through the Proposed Convention

10.4.2.1 More Explicit References to R2P Are Necessary

Where there remains room for expansion is in the Proposed Convention's treatment of R2P. The members of the CAH Initiative expressed awareness of the importance of R2P to the Proposed Convention:

> The Initiative's goal of ending impunity for those who commit crimes against humanity is also linked to the further development of the Responsibility to Protect doctrine. Under international law, States must not commit certain of the most serious international crimes and may have a duty to prosecute those responsible for their commission. The emerging Responsibility to Protect principle may also require States to affirmatively intervene to protect vulnerable populations from nascent or continuing international crimes under certain circumstances. A necessary condition precedent to the invocation of the Responsibility to Protect is a clear definition of the event which triggers that responsibility. A comprehensive crimes against humanity convention could reinforce the normative obligation not to commit crimes against humanity, as well as emphasize the duty of States to prevent the commission of atrocity crimes.[97]

The Proposed Convention is an opportunity to develop the R2P doctrine and create a binding legal obligation on States Parties, under the Proposed Convention, to take steps to implement the principle through prosecuting those alleged to have committed crimes against humanity.

To do so however, requires direct language in the Proposed Convention about the responsibility to protect and the link between prosecution and achieving the R2P mandate. There are several important ways in which the Proposed Convention could re-enforce R2P principles and elevate the doctrine to a binding legal obligation. First, the preambular language, while not forming part of the binding terms of the Proposed Convention, accomplishes an important function of dismissing some of the misconceptions about the concept of R2P – specifically, that it is just political rhetoric or limited to military intervention.

---

[97] Declaration, para. 9, see *supra* note 85.

The Preamble could be expanded to include specific recognition of the deterrent effect that effective prosecution and/or extradition has on the advancement of R2P. The proposed language might read as follows:

> Recognizing that one of the most effective ways to promote the responsibility to prevent crimes against humanity is to demonstrate, through domestic legislative, administrative and judicial measures that those who commit crimes against humanity will be prosecuted and/or extradited without delay [...].

Further, there should be language which reminds States Parties that a failure to act expeditiously to prosecute or extradite suspected war criminals is a breach not only of each State Party's obligations under the Proposed Convention to prosecute or extradite, but a breach of the customary norm recognizing a duty to protect and prevent, sending a clear message that R2P is not an ideal, but a duty and a positive obligation under the Proposed Convention. The language might read as follows:

> Aware that, by failing to prosecute and/or extradite those who commit crimes against humanity, the State Party is in breach of its obligation to punish and prevent crimes against humanity [...].

Connecting the duty to prosecute or extradite with R2P is an important way in which the Proposed Convention can solidify R2P as an essential part of the Proposed Convention's mandate.

Moreover, Article 8 which enumerates obligations of States Parties should make specific reference to the responsibility to protect doctrine and mandate that each State Party endeavour to take measures, in accordance with its domestic legal system, to offer protection to vulnerable populations. The language might include:

> Protection
>
> Recognizing the binding legal obligation on States Parties to protect vulnerable populations, each State Party shall endeavour, in accordance with its domestic legal system and the responsibility to protect principle, to implement strategies to protect vulnerable groups from nascent or continuing international crimes, including but not limited to affirmative intervention and prosecuting those responsible for the commission of crimes against humanity.

Finally, Article 10 ought to specifically recognize R2P and be modified by adding to the beginning of subsection (2), "In recognition of each State Party's obligation to protect vulnerable populations and prevent crimes against humanity [...]". Linking R2P to the State Party's obligation to enact measures to establish competence and jurisdiction creates a meaningful and logical connection between the doctrine and prosecutions.

10.4.2.2 Greater Reporting and Accountability Measures Related to Prosecutions and Extraditions

Article 9 of the Proposed Convention should include an additional paragraph setting out a requirement that all States Parties report to the proposed Committee established pursuant to the Proposed Convention ('the Committee') under Article 19(b). Specifically, the Committee is entrusted, through subparagraph 8 of Article 19(b) to collect information about the plans and practices of States Parties to implement the Proposed Convention and specifies a requirement that States Parties provide data regarding "the number of allegations, investigations, prosecutions, convictions, extraditions and mutual legal assistance".[98] This section might be expanded to include a reporting requirement on States Parties to provide a timeline for dealing with outstanding suspects, including a strategic plan for dealing with suspected perpetrators known to be in the country, but against whom action has not yet been taken.

10.5. Conclusion

Canada's efforts to criminalize core international crimes, coupled with its role in pioneering general international acceptance of R2P, provides very helpful reference points for thinking about how the Proposed Convention could be strengthened to more directly highlight the obligation to prosecute and explicitly link it to R2P.

The current understanding of R2P is misconstrued as pertaining mainly to military or humanitarian interventions. Numerous scholars have observed that prosecutions play an invaluable role in promoting human

---

[98] Proposed Convention, Article 19(b), subparagraph 8(c), see *supra* note 8.

rights by promoting respect for the courts and ensuring that war criminals are brought to justice.[99]

The crucial aspect of implementation of the Proposed Convention will be the actual enforcement: investigations, prosecutions and convictions. The principle of complementarity depends on strong national courts as the forum of first resort.[100] By linking the duty to prosecute with the responsibility to protect, the Proposed Convention has the capacity to push the doctrine of R2P from an ideal to a more binding legal obligation. Explicit universal jurisdiction and an acceptance of R2P as a legal obligation in the Proposed Convention are fundamental components of galvanizing States to act when faced with individuals who have committed the worst crimes imaginable.

---

[99] The National Post, "Issuing an Arrest Warrant is One Thing, Enforcing It is Another", 10 March 2009.

[100] Jann Kleffner, "The Impact of Complementarity on National Implementation of Substantive International Criminal Law", in *Journal of International Criminal Justice*, 2003, vol. 1, no. 1, pp. 86 and 112.

11

U.S. Role in the Prevention and Prosecution of and Response to Crimes Against Humanity

Mary Kate Whalen[*]

> How we as a country treat suspected perpetrators of serious human rights abuses in the United States sends an important message to the world about our commitment to human rights and the rule of law.[1]

11.1. Introduction

In the aftermath of World War II, the international community rallied to implement international law structures to prevent and punish genocide, war crimes and atrocities against civilian populations through enactment of international conventions such as the Convention on the Prevention and Punishment of the Crime of Genocide ('Genocide Convention')[2] and the four Geneva Conventions[3]. Over the past 20 years, international tribunals

---

[*] **Mary Kate Whalen** received her *juris doctor* from Suffolk University Law School and a Masters of Law with a National Security Law certificate from Georgetown University Law School. She has practiced in both the private and public sectors in the United States including the Department of Homeland Security, Transportation Security Administration, and Drug Enforcement Administration. The positions set forth in this chapter are those of the author in her personal capacity and do not necessarily represent official positions of the U.S. government. All Internet references were last accessed on 4 October 2014.

[1] Richard Durbin, U.S. Senator, Chairman, Subcommittee on Human Rights and the Law of the U.S. Senate Judiciary Committee, "No Safe Haven: Accountability for Human Rights Violators in the United States", Hearing before the Subcommittee on Human Rights and the Law of the Committee on the Judiciary, United States Senate, 110th Cong., 1st Sess., Serial No. J-110-63, 14 November 2007 ('No Safe Haven Part I'), Opening Statement of Hon. Richard J. Durbin, A U.S. Senator from the State of Illinois.

[2] U.N. General Assembly, Prevention and Punishment of the Crime of Genocide, 9 December 1948, A/RES/260, in UNTS, vol. 78, p. 277, 12 January 1951.

[3] Geneva Convention for the Amelioration of the Condition of the Wounded and Sick in Armed Forces in the Field of 12 August 1949; Geneva Convention for the Amelioration of the Conditions of Wounded, Sick and Shipwrecked Members of Armed Forces at Sea of 12 August 1949; Geneva Convention Relative to the Treatment of Prisoners of War of 12 August 1949; Geneva Convention Relative to the Protection of Civilian Persons in Time of War of 12 August 1949.

---

and special courts have been established for Rwanda, the former Yugoslavia, Liberia and Sierra Leone, among others, to prosecute individuals and government leadership for commission of atrocity crimes. Despite these efforts, incidents of crimes against humanity and other atrocities continue to emerge and often continue unabated in regions such as Darfur, Kenya, Gaza, Sri Lanka, Myanmar, and the Democratic Republic of the Congo.

Political uprisings such as the Arab Spring, and resulting civil wars by factions battling for leadership or leadership vacuums have resulted in increased incidents of human rights violations in countries like Libya, Syria, Iraq and Yemen – countries with governments either unwilling or unable to prevent attacks against their civilian populations in general or specific groups within the general population. The atrocities committed within these regions do not all fall within the current international legal framework for prosecutions for perpetrators of such crimes or for government officials establishing policies promoting or supporting such crimes. Most recently, atrocities are being committed by transnational terrorist organizations, including the Islamic State of Iraq and the Levant ('ISIL')[4] in Syria and Iraq and Boko Haram in Nigeria.

In August 2010, the Crimes Against Humanity Initiative, a non-governmental initiative comprised of a number of senior experts on international criminal law conducting a study of international law regarding crimes against humanity and drafting a multilateral treaty prohibiting such crimes, unveiled a draft proposed convention.[5] The Proposed International Convention on the Prevention and Punishment of Crimes Against Humanity ('Proposed Convention')[6] would establish a legal framework for prosecution of perpetrators of crimes against humanity as defined under Article 7 of the Rome Statute of the International Criminal Court ('ICC Statute').[7]

---

[4] Also referred to as the Islamic States of Iraq and Syria or ISIS; see, *e.g.*, Washington Post, Ishaan Tharoor, "ISIS or ISIL? The debate over what to call Iraq's terror group", 18 June 2014.

[5] Washington University Law, "Work Begins on Specialized Convention no Crimes Against Humanity", available at http://law.wustl.edu/news/pages.aspx?id=7194.

[6] The Proposed International Convention on the Prevention and Punishment of Crimes Against Humanity, Washington University Law, Whitney R. Harris World Law Institute, Crimes Against Humanity Initiative, see Annex 1.

[7] Rome Statute of the International Criminal Court, U.N. Doc. A/CONF.183/9, adopted 17 July 1998.

In a recent report on the status of the Proposed Convention, the Crimes Against Humanity Initiative noted that the U.S. government had not taken a position on a treaty governing crimes against humanity. The report further noted that the U.S. government "is largely unaware of the work of the initiative and the call for the conclusion and adoption of a new international treaty to prevent and punish the commission of crimes against humanity".[8]

On 18 July 2014, the U.N. International Law Commission voted to add the drafting of a treaty to address crimes against humanity to its active agenda.[9] In its report to the U.N. General Assembly, the International Law Commission directed Member States to report on the following by 30 January 2015:

(a) whether the State's national law at present expressly criminalizes "crimes against humanity" as such and, if so:

(b) the text of the relevant criminal statute(s);

(c) under what conditions the State is capable of exercising jurisdiction over an alleged offender for the commission of a crime against humanity (e.g. when the offense occurs within its territory or when the offense is by its national or resident); and

(d) decisions of the State's national courts that have adjudicated crimes against humanity.[10]

The United States does not yet have a domestic law expressly criminalizing 'crimes against humanity' as defined under Article 7 of the ICC Statute or as contemplated under the Proposed Convention. U.S. federal law, however, provides several options for prosecution of persons suspected of human rights crimes, including underlying offenses in the international law definition of 'crimes against humanity'. This chapter ex-

---

[8] Leila Nadya Sadat, *A Comprehensive History of the Proposed International Convention on the Prevention and Punishment of Crimes Against Humanity*, 2010, Washington University Law, Whitney R. Harris World Law Institute, Crimes Against Humanity Initiative, p. 39, available at http://law.wustl.edu/harris/cah/docs/EnglishTreatyFinal.pdf.

[9] Washington University Law, "UN International Law Commission to Elaborate New Global Convention on Crimes Against Humanity Following Experts Meeting in Geneva", available at http://law.wustl.edu/news/pages.aspx?id=10225.

[10] Report of the International Law Commission, 66th Session, 5 May–6 June and 7 July–8 August 2014, General Assembly Official Records, 69th Session, Supplement No. 10, A/69/10, Chapter III, p. 9, para. 34.

plores the status of U.S. laws and legislative efforts regarding the prevention and punishment of and response to atrocity crimes, as well as the limitations under current U.S. law.

11.2. Proposed Convention and ICC Statute Provisions

The Proposed Convention adopts the definition of 'crimes against humanity' set forth under Article 7 of the ICC Statute, defining the offense to mean:

> any of the following acts when committed as a part of a widespread or systematic attack directed against any civilian population, with knowledge of the attack:
>
> (a) Murder;
>
> (b) Extermination;
>
> (c) Enslavement;
>
> (d) Deportation or forcible transfer of population;
>
> (e) Imprisonment or other severe deprivation of physical liberty in violation of fundamental rules of international law;
>
> (f) Torture;
>
> (g) Rape, sexual slavery, enforced prostitution, forced pregnancy, enforced sterilization, or any other form of sexual violence of comparable gravity;
>
> (h) Persecution against any identifiable group or collectivity on political, racial, national, ethnic, cultural, religious, gender or other grounds that are universally recognized as impermissible under international law;
>
> (i) Enforced disappearance of persons;
>
> (j) The crime of apartheid; or
>
> (k) Other inhumane acts of similar character intentionally causing great suffering or serious injury to body or physical health.

The Proposed Convention, as currently drafted, would extend jurisdiction for prosecution of crimes against humanity beyond the ICC States Parties and the limits of the ICC or international criminal tribunals to provide universal jurisdiction (although not mandatory) for this offense, by allowing any State Party to capture and prosecute a perpetrator of crimes against humanity regardless of the geographic location of the crimes or the nationality of the perpetrator or victim.[11] Further, the Proposed Convention would eliminate immunities from prosecution traditionally available for heads of State and other government officials.[12]

The Proposed Convention would abolish statutes of limitation on prosecution of crimes against humanity.[13] In addition, it would not allow States Parties to ratify the Convention contingent upon any reservation.[14]

11.3. U.S. Legislative Efforts Regarding Human Rights Violations

The United States has long supported international efforts to establish necessary legal frameworks for the prevention and punishment of human rights violations. The United States, along with its allies, established International Military Tribunals at Nuremberg and Tokyo after World War II to prosecute perpetrators of war crimes, crimes against humanity and crimes against the peace.[15] The United States continues to support international tribunals established to address the commission of genocide, crimes against humanity and other human rights violations in places such as the former Yugoslavia, Rwanda, and Sierra Leone.

The United States, however, does not have domestic legislation that expressly criminalizes the commission of 'crimes against humanity', as that term is defined under the ICC Statute and the Proposed Convention. U.S. legislators have attempted to implement federal legislation. Although legislative efforts pertaining to a specific statute for crimes against humanity have not been successful, the United States has established or ex-

---

[11] See *supra* note 6, Article 10(3) of the Proposed Convention states:

> Each State Party shall likewise take such measures as may be necessary to establish its competence to exercise jurisdiction over the offense of crimes against humanity when the alleged offender is present in any territory under its jurisdiction, unless it extradites or surrenders him or her to another State in accordance with its international obligations or surrenders him or her to an international criminal tribunal whose jurisdiction it has recognized.

[12] *Ibid.*, Article 6 and Explanatory Notes.

[13] *Ibid.*, Article 7 and Explanatory Notes.

[14] *Ibid.*, Article 23.

[15] U.S. Department of State, Office of the Historian, "Milestones: 1945–1952", available at https://history.state.gov/milestones/1945-1952/nuremberg.

panded jurisdiction pertaining to the prosecution of perpetrators of certain human rights law violations.

11.3.1. Subcommittee on Human Rights and the Law Hearings Leading to Legislations

The first decade of the 21st century saw significant U.S. legislative activity regarding domestic human rights law. In January 2007, the U.S. Senate Committee on the Judiciary formed a new subcommittee, Human Rights and the Law ('Human Rights Subcommittee'), charged with congressional oversight of U.S. enforcement and implementation of human rights laws.[16] From 2007 through 2009, the Human Rights Subcommittee held a series of hearings regarding U.S. human rights policy and laws.[17]

Several of these hearings illuminated the lack of jurisdiction for U.S. prosecution of crimes against humanity. In particular, during the November 2007 hearing on the enforcement of human rights laws in the United States ('No Safe Haven: Accountability for Human Rights Violators in the United States'), panellists from the U.S. Department of Justice and Immigration and Customs Enforcement, and U.S. Department of Homeland Security were questioned regarding the limitations on their respective agencies to prosecute foreign nationals suspected of committing atrocity crimes when the suspects were located within the United States.[18] To the extent U.S. law criminalized certain international human rights law violations, such as genocide, the jurisdiction of U.S. courts was limited to prosecution of U.S. citizens, nationals, and lawful permanent residents (collectively referred to hereinafter as 'U.S. persons') or to actions committed on U.S. territories or against U.S. persons. U.S. law at that time did

---

[16] The Subcommittee on Human Rights and the Law was created by Patrick Leahy, Chairman of the Senate Judiciary Committee in 2007, available at www.judiciary.senate. gov/about/chairman. The Subcommittee was subsequently subsumed into the current Subcommittee on the Constitution, Civil Rights and Human Rights, see Subcommittee on The Constitution, Civil Rights and Human Rights, available at www.judiciary.senate.gov/ about/subcommittees.

[17] See, *e.g.*, "Genocide and the Rule of Law"; S. Hrg. 110-46, Serial No. J-110-9, 5 February 2007; "Legal Options to stop Human Trafficking", S. Hrg. 110-42, Serial No. J.110-24, 26 March 2007; "Casualties of War: Child Soldiers and the Law", S. Hrg. 110-176, Serial No. J-110-29, 24 April 2007; No Safe Haven Part I, see *supra* note 1; "From Nuremberg to Darfur: Accountability for Crimes Against Humanity", S. Hrg 110-786, Serial No. J 110-102, 24 June 2008.

[18] *Ibid.*, No Safe Haven Part I, Transcript, p. 13.

---

not allow for the prosecution of perpetrators of atrocities committed out-side the U.S. or against non-U.S. persons, even when the perpetrator was located in the United States.

The Subcommittee members were particularly concerned that such limitations in U.S. law not only restricted the United States from holding perpetrators of atrocity crimes accountable, but, more importantly, such loopholes promoted the United States as a safe haven for the perpetrators of such crimes. The Subcommittee members and a number of panellists pointed to the case of Marko Boskić, a Bosnian national who was able to obtain lawful immigration status – first as a refugee and subsequently as a lawful permanent resident – in the United States, despite his involvement in the 1995 Srebrenica massacre in Bosnia.[19] Chairman Durbin of the Subcommittee questioned:

> Why is it that the only thing we could find to charge this man with was visa fraud. It is reiminiscent of convictions of Al Capone for tax fraud. It sounds to me like we were searching for anything to find him guilty of instead of the obvious. [...] Boskic admitted to killing many Bosnian civilians in Srebrenica. Under current law, is it possible to prosecute Boskic for these crimes in the United States?

The U.S. Department of Justice stated:

> If there were no American victims or [the crimes] were not perpetrated by a U.S. national, sitting here today, it is difficult to come up with a potential charge that we could charge him with.[20]

The Subcommittee's concern was echoed by Senator Benjamin Cardin, who noted:

> I hope that we can work together to figure out how we can come up with the strongest possible laws in this country, consistent with our international obligations, to make it clear that the United States will not only [...] prevent a safe haven for those who have committed human rights violations, but will hold accountable indivdiuals who are under our control,

---

[19] See *U.S. v. Boskic*, 549 F. 3d 69, 71, U.S. Court of Appeals for the First Circuit 2008 (af-firming district court conviction for making false statements on his applications for refugee status and permanent residency in the United States).

[20] Sigal P. Mandelker, Deputy Assistant Attorney General, Criminal Division, U.S. Depart-ment of Justice, No Safe Haven Part I, Transcript, p. 13, see *supra* note 1.

> [...] who have violated international norms, committed war
> crimes, genocide and other types of human rights violations.
> I wanted to make sure that the point is clear in our record
> that it is not just departing these individuals or taking away
> their naturalized citizenship. It is holding them accountable
> for the violations of human rights.[21]

In his written statement for the record, David Scheffer, former U.S.
War Crimes Ambassador to the United Nations, expressly recommended,
inter alia, that the United States amend the domestic law to address
crimes against humanity:

> Filling the gaps in American law pertaining to atrocity
> crimes would demonstrate that the United States has the
> confidence to reject impunity for such crimes and to hold its
> own nationals to account as well as foreign nationals over
> whom U.S. courts should be exercising personal jurisdiction.
> The United States would no longer be a safe haven in reality
> or as potential destination for untold numbers of perpetrators
> of atrocity crimes. Amending and thus modernizing [the U.S.
> Criminal Code] in the manner proposed in this testimony
> would signal the end to exceptionalism in atrocity crimes
> and place the United States on equal footing with many of its
> allies which have already recast their criminal law to reflect
> the reality of international criminal and humanitarian law in
> our own time.[22]

These hearings directly resulted in significant changes in U.S. laws
pertaining to human rights through bipartisan legislation including the
Genocide Accountability Act of 2007,[23] the Child Soldiers Accountability
Act of 2008,[24] and the William Wilberforce Trafficking Victim Protection
Reauthorization Act of 2008, which, among other things, closed loopholes
in U.S. law by vesting federal courts with jurisdiction to prosecute indi-

---

[21]   *Ibid.*, p. 17.

[22]   *Ibid.*, Written Testimony, p. 31, David Scheffer, "Gaps in U.S. Law Pertaining to Atrocity
       Crimes"; also Transcript, p. 20 (Recommending, *inter alia*, that the United States "amend
       the Federal criminal code so that it enables federal criminal courts to more effectively and
       unambiguously prosecute crimes against humanity and war crimes that are already codi-
       fied in the statutes of the international and hybrid criminal tribunals and are defined as part
       of customary international law").

[23]   Pub. L. 110–150, 121 Stat. 1821, 10 December 2007.

[24]   Pub. L. 113–340, 3 October 2008.

---

viduals found within the United States for activities occurring outside of
the United States.

In 2008, based on testimony obtained from the prior human rights
hearings, the Human Rights Subcommittee convened the first congressional hearing specifically directed towards U.S. law and policy on crimes
against humanity.[25] As noted by the Subcommittee Chairman:

> By signalling to perpetrators of genocide that they will not
> find a safe haven in the United States, the Genocide
> Accountability Ac moved us a little closer to fulfilling our
> pledge of "never again". We should take the next step and
> make sure that those who commit crimes against humanity
> cannot escape accountability in America, but we must go
> further and ensure the perpetrators of crimes against
> humanity cannot escape accountability anywhere in the
> world.[26]

Testimony presented at the hearings included examples of persons
who obtained safe haven in the United States despite having committed
atrocities. Of particular note was the case of Pol Pot, leader of the Khmer
Rouge who became available for prosecution in 1997 when his military
forces turned on him.[27] As noted by the witness,

> the U.S. government wanted to bring him to justice and
> discovered that our own law didn't make it possible to
> prosecute him here. The administration at that time tried
> desperately to find another government that would prosecute
> Pol Pot and was unable to do so before he died a year later.[28]

11.3.2. Draft Crimes Against Humanity Act of 2009

On 24 June 2009, Senator Richard Durbin introduced to the Senate Judiciary Committee legislation entitled '[A] bill to penalize crimes against

---

[25] "From Nuremberg to Darfur: Accountability for Crimes Against Humanity", Senate Hear-
ing 110-786, Hearing before the Subcommittee on Human Rights and the Law of the
Committee on the Judiciary, United States Senate, One Hundred Tenth Congress, Second
Session, 24 June 2008.

[26] *Ibid.*, Opening Statement of Hon. Richard J. Durbin, A U.S. Senator from Illinois, Transcript, p. 4.

[27] *Ibid.*, Questioning of Professor Diane Orentlicher, Washington College of Law, American
University, Washington, District of Columbia, Transcript, pp. 16–17.

[28] *Ibid.*, p. 17.

humanity and for other purposes'. The bill, referred to as the 'Crimes Against Humanity Act of 2009' ('2009 Act'),[29] proposed to amend the U.S. Federal Criminal Code[30] to establish a new Chapter 25A 'Crimes Against Humanity' for consideration by the U.S. Senate. At that time, the Subcommittee had recently successfully navigated the Genocide Accountability Act of 2007 and the Child Soldier's Accountability Act of 2008 through bipartisan congressional approval and enactment into law. The 2009 Act however did not gain momentum and was not introduced to the full Senate for approval. The provisions of the proposed legislation remain instructive as to potential U.S. direction for future legislation.

The 2009 Act proposed to establish a federal criminal offense making it unlawful for "any person to commit or engage in, as a part of a widespread and systemic attack directed against any civilian population, and with knowledge of the attack", a listing of crimes mirroring, with some exceptions, the activities enumerated under the definition of 'crimes against humanity' set forth in the ICC Statute.[31] Accordingly the definitional language in the 2009 Act also would have generally tracked the language of the Proposed Convention, subject to the exceptions noted below. The 2009 Act proposed criminal penalties of a fine and/or up to 20 years imprisonment for any person convicted of committing one of the enumerated offenses directly or found to have attempted or conspired to commit such offenses.[32] For offenses resulting in the death of an individual would have been subject to imprisonment for any number of years including a life sentence.[33]

11.3.2.1. The 2009 Act: Departures from the 'Crimes Against Humanity' Definition in the ICC Statute and Proposed Convention

The 2009 Act differed from the ICC Statute's definition of 'crimes against humanity' in several aspects. First, where the ICC Statute defines crimes against humanity as pertaining to activities committed "as part of a widespread *or* systematic attack directed against any civilian population",[34] the

---

[29] Senate (S.) 1346, 111th Congress, 1st Sess., 24 June 2009, Congressional Record Vol. 155, No. 96, pp. S7011–S7012.

[30] Title 18 U.S.C. Parts I–V 'Crimes and Criminal Procedure'.

[31] S. 1346, § 519(a); ICC Statute, Article 7, see *supra* note 7.

[32] S. 1346, § 519(b).

[33] *Ibid.*

[34] ICC Statute, Article 7, see *supra* note 7 (emphasis added).

2009 Act would have required a finding that the alleged activities were committed "as part of a widespread *and* systematic attack".[35] By requiring a finding of both factors as a basis for prosecution, the 2009 Act would have set a higher standard than exists under the ICC Statute or as contemplated under the Proposed Convention.

Second, although Article 7 of the ICC Statute includes the crime of "enforced disappearance", the 2009 Act did not prohibit or define "enforced disappearance of persons". Instead, the 2009 Act listed "arbitrary detention" as an underlying offense, defined to mean:

> imprisonment or other severe deprivation of physical liberty except on such grounds and in accordance with such procedure as are established by the law of the jurisdiction where such imprisonment or other severe deprivation of physical liberty took place.[36]

The 2009 Act also limited the definition of "attack directed against any civilian population" to mean "a course of conduct in which a civilian population is a primary rather than an incidental target". Although there is no narrative in the congressional record discussing or debating the specific provisions of the 2009 Act, it is likely that the failure to include "enforced disappearance" as an enumerated offense, the limitation on the definition of "arbitrary detention", and the qualification regarding actions against civilian populations were intended to safeguard U.S. military and civilian government personnel involved in U.S. counterterrorism activities following the 11 September 2001 attacks, U.S. war time efforts in Iraq and Afghanistan during this period, and in particular the detention at the U.S. Naval Station in Guantanamo Bay and other international detention facilities of persons suspected of terrorist activities or support of same against the United States.

11.3.2.2. The 2009 Act: Broad Jurisdiction

The 2009 Act would have provided U.S. prosecutors with relatively broad jurisdictional authority. Jurisdiction for most federal crimes is limited to offenses committed by U.S. citizens, nationals or lawful permanent residents for offenses committed against U.S. persons or property. The 2009 Act, however, would have authorized jurisdiction not only over any U.S.

---

[35] S. 1346, § 519(a) (emphasis added).

[36] *Ibid.*, § 519(e)(1).

citizen, national or lawful permanent resident, but also over an alleged offender who was a stateless person with habitual residence in the United States; persons simply present in the United States regardless of their nationality.[37] The 2009 Act also provided jurisdiction for offenses committed wholly or partially within the United States.[38] Thus, enactment of the Act would have permitted the United States to prosecute suspected perpetrators of crimes against humanity when the suspects were present in the United States regardless of nationality or residence and notwithstanding the geographic location of the crimes as long as the suspect was present in the United States at the time of arrest and prosecution or, regardless of presence at time of arrest, had committed the alleged offenses wholly or partially within the United States. The 2009 Act can be said to have prescribed universal jurisdiction for crimes against humanity as the Proposed Convention would require.

11.3.2.3. Other Aspects Compared with the Proposed Convention

The 2009 Act was silent on, and thus did not expressly authorize, prosecution of military or civilian officials with command authority and responsibility.[39] The 2009 Act also did not seek to eliminate immunities or exceptions for heads of State or other officials.[40]

The 2009 Act, however, would have been consistent with the prohibition against statutes of limitation set forth under Article 7 of the Proposed Convention. Under U.S. federal criminal law, prosecutors must file an indictment to prosecute individuals for non-capital federal crimes no less than five years from the date of the commission of the offense.[41] The 2009 Act would have removed such a time limitation pertaining to the criminal prosecution of offenses defined under the Act.[42]

---

[37]   S. 1346, § 519(c).

[38]   *Ibid.*

[39]   Proposed Convention, Article 5, see *supra* note 6.

[40]   *Ibid.*, Article 6.

[41]   Title 18 U.S.C. § 3282.

[42]   S. 1346, § 519 (d).

11.3.3. Draft Crimes Against Humanity Act of 2010

As noted above, the 2009 Act died in Senate Subcommittee. In July 2010, an amended bill was introduced as a substitute for the 2009 Act.[43] The 'Crimes Against Humanity Act of 2010' ('2010 Act')[44] was introduced to the U.S. Senate on 21 July 2010, with no narrative or discussion set forth in written record. The 2010 Act also died in Committee. To date, there is no congressional record reflecting any further official activity regarding the 2010 Act or any further proposed domestic legislation to criminalize crimes against humanity. The changes to the language of the 2009 bill, however, are informative as to the United States' potential legislative efforts regarding crimes against humanity in the future.

The 2010 Act struck the language in the 2009 Act pertaining to "arbitrary detention" in its entirety. Further, the 2010 Act provided that the Act would not have criminalized activities conducted pursuant to the laws of war.[45] These provisions no doubt were due to concerns that U.S. military personnel or other U.S. government officials could be held liable under that language as a result of U.S. policies of detaining suspects in U.S. military prisons – either in Guantanamo Bay, Baghram Air Base in Iraq, or through the U.S. use of secret CIA detention facilities abroad.

In addition, the 2010 Act if enacted, would have had a more limited jurisdictional reach than the 2009 Act. The 2010 legislation expressly limited the jurisdiction of federal courts to U.S. nationals, resident aliens, and stateless persons who habitually reside in the United States; and struck language authorizing the jurisdiction over non-U.S. persons merely present in the United States. The 2010 provisions thus would not have authorized the United States to prosecute a foreign national present in the United States for crimes committed outside of the United States and therefore would not have served to discourage perpetrators of crimes against humanity from seeking refuge in the U.S. due to safe havens found in gaps in U.S. criminal laws.

The 2010 Act also sought to limit prosecution unless the U.S. Attorney General certified in writing, after consultation with the Secretary of

[43] S. 1346RS (Reported in Senate), 111th Congress, 2d Sess., 21 July 2010, Congressional Record Vol. 156, No.108, p. S6078.
[44] A copy of the text of the 2010 Act is available at https://www.govtrack.us/congress/bills/111/s1346/text.
[45] *Ibid.*

State and Secretary of Homeland Security that no foreign jurisdiction was prepared to prosecute the suspects for the conduct forming the basis of the offense; and that prosecution by the United States "is in the public interest and necessary to secure substantial justice". Further, once these factors were met, prosecution would only be authorized if the Secretaries of State and Homeland Security and the Director of National Intelligence did not object to such prosecution.[46]

The 2010 Act maintained the 2009 Act's language requiring commission of covered offenses as part of a "widespread *and* systematic" attack.[47] However, the 2010 Act defined both terms in a limiting manner. "Systemic" was proposed to mean "pursuant to or in furtherance of the policy of a country or armed group. To constitute a policy, the country or armed group must have *actively* promoted the policy".[48] The proposed legislation would have defined "widespread" to mean "involving not less than 50 victims".[49]

The 2010 Act was consistent with the 2009 Act in its refusal to limit immunities available to foreign heads of State, government officials, or persons with command responsibility for commission of offenses constituting crimes against humanity.

11.4. Existing U.S. Law Authorizing Prosecution of and Other Responses to Human Rights Violations

As demonstrated above, the United States does not have any federal or state law that explicitly criminalizes the offense of crimes against humanity or provides jurisdiction for prosecution of a person charged with commission of crimes against humanity as defined under the ICC Statute or contemplated under the Proposed Convention. Despite the lack of specific legislation, the United States has a number of legal authorities that allow for the prosecution of persons suspected of committing human rights violations, including commission of certain offenses delineated as crimes against humanity under the ICC Statute and thus supporting in part the intent of the Proposed Convention.

---

[46] *Ibid.*, Section 2(e).

[47] *Ibid.*, section 2(a) (emphasis added).

[48] *Ibid.*, section 2(i)(7) (emphasis added).

[49] *Ibid.*, section 2(i)(8).

U.S. law governing the prosecution of human rights violations generally reflect the same core principles and considerations. First, that the responsibility to prevent and respond to crimes against humanity and prosecution of persons suspected of committing atrocities lies first and foremost with the State where the actions are committed. Second, the United States is bound by the terms of the U.S. Constitution and accordingly will not bind itself to a treaty or other international agreement, or enact legislation implementing the same, which is incompatible with constitutional law, including due process protections afforded under the Constitution and the recognition of the laws of the individual U.S. states regarding traditional 'common crimes'. Third, the United States, with control over the largest military forces in the world has a responsibility to its military and support personnel deployed internationally, both in times of war and for those deployed for peacekeeping purposes.

U.S. law, accordingly, looks to the originating States to handle prosecution as the first line of action for punishment for those committing crimes against humanity or related atrocities. Where such States have failed or refused to prosecute these offenses, the United States' first priority is to prevent the use of the territories of the United States as a safe haven by those fleeing prosecution in their own countries for human rights violations. The arsenal available for this purpose includes authorizing: prosecution for a limited number of offenses that constitute human rights violations under international law for perpetrators located within the United States, including U.S. military personnel and contractors; prosecution for immigration and visa fraud; and civil penalties to provide a monetary remedy for victims of human rights abuses against individuals and corporations responsible for such offenses. U.S. immigration laws also bar admission to persons who commit certain human rights violations, including genocide, war crimes, recruitment of child soldiers, and human trafficking.

11.4.1. U.S. Law Criminalizing Genocide

U.S. law authorizes criminal prosecution of certain crimes set forth under treaties to which the United States is a party. Specifically, the U.S. has enacted legislation to implement its responsibilities as a State Party to, among others, the Genocide Convention, the four Geneva Conventions, and the Convention Against Torture and Other Cruel, Inhuman or Degrading Treatment or Punishment ('CAT')[50]. Under these provisions, for example, U.S. federal law authorizes the prosecution of persons who commit genocide, including those who have perpetrated such crimes outside the United States against non-U.S. nationals as long as the perpetrator is present in the territory or jurisdiction of United States. Accordingly, perpetrators of these crimes cannot look to the United States as a safe haven from prosecution for activities conducted outside of the United States.

The Genocide Convention was adopted by the United Nations General Assembly on 9 December 1948, and entered into force on 12 January 1951. The United States signed the treaty on 11 December 1948. Although President Harry S. Truman submitted the treaty to the U.S. Senate for approval in June 1949, the treaty ultimately languished for almost 40 years.[51] The U.S. Senate consented to ratification on 19 February 1986, subject to several conditions, including the declaration that the U.S. President would not deposit the instrument of ratification until the United States enacted implementing legislation. It was not until 4 November 1988 that President Ronald Reagan signed the Genocide Convention Implementation Act of 1987 into law implementing the Genocide Convention and binding the United States to the Genocide Convention, subject to U.S. reservations, understandings and declarations.[52]

The U.S. Genocide Act mirrors the definition of 'genocide' under the Genocide Convention and Article 6 of the ICC Statute – despite the fact that the United States is not a party to the ICC Statute. Under the Genocide Act,[53] as amended by the Genocide Accountability Act of 2007, U.S. courts have jurisdiction to prosecute perpetrators of genocide committed outside of the territory of the United States as long as the alleged offender is present in the United States or the offense is against a U.S. person.[54] The statute, however, does not provide jurisdiction for a U.S. court to prosecute a non-U.S. person located outside of the United States

---

[50] The Convention Against Torture and Other Cruel, Inhuman, or Degrading Treatment or Punishment, 10 December 1984, S. Treaty Doc. No. 100–20 (1988), in UNTS, vol. 1465, p. 85.

[51] New York Times, Steven V. Roberts, "Reagan Signs Bill Ratifying UN Genocide Pact", 5 November 1988, available at http://www.nytimes.com/1988/11/05/opinion/reagan-signs-bill-ratifying-un-genocide-pact.html.

[52] Pub. L. 100-606, § 2(a), 4 November 1988, 102 Stat. 3045.

[53] Title 18 U.S.C. § 1091.

[54] 18 U.S.C. §§ 1091(e), 2242 (c), and 1596.

for actions not directly against a U.S. person. It is not surprising, therefore, that the United States has not prosecuted anyone under this statute to date.

11.4.2. U.S. Laws Authorizing Prosecutions for Crimes Included in Article 7 of the ICC Statute and as Defined in the Proposed Convention

Notwithstanding the lack of U.S. law authorizing prosecution of crimes against humanity, the United States has laws in place to authorize prosecution for a number of offenses enumerated under the definition of 'crimes against humanity' adopted by the ICC Statute and the Proposed Convention.

11.4.2.1. Torture

The United States signed the Convention Against Torture and Other Cruel, Inhuman or Degrading Treatment or Punishment in April 1988 and ratified the treaty in October 1994. The CAT, among other actions, requires its States Parties to take such measures as necessary to criminalize acts falling under the definition of "torture" set forth in the treaty and to prevent acts of torture within their jurisdictions.[55]

The U.S. ratification was subject to a series of reservations, understandings, and declarations, including a declaration that Articles 1 through 16 of the treaty are not self-executing and therefore would require enactment of domestic legislation to implement the treaty.[56] The U.S. ratification also was conditioned upon an understanding that narrows the definition of "torture'" as it applies to the United States. The definition of "torture" under the CAT means "any act by which severe pain or suffering, whether physical or mental, is intentionally inflicted on a person for" purposes enumerated under the treaty. The U.S. Senate's advice and consent in approving the ratification of the CAT was contingent on the express understanding that:

---

[55] CAT, Articles 4 and 5(2), see *supra* note 50.

[56] U.S. reservations, declarations, and understandings, Convention Against Torture and Other Cruel, Inhuman or Degrading Treatment or Punishment, Cong. Rec. S17486-01, 10 October 1990, available at http://www1.umn.edu/humanrts/usdocs/tortres.html.

> [I]n order to constitute torture, an act must be specifically intended to inflict severe physical or mental pain or suffering and that mental pain or suffering refers to prolonged mental harm caused by or resulting from (1) the intentional infliction or threatened infliction of severe physical pain or suffering; (2) the administration or application, or threatened administration or application, of mind altering substances or other procedures calculated to disrupt profoundly the senses or the personality; (3) *the threat of imminent death*; or (4) *the threat that another person will imminently be subjected to death*, severe physical pain or suffering, or the administration or application of mind altering substances or other procedures calculated to disrupt profoundly the senses or personality.[57]

This understanding is implemented in the definition of "torture" codified under U.S. domestic law in the Torture Act, title 18 U.S.C. § 2340 and 2340A. Accordingly, although U.S. law criminalizes torture, one of the enumerated offenses under the ICC Statute and thus meets the spirit of the Proposed Convention, the U.S. definition of torture does not track directly with the scope of criminalized activity under the Proposed Convention.

The Torture Act provides a criminal penalty of fine or imprisonment of not more than 20 years upon conviction of the crime of torture. However, if the victim died as a result of the torture, the potential term of incarceration was limited only to life in prison.[58] Furthermore, an individual who conspires to commit torture also is subject to the same penalties as the individual committing the activity amounting to torture.[59]

The United States has only prosecuted and convicted one individual under the Torture Act. In October 2008, Charles McArthur Emmanuel ('Emmanuel', also known as Chuckie Taylor, Roy M. Belfast, Jr., and Charles Taylor, Jr.) became the first, and at the time of writing only, person convicted by the United States under the Torture Act. Emmanuel, who was born in the United States, is the son of former Liberian dictator Charles Taylor.[60] Emmanuel was convicted of five counts of torture,

---

[57]   *Ibid.* (emphasis added).

[58]   Title 18 U.S.C.§ 2340A(a).

[59]   *Ibid.*

[60]   Charles Taylor resigned in 2003 following the end of the civil war in Liberia. He ultimately left Liberia and subsequently was extradited to The Hague to stand trial for crimes

among other charges, related to offenses he committed as a leader and member of Liberia's Anti-Terrorism Unit ('ATU'), including, *inter alia*, torture of refugees from Sierra Leone seeking refuge in Liberia.[61] The United States Court of Appeals for the Eleventh Circuit upheld Emmanuel's conviction upon appeal finding that he was subject to prosecution under U.S. law implementing the Convention Against Torture, for acts of torture he committed in Liberia before Liberia became a signatory to the CAT: "The Supreme Court made clear long ago that an absent United States citizen is nonetheless personally bound to take notice of the laws [of the United States] that are applicable to him and to obey them".[62] Emmanuel was sentenced to 97 years in prison in the United States.[63]

11.4.2.2. Additional Crimes

The U.S. Criminal Code authorizes prosecution for the following crimes which track with those contained in the internationally accepted definition of 'crimes against humanity':

- Peonage,[64]
- Enticement into Slavery,[65]
- Involuntary Servitude,[66]
- Forced Labor,[67]
- Trafficking with Respect to Peonage, Slavery, Involuntary Servitude, or Forced Labor,[68] and
- Sex Trafficking of Children or by Force, Fraud, or Coercion.[69]

---

against humanity in the Special Court for Sierra Leone. See *Belfast v. United States.*, 2012 WL 7149532, *3 (S.D.Fla., 2012 (unreported) (U.S. District Court for the Southern District of Florida denying Emmanuel's motion to vacate convictions under the Torture Act).

[61] *U.S. v. Belfast*, 611 F.3d 783, 794 (11th Cir., 2010).

[62] *Ibid.*, at 810, citing *Blackmer v. United States*, 284 U.S. 421, 438 (1932).

[63] U.S. Department of Justice, Press Release, 9 January 2009, available at http://www.justice. gov/opa/pr/roy-belfast-jr-aka-chuckie-taylor-sentenced-torture-charges.

[64] Title 18 U.S.C. § 1581.

[65] Title 18 U.S.C. § 1583.

[66] Title 18 U.S.C. § 1584.

[67] Title 18 U.S.C. § 1589.

[68] Title 18 U.S.C. § 1590.

[69] Title 18 U.S.C. § 1591.

The U.S. Federal Criminal Code provides jurisdiction over perpetrators of these crimes who are U.S. nationals or lawful permanent residents or an offender present in the United States regardless of nationality.[70] U.S. courts, however, cannot prosecute a person under this section if a foreign government has prosecuted or is prosecuting person for the same conduct, unless approved by the U.S. Attorney General or his delegate.[71]

11.4.2.3. Limitations to Prosecuting Crimes Against Humanity under U.S. Criminal Law

U.S. jurisprudence has long recognized that the criminal laws of the United States are meant to apply only within the territorial jurisdiction of the United States with very limited exceptions:

> The presumption against extraterritoriality can be overcome only by clear expression of Congress' intention to extend the reach of the relevant Act beyond those places where the United States has sovereignty or has some measure of legislative control.[72]

Thus, the jurisdiction of federal courts to prosecute perpetrators of crimes consistent with international law is understood to be limited to crimes with a nexus to the United States, that is, where a U.S. citizen, national or lawful permanent resident is either the victim or suspected perpetrator, or the offense is committed on U.S. soil, unless the U.S. Congress has expressly provided broader jurisdiction.

Accordingly, although U.S. federal and state laws establish subject matter jurisdiction to prosecute individuals for commission of crimes such as murder, rape and unlawful imprisonment, these courts lack personal jurisdiction over perpetrators unless the victim or suspect is a U.S. person or the offense has been committed within the United States. Further, these so-called "common crimes" are committed by and against individuals and do not have the magnitude contemplated in the ICC Statute and the Proposed Convention.

---

[70] Title 18 U.S.C. § 1596(a).

[71] *Ibid.*, (b).

[72] See *Morrison v. Nat'l Austl. Bank Ltd.*, 561 U.S. 247, 255 (U.S. Supreme Court 2010) (holding that anti-fraud provision of the U.S. Securities Exchange Act did not apply extraterritorially to provide cause of action to foreign plaintiffs suing foreign and American defendants for misconduct in connection with securities traded on foreign exchanges) (citations omitted).

In addition, the U.S. Constitution prohibits enactment of *ex post facto* laws, that is, a law that retroactively criminalizes conducts.[73] U.S. law, therefore, may prevent prosecution of human rights violations preceding their criminalization under the U.S. law despite their criminalization under international treaties, even if the U.S. was a party to those treaties at the time. Similarly, U.S. law limits the ability of a court to prosecute acts committed outside of the time period set by the applicable statute of limitation. Finally, U.S. law traditionally recognizes immunities accorded to foreign heads of State and other foreign government officials[74] and thus would preclude prosecution of those responsible for establishing policies directing or supporting commission of crimes against humanity or those with command responsibility for same.[75]

Notwithstanding these limitations, U.S. law retains substantive legal mechanisms to punish perpetrators of crimes against humanity.

11.4.3. Military Extraterritorial Jurisdiction Act

The United States also has laws in place for the prosecution of violent crimes in occupied countries committed by U.S. military and support personnel. Prior to 2000, a jurisdictional gap existed that allowed former service members to escape prosecution for offenses committed on foreign

---

[73] U.S. Constitution, Article I, section 9, cl. 3 ("No Bill of Attainder or *ex post facto* Law shall be passed").

[74] The U.S. Foreign Sovereign Immunity Act ('FSIA'), 28 U.S.C. § 1604 *et seq.*, codified U.S. common law providing that provides that "a foreign state shall be immune from the jurisdiction of the courts of the United States and of the States" except as provided in the Act. Therefore, if a defendant is a "foreign State" within the meaning of the Act, then the defendant is immune from jurisdiction unless one of the exceptions set forth under the FSIA applies. See *Samantar v. Yousuf*, 560 U.S. 305, 313–314 (U.S Supreme Court, 2010), citing 28 U.S.C. §§ 1605–1607 (enumerating exceptions).

[75] See, *e.g.*, *Manoharan v. Rajapaksa*, 711 F.3d 178, 180 (U.S. Court of Appeals for the District of Columbia Circuit 2013) (holding that the sitting president of Sri Lanka was immune from civil suit under the U.S. Torture Victims Protection Act brought by relatives of alleged victims of extrajudicial killings in Sri Lanka); *Yousuf v. Samantar*, 699 F.3d 763, 769 (U.S. 4th Cir. 2012) (holding high-ranking government official immune from civil action under the TWPA and Alien Tort Statute brought by natives of Somalia seeking to impose liability against and recover damages for alleged acts of torture and human rights violations committed against them by government agents).

service.[76] The Military Extraterritorial Jurisdiction Act ('MEJA')[77] enacted in 2000 provides:

> Whoever engages in conduct outside the United States that would constitute an offense punishable by imprisonment for more than 1 year if the conduct had been engaged in within the special maritime and territorial jurisdiction of the United States –
>
> (1) while employed by or accompanying the Armed Forces outside the United States; or
>
> (2) while a member of the Armed Forces subject to chapter 47 of title 10 (the Uniform Code of Military Justice), shall be punished as provided for that offense.

In 2009, former U.S. Army member Steven D. Green was convicted under MEJA of the sexual assault of a 14-year-old Iraqi girl and the murder of the girl and her family committed by Green and two other service members while stationed in Iraq. Green was sentenced to five consecutive terms of life imprisonment in the United States.[78] He later committed suicide in prison.

11.4.4. Visa/Naturalization Fraud Prosecution

Despite the scorn for reliance on immigration and visa fraud exhibited by U.S. Senate Subcommittee members and witnesses during the human rights hearings in 2007 through 2009, prosecution for such offense continues to be the most prolific prosecutorial tool against perpetrators of crimes against humanity located within the United States. Although prosecution for these crimes has been criticized as a 'slap on the wrist' for such heinous activities, the U.S. has been successful in obtaining criminal convictions and significant prison terms for immigration related offenses. Following conclusion of the perpetrator's sentence, the U.S. may buy time to co-ordinate the extradition of the individual to the country with jurisdiction to prosecute human rights violations. At a minimum, the U.S. can revoke citizenship, lawful permanent residence, or a visa status granted based on fraud, and remove the individual from the United States, thus

---

[76] *United States v. Green*, 654 F.2d 637, 645 (U.S. Court of Appeals for the Sixth Circuit 2011), citing, H.R. Rep. No. 106–778, part 1, at 5 (2000).

[77] Title 18 U.S.C. § 3261.

[78] *Green*, at 645, see *supra* note 76.

deterring individuals from using the United States as a safe haven from prosecution for human rights violations in their countries of origin.

One high profile example was the aforementioned prosecution of Marko Boskić, referenced in the 2007 U.S. Senate Subcommittee hearing 'No Safe Haven: Accountability for Human Rights Violators in the United States'. In 2002, Boskić, while in Germany, submitted an application to the U.S. seeking classification as a refugee.[79] The application asked questions about his past military service, criminal convictions, and basis for seeking admission to the United States as a refugee.[80] Boskić was granted refugee status and admitted to the United States based on the information set forth in his application.[81] He subsequently immigrated to the United States taking up residence in Massachusetts.[82] In 2001, he filed and was approved for an adjustment of status to that of a lawful permanent resident.[83] The application form for that adjustment also included questions about past military service and criminal history.[84]

Following Boskić's admission to the United States, investigators for the International Criminal Tribunal for the former Yugoslavia ('ICTY') uncovered evidence identifying him as a member of a military unit – the 10th Sabotage Detachment of the Army of the *Republika Srpska* – suspected of war crimes and other atrocities during the 1995 Srebrenica massacre in Bosnia.[85] U.S. authorities, acting on the information from the ICTY, subsequently initiated an investigation and determined that Boskić had committed immigration fraud by failing to disclose on his applications seeking refugee status and later adjustment of status to permanent resident by failing to disclose his prior military service in Bosnia and a prior criminal record.[86] Boskić was arrested in August 2004.[87] In 2006, he

---

[79] *United States v. Boskic*, 545 F.3d 69, 73, 1st Cir. 2008 (affirming conviction for immigration fraud).

[80] *Ibid.*

[81] *Ibid.*

[82] *Ibid.*

[83] *Ibid.*

[84] *Ibid.*

[85] *Ibid.*

[86] *Ibid.*

[87] "War crimes suspect charged in Boston, Peabody man tied to Bosnia mass execution", available at http://www.boston.com/news/local/articles/2004/08/27/war_crimes_suspect_charged_in_boston/?page=full.

was convicted in federal court for visa fraud and sentenced to 63 months incarceration in federal prison.[88] The U.S. also revoked his lawful permanent resident status.

Following Boskić's conviction and incarceration, U.S. Immigrations and Customs Enforcement initiated removal proceedings. On 18 February 2010, an immigration judge ordered Boskić removed to Bosnia and Herzegovina,[89] where he was prosecuted and convicted pursuant to a plea bargain for crimes against humanity on 20 July 2010. He is currently serving 10 years in prison.[90]

11.5. U.S. Policy Regarding Crimes Against Humanity

U.S. officials traditionally have viewed genocide, mass atrocities, and other international human rights issues as matters of moral imperative. More recently, U.S. leaders and policy makers have begun to recognize the potential impact of international conflicts and in particular the potential national security vulnerabilities realized from the commission of atrocity crimes. In February 2010, Dennis C. Blair, Director of National Intelligence, for the first time raised the issue of the potential threat to U.S. national security from genocide and mass atrocities in Africa and Asia during congressional testimony on the U.S. government's annual threat assessment.[91] Shortly thereafter, the White House issued the first National Security Strategy for the Administration of President Barack Obama noting the potential threat to U.S. security interests from global instability leading to commission of widespread atrocity crimes. It states:

> From Nuremberg to Yugoslavia to Liberia, the United States has seen that the end of impunity and the promotion of justice are not just moral imperatives; they are stabilizing forces in international affairs. The United States is thus working to strengthen national justice systems and is

---

[88] *Ibid.*

[89] U.S. Immigration and Customs Enforcement, "Bosnian-Serb suspect removed –Suspect participated in murder of thousands of Bosnian Muslim men and boys", 27 April 2010, available at http://www.ice.gov/news/releases/1004/100427washingtondc2.htm.

[90] JURIST, "Bosnia court convicts Serbian war crimes suspect of crimes against humanity", 20 July 2010, available at http://jurist.org/paperchase/2010/07/bosnia-court-convicts-serbian-war-crimes-suspect-for-crimes-against-humanity.php.

[91] Foreign Policy, "How Genocide is a National Security Threat", 28 February 2010, available at http://www.foreignpolicy.com/articles/2010/02/26/how_genocide_became_a_national_security_threat.

maintaining our support for ad hoc international tribunals and hybrid courts. Those who intentionally target innocent civilians must be held accountable, and we will continue to support institutions and prosecutions that advance this important interest. Although the United States is not at present a party to the Rome Statute of the International Criminal Court (ICC), and will always protect U.S. personnel, we are engaging with State Parties to the Rome Statute on issues of concern and are supporting the ICC's prosecution of those cases that advance U.S. interests and values, consistent with the requirements of U.S. law.[92]

On 4 August 2011, U.S. President Barack Obama announced a comprehensive strategy to strengthen the United States' ability to prevent mass atrocities and human rights violations.[93] The strategy included the following:

- Issuance of a Presidential Proclamation suspending entry of immigrants and non-immigrants of persons who participate in serious human rights and humanitarian law violations.[94]

- Creation of an interagency Atrocities Board. In so doing the President noted that "the United States still lacks a comprehensive policy framework and corresponding interagency mechanism for preventing and responding to mass atrocities and genocide. This has left us ill-prepared to engage early, proactively, and decisively, to prevent threats from evolving into large scale civilian atrocities".[95] He further noted the options available to the United States range from economic actions to diplomatic intervention and both non-combat

---

[92] National Security Strategy, The White House, May 2010, p. 48, available at http://whitehouse.gov.

[93] The White House, Office of the Press Secretary, "Fact Sheet: President Obama Directs New Steps to Prevent Mass Atrocities and Impose Consequences on Serious Human Rights Violators", 4 August 2011, available at http://www.whitehouse.gov/the-press-office/2011/08/04/fact-sheet-president-obama-directs-new-steps-prevent-mass-atrocities-and.

[94] The White House, Office of the Press Secretary, "Presidential Proclamation – Suspension of Entry as Immigrants and Nonimmigrants of Persons who Participate in Serious Human Rights and Humanitarian law Violations and Other Abuses", 4 August 2014, available at http://www.whitehouse.gov/the-press-office/2011/08/04/presidential-proclamation-suspension-entry-immigrants-and-nonimmigrants-.

[95] *Ibid.*

military actions or direct military intervention.[96] The Atrocities Prevention Board was launched on 23 April 2012.[97]

In July 2014, President Obama issued an Executive Order to provide additional flexibility for the United States to target persons contributing to the conflict in the Democratic Republic of the Congo, including new criteria to be used to sanction persons involved in the conflict. The Executive Order also conformed U.S. practices to the criteria established in recent Security Council Resolutions.[98]

In September 2014, President Obama took the unusual step of taking the lead on obtaining multi-national approval of a U.N. Security Council Resolution authorizing military action to stop the spread of ISIL – an action with both important national and global security purpose as well as humanitarian intervention.[99] The U.S. Congress subsequently authorized the use of U.S. military force, in conjunction with other international efforts.

11.6. Conclusion

The United States currently does not have a specific federal law criminalizing crimes against humanity. The U.S., however, continues to take steps in law and policy to partner with its international allies to respond to incidents of atrocities committed against civilian populations. Recent legislative attempts to address crimes against humanity, that is, the Crimes Against Humanity Acts of 2009 and 2010, highlight controversies over issues such as inclusion of certain underlying crimes, jurisdiction, command responsibility, and immunities. A delicate balance need to be sought between sovereign interests, including protecting overseas U.S. personnel, and ending impunity. Notably the latest draft Act of 2010 regressed from the 2009 Act in the strength to punish. It is worth emphasizing that those controversial issues must be addressed thoroughly in future legislation to effectuate the fight against impunity.

---

[96]   *Ibid.*

[97]   United States Institute of Peace, "Obama Announces Formation of the Atrocities Prevention Board", available at http://www.usip.org/publications/obama-announces-formation-the-atrocities-prevention-board.

[98]   The White House, Office of the Press Secretary, "Executive Order Regarding the Democratic Republic of the Congo", available at http://www.whitehouse.gov/the-press-office/2014/07/08/executive-order-regarding-democratic-republic-congo.

[99]   U.N. Security Council, S/RES/21768 (2014), 24 September 2014.

12

The Proposed Convention on Crimes Against Humanity and *Aut Dedere Aut Judicare*

Ian Kennedy[*]

12.1. Introduction

International law is a tangle of interacting and overlapping treaties, customs and principles. Developments in one seemingly discrete corner can trigger unforeseen shifts elsewhere. This chapter examines how a new international treaty on crimes against humanity could impact the principle of *aut dedere aut judicare* ('ADAJ'). It argues that the Proposed International Convention on the Prevention and Punishment of Crimes Against Humanity ('Proposed Convention')[1] invites State practices that could prevent an ADAJ response to alleged crimes against humanity ('CAH' and, with regard to the larger concept, 'ADAJ for CAH') from becoming customary international law.

12.2. *Aut Dedere Aut Judicare*

The principle of *aut dedere aut judicare*, meaning 'extradite or prosecute', was first articulated by Hugo Grotius in the early 17th century.[2] It promises to fulfill the goal of the international criminal law: to end impunity for perpetrators of international crimes. The prosecution option, carried out by the State in whose territory the alleged criminal is found, respects State sovereignty, avoids messy jurisdictional issues, often allows greater witness participation, and may make justice more visible to victims. The extradite option accounts for States unwilling or unable to pros-

---

[*] **Ian Kennedy** is a practicing lawyer in Vancouver, Canada, and a Fellow with the Canadian Centre for International Justice. All Internet references were last accessed on 16 September 2014.

[1] Crimes Against Humanity Initiative, "Proposed International Convention on the Prevention and Punishment of Crimes Against Humanity", Washington University School of Law, August 2010, see Annex 1.

[2] Michael Scharf, "*Aut Dedere Aut Iudicare*", in Rüdiger Wolfrum (ed.), *Max Planck Encyclopedia of Public International Law*, Oxford University Press, 2008, online edition.

ecute international crimes; in either case, the ADAJ principle mandates that States extradite the accused to a State that will prosecute. Faithful adherence to these twin principles would ensure that persons accused of international crimes face trial.

The ADAJ principle is regularly included in international criminal law treaties. A study conducted by M. Cherif Bassiouni determined that some 48 treaties incorporate the principle.[3] The Rome Statute of the International Criminal Court ('ICC Statute') adopts the principle of complementarity, a variant of ADAJ. Article 17 of the ICC Statute assigns primary responsibility for investigation and prosecution of crimes to the State with jurisdiction. However, if that State is unwilling or unable to investigate and prosecute, the ICC may take on the case. This is a robust version of the extradite branch of ADAJ.

12.3. ADAJ for CAH as Customary International Law?

With wide acceptance of CAH as serious international crimes and ADAJ as a method to ensure criminal punishment, it has been argued that ADAJ for CAH is customary international law. Unlike treaty law, which is binding only on States Parties, customary law binds all States.[4]

During a 2009 U.N. General Assembly session, delegations from Hungary, Mexico, Cuba, Iran, and Uruguay all expressed that they consider the duty to extradite or prosecute CAH to be a legal obligation.[5] In the case of *Questions relating to the Obligation to Prosecute or Extradite (Belgium v. Senegal)* before the International Court of Justice ('ICJ'), Belgium submitted an extensive argument that ADAJ for CAH and other crimes is a rule of customary international law.[6] Similarly, a number of prominent academics, including M. Cherif Bassiouni, Leila Sadat, Carla Edelenbos, Diane Orentlicher, and Naomi Roht-Arriaza, have argued that there is an international legal duty to prosecute persons accused of CAH.[7]

---

[3] M. Cherif Bassiouni, *International Crimes: Digest/Index of International Instruments 1815–1985*, New York: Oceana, 1986.

[4] The only exception is States that have persistently objected to the customary law during its formation.

[5] Zdzislaw Galicki, "Fourth report on the obligation to extradite or prosecute (*aut dedere aut judicare*)", International Law Commission, Geneva, 31 May 2011.

[6] International Court of Justice, Document CR.2009/08, 6 April 2009, pp. 23–25, available at http://www.icj-cij.org/docket/files/144/15119.pdf.

[7] Scharf, 2008, *supra* note 2.

The argument that ADAJ for CAH is customary law invariably relies on documents like U.N. General Assembly resolutions, declarations of international conferences, and reports of the U.N. Secretary-General.[8] These are not so strong foundations; customary international law is not born from resolutions and declarations. The formation of customary international law has two requirements: general State practice and *opinio juris* – the acceptance of that practice as law.[9] State practice, according to the ICJ, must be "both extensive and virtually uniform".[10] Occasional deviations from the rule will not necessarily compromise its customary legal standing, but such deviations should generally have been treated as breaches of the rule.[11] The *opinio juris* requirement demands that this practice is not only the result of self-interest or accident, but is understood by States to be a legal obligation.

ADAJ for CAH is neither generally adhered to by States nor understood by them to be a legal requirement. Although some States have claimed that ADAJ for CAH is customary law, these statements alone are not State practice. As Mark Villiger has written:

> For written rules to have any value in formative process of customary law, further instances of material practice, in conjunction with the written rules, are required. It is not the written text which contributes towards customary law, but

---

[8]   *Ibid.* See also ICJ Document CR.2009/08, *supra* note 6.

[9]   Statute of the International Court of Justice, 18 April 1946. Article 38(b) describes "international custom, as evidence of a general practice accepted as law" as a source of law that the Court can draw upon.

[10] ICJ, *North Sea Continental Shelf Cases (Federal Republic of Germany v. Denmark; Federal Republic of Germany v. Netherlands)*, Judgment, 20 February 1969, para. 74.

[11] ICJ, *Case Concerning Military and Paramilitary Activities In and Against Nicaragua (Nicaragua v. United States of America)*, Judgment, 27 June 1986, para. 186:

> The Court does not consider that, for a rule to be established as customary, the corresponding practice must be in absolutely rigorous conformity with the rule. In order to deduce the existence of customary rules, the Court deems it sufficient that the conduct of States should, in general, be consistent with such rules, and that instances of State conduct inconsistent with a given rule should generally have been treated as breaches of that rule, not as indications of the recognition of a new rule.

the instances whereby States apply these rules in a concrete case, or refer to them, or vote upon them, which do so.[12]

The words of States must be reinforced by real action before they evidence State practice. In the case of ADAJ for CAH, that real action is missing. Robert Cryer puts it this way:

> There is almost no evidence of any State practice confirming prosecution on a universal jurisdiction basis as a customary duty rather than a right. Even the most ardent supporters of such a duty are forced to concede this point.[13]

Similarly, Michael Scharf observes: "To the extent any State practice in this area is widespread, it is the practice of granting amnesties or asylum to those who commit crimes against humanity, rather than the practice of prosecuting or extraditing them".[14]

The argument that ADAJ for CAH is customary law was definitively quashed by a Separate Joint Opinion of three ICJ judges in 2000, who held:

> While no general rule of positive international law can as yet be asserted which gives states *the right* to punish foreign nationals for crimes against humanity in the same way they are, for instance, entitled to punish acts of piracy, there are clear indications pointing to the gradual evolution of significant principles of international law to that effect.[15]

That the judges were unconvinced that there was a "right" to punish foreign nationals for CAH breaches can only mean that there is no customary legal duty to do so.

Although ADAJ for CAH is not customary international law, it may yet attain that status. The ICJ Separate Joint Opinion noted the "gradual evolution" of a right to punish foreign nationals for international crimes. This evolution may yield a duty. The inclusion of ADAJ in an increasing

---

[12] Mark E. Villiger, *Customary Law and Treaties*, Dordrecht: Martinus Nijhoff Publishers, 1997, p. 26.

[13] Robert Cryer, *Prosecuting International Crimes: Selectivity and International Criminal Law Regime*, Cambridge: Cambridge University Press, 2005, pp. 90–91.

[14] Scharf, 2008, see *supra* note 2.

[15] ICJ, *Case Concerning the Arrest Warrant of 11 April 2000 (Democratic Republic of the Congo v. Belgium)*, Separate Joint Opinion of Judges Higgins, Kooijmans and Buergenthal, 14 February 2002, para. 52 (emphasis added). The majority decision did not address this point.

number of treaties should translate into increased State practice and, perhaps eventually, *opinio juris*. A 2008 International Law Commission ('ILC') report states:

> The number of international treaties containing the obligation *aut dedere aut judicare* is growing every year. That formulation alone cannot serve as sufficient background for the codification of a generally binding customary rule, but the development of international practice based on the growing number of treaties establishing and confirming such an obligation may lead at least to the beginning of the formulation of an appropriate customary norm.[16]

A 2011 ILC report went further still, proposing to add a draft article on "international custom as a source of the obligation aut dedere aut judicare" to its set of draft articles on ADAJ.[17] State practice may shift towards respecting ADAJ for CAH as an obligation. This could eventually qualify ADAJ for CAH as customary international law.

12.4. The Proposed Convention on Crimes Against Humanity

The Proposed Convention on crimes against humanity[18] was authored by a group of international criminal law experts called the 'Crimes Against Humanity Initiative', sponsored by the Washington University School of Law.[19] The Proposed Convention was finalized in 2010, and published in the 2011 book 'Forging a Convention for Crimes Against Humanity'.[20]

Should the Proposed Convention enter into force, it would fill a substantial gap in conventional international criminal law. CAH are currently only covered where the ICC has jurisdiction, and where CAH overlap with other treaties, such as the Geneva Conventions. In the opinion of Bassiouni, one Proposed Convention author, a comprehensive CAH treaty is long overdue. He has written: "It is nothing short of amazing that since

---

[16] Zdzislaw Galicki, "Third report on the obligation to extradite or prosecute (*aut dedere aut judicare*)", International Law Commission, Geneva, 10 June 2008.

[17] Galicki, 2011, see *supra* note 5, p. 24.

[18] See *supra* note 1.

[19] The web site of the Crimes Against Humanity Initiative is available at http://crimesagainsthumanity.wustl.edu/.

[20] Leila Nadya Sadat (ed.), *Forging a Convention for Crimes Against Humanity*, New York: Cambridge University Press, 2011.

World War II, CAH has not been codified in an international conven-tion".[21]

The Proposed Convention contains a provision on ADAJ. Laura Ol-son describes this as having been obligatory: "[A] specialized convention on crimes against humanity must include the obligation to extradite and/or prosecute in order to meet the stated, primary objective of the treaty – ending impunity".[22]

Article 9 of the Proposed Convention, entitled *Aut Dedere Aut Ju-dicare*, binds States Parties to either prosecute or extradite persons ac-cused of CAH:

> 1. Each State Party shall take necessary measures to establish its competence to exercise jurisdiction over crimes against humanity when the alleged offender is present in any territory under its jurisdiction, unless it extradites him or her to another State in accordance with its international obligations or surrenders him or her to the International Criminal Court, if it is a State Party to the ICC Statute, or to another international criminal tribunal whose jurisdiction it has recognized.
>
> 2. In the event that a State Party does not, for any reason not specified in the present Convention, prosecute a person sus-pected of committing crimes against humanity, it shall, pur-suant to an appropriate request, either surrender such a per-son to another State willing to prosecute fairly and effective-ly, to the International Criminal Court, if it is a State Party to the ICC Statute, or to a competent international tribunal hav-ing jurisdiction over crimes against humanity.[23]

It must be read concurrently with Article 8(7), (8) and (9):

> 7. Upon receiving information that a person who has committed or who is alleged to have committed crimes

---

21   M. Cherif Bassiouni, "Revisiting the Architecture of Crimes Against Humanity: Almost a Century in the Making, with Gaps and Ambiguities Remaining – the Need for a Special-ized Convention", in Leila Nadya Sadat (ed.), *Forging a Convention for Crimes Against Humanity, op. cit.*, p. 58.

22   Laura Olson, "Re-enforcing Enforcement in a Specialized Convention on Crimes Against Humanity: Inter-State Cooperation, Mutual Legal Assistance, and the *Aut Dedere Aut Ju-dicare* Obligation", in Leila Nadya Sadat (ed.), *Forging a Convention for Crimes Against Humanity, op. cit.*, p. 326.

23   Article 9, Proposed Convention, see *supra* note 1.

---

against humanity may be present in its territory, the State Party concerned shall take such measures as may be necessary under its domestic law to investigate the facts contained in the information.

8. Upon being satisfied that the circumstances so warrant, the State Party in whose territory the person who has committed or who is alleged to have committed crimes against humanity is present shall take the necessary and appropriate measures under its domestic law so as to ensure that person's presence for the purpose of prosecution or extradition.

9. States Parties shall prosecute or extradite those charged with or suspected of committing crimes against humanity.

States Parties that do not abide by the ADAJ obligation may be challenged by other States Parties under Article 26 of the Convention, initiating arbitration, or, if necessary, a suit before the ICJ.

Article 9 would be unproblematic if identifying "an alleged offender" or "a person suspected of committing crimes against humanity" was an objective exercise. It is not. As discussed below, not all allegations or suspicions can engage the Proposed Convention, and, adding to the difficulty, several aspects of the CAH definition are unsettled.

12.4.1. What Allegations or Suspicions Trigger Article 9?

Accusations of CAH could be made by a variety of actors. It is unclear which should trigger Article 9 of the Proposed Convention and require States to make a prosecute-or-extradite decision. Is it enough that another State raises an allegation or suspicion? A U.N. body? A prominent NGO? A group of victims? In each case, are there circumstances that would make the accusation void?

12.4.2. What qualifies as CAH?

The definition of CAH in the Proposed Convention is the same as the definition set out in Article 7 of the ICC Statute:

'crimes against humanity' means any of the following acts when committed as part of a widespread or systematic attack

> directed against any civilian population, with knowledge of
> the attack [...].[24]

The definition then lists a number of acts, among them murder, torture, and persecution. It also defines "attack" as a "course of conduct involving the multiple commission of acts [...] pursuant to or in furtherance of a State or organizational policy to commit such attack".[25] This definition contains numerous ambiguities that are the subject of disagreement among experts. Bassiouni notes:

> The historical evolution of CAH, slow and tortured as it was,
> has not yet settled into its final form. Its nature, scope, application, and the legal elements are still somewhat unsettled.[26]

Three unsettled aspects of the CAH definition will be examined below.

12.4.2.1. "State or organizational policy"

In order to qualify as CAH, an attack must be connected to a State or organizational policy. What this means is unclear. In particular, does the term "organizational policy" mean that non-State organizations can commit crimes against humanity? This would be a significant departure from the traditional understanding that only State policies can qualify as CAH. Bassiouni maintains:

> [the CAH definition] clearly refers to State policy, and the
> words 'organizational policy' do not refer to the policy of an
> organization, but the policy of a State. It does not refer to
> non-State actors.[27]

He notes that otherwise, the mafia could be charged with CAH, which is not the intended purpose of the CAH provision, at least in the ICC Statute.[28]

Kai Ambos adopts a contrary, and perhaps more intuitive, interpretation of the provision: "[T]he reference to ["organizational policy"] in

---

[24] *Ibid.*, Article 3(1).

[25] *Ibid.*, Article 3(2)(a).

[26] Bassiouni, 2011, p. 56, see *supra* note 21.

[27] M. Cherif Bassiouni, *The Legislative History of the International Criminal Court: Introduction, Analysis, and Integrated Text*, Ardsley, NY: Transnational Publishers, 2005, pp. 151–152.

[28] *Ibid.*

Article 7(2) [of the ICC Statute; Article 3(2)(a) of the Proposed Convention] makes clear that the provision also applies to non-State actors".[29] Ambos qualifies this interpretation by arguing that "these actors must be in a position to act like a State, that is, they must possess a similar capacity of organization and force".[30] This debate leaves an important question unanswered: can non-State actors commit CAH? If so, what structure and capacities must their organizations have? Bassiouni also raises a related question of whether State agents can commit CAH if they are not acting as part of a State policy.[31]

12.4.2.2. "Against any civilian population"

The phrase "against any civilian population" raises two questions. First, how large must a group of civilians be to qualify as a "population"? Second, is "civilian" really intended to exclude acts against armed combatants? This seems inconsistent with the decision made during the drafting of the ICC Statute to remove the requirement of a nexus between CAH and armed conflicts.[32]

12.4.2.3. "Widespread or systemic"

The chapeau of the CAH definition requires that an attack be "widespread or systemic". The disjunctive article "or" suggests that either is sufficient. However, the subsequent definition of attack requires both "the multiple commission of acts" (which seems to have a similar meaning to widespread) and "a State or organizational policy" (which seems to be a proxy for systematic). In other words, the definition of attack suggests that an attack must be widespread *and* systematic to qualify at CAH. This goes against the rulings of international criminal tribunals, which have, Ambos writes, "always opted for a disjunctive or alternative reading".[33] This ambiguity might be resolved in favour of the disjunctive reading by distinguishing "multiple" from "widespread" or "policy" from "systematic".

---

29   Kai Ambos, "Crimes Against Humanity and the International Criminal Court", in Leila Nadya Sadat (ed.), *Forging a Convention for Crimes Against Humanity, op. cit.*, p. 281.

30   *Ibid.*, p. 283.

31   Bassiouni, 2011, p. 56, see *supra* note 21.

32   *Ibid.*

33   Ambos, 2011, pp. 284–285, see *supra* note 30.

Conversely, it could also be interpreted to require that the attack be both widespread and systemic.

The ambiguity embedded in CAH, and therefore also in Article 9 of the Proposed Convention, can be phrased as a single question: which accusations of which crimes by which actors engage Article 9? It would be impossible for a treaty to give a full answer to this question; there are too many variables to account for. But the Proposed Convention could assign the authority to make that determination. That is, since it cannot answer the question, it could say who can. Instead, the current Proposed Convention is silent on the matter, an approach which, as the following section illustrates, may forestall or prevent ADAJ for CAH from becoming customary international law.

12.4.3. The Importance of a CAH Convention for ADAJ for CAH to Become Customary International Law

CAH captures a broader category of crimes than the other core international crimes listed in the ICC Statute, genocide and war crimes. It has the lowest threshold of the three, since it becomes active where there is a "widespread or systematic attack directed at a civilian population".[34] This is a lesser requirement than the 1949 Geneva Conventions, which apply only to international armed conflict;[35] the common Article 3 of the Geneva Conventions, which applies to non-international armed conflicts;[36] and genocide as defined in the ICC Statute, which requires a manifest pattern of conduct similar to acts of genocide.[37]

In addition to the lowest threshold of the core crimes, CAH also has the widest scope. It covers acts that would be war crimes in times of armed conflict – such as murder, rape, and torture – but it also includes the broad category of "persecution against an identifiable group"[38] and the

---

[34] Article 3(1), Proposed Convention, see *supra* note 1.

[35] Common Article 2, Geneva Convention for the Amelioration of the Condition of the Wounded and Sick in Armed Forces in the Field of August 12, 1949; Geneva Convention for the Amelioration of the Conditions of Wounded, Sick and Shipwrecked Members of Armed Forces at Sea of August 12, 1949; Geneva Convention Relative to the Treatment of Prisoners of War of August 12, 1949; Geneva Convention Relative to the Protection of Civilian Persons in Time of War of August 12, 1949.

[36] *Ibid.*, Common Article 3.

[37] Article 6, ICC Statute.

[38] Article 3(1)(h), Proposed Convention, see *supra* note 1.

catch-all clause of "other inhumane acts of a similar character".[39] In short, CAH covers most war crimes and many additional acts. For this reason, CAH has been widely used in international criminal tribunals. Göran Sluiter writes: "Looking at the judgments of the [International Criminal Tribunal for the former Yugoslavia], one notices the difficulty in securing convictions for genocide, but crimes against humanity figure prominently in both the indictments and convictions".[40] At the International Criminal Tribunal for Rwanda, genocide was the focus of nearly all cases, but Sluiter notes that "each genocide accusation is backed up by crimes against humanity accusation".[41]

The breadth of CAH suggests that, if ratified, the Proposed Convention would be regularly invoked by States Parties. Each time someone accused of CAH is prosecuted or extradited it will add to the record of State practice conforming to ADAJ for CAH. With time, such State practice could lead to ADAJ for CAH becoming customary international law. Payam Akhavan argues that "the adoption and widespread ratification of a Convention on Crimes Against Humanity can have a profound impact on expediting [the] process" of ADAJ for CAH crystallizing into customary international law.[42]

Although the inclusion of ADAJ in the Proposed Convention could further its prospects of becoming customary law, this progress may be undermined by the ambiguities in the Article 9 definition. As discussed, under Article 9 it is unclear who decides what qualifies as an accusation of CAH that would engage Article 9. Interpretations are bound to conflict, contrary to the customary law requirement of State practice being "extensive and virtually uniform". This problem and a proposed solution are explored below.

---

39 *Ibid.*, Article 3(1)(k).

40 Göran Sluiter, "'Chapeau Elements' of Crimes Against Humanity in the Jurisprudence of the UN Ad Hoc Tribunals", in Leila Nadya Sadat (ed.), *Forging a Convention for Crimes Against Humanity, op. cit.*, p. 102.

41 *Ibid.*

42 Payam Akhavan, "The Universal Repression of Crimes Against Humanity before National Jurisdiction: The Need for a Treaty-Based Obligation to Prosecute", in Leila Nadya Sadat (ed.), *Forging a Convention for Crimes Against Humanity, op. cit.*, p. 40.

12.5. The Consequences of the Proposed Convention for ADAJ for CAH Becoming Customary Law

In December 2011, former U.S. President George W. Bush visited Zambia.[43] Prior to his visit, Amnesty International released a report claiming that any State George W. Bush visits has an obligation to investigate his alleged involvement in the crime of torture and to arrest him during that investigation.[44] Zambia declined to arrest George W. Bush. Zambian Foreign Affairs Minister Chishimba Kambwili questioned: "On what basis does Amnesty International want us to arrest President Bush?".[45]

Consider a hypothetical scenario where the Proposed Convention is in force, Zambia is a State Party, and the basis that Amnesty International wants Zambia to make an arrest is the crime of torture under Article 3(1)(f) of the Proposed Convention. In this hypothetical, Zambia nevertheless refuses to arrest George Bush, arguing that it is not obligated to prosecute or extradite under Article 9 for two reasons. First, Zambia claims that the accusation of an NGO with a political agenda does not engage Article 9 of the Proposed Convention, which is an agreement open only to States Parties. Second, Zambia claims that the act of torture that George W. Bush is being accused of does not qualify as a CAH, because the alleged torture was perpetrated against enemy combatants in an armed conflict, not "a civilian population".

The response of other States to Zambia's decision could result in one of three scenarios. In Scenario A, all other States Parties to the Proposed Convention accept that Zambia had the right to dismiss Amnesty's accusation. In Scenario B, at least some States Parties claim that Zambia's decision violated its ADAJ obligations under Article 9 of the Convention, but none instigates arbitration with Zambia under Article 26. In Scenario C, another State Party does instigate legal proceedings against Zambia for having breached its ADAJ obligations under Article 9.

---

[43] Lewis Mwanangombe, "Zambia Rejects Rights Group's Call to Arrest Bush", Associated Press, 4 December 2011.

[44] Amnesty International, "Bringing George Bush to Justice", London: Amnesty International Publications, 2011, available at http://www.amnesty.org/en/library/asset/AMR51/097/2011/en/c2a7843c-2340-445e-9770-f33d76bed282/amr510972011en.pdf.

[45] Lewis Mwanangombe, "Zambia rejects rights group's call to arrest Bush", see *supra* note 44.

The current structure of Article 9 invites a Scenario B outcome because it does not say whether Zambia has the right to disregard Amnesty's CAH accusation. This ambiguity permits States that would like to see George W. Bush prosecuted to complain that Zambia's decision violates its ADAJ obligations. Objecting States can be assured that their complaint is credible because Article 9 requires prosecution or extradition and leaves open no third avenue of inaction. In other words, States that might otherwise be cautious about speaking against Zambia are given space to do so by Article 9. This pushes a potential Scenario A result towards Scenario B.

At the same time, under Article 9 there is little incentive for any one State to go beyond empty criticisms and take legal action against Zambia. Arbitration under Article 26 will be time-consuming and resource-expensive. It may seem to one State that it should fall to another to initiate legal proceedings because of some connection to the alleged crime. Most importantly, because Article 9 does not indicate whether Zambia is within its rights to dismiss the accusation, the outcome of arbitration will be uncertain, a sure deterrent to legal action. In this way, Article 9 pushes a possible Scenario C outcome towards Scenario B.

In Scenario B, some States say that Article 9 of the Convention has been violated, but they do not abide by the dispute resolution provisions provided by Article 26. Acknowledging that the Convention is engaged while simultaneously acting outside of its structure undermines the authority of the Convention.

Scenario B is also the most damaging to the chances of ADAJ for CAH becoming customary international law. In Scenario B, Zambia's decision is treated by objecting States as a deviation from the ADAJ rule by their words but not their actions. The ICJ requires that deviations from a customary rule must be "treated as breaches of that rule" in order for the customary status to be maintained.[46] Article 26 demands that breaches of Article 9 should be arbitrated or brought before the ICJ. Empty criticisms are a half-measure. Over time, Scenario B responses would build a record of alleged breaches of ADAJ for CAH that are ultimately accepted by other States. This would be damaging to any prospect of ADAJ for CAH becoming customary international law.

---

[46] ICJ, *Nicaragua v. United States of America*, see *supra* note 11.

In contrast, Scenario A, where States accept Zambia's decision, has no impact on ADAJ for CAH becoming customary international law. States accept that ADAJ was not engaged by Amnesty's accusation, so Zambia's decision cannot be a deviation from the ADAJ obligation. And in Scenario C, although Zambia's decision is treated as a deviation from the ADAJ rule, it is met with a full objection from another State Party. This response will allow the crystallization of ADAJ for CAH into international law to continue unimpeded.

12.6.   A Proposed Solution

The gravity towards Scenario B, the least-desirable result from the perspective of ADAJ for CAH becoming customary international law, can be reversed by restructuring Article 9. More specifically, Article 9 must establish who has the authority to say which accusations of which crimes by which actors engage Article 9. It should do so in the following way. First, the presumption should be that the State with jurisdiction, here Zambia, can determine whether someone has been accused of CAH in a way that engages its Article 9 obligation.[47] Second, this presumption should be overridden when either the U.N. Security Council or another designated U.N. body supports the accusation of CAH.

Of course, under the U.N. Charter, the Security Council can declare actions to be CAH irrespective of the Proposed Convention. But by explicitly providing that such a declaration would engage the Article 9 obligations, the Proposed Convention would bring Security Council resolutions within its framework.

Empowering another designated U.N. body to determine what qualifies as CAH would be complimentary to Article 8(13) of the Proposed Convention, which provides that States Parties may call upon competent organs of the U.N. for the prevention and punishment of CAH. Allowing

---

[47]   Article 8(8) of the Proposed Convention has a related but different function. Article 8(8) mandates only what States should do when they believe allegations of CAH are warranted; it is silent with regard to the opposite situation where States deem allegations unjustified. It does not give States permission to do nothing when they determine nothing is the appropriate response. For example, Zambia's decision not to pursue action against Georgia W. Bush is unsanctioned by the current Proposed Convention. This is particularly clear when Article 8(8) is read alongside Article 8(9), which requires that States shall prosecute or extradited those "suspected of committing crimes against humanity", without qualifying "suspected".

those same U.N. organs to call on States Parties to abide by Article 9 would create a reciprocal right. Further, the authority of a U.N. body would likely put more pressure on the State with jurisdiction to prosecute or extradite than would the accusations of any single State Party.

Returning to our hypothetical, under this proposed solution, Zambia's right to determine what qualifies as an accusation of CAH respects State sovereignty and would attract States to sign and ratify the Convention. It will also push towards a Scenario A outcome. States Parties will be less likely to object to Zambia's decision to do nothing if it clearly has the right to make that decision. Again, this result will have no impact on ADAJ for CAH becoming customary international law because ADAJ is not engaged.

If the Security Council or another U.N. body overrides Zambia's decision not to prosecute, this will militate towards a Scenario C outcome. States Parties will be more likely to take legal action against Zambia for two reasons. One is that the States who backed the Security Council or U.N. body decision may feel compelled to follow through and press for judicial resolution. This is likely to garner positive international attention for those States, because the involvement of a U.N. body will have heightened public interest around the issue. Second, because the revised Article 9 demands that ADAJ be strictly followed when the Security Council or another U.N. body supports the accusation, any State challenging Zambia is likely to be successful at arbitration.

Assigning authority to determine what qualifies as a CAH accusation to the State with jurisdiction over the accused, while limiting this authority in the case of Security Council or U.N. body interventions, pushes away from a Scenario B result and the negative consequences it would entail for the Proposed Convention and for ADAJ for CAH becoming customary law.

12.7. Conclusion

There will be occasions when States Parties to a CAH Convention refuse to prosecute or extradite persons accused of CAH. This chapter has argued that the ADAJ provision of the Convention should guide other States Parties towards either accepting that refusal or making a full objection through judicial proceedings. These results avoid the dithering middle ground of objections without legal action. If this middle ground were to become the default reaction to a State like Zambia seeking to avoid a prosecute-or-extradite decision, the chances of ADAJ for CAH becoming customary international law would be diminished.

Article 9 could be strengthened by allowing States with jurisdiction the right to dismiss a CAH accusation. This would dissuade empty objections from other States Parties. At the same time, Article 9 should give an overriding power to the Security Council or a designated U.N. body. This would help ensure that serious cases attracting the support of either body would be challenged through the proper legal procedures.

These changes would encourage other States to stay silent or take legal action, accordingly. The result would benefit the legitimacy of the Proposed Convention and the prospects of ADAJ for CAH crystallizing into customary international law.

13

The *Aut Dedere Aut Judicare* Provision in the Proposed Convention on Crimes Against Humanity: Assessment from a Chinese perspective

SHANG Weiwei[*] and ZHANG Yueyao[**]

13.1. Introduction

The obligation *aut dedere aut judicare* requires a State to extradite or prosecute a person found in its territory if the person is suspected of certain crimes. It is created to support international co-operation in fighting impunity for those crimes. There are over 60 multilateral treaties that contain an *aut dedere aut judicare* provision.[1] Yet when it comes to core international crimes, there is no treaty with this obligation for genocide, most crimes against humanity, or war crimes other than grave breaches.[2] The proposed International Convention on Prevention and Punishment of Crimes Against Humanity ('Proposed Convention') tends to narrow this gap by prescribing an obligation *aut dedere aut judicare* ('prosecute or extradite') in its Article 9.

---

[*]   **SHANG Weiwei** (LL.B., China University of Political Science and Law), is currently a master candidate in international law at Peking University, China and an intern in the Appeals Chamber of International Criminal Tribunal for the former Yugoslavia (ICTY).

[**] **ZHANG Yueyao** (LL.B., Peking University, M.A., Peking University, LL.M, University of California Berkeley), is currently a Ph.D. candidate in the Max-Planck Institute for Comparative Public Law and International Law, Heidelberg, Germany. During her studies in Peking University, she participated in the Human Rights Master Programme of Peking University Law School and Lund University Raoul Wallenberg Institute of Human Rights and Humanitarian Law. She is an editor of Peking University International and Comparative Law Review and of the Torkel Opsahl Academic EPublisher. All Internet references were last accessed on 25 August 2014.

[1]   Survey of multilateral conventions that may be of relevance for the work of the International Law Commission on the topic: The obligation to extradite or prosecute (*aut dedere aut judicare*), 18 June 2010, U.N. Doc. A/CN.4/630 ('U.N. Secretariat Survey'), para. 4.

[2]   Report of the Working Group on the Obligation to extradite or prosecute (*aut dedere aut judicare*), 22 July 2013, U.N. Doc. A/CN.4/L.829, para. 20.

China is party to 23 multilateral treaties with *aut dedere aut judicare* provisions.[3] While the obligation set out in some of those provisions are similar to that under Article 9 of the Proposed Convention, the latter contains a unique option of extradition to international judicial organs.

Mindful of China's general recognition of the need to ensure punishment of crimes against humanity, this chapter analyzes the relationship between prosecution and extradition, as well as the three alternatives entertained by Article 9 of the Proposed Convention, in light of China's domestic law and positions pronounced in international fora. Then it turns to China's possible concerns that may be caused by other articles in the Proposed Convention in the implementation of Article 9, and predicts that China may be reluctant to accept this regime for punishing crimes against humanity.

13.2. China's General Recognition of the Need to Ensure Punishment of Crimes Against Humanity

The need to ensure punishment of crimes against humanity by prosecution or extradition was declared in U.N. General Assembly Resolution 2840 (XXVI)[4] and Resolution 3074 (XXVIII)[5] in the 1970s. The Security Council has also adopted many resolutions regarding crimes against humanity and other core international crimes. While not usually prescribing an explicit obligation *aut dedere aut judicare*, those resolutions urge

---

[3] See the Annex to this chapter.

[4] Question of the punishment of war criminals and of persons who have committed crimes against humanity, 18 December 1971, U.N. Doc. A/Res/2840 (XXVI). In its para. 1, the resolution "urges all States [...] to put an end to and to prevent war crimes and crimes against humanity and to ensure the punishment of all persons guilty of such crimes, including their extradition to those countries where they have committed such crimes".

[5] Principles of international cooperation in the detection, arrest, extradition and punishment of persons guilty of war crimes and crimes against humanity, 3 December 1973, U.N. Doc. A/Res/3074 (XXVIII). Para. 5 of the resolution provides:

> Persons against whom there is evidence that they have committed war crimes and crimes against humanity shall be subject to trial and, if found guilty, to punishment, as a general rule in the country in which they committed those crimes. In that connection, States shall cooperate on questions of extraditing such persons.

States to put an end to impunity for crimes against humanity.[6] China voted for all of the resolutions above.[7]

In connection with the Draft Code of Crimes against the Peace and Security of Mankind, States discussed in detail the obligation to prosecute or extradite core international crimes, including crimes against humanity.[8] Although China did not submit specific comments regarding this issue, the record shows that the association of this obligation with crimes against humanity was not challenged.[9]

In a 2007 Statement regarding the International Law Commission ('ILC') report, China suggests crimes covered by the obligation *aut dedere aut judicare* should primarily include, among others, international crimes "endangering the common interest of the international community as confirmed by the international law". According to China, if the crime to which this obligation is applied is a crime under customary law *universally* acknowledged by the international community, the obligation to extradite or prosecute may also become an obligation under customary in-

---

[6]   Resolution 1318 (2000) of U.N. Security Council, 7 September 2000, U.N. Doc. S/RES/1318 (2000), at VI; Resolution 1325 (2000) U.N. Security Council, 31 October 2000, U.N. Doc. S/RES/1325 (2000), para. 11; Resolution 1379 (2001) of U.N. Security Council, 20 November 2001, U.N. Doc. S/RES/1379 (2001), para. 9(a); Resolution 1612 (2005) of U.N. Security Council, 26 July 2005, U.N. Doc. S/RES/1612 (2005), Preamble; Resolution 1674 (2006) of U.N. Security Council, 28 April 2006, U.N. Doc. S/RES/1674 (2006), para. 8; Resolution 1820 (2008) of U.N. Security Council, 19 June 2008, U.N. Doc. S/RES/1820 (2008), para. 4.

[7]   Study on relevant State declarations see Raphaël van Steenberghe, "The Obligation to Extradite or Prosecute – Clarifying its Nature", in *Journal of International Criminal Justice*, 2011, vol. 9, pp. 1100–1101.

[8]   Draft Code of Crimes Against the Peace and Security of Mankind, U.N. Doc. A/CN.4/L.532, Corr.1, Corr.3, 26 July 1996, Articles 9 and 18.

[9]   Twelfth Report on The Draft Code of Crimes Against the Peace and Security of Mankind, by Mr. Doudou Thiam, Special Rapporteur, 15 April 1994, U.N. Doc. A/CN.4/460 and Corr. 1, paras. 49–69.

ternational law.[10] In another Statement in 2012, China recognizes crimes against humanity as established international crimes.[11]

Through these documents and declarations, China repeatedly, although in a general sense, supports the application of the obligation *aut dedere aut judicare* to crimes against humanity. That being said, one should bear in mind that China holds a narrow definition and have reservations over the universality of this category of crime.[12]

13.3. Relationship between Prosecution and Extradition

13.3.1. Two Categories of Relationship

The *aut dedere aut judicare* provisions in international treaties ensure prosecution of the alleged offender either by the State requesting extradition or by the State where the individual is present. The relationship between extradition and prosecution in existing treaties can be classified into two categories: (i) an obligation to prosecute arises *ipso facto* when the alleged offender is present in the territory of the State. Once a request for extradition is made, the State concerned may be relieved of the obligation to prosecute by opting for extradition; and (ii) the obligation to prosecute is only triggered by the refusal to surrender the alleged offender following a request for extradition. It is also the obligation *aut dedere aut judicare* in its classic sense of the word.[13]

Examples of Category One *aut dedere aut judicare* obligation can be found in the relevant provisions of the 1949 Geneva Conventions and their 1977 Additional Protocol I, and the Convention against Torture and Other Cruel, Inhuman or Degrading Treatment or Punishment ('Torture

---

[10] "Statement by Mr. DUAN Jielong, Director-General of Treaty and Law Department, Ministry of Foreign Affairs of China, at the Sixth Committee of the 62nd Session of the U.N. General Assembly, on Item 82 'Report of the International Law Commission' (Reservations to Treaties, Shared Natural Resources, Obligation to Extradite or Prosecute)", 1 November 2007 ('DUAN 2007 Statement').

[11] "Statement by Mr. Li Linlin, Chinese Delegate at the Sixth Committee of the 67th Session of the UN General Assembly on Report of the International Law Commission on the Work of its 64th Session on 5 November 2012" ('LI 2012 Statement').

[12] United Nations Diplomatic Conference of Plenipotentiaries on the Establishment of an International Criminal Court Rome, 15 June–17 July 1998, Official Records, Volume II, Summary records of the plenary meetings and of the meetings of the Committee of the Whole ('Rome Conference Records, Volume II'), pp. 149, 299.

[13] U.N. Secretariat Survey, para. 126, *supra* note 1.

Convention').[14] The Draft Code of Offences against the Peace and Security of Mankind also contains a similar provision intended to create an obligation *ipso facto* to prosecute.[15] Article 9 of the Proposed Convention falls into this category:

Aut dedere aut judicare (Prosecute or Extradite)

1. Each State Party shall take necessary measures to establish its competence to exercise jurisdiction over crimes against humanity when the alleged offender is present in any territory under its jurisdiction, unless it extradites him or her to another State in accordance with its international obligations or surrenders him or her to the International Criminal Court, if it is a State Party to the Rome Statute, or to another international criminal tribunal whose jurisdiction it has recognized.

2. In the event that a State Party does not, for any reason not specified in the present Convention, prosecute a person suspected of committing crimes against humanity, it shall, pursuant to an appropriate request, either surrender such a person to another State willing to prosecute fairly and effectively, to the International Criminal Court, if it is a State Party to the Rome Statute, or to a competent international tribunal having jurisdiction over crimes against humanity.

Under the Category One obligation, where there is a lack of request for extradition, the obligation to prosecute is absolute. Once such a request is made, the custodial State has the discretion to choose between extradition and prosecution. The International Court of Justice ('ICJ') held in the *Obligation to Prosecute or Extradite* case that such an interpretation gives certain priority to prosecution by the custodial State.[16] It is in this sense that the term "obligation to prosecute or extradite" is used to

---

14 See Annex. of the Four 1949 Geneva Conventions, in UNTS, vol. 75, p. 287, entered into force on 21 October 1950, Articles 49, 50, 129, 146; 1977 Additional Protocol I, in UNTS, vol. 1125, p. 3, entered into force on 7 December 1979, Article 85; the wording of Article 7 of the Convention Against Torture is ambiguous, but it was interpreted by the Committee Against Torture and the International Court of Justice as imposing an obligation to prosecute independently from any request for extradition, CAT/C/36/D/181/2001, para. 9.7.; *Questions relating to the Obligation to Prosecute or Extradite (Belgium v. Senegal),* Judgment, 20 July 2012 (*'Obligation to Prosecute or Extradite* case'), para. 94. See also U.N. Secretariat Survey, *supra* note 1, paras. 128 and 130.

15 U.N. Secretariat Survey, para. 129, see *supra* note 1.

16 *Obligation to Prosecute or Extradite* case, para. 95, see *supra* note 14.

denote this first category, and "obligation to extradite or prosecute" the second category. The Latin tag *aut dedere aut judicare* may be used to indicate both categories and this type of obligation in general.[17]

13.3.2. Chinese Perspective on the Relationship

As mentioned above, China is party to various international conventions providing for an obligation *aut dedere aut judicare* similar to that under Article 9 of the Proposed Convention, such as the 1949 Geneva Conventions and their Additional Protocol I, and the Torture Convention.[18] Therefore China has no problem accepting the Category One obligation regarding certain crimes. In the meantime, its 2007 Statement on this topic, while supporting the alternative nature of the obligation *aut dedere aut judicare*, specifically points out that the State has free choice between prosecution and extradition.[19] China's position is arguably taken further by Judge XUE Hanqin in her Dissenting Opinion in the *Obligation to Prosecute or Extradite* case.

Judge XUE recognizes that the obligation to prosecute under the Torture Convention arises irrespective of a request for extradition, but considers the majority unduly accord more weight to the prosecution option and overlook the extradition alternative still available to the custodial State. In Judge XUE's view, the majority by restricting their examination to the prosecution option alone, arrive at the premature conclusion that Senegal violates its obligation *aut dedere aut judicare* as a whole. In particular, according to Judge XUE, even after Senegal has opted for prosecution but failed to implement it, so long as Belgium continues to make extradition requests and extradition is still a possibility, Senegal cannot be found in breach of its obligation *aut dedere aut judicare*.[20] It essentially

---

[17] It has been argued that the formula '*prose qui vel dedere*' or '*judicare vel dedere*' embodies more precisely Category One obligation, while '*aut dedere aut judicare*' is reserved for Category Two obligation in the classical sense of the term. This chapter uses '*aut dedere aut judicare*' in a general sense. See Belgium's comments submitted to the International Law Commission regarding the obligation to extradite or prosecute, A/CN.4/612, para. 15; Raphaël van Steenberghe, 2011, p. 1114, footnote 99, see *supra* note 7.

[18] See the list in the Annex to this chapter.

[19] DUAN 2007 Statement, see *supra* note 10.

[20] International Court of Justice, *Questions relating to the Obligation to Prosecute or Extradite (Belgium v. Senegal)*, Dissenting Opinion of Judge Xue Hanqin ('Dissenting Opinion, XUE'), paras. 35–38. A prominent Chinese scholar in extradition law deems the ICJ's interpretation of an *ipso facto* obligation to prosecute inconsistent with the ordinary meaning

means the custodial State can refuse to extradite *and* fail to prosecute, the renewed extradition requests will just keep it from violating the obligation *aut dedere aut judicare*.

Judge XUE's interpretation may or may not predict the evolution of China's position, it certainly expands the connotation of the alternative nature of the obligation. It differs from the classic version as regards *when* does the obligation to prosecute start. In her understanding, the starting time of the obligation to prosecute is at the discretion of the custodial State; whereas in the context of the Proposed Convention, the obligation starts once the alleged offender is found in the custodial State's territory, leaving States limited discretion on when to start the proceedings. Seen in this light, the alternative nature China has consistently emphasized may be sovereign States' discretion as to whether and when to prosecute the alleged offender without any external interference.

13.4. The Prosecution Alternative

13.4.1. Domestic Legislation and Rules in China

In 1992, the obligation *aut dedere aut judicare* was first dealt with in an internal document titled 'Rules Regarding Several Questions Encountered in Processing Extradition Cases' issued jointly by the Ministry of Foreign Affairs, the Supreme People's Court, the Supreme People's Procuratorate, the Ministry of Public Security and the Ministry of Justice of China ('the Rules'). The Rules is not law proper, but may be an important source of reference for extradition-related work within the Chinese government before the adoption of Extradition Law in 2000.[21] It may also be the only domestic document that gives guidance on the implementation of the obligation *aut dedere aut judicare*. According to the Rules, where the decision is made not to extradite the alleged author of crimes for which China has treaty obligations to extradite or prosecute, such alleged offender

---

of the text of the Torture Convention. 《或引渡或起诉》, 黄风著, 中国政法大学出版社, 2013 年, 第 145 页 (HUANG Feng, *Aut dedere aut judicare*, China University of Political Science and Law Press, 2013, p. 145).

[21] 中华人民共和国引渡法 (Extradition Law of the People's Republic of China), adopted on 28 December 2000 at the 19th meeting of the Standing Committee General Assembly by the National People's Congress of the PRC.

should be brought to competent judicial organs with the view to prosecution.[22]

The obligation to prosecute requires strong legal commitments from States Parties. It is conditioned on two premises: (i) the prohibited conduct is criminalized under domestic law; and (ii) the national courts are empowered with necessary jurisdiction over those crimes, which usually implies recognition of extraterritorial jurisdiction, including universal jurisdiction as provided for in the Proposed Convention.[23]

These two premises were missing in the Chinese law for a long time, even after China had entered into international obligations to prosecute certain crimes. For example, genocide and most war crimes are not included in China's Criminal Law, despite of China's ratification of the Convention on the Prevention and Punishment of the Crime of Genocide ('Genocide Convention') in 1983[24] and of the 1949 Geneva Conventions and their Additional Protocol I respectively in 1956 and 1983.[25] Nor did the Criminal Law provide for extraterritorial jurisdiction at the relevant time. Although the Chinese Constitution does not define the relationship between international law and domestic law, which leaves the question open whether international treaties have automatic application in domestic courts, the legislative gap was acutely felt in the actual implementation of

---

[22] 外交部、最高人民法院、最高人民检察院、公安部、司法部关于印发《关于办理引渡案件若干问题的规定》的通知 (Rules regarding Several Questions Encountered in Processing Extradition Cases issued jointly by the Foreign Affairs Ministry, Supreme Court, Supreme Procuratorate, Public Security Ministry, and Justice Ministry of PRC), 23 April 1992, available at http://www.law-lib.com/law/law_view.asp?id=8562; see also 黄风 (HUANG Feng), *supra* note 20, p. 61.

[23] The Proposed Convention, Article 8 'Obligations of States Parties', Section A 'Legislation and Penalties'.

[24] Convention on the Prevention and Punishment of the Crime of Genocide, in UNTS, vol. 78, p. 277, entered into force on 12 January 1951. Although the Genocide Convention does not include an *aut dedere aut judicare* provision, its Articles V and VI require criminalization of genocide offences under national law and prosecution by the territorial State,

[25] 中华人民共和国刑法 (Criminal Law of PRC), entered into force on 1 July 1979, amended on 14 March 1997. Chapter X of the Chinese Criminal Law deals with crimes committed by servicemen in wartime. Some provisions may be said to liken war crimes, but in a very limited manner: Article 444 (abandoning wounded or sick soldiers of Chinese armed forces), Article 445 (refusing to treat serviceman of the Chinese armed forces), Article 446 (attacking or plundering innocent residents), and Article 448 (maltreatment of prisoners of war).

---

the obligation *aut dedere aut judicare*.[26] In order to solve this problem, in 1997, the Criminal Law of China was amended to include Article 9, which reads:

> This Law is applicable to the crimes prescribed in the international treaties concluded or acceded to by the People's Republic of China and over which the People's Republic of China has criminal jurisdiction within its obligation in accordance with the treaties.

It is China's official position that this one-sentence article constitutes the legal basis for the exercise of universal jurisdiction over crimes prescribed in the Torture Convention.[27] In its latest report submitted to the Committee Against Torture, China maintains that the principle *aut dedere aut judicare* laid down in the Torture Convention is in keeping with the Chinese criminal justice system.[28] Chinese scholars have pointed out that Article 9 may solve the problem of universal jurisdiction, but whether it can import singlehandedly treaty crimes for the purpose of prosecution is questionable.[29] Article 3 on principle of legality, added to the Criminal Law at the same time as Article 9, reads as follows: "An act which is explicitly criminalised by law shall be convicted and punished in accordance with law; otherwise, it shall not be convicted or punished". The term "law" may be interpreted as including international treaties China has concluded, so that the crime itself may be established. However, given that international conventions do not prescribe penalty for concerned crimes, the punishment is inevitably left to randomness. It has also been

---

[26] Ma Chengyuan, "The Connotation of Universal Jurisdiction and its Application in the Criminal Law of PRC", in Morten Bergsmo and LING Yan (eds.), *State Sovereignty and International Criminal Law*, Torkel Opsahl Academic EPublisher, Beijing, 2012, p. 181 (www.legal-tools.org/doc/a634d0/).

[27] The Third Periodic Report on Implementation of Convention Against Torture and Other Cruel, Inhuman or Degrading Treatment or Punishment, submitted to Committee Against Torture by the Government of China, 5 January 2000, CAT/C/39/Add.2, para. 15.

[28] 中华人民共和国执行《禁止酷刑和其他残忍、不人道或有辱人格的待遇或处罚公约》的第六次报告 (The Sixth Periodic Report on the Implementation of the Convention against Torture and Other Cruel, Inhuman or Degrading Treatment or Punishment, submitted to Committee Against Torture by the Government of China), 4 April 2014, CAT/C/CHN/5, para. 46, restating the position in the Supplementary Report submitted to Committee Against Torture, 18 January 1993, CAT/C/7/Add.14, para. 90.

[29] See, *e.g.*, MA Chengyuan, 2012, pp. 185–186, *supra* note 26.

argued that prosecution of international crimes under the name of existing ordinary crimes would violate the principle of prohibition of analogy.[30]

13.4.2. Relevant Chinese Practice Regarding Other Crimes and Implications for Crimes Against Humanity

Even before the adoption of Article 9, in a special case, a Chinese court had already applied international treaties directly. In 1985, a Soviet pilot hijacked a civil aircraft to China to seek asylum. China was then party to the Hague Convention for the Suppression of Unlawful Seizure of Aircraft and Convention for the Suppression of Unlawful Acts against Safety of Civil Aviation, both containing *aut dedere aut judicare* provisions. After taking control of this pilot, China chose to prosecute him instead of extraditing him to the Soviet Union. Given that unlawful seizure of aircraft was not criminalized under domestic law,[31] the court relied on the aforementioned treaties and "relevant domestic law" to reach the conviction and sentenced the pilot to eight years in prison.[32]

This case may be one of its kind. It was operated out of a political need to show judicial competence, even with a bit of a stretch for the latter. It would arguably be more difficult for today's courts to do so, with greater consciousness of the principle of legality and under closer watch of the rest of the world. The justification provided by Article 9 has its limitations, as is discussed above.

Combining China's official position and scholar interpretations of Article 9 of the Criminal Law with the case predating it, it can be said that the prosecution of those non-incorporated crimes, including crimes against humanity when need be, would be controversial but not impossible. In any case, interest to incorporate core international crimes into the

---

[30] *Ibid.*, pp. 184–187.

[31] The crime of unlawful seizure of aircraft was criminalized by the 'Decision of the Standing Committee of the National People's Congress Regarding the Punishment of Criminals Engaged in Aircraft Hijacking' in 1992, and subsequently incorporated into the Criminal Law by an amendment in 1997. The Decision is available at http://en.pkulaw.cn/display.aspx?cgid=6078&lib=law; the comparison table of the 1979 and 1997 versions of the Criminal Law is available at http://www.pkulaw.cn/bzk/compare.aspx?cid=186.

[32] 张持坚："揭秘 23 年前苏联客机遭劫持迫降中国事件"，2008 年 11 月 3 日 (ZHANG Chijian, 'Forced Landing of Hijacked Soviet Civil Aircraft in China 23 Years Ago', 3 November 2008). The "relevant domestic law" relied on by the court is not specified in the report. See also 黄风 (HUANG Feng), 2013, p. 63, *supra* note 20.

Criminal Law is lacking because of their unlikely application in China. As there is no domestic legislation on crimes against humanity, an Article 9-based prosecution would be the only choice when such a need arises.

13.4.3. The Obligation to Prosecute and the *Obligation to Prosecute or Extradite* Case Before the ICJ

The discussion over the obligation to prosecute features the *Obligation to Prosecute or Extradite* Judgment by the ICJ. It serves as an important source of reference regarding the scope and extent of this obligation. In this case, since Senegal claims it has opted for prosecution, the Court turns to examine whether measures taken by Senegal fulfil the obligation to prosecute under the Torture Convention, in particular, whether there is undue delay in initiating proceedings against the former Chadian president Hissène Habré.[33]

The Court considers it implicit in the text of Article 7(1) of the Torture Convention that the obligation to prosecute must be implemented within a reasonable time, in a manner compatible with the Convention's object and purpose "to make more effective the struggle against torture".[34] According to the Court, Senegal's delay in initiating proceedings against Habré since the first complaint in 2000 constitutes a breach of such an obligation.[35] Other intervening factors in the interval period, such as referral to the African Union and judgment of the ECOWAS Court, do not justify the delay.[36]

Judge XUE disagrees with this approach. First, she highlights that establishment of universal jurisdiction required by Article 5(2) is the precondition for implementing the obligation to prosecute under Article 7(1). Senegal's violation of the obligation to prosecute before 2007 is the logical consequence of its violation of Article 5(2).[37] Given that Senegal had acknowledged its breach of Article 5(2) before 2007, Judge XUE holds that the relevant time for the consideration whether Senegal has breached

---

[33] *Obligation to Prosecute or Extradite* case, para. 109, see *supra* note 14.

[34] *Ibid.*, para. 115.

[35] *Ibid.*, paras. 114–117.

[36] *Ibid.*, paras. 111–112.

[37] Dissenting Opinion, XUE, paras. 25–27, see *supra* note 20.

its obligation under Article 7(1) should start from 2007, rather than 2000.[38]

Second, she observes that according to the majority opinion, Belgium's request for extradition essentially serves to monitor the implementation of Senegal's obligation to prosecute, which is beyond the legal framework of the Torture Convention. She underlines that Article 7(1) does not entitle the State requesting extradition to *urge* the requested State to prosecute.[39] She also points out that in any event, the decision of the ECOWAS Court constitutes a legal justification for possible delay of proceedings before Senegalese courts.[40]

Indeed, taking the majority's approach, where a State Party has breached Article 5(2), it will usually continue to be in breach of Article 7(1) *after* it establishes the necessary jurisdiction and even commences on the required proceedings – the latter just cannot come soon enough with the time consumed by legislative amendment. Thus for States Parties who are not adequately equipped to implement the obligation to prosecute, acceding to extradition request at the very beginning seems to be the wise choice.

Judge XUE's concern over the monitoring effect of Belgium's claim is inseparable from the issue of States Parties' standing to invoke the responsibility of another State Party for breach of Article 7(1), which will be discussed in section 13.6. Her specific emphasis on the custodial State's discretion in conducting the prosecution, such as deciding its timeframe, coincides with China's position on non-interference. The majority's approach in assessing the obligation to prosecute renders China susceptible to accusations of breaching its obligation to prosecute, in light of the latter's unsatisfying criminalization of conduct prohibited by international treaties.

The comprehensive debate within the ICJ regarding the obligation to prosecute reveals points of contention that may arise in its application. It helps to inform States when positioning themselves in this matter, especially for consideration of future *aut dedere aut judicare* provisions.

In general, China has limited potential to realize the prosecution alternative regarding crimes against humanity – Article 9 of the Criminal

---

[38] *Ibid.*, paras. 27–28.
[39] *Ibid.*, para. 39.
[40] *Ibid.*, para. 43.

Law is more symbolic than plausible. It is all the more reason that China insists on ultimate 'discretion' – whatever that means – in interpreting and applying the *aut dedere aut judicare* provisions.

13.5. The Extradition Alternative

The Extradition Law passed in 2000 sets out China's legal regime for extradition.[41] This section examines provisions in the Extradition Law that are relevant to the current discussion, namely, Article 9 and those on double criminality, non-extradition of nationals, procedure of extradition and authorities involved; and assesses their implications for the extradition alternative provided for in the Proposed Convention.

Article 9 (1) of the Chinese Extradition Law reads as follows:

> If China has criminal jurisprudence over the offence indicated in the request and criminal proceedings are being instituted against the person or preparations are being made for such proceedings, the request for extradition made by a foreign state to China may be rejected.[42]

The commentary of this article explains that if China agrees to extradite the suspect, China shall give up the criminal jurisdiction to the claimed offence and terminate all criminal suits concerning the offense.[43] The Extradition Law requires double criminality for a conduct to be extraditable, that is, the conduct indicated in the request for extradition constitutes an offence under the laws of both China and the requesting State.[44] The decision over the criminality of a conduct for the purpose of extradition is less drastic than an actual conviction. In this sense, Article 9 of the Criminal Law may be a better basis for implementing the obligation of extradition than prosecution regarding conduct prohibited by interna-

---

[41] Before the 1990s, due to lack of domestic regime, China had difficulties in implementing extradition obligations under international treaties. For example, when acceding to the Additional Protocol I of the 1949 Geneva Conventions, China made the following reservation: "At present, Chinese legislation has no provisions concerning extradition, and deals with this matter on a case-by-case basis. For this reason China does not accept the stipulations of Article 88, paragraph 2, of Protocol I". See also 黄风 (HUANG Feng), p. 60, *supra* note 20.

[42] Extradition Law, see *supra* note 21.

[43] National People's Congress Commentary of the Extradition Law of China, Article 9(1), available at http://www.npc.gov.cn/npc/flsyywd/xingfa/2002-07/15/content_297580.htm.

[44] Extradition Law, Article 7(1), see *supra* note 21.

tional treaties to which China is a party but not criminalized under Chinese law. The aforementioned 1992 Rules already declare that crimes towards which China has the obligation *aut dedere aut judicare* under international treaties should be regarded as extraditable.[45] For example, to grant a hypothetical extradition request over genocide offences, the Genocide Convention, to which China is a party, may be relied on in deciding the criminality of the concerned conduct.[46]

The decision whether a request meets conditions for extradition is made by the court, on the basis of the Extradition Law and international treaties. It is subsequently transmitted to the Ministry of Foreign Affairs. When the court adjudicates that relevant conditions are not met, the Ministry shall deny the request for extradition; when the court holds that conditions are met, the case is referred to the State Council for final approval.[47] The question of immunity, which often arises with regard to core international crimes, including crimes against humanity, may emerge already before the court and continue to influence the decision-making if the case goes to the State Council. This issue will be discussed in the last section of this chapter.

Where the court or State Council denies the request for extradition, the law requires the immediate termination of the compulsory measures against the alleged offender.[48] No subsequent proceedings against the alleged offender pursuant to *aut dedere aut judicare* are contemplated in the Extradition Law. Here the aforementioned 1992 Rules should be considered in order to decide whether the end of the extradition procedure may be the beginning of domestic proceedings as a result of application of the obligation *aut dedere aut judicare* regarding certain crimes. In its report to the Committee Against Torture, China specifically mentions that where parties to extradition treaties refuse to extradite their own nationals, the custodial State *must* submit its nationals to competent authorities with the view to prosecution.[49]

---

[45] Rules regarding Several Questions Encountered in Processing Extradition Cases, Article 6, see *supra* note 22.

[46] Although in any event, conducts contemplated in core international crimes may find analogy in ordinary crimes under domestic law, thus satisfy the criminality requirement.

[47] Extradition Law, Articles 22–29, see *supra* note 21.

[48] *Ibid.*, Articles 28–29.

[49] 中华人民共和国执行《禁止酷刑和其他残忍、不人道或有辱人格的待遇或处罚公约》的第六次报告 (The Sixth Periodic Report on the Implementation of the Convention

There is ample Chinese practice of extradition pursuant to the obligation *aut dedere aut judicare* regarding ordinary crimes with an international nexus and transnational offences whose perpetration may affect international communication between States.[50] Judicial co-operation in punishing these crimes is the priority of the domestic authorities. Practice regarding core international crimes seldom has occasion to rise and is not much discussed in the domestic context.

Generally, extradition induces a less strenuous judicial burden than prosecution. The Chinese legislation and practice provide more room for manoeuvre in extradition than prosecution when it comes to crimes set out in treaties to which China is a party but which are not incorporated into Chinese criminal law.

13.6. The Third Alternative of Transfer to International Judicial Organs

Article 9 of the Proposed Convention adds the International Criminal Court ('ICC') and other international criminal tribunals to the destinations of transfers, as does Article 1 of the Draft Rules on the Obligation to Extradite or Prosecute proposed by the Special Rapporteur before the ILC. China expressed caution over this so-called 'third alternative' in its 2007 Statement.[51]

Taking the ICC for example, its States Parties are already under the obligation to give priority to the request of the ICC over that of other States Parties, or even non-States Parties if the requested State has no international obligation to extradite the person to those States. During the negotiation of the ICC Statute, China put forward a proposal requiring the requested State, in case of parallel requests, to give priority to the requesting State over the ICC, unless the matter is referred to the ICC by the Security Council. Notably, China's proposal also underlines the need to ensure prosecution of the alleged offender: the requested State should either

---

Against Torture and Other Cruel, Inhuman or Degrading Treatment or Punishment, submitted to Committee Against Torture by the Government of China), para. 46, *supra* note 28.

[50] 黄风 (HUANG Feng), 2013, pp. 66–69, see *supra* note 20. For a classification of crimes to which the obligation *aut dedere aut judicare* applies, see Raphaël van Steenberghe, pp. 1111–1115, *supra* note 7.

[51] DUAN 2007 Statement, see *supra* note 10.

transfer the person to the ICC or to another State, or refer the case to its competent authorities for the purpose of prosecution.[52]

This Chinese proposal must be viewed in light of China's position on the jurisdiction of the ICC. First, China considers crimes against humanity should be associated with armed conflicts.[53] Second, China repeatedly emphasizes that the ICC's jurisdiction should be conditioned on consent of *both* the State of nationality and the territorial State.[54] China criticized Article 12 of the ultimate ICC Statute, which only requires consent from one of these States to establish jurisdiction, as violating the sovereignty of States Parties and imposing obligations on non-States Parties.[55] Thus the option to transfer the alleged offender to the ICC in the Chinese proposal is premised on the consents of both the State of nationality and the territorial State, without further competing requests for extradition from any other States claiming jurisdiction. Plus the definition of crimes against humanity held by China is much narrower than that set out in the ICC Statute and the Proposed Convention.[56]

True, the 'third alternative' does not increase the risk of jurisdictional claims of the territorial State and State of nationality beyond the existing regime of the ICC Statute. But acceding to such a provision may constitute recognition of the ICC's exercise of jurisdiction over crimes against humanity without consent from the aforementioned States.

To counterbalance such an undesirable effect, China deemed it necessary in its 2007 Statement to set limits to the alternative obligations of States. In particular, China suggested that in opting for extradition or prosecution, States should prioritise territorial jurisdiction and personal jurisdiction.[57]

Additionally, the 'third alternative' may be a well-regarded solution to certain practical difficulties. In her Dissenting Opinion in the *Obligation to Prosecute or Extradite* case, Judge XUE advocated the possibility

---

52 United Nations Diplomatic Conference of Plenipotentiaries on the Establishment of an International Criminal Court Rome, 15 June–17 July 1998, Official Records, Volume III, Reports and other documents, p. 336.

53 Rome Conference Records, Volume II, pp. 124, 149, see *supra* note 12.

54 *Ibid.*, Comments by Mr. LIU Daqun, pp.123, 323 and 362.

55 *Ibid.*

56 Article 7, Rome Statute of the International Criminal Court, in UNTS, vol. 2187, p. 90, entered into force on July 1 2002; Article 3, Proposed Convention.

57 DUAN 2007 Statement, see *supra* note 10.

of extraditing Habré to an *ad hoc* tribunal set up by the African Union.[58] Although the position was taken uniquely under the circumstances of that case, it illustrates a sensible option to garner financial and political support to effectively end impunity.

13.7. Standing of States Parties to Bring Potential Breach of the Obligation Before the ICJ

The ICJ recognizes that States Parties to the Torture Convention have a common interest to ensure those who commit acts of torture do not enjoy impunity. The obligation *aut dedere aut judicare* under Article 7(1), as an essential means to achieve that goal, is owed by any State Party to all the other States Parties to the Torture Convention. It is regarded as an obligation *erga omnes partes*. In reaching this conclusion, the Court also draws analogy to similar provisions in the Genocide Convention.[59]

It is based on the *erga omnes partes* nature of this obligation that the ICJ deduces the entitlement of each State Party to make a claim concerning the cessation of an alleged breach by another State Party, which serves as the foundation of Belgium's claim in that case.[60]

In her Dissenting Opinion, Judge XUE considers the mere fact that States Parties have a common interest in the observance of the obligation *aut dedere aut judicare* does not give them the standing to bring a claim before the Court. Only States "specifically affected" by the breach are qualified to do so.[61]

Where to draw the line in granting the standing has direct bearing on the chances of States Parties being challenged before the ICJ. It is true that if a special interest were required for that purpose, in many cases no State would be in the position to claim a potential breach by a State Party,[62] however grave it is. What may be equally true is that the possibility for every State Party to take a potential breach to the ICJ opens the gate to many claims.

---

[58] *Obligation to Prosecute or Extradite* case, paras. 42–47, see *supra* note 14.
[59] *Ibid.*, para.68.
[60] *Ibid.*, para. 69.
[61] Dissenting Opinion, XUE, paras. 11–23, see *supra* note 20.
[62] *Obligation to Prosecute or Extradite* case, para. 69, see *supra* note 14.

The latter possibility is almost anathema to China, at multiple levels, given its reluctance to engage in international judicial proceedings and its consistent emphasis on non-interference and stability of international order. China's position is made abundantly clear by its reservation to Article 30(1) of the Torture Convention, which provides for compulsory dispute resolution through arbitration or before the ICJ.[63] The dispute resolution clause in the Proposed Convention draws on Article 30(1) of the Torture Convention, its relevance to the current discussion will be examined in the next section.

13.8. Immunity and the Obligation *Aut Dedere Aut Judicare* under the Proposed Convention

In 2005, the Security Council referred the Darfur situation to the ICC.[64] The ICC subsequently issued two arrest warrants for Omar Al Bashir, the President of Sudan, holding that there were reasonable grounds to believe Bashir had committed crimes within the jurisdiction of the ICC, including crimes against humanity.[65] In 2011, Bashir visited China with the arrest warrants for him pending. In defending Bashir's visit, China expressed serious reservations over ICC's prosecution of Bashir and considered it detrimental to the peace and stability of the region.[66]

When discussing the obligation *aut dedere aut judicare*, the question of immunity is the elephant in the room. The Proposed Convention unequivocally lifts any immunity accorded to State officials regarding

---

[63] Article 30(1) reads:

> Any dispute between two or more States Parties concerning the interpretation or application of this Convention which cannot be settled through negotiation shall, at the request of one of them, be submitted to arbitration. If within six months from the date of the request for arbitration the Parties are unable to agree on the organization of the arbitration, any one of those Parties may refer the dispute to the International Court of Justice by request in conformity with the Statute of the Court.

[64] Security Council refers situation in Darfur, Sudan to the Prosecutor of the International Criminal Court (Resolution 1593 Adopted by Vote of 11 in favour to none against, with 4 abstentions of Algeria, Brazil, China, United States), 31 March 2005, S/RES/1593(2005), available at http://www.un.org/News/Press/docs/2005/sc8351.doc.htm.

[65] International Criminal Court, *Prosecutor v. Omar Hassan Ahmad Al Bashir*, Warrant of Arrest, 4 March 2009, ICC-02/05-01/09-1; International Criminal Court, *Prosecutor v. Omar Hassan Ahmad Al Bashir*, Warrant of Arrest II, 12 July 2010, ICC-02/05-01/09-1.

[66] "Foreign Ministry Spokesperson HONG Lei, regular press conference of 28 June 2011", available at http://karachi.chineseconsulate.org/eng/fyrth/t835066.htm.

---

crimes against humanity, either before national or international courts. This principle combined with the obligation to prosecute or extradite, if applied to Bashir's visit, would run counter to Article 11 of the Chinese Criminal Law, which exempts foreign nationals vested with immunity from China's criminal jurisdiction.[67]

On the correlation (or no) between the obligation and immunity, China emphasizes that "the application of the obligation to extradite or prosecute should not compromise the judicial jurisdiction of States, nor should it affect the immunity of State officials from criminal judicial jurisdiction".[68] This position is supported by the ICJ, who holds in the *Obligation to Prosecute or Extradite* Judgment that the obligation to prosecute or extradite regarding serious crimes does not create exception to immunity before national courts.[69]

Specifically on immunity and crimes against humanity, in a 2012 declaration, China, while recognizing crimes against humanity are established international crimes, believes customary international law neither excludes the immunity of State officials from foreign jurisdiction, nor recognizes any exceptions to that immunity. China refers to means provided by the ICJ in the *Arrest Warrant* case to ensure substantive responsibilities of the State official over international crimes.[70]

China's stake in these matters is not imaginary. Among overseas criminal proceedings against current or former Chinese officials, crimes against humanity may be a convenient choice for the prosecution. All those attempts before foreign national courts, like the overwhelming majority of similar cases concerning State officials of other countries, have not been successful or even remotely so.[71] Yet such threat to the dignity of

---

[67] Criminal Law of China, see *supra* note 25, Article 11 reads as follows: "The problem of criminal responsibility of foreigners who enjoy diplomatic privileges and impunity is to be resolved through diplomatic channels".

[68] DUAN 2007 Statement, see *supra* note 10.

[69] *Obligation to Prosecute or Extradite* case, supra note 14, paras. 58–59.

[70] Li 2012 Statement, see *supra* note 11. See also, HUANG Huikang, "On Immunity of State Officials from Foreign Criminal Jurisdiction", in *Chinese Journal of International Law*, 2014, vol. 13, no. 1 (the author is Member of the International Law Commission, former Director-General of the Department of Treaty and Law of the Ministry of Foreign Affairs of China).

[71] Second Report on Immunity of State Officials From Foreign Criminal Jurisdiction, Roman Anatolevich Kolodkin, Special Rapporteur, International Law Commission, 10 June 2010, A/CN.4/631, footnote 19. In Spain in the period 2008–2009, investigations were launched

State certainly contributes to China's sentiment towards crimes against humanity and entrenches its determination to maintain strict immunity.[72] In his comments on the topic 'crimes against humanity' added to the ILC's agenda, the Chinese member underlines "the complexity and sensitivity of this topic", and suggests the Commission to deal with it "in a prudent manner and avoid any pre-determined results before wide consensus is reached by States".[73]

In sum, from the Chinese perspective, it seems the obligation *aut dedere aut judicare* cannot be compatible with the principle of irrelevance of official capacity as defined in the Proposed Convention, either as a matter of domestic law or in terms of her inter-State communications. The recognition of the obligation *aut dedere aut judicare* will only make the need to assert immunity more pressing. In light of the compulsory dispute resolution mechanism in the Proposed Convention,[74] and the general standing of other States Parties to invoke the responsibility of the State Party in breach of this obligation, as sustained by the ICJ,[75] China would be vulnerable to international proceedings under the regime of the Proposed Convention. And the prohibition of reservations in the Proposed Convention provides no exit from this dilemma.[76]

---

in connection with charges of having committed crimes against humanity and genocide in Tibet brought against high-ranking officials and politicians in China (the former President of China JIANG Zemin, Defence Minister LIANG Guanglie and others). In view of changes in Spain's legislation which restricted the scope of 'universal jurisdiction', the cases were abandoned. (*El Pais*, 27 February 2010.) A warrant was also issued in Argentina in December 2009 for the arrest of JIANG Zemin and the head of the security service LUO Gan on charges of crimes against humanity which had manifested themselves in persecution of the Falun Gong movement. See "Argentina judge asks China arrests over Falun Gong", 22 December 2009, available at http://www.reuters.com/article/2009/12/23/us-argentina-china-falungong-idUSTRE5BM02B 2009 1223.

[72] "Foreign Ministry Spokesperson Hua Chunying", regular press conference of 11 Feburary 2014, available at http://si.chineseembassy.org/eng/fyrth/t1127523.htm.

[73] "Statement by Mr. Huang Huikang Director-General of the Department of Treaty and Law of the Ministry of Foreign Affairs of China At the 68th Session of the UN General Assembly On Agenda Item 81 Report of the 65th Session of the International Law Commission (Part 1) on 30 October 2013", available at http://www.china-un.org/eng/hyyfy/t1095251.htm.

[74] Article 26, the Proposed Convention.

[75] See *supra* Section 6.

[76] Article 23, the Proposed Convention.

13.9. Conclusion

China generally considers the obligation *aut dedere aut judicare* an adequate means to ensure punishment of crimes, including crimes against humanity. Article 9 of the Chinese Criminal Law establishes the necessary albeit controversial jurisdiction over crimes set out in international treaties to which China is a party but which are not incorporated into Chinese law. In the implementation of the obligation *aut dedere aut judicare*, China has abundant practice regarding other crimes of international concern, but seldom core international crimes. There is also a lack of interest in taking up the latter matter in China.

China's acceptance of the *aut dedere aut judicare* provision in the Proposed Convention may be limited by China's position on crimes against humanity proper and the 'third alternative' to transfer to international judicial organs. The former depends on the evolvement of China's perspective,[77] and the latter can be cured with further qualification to the 'third alternative'. None of these two represent insurmountable obstacles.

Concerns may be derived from the strict overall regime crafted by the Proposed Convention, where the articles on irrelevance of official capacity and compulsory dispute resolution significantly increase the burden of implementing the obligation *aut dedere aut judicare*, to the extent of contradicting the domestic law and international practice of China.

---

[77] For example, Judge LIU Daqun of the ICTY observed the trend of development of customary international law to recognize crimes against humanity regardless of its association with armed conflicts. 见李世光、刘大群、凌岩主编：《国际刑事法院罗马规约评释》，北京大学出版社，2006 年版，第 79–80 页 (see LI Shiguang, LIU Daqun, LING Yan (eds.), *The International Criminal Court: A Commentary on the Rome Statute*, Peking University Press, 2006, pp. 79–80).

Annex: Twenty-Three Multilateral Treaties With *Aut Dedere Aut Judicare* Provisions to Which China is a State Party

1. Geneva Convention for the Amelioration of the Condition of the Wounded and Sick in Armed Forces in the Field of 12 August 1949, Article 49, ratified by Chinese National People's Congress Standing Committee on 5 November 1956.

2. Geneva Convention for the Amelioration of the Condition of Wounded, Sick and Shipwrecked Members of Armed Forces at Sea of 12 August 1949, Article 50, ratified by Chinese National People's Congress Standing Committee on 5 November 1956.

3. Geneva Convention relative to the Treatment of Prisoners of War of 12 August 1949, Article 129, ratified by Chinese National People's Congress Standing Committee on 5 November 1956.

4. Geneva Convention relative to the Protection of Civilian Persons in Time of War of 12 August 1949, Article 146, ratified by Chinese National People's Congress Standing Committee on 5 November 1956.

5. 1970 Hague Convention for the Suppression of Unlawful Seizure of Aircraft, Articles 4, 6 and 7, ratified by Chinese National People's Congress Standing Committee on 10 September 1980.

6. 1971 Convention for the Suppression of Unlawful Acts against Safety of Civil Aviation, Articles 5, 6 and 7, ratified by Chinese National People's Congress Standing Committee on 10 September 1980.

7. Protocol Additional to the Geneva Conventions of 12 August 1949, and Relating to the Protection of Victims of International Armed Conflicts (Protocol I), of 8 June 1977, Article 88, ratified by Chinese National People's Congress Standing Committee on 2 September 1983.

8. 1971 Convention on Psychotropic Substances, Article 22, ratified by Chinese National People's Congress Standing Committee on 18 June 1985.

9. Single Convention on Narcotic Drugs, 1961, as amended by the 1972 Protocol Amending the Single Convention on Narcotic Drugs, 1961, Article 36, ratified by Chinese National People's Congress Standing Committee on 18 June 1985.

10. 1973 Convention on the Prevention and Punishment of Crimes against Internationally Protected Persons, including Diplomatic Agents, Articles 3, 6 and 7, ratified by Chinese National People's Congress Standing Committee on 23 June 1987.

11. 1984 Convention Against Torture and other Cruel, Inhuman or Degrading Treatment or Punishment, Articles 5, 6 and 7, ratified by Chinese National People's Congress Standing Committee on 5 September 1988.

12. Convention on the Physical Protection of Nuclear Material, Articles 8, 9 and 10, ratified by Chinese National People's Congress Standing Committee on 2 December 1988.

13. United Nations Convention against Illicit Traffic in Narcotic Drugs and Psychotropic Substances of 1988, Articles 4 and 6, ratified by Chinese National People's Congress Standing Committee on 4 September 1989.

14. 1988 Convention for the Suppression of Unlawful Acts Against the Safety of Maritime Navigation, Articles 5, 6, 7 and 10, ratified by Chinese National People's Congress Standing Committee on 29 June 1991.

15. 1988 Protocol for the Suppression of Unlawful Acts Against the Safety of Fixed Platforms Located on the Continental Shelf, Article 3, ratified by Chinese National People's Congress Standing Committee on 29 June 1991.

16. 1979 Convention against the Taking of Hostages, Articles 5, 6, 7 and 8, ratified by Chinese National People's Congress Standing Committee on 28 December 1992.

17. 1997 International Convention for the Suppression of Terrorist Bombings, Articles 6, 7 and 8, ratified by Chinese National People's Congress Standing Committee on 27 October 2001.

18. Optional Protocol to the Convention on the Rights of the Child on the Sale of Children, Child Prostitution and Child Pornography, Articles 4 and 5, ratified by Chinese National People's Congress Standing Committee on 29 August 2002.

19. United Nations Convention Against Transnational Organized Crime, Articles 15 and 16, ratified by Chinese National People's Congress

Standing Committee on 27 August 2003.

20. 1999 International Convention for the Suppression of the Financing of Terrorism, Articles 7, 9 and 10, ratified by Chinese National People's Congress Standing Committee on 28 February 2004.

21. Convention on the Safety of United Nations and Associated Personnel, Articles 10, 13 and 14, ratified by Chinese National People's Congress Standing Committee on 28 August 2004.

22. United Nations Convention Against Corruption, Articles 42 and 44, ratified by Chinese National People's Congress Standing Committee on 27 October 2005.

23. 2005 Convention for the Suppression of Acts of Nuclear Terrorism, Articles 9, 10 and 11, ratified by Chinese National People's Congress Standing Committee on 28 August 2008.

14

_____

The Proposed Convention on the Prevention and Punishment of Crimes Against Humanity: Developments and Deficiencies

Tessa Bolton[*]

Never send to know for whom the bell tolls; it tolls for thee.

– John Donne (1624)

To commit crimes against humanity ('CAH') is to divest the individual of essential dignity of personhood, cheapening the worth of being, and hence disenfranchising the human whole. Each regime of widespread and systematic attacks not only claims personal victims in unbearable numbers, it also victimizes humankind, barbarising and brutalising our nature and extending the realm of our potential cruelty. Wherever the occurrence, crimes against humanity are made universal by the "common conscience of mankind. They are *jus cogens*".[1]

It is therefore difficult to acknowledge that there remains, still, no international convention aimed solely at defining, preventing, and prosecuting CAH, even 60 years after the crime of genocide was accordingly codified. There exist several reasons that necessitate the creation of such a convention, and I shall attempt to detail some of them below.

In the first section, I shall ask why there is a necessity for a convention regarding crimes against humanity, including issues of *nullum crimen*

_____

[*] **Tessa Bolton** works as a U.K. Government lawyer. She holds a master's degree from the University of British Columbia and an LL.B. from King's College London, spending a year at the Centre for Transnational Legal Studies. She has been a criminal paralegal at the Centre for Human Rights, Education, Advice and Assistance in Malawi, interned for Justice Africa, a post-conflict NGO, and researched victims of crime in PEI, Canada. Views expressed in this chapter are not necessarily those of the U.K. Government. All Internet references were last accessed on 14 September 2014.
[1] Gregory H. Stanton, "Why the World Needs an International Convention on Crimes Against Humanity", in Leila Nadya Sadat (ed.), *Forging a Convention for Crimes Against Humanity*, Cambridge University Press, Cambridge, 2011, p. 347.

sine lege, the high occurrence rate of CAH, ineptitudes of the ICC Statute, and the Responsibility to Protect ('R2P') principle. I shall also ask whether a specialized convention is the preferred mechanism for the prevention and punishment of CAH, and bars to the establishment of such a convention.

In the second section, I shall consider the Proposed Convention on the Prevention and Punishment of Crimes Against Humanity ('Proposed Convention') as drafted by the Crimes Against Humanity Initiative, and critique its current form. I will look at issues in defining CAH, including the nexus with an armed conflict, gender and sexuality-based crimes, and terrorism. I shall look at obligations created by the Proposed Convention, including R2P and the prohibition of hate speech. I shall finally consider procedural issues within the Proposed Convention, including immunities and universal jurisdiction.

But first it is required to recognise the work of Leila Nadya Sadat, M. Cherif Bassiouni, and other experts of the Crimes Against Humanity Initiative whose tireless labour has brought the world closer than it has ever been to a multilateral convention on CAH. The Initiative has worked for over ten years with the aim of exploring the law on CAH and elaborating its first ever comprehensive specialized convention. With the aid of a Steering Committee led by Sadat, almost 250 experts contributed to seven major revisions of the draft, culminating in the creation of the final Proposed Convention on Crimes Against Humanity in August 2010.

14.1. Anticipating a Proposed Convention

14.1.1. "Nothing Less Than Our Common Humanity is at Stake"[2]: Why the World Needs a Convention on Crimes Against Humanity

14.1.1.1. *Nullum Crimen Sine Lege*

During the Nuremberg trials, prosecutions of CAH were often the most controversial, as "its foundations in international law were so fragile".[3] CAH became tainted with the perception of 'victor's justice' – the accusation that Allied Powers had orchestrated convictions based on law formu-

---

2. Gareth Evans, "Crimes Against Humanity and the Responsibility to Protect", in Leila Nadya Sadat (ed.), *Forging a Convention for Crimes Against Humanity*, *op. cit.*, p. 7.

3. Richard J. Goldstone, "Foreword", in Leila Nadya Sadat (ed.), *Forging a Convention for Crimes Against Humanity*, Cambridge University Press, *op. cit.*, p. XIX.

lated for their convenience.[4] After so long, an attempt to redeem CAH as authentic law should be made through the definitive enshrinement of its elements. Such an exercise will add legitimacy to the punishment of CAH in both past and future conflicts.

CAH has been critiqued as opportunistic in part because its definition is so untraceable. Twelve multilateral formulations of the offence have been articulated since 1947,[5] and each definition seems to differ. Even the statutes of the International Criminal Tribunals for the Former Yugoslavia ('ICTY') and Rwanda ('ICTR') and International Criminal Court ('ICC') are "different and arguably contradictory".[6] Establishing a majority-ratified international convention specifically on crimes against humanity could provide an overarching definition.

Three benefits would result. Firstly, the principles of legality and due process would be upheld in enforcing the law. Prosecuting an individual for a crime for which there is no widely accepted definition could undermine certainty in law. As Bassiouni puts it: "Concern for legality is never to be taken lightly, no matter how atrocious the violation or how abhorrent the violator".[7] The lasting harm of "an uncurbed spirit of revenge and retribution" is to reduce critical judgements to arbitrary declarations of "higher motives"[8] which are no more infallible than those often espoused by perpetrators of grave and widespread crimes.

Secondly, solidifying the definition of CAH internationally would provide a "strong counterforce against erosion and watering down of the definitions by advocates of 'national security', 'counterinsurgency', and the 'war on terror'".[9] To preserve and retain the worth of CAH prosecutions, it must not be the case that powerful States are free to redefine the offence in situations beneficial to themselves.

---

[4] Francis M. Deng, "Review", in Leila Nadya Sadat (ed.), *Forging a Convention for Crimes Against Humanity, op. cit.*

[5] M. Cherif Bassiouni, *Crimes Against Humanity: Historical Evolution and Contemporary Application*, Cambridge University Press, 2011, pp. 732–733.

[6] Goldstone, 2011, p. XXII, see *supra* note 3.

[7] Bassiouni, 2011, p. 731, see *supra* note 5.

[8] United States Supreme Court, *In Re Yamashita*, Judgment, 4 February 1946, 327 US 1 (Justice Rutledge).

[9] Stanton, 2011, p. 556, see *supra* note 1.

Thirdly, a conventional definition could address the sense that there is a normative *lacuna* surrounding CAH. While a convention exists to deal with Genocide and the Geneva Conventions enshrine the prohibition of war crimes, this is not the case for CAH. The progression of normative societal views of CAH, and the consequential growth of customary law, can be enhanced through treaties which "help guide and construct our thinking".[10]

14.1.1.2. The Continuing Problem of Crimes Against Humanity

Crimes against humanity remain an ongoing concern in the international community. Between 1945 and 2008, 313 documented conflicts took place worldwide, resulting in between 92 and 101 million casualties, or twice the combined number of victims from the two World Wars.[11] Perhaps one of the strongest ways in which the world as a whole can respond to such travesty is through a treaty which describes the offence and defines the role of individuals, States, and international institutions in preventing, investigating, and prosecuting these offences. The Genocide Convention is an example, but it is insufficient. Cases in the Khmer Rouge tribunal of the Extraordinary Chambers in the Courts of Cambodia have demonstrated the need for a clear, treaty-based definition of CAH. Despite the fact that between 1.7 and 2.5 million Cambodians were killed between 1975–1979, most crimes were directed towards political and economic groups, and thus did not fall under the remit of the Genocide Convention.[12] The definition of genocide "just does not reach many of the cases we morally want it to";[13] thus "the international community reached for the Nuremberg precedent only to find that it had failed to finish it".[14]

A specialized convention could respond to crimes against humanity in a number of ways. First, it might act to individually deter potential perpetrators. An example is the NATO bombings in Kosovo in 1999, during which "commanders went to extraordinary lengths to avoid civilian casualties" due in part to their knowledge of the existence and scope of the

---

[10] Leila Nadya Sadat, "A comprehensive History of the Proposed International Convention on the Prevention and Punishment of Crimes Against Humanity", in Leila Nadya Sadat (ed.), *Forging a Convention for Crimes Against Humanity, op. cit.*, p. 489.

[11] Bassiouni, 2011, p. 735, see *supra* note 5.

[12] Stanton, 2011, p. 535, see *supra* note 1.

[13] Evans, 2011, p. 3, see *supra* note 2.

[14] Goldstone, 2011, p. XXII, see *supra* note 3.

ICTY Statute.[15] A public and generally accepted repudiation and treaty-based criminalisation of CAH would at least render unequivocal the international community's mandate to oppose such crimes:

> [Evil] tends to emerge more harmfully when external controls are reduced and inducements offered. Impunity is certainly one of these inducements, as is the prospect of indifference.[16]

As such, a convention could also work towards the alleviation of indifference in the global community, which currently leads to impunity for criminals. Hitler reportedly asked in 1939, "who after all is today speaking about the destruction of the Armenians?".[17] Expressing global reprobation and denunciation of crimes against humanity not only affirms our humanitarian values, it also has a role in deterring those who believe their crimes will go unheeded. Currently, too many crimes of international concern have "regrettably elicited only the most superficial reactions from the international community".[18] Declaring specifically, universally, and finally that crimes against humanity are unacceptable to the world community is the very least we should do to fulfill our oft-forgotten promise of 'never again'.

14.1.1.3. Taking It Further than the ICC Statute

In Article 7, the ICC Statute offers the most recent and comprehensive definition of 'crimes against humanity', a definition applicable to all States who are party to the ICC. However this Statute has limits, and can be no substitute for a specific Convention on the Prevention and Punishment of CAH. Only 122 States have ratified the ICC Statute,[19] leaving more than half of the world's population unprotected. The ICC Statute also refers jurisdiction to the ICC only, and as recent cases have showed, this Court has a very limited scope regarding the number of offenders it can prosecute. Secondly, the ICC Statute does not provide for a specific

---

[15] Sadat, 2011, p. 473, see *supra* note 10.

[16] M. Cherif Bassiouni, "Accountability for International Crime and Serious Violations of Fundamental Human Rights: Searching for Peace and Achieving Justice: The Need for Accountability", in *Law and Contemporary Problems*, 1996, vol. 9, p. 22.

[17] Reported in Bassiouni, 2011, p. 737, see *supra* note 5.

[18] *Ibid.*, p. 737.

[19] The Rome Statute of the International Criminal Court, 1 July 2002.

State obligation to prevent CAH, which a specialized convention could. Thus, unlike the ICC Statute, a specialized convention could not only contribute to more adequate prosecution of CAH at the national level, but also enhance their prevention. Thirdly, the ICC Statute does not confer any direct obligations on States Parties to provide for the domestic outlawing of international crimes. Only 55 States have domestically criminalised CAH.[20] To enhance the principle of complementarity and the overall effectiveness of CAH legislation, States should have an obligation to adopt measures to prevent such crimes, and build up their capacity to prosecute them.[21]

Lastly, there is no explicit mechanism in current international law for holding States to account for the commission of, or complicity in, crimes against humanity.[22] In the case of *Bosnia and Herzegovina v. Serbia and Montenegro* before the ICJ, CAH was held to be outside the jurisdiction of the Court: it was limited to providing remedial damages for genocide alone. Thus of the 200,000 deaths, 50,000 rapes and 2.2 million displaced, only the genocidal massacre of 8,000 at Srebrenica was held to have been proven.[23] The ICC Statute is insufficient in its scope regarding crimes against humanity.

Some argue that a protocol to the ICC Statute would be preferable to a new CAH treaty, as this would be a quicker and more efficient way of achieving the same ends, and would furthermore demonstrate support for the workings of the ICC Statute.[24] However the drawbacks of such an approach outweigh its benefits. States that are not party to the ICC, though able to ratify a separate protocol, would potentially be barred from contributing on an equal footing to early rounds of its negotiation. Secondly, such a protocol could not include provisions on State responsibility or impose duties on States to prevent the occurrence of CAH.[25]

---

[20] Bassiouni, 2011, p. 660, see *supra* note 5.

[21] Goldstone, 2011, p. XVII, see *supra* note 3.

[22] Sadat, 2011, p. 347, see *supra* note 10.

[23] Goldstone, 2011, p. XVI, see *supra* note 3.

[24] Sadat, 2011, p. 464, see *supra* note 10.

[25] Goldstone, 2011, p. XVII, see *supra* note 3.

14.1.1.4. Enhancing the 'Responsibility to Protect' Principle

An emerging principle of international law is the State's 'Responsibility to Protect' civilians from international crimes. It points to growing co-operation between States in turbulent times, including the potential for intervention to protect vulnerable populations in certain situations. However, "a necessary condition precedent to the invocation of the Responsibility to Protect is a clear definition of the event which triggers that responsibility".[26] It is clear that the relationship between this new and growing principle and the Proposed Convention will be significant and may be momentous, as I shall discuss further below.

In sum, there are several important reasons for which "the adoption of a comprehensive international instrument on crimes against humanity is both urgently required and eminently feasible".[27]

14.1.2. "The Politics of Furthering Impunity"[28]: Bars to a Convention on CAH

That a convention preventing and punishing CAH would benefit global society does not necessarily entail that it will be effective. Two current factors which may prevent the progress of the Proposed Convention are a lack of political will, furthered and enabled by a dearth of public interest. Political indifference is enhanced by States' fear of restraints on sovereignty and imposed duties to prevent, protect and intervene regarding CAH. State leaders in particular may fear a loss of immunity that would lead to greater threat of prosecution and a diminution of their power and freedom.

The public indifference towards CAH, however, is more nuanced. There exists a certain apathy towards the semantics of 'crimes against humanity', particularly when read, as it often is, in comparison with genocide, the "crime of crimes".[29] Genocide has wide public concern, in part due to its especially egregious reduction of human diversity: "Genocide is

---

[26] Sadat, 2011, p. 458, see *supra* note 10.

[27] *Ibid.*, p. 501.

[28] Bassiouni, 2011, p. 734, see *supra* note 5.

[29] International Criminal Tribunal for Rwanda, *Prosecutor v. Kambanda*, Case No. ICTR-97-23-A, Appeal Judgment, 4 September 1998, para. 16.

like extinction of a species";[30] but also due to the historical pull of the Holocaust: "the public invocation of the term genocide represents an attempt to make a connection with that unique catastrophe for human dignity and a statement that that is the point at which intervention is morally imperative".[31] By comparison, CAH suffers perhaps from a perception problem, viewed not just as a different, but as "less egregious",[32] less noteworthy, crime. The struggle for advocates of a CAH Convention is to increase the status of crimes against humanity, bringing them to the public table, so that they become perceived as a "resonating legal concept [...] and not just a kind of after-thought category".[33]

14.2. Taking a Closer Look at the Proposed Convention on the Prevention and Punishment of Crimes Against Humanity

14.2.1. Concerns in Defining Crimes Against Humanity

14.2.1.1. Requirement of a Nexus with an International Armed Conflict

The Proposed Convention omits the necessity of a connection with international armed conflict. Though the ICTY Statute upheld the nexus requirement for an international armed conflict, the Rwandan situation did not have an international aspect as such, yet in *Tadić* it was recognised that the law regarding crimes against humanity had progressed to include crimes committed outside of international conflicts.[34] The ICC Statute upheld this notion. The Proposed Convention, with the definition of CAH almost a carbon-copy of that in the ICC Statute, retains the omission.

14.2.1.2. Gender Crimes

Article 3(1)(h) and (3) of the Proposed Convention provides that,

> "crimes against humanity" means any of the following acts
> [...]. Persecution against any identifiable group or

---

[30] Stanton, 2011, p. 347, see *supra* note 1.

[31] Steven R. Ratner, "Can We Compare Evils? The Enduring Debate on Genocide and Crimes Against Humanity", in *Washington University Global Studies Law Review*, 2007, vol. 6, p. 588.

[32] Sadat, 2011, p. 476, see *supra* note 10.

[33] Evans, 2011, p. 3, see *supra* note 2.

[34] ICTY, *The Prosecutor v. Duško Tadić*, Case No.IT-94-1-A, Decision on the Defence Motion for Interlocutory Appeal on Jurisdiction, 2 October 1995, para. 70.

---

collectivity on political, racial, national, ethnic, cultural,
religious, gender as defined in paragraph 3, or other grounds.

[...]

For the purposes of the present Convention, it is understood
that the term 'gender' refers to the two sexes, male and
female, within the context of society. The term 'gender' does
not indicate any meaning different from the above.

When defining CAH, the drafters of the Proposed Convention lifted
almost the exact definition from the ICC Statute, in order to complement
the ICC and not undermine it.[35] In doing so, some imperfections and un-
resolved issues were also transplanted. Particularly, the section on gender
and gender crimes has been regarded as insufficient. The definition of
gender in Article 3(3) of the Proposed Convention is disputed. Admittedly
controversial, this definition was the only one with which drafters of the
ICC Statute could get all parties to agree;[36] nevertheless it is "opaque and
circular".[37] Oosterveld argues that gender is an elusive social structure
which defies definition, and as such should be left undefined in the Convention. Some note that the principle of legality may require the inclusion
of a clarified definition, however the ICC Statute version is unsatisfying
due to its inherent tautology and failure to encompass the social and variable aspects of gender.[38] The definition focuses too exclusively on biological traits. It is notable that the French version of the ICC Statute trans-
lates "gender" as "*sexe*".[39] This conception of gender is too narrow. It
does not adequately reflect social and cultural implications, and may fore-
seeably prevent a persecution being deemed as CAH due to discriminatory categorisations that are not applicable under the Convention. One example might be persecutions or other CAH based on transgender status, or
on not conforming to particular societal conventions pertaining to gender
norms. With a limited definition of gender, such crimes could not be
prosecuted under international criminal law.

---

[35] Sadat, 2011, p. 481, see *supra* note 10.
[36] Julia Martinez Vivancos, "LGBT and the International Criminal Court", 2010, available at
http://www.amicc.org/docs/LGBTandICC.pdf.
[37] Valerie Oosterveld, "Gender-Based Crimes Against Humanity", in Leila Nadya Sadat
(ed.), *Forging a Convention for Crimes Against Humanity*, *op. cit.*, p. 82.
[38] *Ibid.*, p. 83.
[39] Sadat, 2011, p. 482, see *supra* note 10.

Further to the incomplete definition of gender, the Proposed Convention neglects to include certain gender-based acts as crimes against humanity. In particular, forced marriage is a crime which has been proven to have occurred, distinctly from sexual slavery, in emerging cases in the Special Court for Sierra Leone.[40] The Court provided a definition of the crime, and noted specific resulting injuries including physical, sexual, and emotional abuse, the contraction of STIs, forced pregnancy, and long-term social stigma after the events.[41]

The crime of forced marriage is by no means reducible to the Sierra Leone conflict. During the reign of Joseph Kony and the LRA in northern Uganda, thousands of girls were abducted to be used as 'wives' or 'sisters' of LRA troops,[42] suffering from both sexual slavery and the trappings of marital relations, including being required to reside with their abusers and provide domestically for them.[43] Such events lead to a pandemic of forced pregnancy amongst the girls, with 800 babies reportedly being born to LRA 'wives' during the 1990s in the Jabelein LRA camp alone.[44] Young women and girls who had fallen prey to Kony's troops also faced stigma on their return, as up to 83% of husbands subsequently rejected victims of rape.[45] In the conflict in Darfur, too, gender-based crimes went beyond prevalent and continual rape. In some cases, the "intention (was) to change the race of the offspring" and the women involved, with victims reporting being raped, branded and told, "You are now Arab wives".[46] These incidents are not captured within the prohibition of "sexual slavery"; they require a greater emphasis and level of elucidation within the Proposed Convention. Nevertheless, forced marriage

---

[40] Special Court for Sierra Leone, *Prosecutor v. Brima et al.*, Case No. SCSL-04-16-A, Appeal Judgment, 22 February 2008.

[41] Oosterveld, 2011, p. 97, see *supra* note 38; *Prosecutor v. Brima et al., op. cit.*, paras. 187–196.

[42] Press Conference, International Criminal Court, Statement by Chief Prosecutor Luis Moreno Ocampo (14 October 2005), p. 6.

[43] *Ibid.*, p. 5.

[44] Payam Akhavan, "The Lord's Resistance Army Case: Uganda's Submission of the First State Referral to the International Criminal Court", in *American Journal of International Law*, 2005, vol. 99, no. 2, p. 408.

[45] Ruddy Doom and Koen Vlassenroot, "Kony's Message: A New Koine? The Lord's Resistance Army in Northern Uganda", in *African Affairs*, 1999, vol. 98, p. 27.

[46] John Hagan and Wenona Rymond-Richmond, "The Collective Dynamics of Racial Dehumanization and Genocidal Victimization in Darfur", in *American Sociological Review*, 2008, vol. 73, p. 889.

has been omitted from the Proposed Convention, and may only be prosecuted under the category of "other inhumane acts" in Article 3(1)(k). This wording does not reflect the true experiences of many survivors, nor does it emphasize the progressive, updated version of international criminal law which the Proposed Convention ought to emulate.

Secondly, Oosterveld argues that forced abortion or forced miscarriage could be considered as a discrete CAH, due in particular to its similarity to sterilization, a listed crime.[47] The *Lubanga* case adduced evidence in 2009 as to this conduct,[48] although it was not specifically charged. Thus while many acts of sexual violence are included within the definition of CAH in the Proposed Convention, there is scope for the inclusion of other gender, but not necessarily sex-based, acts.[49]

14.2.1.3. Persecution Based on Sexual Orientation

The Proposed Convention omits the crime of persecution based on grounds of sexual orientation. Given the history of continued repression and overt incidents of crimes against humanity on grounds of homosexuality, and in light of the emerging and vulnerable status of empowerment of homosexual people throughout the world, such an omission is at this stage glaring and wrong.

The persecution of people based on their sexual orientation has both historical and contemporary relevance. The most notable and heinous crimes against homosexuals were possibly those committed during the Nazi Holocaust. From 1933 to 1945, between 50,000 and 100,000 individuals were arrested and convicted for homosexuality in Nazi Germany.[50] In the notorious concentration camps, between 5,000 and 15,000 inmates wore the Pink Triangle, designating their status as sexual deviant,[51]

---

[47] Oosterveld, 2011, p. 99, see *supra* note 37.

[48] Beth Van Schaack, "Forced Marriage: A 'New' Crime Against Humanity?", in *Northwestern Journal of International Human Rights*, 2009, vol. 8, p. 53.

[49] Oosterveld, 2011, p. 100, see *supra* note 37.

[50] Robert Plant, *The Pink Triangle: The Nazi War Against Homosexuality*, Holt Paperbacks, New York, 1986, p. 149; Robert Franklin, "Warm Brothers in the Boomtowns of Hell: The Persecution of Homosexuals in Nazi Germany", in *Hohonu Journal of Academic Writing*, 2011, vol. 9, p. 56.

[51] Rüdiger Lautmann, "The Pink Triangle: Homosexuals as 'Enemies of the State'", in Michael Berenbaum and Abraham J. Peck (eds.), *The Holocaust and History: The Known, the*

with such inmates suffering one of the worst death rates, at around 60%.[52] Designated homosexual camp inmates were also sometimes subject to castration and experimental medical operations,[53] while those outside the camps spent years renouncing their desires and living in fear.[54] Similarly repulsive was the fact that immediately after the conclusion of the war, there was no prosecution of crimes based on sexuality at Nuremberg, and no reparations granted to such victims,[55] many of them being forced to serve the remainder of their prescribed sentences in jail.[56]

Contemporarily, many countries retain the death penalty for convictions of homosexuality,[57] while up to 76 States criminalize same sex relations, often with extremely long jail terms.[58] Less formal crimes occur frequently against people based on sexual orientation, including police harassment,[59] involuntary institution and curative 'treatments' such as electroshock,[60] government inaction in response to systematic criminal assaults,[61] 'corrective' lesbian rape,[62] and prohibition of collaboration and

---

Unknown, the Disputed, and the Reexamined, Indiana University Press, Bloomington, 1998, p. 348.

[52] *Ibid.*, p. 348; Franklin, 2011, p. 56, see *supra* note 50.

[53] "Homosexuals – Victims of the Nazi Era 193301945", United States Holocaust Memorial Museum, p. 4, available at http://www.chgs.umn.edu/pdf/homosbklt.pdf.

[54] Plant, 2011, p. 112, see *supra* note 50; Lautmann, 1998, p. 354, see *supra* note 51.

[55] "Homosexuals – Victims of the Nazi Era", p. 6, see *supra* note 54.

[56] Franklin, 2011, p. 57, see *supra* note 50.

[57] "International Lesbian, Gay, Bisexual, Trans and Intersex Association Map", reported in *The Independent*, 25 February 2014: States include Iran, Saudi Arabia, Yemen, southern Somalia, northern Nigeria, and Mauritania.

[58] "Free & Equal: UN for LGBT Equality" Fact Sheet, available at https://unfe-uploads-production.s3.amazonaws.com/unfe-34-UN_Fact_Sheets_v6_-_Criminal ization.pdf. Sentences extend from between 14 years to life imprisonment.

[59] Suzanne Goldberg, "Give me Liberty or Give me Death: Political Asylum and the Global Persecution of Lesbians and Gay Men", in *Cornell International Law Journal*, 1993, vol. 26, no. 2, p. 605.

[60] *Ibid.*, p. 605.

[61] *Ibid.*

[62] ActionAid, *The Rise of 'Corrective Rape' in South Africa*, London, 2009.

demonstrations.[63] There has been a perturbing broadening of existing anti-homosexuality laws in recent years, particularly in Africa.[64]

International criminal law could be a suitable forum in which to address these crimes. The mechanism is powerful and trans-State, capable of transcending cultural partiality and protecting vulnerable groups from systematic persecution. It also retains undeniable rhetoric power. While many argue that States ought to retain the autonomy to determine their social policy, this ability cannot supersede the liberty of individuals and groups to enjoy their most basic rights and protections. We should not ignore crimes meted out against innocent people whom it is simply not convenient to protect.

Under the CAH definitions, 'persecution' appears to be the crime which most directly applies to the situations of life suffered by many LGBT individuals and groups around the world. Justice Ponsor, in a recent non-binding pre-trial statement in the U.S. District Court of Massachusetts case of *Sexual Minorities Uganda v. Scott Lively*, stated that "widespread, systematic persecution of LGBT people constitutes a crime against humanity that unquestionably violates international norms".[65]

As it stands, there remains no explicit inclusion of sexual orientation as a protected ground under the persecution definition of CAH in the ICC Statute. A convention on CAH should attempt to include it, for the avoidance of doubt, and as a symbolic statement that progress has been made to the extent that such persecution should no longer be tolerated.

Short of specifically including sexual orientation as grounds for persecution within the definition of CAH, there exist at least two mechanisms through which jurisdiction over crimes against humanity committed on the basis of sexual orientation may arise.

The first is through an expansive interpretation of the definition of "gender" in Article 3(3). As discussed above, the definition is vague and

---

[63] Amnesty International, *Making Love a Crime: Criminalization of Consensual Same-Sex Behaviour in Sub-Saharan Africa*, London, 2013, p. 7.

[64] *E.g.*, in Nigeria and Uganda, see The Anti-Homosexuality Act (Nigeria), 2014; The Anti-Homosexuality Act (Uganda) 2014; Al Chukwuma Okoli, "Betwixt Liberty and National Sensibility: Implications of Nigeria's Anti-Gay Law", in *International Affairs and Global Strategy*, 2014, vol. 19.

[65] Justice Ponsor, *Sexual Minorities Uganda v. Scott Lively*, District Court of Massachusetts, Memorandum and Order denying Defendant's Motion to Dismiss, 14 August 2013, p. 20.

there is no consensus as to whether it provides for persecution on the grounds of sexual orientation.[66] Some argue that it was left open for the courts to decide, case-by-case, whether particular persecution was "gen-der"-based,[67] whereas others say this aspect of the statute purposefully omitted persecution on the grounds of sexual orientation. Martinez contends that "conceptions of gender and sexual orientation are linked [...]. The term 'gender' must be broad enough to capture any group challenging traditional defined gender roles".[68]

Key to the argument is Article 21(3) of the ICC Statute, and to a similar extent Article 25 of the Proposed Convention, both of which purport to include the necessity to interpret provisions consistent with "internationally recognised human rights" norms. As such, when facing this ambiguity of definition, a judge ought to take into account international human rights norms. Previously, deference to Article 21(3) has included references to the ICCPR and ECHR rulings.[69] It is notable that these and other international institutions are becoming increasingly vocal in their support of protections for vulnerable groups defined by their sexual orientation. The European Court of Human Rights has in several cases promoted the rights of homosexual individuals and groups,[70] as have key U.S. courts[71] and the U.N. Human Rights Committee dealing with the ICCPR.[72] The Organisation of American States and the U.N. Human Rights Committee have both issued declarations of support for LGBT rights,[73] while a U.N. General Assembly Statement in 2008 was supported by 66

---

[66] Vivancos, 2010, p. 2, see *supra* note 36.

[67] Oosterveld, 2011, p. 96, see *supra* note 37.

[68] Vivancos, 2010, p. 3, see *supra* note 36.

[69] See, *e.g.*, International Criminal Court, *Prosecutor v. Lubanga*, Judgment Pursuant to Article 74, 14 March 2012, para. 604.

[70] See, *e.g.*, European Court of Human Rights, *Dudgeon v. UK*, Judgment, 22 October 1981, rendering anti-homosexuality laws illegal; and European Court of Human Rights, *L and V v. Austria*, 9 January 2003, equalising sexual ages of consent for homosexual and heterosexual relations.

[71] See, *e.g.*, *United States v. Windsor*, USSC 2013, modifying the Defence of Marriage Act and dissolving federal blocks to same-sex marriage; and *Lawrence v. Texas*, USSC 2003, prohibiting anti-sodomy laws.

[72] See in particular *Toonen v. Australia* (488/1992) HRC, declaring prohibitions on homosexual behaviour to be in violation of the ICCPR.

[73] See Organisation of American States AG/RES. 2435 (XXXVIII-O/08) OAS 2008; U.N. HRC Resolution, 14 July 2011, 34th meeting on 17 June 2011.

States.[74] The non-legal Yogyakarta Principles, too, detailed comprehensive rights of LGBT individuals and groups in 2006-7.[75]

Secondly, persecution on grounds of sexual orientation may be incorporated as a CAH through the absorption clause of Article 3(1), as an example of "other grounds that are universally recognised as impermissible under international law". However, this threshold is higher than the previous. International law "has not yet universally recognized (sexual orientation) as a prohibited ground of discrimination".[76] There are some examples of international recognition of the adverse potential for persecution on sexual grounds, for example in the Convention Relating to the Status of Refugees, "international law recognizes a well-founded fear of persecution on the basis of sexual orientation as a basis for refugee status".[77] In this case the U.N. High Commissioner for Refugees interpreted "social group" to include those grounded on LGBT delineations.[78] However, international law is not yet at a sufficiently consolidated level to permit this ambiguity being resolved in favour of protecting vulnerable groups.

The 'constructive ambiguities' of the definition of CAH in the Proposed Convention are, in this instance, insufficient. The rights of vulnerable LGBT groups would be inadequately protected by a convention that has taken too regressive an outlook. Though the international community may find it controversial and, for some, unacceptable, the addition of persecution on grounds of sexual orientation in the Proposed Convention would at least bring this neglected issue to the fore of global debate. Such an inclusion "is not only desirable, but also necessary to prosecute the kind of homophobic persecution that had occurred in World War II".[79]

14.2.1.4. Terrorism and CAH

There is no inclusion of terrorist acts specifically within the definition of CAH in the Proposed Convention. Terrorist activities often consist of

---

[74] UNGA Statement on Sexual Orientation and Gender Identity, 2008.

[75] Yogyakarta Principles on the Application of International Human Rights Law in Relation to Sexual Orientation and Gender Identity, U.N. Human Rights Council, 2007.

[76] Vivancos, 2010, p. 3, see *supra* note 36.

[77] Douglas Sanders, "Human Rights and Sexual Orientation in International Law", in *International Journal of Public Administration*, 2002, vol. 25, no. 1, p. 14.

[78] Vivancos, 2010, p. 3, see *supra* note 36.

[79] Oosterveld, 2011, p. 96, see *supra* note 37.

CAH, and are intrinsically linked with them in many ways. Nevertheless, this seems overall a correct conclusion of the drafters. Though there is a proliferation of treaties dealing with terrorist activities, some argue that the Proposed Convention ought to include a CAH of terrorism to fill gaps between peacetime terrorism conventions,[80] to entail "uniformity of jurisdiction and prosecutorial obligation",[81] and to enable prosecution of these crimes by the ICC.[82] Scharf and Newton demonstrate that, for example, the terrorist attacks in the U.S. on 11 September 2001 could have fulfilled the common elements of CAH. The attacks were "widespread and systematic" in that they resulted in almost 3,000 deaths, were "part of a string of attacks" (including bombings of the World Trade Center in 1993 and in Saudi Arabia in 1995-1996), and "constituted a systematic attack" on at least three separate targets.[83] It is also clear that the high number of terrorism treaties has failed to abate "the persistence of transnational terrorism as a feature of the international community".[84] It seems that more international co-operation and effort are required.

Inclusion of terrorism as a CAH would face difficulties in particular due to the absence of international consensus regarding a definition of the crime.[85] The concept is "caught in a kaleidoscope of conflicting sociological, political, psychological, moral, and yes, legal perspectives".[86] The term 'terrorism', too, is deemed politicised and emotive; it thus lacks legal certainty and would undermine the value of existing prohibitions.[87] Furthermore, the existing patchwork of norms and prohibitions regarding 'terrorism' means that most specific crimes are already covered. Terrorist acts could fall within the scope of the Proposed Convention under "murder" in Article (3)(1)(a) or "other inhumane acts" in Article (3)(1)(k). The determination of whether a specific act comes under the Proposed Convention is perhaps best decided judicially on a case-by-case basis, rather

---

[80] Michael P. Scharf and Michael A. Newton, "Terrorism and Crimes Against Humanity", in Leila Nadya Sadat (ed.), *Forging a Convention for Crimes Against Humanity*, *op. cit.*, p. 273.

[81] *Ibid.*, p. 277.

[82] *Ibid.*, p. 278.

[83] *Ibid.*, p. 274.

[84] *Ibid.*, p. 263.

[85] Sadat, 2011, p. 469, see *supra* note 10.

[86] Scharf and Newton, 2011, p. 266, see *supra* note 80.

[87] *Ibid.*

than through a casuistic legislative process seeking to identify a universal definition of "terrorist acts".

14.2.2. Obligations Created by the Proposed Convention

14.2.2.1. The Responsibility to Protect

Articles 2(1), (2)(a), and 8(1) and (13) of the Proposed Convention provide:

> The States Parties to the present Convention undertake to prevent crimes against humanity and to investigate, prosecute, and punish those responsible for such crimes.
>
> [...]
>
> each State Party agrees: To cooperate, pursuant to the provisions of the present Convention, with other States Parties to prevent crimes against humanity.
>
> [...]
>
> Each State Party shall enact necessary legislation and other measures as required by its Constitution or legal system to give effect to the provisions of the present Convention and, in particular, to take effective legislative, administrative, judicial and other measures in accordance with the Charter of the United Nations to prevent and punish the commission of crimes against humanity in any territory under its jurisdiction or control.
>
> [...]
>
> States Parties may call upon the competent organs of the United Nations to take such action in accordance with the Charter of the United Nations as they consider appropriate for the prevention and punishment of crimes against humanity.

The 'Responsibility to Protect' is an emerging principle of international law which has evolved as a result of an international Commission which in 2000 aimed at finding "a conceptual and practical answer"[88] to respond to and prevent core international crimes. The culmination of the Commission's work was the U.N. General Assembly's endorsement of

---

[88]   Evans, 2011, p. 2, see *supra* note 2.

the Responsibility to Protect in a resolution at the 2005 World Summit.[89] In its essence, R2P is "the logical extension of the concept of popular sovereignty".[90] It re-defines sovereignty as the duty of States to protect civilians within and beyond their territorial borders.[91] R2P provides that States are required to "affirmatively intervene to protect vulnerable populations from nascent or continuing international crimes"[92] in specific situations.

International criminal law has a significant role to play in the establishment and fulfilment of R2P. Of the four categories of core international crimes, R2P is most relevant to CAH, because they are systematic, typically take place over a long period of time, and likely become known to the outside community before or during their perpetration, often unlike crimes of genocide.[93]

Paragraph 138 of the U.N. Resolution states that "each individual State has the responsibility to protect its populations from genocide, war crimes, ethnic cleansing and crimes against humanity".[94] Paragraph 139 goes further:

> the international community [...] also has the responsibility to use appropriate diplomatic, humanitarian and other peaceful means [...] to help to protect populations from genocide, war crimes, ethnic cleansing and crimes against humanity. In this context, we are prepared to take collective action [...] through the Security Council [...] should peaceful means be inadequate.[95]

Article 8(1) of the Proposed Convention obliges States to protect civilians within their territory or within territory under their jurisdiction or control, but unlike the U.N. Resolution does not provide an explicit duty to protect all vulnerable populations of the world.[96] It is nevertheless

---

[89] United Nations General Assembly, "World Summit Outcome Document", 24 October 2005, see particularly paras. 138–139.

[90] Stanton, 2011, p. 357, see *supra* note 1.

[91] Evans, 2011, p. 2, see *supra* note 2.

[92] Sadat, 2011, p. 458, see *supra* note 10.

[93] *Ibid.*, pp. 494–495.

[94] United Nations General Assembly, "World Summit Outcome Document", 2005, see *supra* note 89.

[95] Sadat, 2011, pp. 494–495, see *supra* note 10.

[96] *Ibid.*

broader than the ICC Statute. The Proposed Convention, unlike the ICC Statute, does not explicitly forbid the interference of foreign States in the internal affairs or territorial integrity of another State.[97] The R2P is also more fully realised by the call in Article 8(13) for States to call upon the U.N. in dealing with CAH, rather than operating a unilateral 'State v. State' approach.[98]

There is, however, debate on whether the Proposed Convention should go further in promoting the R2P principle, including a clause of collective responsibility to intervene where early-warning systems indicate that CAH may occur imminently. States "should not wait until the eleventh hour to intervene".[99] Furthermore, States may be held responsible before the ICJ for failing to adequately intervene for reasons of negligence in situations where citizens are harmed. Such intervention need not necessarily be military or by physical force, but may involve economic or political measures.[100] Such an obligation is so comprehensive and complex that the Proposed Convention on CAH may be the wrong forum. The complex duty of intervention in territories outside the State's jurisdiction requires a much stronger legal basis and a separate process of negotiation and exploration.

14.2.2.2. Prohibiting Hate Speech

Article 8(12) of the Proposed Convention provides:

> Each State Party shall endeavour to take measures in accordance with its domestic legal system to prevent crimes against humanity. Such measures include, but are not limited to, ensuring that any advocacy of national, racial, or religious hatred that constitutes incitement to discrimination, hostility, or violence shall be prohibited by law.

Requiring States to domestically prohibit incitement and hate speech is controversial. It conflicts with fundamental rights to freedom of expression and, because it is difficult to prove a direct link between incitement and later events, is open to abuse and prejudicial use.[101] It is no-

---

[97] *Ibid.*
[98] *Ibid.*
[99] *Ibid.*
[100] *Ibid.*, p. 497.
[101] *Ibid.*

table that, in negotiating the ICC Statute, States refused to include the prohibition of incitement for CAH, but limited such prohibition to genocide.[102] There is, however, strong precedent for including incitement clauses in human rights conventions. The International Convention on the Elimination of All Forms of Racial Discrimination specificially prohibits incitement[103] and has 177 States Parties.[104] The International Covenant on Civil and Political Rights ('ICCPR') provides that "[a]ny advocacy of national, racial or religious hatred that constitutes incitement to discrimination, hostility or violence shall be prohibited by law".[105] It is from this language that Article 8(12) of the Proposed Convention was drafted.[106]

Whether Article 8(12) will survive the negotiation process depends on the willingness of States to move towards the progress achieved in other international treaties. A brief review of State practice in implementing provisions prohibiting incitement may shed some light on the potential reception of proposed Article 8(12).

The general picture suggests that States have applied these prohibitions haphazardly, incompletely, or not at all. There is a marked "absence of the legal prohibition of incitement to hatred in many domestic legal frameworks around the world".[107] Researchers have found that "the legislation of a number of States Parties did not include the provisions envisaged in Article 4 (a) and (b) of the Convention [on the Elimination of All Forms of Racial Discrimination]",[108] while "States vary greatly in their

---

[102] *Ibid.*

[103] International Convention on the Elimination of All Forms of Racial Discrimination, 4 January 1969, Article 4.

[104] United Nations Treaty Collection Database, available at https://treaties.un.org/pages/ViewDetails.aspx?src=TREATY&mtdsg_no=IV-2&chapter=4&lang=en.

[105] International Covenant on Civil and Political Rights, 19 December 1966, Article 20(2).

[106] Sadat *et al.*, "Proposed International Convention on the Prevention and Punishment of Crimes Against Humanity (explanatory notes)", in Leila Nadya Sadat (ed.), *Forging a Convention for Crimes Against Humanity*, *op. cit.*

[107] "Rabat Plan of Action on the Prohibition of Advocacy of National, Racial or Religious Hatred that Constitutes Incitement to Discrimination, Hostility or Violence: Conclusions and Recommendations Emanating from the Four Regional Expert Workshops Organised by OHCHR, in 2011, and Adopted by Experts in Rabat, Morocco on 5 October 2012", p. 3.

[108] Atsuko Tanaka with Yoshinobu Nagamine, "The International Convention on the Elimination of All Forms of Racial Discrimination: A Guide for NGOs", Minority Rights Group International and IMADR, 2001, p. 26, available at http://www.minorityrights.org/894/guides/icerd-a-guide-for-ngos.html.

---

approach to and interpretation of the obligation set out in Article 20(2) of the ICCPR".[109] Legislation, where it exists, often does not follow the precise prescription of either instrument, using instead "variable terminology (which) is often inconsistent"[110] with the instruments' aims. Frequently, "domestic laws fail to refer to 'incitement' as such, using comparable terms such as 'stirring up' (the U.K.), 'provocation' (Spain) or 'threatening speech' (Denmark)".[111] There is a lack of "conceptual discipline or rigour" in States' judicial interpretations,[112] and concern for the potential adverse effects of over-expansive interpretations in restricting rights to freedom of expression.[113]

It is highly likely that the requirements in proposed Article 8(12) may face both resistance and inconsistent application at the domestic level. Drafters should clarify the elements and steps required for an incitement to occur, both to aid domestic implementation and to prevent potential overreach of anti-incitement laws. The 2012 'Rabat Plan of Action on the Prohibition of Advocacy of National, Racial or Religious Hatred that Constitutes Incitement to Discrimination, Hostility or Violence' provides a useful framework for assisting States in adopting and utilising laws which prohibit incitement.[114]

Another alternative that may both render the draft Article more effective, and provide a level of added value outside of already-existing anti-incitement protocols, may be to remove "by law" and instead allow an expansion of methodologies for domestic approaches to incitement. Such flexibility may increase ultimate State compliance with the Proposed

---

[109] Article 19: Policy Brief, "Prohibiting Incitement to Discrimination, Hostility or Violence", December 2012, p. 25, http://www.article19.org/data/files/medialibrary/3548/ ARTICLE-19-policy-on-prohibition-to-incitement.pdf.

[110] Rabat Plan of Action, 2012, p. 3, see *supra* note 107.

[111] Article 19 Global Campaign for Free Expression, "Towards an Interpretation of Article 20 of the ICCPR: Thresholds for the Prohibition of Incitement to Hatred" (A study prepared for the regional expert meeting on article 20, organised by the Office of the High Cimmissioner for Human Rights, Vienna, 8–9 February 2010), p. 3, available at http://www.ohchr.org/Documents/Issues/Expression/ICCPR/Vienna/CRP7Callamard.pdf.

[112] Article 19: Policy Brief, 2012, p. 25, see *supra* note 109.

[113] See, *e.g.*, "Statement of the Special Rapporteur on Freedom of Religion or Belief", Heiner Bielefeldt, during the 25th session of the Human Rights Council, 11 March 2014, available at http://www.ohchr.org/EN/NewsEvents/Pages/DisplayNews.aspx?NewsID=14398&LangID=E.

[114] Rabat Plan of Action, 2012, see *supra* note 107.

Convention. One author notes that, regarding Article 20 of the ICCPR, "[w]hile the overall goal is to preserve freedom, a particular course of conduct, that is the adoption of legislation prohibiting propaganda for war, is mandated".[115] This approach potentially limits the freedom of States to find more culturally and socially appropriate responses to incitement, and is reflected in draft Article 8(12).

Secondly, the Proposed Convention could expand the grounds on which incitement is prohibited outside of "national, racial, or religious" hatred. It is laudable that the proposed Article already contains the "not limited to" non-exhaustion clause, but the phrasing could go further to include, for example, prohibitions of hatred based on gender, sexual orientation, or disability. Indeed, the ICCPR has already been criticised for not extending its reach far enough towards encompassing all forms of hate speech.[116] Expansion to further grounds would demonstrate a recognition of progress and advancement in the international legal sphere.

14.2.3. Procedural Issues within the Proposed Convention

14.2.3.1. Immunities

Article 6(1) and (2) of the Proposed Convention provide:

> The present Convention shall apply equally to all persons without any distinction based on official capacity. In particular, official capacity as a Head of State or Government [...] shall in no case exempt a person from criminal responsibility
>
> [...]
>
> Immunities or special procedural rules which may attach to the official capacity of a person, whether under national or international law, shall not bar a court from exercising its jurisdiction over such a person.

In the Explanatory Note to the Proposed Convention, it is stated that Article 6(2) "draws upon the dissenting opinion of Judge Van den Wyngaert from the ICJ's judgement in the Case Concerning the Arrest

---

[115] Anja Seibert-Fohr, "Domestic Implementation of the International Covenant on Civil and Political Rights Pursuant to its Article 2 Para. 2", in *Max Planck United Nations Law*, 2001, vol. 5, p. 402, footnote 10.

[116] Office of the High Commissioner for Human Rights, "Draft General Comment 34", October 2010, para. 54.

Warrant of 11 April 2000 (*Democratic Republic of the Congo v. Belgium*), 14 February 2002, and supports a different and more expansive principle than Article 27(2) of the Rome Statute".[117] However, in looking at the ICC Statute, Article 27(2) uses almost identical wording:

> Immunities or special procedural rules which may attach to the official capacity of a person, whether under national or international law, shall not bar the Court from exercising its jurisdiction over such a person.

The only distinction is changing of the words "the Court" in the ICC Statute to "a court" in the Proposed Convention. In removing immunities for all courts, not just the ICC, the scope of the Convention is expanded in a simple but distinct way. By ratifying such a provision, States would abrogate the immunities *rationae personae* that their officials would otherwise enjoy, not just before the ICC, but all national and international courts and tribunals with jurisdiction over cases of CAH.[118]

In Judge Van den Wyngaert's dissent, she stated that

> there is no rule of customary international law protecting incumbent Foreign Ministers against criminal prosecution. International comity and political wisdom may command restraint, but there is no obligation under positive international law on States to refrain from exercising jurisdiction in the case of incumbent Foreign Ministers suspected of war crimes and crimes against humanity.[119]

Judge Van den Wyngaert also discussed the "the general tendency toward the restriction of immunity of the State officials (including even Heads of State)",[120] and the "recent movement" in favour of "the principle of individual accountability for international core crimes".[121]

While applauding the noble intentions of the drafters of the Proposed Convention to incorporate this development in the theory of inter-

---

[117] Sadat *et al.*, "Proposed International Convention on the Prevention and Punishment of Crimes Against Humanity (explanatory notes)", 2011, see *supra* note 106.

[118] Diane Orenticher, "Immunities and Amnesties", in Leila Nadya Sadat (ed.), *Forging a Convention for Crimes Against Humanity*, *op. cit.*, p. 216.

[119] International Court of Justice, *Arrest Warrant of 11 April 2000 (Democratic Republic of the Congo v. Belgium)*, Dissenting Opinion of Judge Van den Wyngaert, 14 February 2002, para. 10.

[120] *Ibid.*, para. 23.

[121] *Ibid.*, para. 27.

national criminal law, it is also important to note reservations regarding the likelihood of State acceptance. State officials have suffered considerable assaults on their immunity during the evolution of international criminal law, and are generally reticent about tolerating further diminution.[122] States' trepidation is revealed in the International Law Commission's study on the immunity of State officials from foreign criminal jurisdiction.[123]

This ambition of the Proposed Convention is a departure from the current state of international law, and runs against recent attempts to shore up the definition and scope of head of State immunity by the International Law Commission.[124] There remains significant disagreement as to whether the "overall objective to avoid impunity for atrocity crimes [... ultimately supersedes] the desire to allow for the peaceful conduct of international relations between senior government officials".[125]

The international community appears to have come to the fragile consensus that immunity *ratione personae* generally no longer applies in the context of international criminal tribunals. The rationale for this shift, though, very much stems from the status of these venues as being outside of the usual State diplomatic and political functions. Immunity *ratione personae* has traditionally been confered because of the 'representative' nature of the individual as "the personal embodiment of the state itself"[126] (responding to the legal metonymy: "*L'État, c'est moi*").[127] Whereas the 'functional' need for such an individual requires immunity as a means of ensuring inter-state sovereign equality,[128] such logic does not apply under

---

[122] Orenticher, 2011, p. 217, see *supra* note 118.

[123] United Nations General Assembly, "Immunity of State Officials from Foreign Criminal Jurisdiction", 31 March 2008.

[124] Sean D. Murphy, "Immunity *Ratione Personae* of Foreign Government Officials and Other Topics: The Sixty-Fifth Session of the International Law Commission", in *American Journal of International Law*, 2014, vol. 108, no. 1, pp. 41 and 42, discussing the ILC's recent 2013 preliminary adoptions of three draft articles confirming head of State immunity from criminal jurisdiction.

[125] *Ibid.*, p. 47.

[126] Lord Millett, Judgment of the House of Lords, *Regina v. Bartle and the Commissioner of Police for the Metropolis and Others Ex Parte Pinochet* (U.K.), 1999, para. 49.

[127] David Luban, "State Criminality and the Ambition of International Criminal Law", in Tracy Isaacs and Richard Vernon (eds.), *Accountability for Collective Wrongdoing*, Cambridge University Press, Cambridge, 2011, p. 68.

[128] HUANG Huikang, "On Immunity of State Officials from Foreign Criminal Jurisdiction", in *Chinese Journal of International Law*, 2014, vol. 13, p. 2.

---

the purview of international criminal tribunals. It has been argued that "concerns of sovereign equality are irrelevant before international tribunals [... because such] courts derive their mandate from the international community which safeguards against unilateral judgment by one state".[129] The eminent immunity justification *par in parem non habet imperium* as such "has no application to international tribunals".[130]

Such a justification for removing immunity does not apply, however, to the context of national jurisdictions attempting to try international crimes. It "remains unclear" whether the new vitiation of immunity *ratione personae* has been extended to the national level,[131] in particular since the traditional fears of destabilising sovereign equality stands in this context. Even the ICC, in a Pre-Trial Chamber Decision in the Al Bashir case, declined to suggest that an exception to such immunity existed anywhere except "when *international* courts seek a Head of State's arrest for the commission of international crimes".[132] With regards to immunities, international criminal justice already "mounts a dramatic challenge to the prevailing idolatry of the state".[133] It is highly likely that this expansive attempt may be a leap too far, too soon.

Nevertheless, these issues do not diminish the need for a strong non-immunity declaration within the Proposed Convention. Taking a strong stand against immunities allows States negotiation space so that the provisions may retain their strength after watering down during the process.[134] It is also important to recall that the crimes at hand violate *jus cogens* norms, and as such immunity ought not to apply,[135] yet the time for such an advancement may not yet be here. Hopefully, in the future, international lawyers and commentators will have greater sympathy for the

---

[129] Jessica Needham, "Protection or Prosecution for Omar Al Bashir? The Changing Face of Immunity in International Criminal Law", in *Auckland Law Review*, 2011, vol. 17, p. 231.

[130] Luban, 2011, p. 69, see *supra* note 127.

[131] HUANG Huikang, 2014, p. 3, see *supra* note 128.

[132] International Criminal Court, *The Prosecutor v. Omar Hassan Ahmad Al Bashir*, Decision Pursuant to Article 87(7) of the ICC Statute on the Failure by the Republic of Malawi to Comply with the Cooperation Requests Issued by the Court with Respect to the Arrest and Surrender of Omar Hassan Ahmad Al Bashir, No. ICC-02/05-01.09, 12 December 2011, para. 43 (emphasis added).

[133] Luban, 2011, p. 70, see *supra* note 127.

[134] Sadat, 2011, p. 497, see *supra* note 10.

[135] Needham, 2011, p. 230, see *supra* note 129.

removal of such immunity in the cases of vast international crimes, and we will see more spectacles of heads of State facing criminal justice where, "strikingly, they stand revealed as bodies natural, not bodies politic".[136]

14.2.3.2. Universal Jurisdiction

Article 10(3) of the Proposed Convention provides:

> Each State Party shall likewise take such measures as may be necessary to establish its competence to exercise jurisdiction over the offense of crimes against humanity when the alleged offender is present in any territory under its jurisdiction, unless it extradites or surrenders him or her to another State in accordance with its international oligations or surrenders him or her to an international criminal tribnal whose jurisdiction it has recognized.

The importance of filling the jurisdictional *lacuna* for CAH is evident considering the gargantuan length and cost of trials in the ICTY, ICTR and ICC.[137] Furthermore, the normative incongruence between universal jurisdiction regarding different international crimes creates uneasiness in the operation of international law. Crimes of torture and war crimes, by virtue of the Torture Convention and the Geneva Conventions respectively, entail obligation of prosecution by the State where a suspected criminal is present; crimes against humanity do not. This manifests a "significant loophole" in international law.[138]

Customary law, and to an extent international conventions, have certainly been moving towards the establishment of a duty of exercising universal jurisdiction, but they have not yet accomplished that goal. The ICC Statute pronounces a duty of States to exercise jurisdiction in the preamble, but such duty is not addressed in the operative provisions. Therefore, beyond the two situations where the conduct occurred on the territory of the State, or where the person accused is a national of the State, "mere custody of a person accused of CAH does not entail any ob-

---

[136] Luban, 2011, p. 70, see *supra* note 127.

[137] Payam Akhavan, "The Universal Repression of Crimes Against Humanity before National Jurisdictions: The Need for a Treaty-Based Obligation to Prosecute", in Leila Nadya Sadat (ed.), *Forging a Convention for Crimes Against Humanity*, *op. cit.*, p. 30.

[138] *Ibid.*, p. 31.

---

ligations under the Rome Statute".[139] Customary law seems to support the view that States have a right to exercise universal jurisdiction in CAH cases, but not the obligation to do so.[140] Judges in the ICJ, however, spoke recently of the "clear indications pointing to a gradual evolution" of universal jurisdiction for CAH.[141]

The value of the inclusion of universal jurisdiction obligations in the Proposed Convention cannot be overstated. In Article 10(3), the Proposed Convention effectively imposes a duty on States to prosecute individuals accused of CAH whenever that person is under the country's control, and thus significantly expands the State's remit for prosecution. Obliging States to operate universal jurisdiction is substantially more powerful than the option to do so. For instance, despite their 'no safe haven' policy, Canadian courts have demonstrated that the cost and difficulty of obtaining convictions in international CAH cases remarkably reduces the incentive to prosecute crimes with no direct connection to the State.[142] Moreover, Akhavan has discussed the benefits of crystallising and entrenching current 'soft law' into an established international norm, with the Proposed Convention having a "profound impact on expediting this process of convergence".[143] The ambitious effort of drafters of the Proposed Convention has finally instigated "a first step in a long and tortuous road to universal accountability".[144]

14.3. Concluding Remarks

Crimes Against Humanity are patently heinous, and the need for providing an international convention to deal with them is strong. While individual aspects of the Proposed Convention may be criticised, the negotiation process is unpredictable. The preservation of individual tenets cannot be guaranteed. I particularly hope that this opportunity is grasped by legislators to offer a more in-depth definition of 'crimes against humanity'

---

[139] *Ibid.*, p. 33.

[140] *Ibid.*, p. 31.

[141] International Court of Justice, *Arrest Warrant of 11 April 2000 (Democratic Republic of the Congo v. Belgium)*, Joint Separate Opinion of Judges Higgins, Koojimans and Buergenthal, 14 February 2002, para. 52.

[142] Akhavan, 2011, p. 32, see *supra* note 137.

[143] *Ibid.*

[144] *Ibid.*

with regard to gender crimes and, to an even greater extent, persecution on the grounds of sexuality. While far from perfect, the Proposed Convention represents a milestone and building block on the road to ending impunity for core international crimes and, ultimately, preventing such crimes.

> Law, like blueprints written on paper, must be built into the structures of human life. The nations of the world must enact the provisions of this international Convention into their national laws. Using national courts, the nave and the transept of the cathedral of international criminal law will be built, block by national block. And someday, after our lifetimes, great windows will light it, not with the colour of human blood, but with the green of the grass, the blue of the sky, and the gold of the sun.[145]

---

[145] Stanton, 2011, p. 358, see *supra* note 1.

ANNEX 1

Proposed International Convention on the Prevention and Punishment of Crimes Against Humanity[1]

Preamble

The States Parties to the present Convention,

Conscious that all people are united by common bonds and share certain common values,

Affirming their belief in the need to effectively protect human life and human dignity,

Reaffirming their commitment to the purposes and principles of the United Nations, outlined in its Charter, and to the universal human rights norms reflected in the Universal Declaration of Human Rights and other relevant international instruments,

Mindful of the millions of people, particularly women and children, who over the course of human history have been subjected to extermination, persecution, crimes of sexual violence, and other atrocities that have shocked the conscience of humanity,

---

[1] © Leila Nadya Sadat, 2011. Reprinted with the permission of Professor Leila Nadya Sadat, Washington University School of Law, Whitney R. Harris World Law Institute. The *Proposed International Convention on the Prevention and Punishment of Crimes Against Humanity* is a product of a multi-year project (the 'Crimes Against Humanity Initiative'), and has been translated from the original English into six languages: Arabic, Chinese, French, German, Spanish and Russian. These translations are available on the Initiative's web site http://crimesagainsthumanity.wustl.edu/. The *Proposed Convention* was originally published in *Forging a Convention for Crimes Against Humanity*, *op.cit*. This version of the text was issued in February 2012 and contains minor corrections of the original text from August 2010. The corrections are listed in a corrigendum published on 17 February 2012.

Emphasizing their commitment to spare the world community and their respective societies the recurrence of atrocities, by preventing the commission of crimes against humanity, and prosecuting and punishing the perpetrators of such crimes,

Determined to put an end to impunity for the perpetrators of crimes against humanity by ensuring their fair and effective prosecution and punishment at the national and international levels,

Recognizing that fair and effective prosecution and punishment of the perpetrators of crimes against humanity necessitates good faith and effective international cooperation,

Recognizing that effective international cooperation is dependent upon the capacity of individual States Parties to fulfill their international obligations, and that ensuring the capacity of each State Party to fulfill its obligations to prevent and punish crimes against humanity is in the interest of all States Parties,

Recalling that it is the duty of every State to exercise its criminal jurisdiction over those responsible for international crimes, including crimes against humanity,

Recalling the contributions made by the statutes and jurisprudence of international, national, and other tribunals established pursuant to an international legal instrument, to the affirmation and development of the prevention and punishment of crimes against humanity,

Recalling that crimes against humanity constitute crimes under international law, which may give rise to the responsibility of States for internationally wrongful acts,

Recalling Article 7 and other relevant provisions of the Rome Statute of the International Criminal Court,

Declaring that in cases not covered by the present Convention or by other international agreements, the human person remains under the protection and authority of the principles of international law derived from established customs, from the laws of humanity, and from the dictates of the public conscience, and continues to enjoy the fundamental rights that are recognized by international law,

Have agreed as follows:

Explanatory Note

What follows are cross-references to other international instruments. For full commentary on the Convention and description of the choices made therein, see the Comprehensive History of the Proposed CAH Convention.

1. *The word "Punishment" tracks the Genocide Convention.*

2. *Preambular paragraphs 1, 4, 6 and 9 draw heavily from the Preamble to the Rome Statute of the International Criminal Court.*

3. *Preambular paragraph 3 draws upon the Preamble to the Enforced Disappearance Convention.*

4. *Preambular paragraphs 5, 6 and 7 include language specifically directed at both prevention and punishment.*

5. *Preambular paragraph 8 is intended to forcefully emphasize the importance of capacity building to ensuring the effective operation of the present Convention.*

6. *The reference in preambular paragraph 10 to "other tribunals established pursuant to an international legal instrument" includes mixed-model tribunals such as the Special Court for Sierra Leone.*

7. *Preambular paragraph 11 acknowledges that crimes against humanity may give rise to the responsibility of States for internationally wrongful acts. This does not mean that State responsibility necessarily attaches. See Article 1 and accompanying Explanatory Note.*

8. *Preambular paragraph 13 is inspired by the Martens Clause appearing in the Preamble to the Hague Convention of 1907 and by Article 10 of the Rome Statute.*

Contents

Article 1
Nature of the Crime

Crimes against humanity, whether committed in time of armed conflict or in time of peace, constitute crimes under international law for which there is individual criminal responsibility. In addition, States may be held responsible for crimes against humanity pursuant to principles of State responsibility for internationally wrongful acts.

Explanatory Note

1. *States Parties to the present Convention who are also Parties to the Rome Statute are bound by their obligations under that Statute. The obligations arising under the present Convention are therefore compatible with the Rome Statute. In addition, the provisions of the present Convention regulate the bilateral relations between the States Parties to the Rome Statute. The present Convention also offers an opportunity for States that are not parties to the Rome Statute to regulate their bilateral relations with other States, whether Parties to the Rome Statute or not.*

2. *The prohibition against crimes against humanity exists under customary international law and this provision incorporates the customary international law development, which recognizes that crimes against humanity may be committed in time of armed conflict and in time of peace.*

3. *Article 1, like preambular paragraph 11, acknowledges that crimes against humanity may give rise to the responsibility of States for internationally wrongful acts should breaches of the present Convention be attributable to a State Party in accordance with the International Law Commission's Draft Articles on Responsibility of States for Internationally Wrongful Acts adopted in 2001.*

4. *Specific reference to State responsibility underscores the applicability of State responsibility principles to the present Convention.*

Article 2
Object and Purposes of the Present Convention

1.   The States Parties to the present Convention undertake to prevent crimes against humanity and to investigate, prosecute, and punish those responsible for such crimes.

2.   To these ends, each State Party agrees:

   (a)   To cooperate, pursuant to the provisions of the present Convention, with other States Parties to prevent crimes against humanity;

   (b)   To investigate, prosecute and punish persons responsible for crimes against humanity fairly and effectively;

   (c)   To cooperate, pursuant to the provisions of the present Convention, with other States Parties, with the International Criminal Court if the State is a Party to the Rome Statute, and with other tribunals established pursuant to an international legal instrument having jurisdiction over crimes against humanity, in the fair and effective investigation, prosecution and punishment of persons responsible for crimes against humanity; and

   (d)   To assist other States Parties in fulfilling their obligations in accordance with Article 8 of the present Convention.

Explanatory Note

1.   *This provision highlights the three core "pillars" of the present Convention: prevention, punishment, and effective capacity building to facilitate such prevention and punishment.*

2.   *The reference in paragraph 2(c) to other international tribunals includes the ad hoc tribunals such as the International Criminal Tribunal for the former Yugoslavia and the International Criminal Tribunal for Rwanda, as well as mixed-model tribunals established pursuant to an international legal instrument, such as the Special Court for Sierra Leone, and the Extraordinary Chambers in the Courts of Cambodia. With regard to this provision's reference to a State Party cooperating*

with the International Criminal Court, it should be noted that States Parties to the Rome Statute may have such an obligation. States which are not Party to the Rome Statute have no such obligation absent a referral by the Security Council or voluntary acceptance of the Court's jurisdiction, but may co-operate with the International Criminal Court. This provision recognizes that such States may cooperate with the International Criminal Court, but does not impose an independent obligation to do so.

3. *The reference in Article 2(d) to assisting "States Parties in fulfilling their obligations" includes the obligations in Article 8 to facilitate State capacity building.*

Article 3
Definition of Crimes Against Humanity

1. For the purpose of the present Convention, "crimes against humanity" means any of the following acts when committed as part of a widespread or systematic attack directed against any civilian population, with knowledge of the attack:

    (a) Murder;

    (b) Extermination;

    (c) Enslavement;

    (d) Deportation or forcible transfer of population;

    (e) Imprisonment or other severe deprivation of physical liberty in violation of fundamental rules of international law;

    (f) Torture;

    (g) Rape, sexual slavery, enforced prostitution, forced pregnancy, enforced sterilization, or any other form of sexual violence of comparable gravity;

    (h) Persecution against any identifiable group or collectivity on political, racial, national, ethnic, cultural, religious, gender as defined in paragraph 3, or other grounds that are universally recognized as impermissible under international law, in connection with any act referred to in this paragraph or in connection with acts of genocide or war crimes;

    (i) Enforced disappearance of persons;

    (j) The crime of apartheid;

    (k) Other inhumane acts of a similar character intentionally causing great suffering, or serious injury to body or to mental or physical health.

2. For the purpose of paragraph 1:

    (a) "Attack directed against any civilian population" means a course of conduct involving the multiple commission of acts referred to in paragraph 1 against any civilian population, pursuant to or in furtherance of a State or organizational policy to commit such attack;

(b) "Extermination" includes the intentional infliction of conditions of life, *inter alia* the deprivation of access to food and medicine, calculated to bring about the destruction of part of a population;

(c) "Enslavement" means the exercise of any or all of the powers attaching to the right of ownership over a person and includes the exercise of such power in the course of trafficking in persons, in particular women and children;

(d) "Deportation or forcible transfer of population" means forced displacement of the persons concerned by expulsion or other coercive acts from the area in which they are lawfully present, without grounds permitted under international law;

(e) "Torture" means the intentional infliction of severe pain or suffering, whether physical or mental, upon a person in the custody or under the control of the accused; except that torture shall not include pain or suffering arising only from, inherent in or incidental to, lawful sanctions;

(f) "Forced pregnancy" means the unlawful confinement of a woman forcibly made pregnant, with the intent of affecting the ethnic composition of any population or carrying out other grave violations of international law. This definition shall not in any way be interpreted as affecting national laws relating to pregnancy;

(g) "Persecution" means the intentional and severe deprivation of fundamental rights contrary to international law by reason of the identity of the group or collectivity;

(h) "The crime of apartheid" means inhumane acts of a character similar to those referred to in paragraph 1, committed in the context of an institutionalized regime of systematic oppression and domination by one racial group over any other racial group or groups and committed with the intention of maintaining that regime;

(i) "Enforced disappearance of persons" means the arrest, detention or abduction of persons by, or with the authorization, support or acquiescence of, a State or a political organization, followed by a refusal to acknowledge that deprivation of freedom or to give information on the fate or whereabouts of those persons, with the intention of removing them from the protection of the law for a prolonged period of time.

3.   For the purposes of the present Convention, it is understood that the term "gender" refers to the two sexes, male and female, within the context of society. The term "gender" does not indicate any meaning different from the above.

Explanatory Note

1. *The text of paragraphs 1 and 2 incorporates the definition contained in Article 7 of the Rome Statute, with two necessary modifications of language specific to the International Criminal Court in subparagraph 1(h), whereby the following language was used: "gender as defined in paragraph 3," and "or in connection with acts of genocide or war crimes."*

2. *No substantive changes to Article 7 of the Rome Statute have been made.*

3. *As used in paragraph 1(k) of the present Convention, "[o]ther inhumane acts of a similar character" could be interpreted, in keeping with Articles II(b) and II(c) of the Genocide Convention, as including acts which cause the same harmful results as the acts listed in subparagraphs (a) through (j).*

Article 4
Individual Criminal Responsibility

1. A person who commits a crime against humanity shall be individually responsible and liable for punishment in accordance with the present Convention.

2. In accordance with the present Convention, a person shall be criminally responsible and liable for punishment for a crime against humanity if that person:

    (a) Commits such a crime, whether as an individual, jointly with another or through another person, regardless of whether that other person is criminally responsible;

    (b) Orders, solicits or induces the commission of such a crime which in fact occurs or is attempted;

    (c) For the purposes of facilitating the commission of such a crime, aids, abets or otherwise assists in its commission or its attempted commission, including providing the means for its commission;

    (d) In any other way contributes to the commission or attempted commission of such a crime by a group of persons acting with a common purpose. Such contribution shall be intentional and shall either:

        (i) Be made with the aim of furthering the criminal activity or criminal purpose of the group, where such activity or purpose involves the commission of a crime against humanity; or

        (ii) Be made in the knowledge of the intention of the group to commit the crime;

    (e) Directly and publicly incites others to commit crimes against humanity;

    (f) Attempts to commit such a crime by taking action that commences its execution by means of a substantial step, but the crime does not occur because of circumstances independent of the person's intentions. However, a person who abandons the effort to commit the crime or otherwise prevents the completion of the crime shall not be liable for punishment under the present Convention for the attempt to commit that crime if that person completely and voluntarily gave up the criminal purpose.

3.   No provision in the present Convention relating to individual criminal responsibility shall affect the responsibility of States under international law for internationally wrongful acts.

Explanatory Note

This provision draws upon Article 25 of the Rome Statute.

Article 5
Responsibility of Commanders and other Superiors

In addition to other grounds of criminal responsibility under the present Convention for crimes within the jurisdiction of a court:

1. A military commander or person effectively acting as a military commander shall be criminally responsible for crimes within the jurisdiction of a court committed by forces under his or her effective command and control, or effective authority and control as the case may be, as a result of his or her failure to exercise control properly over such forces, whereas,

    (a) That military commander or person either knew or, owing to the circumstances at the time, should have known that the forces were committing or about to commit such crimes; and

    (b) That military commander or person failed to take all necessary and reasonable measures within his or her power to prevent or repress their commission or to submit the matter to the competent authorities for investigation and prosecution.

2. With respect to superior and subordinate relationships not described in paragraph 1, a superior shall be criminally responsible for crimes within the jurisdiction of a court committed by subordinates under his or her effective authority and control, as a result of his or her failure to exercise control properly over such subordinates, where:

    (a) The superior either knew, or consciously disregarded information which clearly indicated, that the subordinates were committing or about to commit such crimes; and

    (b) The crimes concerned activities that were within the effective responsibility and control of the superior; and

    (c) The superior failed to take all necessary and reasonable measures within his or her power to prevent or repress their commission or to submit the matter to the competent authorities for investigation and prosecution.

Explanatory Note

This provision is from Article 28 of the Rome Statute.

Article 6
Irrelevance of Official Capacity

1.   The present Convention shall apply equally to all persons without any distinction based on official capacity. In particular, official capacity as a Head of State or Government, a member of a Government or parliament, an elected representative or a government official shall in no case exempt a person from criminal responsibility under the present Convention, nor shall it, in and of itself, constitute a ground for reduction of sentence.

2.   Immunities or special procedural rules which may attach to the official capacity of a person, whether under national or international law, shall not bar a court from exercising its jurisdiction over such a person.

Explanatory Note

1.   *This language draws heavily upon Article 27 of the Rome Statute. However, in paragraph 2 of this Article, "the Court" has been changed to "a court," meaning any duly constituted judicial institutions having jurisdiction.*

2.   *Paragraph 2 draws upon the dissenting opinion of Judge Van den Wyngaert from the ICJ's judgment in the Case Concerning the Arrest Warrant of 11 April 2000 (Democratic Republic of the Congo v. Belgium), Judgment of 14 February 2002, and supports a different and more expansive principle than Article 27(2) of the Rome Statute.*

Article 7
Non-applicability of Statute of Limitations

Crimes against humanity as defined by the present Convention shall not be subject to any statute of limitations.

Explanatory Note

1. *This language draws upon Article 29 of the Rome Statute.*

2. *States Parties to the present Convention undertake to adopt, in accordance with their respective constitutional processes, any legislative or other measures necessary to ensure that statutory or other limitations shall not apply to the prosecution and punishment of crimes against humanity as defined in the present Convention and that, where they exist, such limitations shall be abolished.*

Article 8
Obligations of States Parties

1. Each State Party shall enact necessary legislation and other measures as required by its Constitution or legal system to give effect to the provisions of the present Convention and, in particular, to take effective legislative, administrative, judicial and other measures in accordance with the Charter of the United Nations to prevent and punish the commission of crimes against humanity in any territory under its jurisdiction or control.

A. Legislation and Penalties

2. Each State Party shall adopt such legislative and other measures as may be necessary to establish crimes against humanity as serious offenses under its criminal law, as well as its military law, and make such offenses punishable by appropriate penalties which take into account the grave nature of those offenses, the harm committed, and the individual circumstances of the offender. In addition, such a person may be barred from holding public rank or office, be it military or civilian, including elected office.

3. Each State Party shall adopt such legislative and other measures as may be necessary to ensure that a military commander or person effectively acting as a military commander shall be criminally responsible for crimes against humanity as set forth in Article 5, paragraph 1.

4. Each State Party shall adopt such legislative and other measures as may be necessary to ensure that, with respect to superior and subordinate relationships not described in paragraph 3, a superior shall be criminally responsible for crimes against humanity as set forth in Article 5, paragraph 2.

5. Each State Party shall adopt such legislative and other measures as may be necessary to ensure in its legal system that the victims of crimes against humanity have the right to equal and effective access to justice, and the right to adequate, effective and prompt reparation for harm suffered, including, where appropriate:

    (a)   Restitution;

(b)   Compensation;

(c)   Rehabilitation;

(d)   Satisfaction, including restoration of reputation and dignity; and

(e)   Measures to ensure non-repetition.

Each State Party shall ensure that, in the event of the death of a victim of crimes against humanity, his or her heirs shall be entitled to the same rights to equal and effective access to justice, and to adequate, effective and prompt reparation.

6.   Each State Party shall adopt such legislative and other measures as may be necessary, consistent with its legal principles, to establish the liability of legal persons for participation in crimes against humanity. Subject to the legal principles of the State Party, the liability of legal persons may be criminal, civil or administrative. Such liability shall be without prejudice to the criminal liability of the natural persons who have committed the offense. Each State Party shall, in particular, develop administrative measures designed to provide reparation to victims, and to ensure that legal persons held liable in accordance with this article are subject to effective, proportionate and dissuasive criminal or non-criminal sanctions, including monetary sanctions.

B. Investigation and Prosecution

7.   Upon receiving information that a person who has committed or who is alleged to have committed crimes against humanity may be present in its territory, the State Party concerned shall take such measures as may be necessary under its domestic law to investigate the facts contained in the information.

8.   Upon being satisfied that the circumstances so warrant, the State Party in whose territory the person who has committed or who is alleged to have committed crimes against humanity is present shall take the necessary and appropriate measures under its domestic law so as to ensure that person's presence for the purpose of prosecution or extradition.

9. States Parties shall prosecute or extradite those charged with or suspected of committing crimes against humanity.

10. Each State Party shall ensure that any individual who alleges that he or she has been subjected to crimes against humanity in any part of the territory under its jurisdiction has the right to complain to the competent legal authorities and to have his or her case promptly and impartially examined by the competent judicial authorities.

11. Each State Party shall take appropriate measures in accordance with its domestic legal system and within its means to provide effective protection from potential retaliation or intimidation for witnesses and experts who give testimony concerning crimes against humanity and, as appropriate, for their relatives and other persons close to them. Such measures may include, *inter alia*, without prejudice to the rights of the accused, including the right to due process:

    (a) Establishing procedures for the physical protection of such persons such as, to the extent necessary and feasible, relocating them and permitting, where appropriate, non-disclosure or limitations on the disclosure of information concerning the identity and whereabouts of such persons;

    (b) Providing evidentiary rules to permit witnesses and experts to give testimony in a manner that ensures the safety of such persons, such as permitting testimony to be given through the use of communications technology such as video or other adequate means.

C. Prevention

12. Each State Party shall endeavor to take measures in accordance with its domestic legal system to prevent crimes against humanity. Such measures include, but are not limited to, ensuring that any advocacy of national, racial, or religious hatred that constitutes incitement to discrimination, hostility, or violence shall be prohibited by law.

13. States Parties may call upon the competent organs of the United Nations to take such action in accordance with the Charter of the

United Nations as they consider appropriate for the prevention and punishment of crimes against humanity.

14.   States Parties may also call upon the competent organs of a regional organization to take such action in accordance with the Charter of the United Nations as they consider appropriate for the prevention and punishment of crimes against humanity.

15.   States Parties shall develop educational and informational programs regarding the prohibition of crimes against humanity including the training of law enforcement officers, military personnel, or other relevant public officials in order to:

(a)   Prevent the involvement of such officials in crimes against humanity;

(b)   Emphasize the importance of prevention and investigations in relation to crimes against humanity;

16.   Each State Party shall ensure that orders or instructions prescribing, authorizing, or encouraging crimes against humanity are prohibited. Each State Party shall guarantee that a person who refuses to obey such an order will not be punished. Moreover, each State Party shall take the necessary measures to ensure that persons who have reason to believe that crimes against humanity have occurred or are planned to occur, and who report the matter to their superiors or to appropriate authorities or bodies vested with powers of review or remedy are not punished for such conduct.

D. Cooperation

17.   States Parties shall cooperate with States or tribunals established pursuant to an international legal instrument having jurisdiction in the investigation, prosecution, and punishment of crimes against humanity.

18.   States Parties shall afford one another the greatest measure of assistance and cooperation in the course of any investigation or prosecution of persons alleged to be responsible for crimes against humanity irrespective of whether there exist between said States Parties any treaties on extradition or mutual legal assistance.

E. Capacity Building

19.　States Parties shall to the extent possible provide one another capacity building assistance on an individual basis or through the mechanisms outlined in Article 19.

Explanatory Note

1.　This provision draws upon similar language from other international criminal law conventions. Paragraph 1 of this provision provides that measures taken by States Parties to prevent and repress crimes against humanity must be in accordance with the Charter of the United Nations. It should also be understood, however, that the obligation to prevent crimes against humanity includes the obligation not to provide aid or assistance to facilitate the commission of crimes against humanity by another State. See ILC Draft Articles on Responsibility of States for Internationally Wrongful Acts, Article 16, commentary paragraph (9). See also the ICJ's judgment in the Application of the Convention on the Prevention and Punishment of the Crime of Genocide (Bosnia and Herzegovina v. Serbia and Montenegro), Judgment of 26 February 2007, paragraphs 425-38. This is consistent with Article 1 of the present Convention.

2.　With regard to paragraph 2, it is understood that the obligations of States Parties apply to all institutions and organs of the State without exception including, inter alia, military courts and any other special proceedings. The language regarding penalties is drawn from Article 4(1) of the Torture Convention. The current provision acknowledges, however, that States Parties may have different obligations arising under regional human rights conventions, and earlier language requiring penalties to be no less severe than those applicable for the most serious crimes of a similar nature has been removed. With regard to barring individuals found responsible for crimes against humanity from holding public rank or of-

fice, the permissive "may" was included to avoid possible contradiction with the jurisprudence of the European Court of Human Rights. There is, however, language in Velásquez Rodríguez v. Honduras (Merits), Inter-Am. Ct. H.R., 29 July 1988, Ser. C, No. 4, to support the proposition that persons who abused power to commit crimes against humanity could be barred from holding public office.

3. Paragraphs 3 and 4 require States Parties to enact legislation to ensure that military commanders and other superiors are criminally responsible for crimes against humanity committed by subordinates under their effective command and control, or effective authority and control as the case may be, as a result of the commander or superior's failure to exercise control over such subordinates.

4. Paragraph 5 draws upon the General Assembly's Resolution adopting Basic Principles and Guidelines on the Right to a Remedy and Reparation for Victims of Gross Violations of International Human Rights Law and Serious Violations of International Humanitarian Law, UN Doc. A/RES/60/147 (March 21, 2006).

5. In order to avoid impunity or de facto immunity for those persons who act collectively or within a legal structure, States Parties should enact legislation capable of reaching such entities. Paragraph 6 draws heavily upon Article 26 of the UN Convention Against Corruption to oblige States Parties to adopt appropriate legislation and develop administrative measures designed to provide reparation to victims.

6. Paragraph 7 is from Article 7(1) of the Terrorist Bombing Convention. It also covers persons who have committed crimes against humanity or alleged to have done so.

7. Paragraph 8 is from Article 7(2) of the Terrorist Bombing Convention.

8. Paragraph 9 recognizes the obligation of aut dedere aut judicare.

9. Paragraph 10 draws upon Article 13 of the Torture Convention but includes language clarifying that the State Party's ob-

ligation extends to "*any part of the*" *territory under its jurisdiction.*

10. *Paragraph 11 draws upon Article 32 of the UN Convention Against Corruption.*

11. *The language of paragraph 12 is from Article 20 of the ICCPR.*

12. *Paragraph 13 is from Article VIII of the Genocide Convention. This is consistent with paragraph 1 of the present provision, which provides that any measures taken by States Parties to prevent and punish crimes against humanity must be in accordance with the Charter of the United Nations.*

13. *The term competent used here means the appropriate body within the regional instrument and also those bodies acting within its constituent instrument.*

14. *Paragraphs 15 and 16 oblige States Parties to develop education and training sessions in order to give effect to the obligation to prevent crimes against humanity. These paragraphs draw heavily upon Article 23 of the Enforced Disappearance Convention.*

15. *The Summary of Recommendations of the Genocide Prevention Task Force Report sets forth specific policy measures for education and prevention, which cannot be incorporated into normative provisions of the present Convention. However, if the present Convention has a treaty body that recommends specific measures to States Parties, such a body may use these recommendations.*

16. *Recognizing that capacity building is one of the core functions of the present Convention, paragraph 19 provides that States Parties, to the extent possible, shall provide one another capacity building assistance. Providing capacity building technical assistance to States Parties is one of the mandated functions of the permanent Secretariat to be established pursuant to Article 19, paragraphs 10 and 11.*

17. *Although it defines the obligations of States Parties, this article makes no explicit reference to State responsibility. Both preambular paragraph 11 and Article 1 explicitly recognize that crimes against humanity are crimes under international*

law which may give rise to the responsibility of States for internationally wrongful acts.

Article 9
Aut Dedere Aut Judicare (Prosecute or Extradite)

1. Each State Party shall take necessary measures to establish its competence to exercise jurisdiction over crimes against humanity when the alleged offender is present in any territory under its jurisdiction, unless it extradites him or her to another State in accordance with its international obligations or surrenders him or her to the International Criminal Court, if it is a State Party to the Rome Statute, or to another international criminal tribunal whose jurisdiction it has recognized.

2. In the event that a State Party does not, for any reason not specified in the present Convention, prosecute a person suspected of committing crimes against humanity, it shall, pursuant to an appropriate request, either surrender such a person to another State willing to prosecute fairly and effectively, to the International Criminal Court, if it is a State Party to the Rome Statute, or to a competent international tribunal having jurisdiction over crimes against humanity.

Explanatory Note

1. *Paragraph 1 draws upon Article 9(2) of the Enforced Disappearance Convention.*

2. *Paragraph 2 reflects the principle aut dedere aut judicare.*

3. *With regard to this provision's reference to a State Party surrendering an accused individual to the International Criminal Court, it should be noted that States Parties to the Rome Statute may have such an obligation. States which are not Party to the Rome Statute may have no such obligation, but may cooperate with the International Criminal Court. This provision recognizes that such States may cooperate with the International Criminal Court, but does not impose an independent obligation to do so.*

Article 10
Jurisdiction

1. Persons alleged to be responsible for crimes against humanity shall be tried by a criminal court of the State Party, or by the International Criminal Court, or by an international tribunal having jurisdiction over crimes against humanity.

2. Each State Party shall take the necessary measures to establish its competence to exercise jurisdiction over persons alleged to be responsible for crimes against humanity:

    (a) When the offense is committed in any territory under its jurisdiction or onboard a ship or aircraft registered in that State or whenever a person is under the physical control of that State; or

    (b) When the person alleged to be responsible is one of its nationals; or

    (c) When the victim is one of its nationals and the State Party considers it appropriate.

3. Each State Party shall likewise take such measures as may be necessary to establish its competence to exercise jurisdiction over the offense of crimes against humanity when the alleged offender is present in any territory under its jurisdiction, unless it extradites or surrenders him or her to another State in accordance with its international obligations or surrenders him or her to an international criminal tribunal whose jurisdiction it has recognized.

4. The present Convention does not preclude the exercise of any other competent criminal jurisdiction compatible with international law and which is exercised in accordance with national law.

5. For purposes of cooperation, jurisdiction shall be deemed to exist whenever the person responsible for, or alleged to be responsible for, crimes against humanity is present in the State's territory or the State Party is in a position to exercise physical control over him or her.

Explanatory Note

1. *It is understood that the reference in paragraph 1 to "an international tribunal having jurisdiction," is with respect to any State Party that shall have accepted the jurisdiction of such tribunal. This provision also recognizes the principle of complementarity embodied in the Rome Statute.*

2. *Paragraph 2 draws upon the language of Article 9(1) of the Enforced Disappearance Convention. This provision is intended to avoid litigation over the scope of territorial application.*

3. *Paragraph 3 draws upon Article 9(2) of the Enforced Disappearance Convention and Article 5(2) of the Torture Convention.*

4. *Paragraph 4 draws upon Article 9(3) of the Enforced Disappearance Convention.*

5. *Paragraph 5 is intended to ensure that there exists no jurisdictional gap in a State Party's capacity to exercise jurisdiction over a person who is responsible for, or is alleged to be responsible for, crimes against humanity, and would apply to persons transiting a State Party's territory even where the State Party is not in a position to exercise physical control over the person.*

Article 11
Evidence

1. The rules of evidence required for prosecution shall be those in existence under the national laws of the State Party conducting the investigation, prosecution, or post-trial proceedings but shall in no way be less stringent than those that apply in cases of similar gravity under the law of said State Party.

2. States Parties may, for purposes of the present Convention, recognize the validity of evidence obtained by another State Party even when the legal standards and procedure for obtaining such evidence do not conform to the same standards of a given State Party. Such non-conformity shall not be grounds for exclusion of evidence, provided that the evidence is deemed credible and that it is obtained in conformity with international standards of due process. This paragraph shall apply to all aspects of the present Convention including, but not limited to: extradition, mutual legal assistance, transfer of criminal proceedings, enforcement of judicial orders, transfer and execution of foreign penal sentences, and recognition of foreign penal judgments.

3. In relation to the collection of evidence, States Parties shall endeavor to conform with international standards of due process.

Explanatory Note

1. *Paragraph 1 recognizes that in multilateral and bilateral treaties the law of evidence that applies is the law of the forum State.*

2. *In connection with mutual legal assistance and as currently reflected in Article 13 and Annex 2, it is also possible for requesting States to ask that specific conditions be employed or procedures followed in the taking of evidence by the requested State. Paragraph 2 permits States to recognize the validity of evidence obtained by another State Party, even where the requested conditions or procedures are not followed, provided that the evidence is deemed credible and that it is obtained in conformity with international standards of due process, in-*

cluding the obligation under Article 15 of the Torture Convention, which would exclude any statement made as a result of torture.

3. *Paragraph 3 obliges States to endeavor to conform to international standards of due process in the collection of evidence.*

Article 12
Extradition

States Parties shall afford one another the greatest measure of assistance in connection with extradition requests made with respect to crimes against humanity in accordance with the provisions of Annex 2.

Explanatory Note

The obligation to extradite or prosecute persons responsible for, or alleged to be responsible for, crimes against humanity is found in Article 8, paragraph 9 and Article 9 of the present Convention. Applicable modalities are provided in Annex 2.

Article 13
Mutual Legal Assistance

States Parties shall afford one another the greatest measure of assistance in connection with investigations, prosecutions and judicial proceedings brought with respect to crimes against humanity in accordance with the provisions of Annex 3.

Explanatory Note

The modalities by which States Parties are obliged to afford one another mutual legal assistance are outlined in Annex 3, which is drawn from the mutual legal assistance provisions of Article 46 of the UN Convention Against Corruption.

Article 14
Transfer of Criminal Proceedings

States Parties having jurisdiction in a case involving crimes against humanity may engage in a transfer of criminal proceedings in accordance with Annex 4.

<u>Explanatory Note</u>

The modalities by which States Parties may engage in a transfer of criminal proceedings under the present Convention are contained in Annex 4, which is based on the European Transfer of Proceedings Convention and its Protocol.

Article 15
Transfer of Convicted Persons for the Execution of Their Sentences

States Parties may transfer to one another a person convicted of crimes against humanity in their respective legal systems for purposes of the execution of such convicted person's sentence in accordance with the provisions of Annex 5.

Explanatory Note

The modalities by which States Parties may transfer persons convicted of crimes against humanity for the execution of their sentences are outlined in Annex 5, which is based on the European Convention on the Transfer of Sentenced Persons as well as the Inter-American Criminal Sentences Convention.

Article 16
Enforcement of the Effects of States Parties' Penal Judgments

A State Party may recognize and enforce the effects of another State Party's penal judgments in accordance with the provisions of Annex 6.

<u>Explanatory Note</u>

This provision acknowledges that States may recognize and enforce the effects of another State Party's penal judgments. The modalities for such recognition and enforcement are found in Annex 6, which is based on the European Convention on the International Validity of Criminal Judgments.

Article 17
Ne Bis in Idem

A person effectively prosecuted for crimes against humanity and convicted or acquitted cannot be prosecuted by another State Party for the same crime based on the same or substantially same facts underlying the earlier prosecution.

Explanatory Note

1. *This provision recognizes the ne bis in idem principle, which is found in many international instruments, including Article 14(7) of the ICCPR, Article 20 of the Rome Statute, Article 10 of the ICTY Statute, and Article 9 of the ICTR Statute.*

2. *This provision recognizes that for the ne bis in idem principle to apply as a bar to a subsequent prosecution, the first prosecution must have been conducted "effectively." Pursuant to Annex 1(b), "effectively" means diligently, independently and impartially in a manner not designed to shield the person concerned from criminal responsibility for crimes against humanity and consistent with an intent to bring the person concerned to justice, bearing in mind respect for the principle of the presumption of innocence.*

Article 18
Non-refoulement

1. No State Party shall expel, return (*"refouler"*) or extradite a person to another State where there are substantial grounds for believing that such a person would be in danger of being subjected to crimes against humanity.

2. For the purpose of determining whether there are such grounds, the competent authorities shall take into account all relevant considerations including, where applicable, the existence in the State concerned of a consistent pattern of gross, flagrant or mass violations of human rights or of serious violations of international humanitarian law.

<u>Explanatory Note</u>

1. *This provision draws upon Article 16 of the Enforced Disappearance Convention, which is in turn drawn from Article 8 of the Enforced Disappearance Declaration. A similar obligation, specific to torture, is found in the Torture Convention.*

2. *Paragraph 1 also draws upon Article 3(1) of the Torture Convention.*

3. *The non-refoulement provision of the present Convention is limited to situations involving crimes against humanity because such crimes form the core subject matter of the present Convention. In this regard, the present Convention follows the approach of the Enforced Disappearance Convention and the Torture Convention.*

Article 19
Institutional Mechanisms

A. Conference of States Parties

1.   A Conference of States Parties to the present Convention is hereby established to improve the capacity of and cooperation between States Parties to achieve the objectives set forth in the present Convention and to promote and review its implementation.

2.   The Secretary-General of the United Nations shall convene the Conference of States Parties not later than one year following the entry into force of the present Convention. Thereafter, regular meetings of the Conference of States Parties shall be held every three years. With regard to the first convening of the Conference of States Parties by the Secretary-General of the United Nations, the Secretary-General shall provide the necessary secretariat services to the Conference of States Parties to the Convention. The secretariat provided by the Secretary-General of the United Nations shall:

     (a)   Assist the Conference of States Parties in carrying out the activities set forth in this article and make arrangements and provide the necessary services for the sessions of the Conference of States Parties;

     (b)   Upon request, assist States Parties in providing information to the Conference of States Parties as envisaged in paragraphs 5 and 6; and

     (c)   Ensure the necessary coordination with the secretariats of relevant international and regional organizations.

3.   Each State Party shall have one representative in the Conference who may be accompanied by alternates and advisers. The Conference of States Parties shall adopt rules of procedure and rules governing the functioning of the activities set forth in this article, including rules concerning the admission and participation of ob-

servers and the payment of expenses incurred in carrying out those activities.

B. <u>Committee</u>

4. For the purpose of achieving the objectives set forth in paragraph 1 of this article, the Conference of States Parties shall establish the "Committee Established Pursuant to the International Convention on the Prevention and Punishment of Crimes Against Humanity" (the Committee).

5. The Committee shall have ten members. The members of the Committee shall be experts in matters relevant to the present Convention who are designated by the States Parties and elected by the Conference of States Parties. The members of the Committee shall be elected for a term of four years. They shall be eligible for re-election once. However, the term of five of the members elected at the first election shall expire at the end of two years. Immediately after the first election, the names of these five members shall be chosen by lot in a manner designated by the Conference of States Parties.

6. The Committee shall establish its own rules of procedure and shall agree upon activities, procedures and methods of work to achieve the objectives set forth in paragraph 1, including:

    (a) Facilitating activities by and between States Parties under the present Convention;

    (b) Facilitating the exchange of information among States Parties on successful practices for preventing and punishing crimes against humanity;

    (c) Cooperating with relevant international and regional organizations and mechanisms and non-governmental organizations;

    (d) Making appropriate use of relevant information produced by other international and regional mechanisms for preventing and punishing crimes against humanity in order to avoid unnecessary duplication of work;

(e) Making recommendations to improve the present Convention and its implementation;

(f) Taking note of the technical assistance requirements of States Parties with regard to the implementation of the present Convention and recommending any action it may deem necessary in that respect;

(g) Establishing financial rules and regulations for the functioning of the Committee and the Secretariat; and

(h) Managing the Voluntary Trust Fund established by the States Parties pursuant to paragraph 14.

7. For the purpose of paragraph 6, the Committee shall acquire the necessary knowledge of the measures taken by States Parties in implementing the present Convention and the difficulties encountered by them in doing so through information provided by States Parties and through such supplemental review mechanisms as may be established by the Committee.

8. The Committee shall examine the most effective way of receiving and acting upon information, including, *inter alia*, information received from States Parties and from competent international organizations. Input received from relevant non-governmental organizations duly accredited in accordance with procedures to be decided upon by the Committee may also be considered. Each State Party shall provide the Committee with information on its programs, plans and practices to implement the present Convention, including:

(a) The adoption of national implementing legislation;

(b) The establishment of administrative mechanisms fulfilling the prevention requirements contained in the present Convention;

(c)   Reports on data gathering regarding its obligations under the present Convention including, but not limited to, the number of allegations, investigations, prosecutions, convictions, extraditions and mutual legal assistance requests.

9.   The information provided by the States Parties shall be considered by the Committee, which shall issue such comments, observations or recommendations as it may deem appropriate. The comments, observations or recommendations shall be communicated to the State Party concerned, which may respond to them on its own initiative or at the request of the Committee. The Committee may also request States Parties to provide additional information on the implementation of the present Convention.

10.   The Committee shall establish a permanent Secretariat to facilitate its activities, procedures and methods of work to achieve the objectives set forth in paragraphs 1, 5, 6 and 7. The Committee may establish such other subsidiary bodies as may be necessary.

C. Secretariat

11.   The Secretariat's functions shall be:

(a)   Providing technical assistance to States in the process of acceding to the present Convention;

(b)   Providing technical assistance, including appropriate capacity building assistance, to States Parties in fulfilling their obligations under the present Convention;

(c)   Disseminating information between States Parties;

(d)   Facilitating mutual legal assistance and other aspects of cooperation between States Parties, including facilitating cooperation in matters involving the appearance of witnesses and experts in judicial proceedings, and in effectively protecting such persons;

(e)   Receiving and compiling information from States Parties as required by the Committee; and

(f)   Ensuring the necessary coordination with the secretariats of relevant international and regional organizations.

12.   The Secretariat shall be headquartered at _____.

D. Expenses

13.   The expenses of the Conference of States Parties, the Committee, the Secretariat, and any other subsidiary bodies shall be provided from the following sources:

(a)   Contributions of States Parties assessed in accordance with an agreed scale of assessment, based on the scale adopted by the United Nations for its regular budget and adjusted in accordance with the principles on which that scale is based;

(b)   Funds contributed on a voluntary basis by governments, inter-governmental organizations, non-governmental organizations, private organizations, foundations, and individuals.

E. Voluntary Trust Fund

14.   The States Parties shall establish a Voluntary Trust Fund managed by the Committee to provide States Parties with technical assistance and capacity building needed in support of efforts to carry out the obligations arising under the present Convention.

Explanatory Note

1. *This article draws heavily upon Articles 112, 116 and 117 of the Rome Statute, Articles 63 and 64 of the UN Convention Against Corruption, and Articles 26 and 29 of the Enforced Disappearance Convention.*

2. *Paragraph 2 of this provision will be subject to approval by the competent organs of the United Nations, including reimbursement by the States Parties to the United Nations for expenses incurred by the organization.*

3. *The experience of States Parties with this body and its functions will determine how it will evolve in the future and what role it will assume over and above the mandate mentioned in the Convention such as fact-finding for purposes of developing an early warning system.*

4. *With regard to paragraph 12, an appropriate Headquarters Agreement will need to be negotiated with the host country, subject to approval by the Conference of States Parties.*

Article 20
Federal States

The provisions of the present Convention shall apply to all parts of federal States without any limitations or exceptions.

Explanatory Note

This language is from Article 41 of the Enforced Disappearance Convention.

Article 21
Signature, Ratification, Acceptance, Approval, or Accession

1. The present Convention shall be open for signature by all States at _____ until _____.

2. The present Convention shall be subject to ratification, acceptance or approval by signatory States. Instruments of ratification, acceptance or approval shall be deposited with the Secretary-General of the United Nations.

3. The present Convention shall be open to accession by all States. Instruments of accession shall be deposited with the Secretary-General of the United Nations.

<u>Explanatory Note</u>

This article draws upon Article 125 of the Rome Statute.

Article 22
Entry into Force

1. The present Convention shall enter into force on the thirtieth (30th) day following the date of deposit of the twentieth (20th) instrument of ratification, acceptance, approval, or accession with the Secretary-General of the United Nations.

2. For each State ratifying, accepting, approving, or acceding to the present Convention after the deposit of the twentieth (20th) instrument of ratification, acceptance, approval, or accession, the Convention shall enter into force on the thirtieth (30th) day after the deposit by such State of its instrument of ratification, acceptance, approval, or accession.

Explanatory Note

Paragraphs 1 and 2 draw upon Article 126 of the Rome Statute.

Article 23
Reservations

No reservations may be made to the present Convention.

<u>Explanatory Note</u>

1. *This language is from Article 120 of the Rome Statute.*

2. *It is understood that national legislative systems vary and that these variances will apply to modalities of aut dedere aut judicare and that States may make declarations about their respective national legal systems and procedures. This applies particularly to Articles 9, 10, 11, 12, 13, 14, 15, and 16 of the present Convention.*

Article 24
Amendment

1. Any State Party to the present Convention may propose amendments thereto. The text of any proposed amendment shall be submitted to the Secretary-General of the United Nations, who shall promptly circulate it to all States Parties.

2. No sooner than three months from the date of notification, the Conference of States Parties, at its next meeting, shall, by a majority of those present and voting, decide whether to take up the proposal. The Conference may deal with the proposal directly or convene a Review Conference if the issue involved so warrants.

3. The adoption of an amendment at a meeting of the Conference of States Parties or at a Review Conference on which consensus cannot be reached shall require a two-thirds majority of States Parties.

4. Amendments to the present Convention shall enter into force one year after instruments of ratification or acceptance have been deposited with the Secretary-General of the United Nations by two-thirds of the States Parties and shall be binding on those States Parties that have accepted them; other States Parties who have not accepted the amendments shall continue to be bound by the provisions of the present Convention and any earlier amendments that they have accepted.

5. The Secretary-General of the United Nations shall circulate to all States Parties any amendment adopted at a meeting of the Conference of States Parties or at a Review Conference.

Explanatory Note

This article draws heavily upon Article 121 of the Rome Statute.

Article 25
Interpretation

The terms of the present Convention shall also be interpreted in the light of internationally recognized human rights standards and norms.

Explanatory Note

It is self-evident that the customary international law of treaty interpretation applies (codified in the Vienna Convention on the Law of Treaties). This article is also intended to ensure that the terms of the present Convention are interpreted in accordance with the regional human rights obligations of States Parties under the European Convention on Human Rights, the American Convention on Human Rights, and the African Charter on Human and Peoples' Rights, as well as in accordance with specific obligations established by treaty bodies with respect to different human rights conventions.

Article 26
Dispute Settlement Between States Parties

Any dispute between two or more States Parties concerning the interpretation or application of the present Convention, including those relating to the responsibility of a State for alleged breaches thereof, that cannot be settled through negotiation shall, at the request of one of them, be submitted to arbitration. If within six months from the date of the request for arbitration the Parties are unable to agree on the organization of the arbitration, any one of those Parties may refer the dispute to the International Court of Justice for a final and binding decision by a request in conformity with the Statute of the Court.

Explanatory Note

This provision draws upon Article 30(1) of the Torture Convention, Article 42(1) of the Enforced Disappearance Convention, and Article IX of the Genocide Convention.

Article 27
Authentic Texts

The original of the present Convention, of which the Arabic, Chinese, English, French, Russian, and Spanish texts are equally authentic, shall be deposited with the Secretary-General of the United Nations, who shall send certified copies thereof to all States.

<u>Explanatory Note</u>

This language is from Article 128 of the Rome Statute.

Annex 1
Use of Terms

For the purposes of the present Convention:

(a)   "Fair," "fairly" or "fairness" means in accordance with norms of due process recognized by international law, consistent with the minimum guarantees in criminal proceedings, as contained in the International Covenant on Civil and Political Rights;

(b)   "Effective," "effectively" or "effectiveness" means diligently, independently and impartially in a manner not designed to shield the person concerned from criminal responsibility for crimes against humanity and consistent with an intent to bring the person concerned to justice, bearing in mind respect for the principle of the presumption of innocence.

(c)   "Person" means a natural person or legal entity.

Explanatory Note

The definitions of "fair" and "effective" in paragraphs (a) and (b) are designed to ensure that States may not use sham investigations or legal proceedings to thwart their obligations to investigate, prosecute or extradite. The definition in paragraph (b) draws heavily upon the ne bis in idem principle articulated in Article 10 of the ICTY Statute and Article 20 of the Rome Statute.

Annex 2
Extradition

A. Crimes Against Humanity as Extraditable Offenses

1. Crimes against humanity shall be deemed to be included as an extraditable offense in any extradition treaty existing between States Parties before the entry into force of the present Convention.

2. States Parties undertake to include crimes against humanity as an extraditable offense in any extradition treaty subsequently to be concluded between them.

B. Legal Basis for Extradition

3. In the absence of relevant national legislation or other extradition relationship, States Parties shall consider the present Convention as the legal basis for extradition in order to fulfill their obligation to prosecute or extradite persons alleged to be responsible for crimes against humanity pursuant to Article 8, paragraph 9 and Article 9.

C. Modalities of Extradition

4. In the absence of relevant national legislation or other extradition relationship, States Parties may use all or some of the following modalities provided in this Annex.

D. Grounds for Refusal of Extradition

5. For the purposes of extradition between States Parties, crimes against humanity shall not be regarded as a political offense or as an offense connected with a political offense. Accordingly, a request for extradition for crimes against humanity may not be refused on this ground alone, nor shall extradition be barred by claims of official capacity subject to Article 6, paragraph 1.

6. It shall be grounds for denial of extradition that the person sought is being tried for crimes against humanity or for another crime under the laws of the requested State based on facts which constitute one or more of the constituent acts listed in Article 3, paragraph 1, or that the person sought has already been tried for such crime or crimes and acquitted or convicted, and has fulfilled the penalty for said conviction. It shall also be grounds for denial of extradition if the requested State Party ascertains that the person sought for extradition may be subjected to crimes against humanity in the requesting State as provided for in Article 18.

7. It shall be grounds for denial of extradition that the requested State has substantial grounds for believing that the request for extradition has been made for the purpose of prosecuting or punishing a person on account of that person's race, religion, nationality, ethnic origin, political opinions, sex or status, or that the person's right to a fair and impartial trial may be prejudiced for any of those reasons.

8. It shall be grounds for denial of extradition that the judgment of the requesting State has been rendered *in absentia*, the convicted person has not had sufficient notice of the trial or the opportunity to arrange for his or her defense, and the person has not or will not have the opportunity to have the case retried in his or her presence.

9. It shall be grounds for denial of extradition that the person has not received or would not receive the minimum guarantees in criminal proceedings, as contained in Article 14 of the International Covenant on Civil and Political Rights.

10. Extradition may be refused if the offense of crimes against humanity carries a penalty not provided for in the requested State, unless the requesting State gives such assurance as the requested State considers sufficient that the penalty not provided for in the requested State will not be imposed or, if imposed, will not be carried out.

E. Rule of Specialty

11. No person extradited for crimes against humanity shall be tried in the requesting State for any other crime than that for which extradition was granted unless the requested State or person extradited so consents.

F. Multiple Requests for Extradition

12. In cases of multiple requests for extradition, the State Party in whose territory the person alleged to be responsible for crimes against humanity has been found may take into consideration the following factors in determining priority:

   (a) The territory where one or more of the constitutive acts considered part of the crime has taken place;

   (b) The nationality of the offender(s);

   (c) The nationality of the victim(s); and

   (d) The forum most likely to have the greater ability and effectiveness in carrying out the prosecution, and which provides greater fairness and impartiality.

Explanatory Note

1. *Paragraph 1 draws upon Article 13(2) of the Enforced Disappearance Convention.*

2. *Paragraph 2 draws upon Article 13(3) of the Enforced Disappearance Convention.*

3. *Paragraph 3 ensures that, in the absence of relevant national legislation or an existing bilateral or multilateral extradition relationship, the present Convention shall provide the legal basis upon which a State Party may fulfill its obligation to extradite or prosecute in accordance with Article 8, paragraph 9 and Article 9.*

4. *Paragraph 4 ensures that, in the absence of relevant national legislation or an existing bilateral or multilateral extradition relationship, the present Convention may define the modalities by which a State Party may fulfill its obligation to extradite or*

prosecute in accordance with Article 8, paragraph 9 and Article 9.

5. *Paragraph 5 draws upon Article 13(1) of the Enforced Disappearance Convention with regard to political offenses. With regard to claims of official capacity, this paragraph is consistent with Article 6, paragraph 1 of the present Convention, which precludes any official capacity as an applicable defense.*

6. *With regard to paragraph 6, in order to uphold the substance of the principle ne bis in idem, it should not matter whether a State or a State Party has tried a person. In any event, the requested State will have to determine whether the prosecution was fair and effective.*

7. *Paragraph 7 draws upon Article 3(b) of the UN Model Treaty on Extradition.*

8. *Paragraph 8 draws upon Article 3(g) of the UN Model Treaty on Extradition.*

9. *Paragraph 9 is draws upon Article 3(f) of the UN Model Treaty on Extradition.*

10. *Paragraph 10 is similar to, but broader than, Article 4(d) of the UN Model Treaty on Extradition, and recognizes that States may have differing obligations with respect to regional human rights treaties.*

11. *Paragraphs 6 through 9 provide mandatory grounds for refusal of extradition, while paragraph 10 provides an optional ground for refusal. Potential additional optional grounds for refusal are provided in the UN Model Treaty on Extradition, Article 4.*

Annex 3
Mutual Legal Assistance

1.   Legal assistance between States Parties shall be afforded to the fullest extent possible under relevant laws, treaties, agreements, and arrangements of the requested State Party and may be afforded on the basis of the present Convention and without the need for reliance on a bilateral treaty or national legislation.

A. Types of Mutual Legal Assistance

2.   Legal assistance to be afforded in accordance with this Annex may be requested for any of the following purposes:

(a)   Taking evidence or statements from persons;

(b)   Effecting service of judicial documents;

(c)   Executing searches and seizures, and freezing of assets;

(d)   Examining objects and sites;

(e)   Providing information, evidentiary items and expert evaluations;

(f)   Providing originals or certified copies of relevant documents and records, including government, bank, financial, corporate or business records;

(g)   Identifying or tracing proceeds of crime, property instrumentalities or other things for evidentiary purposes;

(h)   Facilitating the voluntary appearance of persons in the requesting State Party;

(i)   Any other type of assistance that is not contrary to the domestic law of the requested State Party.

B. Transmission of Information

3.   Without prejudice to domestic law, the competent authorities of a State Party may, without prior request, transmit information relating to crimes against humanity to a competent authority in another

State Party where they believe that such information could assist the authority in undertaking or successfully concluding inquiries and criminal proceedings or could result in a request formulated by the latter State Party pursuant to the present Convention.

4.   The transmission of information pursuant to paragraph 3 of this Annex shall be without prejudice to inquiries and criminal proceedings in the State of the competent authorities providing the information. The competent authorities receiving the information shall comply with a request that said information remain confidential, even temporarily, or with restrictions on its use. However, this shall not prevent the receiving State Party from disclosing in its proceedings information that is exculpatory to an accused person. In such a case, the receiving State Party shall notify the transmitting State Party prior to the disclosure and, if so requested, consult with the transmitting State Party. If, in an exceptional case, advance notice is not possible, the receiving State Party shall inform the transmitting State Party of the disclosure without delay.

C. Obligations Under Other Applicable Treaties

5.   The provisions of this Annex shall not affect the obligations under any other treaty, bilateral or multilateral, that governs or will govern, in whole or in part, mutual legal assistance.

D. Transfer of Detained Persons

6.   A person who is being detained or is serving a sentence in the territory of one State Party whose presence in another State Party is requested for purposes of identification, testimony or otherwise providing assistance in obtaining evidence for investigations, prosecutions or judicial proceedings in relation to crimes against humanity may be transferred if the following conditions are met:

    (a)   The person freely gives his or her informed consent;

    (b)   The competent authorities of both States Parties agree, subject to such conditions as those States Parties deem appropriate.

E. Form of Requests for Mutual Legal Assistance

7.   Requests for legal assistance shall be made in writing or, where possible, by any means capable of producing a written record, in a language acceptable to the requested State Party, under conditions allowing that State Party to establish authenticity. The Secretary-General of the United Nations shall be notified of the language or languages acceptable to each State Party at the time it deposits its instrument of ratification, acceptance or approval of or accession to the present Convention. In urgent circumstances and where agreed by the States Parties, requests may be made orally but shall be confirmed in writing forthwith.

8.   A request for legal assistance shall contain:

(a)   The identity of the authority making the request;

(b)   The subject matter and nature of the investigation, prosecution or judicial proceedings to which the request relates and the name and functions of the authority conducting the investigation, prosecution or judicial proceedings;

(c)   A summary of the relevant facts, except in relation to requests for the purpose of service of judicial documents;

(d)   A description of the assistance sought and details of any particular procedure that the requesting State Party wishes to be followed;

(e)   Where possible, the identity, location and nationality of any person concerned; and

(f)   The purpose for which the evidence, information or action is sought.

9.   The requested State Party may request additional information when it appears necessary for the execution of the request in accordance with its domestic law or when it can facilitate such execution.

F. Execution of Requests for Mutual Legal Assistance

10.   A request shall be executed in accordance with the domestic law of the requested State Party and, to the extent not contrary with

the domestic law of the requested State Party and where possible, in accordance with the procedures specified in the request.

G. Witnesses

11. Wherever possible and consistent with fundamental principles of domestic law, when an individual is in the territory of a State Party and has to be heard as a witness or expert by the judicial authorities of another State Party, the first State Party may, at the request of the other, permit the hearing to take place by video conference if it is not possible or desirable for the individual in question to appear in person in the territory of the requesting State Party. States Parties may agree that the hearing shall be conducted by a judicial authority of the requesting State Party and attended by a judicial authority of the requested State Party.

H. Limited Use of Information

12. The requesting State Party shall not transmit or use information or evidence furnished by the requested State Party for investigations, prosecutions or judicial proceedings other than those stated in the request without the prior consent of the requested State Party. Nothing in this paragraph shall prevent the requesting State Party from disclosing in its proceedings information or evidence that is exculpatory to an accused person. In the latter case, the requesting State Party shall notify the requested State Party prior to the disclosure and, if so requested, consult with the requested State Party. If, in an exceptional case, advance notice is not possible, the requesting State Party shall inform the requested State Party of the disclosure without delay.

I. Refusal of Requests for Mutual Legal Assistance

13. States Parties shall not decline to render mutual legal assistance pursuant to this Annex on the ground of bank secrecy.

14. Legal assistance may be refused if the request is not made in conformity with the provisions of this Annex.

15. Legal assistance may not be refused based upon claims of official capacity subject to Article 6, paragraph 1, or that the crime was of a political nature.

16. Legal assistance shall be refused if the person who is the subject of the request is being tried for crimes against humanity or for another crime under the laws of the requested State based on facts which constitute one or more of the constituent acts listed in Article 3, paragraph 1, or if the person has already been tried for such crime or crimes and acquitted or convicted, and has fulfilled the penalty for said conviction. It shall also be grounds for refusal of mutual legal assistance if the requested State Party ascertains that the person who is the subject of the request may be subjected to crimes against humanity in the requesting State.

Explanatory Note

1. *Much of the text of this Annex draws upon the mutual legal assistance provisions of Article 46 of the UN Convention Against Corruption.*

2. *For additional modalities of effectuating mutual legal assistance, States Parties may look to model legislation such as the UN Model Treaty on Mutual Assistance in Criminal Matters or to the relevant conventions of regional bodies.*

Annex 4
Transfer of Criminal Proceedings

1. Whenever a State Party, having jurisdiction over a person charged with crimes against humanity, agrees with another State Party, also having jurisdiction pursuant to Article 10, to cede jurisdiction and to transfer the record of the proceedings undertaken to the requesting State Party, the transfer procedure shall be established by agreement between their respective competent authorities. Such a procedure shall be based on the present Convention and shall not require the existence of a bilateral treaty between the respective States Parties or national legislation.

2. A transfer may occur when it is in the best interest of justice, and when it enhances fair and effective prosecution.

3. A State Party may request another State Party to take over proceedings in any one or more of the following cases:

    (a) If the suspected person is ordinarily resident in the requested State;

    (b) If the suspected person is a national of the requested State or if that State is his or her State of origin;

    (c) If the suspected person is undergoing or is to undergo a sentence involving deprivation of liberty in the requested State;

    (d) If proceedings for the same or other offenses are being taken against the suspected person in the requested State;

    (e) If it considers that transfer of the proceedings is warranted in the interests of arriving at the truth and in particular that the most important items of evidence are located in the requested State;

    (f) If it considers that the enforcement in the requested State of a sentence, if one were passed, is likely to improve the prospects for the social rehabilitation of the person sentenced;

    (g) If it considers that the presence of the suspected person cannot be ensured at the hearing of proceedings in the requesting State and that his or her presence in person at the hearing of proceedings in the requested State can be ensured;

(h)   If it considers that it could not itself enforce a sentence if one were passed, even by having recourse to extradition, and that the requested State could do so.

Explanatory Note

1. *This provision draws upon the European Transfer of Proceedings Convention and includes in paragraph 3 the situations listed in Article 8 of that convention defining when States may make such transfer requests.*

2. *Grounds for refusal have not been included in light of the diversity of national legal systems.*

Annex 5
Transfer of Convicted Persons for the Execution of Their Sentences

1. States Parties may transfer to one another a person convicted of crimes against humanity in their respective legal systems for purposes of the execution of such convicted person's sentence on the basis of the present Convention and without the need for a bilateral treaty between the States Parties or national legislation.

2. The transfer shall require the consent of the transferring State Party, the transferred-to State Party, and the person to be transferred, who shall waive any rights to challenge his or her conviction in the transferring State, along with the agreement of the transferred-to State Party to execute the sentence as decided in the transferring State in accordance with its penal laws and applicable regulations.

3. Conditional release and other measures provided for in the transferred-to State shall be in accordance with its laws and applicable regulations. No pardon or other similar measure of clemency, however, shall be extended to the transferred person without the consent of the transferring State.

Explanatory Note

This provision draws upon the Convention on the Transfer of Sentenced Persons as well as the Inter-American Criminal Sentences Convention. States Parties may also wish to look to model legislation of relevant organizations, to regional directives, and to subregional agreements.

Annex 6
Enforcement of the Effects of States Parties' Penal Judgments

1. Recognition and enforcement of a State Party's penal judgment shall be based on the present Convention and shall not require a bilateral treaty between the respective States Parties, or national legislation, other than that which may be required under the Constitution or national law of each State Party to implement the present Convention.

2. Cooperation and assistance between States Parties, particularly with regards to giving effect to Annexes 3 through 6, and which, in accordance with the laws of a given State Party, are barred if predicated on a foreign penal judgment or which require a treaty or national legislation having for effect the recognition of a foreign penal judgment, shall instead rely on the present Convention with respect to the enforcement or reliance upon a foreign penal judgment.

3. A State Party may, however, refuse to execute, enforce, give effect to, or rely on another State Party's penal judgments if the judgment in question was obtained by fraud or duress, or was issued on the basis of procedures that violate international standards of due process, or are in conflict with domestic public policy.

Explanatory Note

This provision draws upon the European Convention on the International Validity of Criminal Judgments.

International Convention on the Prevention and Punishment of Crimes Against Humanity

Table of Abbreviations and Instruments Cited in the Convention and Explanatory Notes

African Charter	**African [Banjul] Charter on Human and People's Rights,** 1982, 1520 U.N.T.S. 217 (entry into force Oct. 21, 1986).
Apartheid Convention	**International Convention on the Suppression and Punishment of the Crime of *Apartheid,*** 1973, G.A. Res. 3068 (XXVIII) of Nov. 30, 1973, UN Doc. A/9030, 1015 U.N.T.S. 243 (entry into force July 18, 1976).
American Convention on Human Rights	**American Convention on Human Rights,** 1969, O.A.S.T.S. No. 36, 1144 U.N.T.S. 123 (entry into force July 18, 1978).
CAH	Crime(s) Against Humanity.
Comprehensive History of the Proposed CAH Convention	**Leila Nadya Sadat, *A Comprehensive History of the Proposed International Convention on the Prevention and Punishment of Crimes Against Humanity,* in FORGING A CONVENTION FOR CRIMES AGAINST HUMANITY** (Cambridge Univ. Press, 2011). For the website of the Washington University School of Law Whitney R. Harris World Law Institute Crimes Against Humanity Initiative, see http://law.wustl.edu/crimesagainsthumanity/.
European Convention on the Transfer of Sentenced Persons	**Convention on the Transfer of Sentenced Persons,** 1983, Europ. T.S. No. 112, Strasbourg (Mar. 21, 1983) (entry into force July 1, 1985).

ECHR	**European Convention for the Protection of Human Rights and Fundamental Freedoms,** 1950, Europ. T.S. No. 5, 213 U.N.T.S. 222, Rome, (Sep. 4, 1950) (entry into force Sep. 3, 1953).
Enforced Disappearance Convention	**International Convention on the Protection of All Persons from Enforced Disappearance,** 2006, G.A. Res. 61/177, UN GAOR 61st Sess., Supp. No. 49, at 207, UN Doc. A/RES/61/177 (Dec. 20, 2006) (not yet in force).
Enforced Disappearance Declaration	**Declaration on the Protection of All Persons from Enforced Disappearance,** 1992, G.A. Res. 47/133, UN GAOR 47th Sess., Supp. No. 49, at 207, UN Doc. A/47/49 (1992).
European Convention on the International Validity of Criminal Judgments	**European Convention on the International Validity of Criminal Judgments,** 1970, Europ. T.S. No. 70, Criminal Judgments, The Hague, (May 28, 1970) (entry into force July 26, 1974).
European Evidence Warrant	**Council Framework Decision on the European Evidence Warrant for the purpose of obtaining objects, documents and data for use in proceedings in criminal matters,** 2008, O.J. (L 350) 72, Council Framework Decision 2008/978/JHA (entry into force Feb. 8, 2009).
European Mutual Assistance Convention	**European Convention on Mutual Assistance in Criminal Matters,** 1959, Europ. T.S. No. 30, Mutual Assistance in Criminal Matters, Strasbourg, (April 20, 1959) (entry into force 12 June 1962).
European Statutory Limitations Convention	**European Convention on the Non-Applicability of Statutory Limitation to Crimes against humanity and War Crimes,** 1974, Europ. T.S. No. 82, Crimes against humanity and War Crimes, Strasbourg (Jan. 25, 1974) (entry into force June 26, 2003).
European Transfer of Proceedings Convention	**European Convention on the Transfer of Proceedings in Criminal Matters,** 1972, Europ. T.S. No. 73, Criminal Proceedings, Strasbourg, (May 15, 1972) (entry into force Mar. 30, 1978).

Genocide Convention	**Convention on the Prevention and Punishment of the Crime of Genocide,** 1951, G.A. Res. 260 (III), UN Doc. No. A/180, 78 U.N.T.S. 277 (Dec. 9, 1948) (entry into force Jan. 12, 1951).
Genocide Prevention Task Force Report	**Madeleine Albright & William Cohen, Preventing Genocide: A Blueprint for U.S. Policymakers (2008),** *available at:* http://www.usip.org/genocide_taskforce/report.html.
Hijacking Convention	**Convention for the Suppression of Unlawful Seizure of Aircraft,** 1970, (The Hague, Dec. 18, 1970), T.I.A.S. No. 7192, 22 U.S.T. 1641, 860 U.N.T.S. 105 (entry into force Oct. 14, 1971).
ICCPR	**International Covenant on Civil and Political Rights,** 1976, G.A. Res. 2200 (XXI), Supp. No. 16, UN Doc. A/6316 (Dec. 16, 1966) (entry into force Mar. 23, 1976).
ICJ	**International Court of Justice**
ICTR Statute	**Statute of the International Criminal Tribunal for the Prosecution of Persons Responsible for Genocide and Other Serious Violations of International Humanitarian Law Committed in the Territory of Rwanda and Rwandan Citizens Responsible for Genocide and Other Such Violations Committed in the Territory of Neighbouring States, between 1 January 1994 and 31 December 1994,** 1994, S.C.Res. 955, UN Doc. S/RES/955 (Nov. 8, 1994), as amended by S.C.Res. 1431, UN Doc. S/RES/1431 (Aug. 14, 2002).
ICTY Statute	**Statute of the International Criminal Tribunal for the Prosecution of Persons Responsible for Serious Violations of International Humanitarian Law Committed in the Territory of the Former Yugoslavia since 1991,** UN Doc. S/25704 at 36, annex (1993) & S/25704/Add.1 (1993), adopted by Security Council on May 25, 1993, UN Doc. S/RES/827 (1993).

ILC Draft Articles on the Responsibility of States for Internationally Wrongful Acts	Report of the International Law Commission on the work of its fifty-third session, 23 April – 1 June and 2 July – 10 August 2001, 2001, UN GAOR, 56th Sess., UN Doc. A/56/10 (2001).
Inter-American Criminal Sentences Convention	Inter-American Convention on Serving Criminal Sentences Abroad, 1993, O.A.S.T.S. No. 76 (June 9, 1993) (entry into force April 13, 1996).
Inter-American Extradition Convention	Inter-American Convention on Extradition, 1981, O.A.S.T.S. No. 60 (Feb. 25, 1981) (entry into force Mar. 28, 1992).
Inter-American Mutual Assistance Convention	Inter-American Convention on Mutual Assistance in Criminal Matters, 1992, O.A.S.T.S. No. 75 (May 23, 1992) (entry into force April 14, 1996).
Nuclear Terrorism Convention	International Convention for the Suppression of Acts of Nuclear Terrorism, 2005, G.A. Res. 59/290 (LIX), Annex, UN Doc. A/59/766 (April 13, 2005) (entry into force July 7, 2007).
Nürnberg Principles	Principles of International Law Recognized in the Charter of the Nürnberg Tribunal and in the Judgment of the Tribunal, 1950, Int'l Law Comm'n, delivered to the General Assembly, UN Doc. A/1316 (1950).
Rabat Declaration	Convention on Extradition and Mutual Legal Assistance in Counter-Terrorism, 2008, annex to the letter dated 14 August 2008 from the Chargé d'affaires a.i. of the Permanent Mission of Morocco to the United Nations addressed to the Secretary-General. A/62/939 – S/2008/567 (08-47023) (not in force).
Rome Statute	Rome Statute of the International Criminal Court, 1998, 2187 U.N.T.S. 90 (entry into force July 1, 2002).

Statutory Limita-tions Convention	**Convention on the Non-Applicability of Statutory Limitations to War Crimes and Crimes Against Humanity**, 1970, G.A. Res. 2391 (XXIII) UN Doc. A/7218, 754 U.N.T.S. 73 (Nov. 26, 1968) (entry into force Nov. 11, 1970).
Terrorist Bomb-ings Convention	**International Convention for the Suppression of Terrorist Bombings**, 1997, G.A. Res. 52/164, UN Doc. A/RES/52/164 (Jan. 12, 1998) (entry into force May 23, 2001).
Torture Conven-tion	**Convention against Torture and Other Cruel, In-human or Degrading Treatment or Punishment**, 1987, G.A. Res. 39/46, annex, UN GAOR, 39th Sess., Supp. No. 51, at 197, UN Doc. A/39/51 (1984) (entry into force June 26, 1987).
UN Charter	**Charter of the United Nations**, 1945, 1 U.N.T.S. 16 (Oct. 24, 1945).
UN Model Assis-tance Treaty	**United Nations Model Treaty on Mutual Assistance in Criminal Matters**, 1990, G.A. Res. 45/117, UN Doc. A/RES/45/117 (Dec. 14, 1990).
UN Convention Against Corrup-tion	**United Nations Convention Against Corruption**, 2003, G.A. Res. 58/4, UN Doc. A/58/422 (Oct. 31. 2003) (entry into force Dec. 14, 2005).
UN Convention Against Transna-tional Organized Crime	**United Nations Convention Against Transnational Organized Crime**, 2001, G.A. Res. 25/55, annex I, UN GAOR, 55th Sess., Supp. No. 49, at 44, UN Doc. A/45/49 (Vol. I) (2001) (entry into force Sept. 29, 2003).
UN Model Ex-tradition Treaty	**United Nations Model Treaty on Extradition**, 1990, G.A. Res. 45/116, Annex, UN Doc. A/RES/45/49 (Dec. 14, 1990).
World Summit Outcome Docu-ment	**General Assembly Resolution 60/1: 2005 World Summit Outcome**, 2005, G.A. Res. A/RES/60/1, UN Doc. A/RES/60/1 (Oct. 24, 2005).

INDEX

A

A. v. the United Kingdom, 271
ABA House of Delegates, 33
abduction, 250
Abidjan, 90
absolute power, 269
access to justice for victims, 216
acts of genocide, 338
administrative orders, 206
adoption of legislation prohibiting
    propaganda for war, 390
Afghanistan, 313
Africa, 248, 381
aggression, 14
Akayesu case, 235, 263, 270
Akhavan, Payam, 339
Allied Powers, 370
Ambos, Kai, 336
American Society of International Law,
    20
American South, 252
Amnesty International, 340
Annan, Kofi, 281
apartheid, 5
Arab Spring, 304
arbitrary criterion, 231
Argentina, 23, 43
armed conflict, 3, 18, 40
armed conflicts, 337
Arrest Warrant case, 363
asylum, 354
atrocities against civilian populations, 303
atrocity, 31
atrocity crimes, 309, 326
attack, 94, 96, 98, 118, 260
Austria, iv
aut dedere aut judicare, v, 8, 12, 41, 216,
    297, 329, 345
autonomous implementation, 293

B

Baghram Air Base in Iraq, 315

Bales, Kevin, 248
Ban, Ki-moon, 283
Bangladesh, 248
Banković case, 150
Barayagwiza, Jean-Bosco, 239
Barbie, Klaus, 23
bars, 370
Bashir case, 68, 71, 93, 393
Bashir, Omar Al, 63, 362
Bashir's visit (to China), 363
basic human rights, 78
basic human values, 77, 98
Bassiouni, M. Cherif, 27, 36, 330, 370
Belgium, 294, 330, 356, 361
Belgium v. Senegal, 29
Bemba case, 66
Blair, Dennis C., 326
Blaškić decision, 122
Boko Haram, 187
Boskić, Marko, 325
Bosnia, 164, 309
Bosnia and Herzegovina, 164
Bosnia and Herzegovina case, 8, 177,
    180, 184, 186, 190, 204, 374
Bosnia v. Serbia, 30, 42
Brown, James Scott, 20
Bush, George W., 340
bystander State, 207

C

Canada, 23, 231, 275, 280
capacity to influence, 182
Cardin, Benjamin, 309
*Case Concerning the Application of the
    Convention on the Prevention and
    Punishment of the Crime of Genocide*,
    136
Cassese, Antonio, 126
Central African Republic, 49, 62
central criminal moneymaking activity,
    267
certainty in law, 371

Convention for the Suppression of
Unlawful Acts against Safety of Civil
Aviation, 354
Convention for the Suppression of
Unlawful Seizure of Aircraft, 9
Convention on the Elimination of All
Forms of Racial Discrimination, 388
Convention on the Prevention and
Punishment of Crimes Against
Humanity, 36
Convention on the Prevention and
Punishment of the Crime of Genocide,
v
Convention Relating to the Status of
Refugees, 222, 223, 383
conventional international criminal law,
333
Conventions on Corruption and
Organized Crime, 36
core crimes of international concern, 218
core international crimes, 1, 3, 4, 10, 202,
205, 219, 345, 354, 386, 396
genocide, 1
war crimes, 1
correlation (or no) between the obligation
and immunity, 363
Côte d'Ivoire, 90
Cotler, Irwin, 285
Council of Europe, 209
counterinsurgency, 371
countries of origin, 325
creative judicial interpretation, 235
crime of apartheid, 166
crime of crimes, 375
Crime of Crimes' claims, 233
crime of genocide, 369
crime under international law, 144
crimes against humanity, 307
contextual elements, 11, 91
definition, 373
definitive enshrinement of its
elements, 371
ICC definition, 31
normative foundations, 17
raison d'être, 100
statutory definition, 48
Crimes Against Humanity
definition, 3

Crimes Against Humanity Act of 2010
(U.S.), 315
Crimes Against Humanity and War
Crimes Act, 278
Crimes Against Humanity Initiative, v, 2,
34, 295, 304, 333, 370
crimes against humantiy
practical application, 17
crimes against peace, 25, 40, 137
crimes against the peace, 307
crimes contre l'esprit, 18
criminal activity, 186
criminal jurisdiction, 211, 214
criminal justice, iii
criminal justice system, 268
criminal liability, 241
criminal responsibility, 213
criminalization, 323
criteria of stability and permanence, 235
Croatia, iii
cross-border human trafficking, 265
Cryer, Robert, 332
CSCE Moscow Human Dimension
Mechanism to Bosnia-Herzegovina
and Croatia, iv
cultural backgrounds, 166
cultural genocide, 231
custodial State, 349
custom, 110
customary international law, 12, 18, 20,
23, 25, 27, 29, 31, 162, 191, 210, 290,
329, 333, 338, 341, 344, 348, 363
Cypriot cases, 141, 160

D

Darfur, 63, 304, 378
Darfur situation, 362
death penalty for convictions of
homosexuality, 380
debt bondage, 250
deception, 250
Declaration on the Protection of All
Persons from Enforced Disappearance,
6
deliberate inaction, 112, 130
deliberate State action, 170
delicate balance, 328
delictum iuris gentium, 79

G

H

L

M

N

FICHL Publication Series

Editors
Professor Morten Bergsmo, Editor-in-Chief
Professor Olympia Bekou, Editor
Mr. Mats Benestad, Editor
Mr. Alf Butenschøn Skre, Senior Executive Editor
Assistant Professor CHEAH Wui Ling, Editor
Ms. FAN Yuwen, Editor
Professor Håkan Friman, Editor
Dr. Kishan Manocha, Editor
Ms. ZHANG Xin, Editor
Ms. ZHANG Yueyao, Editor
Mr. Nikolaus Scheffel

Editorial Assistant
Ms. Marquise Lee Houle

Scientific Advisers
Professor Dan Sarooshi, Principal Scientific Adviser for International Law
Professor Andreas Zimmermann, Principal Scientific Adviser for Public International Law
Professor Kai Ambos, Principal Scientific Adviser for International Criminal Law
Dr.h.c. Asbjørn Eide, Principal Scientific Adviser for International Human Rights Law

Editorial Board
Dr. Xabier Agirre, International Criminal Court
Dr. Claudia Angermaier, Austrian judiciary
Ms. Neela Badami, Narasappa, Doraswamy and Raja
Dr. Markus Benzing, Freshfields Bruckhaus Deringer, Frankfurt
Associate Professor Margaret deGuzman, Temple University
Dr. Cecilie Hellestveit, International Law and Policy Institute
Fellow Pablo Kalmanovitz, Yale University
Mr. Sangkul Kim, Korea University
Associate Professor Jann K. Kleffner, Swedish National Defence College
Professor Kjetil Mujezinović Larsen, Norwegian Centre for Human Rights
Mr. Salím A. Nakhjavání, Extraordinary Chambers in the Courts of Cambodia
Professor Hector Olasolo, Universidad del Rosario
Ms. Maria Paula Saffon, Columbia University
Dr. Torunn Salomonsen, Norwegian Ministry of Justice
Professor Carsten Stahn, Leiden University
Professor Jo Stigen, University of Oslo
Dr. Philippa Webb, King's College London
Ms. WEI Xiaohong, Renmin University of China

Advisory Board

Mr. Hirad Abtahi, Legal Adviser of the Presidency of the International Criminal Court
Ms. Silvana Arbia, former Registrar of the International Criminal Court
Professor Emeritus M. Cherif Bassiouni
Professor Olympia Bekou, University of Nottingham
Mr. Gilbert Bitti, Senior Legal Adviser, Pre-Trial Division, International Criminal Court
Research Professor J. Peter Burgess, PRIO
Former Judge Advocate General Arne Willy Dahl, Norway
Professor Emeritus Yoram Dinstein, Tel Aviv University
Professor Jon Elster, Columbia University and Collège de France
Mr. James A. Goldston, Open Society Institute Justice Initiative
Mr. Richard Goldstone, former Chief Prosecutor,
    International Criminal Tribunal for the former Yugoslavia
Judge Hanne Sophie Greve, Gulating Court of Appeal, formerly
    European Court of Human Rights
Dr. Fabricio Guariglia, Office of the Prosecutor,
    International Criminal Court
Professor Franz Günthner, Ludwig-Maximilians-Universität
Mr. Wolfgang Kaleck, European Center for Constitutional and Human Rights
Professor Emeritus Frits Kalshoven, Leiden University
Judge Erkki Kourula, International Criminal Court
Prof. Claus Kreß, Cologne University
Professor David Luban, Georgetown University
Mr. Juan E. Méndez, Special Adviser to the ICC Prosecutor on Crime Prevention, former President, ICTJ
Dr. Alexander Muller, Director, The Hague Institute for the Internationalisation of Law
Judge Erik Møse, European Court of Human Rights, former President,
    International Criminal Tribunal for Rwanda
Dr. Gro Nystuen, International Law and Policy Institute
Mr. William Pace, Convener, Coalition for the International Criminal Court
Ms. Jelena Pejić, International Committee of the Red Cross
Mr. Robert Petit, former International Co-Prosecutor,
    Extraordinary Chambers in the Courts of Cambodia
Dr. Joseph Rikhof, Department of Justice, Canada
Maj-Gen (ret'd) Anthony P.V. Rogers, Cambridge University
Professor William A. Schabas, Middlesex University
Professor James Silk, Yale Law School
Professor Emeritus Otto Triffterer, Salzburg University
Associate Professor YANG Lijun, Chinese Academy of Social Science
Professor Marcos Zilli, University of Sao Paulo

OTHER VOLUMES IN THE
FICHL PUBLICATION SERIES

Morten Bergsmo, Mads Harlem and Nobuo Hayashi (editors):
Importing Core International Crimes into National Law
Torkel Opsahl Academic EPublisher
Oslo, 2010
FICHL Publication Series No. 1 (Second Edition, 2010)
ISBN 978-82-93081-00-5

Nobuo Hayashi (editor):
National Military Manuals on the Law of Armed Conflict
Torkel Opsahl Academic EPublisher
Oslo, 2010
FICHL Publication Series No. 2 (Second Edition, 2010)
ISBN 978-82-93081-02-9

Morten Bergsmo, Kjetil Helvig, Ilia Utmelidze and Gorana Žagovec:
The Backlog of Core International Crimes Case Files in Bosnia and Herzegovina
Torkel Opsahl Academic EPublisher
Oslo, 2010
FICHL Publication Series No. 3 (Second Edition, 2010)
ISBN 978-82-93081-04-3

Morten Bergsmo (editor):
Criteria for Prioritizing and Selecting Core International Crimes Cases
Torkel Opsahl Academic EPublisher
Oslo, 2010
FICHL Publication Series No. 4 (Second Edition, 2010)
ISBN 978-82-93081-06-7

Morten Bergsmo and Pablo Kalmanovitz (editors):
Law in Peace Negotiations
Torkel Opsahl Academic EPublisher
Oslo, 2010
FICHL Publication Series No. 5 (Second Edition, 2010)
ISBN 978-82-93081-08-1

Morten Bergsmo, César Rodríguez Garavito, Pablo Kalmanovitz and Maria Paula Saffon (editors):
Distributive Justice in Transitions
Torkel Opsahl Academic EPublisher
Oslo, 2010
FICHL Publication Series No. 6 (2010)
ISBN 978-82-93081-12-8

Morten Bergsmo (editor):
Complementarity and the Exercise of Universal Jurisdiction for Core International Crimes
Torkel Opsahl Academic EPublisher
Oslo, 2010
FICHL Publication Series No. 7 (2010)
ISBN 978-82-93081-14-2

Morten Bergsmo (editor):
Active Complementarity: Legal Information Transfer
Torkel Opsahl Academic EPublisher
Oslo, 2011
FICHL Publication Series No. 8 (2011)
ISBN 978-82-93081-55-5 (PDF)
ISBN 978-82-93081-56-2 (print)

Sam Muller, Stavros Zouridis, Morly Frishman and Laura Kistemaker (editors):
The Law of the Future and the Future of Law
Torkel Opsahl Academic EPublisher
Oslo, 2010
FICHL Publication Series No. 11 (2011)
ISBN 978-82-93081-27-2

Morten Bergsmo, Alf Butenschøn Skre and Elisabeth J. Wood (editors):
Understanding and Proving International Sex Crimes
Torkel Opsahl Academic EPublisher
Beijing, 2012
FICHL Publication Series No. 12 (2012)
ISBN 978-82-93081-29-6

Morten Bergsmo (editor):
Thematic Prosecution of International Sex Crimes
Torkel Opsahl Academic EPublisher
Beijing, 2012
FICHL Publication Series No. 13 (2012)
ISBN 978-82-93081-31-9

Terje Einarsen:
The Concept of Universal Crimes in International Law
Torkel Opsahl Academic EPublisher
Oslo, 2012
FICHL Publication Series No. 14 (2012)
ISBN 978-82-93081-33-3

莫滕·伯格斯默 凌岩（主编）：

国家主权与国际刑法
Torkel Opsahl Academic EPublisher
Beijing, 2012
FICHL Publication Series No. 15 (2012)
ISBN 978-82-93081-58-6

Morten Bergsmo and LING Yan (editors):
State Sovereignty and International Criminal Law
Torkel Opsahl Academic EPublisher
Beijing, 2012
FICHL Publication Series No. 15 (2012)
ISBN 978-82-93081-35-7

Morten Bergsmo and CHEAH Wui Ling (editors):
Old Evidence and Core International Crimes
Torkel Opsahl Academic EPublisher
Beijing, 2012
FICHL Publication Series No. 16 (2012)
ISBN 978-82-93081-60-9

YI Ping:
戦争と平和の間——発足期日本国際法学における「正しい戦争」
の観念とその帰結
Torkel Opsahl Academic EPublisher
Beijing, 2013
FICHL Publication Series No. 17 (2013)
ISBN 978-82-93081-66-1

Morten Bergsmo (editor):
Quality Control in Fact-Finding
Torkel Opsahl Academic EPublisher
Florence, 2013
FICHL Publication Series No. 19 (2013)
ISBN 978-82-93081-78-4

All volumes are freely available online at http://www.fichl.org/publication-series/.
Printed copies may be ordered from distributors indicated at http://www.fichl.org/
torkel-opsahl-academic-epublisher/distribution/, including from http://www.amazon.
co.uk/. For reviews of earlier books in this Series in academic journals, please see
http://www.fichl.org/torkel-opsahl-academic-epublisher/reviews-of-toaep-books/.

www.ingramcontent.com/pod-product-compliance
Lightning Source LLC
Chambersburg PA
CBHW070808300326
41914CB00078B/1907/J

* 9 7 8 8 2 9 3 0 8 1 9 6 8 *